A DOCUMENTARY HISTORY

of

UNITARIAN
UNIVERSALISM

FROM 1900 TO THE PRESENT

Edited by Dan McKanan

EDITORIAL COMMITTEE
Mark W. Harris
Peter Hughes
Nicole C. Kirk
Emily Mace
Natalie Malter
Mark D. Morrison-Reed
Susan Ritchie

Skinner House Books
BOSTON

skinnerhouse.org

Printed in the United States

Cover design by Suzanne Morgan
Text design by Jeff Miller

print ISBN: 978-1-55896-791-5
eBook ISBN: 978-1-55896-792-2

6 5 4 3 2
22 21 20

Library of Congress Cataloging-in-Publication Data is available

We are grateful for permission to reprint the following copyrighted material:

Curtis W. Reese, *Humanism*, © 1926 by Open Court Publishing Company; John H. Dietrich, "Unitarianism and Humanism," © 1927 by Open Court Publishing Company; Charles Hartshorne, *A Natural Theology for Our Time*, © 1967 by Open Court Publishing Company. Reproduced with permission.

Marjorie Bowens-Wheatley, "Cornrows, Kwanzaa and Confusion: The Dilemma of Cultural Racism and Misappropriation." This article originally appeared in the Fall 1995 edition of the Liberal Religious Education Journal entitled *Bridges to the Future: From Assimilation to Pluralism*, published by the Liberal Religious Educators Association, www.lreda.org. Used with permission of the Liberal Religious Educators Association.

Jason Shelton, "Standing on the Side of Love," in *Singing the Journey: A Supplement to Singing the Living Tradition* (Boston: UUA, 2005), #1014. Copyright Yelton Rhodes Music, www.yrmusic.com. Used with permission of Yelton Rhodes Music.

"Constitution of the Unitarian Universalist Church of the Philippines, Inc.," in Fredric John Muir, *Maglipay Universalist: The Unitarian Universalist Church of the Philippines* (self-published, 2001). Used with permission of Fredric Muir.

"Constitution and By-Laws of the First Icelandic Unitarian Church of Winnipeg," in V. Emil Gudmundson, *The Icelandic Unitarian Connection: Beginnings of Icelandic Unitarianism in North America, 1885–1900* (Winnipeg, Manitoba: Wheatfield Press, 1984). Used with permission of Marti Gudmundson.

Magnús Skaptason, "Sermon delivered at Gimli," in V. Emil Gudmundson, *The Icelandic Unitarian Connection: Beginnings of Icelandic Unitarianism in North America, 1885–1900* (Winnipeg, Manitoba: Wheatfield Press, 1984). Used with permission of Marti Gudmundson.

James Luther Adams, "The Indispensable Discipline of Social Responsibility," in *Journal of the Liberal Ministry 6* (Spring 1966). Used with permission of the Unitarian Universalist Ministers Association.

James Luther Adams, "Why Liberal?" in *Journal of Liberal Religion 1/2* (Autumn 1939). Used with permission of Meadville Lombard Theological School.

James Luther Adams, "The Changing Reputation of Human Nature," in *Journal of Liberal Religion 4* (Autumn 1942 and Winter 1943). Used with permission of Meadville Lombard Theological School.

William G. Sinkford, "The Language of Faith," in Dean Grodzins, ed., *A Language of Reverence* (Chicago: Meadville Lombard, 2004). Used with permission of William G. Sinkford.

Betty Bobo Seiden, "Sojourner Truth to Shirley Chisholm," Unitarian Universalist Sankofa Special Collection, Meadville Lombard Library. Used with permission of Sankofa Special Collection.

Credit lines continued on p. 565.

Contents

Introduction to the Collection

Primary sources are the building blocks of history. By reading sermons, letters, journal entries, meeting minutes, hymns, and other written sources from the past— as well as by examining buildings, paintings, and other physical objects—we get a glimpse of how historical events appeared to the people who created and experienced them. Sermons preached in rural Iowa in 1900 or in Harlem in 1925, for example, illumine the diverse ways in which ordinary people were introduced to liberal faith in those contexts, just as the founding documents of the Universalist Convention (1790), the American Unitarian Association (1825), and the Unitarian Universalist Association (1961) represent three different visions of how people of liberal faith should sustain their shared work. The selections included in this volume represent only a tiny slice of the sources available for the study of Unitarian Universalist history, but it is—to the best of our ability—a representative slice. Within this volume, you can explore Unitarian Universalist theology, polity, worship, religious education, missionary outreach, and social witness from multiple generations. You can also hear the voices of leaders and followers, institution builders and rebels, scholars and activists.

We have chosen to arrange the sources in strictly chronological order, rather than organizing them by theme or genre. Our hope is that this will help readers understand the context for each selection, and that the juxtaposition of Unitarian and Universalist texts, or of hymns and theological treatises, will spark new insights about how different traditions or genres may have influenced one another, or failed to do so. Early nineteenth-century Unitarians and Universalists could work just steps from one another without every becoming acquainted, as was the case for William Ellery Channing and Hosea Ballou. Readers should not feel obliged to read the selections in the order we have presented them; for those who prefer a more thematic ordering, we have included an index of sources by genre and topic.

Relatively few of the sources included in this collection appear in their entirety. We have excerpted sources in order to present a variety of voices within two volumes, and to highlight the ideas and phrases that have exerted the most historical influence. Readers should not assume that the beginning and end of the texts presented here correspond to the beginning and end of the original sources; in many cases, the selection we offer has been taken from the middle. Within each selection, we have used ellipses to indicate deletions of a paragraph or less, and three asterisks to mark longer deletions. Many, though not all, of the sources are available in their entirety through Google Books and other public resources, and readers who become interested in a specific text should use these resources to read it in its entirety.

We anticipate that most readers will use this volume alongside a narrative history of Unitarian Universalism. Several of these are listed in the bibliography, along with several of the primary source collections that preceded this one. Readers who are just discovering Unitarian Universalist history should be aware that there is no consensus about how to tell the story. Some scholars stress the ancient roots of "unitarian" and "universalist" ideas, claiming such early Christians as Arius and Origen as part of our common heritage; others accent the distinctively American character of the denominations founded in the United States in the decades just after the Revolution. Likewise, some place primary emphasis on the ideas and leaders that were dominant in each historical epoch, while others prefer to stress the visionaries who may have been neglected in their own time but cherished by subsequent generations. This volume is doubtless shaped by the biases of its editors, but our conscious intent has been to avoid taking sides in such historiographical debates and to provide readers with the resources needed to begin reaching their own conclusions.

History changes with each generation. This collection differs from its predecessors not only by including sources from the years 1960 to 2015, and not only because it includes Unitarian and Universalist sources alongside one another, but also because it reflects the commitments and curiosities of Unitarian Universalists, and of historians, over the past two generations. Recognizing that Unitarian Universalism has always been shaped by both lay and ordained persons of diverse ethnicities and genders, we have sought a balanced mix of voices throughout the collection, even as we recognize that ordained white men have held a preponderance of institutional power until recently. The exemplars and "saints" who are part of our living heritage are featured prominently in this collection, but we have also included many voices that Unitarian Universalists have forgotten, or have tried to forget. We have also included a sampling of documents from Unitarian, Universalist, and related traditions outside the United States, while keeping a primary focus on the Unitarian Universalist Association and its predecessors.

The majority of individuals included in this collection were members of Unitarian, Universalist, or Unitarian Universalist congregations, but some were not. Our tradition has always cherished rebellious responses to inherited institutions, and as a result the living heritage of Unitarian Universalism includes such people as Margaret Fuller and Abner Kneeland, both of whom repudiated Unitarian or Universalist churches on behalf of values that would be embraced by those same churches generations later. It also includes such precursors as Michael Servetus and George de Benneville, who articulated liberal religious beliefs long before the creation of liberal denominations. Nevertheless, ideas and values rarely survive without institutional support, and so we have been careful to balance individual voices with documents that reflect the policies and practices of institutions.

Each selection contains a very brief, scholarly introduction, and most include recommendations for further reading. Some of the authors featured here are the subjects of book-length biographies; most also appear in the online *Dictionary of Unitarian & Universalist Biography*, which is an indispensable resource for historians of Unitarian Universalism. Several of the volumes listed in the bibliography also provide biographical information on the persons featured in this collection.

Introduction to Volume Two

As the second half of our *Documentary History of Unitarian Universalism*, this volume covers Unitarian, Universalist, and Unitarian Universalist history from 1900 to the present. This was a time of theological change and institutional consolidation, as Unitarians and Universalists came together, transformed their relationship to their Christian roots, and deepened their commitment to social justice.

After a century of rapid theological development and controversy, both the Unitarians and the Universalists entered the twentieth century fully committed to their non-creedal identities. At Saratoga in 1894, the National Conference of Unitarian Churches revised its constitution to specify that "nothing in this constitution is to be construed as an authoritative test" and to welcome "any who, while differing from us in belief, are in general sympathy with our spirit and our practical aims." And in Boston in 1899, the Universalist General Convention reaffirmed its historic Winchester Profession alongside an updated list of five principles, adding that "neither this, nor any other precise form of words, is required as a condition of fellowship." Over the decades that followed, these commitments allowed both denominations to absorb theological changes even more radical than those they had experienced in the nineteenth century, without suffering major schisms. They also increased the sense of affinity between Universalists and Unitarians, preparing the way for denominational consolidation in 1961.

This new unity and clarity provided a foundation for global outreach. Over the course of the nineteenth century, Unitarians in the United States had deepened relationships with their coreligionists in Canada, the United Kingdom, and Transylvania, as well as with a newborn Unitarian movement in the Khasi Hills of India. They had also made contact with religious liberals rooted in other world faiths at the World's Parliament of Religions in 1893. At the dawn of the new century, American Unitarian Association president Samuel Atkins Eliot II called a meeting that led to the founding of the International Council of Unitarian and Other Liberal Religious Thinkers and Workers (now the International Association for Religious Freedom), an inclusive organization for religious liberals of many stripes. This period also marked a high point of Unitarian and Universalist missionary activity. The Unitarians and Universalists launched missions to Japan in 1887 and 1890, respectively, and these briefly took center stage in the liberal religious consciousness during the period of intense Japanese suffering that followed the 1904–1905 Russo-Japanese War. And when the United States seized control of the Philippines after the Spanish American war, Philippine governor William Howard Taft, a Unitarian layman, galvanized a partnership between Unitarianism and a local movement that blended religious reform with opposition to Spanish rule.

Back in the United States, the most significant theological impulse of the century's first two decades was the social gospel, a pan-Protestant movement that reinterpreted traditional doctrines in social rather than individual terms. "Sin" now referred to the structural evils of poverty, exploitation, and racism, while "salvation" meant the creation of a society based on the Golden Rule. Some social gospelers saw this new theology as a supplement to the old, while others wanted to dispense with individualistic and otherworldly theology altogether. Likewise, some believed it was possible to Christianize capitalism, while others regarded socialism as a more faithful embodiment of Jesus's social vision. Virtually all social gospelers, and indeed virtually all Unitarians and Universalists, accepted the Darwinian account of human origins as an integral part of their new theology. They also believed that an evolutionary process within society and culture would produce a universal religion of the future that would look remarkably similar to the liberal religion of the present. This viewpoint is vigorously argued in this volume in the selections by Charles Eliot and Clarence Skinner.

In many ways, the Unitarian and Universalist social reformers of the nineteenth century had prepared the way for the social gospel. What was new in the twentieth century was that Methodists, Congregationalists, Presbyterians, and Episcopalians were thinking and acting similarly. Every major denomination created a commission or federation for social service and justice, and the Unitarians and Universalists were no exception. John Haynes Holmes and Clarence Skinner, two friends who were active within the radical wing of the social gospel, were the major organizers of the Unitarian Fellowship for Social Justice and the Universalist Commission on Social Service. The ecumenical organizations that mainline Protestants created to coordinate their social justice work usually excluded Unitarians and Universalists, who wound up directing much of their energy to superficially secular organizations. Unitarians, most of them white, were prominent among the founders of the National Association for the Advancement of Colored People and the American Civil Liberties Union, while ordained and lay women in both denominations played leading roles in the reunited and revitalized women's suffrage movement of the early twentieth century. Eleanor Elizabeth Gordon, Anna Garlin Spencer, May Wright Sewall, and Olympia Brown were among dozens of women who blended religious leadership with advocacy for women's rights and direct service to people in need, while Charlotte Perkins Gilman, who had been raised Universalist, was the central intellectual of the new "feminist" movement that called for cultural transformation as well as legal rights for women.

The long simmering tension between the moderate and radical wings of the social gospel movement boiled over during World War I, which the radicals regarded as an unchristian display of nationalism, worked up by capitalists who stood to profit from the manufacture of arms. Though such prominent figures as Jenkin Lloyd Jones, John Haynes Holmes, and Clarence Skinner all took this position, the vast majority of Unitarians and Universalists disagreed. Skinner lost his pulpit but retained his teaching position at Tufts; Holmes retained the support of his congregation but broke with the Unitarian denomination after bitterly debating former U.S. president William Howard Taft at the Unitarian General Conference meeting that occurred just as the United States was entering the war. Holmes reorganized his New York City congregation as a "Community Church," then joined with Skinner to found a sister congregation in Boston.

The years after World War I were marked by the most significant development within Unitarian and Universalist theology in the twentieth century: the rise of religious humanism. The idea that even people who didn't believe in God might value covenantal religious community was not entirely new; this was the premise of both the freethought congregations of the 1830s and the Ethical Culture movement initiated in 1877. But Curtis Reese, John Dietrich, and their allies took the new step of cultivating religious humanism within existing Unitarian congregations. They also partnered with academic philosophers, especially those influenced by John Dewey, to produce the "Humanist Manifesto," a widely circulated document that has been updated twice and still serves as a touchstone for those who define religion as a "means for realizing the highest values of life" and who regard the scientific method as the surest path to truth.

Dewey's influence on progressive education was as great as his influence on philosophical humanism, and the religious educators among his students led a thorough reinvention of Unitarian and Universalist religious education during the middle decades of the century. The Unitarians' New Beacon Series, developed by Sophia Lyon Fahs, led the way with storybooks that sought to draw out children's inherent religiosity rather than imposing doctrines or traditions on them. Dorothy Spoerl and Angus MacLean brought the same approach into Universalism and fostered curricular collaboration between the two denominations.

Humanism drove a sharp wedge between religious liberals and their former social gospel allies within the Protestant mainstream. The rise of humanism coincided with a series of Protestant schisms that divided fundamentalists from modernists, prompting ecumenical leaders to seek the safety of middle ground. (Both Reese and Dietrich began their careers as Protestant modernists who avoided heresy trials by becoming Unitarian.) After separating from the fundamentalists, many in the Protestant mainline were attracted to the neo-orthodox theology promulgated by Karl Barth in Switzerland and the Niebuhr brothers in the United States. Neo-orthodox theologians accepted liberalism's historical approach to the Bible and concern for social justice, but argued that liberals' faith in progress and antipathy to dogma made them captive to contemporary culture and susceptible to the radical evil represented by fascism. Their antidote was a return to biblical narratives and classical doctrines.

This was the context in which the Federal Council of Churches twice denied the Universalist Church of America's application for membership, prompting Universalists to think more seriously about merger with Unitarianism. It was also the context in which some Unitarians began to question their inherited faith in progress. The most influential of these chastened liberals was James Luther Adams. Building on the earlier insights of Harvard Divinity School dean William Wallace Fenn, as well as on his personal friendship with Paul Tillich, Adams argued that liberalism should be distinguished not by a naïve faith in progress but by continuous self-criticism and the cultivation of voluntary, democratic communities.

Alfred North Whitehead's process philosophy, which held that reality is composed of evolutionary processes rather than static substances, influenced two other mid-century developments in liberal theology, both developed by scholars who converted to Unitarianism late in their careers. Henry Nelson Wieman's "religious naturalism" shared humanism's emphasis on working within the limits of the scientific method, but sometimes used the term *God* to designate the "creative good" that transcends and relativizes even the most precious "created goods." And Charles Hartshorne's "process theology" offered a radically relational picture of a God who is continually growing and changing in relation to the world. Half a century later, process thought is an even stronger component of the Unitarian Universalist theological mix, especially as blended with feminist theology in the work of Rebecca Parker, Thandeka, and others.

These theological developments occurred more or less in tandem among Unitarians and Universalists, though the Universalist embrace of humanism was slightly later and more limited in scope. Institutionally, the two traditions charted different courses. The Universalists struggled to create strong national structures even as they faced a daunting demographic challenge: The rural communities of New York and New England that had been their heartland were rapidly depopulating, as agriculture shifted to flatter and more fertile lands farther west. Neither the fundraising prowess of women's mission circles nor the church-planting enthusiasm of "grasshopper missionary" Quillen Shinn were enough to offset the dwindling of Universalism's historic congregations. The Universalists had begun the century with roughly sixty thousand members, almost as many as the Unitarians; by the time of consolidation, they had declined to thirty-seven thousand.

Unitarianism experienced alternating periods of growth and decline, but managed to exceed one hundred thousand members just before consolidation. American Unitarian Association president Samuel Atkins Eliot II restored that body's role as the central Unitarian denominational structure early in the century. He was a shrewd manager who knew that Unitarianism would prosper nationally if it invested in congregations in professional neighborhoods and rapidly growing cities. This policy came with a cost: Most ordained women served isolated rural congregations—that is, those congregations that could not afford to recruit a seminary-educated man—and these congregations, like their Universalist counterparts, fared poorly in the twentieth century. The numbers of ordained women actually declined throughout the first half of the century. Eliot was no more sympathetic to the innovative ministry of Jamaican-born Egbert Ethelred Brown, who founded and led the Harlem Unitarian Church during the height of the Harlem Renaissance.

Unitarianism, like Protestantism generally, entered the doldrums during the Great Depression but rebounded during the dynamic presidency of Frederick May Eliot (scion of a different but equally prominent family of Unitarian Eliots), who served from 1937 until his death in 1958. Eliot's leadership began when he chaired the first Commission of Appraisal, whose review of Unitarian institutions pushed the denomination toward a more truly national, less Boston-centered identity. As denominational president, he effectively framed religious liberalism as the antithesis of fascist totalitarianism, allowing wartime patriotism to coexist with conscientious objection, interracial activism, and even support for Communism. Eliot encouraged the courageous ministry of Norbert Čapek in Prague and supported the development of the Unitarian Service Committee, whose first task was to help Jewish children and other refugees escaping the Nazis. Eliot's version of religious liberalism was capacious enough to be shared by such diverse individuals as ethicist James Luther Adams, Mills College president Aurelia Henry Reinhardt, Supreme Court Justice William O. Douglass, Popular Front radical Stephen Fritchman, Gandhian activist Homer Jack, and even Eliot's rival for denominational leadership, A. Powell Davies. Both American Unitarian Youth and the General Alliance of Unitarian Women took on more activist, outwardly focused identities during the Second World War. Just after the war, Eliot's coalition teetered but did not collapse when Fritchman was fired as editor of the *Christian Register*. Fritchman went on to a well-respected ministry at First Unitarian of Los Angeles. Eliot strengthened Unitarianism by supporting a proposal offered by Lon Ray Call and Munroe Husbands just after World War II. Rather than paying ordained church planters to establish congregations in new communities, they suggested, why not provide local laypeople with the resources they need to start congregations on their own? The resulting fellowship movement was perfectly timed to coincide with suburbanization, the Baby Boom, and the GI Bill's expansion of higher education. All of these factors increased interest in religious liberalism in areas previously unserved by the Unitarians (or the Universalists), and within two decades more than four hundred fellowships had been planted, mostly in college towns and new suburbs.

Frederick Eliot's lifelong dream was the creation of a United Liberal Church of America, something he hoped would unite Unitarians with Quakers, Ethical Culturists, Reform Jews, and Universalists. It quickly became apparent that only the Universalists shared Eliot's enthusiasm. One leading Universalist, Clinton Lee Scott, went so far as to recruit a leading Unitarian humanist, Kenneth Patton, to lead an experimental congregation intended to revitalize Universalism in Boston. The first institutional fruit of the new interest in merger was the joint hymnal *Hymns of the Spirit*, published in 1937, followed by the creation of Liberal Religious Youth, a fully merged youth organization developed by Unitarian and Universalist teenagers between 1950 and 1952. The formal merger process began with a Joint Merger Commission in 1956. Under the able leadership of William B. Rice, the Commission collected data, produced study documents, encouraged open debate, and finally conducted a series of plebiscites in which both denominations overwhelmingly supported consolidation (a legal form that was judged less vulnerable to litigation than merger).

Dana Greeley, who had succeeded Frederick Eliot as president of the American Unitarian Association, became the first president of the Unitarian Universalist Association, and his presidency was marked by numerical growth and energetic participation in all the social movements of the day. The greatest of these movements was the Southern freedom struggle that had begun with the Montgomery Bus Boycott of 1955–1956. That movement built on the earlier work of the National Association for the Advancement of Colored People, the Congress of Racial Equality, and the Urban League—all groups with significant Unitarian connections. Unitarian Universalist engagement with civil rights extended to the 1965 march in Selma, during which minister James Reeb and laywoman Viola Liuzzo, both European Americans, joined an already lengthy list of those who laid down their lives for the cause of racial justice.

Unitarian Universalists were deeply divided when the emphasis of the freedom struggle shifted from freedom to empowerment. Advocates of black power, with Hayward Henry as their eloquent spokesperson, created a Black Caucus and twice persuaded the General Assembly to allocate one million dollars, spread over four years, to empowerment projects controlled by the African-American community. The newly militant members of Liberal Religious Youth endorsed this cause and made their own demands for self-determination. But other Unitarian Universalist advocates of racial justice were not persuaded that the time for integration had passed, and the denomination's remaining moderates and conservatives were simply horrified. Frederick Eliot's wartime coalition of liberals and radicals had survived the McCarthy period but now it collapsed, resulting in a precipitous membership decline and a budget crisis that exacerbated the conflict and eventually prevented most of the empowerment money from being delivered.

The empowerment controversy reached its crisis at the 1969 General Assembly in Boston, when supporters of the Black Caucus staged an extended walkout. One year later, the UU General Assembly passed its first social statement related to sexual orientation, calling for "an end to all discrimination against homosexuals, homosexuality, bisexuals, and bisexuality." It also affirmed support for the feminist movement for the first time, though it had endorsed abortion rights on several previous occasions. Suddenly two groups that had often been ignored by the social movements of the 1960s were at center stage, and over the next decades women and LGBTQ persons would transform the leadership and vision of Unitarian Universalism.

In the 1970s women were well represented among seminarians, but still a tiny minority of ordained clergy. In the succeeding decades the numbers of women clergy were augmented by young women embracing ministry as their first career and by an even larger cohort of second-career women for whom ordination had not been a viable option when they were younger. By the end of the century, women were the majority of Unitarian Universalist clergy, and they had transformed theologies, worship styles, and modes of delivering pastoral care. Lay and ordained women worked together to pass the Women and Religion resolution in 1977, which called on Unitarian Universalism not merely to include women in its existing power structure, but to root sexism out of its liturgy, theology, and culture. Inclusive language, Goddess spirituality, and feminist poetry quickly became as central to Unitarian Universalist culture as the scientific vocabulary of humanism. The Women and Religion resolution in turn catalyzed the revision of the Unitarian Universalist Principles and Sources, creating in 1985 a beloved and unifying (but still resolutely non-creedal) document. But some glass ceilings remained hard to break: At the time of this writing, the Unitarian Universalist Association had never elected a female president, and very few of the largest congregations were served by female senior ministers. In this collection, Marilyn Sewell, Laurel Hallman, and Christine Robinson represent the experiences of female senior ministers; Sandra Caron and Denny Davidoff illustrate the leadership of laywomen who served as UUA moderator; and Lucile Longview and Carolyn McDade represent radical feminist laywomen with a warier approach to institutional power. Rebecca Parker, who served twenty-five years as president of Starr King School for the Ministry, was one of several theological educators who ensured that all ministers were introduced to feminist theology.

Unitarian Universalism's transformation with regard to sexuality proceeded in tandem with its feminist evolution. Already in the 1950s some Unitarian ministers had performed same-sex weddings, and soon after the Stonewall uprising of 1969 it became clear that the majority of Unitarian Universalists supported full inclusion of people of all sexual orientations. Previously closeted individuals came out, created a Gay Caucus modeled on the Black Caucus of the previous decade, and demanded that the denomination translate vague sympathy into institutional support. The pioneering sexuality education curriculum "About Your Sexuality" was updated to affirm diverse sexualities. Most congregations participated in the Welcoming Congregation process initiated in 1989, and LGBTQ persons were soon proudly visible throughout the denomination. Unitarian Universalism was thus able to participate energetically in the AIDS activism of the 1980s and, even more so, in the triumphant campaign for marriage equality of the early twenty-first century.

Feminism and LGBTQ liberation were, for the most part, unifying causes for Unitarian Universalists. But they divided mainline Protestantism. Several mainline churches took four decades to reach consensus on sexual orientation, and several more have still not reached consensus. With the rise of the Moral Majority and the election of Ronald Reagan, previously marginal evangelical denominations superseded a divided mainline as the informal religious establishment of the United States. This turned out to be good news for Unitarian Universalist growth, since Unitarian Universalist congregations, especially in the Sunbelt, could position themselves as clear alternatives. As the mainline continued to decline numerically, Unitarian Universalism entered a period of steady albeit modest growth that lasted, roughly, from Reagan's election to the beginning of the Great Recession of 2008.

Unitarian Universalist theologies became more diverse during this time of growth. In the early years of the UUA, humanism had been the clearly dominant position, but now the pendulum began to swing back toward process theism and liberal Christianity. At the same time, rapidly increasing numbers of Unitarian Universalists identified as Buddhists or pagans. Unitarian Universalism had long offered a welcoming home to interfaith families, but in this period more and more people felt comfortable bringing their previous religious identities into their lives as Unitarian Universalists. Organizations such as UUs for Jewish Awareness, the UU Buddhist Fellowship, and the Covenant of UU Pagans proliferated.

Relations between Unitarian Universalists in the United States and their coreligionists around the world took on new forms at the end of the twentieth century. The Unitarian Universalist Partner Church Council, created in 1993, fostered direct ties between congregations in the United States and those in Transylvania, the Khasi Hills, and elsewhere. Recognizing that the International Association for Religious Freedom had evolved into an interfaith rather than Unitarian Universalist organization, representatives of many churches created the International Council of Unitarians and Universalists in 1995. Brand new Unitarian Universalist congregations sprouted in places as diverse as the Philippines, Burundi, and Bolivia, each with its own unique pedigree.

Gradually, Unitarian Universalists returned to the work of racial justice that had been disrupted by the 1960s controversy over empowerment. People of color working as ministers, theologians, historians, and religious educators—among them Mark Morrison-Reed, Jacqui James, Betty Bobo Seiden, Margaret Williams Braxton,

William Jones, Marjorie Bowens-Wheatley, and Rosemary Bray McNatt—revealed the ways in which racism is embedded in the institutional history of Unitarian Universalism, in its language of worship, and in its habit of appropriating resources from other cultures. Both identity-based and ally organizations pioneered new models of solidarity in justice work. In 1997, the General Assembly pledged to make the UUA a truly anti-racist organization through "an ongoing process for the comprehensive institutionalization of anti-racism and multi-culturalism, understanding that whether or not a group becomes multi-racial, there is always the opportunity to become anti-racist." Before and after that assembly, hundreds of congregations and other groups participated in anti-racist work under the rubric of "Journey Toward Wholeness."

During the presidency of Peter Morales, the black-and-white paradigm that had once dominated Unitarian Universalist thinking about race began to disappear. Activism in solidarity with immigrants, who faced harsh repression in many states, took center stage alongside marriage equality in the "Standing on the Side of Love" campaign, which (among other things) encouraged Unitarian Universalists to engage in activism *as* Unitarian Universalists, wearing bright yellow T-shirts that identified them as the "love people." Activism around reproductive justice, mass incarceration, police violence, and the Doctrine of Discovery all followed a paradigm of deep partnership with non-UU organizations that had flowered at the 2012 "Justice General Assembly" in Phoenix. And a longstanding tradition of environmentalism led congregations to receive accreditation as "Green Sanctuaries" and the UUA to divest itself of investments in fossil fuels.

Unitarian Universalism in 2017, as throughout its history, is more than the sum of its activist commitments. But for many, "Standing on the Side of Love" is an apt summary of Unitarian Universalism as a whole. Interreligious, interracial, and LGBTQ families have embraced Unitarian Universalism as one of the few religious traditions willing to recognize the holiness of their diverse loves. Unwilling to impose doctrinal beliefs on one another, Unitarian Universalists remain bound together in a covenant of love that, in turn, empowers them to embody the Unitarian Universalist principles in their lives and in the world.

ELEANOR ELIZABETH GORDON

"Our Mission to Save by Culture"

1900

Eleanor Elizabeth Gordon (1852–1942) was a member of the "Iowa Sister-hood," an informal but influential group of Unitarian women ministers, and a partner in ministry with Mary Safford. Because Safford was the more dominating personality, Gordon learned what it was to be assigned the role of assistant and housekeeper, even when living with another woman. To assert her own personality she ultimately had to set out on her own in ministry. She promoted the education of women, the entry of women into ministry, and women's right to vote and to engage in politics. Portraying church as a kind of school, she argued that the best of human culture was the proper material for religious discussion and inspiration. She preached that a woman "must believe herself a human mind with only the limitations of a human mind, a part of the universal mind, with all possibilities of growth and development." Further Reading: Cynthia Grant Tucker, Prophetic Sisterhood: Liberal Women Ministers of the Frontier, 1880–1930 *(Boston: Beacon Press, 1990).*

—Peter Hughes

Without criticizing the work of other organizations, with no suggestions as to what may be or as to what may not be their work, it seems to me our duty is plain. Our work is mapped out for us. Our ideal is clear before us—to make truth, goodness and beauty the supreme things in the world by the slow process of education, by the slow process of line upon line, precept upon precept, by training the children, by inspiring young men and women, by making religion the one *real* thing in the world, by making the religious life the all-inclusive life. Shall I make this still more concrete? Shall I speak more plainly? I recently visited a village for Sunday services. As I went from the station I was compelled to make my way through cigarette smoking, tobacco spitting, and a crowd of uncouth looking men and boys on the platform. There was evidence of thrift in the village on every hand, but everything was hopelessly, drearily dull and homely.

I was in the place two days and the following is the substance of many conversations held with different residents:

"Why do you not have a Village Improvement Society and cut these weeds and sprinkle the streets and plant trees and improve the yards and do many things to make the place more attractive?" "There is no one to be interested or take the lead."

1

"How many ministers in the place?" "Four." "Why can not they do it?" "Oh, they wouldn't; that isn't religious work." "Have you a humane society?" "No." "Do you not need one?" "Yes—very much." "Why do not the churches unite for this work?" "Oh, they wouldn't think that religious work." "Have you a literary club, or debating club, or a reading room, or anything to make life beautiful or interesting to the boys and girls?"—and I thought with a shudder of the boys I had seen on the station platform. "No, *there is no one to take the lead* in such things. Our teachers are too young." "What do your ministers do?" "They preach sermons and lead the prayer meetings." "What do they preach about?" "Doctrines. The Methodist is a mighty good hand to show that the Baptists and Presbyterians are wrong and the others do about the same." "What do you do at prayer meetings?" "Why, *pray, of course.*"

Four church buildings, each one homelier than the others, four ministers, four Sunday schools, four prayer meetings, and the emphasis in one and all on certain little narrow interpretations of certain texts of the Bible! Nothing from one week's end to another that made for life in the highest, broadest, sense of the word. Everything that makes life beautiful, rich, pure, humane, left out. Art and literature a dead letter. Poetry an unknown tongue. Kindness and mercy only dimly hinted. Grace and refinement of speech or bearing utterly neglected.

This village, added to or subtracted from, is your problem and mine. Not the slums of the city, not the desperately wicked or abandoned,—although they may be found in places such as these,—are so much for your consideration.

These people had plenty to eat, lived in comfortable homes, the tyranny of trusts or the evil of unjust discrimination did not much affect their lives; but think you not that they hungered and thirsted not for the bread and water of life? The Liberal minister that will go into such a place as this and unite with the men and women who are waiting for such a leader to make life there beautiful, good and true; to make life pure, refined, humane; to reveal the inspiration of art, the marvel of music, the glory of literature; to lift men and women into the atmosphere of a rational religion and noble ethics—such a minister is doing the noblest work that can be given to a child of God to do.

It may have been a religious act for Rachel Winslow to renounce forever the artist's life and dedicate her voice to the cause of the poor, but that religious impulse is dwarfing and in so far not to be trusted that would confine the voice of the trained singer to the singing of gospel hymns at revival meetings. The great masters of music and poetry have their message too for the sorrowful of earth. To sing "Follow Me" or some other simple religious music, and by the singing to move men and women to resolve to be better and do better, is religious work; but the artist who sings the compositions of the great masters to an audience of cultivated people may be doing a far more beautiful thing. In the one audience, as in the other, there may be aching hearts needing comfort, stolid souls that need to be awakened, deeper feelings that need to be stirred. It depends upon the motive with which one sings whether it is religious work or not. The voice may sing "Oh to be nothing, nothing," at a revival meeting and the heart may be filled with arrogance and self-conceit.

To win for ourselves and to win for others, in so far as one soul can win for another the life that is true, good and beautiful—this is our ideal. And whence our inspiration? All the truth that the past has won, in bibles, books of science, history, we will search for the word of God, test what we find, claiming to be this word by your own experience and hold fast to that which seemeth true. All the goodness of the past, the devotion of the humble as well as the exalted, the earnestness of the ignorant as well as that of the learned, all that made for noble living, for brave daring, is for our heritage. All that is fair of form or face,—the music of childhood and of birds and of artists, the color of sunset sky and painted canvas, the revelation of poem and tale,—from one and all we shall draw our inspiration until our hearts give glad recognition that "all truth when fully realized is beautiful, that all beauty when fully realized is good, and all goodness, when fully recognized, is both truthful and beautiful."

Is this a hard saying? Would some of us choose the easier way? Do we still question our strength and wisdom? One thing, and one only, we need to remember and we are strong again—from whence our strength? A great artist once stood before the masterpiece of the great genius of his age, and whom he could never hope to equal or even rival. And yet the beautiful creation before him only elevated his feeling, for he saw realized there those conceptions which had floated before him dim and unsubstantial.

In every line and touch he felt a spirit immeasurably superior to his own, and yet kindred. As he looked upon the great picture before him he exclaimed with dignified humility, "And I too am a painter!"

Is not this our spirit as we stand before the great responsibilities of our work? We pass in review the history of humanity. We trace step by step the steady gain of the true, the good, and the beautiful. Our hearts thrill in response to the brave deeds of the past, throb with exultation as we learn more of the devotion of patriot, of the heroism of reformer and martyr, more of the earnestness of saint, prophet, and poet.

As we read of what they did we know that we can not win what they succeeded in winning; and yet, in the presence of their success and proud achievement, in dignified humility we recognize our kinship and each can say, "I too am a human soul. I too am a child of God. I too am an heir of all that has been won. I stand in the long line of succession and claim as my own all that I am worthy to have to hold."

SOURCE: Eleanor Gordon, "Our Mission to Save by Culture," *Old & New* 9 (September 1990): 7.

QUILLEN SHINN

"Affirmations of Universalism"

1900

Quillen Shinn (1845–1907) revived the practice of Universalist circuit-riding in the final decades of the nineteenth century and planted at least forty churches. A native of West Virginia who fought for the Union during the Civil War, Shinn graduated from the Canton Theological School at St. Lawrence University in 1870, served churches mostly in New England for twenty years, and then devoted himself full-time to church planting, serving the Universalist General Convention as "General Missionary" and then as "Missionary to the Southern States." Called the "Grasshopper Missionary" because of the brevity of his time in each locale, Shinn established several enduring congregations and expanded his denomination's geographical range, but failed to reverse its steady numerical decline. As this selection demonstrates, Shinn's theology was enthusiastically Universalist and solidly Christian, occupying a middle space between mainline liberalism and an increasingly post-Christian Unitarian movement. Further Reading: William H. McGlauflin, Faith with Power: A Life Story of Quillen Hamilton Shinn, D.D. (Boston: Universalist Publishing House, 1912).

— Dan McKanan

The word Destiny distinguishes us from Christians of other churches. We believe in a good destiny for all. We believe God will make all his bad children good; he wants to, and he can. He has the disposition, the power, the means, and the time. If love is all conquering, there is no foe it will not subdue, not even the rebellious will of man. We believe *more* than our brethren of other churches, not less. No faith is so grand or complete as ours, and yet so misunderstood. All benevolent people want it to be true, but think it is too good to be true. The selfish man hopes for something better, and looks forward to it, for himself. The benevolent man—and every Christian is one—is looking forward to something better for all the other members of the great family; and he will never be satisfied and perfectly happy until there is something better for all. Questions asked every day betray the general ignorance prevailing as to the beliefs of Universalism. People ask if we believe in God, if we believe in Christ, if we believe in the Bible, if we believe in a hereafter, if we believe in prayer, and even if we believe in *punishment*,—when I know of no Christian people who emphasize as strongly as we do the absolute certainty of punishment. It seems to be the

4

opinion of most all Christian people that our church is founded upon negations, whereas our affirmations express stronger faith than that professed by any other church on earth. And now it is my purpose to call attention to some of these great affirmations.

The text will be found in John's Gospel, 6: 44, 45: "No man can come to me, except the Father which hath sent me draw him; and I will raise him up at the last day. It is written in the prophets, and they shall be all taught of God. Every man, therefore, that hath heard, and hath learned of the Father, cometh unto me."

According to this declaration of our Master, no man can come to him until moved upon by the divine spirit; he can do nothing of himself, nothing till drawn by the Father. This completely explodes the free-will doctrine we hear so much about. Then Jesus declares that all shall be taught of God—*shall*—and tells what the result will be: "Every man that hath heard,"—all shall hear,—"and hath learned of the Father,"—all shall learn,—"cometh unto me." Do you observe that the doom of all sinful men is here pronounced? They are doomed to come unto him. When he said, "I will draw all men unto me," he pronounced the same doom. Speaking of those outside the fold, he said: "Them also I must bring, and they *shall* hear my voice, and there shall be one fold and one shepherd." He dooms them to come in! Most all our preachers doom them to stay out. I know you may refer me to his words in Matthew 26, where he says, "These shall go away into everlasting punishment," and "Depart from me ye cursed into everlasting fire prepared for the Devil and his angels." As I understand these words, they are in perfect harmony with the text I have quoted. What is the significance of the word "everlasting" in the Bible? It is applied to things which have come to an end, and to things which must in their nature come to an end. Therefore it does not signify endless duration. Besides, the word "everlasting," or "eternal," is from *aion*, which means age; and frequently our Savior spoke of the *end* of the *aion*, or age. Surely he would not speak of the end of a period of time that has no end. This is the significance of these threats uttered against those who were so shriveled in selfishness that they refused bread to the hungry and water to the thirsty, refused to take the stranger in, clothe the naked, visit the sick, and go to those in prison. They must be cured! Punishment is administered to cure, and must last till it has accomplished its purpose. This is the full meaning of the everlasting punishment in the passage under consideration. And the everlasting fire has great significance. It means that the selfishness of those people was to be destroyed, burned out. "Devil and his angels" are figurative terms, to intensify the burning process, the fires of remorse that would continue until those guilty souls were cleansed, purged, purified. Remember, the fire symbol in the Bible means this. Fire is an agent of destruction and an emblem of purification. See First Corinthians 3: 11–15 and Hebrews 12: 29. So, then, these threats, that seem so awful, mean what the promises mean, namely that all sinful souls *shall be cured.*

5

* * *

All means universal, Universalism means all. It is from the word universe. There is nothing good in the universe which it does not include. As a system of belief it includes all that is good and true in all religions ancient and modern, in all systems, in all philosophies, in all churches, in all worlds, and in all the universe. I accept the Christian religion as the infallible, the authoritative religion, because it takes up into itself and embodies all that is good and true; excludes only that which is false. There are but few Christians to-day who will not agree with us in the universality of the Christian religion in respect to its provisions. Its provisions, they say, are universal, but not its results. We affirm that it will be universal in its results. If not so, the provisions are inadequate, therefore not universal. And until all Christians shall come to believe that the religion of Christ will be universal in its results, the denominational name we bear must be retained, distinguishing us from Christians of other sects. Only in this sense, therefore, are we under obligation to remain sectarian. Loyalty to truth demands it of us.

There is truth in all churches, and error too. If any church assumes infallibility, that it is right and all others are wrong, that church is guilty of colossal egotism. There is no infallible church. If a man assumes he knows all there is worth knowing, and shuts himself against all the open avenues of truth and knowledge, he is guilty of monumental conceit! How superficial such a man! Great thinkers, the ripest scholars, are humble men because they know so little. They are men who know enough to know how little they know. I believe the Methodists have some truth, and the Baptists and the Presbyterians and the Episcopalians, and possibly the Catholics. I believe the Universalists have a little, not much. But Universalism, this system of faith, includes all the truth that all churches have. Do not misunderstand me. I am not saying that we have all the truth. We know but little. Universalism includes the little we have learned and all there is to be learned. It includes all that all men know and all that they don't know. Now, if a partialist ever suffers himself to say a word against Universalism, he says that word against all the truth he has; for it is part of the whole. I am sure that I cannot be misunderstood when I say we believe more than any other Christians. We do if the whole is greater than a part. We stand for the *whole*. Our system of faith must include all truth that has been discovered, and all that is yet to be discovered. Hence it is a progressive faith.

I trust the way is now prepared for a more specific statement of our affirmations.

1. We believe in this world, in the book of nature. All the laws of nature are God's laws, and are working out his purposes. They point to fulfillment, to victory, and not to defeat. This glorious prophecy is in every movement and evolution witnessed by the eye of science. The divine writing is on every page of this great volume; earth and cloud and sky all teaching the ways of God. Everywhere is the

6

impress of benevolence and radiance of eternal beauty. What a joy to live in God's beautiful world, with its teeming fields and waving forests and fruitful valleys and towering mountains and flowing streams! How thankful must we be for the thronging delights in this lower mansion of our Father's House. Let us cultivate a love for this world, and try to live here and enjoy it as long as we can. Its victories will fit us for higher victories, and there will be compensations for its defeats. Restorative and compensating laws are ever active, making good the losses. Science, penetrating to the heart of nature and unsealing its hidden laws, teaches man that there is but one force, with different manifestations. It manifests itself in magnetism, in electricity, in heat and motion, in chemical affirmity, etc.; but there is but one great central force, and that is good. Way back in the benighted past, man, lacking foresight to see how the discords and conflicts of nature would result in harmony, came to ascribe things he called evil to evil beings; hence the world's belief in devils, ghosts, hobgoblins, and witches. All these are perishing; the light of science is killing them.

Should one atom get beyond the reach of this one force, there would be endless discord in the universe. Should one soul get beyond the reach of this one force — and what shall we call it now? The force behind all forces and all worlds is love; if God is love, should one soul get beyond the reach of this Almighty force of love so that it is unable to draw it back, win it back, then there would be two forces in the universe, eternal discord. We believe no such catastrophe can happen. Nature means victory. Therefore we read Universalism from this book. Every law operative here, and all the laws relating our world to other worlds, are prophetic of victory. Nowhere in this universe do we read a prophecy of defeat.

2. Universalism affirms belief in human nature, another book whose writings point to victory. We stand for the worth of man. Fashioned in God's image, man is of infinite value, worth more in the sight of God than all the stars of heaven. The divine Fatherhood means this. Though yet a child, incomplete, imperfect, wayward, man bears the image of God, which image God himself cannot destroy or lose; God cannot destroy a thing that is indestructible. Wrapped up in this divine embryo are capacities and powers that fit man for endless growth and progress; for, between man the finite, and God the infinite, there is scope for a progression that can never end. What joy in believing this; for man is truly happy only when he is growing, and here is assurance of endless growth. In this sense the spiritual perfection reached by God's children will be relative, not absolute. There is but one absolute Being, and we may approximate his perfection forever.

Man is not made, he is making. Those who have made greatest progress are still in the Father's primary school. There will be higher departments, one grade leading to another, on and up forever. The school of God will never let out.

* * *

7

We need only to know the meaning of Fatherhood to be assured of God's regard for his children. In his Sermon on the Mount, our Savior calls the Supreme Being Father or Heavenly Father sixteen times. Some take the position that God is not the Father of evil men, but in this sermon the Master says he is. If he is not, we are all spiritual orphans, and have no right to say the Lord's Prayer; and how guilty of inconsistency when we go down among the wicked, teaching them to say this prayer if God is not their Heavenly Father.

Universalism affirms belief in inherent immortality. Without this divine inheritance what can man do to become immortal? No more than a tree. The trouble is, Christian people have failed to make a distinction between immortal life and eternal life. It was a part of Christ's mission to *reveal* immortality, but no part of his mission to create it. Immortal life has reference to duration; eternal life to quality. Said Jesus, "This is life eternal, to know thee the only true God and Jesus Christ whom thou hast sent." Then it is spiritual knowledge, or love in the soul. This it was Christ's mission to create. Were this simple fact understood the doctrine of conditional immortality, that it is acquired through faith in Christ, would soon vanish from the minds of men.

*   *   *

3. There is another book Universalists believe in. Most heartily we believe in the Bible, and we stand for the spiritual interpretation of the sacred volume. We go beneath figurative speech, metaphor, symbol, parable. Surface students, by literalizing these, have missed the deep meanings, and built up doctrines contrary to the great principles disclosed in this book. When reasoning from these three great books, the book of nature, the book of human nature, and the book of revelation, we get our ideas of life and destiny, and proclaim them to the world, convinced that these three books agree. How often we meet with such words as these: "Oh, yes, your doctrines are grand, I would like to believe them; but how can I! for there is the Bible." Then the Bible, they think, contradicts the book of human nature. If this is correct, God writes one revelation in the hearts of his children and on the pages of nature's volume, and another in a book; divided against himself. Friends, when interpreted by its general tone and spirit, the Bible supports Universalism most strongly. It is a book of hope, a book of victory. From beginning to end its Universalism shines forth. Temporary defeats are recognized as coming to men, but not final. And when God is recognized, when his guiding hand is seen, there is no such thing intimated as defeat or failure. The whole trend is toward victory. Notes of melody, strains of hope, songs of victory, rise and throb, and blend in anthems of rapture, and the glad refrain goes pulsing on. In the first pages we have a prophecy of victory. The truth, symboled by the seed of the woman, should crush the serpent's head; symbol of all that is bad in man. In the very last chapter, in that book of visions, that same prophecy glows in more exultant strains. We see standing by the river, clear as crystal, the tree of life,

8

called the tree of life because it will never die. "And its leaves are for the healing of the nations." That means final Universal cure.

✻ ✻ ✻

4. Universalism affirms a perfect God. He is good. He is perfectly good. He is love. He is perfect love. He is Father. He is a perfect Father. He is perfect in all his attributes. Calvinism limits his goodness. Simplified, it says: God can save all men, but he does not want to. Arminianism limits his power. It says: he wants to save all men, but cannot. And how glaring is the limitation of his wisdom according to the superficial free-will argument so often met with! We are told that God will not save a man against his will, that he cannot save an unwilling soul. What Universalist ever taught that God will save a man against his will? He does not save men that way, by arbitrary force; that is not his method. He saves men by their wills, through moral influence. Strange people cannot be made to understand that God has resources in his universe, the all-conquering agencies of love, to make the unwilling soul willing! He has light enough to make the blind see, and love enough to melt the hardened heart. See now how the free-will argument limits the wisdom of God. He is omniscient, all-knowing. Then from the beginning he knew when he made man a free moral agent that he was giving him power to defeat the divine purpose, giving his child power to work out his own eternal ruin and shatter the throne of Heaven; knew that he was giving his child a power which he himself could not control. In other words, a power was bestowed on man mightier than the Almighty. That is, God made man stronger than himself. What are we to think of his wisdom? Doesn't this limit the divine wisdom? Now, then, when we limit God's goodness or power or wisdom, we made him an imperfect God. If God is not perfect, there is no God. So this is atheism. Make what else of it you can.

✻ ✻ ✻

5. Universalists believe in a victorious Savior. We do not believe in the Deity of Christ, but in his divinity. If he were the "very God" how could he *increase* in wisdom? And we would have no example, no spiritual pattern. An absolute being cannot be an example for a finite being. Knowing we cannot reach the infinite, we have nothing to stimulate us to strive for perfection. The mission of Christ was to disclose the Heavenly Father to his children, and make his love a saving power. He did not create the Father's love. He revealed it. It was his mission to *make* Christians, not to save them. To become a Christian is to be saved. It is not going somewhere; it is *becoming something*. To express it all in a sentence, the mission of Christ was to *cure all men of sin*. We are Universalists because we believe he will accomplish the work he came to do; he will *succeed*. We believe it for three reasons: (*a*) He has medicine enough to cure all. (*b*) He has sufficient skill to administer the medicine. (*c*) He has sufficient time to administer the medicine in. So we can sing consistently about the good physician. He will never save a good man. To become good is to be saved. He

9

will never save a righteous man. To be saved is not going somewhere after one becomes righteous; it is *becoming* righteous. Christ has no more to do with getting men to heaven, in the sense of a *place* in another world, than he has to do with getting them across the Mississippi River. To believe, then, in a Universal Savior, a triumphant Savior, is to believe more in Christ than any other Christian people. And so we sing our glad song of victory. The lost, Christ came to seek and save; but these the very people he came to save, and needing salvation most, some Christians think he will lose. Universalism makes its strong affirmation that Jesus will save, redeem from sin, all the lost!

6. Universalism affirms a good destiny for the entire human race. At the outset I dwelt upon this distinguishing feature of our faith. A few additional words I think are necessary for the reason that, however clear we make to ourselves our views touching destiny, we are still confronted, and how frequently, with the old question, "What will become of wicked people who die in their sins?" The idea seems fixed in the minds of people that God can do nothing for his sinful children after they leave this world. Now, the relationship existing between the spiritual Father and his children is spiritual. Death cannot change it. Death cannot separate us from the love of God, said the great apostle. Has redeeming love physical limitations? Will we get beyond its reach by going to another world? It would be as reasonable to confine its action to New York, or even to Rhode Island, as to confine it to this world.

What, then, is our answer to this question so perplexing to many anxious souls? This: Those who are not cured in this world, and none are completely cured here, will be cured in the next. Old Orthodoxy says they will be sent to an eternal penitentiary. New Orthodoxy says they will establish themselves in endless rebellion against God, become eternal anarchists. The doctrine of annihilation, another phase of New Orthodoxy, says they will be blotted out of existence. Which answer can you best harmonize with the will and purpose and character of an infinitely good God? Universalism answers, *They will be cured.*

The doctrine of endless brutality, politely called eternal punishment, must be utterly abhorrent to every thinking mind, revolting to every benevolent instinct. It is a hideous, ghastly, fiendish doctrine, heart-paralyzing, soul-stifling. It makes God infinitely worse than Nero, his malignancy transcending that of all the fiends of cruelty that ever lived. If true for only one soul, then that soul will receive more pain from the hands of God than the whole human family have received from all the monsters of brutality that have cursed our world; because there is no end to it. This doctrine is the great satanic blasphemy of the ages. Its ghastliness is monumental. It out-pagans the blackest paganism! It ought to be a disgrace to preach the colossal infamy! It should cause the most brutal savage to blush with shame to listen to it! It has crushed more hearts, darkened more homes, caused more insanity and suffering and pain, it has made more infidels and atheists, than all other scourges that have ever desolated our fair world! Oh, friends! I can't do it just could make all men see its hideousness as I see it, and hate the it. I hate it!

How sad to hear good, generous, kind-hearted people say they be would be insane if they did. They are phonograph-Christians. They sii what has been talked into them. No benevolent man, no man who has a s ... in him, can sit down and think of the doctrine five minutes without discarding it forever. How benumbing to the sensibilities of good people! When we ask them how they expect to be happy in heaven when their fellowmen, and possibly their own loved ones, are suffering in torment, and doomed to remain and suffer endless pain, they answer, "Oh, we will be so changed!" This is the saddest thing I ever heard. Think what it means! It means ossification of the heart. It means that they are to undergo a process of hardening, that they are to be robbed of love, robbed of all feeling and sympathy and tenderness and pity! What a change! Hearts tender here with Christ's compassion there will turn to stone. It means a world of eternal heartlessness. Whittier says, "If man goes to heaven without a heart, God knows he leaves behind his better part."

Friends, I am more concerned about the destiny of saints, such as are to undergo this change, than the most wicked sinners that leave this world unsaved. In all reverence I ask, would you not ten thousand times rather be an asbestos sinner in the lowest hell with some feeling left than to be a petrified saint in heaven? According to this common answer, holiness in heaven will consist in being wholly selfish!

Finally, we believe in a good destiny for all; that God will cure all his sinful children, because He has the *disposition*, the *power*, the *means*, and the *time*. Four good reasons. A million more might be given; and no man can think of one single reason why he should not cure them.

So we sing the glad song of victory. All the resources of the universe are pledged to the great consummation, God's character, and his infinite love. I love to think of the agencies we see now at work. Every exertion you put forth to make this world better is so much done to make our doctrine true. God works though instrumentalities. We are all to be agents. A Universalist who is idle, doing nothing to make his doctrine true, is a counterfeit.

* * *

Oh! friends, stand on these heights, catch this vision, sing this song, this glad new song; voice it with the pæans of angelic choirs; let your glad and joyous strain blend with the music of the stars. Come down and sing it with the prophets of a larger day; sing it with the poets of a sweeter tune.

SOURCE: Quillen Shinn, "Affirmations of Universalism," in *Good Tidings*, compiled by Q. H. Shinn (Boston and Chicago: Universalist Publishing House, 1900), 68–79, 81, 83–89.

MARION SHUTTER

Applied Evolution

1900

Marion D. Shutter (1853–1939) served as minister of the Church of the Redeemer (now First Universalist) in Minneapolis from his 1891 graduation from St. Lawrence University and the University of Chicago until his death. A vigorous social gospeler, Shutter founded Minneapolis's first settlement house, participated actively in city politics, and served as president of the Universalist General Convention from 1911 to 1915. Like many Unitarian and Universalist ministers of his generation, Shutter enthusiastically embraced Darwinian evolution as a vindication of liberal theology. His approach to the unity of science and theology was indebted to the work of historian and philosopher John Fiske, to whom he dedicated Applied Evolution. *Further Reading: Russell E. Miller,* The Larger Hope: The Second Century of the Universalist Church in America, 1870–1970 *(Boston: Unitarian Universalist Association, 1985), 94–108.*

—Dan McKanan

Let us be perfectly candid. Let us not blind ourselves to facts. Let us not refuse to look with open eyes at the universe under the new light that has been thrown upon it. It will be time enough to give up God when we must. Meanwhile, how stands the case? The planet on which we live rolled, after incalculable ages, out of the original fire-mist. The plants and flowers that wreathe its brown have developed from the fewest and simplest germs, into equatorial pomp and splendor. From the ooze of the ocean, one form of life after another, came the animal kingdoms. From stage to stage, along the upward ascent of being, has crept the ancestral line of man. The final product of this ascending energy, he stands at the summit of the mountain up which the slow and painful ages have toiled. These are the facts that are almost universally accepted among scholars and thinkers to-day.

There are three ways of considering these facts. The agnostic looks upon this sublime spectacle and says, "I can make nothing out of it. I do not know how it has been produced and kept in progress." The materialist says, "The forces in matter were themselves sufficient. There is nothing more!" Now the religious man, if he is wise, will turn to those who have discovered these facts, and say, "I accept the situation. I cannot gainsay your evidence. I am convinced by your arguments. I believe in Evolution as thoroughly as you. I go the whole length of the doctrine and include body and soul in the process. But I cannot stop here. This is not the whole story. I demand an explanation, and an explanation that shall be adequate to the problem, and worthy of the magnificent scheme you have so amply demonstrated." . . .

We have not lost God; we have only lost an old idea of His way of doing things. I have already spoken of the goal of Evolution. I want to speak now of the God of Evolution, who is in the process, guiding it to the glorious culmination.

The God of Evolution is inside of Nature and not outside of it. And when we consider that man himself is a part of Nature, and the best part of it, we must find God also in him, preeminently in him.

1. The view that has hitherto prevailed represents God as a great master mechanic, far away above us and beyond our reach, who once upon a time, long ago, and once for all, worked, created matter, endowed it with necessary properties and powers, "constructed at once out of hand this wonderful cosmos, with its wheels within wheels, put springs into it, set it a-going and then rested."

So far as having anything further to do with it is concerned, except to interfere now and then with its working, He might have been sleeping or dead since the first Sabbath. God is external to Nature and man and only comes in contact with them when he wishes to work a miracle or answer a prayer. The imagery under which God is so often represented comes to us from a pre-scientific age, and is drawn from the human workman and the fabric he constructed. The workman was outside of the table or couch or implement which he shaped; outside of the stone which he fashioned for the temple. So God was conceived as being outside of His universe, something or someone as much apart from it as the carpenter from his block of wood, or the mason from his block of granite. Other imagery—especially that relating to the administration of the universe—has come from the times in which the king or emperor was absolute and supreme. Hence, the God of our theology is a royal personage, a magnified earthly monarch upon his throne,—a throne in the distant heavens,—surrounded by his attendants and courtiers in the shape of archangels; indeed, it was through these that he generally communicated with that outlying territory, the earth, and rarely deigned to visit its inhabitants in person. Caesar had business in Rome; his emissaries must look after the provinces. Even now many Christians feel that they cannot approach God directly, cannot speak to Him face to face, but must come to Him through His Son, or Mary, or some of the saints. As for God Himself, He sits upon His solemn throne, wrapped in robes of seclusion, dwelling in unapproachable grandeur. There is a chasm, wide and deep, between Him and His universe, between Him and man!

On the other hand, the scientific theory of resident forces compels us to find intelligence, purpose, and righteousness in some power within the universe itself and not apart from the universe; we must find "God resident in nature, at all times and in all place, directing every phenomenon,—a God in whom, in the most literal sense, not only we, but all things have their being, in whom all things exist, and without whom there would be and could be nothing."

Perhaps the best illustration we can find is that of the relationship between body and soul in man. Within the body, controlling and directing all its movements and forces, is the mind or spirit. Take this away, and the body lies stark and dead. There is no longer activity. No thought leaps forth from the brain, the tongue is silent, the right hand has lost its cunning. So within nature, controlling and directing all its movements and energies, is God. All outward phenomena are but the manifestations of His thought, all force is but the exercise of His will, all laws are but the regular modes of His activity. As Martineau has very finely said: "The laws of nature are the habits of God." And these are uniform and unchangeable, because He Himself is immutable,—the One with whom there is no variableness, neither "shadow of turning." Thus the law of gravitation resolves into the divine methods of sustaining the universe, holding its planets in place, keeping them within their orbits,—as the laws of cohesion and chemical affinity are the pressure of his hand-clasp upon the materials of which the planets themselves are composed. And thus the processes of evolution become the divine method of originating and developing the universe itself. Take Him away and the universe crumbles. The sun no longer shines. The stars are dead. The earth turns to ice. The planets dash from their orbits in confusion. And man himself perishes amid the "wreck of matter and the crush of worlds!" It is only in Him that we live and move and have our being. One cannot hold on to the old idea of God, as outside of His universe; he is compelled to find Him inside of nature, as he finds the human soul within the human body. To one who takes this view, as John Fiske says: "No part of the universe is Godless."

SOURCE: Marion D. Shutter, *Applied Evolution* (Boston: Eugene F. Endicott, 1900), 246–52.

FRANCIS GREENWOOD PEABODY

Jesus Christ and the Social Question

1900

Unitarian minister and Harvard professor Francis Greenwood Peabody (1847–1936) was a moderate social gospeler and a founder of the academic discipline of social ethics. The son of King's Chapel minister Ephraim Peabody, he was brother-in-law to both Henry Whitney Bellows and Harvard president Charles Eliot and uncle to American Unitarian Association president Samuel Atkins Eliot. At Harvard, Peabody made case-based courses on social problems an integral part of the Divinity School curriculum; one offering was popularly known as "Peabo's Drainage, Drunkenness, and Divorce." As Preacher to the University, he persuaded Harvard to become the first major college to make chapel attendance optional for students. His book Jesus and the Social Question *was both an invitation to Christians to take social problems seriously and a rebuttal to socialists and anarchists who claimed Jesus as one of their own. Further Reading: Gary Dorrien,* Social Ethics in the Making: Interpreting an American Tradition *(Malden, MA: Wiley-Blackwell, 2009), 7–20.*

—Dan McKanan

Here, then, is a perplexing situation. To a vast majority of those who are most concerned with the social question, the Christ of the churches is an object of complete indifference, if not of positive scorn; while to a Christ far removed from the traditions and creeds of Christian worship,—an unmysterious, human leader of the poor,—there is given an honor which as a supernatural being he no longer receives. On the other hand, to the vast majority of Christian worshippers this conception of Jesus as a labor-leader and social revolutionist appears a most inadequate and unhistorical picture of the Christ of the gospels. What have we here but a clean break between the tradition of the past and the need of the present? On the one hand is the ancient and precious story of the relation of Jesus to the individual soul, his revelation of the Father to the child, and his revelation of the child to himself, his message to the religious life in its experiences of sin, repentance, and spiritual peace; and on the other hand is this new and unprecedented appreciation of the external ills of environment and misfortune, of social wrong and injustice, and the discovery that here also Jesus Christ has a message of stern rebuke and pitying love. Is there, then, a permanent chasm set between the work of the Christian Church and the need of the modern world? Is there not unity to be discovered beneath these diverse conceptions of the teaching of Jesus? Must it happen that the force of the Christian religion shall be limited to spiritual and personal renewal, and shall have no part in directing the social movement of the time; or if, on the other hand, the person of Jesus finds a place in the social question, must it be at the cost of his spiritual leadership and religious significance? Must we choose between Christ the Saviour and Jesus the Demagogue; or is there in the religion of Jesus a quality and character which of themselves create a social message such as the modern world needs to hear? These are the questions which confront one as he observes the alienation between Christian teaching and social needs, and which invite to fresh inquiry concerning the social teaching of the gospel.

*　*　*

There are, however, several aspects of his ministry which must be clearly recognized before this teaching can be interpreted in its full significance or scope. In the first place, as one sums up his general impression of the gospels, it becomes obvious that, whatever social teaching there may be in them, and however weighty it may be, the mind of the Teacher was primarily turned another way. The supreme concern of Jesus throughout his ministry was, — it may be unhesitatingly asserted, — not the reorganization of human society, but the disclosure to the human soul of its relation to God. Jesus was, first of all, not a reformer but a revealer; he was not primarily an agitator with a plan, but an idealist with a vision. . . .

Still further, there was at times in the spiritual attitude of Jesus a certain quality of remoteness and detachment from the social problems which were presented to his mind. He refused to be entangled in them. Distribution of property was not within his province: "Man," he says, "who made me a judge or a divider over you?" Forms of government were not for him to change: "Render therefore unto Caesar the things that are Caesar's." There was political oppression about him to be remedied, there were social unrighteousness and iniquity to be condemned; but Jesus does not fling himself into these social issues of his time. He moves through them with a strange tranquility, not as one who is indifferent to them, but as one whose eye is fixed on an end in which these social problems will find their own solution.

*　*　*

Here, then, are two characteristics of the gospel which would seem in some degree to obscure its social teaching, — an evident subordination of social problems, and an equally evident limitation of instruction to specific instances and occasions. Jesus speaks chiefly of God, and speaks chiefly to the individual. It would seem, then, as if we must have been misled in anticipating from him a clear and impressive teaching concerning the social world. If Jesus was not primarily devoted to the social question, and if again his teaching was chiefly personal and occasional instead of systematic and universal, is it not difficult to derive from it any general principles

16

which shall be applicable to the problems of modern social life? On the contrary, one must answer, it is precisely these two characteristics, his relation to God and his relation to the individual, the loftiness of his Theism and the precision of his occasionalism, which open, as we consider them, into the social principles of the teaching of Jesus.

SOURCE: Francis Greenwood Peabody, *Jesus Christ and the Social Question: An Examination of the Teaching of Jesus in Its Relation to Some of the Problems of Modern Social Life* (New York: The MacMillan Company, 1900), 65–67, 77–78, 83–84.

CHARLES W. WENDTE

Report of the General Secretary of the International Council of Unitarian and Other Liberal Religious Thinkers and Workers

1901

The International Council of Unitarian and other Liberal Religious Think-
ers and Workers was organized in 1900 to bring together a global community
of Unitarians and like-minded religious liberals. This was a time of increas-
ing denominational centralization and confidence. Samuel Atkins Eliot had
just persuaded the American Unitarian Association—once again the central
denominational body—to create a stronger presidency, and liberals around
the world were eager to be connected to the growing American movement. The
Council's leading figure for its first two decades was Charles W. Wendte
(1844–1931), a minister who had previously served as AUA missionary super-
visor for the West Coast, helped organize what would become the Starr King
School for the Ministry, and participated in the 1893 Parliament of World
Religions. The Council changed its name repeatedly as it sought to balance
its role in uniting Unitarians worldwide with its aspiration to be a truly inter-
faith organization. Since 1969 it has been known as the International Associ-
ation for Religious Freedom (IARF), and it remains an interfaith body with
a strong Unitarian contingent today. Since 1995, specifically denominational
work in the global context has shifted to the International Council of Uni-
tarians and Universalists (ICUU). Further Reading: Robert Traer, "A Short
History of the IARF," and Josef Boehle, "Inter-religious Co-operation in a
Global Age," both available online at iarf.net/about/history/

—Dan McKanan

Representatives of many nationalities and churches, we are met here in friendly
conference at the invitation of the International Council of Unitarian and other
Liberal Religious Thinkers and Workers.

This Council was organized on May 25th, 1900, at Boston, in the United States,
by Foreign Delegates and others in attendance at the seventy-fifth anniversary of the
founding of the American Unitarian Association.

The mutual interchange of liberal ideas and friendly sentiments among the
free-thinking men and women, of diverse nationalities and religious antecedents,
who had been thus brought together, created among them a general desire for more

18

frequent reunions of like nature, and a continuance of the fraternal and inspiring relations so auspiciously begun. It was agreed that a permanent organization should be effected to bring into closer union, for exchange of ideas, mutual service, and the promotion of their common aims, the scattered liberal congregations, and isolated thinkers and workers for religious freedom, in many lands.

*　*　*

A committee, consisting of Messrs. Batchelor, Boros, Bowie, Eliot, Hocart, and Wendte, was appointed to prepare a plan of organization.

This committee reported the following day, May 25th, 1900, to the re-assembled delegates, their recommendations as follows:—

First.—That the proposed association be called "The International Council of Unitarian and other Liberal Religious Thinkers and Workers."

Second.—That the object of this Council shall be to open communication with those who, in all lands, are striving to unite pure Religion and perfect Liberty, and to increase fellowship and co-operation among them.

Third.—That as this purpose demands neither a fixed constitution nor an elaborate official organization, the foregoing provisions be the only stated Articles of the Association, and that all questions concerning the best methods to be employed in the conduct of the interests committed to the said Council be left to the future to determine, as experience, opportunity, correspondence and conference shall disclose the scope and possibilities of its work.

Fourth.—That the officers of the Council consist of a president and a general secretary, who, together with an executive committee, shall be chosen at each meeting to carry out its objects.

*　*　*

With so large and widespread a response, it has become more and more apparent to us during the year, that the formation of this Council was timely and needed, and that we are inaugurating a movement of profound significance, and great promise of usefulness on behalf of Liberal Religion. The remarkable advance in civilization during the past century has brought the nations of the earth into closer and more complex relations, and made them conscious, as never before, of their interdependence and mutual obligations. The ultimate "Federation of the World" for ideal and fraternal ends is no longer merely a poet's dream; it is an axiom of sound political ethics. The organization of international effort, which has already accomplished so much in the interests of industry and commerce, learned scholarship, scientific research, and political action, should, with even greater reason, be extended to the field of religion. It should be recognized more universally, that nativity and language and religious antecedents form no insurmountable barrier to an international union of hearts and hands for the religious enlightenment and emancipation of mankind.

Already this conviction has led to great International Assemblies of Orthodox Christian Believers in the interest of their particular church or sect.

*   *   *

The same conviction and fraternal impulse have led to the organization of the International Council of Unitarian and other Liberal Religious Thinkers and Workers. It is believed that its sessions, held every two or three years in different countries, will attract public attention and lend influence to its united testimony for advanced religious and ethical ideas. It is believed furthermore, that it will strengthen the hearts and hands of lonely workers for religious truth and freedom in many lands, and that the religious bodies who may unite with it will feel themselves growing in power and influence by the consciousness of larger fraternal relations and a broader organic life. In this good hope we meet to-day, under these happy auspices, to inaugurate what we trust will become a permanent and influential movement for the union in all lands and among all peoples of pure religion and perfect liberty.

SOURCE: Charles W. Wendte, "The Report of the General Secretary," in W. Copeland Bowie, ed., *Liberal Religious Thought at the Beginning of the Twentieth Century* (London: Philip Green, 1901), 321–23, 327–29.

HAJOM KISSOR SINGH

Preamble to the Constitution of the Unitarian Union of North East India

1901

In the mid-nineteenth century, Welsh Calvinists introduced Christianity to the Khasi people of northeast India, a minority ethnic group that had never practiced Hinduism. One early convert, Hajom Kissor Singh (1865–1923) soon rebelled against aspects of Calvinism that he viewed as incompatible with both traditional Khasi values and the teachings of Jesus. Singh developed his own distinctive theology and gathered a worshipping community, after which a member of the Brahmo Samaj referred him to the Unitarian missionary Charles Dall (1816–1886) and then to Jabez Sunderland, who visited the Khasi Hills in 1896. Khasi Unitarianism has been in dialogue and partnership with Unitarians in other parts of the world ever since. This preamble was translated from Khasi to English in 1999 by D. K. B. Mukhim, working with John Rex. Further Reading: Spencer Lavan, Unitarians and India: A Study in Encounter and Response *(Boston: Skinner House, 1977).*

—Dan McKanan

In the establishment of the Union (or meeting) the members in a joint decision with the Unitarian Elders from this country and with J. D. Sunderland and with the Committee of the Unitarian Union from this country, the British and Foreign Unitarian Association in 1896 made the rules of our UNION. Since then they have been amended time and again according to the demands of the times and the progress in the understanding of the members. In these later years a necessity has been felt to print them so that all friends may read them with understanding. Therefore they have been considered in detail and amended and approved as printed in the following pages, by the Unitarian Union in April, 1901.

Now we want every Unitarian, male or female, to study them in detail till they understand clearly their meanings.

In the management of the Committee or the Board, when there is any consideration, if there are some people who do not agree with the majority, it is not for them who are a minority to feel disappointed, to sulk, and to withdraw support, but to resolve together with a liberal and compassionate spirit, as the majority feels satisfied, and to share the burden of that resolution as if it were their very own.

Being a Member or Elder does not mean to be arrogant or to issue discretionary orders, but it is the work to do and to serve and to give one's self and from one's self the energy, the spirit, and the time, so that the Union will flourish.

The general members are to work together to support, to instruct/inspire, and to be faithful to the Elders by remembering that togetherness is strength, without relying too much on the Elders alone. For if every man simply looks up to the Elders, the work will not progress. It is necessary to have uniformity and faithfulness of the followers so that the work will progress well. If every man considers himself an Elder and feels it is difficult to obey and to be uniform together, then who will the Elders command and how will the work progress? Nonuniformity always shows arrogance, and arrogance shows foolishness and irresponsibility.

About the Collections: It is necessary for every Unitarian, however poor they may be, to take the responsibility and to pay certain and regular collections to the Church and the Union and the MISSION FUND according to their earning besides collections set in Rule IX. It is a better way for members to give the collections to the Union at the time of naming children and at the time of marriage for their subscription in such times is a token to express their special thankfulness to GOD.

SOURCE: John Rex, "Khasi Unitarians of North East India: A Presentation to the Harper's Ferry Ministerial Study Group," unpublished paper, November 1999, 19–20.

HAJOM KISSOR SINGH AND ROBIN ROY

The Booklet of Brief Questions about Unitarianism

c. 1901/1960

This catechism was written by Hajom Kissor Singh and his associate Robin Roy around the turn of the twentieth century, then published (and perhaps rearranged) in the Khasi language in 1960 and 1974. It reveals the distinctive features of Khasi Unitarian theology: an emphatic monotheism, a stress on duty as the essential element of religious practice, and a willingness to cite biblical authority despite the fact that many Khasi Unitarians have never understood themselves as Christians. It was translated into English by D. K. B. Mukhim, working with John Rex, and was revised and approved by the board of the Unitarian Union.

—Dan McKanan

1. *Who made you?* God made us and all things, seen and unseen, in the heavens and on earth.
2. *What has God given us?* All things, whatever we have or obtain have been given by God.
3. *Does God see us?* Yes. God sees and hears us unceasingly, night and day, and He knows all that we propose and think because He is within us and outside us, in all places and in all things.
4. *How many Gods are there?* There is only one God, and none others except Him.
5. *Who or what is God?* God is an everlasting Spirit, Life, Source, Designer and Creator, and Administrator of all things.
6. *What is the soul?* The soul is that which feels, loves, thinks, judges, understands, and wills; but human eyes cannot see it, nor hands touch it.
7. *Where do we find God?* God is within us; He is also there in the sky above, and in the earth below, and He is present in and pervades all places and all things. "In him we live and move and have our being." (Acts 17:28)

* * *

9. *What are the sources of knowledge about God?* (1) From our own conscience. (2) From our parents and friends. (3) From the teachings of Jesus and all saintly people. (4) From all the religious scriptures. (5) From all the things in this universe like the sun, the moon, the stars, and from all things above and beneath,

which are the true holy inscriptions from which we can learn about God, because they are all His creations. (Psalm 19:1–2)

10. *What is our relationship with God, which makes us feel closest to Him, etc.? (See question #5)* That God is our Father-Mother and that all people are His/Her children.

*   *   *

16. *(1) What is duty?* Duty is that which God has instilled in us and enabled us to do it. . . .

17. *What is our duty to God?* Our duty to God is: (1) To love, to obey, and to fear and revere Him with all our body and soul—in public or in private. (2) To worship Him; not to take the name of God in vain. (3) To feel that He is constantly with us at all times, in all places, and through all events.

*   *   *

24. *What is our duty to our fellow-human-beings?* Our duty to our fellow human-beings is to love them. (John 13:34–35)

25. *How do we love our fellow human-beings?* (1) To love our fellow human-beings means that we should not be suspicious of, speak ill of, do something wrong to, or speak rudely to anybody. (2) That we should not have ill feeling for, or be jealous of anybody, or sulk or quarrel with anybody; that we should not covet others' property or be selfish. (3) That we should not think in terms of our prosperity at the expense of others; but we ought to help, to co-exist in peace, and keep good will with all fellow human-beings. (4) In short—that we do unto others as we wish others to do to us without expecting reciprocation. This is the Golden Rule.

*   *   *

35. *What is our duty to ourselves?* (1) It is for us to be ready to devote ourselves to hard work in all our tasks; and to strive to improve ourselves in all our thoughts, words, and deeds. (2) We ought to avoid all forms of wrongdoing, or evil, and association with bad company, or allow temptations that would bring us a bad name, but to overcome and rid them by praying to God. (3) We must not have negative attitudes, or be ill hearted or ill tempered. (4) We ought to follow the dictates of our conscience.

SOURCE: John Rex, "Khasi Unitarians of North East India: A Presentation to the Harper's Ferry Ministerial Study Group," unpublished paper, November 1999, 24–28.

NELLIE M. STOUDER

"Value of the Mission Circle"

1905

*As Universalists and Unitarians developed stronger institutions in the wake
of the Civil War, both denominations created national women's organizations. The Woman's Centenary Association began when Universalist women
united to raise funds during the hundredth anniversary of John Murray's
arrival in North America. Formally established in 1871, its work was "to assist
weak parishes, foster poor Sunday-schools, help to educate worthy women
students for the ministry, relieve the wants of sick or disabled preachers, ministers' widows and orphans, distribute denominational literature, and do both
home and foreign missionary work." Lay and ordained women worked side
by side in the Association; its founding president was Caroline Soule, a minister. Early in the twentieth century, the renamed Woman's Universalist
National Missionary Association played a central role in both the mission to
Japan and the planting of a vigorous network of congregations in North Carolina. In this essay, published on the eve of the Association's name change,
corresponding secretary Nellie M. Stouder described the role of each local
Mission Circle. Further Reading: Centenary Voices; or, A Part of the Work
of the Women of the Universalist Church, from Its Centenary Year to the
Present Time (Philadelphia: Woman's Centenary Association, 1886).*

—Dan McKanan

The following extract from the report of the Atlanta church. . . . was made by Mr.
J. C. Bond at the recent Y.P.C.U. Convention:

"The Woman's Mission Circle of our church may be compared to any Circle
in the country. A braver band of loyal, devoted, consecrated Christian women is
not to be found anywhere. They hold their meetings regularly and have since they
organized, which was near the beginning of the movement for a church in Atlanta.
They have never failed to be the staunchest and strongest auxiliary we have and the
existence of our church today is due, in large measure, to their faithfulness and
consecration. . . ."

What is true of this Mission Circle may be said of most Circles throughout the
whole Church. The possibilities of the Mission Circle work are beyond measure,
and, we are glad to say, most of our women are beginning to realize this. Wherever
we find women banded together for church work, there we find the desire growing

for something more permanent than mere material gain. The need of spiritual growth manifests itself at once.

At the recent Convention of California, a most valuable paper was read by Mrs. Lena D. Skeels. . . . She says in part: "And to-day I want to plead for greater attention to the moral and spiritual good we as an organized body of women may do. Speaking of joining our Women's Association, I have heard it said, 'You pay your dollar and then what do you belong to? The association does nothing except collect the dues and use them for doing the good it can. Why not just as well give your money and not have the organization?' This may be true or no. However, let us have something else so plain that no person can help seeing what we have and do. Can we not . . . put into execution some measure whereby the lonely Universalist families may be saved from having to go to another household of faith to receive that bread of life of which all so need to eat, and save to our church and their church the power and energy and wealth that now flows to another?

"There are places in California where we haves several Universalist families and no services. If we could form a local circle of the Women's Association in these places might it not be the seed which in time shall germinate and grow into the large and flourishing tree? . . . Let us organize local branches of our association. As a suggestion for such meetings could we not in the afternoon have the ladies meet at some member's house, have a short Scripture reading, prayer, sacred song, singing and a paper or address or reading upon some spiritual, moral, charitable or other theme, with discussion afterward? Some such scheme as this would so promote the social and spiritual side of our life. And would it not intensify the denominational spirit within us? . . . I am so proud to be a Universalist! Are not you?

SOURCE: Nellie M. Stouder, "Value of the Mission Circle," *Universalist Leader*, September 9, 1905, 1138–39.

SEMPO ITO

"My Religion"

1905

The Universalist mission to Japan began in 1890, three years after the arrival of Unitarian missionaries in that country. Missionaries George Perin, Isaac Cate, and Margaret Shouler planted multiple congregations and a girls' school, and the Universalist presence in Japan continued for more than a century. Interest in the Japanese mission intensified during the Russo-Japanese War of 1904–1905, and in November 1905 the Leader *published a special Japan issue that featured the writings of several of the Japanese ministers serving mission congregations. In this piece, Sempo Ito, pastor of the church in Shidzuoko, offered his version of the Universalist message. Further Reading: Carl Seaburg,* Dojin Means All People: The Universalist Mission to Japan, 1890–1942 *(Boston: Universalist Historical Society, 1978).*

—Dan McKanan

Shukyo, the Japanese for religion, is a very familiar word, commonly used by almost every person in spoken as well as written language, but no word is there so much abused in that it is understood differently by different persons. . . .

Religion in its most comprehensive sense is what man thinks (intellect), feels (feeling), and does (volition), under the consciousness of relationship to a superior and mysterious power in the universe, that is to say, God. In short religion is man's relation to God. . . .

Now, making the controlling idea of God or gods the standard of distinction, there are four forms, viz., dualism, polytheism, pantheism and monotheism. Of these monotheism, which is represented by Judaism, Mohammedanism and Christianity, is the most scientific from every point of view in its conception of God. . . .

Christianity is indeed the most perfect religion of God that has ever been found for the whole human race. All the other religions have no doubt some truth, but Christianity has the absolute truth. No further truth of God than that of Christianity can ever be found. Unfortunately there are many people everywhere, and especially in Japan, who think that not only idol worship but even Christianity is nothing more than mere superstition. They think even the idea of God is man's imagination or an idler's dream, and is not worthy of any attention. This is, however, far from the truth. Christianity is the most rational religion of all and is consistent with the most advanced truth of modern science. Its doctrines and facts are indeed above, but not against reason, and the more scientific truth is discovered the nearer it approaches to Christian truth.

It is reasonable to believe in the existence of one supreme, self-existent Being, who is infinite in power, wisdom, holiness, goodness and love, of whom, by whom, in whom and through whom we have our being; and . . . every phenomenon of the universe is nothing but the self-manifestation or revelation of God if only we have the eyes of the poet or prophet. But a belief in a merely theistic God is not sufficient for our want. The goodness, wisdom, justice and power of God ought to be combined with another attribute, that is, a fatherly love, which alone satisfies the deepest want of the human heart. It is only in the religion of Christ that the Creator of the universe is called by the name of the heavenly Father, and no other religions have ever taught the Fatherhood of God and the brotherhood of man. . . . Universalism is nothing but the logical process of the Fatherhood of God and the brotherhood of man. There are no Christian denominations that do not believe the doctrine that God is our Father and that we are all brethren. But if there is any point to distinguish our special faith from all the other Christian denominations it is simply to give more emphasis and bring out into clearer light that God is the Father of all. . . .

Now what effect does this belief have upon human life? We should never say that it makes no difference whether we have this belief or not. I noticed once the wonderful courage of a little dog. Usually he was very cowardly when he was alone in the street, always running away from other dogs. . . . When he was at the gate of his master's house, or when he was walking after his master in the street he was an entirely different dog—so courageous that he did not run away; and sometimes he himself began to attack other dogs, even dogs much larger than he. Why did he have this courage which he did not possess in other circumstances? I think it was his belief that he was not alone but with his master, who always loved and protected him from any harm. Just so we are. . . . The faith in our Father in heaven is all in all. We are only to live just as a baby with its mother, trusting in whatever circumstances her benevolence may deem right. This is the secret source of Christ's great strength. Christ did not anything by his own power. All he did was by the faith that he was not alone but with the Father in heaven. All Christian strength comes out of this faith.

Moreover if God is the Father of all, and we are all his children, then we have a common relationship with one another as well as with God. We are all brethren; that is to say we are but one great family of all nations, colors, languages and conditions. . . .

This is the spirit in which I live under any and every circumstance through all my life. This is the reason why I am a Universalist Christian. Now I will conclude with the words: "God is love, and he who dwelleth in love dwelleth in God, and God in him."

SOURCE: Sempo Ito, "My Religion," *Universalist Leader*, November 4, 1905, 1390–91.

CHARLES W. ELIOT

"The Religion of the Future"

1909

Harvard president Charles W. Eliot (1834–1926) was the son of a mayor of Boston and the father of an American Unitarian Association president, both of them named Samuel Atkins Eliot. During his forty years as Harvard president, Eliot built the school into a modern research university with an elective-based undergraduate curriculum that emphasized the sciences more than the classics. In part because mandatory chapel was abolished during his presidency, Eliot is often seen as a champion of the secularization of the university, but he was also a committed Unitarian layman. Eliot's address to the Harvard Summer School of Theology epitomized the religious liberalism of the early twentieth century: expansive, optimistic, and confident in its place at the leading edge of religious evolution. Further Reading: Stephen P. Shoemaker, "The Theological Roots of Charles W. Eliot's Educational Reforms," Journal of Unitarian Universalist History 31 (2006–2007): 30–45.

—Dan McKanan

(1) The religion of the future will not be based on authority, either spiritual or temporal. The decline of the reliance upon absolute authority is one of the most significant phenomena of the modern world. This decline is to be seen everywhere — in government, in education, in church, in business, and in the family. The present generation is willing, and indeed often eager, to be led; but it is averse to being driven, and it wants to understand the grounds and sanctions of authoritative decisions. As a rule, the Christian churches, Roman, Greek, and Protestant, have heretofore relied mainly upon the principle of authority, the Reformation having substituted for an authoritative church an authoritative book; but it is evident that the authority both of the most authoritative churches and of the Bible as a verbally inspired guide is already greatly impaired, and that the tendency towards liberty is progressive, and among educated men irresistible.

(2) It is hardly necessary to say that in the religion of the future there will be no personifications of the primitive forces of nature, such as light, fire, frost, wind, storm, and earthquake, although primitive religions and the actual religions of barbarous or semi-civilized peoples abound in such personifications. The mountains, groves, volcanoes, and oceans will no longer be inhabited by either kindly or malevolent deities; although man will still look to the hills for rest, still find in the ocean a

symbol of infinity, and refreshment and delight in the forests and the streams. The love of nature mounts and spreads, while faith in fairies, imps, nymphs, demons, and angels declines and fades away.

(3) There will be in the religion of the future no worship, express or implied, of dead ancestors, teachers, or rulers; no more tribal, racial, or tutelary gods; no identification of any human being, however majestic in character, with the Eternal Deity. In these respects the religion of the future will not be essentially new, for nineteen centuries ago Jesus said, "Neither in this mountain, nor in Jerusalem, shall ye worship the Father . . . [ellipsis in original]. God is a Spirit; and they that worship him must worship in spirit and truth." . . .

(4) In the religious life of the future the primary object will not be the personal welfare or safety of the individual in this world or any other. That safety, that welfare or salvation, may be incidentally secured, but it will not be the prime object in view. The religious person will not think of his own welfare or security, but of service to others, and of contributions to the common good. The new religion will not teach that character is likely to be suddenly changed, either in this world or in any other,—although in any world a sudden opportunity for improvement may present itself, and the date of that opportunity may be a precious remembrance. The new religion will not rely on either a sudden conversion in this world or a sudden paradise in the next, from out a sensual, selfish, or dishonest life. It will teach that repentance wipes out nothing in the past, and is only the first step towards reformation, and a sign of a better future.

(5) The religion of the future will not be propitiatory, sacrificial, or expiatory. In primitive society fear of the supernal powers, as represented in the awful forces of nature, was the root of religion. . . .

(6) The religion of the future will not perpetuate the Hebrew anthropomorphic representations of God, conceptions which were carried in large measure into institutional Christianity. It will not think of God as an enlarged and glorified man. . . .

(7) The religion of the future will not be gloomy, ascetic, or maledictory. It will not deal chiefly with sorrow and death, but with joy and life. It will not care so much to account for the evil and the ugly in the world as to interpret the good and the beautiful. It will believe in no malignant powers—neither in Satan nor in witches, neither in the evil eye nor in the malign suggestion. When its disciple encounters a wrong or evil in the world, his impulse will be to search out its origin, source, or cause, that he may attack it at its starting-point. He may not speculate on the origin of evil in general, but will surely try to discover the best way to eradicate the particular evil or wrong he has recognized.

Having thus considered what the religion of the future will not be, let us now consider what its positive elements will be.

The new thought of God will be its most characteristic element. This ideal will comprehend the Jewish Jehovah, the Christian Universal Father, the modern physicist's omnipresent and exhaustless Energy, and the biological conception of a Vital Force. The Infinite Spirit pervades the universe, just as the spirit of a man pervades his body, and acts, consciously or unconsciously, in every atom of it. The twentieth century will accept literally and implicitly St. Paul's statement, "In Him we live, and move, and have our being," and God is that vital atmosphere, or incessant inspiration. The new religion is therefore thoroughly monotheistic, its God being the one infinite force; but this one God is not withdrawn or removed, but indwelling, and especially dwelling in every living creature. God is so absolutely immanent in all things, animate and inanimate, that no mediation is needed between him and the least particle of his creation. In his moral attributes, he is for every man the multiplication to infinity of all the noblest, tenderest, and most potent qualities which that man has ever seen or imagined in a human being. In this sense every man makes his own picture of God. Every age, barbarous or civilized, happy or unhappy, improving or degenerating, frames its own conception of God within the limits if its own experiences and imaginings. In this sense, too, a humane religion has to wait for a humane generation. The central thought of the new religion will therefore be a humane and worthy idea of God, thoroughly consistent with the nineteenth-century revelations concerning man and nature, and with all the tenderest and loveliest teachings which have come down to us from the past.

*   *   *

Finally, this twentieth-century religion is not only to be in harmony with the great secular movements of modern society—democracy, individualism, social idealism, the zeal for education, the spirit of research, the modern tendency to welcome the new, the fresh powers of preventative medicine, and the recent advances in business and industrial ethics—but also in essential agreement with the direct, personal teachings of Jesus, as they are reported in the Gospels. The revelation he gave to mankind thus becomes more wonderful than ever.

SOURCE: Charles W. Eliot, "The Religion of the Future," *Harvard Theological Review* 2 (October 1909): 391–95, 407.

ANNA GARLIN SPENCER

"The Vocational Divide," in
Woman's Share in Social Culture

1913

Anna Garlin Spencer (1851–931) was a minister, pacifist, writer, and educator about feminism, social ethics, and religious liberalism. She served as the minister of the liberal, independent Bell Street Chapel and as an associate leader of the New York Society for Ethical Culture, and she taught courses on social ethics and issues of women, family, marriage, and sexuality at the New York School of Philanthropy (now Columbia University's School of Social Work), the University of Wisconsin, the University of Chicago, Meadville Theological School, and Columbia's Teachers College. It was in this context of writing, speaking, and teaching that she published Woman's Share in Social Culture. *The book surveyed the role of women in society from prehistory through the present day, arguing persuasively on behalf of women's full involvement in society for the betterment of women as well as society as a whole. As a wife and mother herself, Spencer's insights into what she called "The Vocational Divide" between women who chose to work and women who chose to devote their efforts to their families remain insightful and useful commentaries today. Further Reading: Emily Mace, "'Citizens of All the World's Temples': Cosmopolitan Religion at Bell Street Chapel," in Leigh E. Schmidt and Sally M. Promey, eds.,* American Religious Liberalism *(Bloomington: Indiana University Press, 2012), 141–61.*

—Emily Mace

The spinster of to-day, educated and successful in vocational choice and work, is following after men in new fields of individual achievement and playing her part well. The wife and mother of to-day, educated and equally successful before marriage in vocational choice and work, is doing something far more significant, if less picturesque. She is blazing a new way of life-adjustment. She is experiencing far more than she understands; is experimenting with far greater success than clearness of interpretation; is feeling her way to the future double "sphere" of womanhood, led by a sure instinct of love and duty. Her heroism of pioneer adventure in a new way of social service will be appreciated only after the "woman movement" becomes past history.

The approach of man to vocational effort is single. Into the life of every woman who attains full experience of the possibilities of her nature there comes a vocational divide. On one side is the road leading to uninterrupted advance in her chosen career or accepted work; on the other side is the road leading to the hearth fire which most often she must tend if it is to be kept bright; and to the voices of children clamoring for admission to the gates of life she alone can open. At the upmost reach of choice on that vocational divide, she must balance the claims for self-expression on the one side, for family service on the other. Physical motherhood itself, among healthy women who live wisely, presents small obstacles to continuous vocational work. As a distinguished sociologist, a man, has said: "These experiences need cause no more interruption than the occasional illnesses or need for occasional rest on the part of men." Most women of to-day are not invalids, and childbearing is a natural process; and the present attention to the muscular development of girls and the checking of tendencies that make for "nerves" will, and do now, insure for the average woman a safe and comparatively easy maternity. The pathological conditions of much manual work that still give women disease and prevent healthy motherhood do, indeed, present social problems. But it is not physical motherhood that makes it difficult for the teacher or other professional woman, or the woman in the counting-room or secretary's position, to keep on with her chosen work after marriage and maternity. Several reasonable "leaves of absence" would adjust that matter. What constitutes the difficulty is not getting the children here, but taking care of them properly after they are born. Neither are the most serious problems of adjustment, in this country at least, those that concern the willingness of the husband to have his wife retain the freedom and joy of her own self-expression and its convenient reward in cash.

SOURCE: Anna Garlin Spencer, *Woman's Share in Social Culture* (New York: M. Kennerley, 1913), 150–51.

WILLIAM WALLACE FENN
"Modern Liberalism"
1913

In the years just before World War I, American religious liberalism was confident of its place in the vanguard of human history. But Harvard Divinity School dean William Wallace Fenn (1862–1932) offered a cautionary note that anticipated the postwar development of neo-orthodox theology and the awkward liberal attempts to respond to its challenge. Educated at Harvard— where he converted from orthodox Congregationalism to Unitarianism— Fenn served congregations in Pittsfield, Massachusetts, and Chicago and taught at Meadville Theological School before returning to his alma mater as professor and then dean. Fenn's overview of "modern liberalism" and its critics was acknowledged by James Luther Adams as a significant inspiration for his own work.

—Dan McKanan

Whether we like it or not, the fact is that there is a certain type of religious thinking now often called Modernism but formerly called Modern Liberalism, which the editors of the *American Journal of Theology* wish the present article briefly to describe and criticize.

The first characteristic, then, of this Modern Liberalism is its free attitude toward traditionalism whether in cult or in creed. . . .

So understood, Liberalism in religion is of a piece with contemporary life in many of its social and intellectual phases.

* * *

In its positive aspect, however, Liberalism is distinguished by an absorbing passion for unity—unity of the mind in itself and with the whole being of man including the feelings and the will, and unity in a world-view of which the unity of man in his completeness gives indications and approximations.

* * *

That it represents a distinct advance in Christian thinking may be freely conceded, but our present duty is criticism rather than appreciation and therefore we must raise the question whether in the system thus briefly outlined there are not faults and deficiencies which point the way of further advance.

These criticisms are of two kinds: some are polemic, directed against it by opponents; and others are dialectic arising from its own creative principle confronted by

34

urgent problems of thought and experience. . . . The adversaries of Liberalism think that it has been trapped in a salient where the only alternatives are unconditional surrender or complete annihilation. Briefly put, the situation is this: Liberalism has made constant and consistent appeal to Jesus, presenting him as Divinity's real and humanity's ideal, identifying pure Christianity with the religion of Jesus himself which it has sought to reproduce and propagate. From the doctrines and practices of the historic church it has appealed to the Jesus of history and from one point of view its appeal has been wholly successful. That the Man of Nazareth said nothing about the cardinal doctrines of traditional Christianity is now pretty generally admitted; but having made its appeal to the Jesus of history it is now triumphantly proclaimed that Liberalism must take the full consequences of that appeal. If it be granted that the Synoptic Gospels alone give us true information concerning him, provided indeed he ever existed, the Jesus whom they disclose is not a Greek Logos but a Jewish Messiah of the apocalyptic sort, quite incompetent to fill the place which Liberalism has accorded him. Therefore Liberalism is imperiously challenged either to relinquish its Jesus, with all that logically must follow such a surrender, or to transfer its allegiance to the Christ of tradition couched for by the testimony of the church on the one had and by the mystical experience of the individual on the other. . . .

In any event, the Liberal has no inclination to return to traditional Christianity, still less to the church which anathematized his departure and now arrogantly commands or patronizingly invites his submission. . . . If Jesus be not the divine ideal of humanity perfectly manifest in the flesh, then Liberalism will find that ideal in the growing hopes of humanity animated and guided by the indwelling spirit. It really matters very little whether or no that ideal has found full expression yet in any single individual; it certainly found large and inspiring expression in the historic Jesus whose very limitations bring him even closer to our hearts. Therefore the Liberal may feel all the nearer to the Jesus whose apocalyptic hopes were vain but whose love of God and Man was not thereby diminished.

*　*　*

Turning now to the criticism of Liberalism from within, to which its own creative principle gives rise, we must seriously raise the question whether it can bear the weight of the tragedies of human experience. Does not its amiable faith in inherent goodness appear but ghastly mockery when confronted by the facts of life? Believing in the immanent God, it must seriously consider what sort of God it is that nature reveals. If God is in all, then he must be in tornado and earthquake as well as in the serene heavens and the smiling earth. If he is in the ripening crops, he must be likewise in the devastating tempest which brings famine to thousands. We cannot be so enamored of the loveliness of nature as to be blind to its terrible aspects. And what of human sin? Here more than anywhere else the weakness of Modern Liberalism shows itself. It may be conceded that traditional theology made too much of sin, but surely that was better than to make light of it. The prophetic curse is against those who call evil good no less than against those who call good evil, and if a Jesus rebukes the doctrine of original sin, a Judas similarly condemns that of original righteousness. . . . A religious doctrine which cannot bear the weight of the heart-breaking disasters of life will prove a broken reed piercing the hand of him who leans upon it. Every fall is a fall upward—tell that to a man who by his sin has fallen from a position of honor and power into deep and damning disgrace. If all's right with the world, something is wrong with man's moral sense. . . . The saviors of the world have always been and always will be men of sorrows and acquainted with grief.

This means—and here we pass to a second criticism—that Modern Liberalism will have to revise its favorite concept of unity. . . . Unity conceived in terms of mechanism has yielded to the organic concept, and it remains to abandon unity construed logically in behalf of unity interpreted in terms of purpose. It is against logical unity which permits no contradictions or inconsistencies, and against mechanical unity which forbids possibilities and knows only of necessity, that pragmatism and pluralism inveigh, and justly. But unity conceived as purpose not only admits of contradictions and possibilities but would even seem to require them, since otherwise purpose would have no possible significance, no sphere of operation. Purpose exists because something, as it now is, is not as it should be, and its fulfillment means the bringing of these contradictions into harmony with the ideal which the purpose makes effective. If then monism be taken purposefully, the principle of divine immanence will mean, not that absolute goodness is now manifest in all, but that in and through all is a power which *makes for* righteousness, a purpose toward the good, even the perfect. . . .

A third criticism must be passed upon Modern Liberalism, less searching and more superficial than the two already made but perhaps more important with reference to its chance of wide acceptance. So far it has been too often an endeavor to adapt old phrases and usages to fit the religious life of today, whereas the urgent need is to aid that religious life in creating its own forms of expression. The motive for this attempt is clear and from one point of view praiseworthy. Language which has been employed for many generations to express the deeper life of man becomes saturated with religious feeling and hence sacred, with the sacredness of the experience which it relates, and moving, through its rich and powerful inheritance of association. To give up the verbal form seems like renouncing the reality which originally fashioned it. But Protestantism has bravely insisted that the Bible must be rendered into the vernacular, and it must now face the necessity of translating the sacred page of the soul into contemporary speech at whatever hazard or cost. . . . The oracular speech of current theology arises from mental confusion which it still further deepens, and thus widens the gulf between itself and the real religious life of today which is already beginning to express itself after its own fashion and not in bygone modes. No one can fail to be impressed with the fact that there is now a large amount of extra-confessional and extra-ecclesiastical religious life which does not and apparently will not run into the traditional molds. Modern Liberalism is reaching out toward men of this sort and marvels that it seems to reach in vain. It may be that its only hope of success lies in so complete and sympathetic an identification with the new religious spirit already moving in the hearts of technically irreligious men as to become capable of interpreting that life in forms appropriate and intelligible to itself.

SOURCE: W. W. Fenn, "Modern Liberalism," *American Journal of Theology* 17 (October 1913): 509–19.

CLARENCE SKINNER

Social Implications of Universalism

1915

Clarence Russell Skinner (1881–1949) wrote his first book, The Social Implications of Universalism, *to address what he saw as religion's failure to address
social inequities, by casting Universalist theology into an optimistic social
gospel framework. A Universalist minister, theologian, and educator, Skinner
organized the denomination's Commission on Social Service, served several
congregations, taught at Crane Theological School of Tufts College, and
founded the Community Church of Boston. He was the most influential
leader guiding twentieth-century Universalism's evolution from a theological
doctrine that focused on the afterlife to a practical philosophy that promoted
social engagement. His book, published in 1915 and also in serial form in the
the* Universalist Leader, *influenced the adoption of the 1917 Declaration of
Social Principles and Social Program by the Universalist General Convention. Further Reading: Charles A. Howe, ed.,* Clarence R. Skinner: Prophet
of a New Universalism *(Boston: Skinner House, 1998).*

—Nicole C. Kirk

How to transform this old earth into the Kingdom of Heaven—that's the primal
question. For thousands of years sad-eyed men have looked upon this war-wracked
and greed-broken world, yearning to gather it into their great healing love. Many
have gazed with amazement at the sorrow and misery of humanity and have wondered. Some have climbed into the high places, searching the heavens for an answer;
others have gone down into the deep places for the secret. Prophets have caught a
various vision, their eyes have been lighted by many and devious enthusiasms which
have sent them into the world to labor and to serve.

For some, the answer has been the individualistic revival of religion stressing the
value of emotional excitement and confession. . . . To others the scheme resolves
itself into a program of reform which would solve all problems through the increase of
income. . . . To increasing multitudes the final answer to this perplexity lies between
the extremes, in a great religious awakening which is not merely emotional, but which
combines spiritual inspiration with the vision of a constructive, working program.

May the humblest of these seekers after truth set forth the talismanic word
which fires him with hope and urges him to whatever service he can render. It is
Universalism—the universal faith and hope in the universal love. . . .

The Challenge

Let us meet the issues of our time with intellectual frankness and with moral courage. Let us recognize the challenging facts of our day, and answer them with truth and with reason.

The fact is that the traditional Protestant Church is dying, dying hard with colors flying, and battling heroically, but nevertheless dying. It ought to be so. The theology upon which it is built is dying; the individualism which called it into being is dying; the social order which it expressed is dying. Why should it not also die?

Our political systems decay, our educational systems perish, our sciences become fossilized in a decade. . . .

When political systems decay it does not mean that man ceases to be a political animal; it merely means that man has discovered an instrument which more perfectly expresses his political needs and instincts. The death of an institution means more life, not less. An outworn creed means more truth, not less. Every death means a larger life.

The passing of the traditional Protestant Church does not mean that man has ceased to be religious, it means that he is more religious, and that he wants his religion in bigger and more vital terms. . . .

The change may come violently, with dramatic cataclysm. . . . It may come as subtly as the pine adds her new leaves to the old. But certain we are that by evolution or by revolution, the Christian church is being daily transformed to more sensitively reflect the life of the age and to exercise a more commanding influence in shaping our spiritual destinies.

The fact that historical ecclesiasticism is crumbling should in no wise cause us to be hysterical or morbid. Organized Christianity has died and has been born again a multitude of times since Jesus of Nazareth preached in Palestine. The religion of Christ was conceived in stormy times; it has been the storm center of advanced civilization for nineteen hundred years; it is the vortex of a world urge and stress to-day. . . .

The fiercest, most barbaric, most bewildering forces have been hurled at the church. It is constantly quivering under the impact. No sooner has it conquered one forced than it has been beset by another. No sooner has it formulated a creed than science has shaken it. . . .

Contradictory as it may seem to some of our platitudinous theories, religion is most dominant and gripping when it is most contemporaneous and most intensely local. The preacher may and ought to thunder his eternal verities, and the cathedral spire may point to the serene empyrean above all jarring discords of earth. But the mind of the common man hungers to have those eternal verities interpreted in terms of his own clime and time, adaptable to his own personal experience. Religion is a spiritual interpretation of the whole of life. That part of life which is the most confusing and bewildering is the immediate present; that part of life which influences man most is that in which he is most intensely engaged—the present. Therefore the Christian Church must be of the moment. . . .

It is unthinkable that this regal function of spiritual interpreter should ever become unnecessary to society. . . .

There is no danger that religion should pass out of life. There *is* danger that the Church may cease to be the voice of religion. The challenge of our day to the Christian Church is evidence of society's need of religion, but of religion in terms of contemporary life, a religion which will be founded upon a twentieth century psychology and theology, a religion which is throbbing with the dynamic of democracy, a spirituality which expresses itself in terms of humanism, rather than in terms of individualism.

Universalism meets the demands of the new age, because it is the product of those forces which created the new age. It does not send its roots down into a medieval civilization, interpreting past history. It does not come to the present weighted down with incrustations of traditionalism or of formalism, which inhibit spontaneous and contemporary action. Its theology expresses the modern conception of the nature of God and man. Its motive power arises out of the new humanism. Its axioms are the assumptions of the great social and psychical movements of the twentieth century. It is the real religion which the masses consciously or unconsciously are adopting. It is the philosophy and the power which under one name or another the multitudes are laying hold upon to swing this old earth nearer to the Kingdom of Heaven. It is the religion of the people, for the people, by the people. It is the faith of the new world life, sweeping upward toward spiritual expression.

Let us see if this be not so.

A Free Church

A great historian has declared that organized religion has been the foe to intellectual, political and social progress. He has beheld, in the panorama of world events, the great institutionalized Church combatting the discoveries of science, tearing the prophet limb from limb and shackling the emancipator. But the historian fails to make the necessary distinction between the free and the traditional forces of religion.

Churches have always been of two groups. The first contains those which have developed a vast and cumbersome organization which makes inertia almost inevitable. They have fulfilled the function of conservators of static racial, social and ethical ideals. They have acted as the bulwarks of industrial and political systems. Their religion is a religion of authority; their theology is a theology of a divine hierarchy; their organization stresses the value of ecclesiastical rites and ceremonies.

The other group of churches contains those fiercer, braver souls who passionately hunger after freedom of mind and soul, who are impatient of metes and bounds, and who are constantly endeavoring to push back the periphery of human experience closer to the universal and the divine. These are the freemen of religion, the pioneers of God. To them a creed is not a tombstone marking the resting place of truth, but is rather a milestone on the long arduous journey to the truth. The man who is spiritually and mentally emancipated never accepts tradition because it is tradition, is never unquestioningly obedient to the institutions and authorities of man, is never comfortably satisfied, but is ever on the alert for high adventurings. In the words of Emerson, "He who would gather immortal palms must not be hindered by the name of goodness, but must explore if it be goodness." A free religion is constantly endeavoring to surpass itself, to outgrow itself, to challenge the fundamentals of existence, to adapt itself to whatever new revelations may come with the dawn.

The social implications of a free religion are apparent. Freedom in religion contributes to freedom in social life. Those who are inspired and encouraged to question the accepted traditions and creeds perpetuated by ecclesiasticism, are the men who naturally and inevitably search for the true bases of the social good. If they are taught to be dissatisfied with the *status quo* in theology, their logic will inexorably drive them to the same dissatisfaction with the *status quo* of politics, or of industry. Light the fuse and the fire will reach the bomb. Emancipate a man's spirit and he will carry his freedom into all he says and does. From defying authority in ecclesiasticism he will progress to defying authority in politics. From fighting tyrannies in theology he will lean on to the fight against the tyrannies of the commercial oligarchies.

The new interpretation of church history is bearing tardy witness to the fact that the men who fought the crucial battles of religious emancipation were foremost among the leaders of intellectual and social revolutions. The great religious leaders from Moses to this day have discovered that in order to impress spiritual ideals upon humanity, the unspiritual economic systems must be transformed. . . .

The genius of Universalism is liberty. Its fathers dared to challenge the olden tyrannies of ecclesiastical authority, and interpret life in larger, more triumphant terms. Its beginnings are linked with the stormy days of political and industrial revolution. Its prophets were stoned in the streets for their daring, they were ostracized by their contemporary complacent fellow religionists. But they fought the battles of religious and civil freedom, and to-day one of the most splendid characteristics of the Universalist Church is the unchallenged right of every individual to interpret the fundamentals of religion according to his conscience. Absolute freedom of utterance and latitude for adventure is secured for preacher and layman in the articles of faith which declare that no form of words and no precise phraseology shall be required of any member of the church.

Such intellectual liberalism and such broad fellowship, after winning the battle for theological freedom, have put Universalists in the forefront among defenders of the new science. They have been among the pioneers who have helped to harmonize that science with religion. When it was heresy to believe in evolution, our fathers dared to proclaim it as a doctrine which would save religion, not destroy it, which would reveal God, not abolish Him.

But the fight for freedom is never won. Inherited liberty is not liberty but tradition. Each generation must win for itself the right to emancipate itself from its own tyrannies, which are ever unprecedented and peculiar. Therefore those who have been reared in freedom, bear a tremendous responsibility to the world to win an ever larger and more important liberty.

Universalists are freemen. Therefore they should be in the front rank of the daring few who are fighting the battles of social emancipation. . . . The logic is relentless, the implication clear. Universalism, by its very genius, is led into the great social maelstrom, because it is essentially a battle for the freedom of the common man. It is a struggle for complete emancipation.

It is easy to gain the right to palliate when charity is popular. It is easy to boast of the similitude of social freedom, to hide slavery behind the mask of relief. But it is hard to win the freedom to eradicate, to blaze the trail, to risk prestige, popularity, ease, in a fight against the causes of misery. . . .

The Universalist Church, though small in numbers, has ever been alive to the championing of social rights. In 1790 the Universalists put themselves on record against the holding of human beings as slaves. This is one of the first actions by a religious body in America. A slave was a charter member of the first Universalist Church in America.

One of the first and most effective champions of industrial freedom was Rev. Adin Ballou. . . .

The cause of woman's liberation has been splendidly upheld. The first journal devoted to working women in this country was organized by a Universalist minister in the city of Lowell. The first National body of women organized in the United States were Universalists, and this denomination was the first to actively promote a woman ministry. The second college in America to introduce coeducation was Lombard.

The cause of the prisoner has been especially upheld by the prophets of the larger faith before the science of penology was developed. The first great agitation against capital punishment, the first proposal of parole and the first prison paper were instituted by Universalists.

They have been among the first agitators for Universal Peace in the modern world. The services of Clara Barton are famed throughout the world.

One of the first, if not the first resolution for total abstinence for individual and State, passed by a religious convention, was proposed in a body of Universalists, and one of the first temperance papers was run by a Universalist.

One of the first movements for the care and education of neglected children eventuated in the first Sunday school in America formed by Benjamin Rush, a Universalist.

Such has been the prophetic vision of Universalism.

※   ※   ※

God and Democracy

All great social problems involve theological conceptions. We may divorce church from state, but we cannot separate the idea of God from the political life of the people. So intimate is the connection between religious and social development, that the history of tribal and National evolution reveals the fact that a particular type of theology is an almost inevitable concomitant of a particular type of society. . . . As man attains increasing democracy, he conceives God as being more universal, more just and more intimately associated with life; and as God is conceived to be more universal, just and intimate, the idea begets more democracy among men. . . .

In the olden times God was conceived to be aristocratic, imperious, partial, because the people were so; and the commonly accepted notions of deity never rise higher than the common social experience. . . .

The Old Testament record of the dramatic struggle between the worshipers of Yahweh and Baal is illustrative of the clash between a democratic people with a democratic idea of God and an aristocratic people with an exploiting God. . . .

So the struggle has gone on through the course of history, a democratic people projecting into their idea of the deity those social and spiritual qualities which were most highly developed in themselves. Each nobler and more just conception of God, therefore, becomes evidence of a new level of political life, and is in turn a *magna carta* of liberties yet to be won. . . .

The old ideas of a God who created a spiritual aristocracy, who maintained partiality, whose sympathies were not as wide as the whole of humanity, are patently inadequate to meet the new needs. There is no mistaking the democratic instinct in wthe new man. He passions after freedom and brotherhood. He lays bare his heart and mind to the great human currents and exults in the tides of feeling which pour upon him, enriching and enlarging him. There is no mistaking the widening of sympathies, the greater sense of inclusiveness, the new solidarity of humanity. Such a humanity will no longer brook the imperious and fastidious God who has scorned the fellowship of most of his creatures in the past. A democratic people demand a democratic God, a robust deity who likes his universe, who hungers for fellowship, who is in and of and for the whole of life. . . .

43

The Universalist idea of God is that of a universal, impartial, immanent spirit whose nature is love. It is the largest thought the world has ever known; it is the most revolutionary doctrine ever proclaimed; it is the most expansive hope ever dreamed. This is the God of the modern man, and the God who is in modern man. This is no tribal deity of ancient divisive civilization, this is no God of the nation or of a chosen people, but the democratic creator of the solid, indivisible world of rich and poor, black and white, good and bad, strong and weak, Jew and Gentile, bond and free. Such a faith is as much a victory for the common people as was the passage of the Fourteenth Amendment to the Constitution. It carries with it a guarantee of spiritual liberties which are precedent to outward forms of governmental action. . . .

And not only is the Universalist conception of the Universal Fatherhood of God a response to the hunger for a larger, more democratic Creator, but it in turn begets a higher level of social life. A universal faith demands a universal application. This vast idea cannot be confined in one human mind, or in one favored class, but escapes beyond the narrow limitations of individualism into every conceivable relation of life. It cannot be calmly accepted by one and denied to the many. The Universal God means universal life, universal opportunity. It means the destruction of the olden tyrannies and the emancipation of the common man, Christ-like, free. It means the wreck of exploitation, the ruin of aristocracy; it means the exaltation of the meanest and weakest of God's creatures to the height of fulfilment. It means democracy.

Some timid folk shudder at the thought of their own innate greatness. From such the shackles of slavish thought would be struck. . . .

The Universal Fatherhood of God, which clearly implies democracy, does not imply equality, for equality does not appear in nature. The infinite variety of the forms of life is occasion for perennial astonishment. Human beings exhibit the widest conceivable variety of physical and temperamental differences, which are not merely accidents of clime, but which are innate, and, so far as we can perceive, a part of the design of creation. Just as there are no two grains of sand alike and no two leaves alike, so there are no two men alike, and where there is no similarity there can be no equality. Democracy does not mean equality. . . . Democracy is an attempt to preserve whatever differences are innate and divine in human personality, and to secure to all absolute freedom to become their own best selves.

The Universal Fatherhood of God recognizes the difference between the black and the white, but it declares that the fact of the difference is no ground for exploitation, but is rather an occasion for mutual respect and mutual self-fulfilment. The whole pith of the matter is this: that the differences which are innate in humanity are just, and must be clearly differentiated from the artificial distinctions which are superimposed upon humanity unjustly by men.

*　*　*

The Nature of Man

There are two avenues of approach to the process of social melioration. One is through the philosophy of economic determinism which is being reinforced and reemphasized to-day with apostolic zeal by Socialism and allied movements. . . . It is undoubtedly a true philosophy. History marshals overwhelming evidence that economic motive lies at the root of many great world movements. . . .

But economic determinism is not a complete philosophy of life. It is an ally rather than a substitute for religion, which is the philosophy of spiritual determinism. Religion approaches the problem of social reorganization through inward motives, which, when aroused, mold outward forces. . . .

Universalism contributes to this social incentive, the dynamic and urgent idea of the universal spirituality of man. The pivotal point of the Universalist theology is the Universal Fatherhood of God. Grant the existence of a universal spirit whose nature and purposes are beneficent, who reveals Himself through universal laws, then the whole cosmic philosophy of Universalism follows with flawless logic, and the social implications become inexorable.

The Universal Fatherhood of God means the innate spirituality and worth of man. If God is literally the Universal Father, then man must be the inheritor of a God-like nature.

In the words of Channing: "What is it to be a Father? It is to communicate one's own nature, to give life to kindred beings."

* * *

This thought exalts human nature, enriches it, makes it of infinite worth, and deepens its significance. Whatever most elevates our conception of man is the supreme social service, be it a theological concept, a social custom or a legislative decree.

* * *

This thought was undoubtedly one of the supreme contributions of Jesus to the world. His sympathies reached out beyond narrow ethnic boundaries and included all humanity in his vision of a unified world under God. The apostles caught the fire of this great vision, and spread the glad tidings of man's sonship to God to barbarian and Jew, bond and free. . . .

This was the lever whereby the world raised itself out of the slough of despair and slavery which had settled down upon it under the Roman dominance. . . .

It is this thought of the preciousness and innate nobility of human nature which forms the distinctive characteristic of the great humanitarian movements of the nineteenth and twentieth centuries. . . .

No social problem can ever be completely solved until it is spiritually solved, for every social problem involves a spiritual content. No matter how gross a fact may seem, it yet impinges upon the human, and it must be interpreted in terms of its effect upon the inner life of humanity.

We may approach child labor from the economic aspect. We ought to recognize that it does not pay in terms of dollars and cents, and we ought to drive home the argument with all the oratorical sledge hammers we can command. Yet this in itself is insufficient. . . .

Let us trumpet abroad the transforming faith in man's innate worth and rouse society to its noblest endeavors by appeal to the divine nature. This is the ultimate incentive to the salvation of the world, and to the building of the new social order.

*   *   *

Brotherhood

Faith in the transforming power of Brotherhood is growing great. It is swiftly girdling the earth. It is infusing old and decadent civilizations with fresh impulses, and is waking sleeping millions to mighty visions. This marvelous spirit seizes the world, enflames it, commands it; folk-hunger throbs and pulses through our veins. We forsake our petty dilettantism, our corroding materialism. Brotherhood has become our passion, our bread and meat, our shining faith. We follow its gleam through the sorrow and misery of this life to the radiant sun-lit hills of hope.

The new religion must reflect this growing fraternalism in a new form.

Universalism in fact clearly implies these conceptions which are the very stuff of brotherhood.

The Universal Fatherhood of God means the universal brotherhood of man. A common origin means a common relationship. If two children are the offspring of the same parents they are brothers or sisters. We may deny the fact, as many have denied it. We may exalt one brother to kingship and reduce the other to beggary. But the fact of the brotherly relation persists through all denial and partiality. . . .

This fact has been established by the physical and chemical sciences. It is the witness of anthropology. It is the creed of all universal religion. It is the burden of sociology. The unbreakable fraternity of all men, black or white, red or yellow, rich or poor, strong or weak, has become established as a necessary postulate of all clear thinking.

*   *   *

The idea of the Universal Brotherhood is the great social dynamic of the twentieth century. Sometimes it is dynamite. It fires our hopes, builds our dreams, unfolds before us the Messianic vision of an imminent kingdom of heaven on earth. Society to-day is in a state of expectancy where it now believes in the possible solution of its hardest problems by the infusion of the spirit of brotherhood that shall cover the earth as the waters cover the sea.

46

And Universalism inspires this faith not only because it teaches the divine origin of all men, but likewise because of its belief in the common destiny of humanity in all times and in all stations of life. Universalism triumphantly holds to the universal salvation of all mankind. It believes that all human souls are children of God with a spark of the divine in their nature, and that eventually, after the varied experiences of this world and the next, those souls will reach a perfect harmony with God.

Never was there such a bold proclamation of brotherhood as this; never such implicit faith in the solidarity of the human race. It is the largest, most astonishing evidence of the new social consciousness.

✻   ✻   ✻

Social Motive

Religion is the product of human nature and of the reaction of human nature to its environment. In order to discover religious motives, therefore, it becomes necessary to study human nature in its relation to historic backgrounds and environments.

The fact that the traditional churches of the modern era have been so feeble in social dynamic, is due to inertia inherited from the medieval ages when humanity lacked social dynamic. . . .

In the first place the old theology is grounded in and springs out of a sense of the hopelessness and worthlessness of life. It defines earthly existence as being a deplorable failure and an absolute disaster. . . .

This gloomy interpretation of life had ample reason for being, as it was but a reaction from economic and psychological conditions which obtained through long periods of Roman decadence and of the Dark Ages. Civilization was based on a deficit of natural resources which eventuated in hopeless poverty, despotism and slavery. Few men attained, or hoped to attain, freedom. Castes were severe and self-perpetuating. Homes were squalid. Famine and plagues were frequent. Unremitting toil and suffering was the lot of the common people. Small wonder that life was despised and held cheap, and that theology was constrained to interpret the world in terms of tragic disaster.

Universalism was born out of the new humanity; it is the gospel of the new heaven and the new earth. It throbs with hope. It was part of the great world movement to reinterpret life in terms of a regenerated, buoyant, self assertive human nature. Universalism believes in the world and in its potential goodness. It repudiates the gloomy and disastrous outlook of the old anti-social theology. It is not frantically searching for an escape from life. It believes that God is the Creator and that He is love; therefore in giving us life He gives us love, power and joy. This is the only interpretation of life which furnishes a real and indigenous social motive. Only those theologies which frankly and persistently align themselves with the world, and openly champion its potential goodness, can logically enter the great reformation of the

47

twentieth century. They alone believe that salvation comes in, by and through a saved world. This is social salvation. All others believe that salvation comes by escaping from a world which is inherently unsavable. That is the individualistic, anti-social, medieval faith.

*　*　*

The Leadership of Jesus

After the first two or three centuries of the Christian era, theology became so concerned with the person of Jesus that it almost completely forgot his program. . . .

When the Master spoke to the contemporaries of his own country about the burning issues of his time he was understood. . . .

His was a soul-stirring message of mighty social import.

But when this fresh, invigorating, life-giving stream of Christianity poured out over the Greeks, it was diverted. To the philosophically minded, the all absorbing question became the relation of Jesus' personality to the triune God-head. It is for this reason that three hundred and fifteen years after the prophet of Nazareth was born, the Christian Church was wrangling over Athanasianism and Arminianism. For sixteen hundred years the theologians have continued to wage battle over the person of Christ, and the world has consequently been blinded to his program.

*　*　*

To grasp the full meaning of the change which has come over civilization and the tragic misunderstanding of Christ which it entails, we have but to behold the appalling spectacle of Christian priests blessing armies accoutered to the teeth and dragging their hell machines behind them. The same travesty exists in commercial ethics, which for centuries condoned exploitation. It exists in the artificial distinctions by which we separate men into caste and class strata. Such travesty exists because men have been taught the saving power of Christ's personality dissociated from his principles. Christ has been held forth as a Savior to be received rather than a leader and teacher to be followed.

*　*　*

The great social passion of to-day is not concerned with beliefs *about* Jesus, but it is mightily concerned with belief *in* Jesus. It is not interested in perpetuating an ecclesiastic *régime* or hierarchy built upon a dead Roman imperialism, but is interested in perpetuating a living power which can flood the earth with brotherhood and provide an authoritative program for social reconstruction. The great social movement looks to Christ as to one who has discovered an emancipating truth, which has the power to set men free from the burdens of misery, greed and exploitation which have enslaved the nations since the beginning of history. The social movement is going to look to Christ as the inspirer of those great sympathies and humanitarian impulses which are the high springs from which all streams of healing flow.

48

Universalism is an endeavor to restore the Christ of the first two centuries to the world, and to put into Christianity its pristine vigor of principle and discipline. Any sincere attempt to discover the real Jesus, the visionary, the emancipator, the great teacher, will inevitably lead to a rediscovery of the social gospel. And the rediscovery of the social gospel with its general acceptance will liberate for the world's redemption the great power which is the power unto salvation.

Hell and Salvation

The old ideas regarding hell and salvation, which swayed the imaginations of men for centuries, have deeply affected the attitude of the churches toward the problem of social amelioration. . . . It has not only been true in the past, but it is true to-day, that those who believe in an avenging God and a substitutional atoning Christ are individualistic, and consistently oppose the new social emphasis in religion. The old theology of Heaven and Hell has been among the strongest deterrents to social service, and the reorganization of religious forces for modernized activity.

The very corner-stones of the old structure of theology were caprice and injustice. A human being might be condemned to hell by a wrathful God, for punishment of an act which was not in itself immoral, and hope for that individual's salvation might be eternally lost. On the other hand, a person might commit a most heinous crime, involving the worst possible sin against the moral nature, yet escape from hell and punishment by accepting the vicarious atonement of Christ. Hell never was pictured in the old theology as an inevitable consequence of breaking the innate laws of being. There were always trapdoors out of which the one who was wise could climb at the last moment. Punishment and reward were not in the exact and inescapable relation of cause and effect. Hell and salvation were both arbitrary and non-human in origin.

The lot of men here, and their destiny hereafter, was supposed to be determined without reference to social causes. . . .

There are few men whose opinions really count in the modern world, who have the temerity to preach the old idea of a wrathful God and a brimstone hell. The Liberal theology has successfully driven these nightmares from the minds of enlightened men.

But Universalism has not tried to abolish the scheme of suffering and punishment from life. It has not done away with moral accountability. The idea of hell and heaven is just as potent in the modern theology as in the old. They are essential elements in religion. Universalism has not abolished the idea of hell.

It has humanized and socialized it. It has established human misery as the direct effect or consequence of human action. The existence of such a hell can be demonstrated, the sting of its lash can be felt, the horror of it can be seen. The broken nerves of the *roue*, the rotting flesh of the prostitute, the moral degeneracy of the sensualist, the blood-red conscience of the murderer, are hell. There is no caprice in its operation, there is no trap door for escape. It is the most real, the most inevitable fact conceivable. To believe that every individual will suffer the just consequences of sin is the hardest, most disciplinary faith known.

And everywhere men are seen not merely suffering the consequences of their own actions, but writhing in the meshes of sin woven about them by others. The horrors of war are suffered as much by the innocent men, women and children as by those who murder and are murdered on the field of battle. The most dreaded feature of intemperance is its deadly power to destroy the homes and blast the hopes of those who remain temperate. Insane asylums, hospitals and clinics tell the awful tale of the havoc wrought by congenital syphilis. Youths are wrecked by institutionalized vice pandering to passion. Vampires still live and grow fat on the blood of human beings, throwing the anemic, skeleton forms into the teeming city to crawl out a wretched death-in-life.

All this is hell—*social hell*—men suffering from instituted customs and practices for which society is responsible, which can be eradicated out of the world.

And Universalism has not only humanized and socialized hell, but it has humanized and socialized salvation. If a man must suffer the consequences of his own sin, he must likewise make his own reparation. The only way out is by an absolutely reformed character, either in this world or in the next. He can not receive salvation, but must achieve it. He must work his way to perfection. God in His infinite mercy is ready to assist, Christ reveals the way, but the man must go that way and avail himself of that mercy. There is no royal road to salvation. Salvation is as much subject to the natural law of cause and effect as is punishment. It can not be arbitrary or capricious. This faith, again, is the most rigorous and disciplinary the world has ever known.

And a man must not only work out his own salvation; he must work out the salvation of the world. He is enmeshed in a world of humanity from which he can by no means wholly disentangle himself. He is a part of the marvelous solidarity of life. . . .

Such a view of the theological problem of punishment and reformation is fundamental to the new social religion; in fact, the social emphasis grows out of this view. The old ideas of hell and salvation were anti-social, and must perforce be discarded before the new religion can gain the allegiance of the people. Let a single illustration suffice.

A prominent Boston clergyman recently told with evident pride his professional experience with a sinning woman. He was called into a brothel to attend the death-bed confession of a woman of the streets who was in fear and terror of the final reckoning and judgment. The minister told her the story of Jesus' atoning sacrifice, which was able to obtain for her forgiveness and salvation. Her sins were wiped away by her acceptance of the Savior, and the minister a few days later had the satisfaction of folding her hands and closing her eyes in peace. The terrors of hell which got hold upon her, were assuaged by the blessed assurance of an immediate heaven.

It does not require a great amount of penetration to see that this system of salvation undermines the whole social process, and discourages the social motive. . . . This scheme furnishes no mighty, all compelling incentive for the organization of the social forces of a community for a radical attack on the social conditions which breed vice and crime.

The New Unity

The unity of religions is no mere academic question, but is fraught with tremendous social consequences. Nothing is of deeper and more immediate import than that the social conscience should have some recognized mode and commonly accepted instrumentality for self-expression. There is urgent need for some universal, democratic faith which will be a true spiritual interpretation of contemporary life, and which will effectively organize and mobilize the forces of community idealism.

The sectarian divisiveness of to-day is more than theologically deplorable; it is a social sin. The churches of the Protestant nations have become so torn and scattered by internecine strife, that they no longer express the common ideals of contemporary humanity, and are no longer able to effectively mobilize against the social evils. . . .

This disruption of the unity of Christendom was probably an inevitable phase of religious development. . . . A new unity, more effective because more spontaneous and more democratic, must germinate through the long years of individualism.

But it is coming. This unity has the inevitableness of destiny, for it is the unforced and unpreventable expression in terms of religion, of that larger unity which is sweeping through the world. . . .

Religion feels and voices the new social solidarity. It is straining at the leash of the old chaotic individualism, and is trying to so reconstruct its machinery and rephrase its message that it may be in increasing measure the certain trumpet of the larger life. The growing sense of social integrity will create its spiritual interpreter. As the idealized common life becomes the recognized goal of religious endeavor, and as religion is recognized as being the highest reach of the common life, the community will learn to function spiritually as a unit. . . .

Before such a consummation of the Protestant sects is achieved two processes must be fulfilled. First, a growing out of the petty sectarian views of the past; and second, the normal growth of a larger, more inclusive faith.

It is inconceivable that the new democratic churches should be built on the sacraments and symbols which have had so important a part in disrupting Christendom. One can not imagine this unity coming through creeds or dogmas about baptism, transubstantiation, apostolic succession, definitions of a personality, views of a book, or forms of prayers. . . .

In fact, denominationalism in the old seclusive and divisive sense is a dying issue.

Man's mind shall become more inclusive, his spirit more democratic, his intuitions more cosmic. Larger views of life shall make the prison-house of ancient creeds become abhorrent. Freer fellowship with God and with man shall break down the old bars and open glimpses into the infinite. There will be a free trade of truth, an untrammeled comradery of soul.

Universalism is the expression in terms of religion of the larger life that is dawning upon man. It is the largest statement of faith ever made, it exhibits the most democratic inclusive spirit, it is the new humanity trumpeting its belief in the universals. Its faith is in the universal Fatherhood of God—a God as wide as the universe, who is impartial, unlimited, yet intensely in and of humanity. Nothing bigger or finer can be conceived than this idea of God. Universalism declares for the universal brotherhood of man. Its faith can not harbor the old systems of spiritual aristocracies, of divisive castes, but includes the whole of society, Christian or heathen, good or bad, rich or poor, in its unshaken faith in brotherhood. Universalism believes in the universal revelation of truth. It can not be shut up in one mind, one book, or one personality, but streams from the stars, springs from the earth, grows great in the heart of the whole of humanity. Its faith is in democratized truth. Universalism believes in Christ, believes that the truth which he revealed and the power which he generated are for world service. Universalism believes in salvation, not in narrow bounds, but as universal, ultimately compelling. Universalism sees the life of the world as an indivisible unit moving on to one common destiny. It is faith in terms of the universal.

Therefore Universalism has more to contribute to the new unity of religious forces than any system of belief yet given to the world. Man can not unite on the old dogmatic fragmentary views of religion of the past. They have outgrown them. The newer, larger life is dawning. The cosmic surge is rallying through the world. The new eyes see the new heaven and the new earth. The religion of the universals— Universalism—is the religion of that new life, is the revelation of that new vision. In it the whole of humanity can be gathered as a unit, each individual with his custom, creed and personality guaranteed freedom and democratic respect, but each individual enlarged and expanded so as to meet all other individuals on the common ground of mutual needs and universal interests.

The new faith of the new unity of man will be the new Universalism.

The Final Triumph

The most distinctive contribution which Universalism has made to the development of theology and religion is the idea of the universal salvation of all souls and its concomitant of the final triumph of good over evil. . . .

The old theology, which conceived evil as being the normal and essential nature of life and good as being supernatural and abnormal, gave way to the Universalist belief that good is the natural and inevitable essence of life; evil being the abnormal and temporary. This newer faith is the faith of humanity in the twentieth century. Pessimism can no longer be successfully superimposed upon the modern mind. The increasing acceptance of the Universalist belief in the ultimate salvation of all souls, and the final triumph of good over evil are indications of the optimism which is galvanizing all the interests and activities of man.

This triumphant hope in the ultimate salvation of humanity does not arise out of blindness to the hard facts of reality. . . . It interprets the present in the light of potentialities.

The vision of the Universalist is founded upon the marvelous discoveries and inventions which have taken place during the past century in the field of medicine, education, economics, industry and above all in social work. Gathering all the evidence from these sources, weighing it, and considering it in its relation to the future of humanity, we learn that the hope which was instinctive and impulsive in the new religion rests upon the "reasoned optimism" of factual revelation.

Medicine lights the future of our race with a vision of preventable and prevented disease. Criminology brings incontrovertible evidence that delinquency finds its roots in congenital defect and preventable neglect, and eugenics holds forth an alluring picture of a perfected race produced through social control of birth. Alcoholism, ignorance, bad housing are preventable and can be eradicated when the conscience of men becomes sufficiently sensitized, socialized and energized. Poverty is no longer considered the inexorable lot of the many, but is conceded to be the result of maladjustments of temporary character. Wars no longer have their roots in the old condition of primitive tribes or nations which battled for wealth-producing territory, but rather in a more easily adjusted misunderstanding and injustice as to the exchange of surplus products.

The facts of the new life, seen in their radical significance make this century preeminently the age of social idealism. Never before have we had such basis for our hope that this old earth may be transformed into a veritable Kingdom of God where there shall be no more misery or sin. The faith of all Universalism in the great salvation of all souls is but an extension into the infinite of the "reasoned optimism" of our present social life. From the opening gates of the morning we catch this vision of the dawn-swept mountains of God.

* * *

53

Is it reasonable to expect that faith in the final triumph of good over evil will operate otherwise? This most splendid of all hopes, radiant, joyful, pulls men into the battle line against evil, and puts into their souls that unshakable trust which makes their onrush like that of a thousand storms. It is said that in the days of anti-slavery discussion, the senate was once crowded to hear a famous abolitionist deliver an oration. He became pessimistic and expressed doubt in the final outcome of his cause, when Sojourner Truth, a negro woman, arose in the assembly and challenged the speaker by crying out: "Is God dead?" That is all she said. But an electrical thrill ran through the crowd, and turned the tide from doubt to victorious faith.

So the belief that God is tremendously in every social movement for the liberation of humanity, strengthens the arm of right. To know that one is battling for justice is to know that the everlasting stars are battling at his side; it is to know that the tides of the universe are flowing at his command. The knowledge of the ultimate triumph of good makes one serve the good with the passion and the calm of æons of time.

* * *

The Larger Faith

Every great development of religion consists of two complementary processes; namely, a denial of limitations, and an assertion of a larger spiritual content. . . .

Critics of the Liberal faith have often scored Universalism as being a negative religion, receiving its initial impulse from denial. The criticism is true in so far as all great religious movements are motived by reaction from contemporaneous limitarianism. But such critics fail to see that the only denial made by Universalism is against some form of partialism which is itself a denial of the unity, integrity or universality of religion. Universalism negatives only the negative, and thus produces a positive faith.

Universalism was one of the early manifestations of that great movement which swept away the barriers of narrow vision which belonged to the olden days, opening vistas into the larger faith. . . .

The Liberal movement, led by Universalists, Unitarians, and Friends made a distinctive contribution to the larger life of humanity by contributing to it a larger faith. It gave a larger outlook to men's intellectual conceptions of the universe; it meant the deepening and enriching of spiritual experience by liberating ideas and emotions of infinite love; it bound men together in a new unity of divine origins; it dignified common humanity with the potentialities of the Christ life. The larger faith gave sweep, vision, cosmic consciousness to the individual by pouring into his nascent soul the infinitudes of a universal religion. It came "that men might have life and have it more abundantly."

* * *

Universalism and the social movement are thus of the same genius, as their ends are identical. The one contributes to the enlarging life by an expansive hope and a cosmic faith, the other by making available the resources of science, education and industry. As a matter of fact, religion and the social movement are inseparable, for they are inter-active and complementary. Man cannot be conveniently divided into the material, the social and the religious, for all the apparently diversified interests are but varying functions of a psychic unity. The mental, physical and social are so closely locked, that the stimulus of one wakens a train of stimulated activities in every other sphere of personality. Just as coal is convertible into steam, steam into power, and power into light, so the physical is convertible into the emotional, the emotional into the ideational, the ideational into activity, and back again in an unbroken circle.

Those who have deepest insight into the nature of the social movement and who are directing it to its noblest ends have clear vision of this truth. The social and religious progress must be mutually contributory and reactive. Each must be converted into terms of the other and both must make for the progressive expansion of the life of the individual. We must have better conditions that we may have better men; we must have better men that we may have better conditions.

The new passion for humanity therefore comes not to destroy, but to fulfill; it promises not less religion, but a religion more complete. It is not a problem of subtraction but of addition or multiplication. It is the expansion of the ideal values of religion into all social values. It seizes upon the vast mechanism of civilization's resources and spiritualizes them into terms of larger hope for men, deeper faith in men and more transforming love by men.

With such enlargement of the function of religion and with such enrichment of the personal life, Universalism is generically allied; for its whole passion is to bring the human soul into the realization of all its potentialities until it attains the stature of the perfect man. To that divinely human end, it unfolds before our vision the unities, the eternities and the universals, and bids us live in conscious communion with them.

SOURCE: Clarence Skinner, *The Social Implications of Universalism* (Boston: Universalist Publishing House, 1915), vii–viii, 1–36, 38–39, 42–44, 48–49, 51–52, 54, 57–58, 60–79, 81–82, 84–86, 88–90.

MAY WRIGHT SEWALL

Women, World War and Permanent Peace

1915

May Wright Sewall (1844–1920) was a leading figure in both women's and peace organizations at the turn of the twentieth century. An educator by training, Sewall taught for more than thirty years in Indianapolis, where she belonged to the local Unitarian congregation. She was active in the National Woman Suffrage Association and served as president of both the National Council of Women and the International Council of Women. Twice widowed, Sewall devoted her retirement years to the causes of spiritualism and peace—the latter by sailing on Henry Ford's "Peace Ship" during World War I and organizing a women's conference on peace. Further Reading: Ray E. Boomhower, Fighting for Equality: A Life of May Wright Sewall (Indianapolis: Indiana Historical Society Press, 2007).

—Dan McKanan

On April 7th, 1914, by request, I presented to the Panama-Pacific International Exposition authorities at San Francisco a plan for convening, under their auspices at some time during the year 1915, an International Conference of Women Workers whose object should be to promote that COÖPERATIVE INTERNATIONALISM on which along for many years it has been my conviction that the foundations of PERMANENT PEACE can be laid.

The original plan contemplated inviting only presidents, past presidents and other leading officials of all existing international societies of women for whatever purpose organized or in whatever country their headquarters may be established, in the hope that through their experience in working for any object in which women of more than one nationality are already interested, women of all nationalities may have learned that what is needed more than any other one thing to advance all the various social, moral and civic reforms that are involved in present international effort, is a heartily affectionate understanding of one another by different peoples. This means the abatement of all those elements of patriotism which tend toward the inculcation of a sense of superiority in any people over other people, and the cultivation of a sympathy that can come only out of actual knowledge of what is interesting in the origin and good in the customs, the habits, the life and the ideals of other peoples.

*   *   *

56

Resolutions Constituting the Platform of the International Conference of Women Workers to Promote Permanent Peace.

This conference, organizing no new movement, represents the Spirit of Co-operation; and its members, adopting the Women's Peace Party as their specific channel of influence, declare their desire to work with and in all existing societies whose object is the PEACE of the world.

I. We women workers here assembled declare that this Conference is a protest against the fallacious doctrine that any nation can secure Peace by preparing for War.

II. We demand that PATRIOTISM be redefined, and that Greed, Arrogance and Rivalry, which are considered vices in individuals, be not accepted as virtues in nations, and to this end such changes in school books, in instruction and in patriotic observances as will induce loyalty to an international ideal.

III. We protest against the misuse of public funds in all countries for the glorification of war, and against all insidious agencies through which militarism is encouraged in youth.

IV. We protest against military drill in all schools and academic institutions.

V. We declare that the time has arrived for crystalizing international sentiment into international institutions. Inasmuch as International Law is now only nominal, we demand that:

(a) The people of the nations shall create an international legislative body, necessitating an international court and international police.

(b) That there be further created an International Council of Investigation and Conciliation to which all international disputes must be submitted.

VI. This Conference endorses that resolution adopted by the recent International Congress at The Hague which provides for an international meeting of women in the same place and at the same time as the Conference of the Powers which shall frame the terms of the peace settlement after this war, for the purpose of presenting practical proposals to that Conference.

VII. We protest against secret treaties and demand that in future all treaties proposed between governments be made public before being ratified.

VIII. This Conference urges that women be permitted to share political rights and responsibilities both nationally and internationally.

IX. This International Conference urges a general, gradual disarmament of the nations.

x. This Conference recommends that the right of capture be abolished and that no disposition of territory be made contrary to the expressed interests and wishes of its inhabitants.

xi. This Conference urges that the governments of the neutral nations create a Conference of the Neutral Nations for the purpose of mediating between the warring Powers until Peace can be secured.

SOURCE: May Wright Sewall, *Women, World War and Permanent Peace* (San Francisco: J. J. Newbegin, 1915), xi, 164–65.

JOHN HAYNES HOLMES

"A Statement To My People On the Eve of War"

1917

The vast majority of Unitarians and Universalists, both lay and ordained,
supported the United States' entry into World War I in April 1917. John
Haynes Holmes (1879–1964), a leading advocate of the social gospel, did not.
Just days before the declaration of war, he reaffirmed his pacifist commitment
in this sermon to his congregation, then known as the Church of the Messiah
in New York City. He also articulated his theology of ministry and made an
eloquent case for what are now the fifth and sixth Unitarian Universalist
principles. Most of his congregants disagreed with his position on the war but
supported his freedom of the pulpit. After Holmes resigned his Unitarian
ministerial fellowship in protest of the denomination's hostility to pacifist
ministers, the congregation agreed to reorganize itself as the Community
Church of New York, while remaining in fellowship with the American Uni-
tarian Association. Decades later, Holmes agreed to be listed once again in
the Unitarian yearbook. Further Reading: Ray H. Abrams, Preachers Present
Arms: The Role of the American Churches and Clergy in World Wars I and
II, with Some Observations on the War in Vietnam *(Scottdale, PA: Herald*
Press, 1969); Patricia Appelbaum, Kingdom to Commune: Protestant Pacifist Culture between World War I and the Vietnam War *(Chapel Hill: Uni-*
versity of North Carolina Press, 2009).

—Dan McKanan

It is in anticipation of the world-shaking events which a week or a day may bring
upon us in this country, and in fulfillment of the duty which I conceived these probable events impose upon me as a religious teacher, that I have chosen this morning,
as on the Sunday following the severance of diplomatic relations with Germany, to
lay aside my sermon, and speak to you as simply and directly as possible upon the
state of the nation. . . . At the moment when I was ordained to be a minister of God,
I conceive that I was commanded to throw wide open the portals of my heart, that
all who cared might see its innermost recesses of conviction; and I do not propose
that even the terror of this hour shall bar that threshold from the public gaze. Furthermore, I cannot forget what I owe to you, my beloved people. You have a right to
know what I shall say and do in the event of war, upon what road of doctrine I shall
set my feet, into what hazards of pain and peril I shall lead this church. The pew is

always entitled to the full confession of the pulpit, but never so urgently as at the time when such confession touches the deep issues of life and death. . . .

On the morning of Sunday, March 7, 1915, I declared in this church my absolute and unalterable opposition to war. "War," I said, "is never justifiable at any time or under any circumstances. No man is wise enough, no nation is important enough, no human interest is precious enough, to justify the wholesale destruction and murder which constitute the essence of war . . . [ellipsis in original]. War is hate, and hate has no place within the human heart. War is death, and death has no place within the realm of life. War is hell, and hell has no more place in the human order than in the divine." . . .

These words spoken in this place more than two years ago, I must reaffirm this day. Nothing has happened in this period of time to change my opinion of war. On the contrary, much has happened to strengthen and confirm it. I do not deny that war, like polygamy, slavery and cannibalism, was inseparable from early and low stages of social life. I do not deny that war, like pestilence, famine and conflagration, has often helped forward the civilization of mankind, for thus does God make the wrath, as well as the agony of men, to praise him. I do not even deny that there have been times in the past when war, like the storms of the sea, has seemed to be unavoidable. What I do deny is that these facts of history touch in any remotest way the judgment of ethics and religion that war is wrong, or should swerve by so much as a hair's breadth the decision of any one of us to have nothing to do with it. War is in open and utter violation of Christianity. If war is right, then Christianity is wrong, false, a lie. If Christianity is right, then war is wrong, false, a lie. . . .

But I must go farther—I must speak not only of war in general, but of this war in particular. Most persons are quite ready to agree, especially in the piping times of peace, that war is wrong. But let a war cloud no bigger than a man's hand, appear on the horizon of the nation's life, and they straightway begin to qualify their judgment, and if the war cloud grow until it covers all the heavens, they finally reverse it. This brings the curious situation of all war being wrong in general, and each war being right in particular.

* * *

In its ultimate causes, this war is the natural product and expression of our unchristian civilization. Its armed men are grown from the dragon's teeth of secret diplomacy, imperialistic ambition, dynastic pride, greedy commercialism, economic exploitation at home and abroad. In the sowing of these teeth, America has had her part; and it is therefore only proper, perhaps, that she should have her part also in the reaping of the dreadful harvest. In its more immediate causes, this war is the direct result of unwarrantable, cruel, but none the less inevitable interferences with our commercial relations with one group of the belligerents. Our participation in the war, therefore, like the war itself, is political and economic, not ethical, in its character.

And how shall I, a pacifist, serve my country in time of war?

When hostilities begin, it is universally assumed that there is but a single service which a loyal citizen can render to the state—that of bearing arms and killing the enemy. Will you understand me if I say, humbly and regretfully, that this I cannot, and will not, do. If any man or boy in this church answers the call to arms, I shall bless him as he marches to the front. When he lies in the trenches, or watches on the lonely sentinel-post, or fights in the charge, I shall follow him with my prayers. If he is brought back dead from hospital or battlefield, I shall bury him with all the honors not of war but of religion. He will have obeyed his conscience and thus performed his whole duty as a man. But I also have a conscience, and that conscience I also must obey. When, therefore, there comes a call for volunteers, I shall have to refuse to heed. When there is an enrollment of citizens for military purposes, I shall have to refuse to register. When, or if, the system of conscription is adopted, I shall have to decline to serve. If this means a fine, I will pay my fine. If this means imprisonment, I will serve my term. If this means persecution, I will carry my cross. . . .

And this resolution applies, let me now be careful to state, quite as much to my professional as to my personal life. Once war is here, the churches will be called upon to enlist, as will every other social institution. Therefore would I make it plain that, so long as I am your minister, the Church of the Messiah will answer no military summons. Other pulpits may preach recruiting sermons; mine will not. Other parish houses may be turned into drill halls and rifle ranges; ours will not. Other clergymen may pray to God for victory for our arms; I will not. In this church, if nowhere else in all America, the Germans will still be included in the family of God's children. . . .

But if I will not, or cannot, either as man or minister, have part in the operations of war, how can I talk of such a thing as serving the nation? When the enemy is at the gates, what is there to do but to snatch up a sword, and fight? Let me tell you what there is to do. Let me specify at least four things which I propose to do.

First of all, I shall make it my duty to fulfill in word and deed the gracious tasks of what may be called the ministry of reconciliation. In a time of raging hate and brutal passion, I will keep alive that spirit of goodwill toward men, through which alone a durable peace on earth may some day be established. . . .

Secondly, I will serve my country in war time by serving the ideals of democracy which constitute the soul and center of her being. War and democracy are incompatible. When war comes, democracy goes. England, fighting nobly to conquer Prussianism, is herself in process of being conquered by the Prussian spirit. Already in our own country, before the beginning of war, the dread work of militarism is under way. Already freedom of thought is being denied, and liberty of conscience challenged. Already we are in the midst of such an orgy of bigotry, intolerance and persecution for opinion's sake, as American has not seen since the days of the Salem witches. . . .

One such assault is now being made in the movement for universal military training. So long as I have breath to speak, or hand to lift a pen, I will oppose this monstrous thing. By conscription the autocracies of Europe have stood thus long. . . .

Thirdly, I will serve my country at this time by preparing the way, so far as I am able, for the establishment of that peace which sooner or later must follow upon war. . . .

Lastly, I will serve my country in war time, by serving the dream of international brotherhood. No nation is worthy the allegiance of even the meanest of her citizenry, which is not dedicated to the establishment of that larger and more inclusive life of universal association, which is the glad promise of mankind. America, for more than a hundred years, has been first among the countries of the world, in recognition and service of this ideal. She has been a gathering place of all the tribes of earth — a melting-pot into which the ingredients of every race, religion and nationality have been poured. And out of it has come not so much a new nation as a new idea — the idea of brotherhood. This idea has stamped our people as a chosen people. It has set our land apart as a holy land. It has exalted our destiny as a divine destiny. . . .

This is my service for the days of war — the ministry of reconciliation, the defence of democracy, the preparation of the gospel of peace, the quest of brotherhood. . . .

That you will follow me upon this road of travail, I cannot command and will not ask. I reverence too deeply and cherish too tenderly not only my freedom but your own, to venture such an appeal to your good nature. But that you will be not unwilling to have your minister lead your church upon this road, I dare to hope. When confusion, death and terror are about us, I like to think that you will be glad to find in the refuge of this place, "those things which cannot be shaken." When cries of hate and lust are burdening the air, I like to think that you will rejoice to hear within this sanctuary the words that tell of "peace on earth, goodwill toward men." Even when the boys of this church, moved by exalted sense of duty, march to the front, there to slay and to be slain, I like to think that they will look back fondly to this altar and its priests, and thank God there is some witness still of better days and happier peoples. It is because I like to think these things that I hope my resignation as your minister will be neither expected nor demanded. It is because I have faith in your understanding of the church of God and its high mission upon earth, that I hope to continue to bear truthful witness in this pulpit, in war as in peace, to what I feel to be the will of God. It is because I have great love for you as friends and comrades, and no other desire upon earth than to serve you and the cause of free religion which you committed to my charge ten years ago, that I hope God will be kind to me, and keep me still in the grace of your affection.

SOURCE: John Haynes Holmes, "A Statement To My People On the Eve of War," *Messiah Pulpit*, May 1917, 4–6, 9, 11–18.

Debate over World War I at the Unitarian General Conference

1917

Five months after Holmes's sermon protesting World War I, Holmes found himself called upon to draft a denominational statement in response to the war for the General Conference meeting in Montreal. Knowing his own position to be that of a small minority, Holmes wrote a report that described several valid responses to the war and called for mutual tolerance and common preparation for peace. Former U.S. president William Howard Taft (1857– 1930), then serving as president of the conference, offered a pro-war substitute motion that ultimately carried with a vote of 236 to 9. The debate on Taft's motion revealed a variety of positions on freedom of conscience in wartime. Two months later, in November 1917, the Universalists avoided a similar debate by unanimously resolving "that this Convention records its complete devotion to the American ideals, and pledges its loyal support in 'making the world safe for democracy,'" without taking a position on the appropriate means to that end.

—Dan McKanan

The president, Mr. Taft, asked the secretary to take the chair and moved the suspension of the rules that he might make a further motion. The motion was carried.

Mr. TAFT.—As a literary effort this paper is beautiful. As describing the functions of the church and the churches in the next century as we struggle on to better things, it is admirable; but as the expression of this body at this time, when our nation is in danger, when the war must be carried on in order to have world peace, it is an insidious document. Are we, as Unitarians, in favor of winning this war, or are we not? Are we going to set out before the world, as Unitarians, four different views on this war, the last one argued with more emphasis and force than any of the others?— that is the question. Now, I would like to have it determined in this Conference where we stand, and I make this motion:—

Resolved, That it is the sense of this Unitarian Conference that this war must be carried to a successful issue to stamp out militarism in the world; that we, as the Unitarian body, approve the measures of President Wilson and Congress to carry on this war, restrictive as they may be; and that these resolutions be sent to President Wilson, as expressive of the sentiment of this body. . . .

Rev. Richard W. Boynton. — . . . Now I have this to say. I personally assent to what Mr. Taft said earlier; I am willing personally to make sacrifice of my freedom of speech, and I do not assent to the idea that this is a practical time to assert that freedom. If I had been writing this report I should not have written it in this way, but while I am willing to see this motion passed and shall vote for it, let it be understood that this Conference through its regular mode of procedure and in due form committed this word to-day to Mr. Holmes; and, while Mr. Taft expresses and has received in return a support from this audience which shows the feeling of the Conference, let us proceed in such manner that it may be said that somewhere in Christendom there is a religious denomination, not great in numbers but high in influence, which is willing, as you have been willing to-day, to listen with appreciation and with honor to the fearless voice of its smallest minority. I would not belong to this body if any motion passed should carry with it the implication of the suppression not so much of freedom of speech as of freedom of thought.

* * *

Mr. Percy A. Atherton. — . . . Liberty of speech is precious to a democracy, but I conceive that even liberty of speech must have its limitations in time of great national disaster. I honor and I love the chairman of our Council. I have worked with him from the days of college debates twenty years ago, and I respect his insight and his sincerity, but it is untimely at this great moment of catastrophe to present such statements as the view of this body.

Rev. John H. Lathrop. — Friends, it seems to me, as a member of the Council, obliged to study the report pretty carefully, three or four times alone, and in council yesterday all day, that you have missed the point entirely. I do not care which side of the general discussion you are on; I see no relation in this discussion to the main contention of the paper. The paper's effort is just to recognize the fact that we are not all of one mind, and, recognizing that fact, to try and find out whether there is something that we all, divided as we may be in opinion, can nevertheless do as a religious organization. None of you, by anything you vote at this hour, can obliterate the fact that we are not all of one mind; and is it not worth while to find out what we can do together as one religious organization at a time like this? That is the whole effort of the report of the Council, over which the Council was divided in opinion, as you are. We commend our chairman's effort to find one great common religious Christian task for men and women who are not in absolute agreement on the present situation. In other words, I ask, have we a religious purpose that gives us a common task for building the future world, whether we agree as to the war or not? It seems to me that your chairman, Mr. Holmes, undertook an important effort, and carried it out successfully.

* * *

Mr. BATES of Austin, Tex.—I am absolutely in favor of this motion. I enjoyed every word of the report, and admired the courage of a man who dared to make such a statement when he knew the opinion of this body. . . .

Everybody believes in peace. No one denies that war is the sum of all iniquity; and it is the duty of every American citizen to stop this war. It is not England, or Canada, or France, or the United States that has shot defenceless women or sent women and children to the bottom of the ocean, torn up treaties, or sent diplomats back with safeguard and found bombs on him for neutral ships. A report that cannot distinguish between the kind of diplomacy in Germany to-day and that illustrated in the state papers of our President is not a report to adopt, but we are not Unitarians or Christians if we refuse to any one the opportunity to be heard, if it takes all day or all night!

* * *

Mr. TAFT.—A resolution passed, a report made, may mean one thing at one time, and another thing at another time. The Government of the United States and the people of the United States have determined to send to Europe, to France, two millions of men if need be, and to expend billions of dollars, in an issue that we may properly assume the people of the United States believe to be vital to world civilization. Now when you carry on righteous war, you must win; and it is not a time for a great body like this Unitarian Conference to permit its appointed committee, called a Council, to send out to the world a declaration that means nothing in the way of decisiveness as to the policy to be pursued in this war.

It is not a question of the personal feeling that Mr. Holmes brought in trying to state impartially four different opinions on the war. It is not to be expected of any man, even a judge, that he should be able to state all views impartially. There is always an unconscious pressing on the last conclusion, that is to be his. It is not a question of Mr. Holmes's personal feeling. It is a question of our unity as Americans, as Canadians, as citizens of the world, to stamp out the evil that every one recognizes. It is not a question whether a hundred years hence we may hope that things may be better through the inspiration of the action of the churches. We all believe that. But we have two millions of men, our own boys, preparing to go to France to fight for something—and are we Unitarians in this country to say now through our Council that we do not know whether they are fighting for anything that is good or not? It is beyond everything personal, beyond everything theoretical, beyond everything hopeful of the millennium. We are in a war that is fierce, a war in which our enemies have used the highest known discoveries of science in support of principles that would almost disgrace a Hun, and yet now we are to stand before the world impartially, and appear as if we were judges above all of them, and felt no call to respond to the necessities of civilization? Our house is afire and we must put it out, and it is no time for considering whether the firemen are using the best kind of water.

I have no doubt Mr. Holmes tried to be fair, but he wrote the report, and we have the testimony of the Council that they took the report and cut it down, and then one of them was not satisfied; and Mr. Holmes is the minority member on that report. Now an opinion that did not concur with the judgment of the court is likely, just from human nature, not to state strongly the conclusion of the majority.

We represent not a large body, but a very important body, of Americans and Canadians. The question is now whether, when there are four hundred thousand Canadians on the front being killed and wounded and captured, and suffering in a cause that the great majority of both countries believes to be just, believes to be necessary in order to stamp out the evil of militarism, in order to stamp down a militaristic dynasty that looks forward to conquering the destines of the world—the question is, I say, whether we, as Americans, are to divide ourselves into four different parts on this report and say some of us believe this or that or the other or the last part, or whether we are going to act like Americans and Canadians, responding to the demands of the great issue that is being fought for, for which the blood of our dearest is being shed or to be shed, or are we going to occupy a high transcendental position of not deciding anything? That is the question.

If those gentlemen who subscribe to the report think it can be reconciled with the resolutions I have moved, then it does not reflect on the report, but as a Unitarian I want no doubt about it. I am not a pacifist. I have struggled during my career to do as much for international peace as I could, but the way to international peace now is to win this war. Therefore we must not be behind the ranks, behind the trenches, behind our guns, saying to the boys who are shedding their blood and giving up their lives, "We do not know whether you are right or not; we are divided into four parts."

That is the issue, and I say that, without dealing with what the report may mean if you go through it with a microscope, we ought to vote for a positive, a patriotic, a world saving resolution that this Unitarian church is back of the fight in which millions of lives are likely to be lost for a righteous cause and for which millions of lives have already been lost. We represent as high an average of the intelligence of the country as any church—I could go further, but I won't! But let us stand up. If our character and our intelligence does not give us the conviction that the country that is fighting for the right will win, then let us go in and go back of the line that is fighting, whether to win or not, for the highest cause that was ever fought for.

SOURCE: *Official Report of the Proceedings of the Twenty-Seventh Meeting of the General Conference of Unitarian and Other Christian Churches Held at Montreal, Canada, Sept. 25–28, 1917* (Boston: George Ellis, 1918), 3–6, 8–9, 12–14.

"A Declaration of Social Principles"

1917

*During the first two decades of the twentieth century, most Protestant denom-
inations established commissions intended to put social gospel ideals into
practice. The Methodist Federation for Social Service (1907) was one of the
earliest; it helped inspire the Unitarian Fellowship for Social Justice (1908)
and the Universalist Commission on Social Service (1909). The Methodists
also led the way in crafting a "Social Creed" (1908) that expressed opposition
to child labor and the "sweating system," along with support for a living wage,
a shorter workweek, labor arbitration, and acceptance of the Golden Rule "as
the supreme law of society." The Federal Council of Churches adapted and
adopted the Methodist Creed as its own. The Universalists, who did not
belong to the Federal Council, did not compose their own statement until the
end of World War I, but when it came, the statement (largely penned by Clarence Skinner) was more comprehensive and more radical than its predecessors. It was adopted by the General Convention as part of the report of the
Social Service Commission. Further Reading: Donald K. Gorrell,* The Age of
Social Responsibility: The Social Gospel in the Progressive Era, 1900–1920
(Macon, GA: Mercer University Press, 1988).

— Dan McKanan

In the present general confusion of thought we deem it wise to restate the essential principles of the Universalist faith and their social implications in relation to
modern life.

We proclaim the doctrine of the essential divinity of man, of God's universal
Fatherhood, and of man's universal brotherhood. Upon this we build our claims to
the divine and inherent right of democracy, which does not mean the pulling down
of the few to the level of the many, but implies the giving to the many the culture,
the responsibilities which beget self-restraint and rulership, and the arts and refine-
ments of life which are now the possession of the few.

While in no wise minimizing the responsibility of the individual for his own
life, we denounce as superstition the teaching that men are led into sin by inherent depravity and by devils of an unseen world; but we hold it to be self-evident
that mankind is led into sin by evil surroundings, by the evils of unjust social and

economic conditions, which condemn one to be born in the squalor and filth of the slums, and another amidst the equally demoralizing influences of unearned luxury. We hold, therefore, that all systems that attempt to load the blame upon Adam, upon Satan, or upon human depravity, tend to weaken human self-respect, and to lead men away from the discovery and cure of the real causes of human sin and misery.

In view of these conclusions, which we believe were plainly taught by the great Founder of Christianity, we insist that we should not judge one another any more, but rather, that we should remove the stumbling block and the barriers to the kingdom of heaven out of our brother's way.

We conclude also that democracy is not only an inherent right, but also a divinely imposed duty. We find that none of us liveth or dieth to himself, and that true men and women should consider nothing foreign to them which is common to humanity.

Specifically, therefore, we urge that a full and free democracy be set up in our country, and that every man and woman be allowed to exercise the divine right and duty of personal responsibility in the acts of government, first, by the full extension of the franchise to women, and second, by granting each citizen a direct vote in the vital affairs of his own government.

We brand as infamous the practice of subordinating human interests to "business interests," and we urge that the National Government should not hesitate to assume immediate control of the management of the production and distribution of the necessaries of life to prevent want and starvation and the economic enslavement of the people to predatory interests in time of a crisis.

We assert that the claims of the religion of Jesus, the religion of democracy and of international brotherhood, transcend all the claims of race and of nationality, and that the highest form of patriotism demands that we endeavor to place our nation in the position of one that seeks its permanent glory in subordinating selfish interests to those of the coming Federation of the World, in which "the common sense of most shall hold a fretful realm in awe."

We confidently affirm our faith in God with us and in us, the assurance of the ultimate triumph of good. As our great Teacher has taught us to respect and reverence him in the very lowliest of humanity, and as one of his disciples wrote that love of God is shown in love of man, so we urge a higher and better morality than that based upon escaping hell and winning a selfish heaven. We assert the old maxim, "Whatsoever ye do, whether ye eat or drink, do all to the glory of God"—the welfare of His children. We believe it to be the duty and the privilege of each one to be a co-worker with God towards that "long desire of the nations." It is our duty, and our privilege, to keep ourselves at our best in body, mind, and spirit for the sake of the service which it is ours to give. In this faith and in this service we invite the co-operation of all.

Program

The Universalist Church recognizes the fact that no individual and no nation can live a completely effective Christian life in an unchristian social order. We therefore declare the primal task of the church of to-day to be the reconstruction of the world's civilization in terms of justice, peace and righteousness, so that the spiritual life of all may develop to its fullest capacity.

To this end we submit the following working program:

Through all the agencies of the church we shall endeavor to educate and inspire the community and the nation to a keener social consciousness and a truer vision of the kingdom of God on the earth.

We want to safeguard marriage so that every child shall be born with a sound physical, mental and moral heritage.

We want to guarantee to every child those conditions of housing, education, food and recreation which will enable him to become his best.

The standard and plane of living for all should be such that deterioration becomes impossible and advancement becomes limited only by capacity.

Democracy, in order to be complete, must be economic and social as well as political. We therefore declare for the democratization of industry and of land, and for the establishment of co-operation.

We would condemn those forms of private monopoly which make it difficult or impossible for men to attain their common share of the common heritage of earth, and especially do we condemn those forms of exploitation which in time of national stress and suffering make the few wealthy at the cost of the many.

No democracy can be real which shuts out half the people. Women should therefore have equal economic, social and political rights with men.

Free discussion is the soul of democracy and the guarantee of our liberties. It should therefore be maintained in our churches, colleges and public platforms, and limited only by mutual self-respect and courtesy.

We recognize in the use of narcotic habit-forming drugs an imminent peril to social welfare, and we are particularly alarmed at the extent to which tobacco, in the form of cigarettes, is undermining the health and character of American youth. We therefore recommend action toward securing national prohibition of the manufacture and sale of alcoholic liquors, and such progress in restriction of the manufacture of cigarettes and the sale of tobacco as public welfare shall require and public sentiment support. We particularly commend the tobacco laws of Kansas as a model for all the states.

While co-operating to the fullest extent possible with the various forms of charity, relief and correction, we recognize that they do not eradicate fundamental causes. We would mobilize the forces of our church against the causes which create misery, disease, accidents, ignorance and crime, and summon all our strength to the establishment of justice, education and social righteousness.

Some forms of social insurance should gradually replace the present individualistic and inadequate methods of charitable relief.

War is brutalizing, wasteful, and ineffective. We therefore pledge ourselves to work for the organization and federation of the world, that peace may be secured at the earliest possible date consistent with justice for all.

The Universalist Church offers a complete program for completing humanity:

First. An Economic Order which shall give to every human being an equal share in the common gifts of God, and in addition all that he shall earn by his own labor.

Second. A Social Order in which there shall be equal rights for all, special privileges for none, the help of the strong for the weak until the weak become strong.

Third. A Moral Order in which all human law and action shall be the expression of the moral order of the universe.

Fourth. A Spiritual Order which shall build out of the growing lives of living men the growing temple of the living God.

SOURCE: "A Declaration of Social Principles," *Universalist Leader*, November 3, 1917, 759–60.

OLYMPIA BROWN

"The Opening Doors"

1920

After serving Universalist congregations in Weymouth Landing, Massa-
chusetts; Bridgeport, Connecticut; and Racine, Wisconsin, Olympia Brown
(1835–1926) turned her primary professional energies to women's suffrage. She
served for many years as president of the Wisconsin Suffrage Association and
vice president of the National Woman Suffrage Association. In 1913, at age
78, she became a charter member of the Woman's Party, participating in
such militant tactics as the public burning of President Woodrow Wilson's
speeches. Unlike most suffrage pioneers, she lived to see the triumph of the
cause, and preached this sermon to her former congregation in Racine soon
after the passage of the Nineteenth Amendment to the United States Con-
stitution. Further Reading: Beverly Ann Zink-Sawyer, From Preachers to
Suffragists: Woman's Rights and Religious Conviction in the Lives of Three
Nineteenth-Century American Clergywomen *(Louisville, KY: Westminster*
John Knox Press, 2003).

— Dan McKanan

"Lift up your heads O ye gates and be ye lifted
up ye everlasting doors." — Ps. 24:7

It is now thirty years since I resigned my pastorate in this church. That is a long time
and many things have happened, but the grandest thing has been the lifting up of
the gates and the opening of the doors to the women of America, giving liberty to
twenty-seven million women, thus opening to them a new and larger life and a
higher ideal. The future opens before them, fraught with great possibilities of noble
achievement. It is worth a lifetime to behold the victory. Then there have been other
changes; Racine has grown larger and richer and the population has changed; many
have come and some have gone. The everlasting doors have opened to some of our
dearest and they have been permitted to behold the mysteries that lie beyond. We
see them no more. We miss their ready cooperation and sympathy and love, but we
know that wherever they are, they are in God's universe and they are safe and all is
well with them. We have had our struggles and our triumphs, our labors and our
victories, our sorrows and our joys and some of us are growing old, but I would say in
the words of Browning,

Grow old along with me
The best is yet to be. . . .

Meantime, new proofs of the truths which we advocate have been accumulating, sustaining the faith in which we have lived, for which we have worked, and which has bound us together as a church. New and wonderful evidences of the truth of Universalism have come to us. We formerly were glad to be able to point to texts of Scripture as proof of our doctrines, showing to the people the impossibility of an endless hell. . . .

We relied on the promises of revelation and we still cherish these grand old texts. They are dear to our hearts and they will ever remain in our memories a precious possession.

But now they are fortified and confirmed by the promises that come to us from nature "new every morning and fresh every evening." Today we are not dependent upon any text or the letter of any book. It is the spirit that giveth life and the spirit speaks to our souls with every breath that blows. Science has been unraveling the mysteries of the universe and has brought to light new examples of the Divine power and purpose. Burbank and Edison and Madame Curie have lifted up the everlasting doors and revealed the Father's countenance, all radiant with love. Madame Curie, by working long in the laboratory has unlocked the rocks and released radium, a substance fraught with incalculable benefit to humanity. Creative chemistry has been at work and by its reactions and combinations has brought to light new powers in the earth and in the air for the use of men. . . . Thus earth and air are filled with proofs of Divine love, goodness and power. . . . The Opening Doors lead to no dark dungeons, open upon no burning lake, give no evidence of everlasting punishment.

* * *

But more significant than even the voices of the natural world is the evidence of Divine life which we see in man himself. When a great heroic deed is done humanity is lifted up and ennobled and we have the assurance that there is a spirit in man and the Lord God giveth him understanding. Oh, what grand acts of self-sacrifice and high courage, what heroism, have we seen in innumerable instances during the last few sorrowful years, all showing that there is a soul in man partaking in the Divine life. A thousand instances of depravity are forgotten in our admiration of one great heroic action by which human nature is lifted to a higher level, by which we know that man has a soul which is immortal and which enables him to utilize and make his own the wonderful resources with which the earth with all its glories is fitted up for his uses.

When the other day I saw crowds of women of all conditions coming into the polling booth all filled with great enthusiasm, forgetting old prejudices, old associations and former interest, only seeking to know how to serve the state, ready to leave their usual amusements and associations and give themselves to new subjects of study, not to serve any particular party, but only to learn to help the world I said, they are grander than I thought. They have "meat to eat that the world knows not of," there is a Divine Life in them which this new experience is revealing.

The greatness of men, the grand capabilities of women attest the worth of the human being fashioned in the image of God.

It is true that the ignorance of men and the awful mistakes they make, the wrongs they do and the sins they commit, bringing with them, even here, terrible punishment and embittering life, might cause us to doubt were it not that we see that there is a pardoning power in the spiritual world as there is healing in nature.

The river rock soon covers itself with moss and becomes a thing of beauty. The tree deformed and disfigured puts out new twigs and branches and covers itself with verdure and so the warped and travel-stained, sorrow-stricken souls of men shall at last put on the garments of Holiness. Men shall find remedies for their weakness, enlightenment for their ignorance and so rise out of their degradation and their sin.

One of our noted political prisoners said the other day in an interview, "I have never been more hopeful and more confident of the future than I am today. Nor have I ever had so great a faith in the moral order of the universe as I have today."

"There is a kinship of misery that generates the true sweetness of human nature, the very milk of human kindness." Thus the sins of men and their sorrows come at last to confirm the great truths revealed in the natural world.

And so Science: the beauties of nature and the grand possibilities of humanity furnish overwhelming proofs of the final victory of the good and the ultimate purification of every human soul.

And this is Universalism: the grandest system of religious truth that has ever been revealed to man. The doctrine for which the world waits.

* * *

We talk of reforms. We have hoped to make the world safe for democracy; to establish a league of peace; but the very first necessity in reform work is the recognition of Divine capabilities in man. The foundation of democracy is the realization that every human being is a child of God, entitled to the opportunities of life, worthy of respect, and requiring an atmosphere of justice and liberty for his development.

We can never make the world safe for democracy by fighting. Rather by showing the power of Justice done to each humble individual shall we be able to create a firm basis for the state. We can establish a league of peace only by teaching the nations the great lesson of the Fatherhood of God and the Brotherhood of Man.

Every nation must learn that the people of all the nations are children of God and must all share the wealth of the world. You may say that this is impracticable, far away, and can never be accomplished. But this is the work which Universalists are appointed to do. Universalists sometimes, somehow, somewhere, must ever teach this great lesson.

We are not alone. There is always an unseen power working for righteousness. The Infinite is behind us. The eternal years of God are ours.

And that is the message which I bring you today. Stand by this great faith which the world needs and which you are called to proclaim.

It is not necessary to go far away to tell the story of God's love or even to win the nations. God has given us the heathen for an inheritance. Here they come to our own city from far away countries and from the islands of the ocean. And here in Racine we may illustrate the great principles of our faith by our charity, by our kindliness and consideration for all. We shall speak the language of Universal love, and it will be heard and the message will be carried far and wide.

What signifies that your numbers are few today when you are inspired by truths that are everlasting and have before you ever the vision of final victory, the assurance of the salvation of all souls?

Universalism shall at last win the world.

Dear friends, stand by this faith. Work for it and sacrifice for it. There is nothing in all the world so important to you as to be loyal to this faith which has placed before you the loftiest ideals, which has comforted you in sorrow, strengthened you for noble duty and made the world beautiful for you. Do not demand immediate results but rejoice that you are worthy to be entrusted with this great message and that you are strong enough to work for a great true principle without counting the cost. Go on finding ever new applications of these truths and new enjoyments in their contemplation, always trusting in the one God which ever lives and loves. "One God, one law, one element, and one far-off divine event to which the whole creation moves."

SOURCE: Olympia Brown Papers, ca. 1849–1963; "Opening Doors," September 12, 1920. A–69, folder 36. Schlesinger Library, Radcliffe Institute for Advanced Study, Harvard University, Cambridge, MA. Reprinted in Dana Greene, ed., *Suffrage and Religious Principle: Speeches and Writings of Olympia Brown* (Metuchen, NJ: Scarecrow Press, 1983), 167–73.

His Religion and Hers

1923

Charlotte Perkins (Stetson) Gilman (1860–1935) was a writer and lecturer on feminism and women's roles in society, particularly as related to economic independence and the challenges of maintaining both career and family commitments. Gilman was related through her father to the famous Beecher family, including Henry Ward Beecher and Harriet Beecher Stowe. Although she is perhaps better remembered today as the author of the story "The Yellow Wallpaper," she was more well known in her time for her work on behalf of women's independence. In His Religion and Hers, *Gilman looks beyond suffrage and other rights as the answer to women's secondary status in society and examines the role played by male-dominated organized religion in holding back the development of human society. The work makes an interesting comparison to earlier critiques found in Elizabeth Cady Stanton's* The Woman's Bible *and Matilda Joslyn Gage's* Woman, Church, and State. *Further Reading: Cynthia J. Davis,* Charlotte Perkins Gilman: A Biography *(Stanford, CA: Stanford University Press, 2010); Judith A. Allen,* The Feminism of Charlotte Perkins Gilman: Sexualities, Histories, Progressivism *(Chicago: University of Chicago Press, 2009).*

—Emily Mace

The most powerful group of concepts governing conduct are those forming a religion. Here is a lever to move the world.

If a religion is based on fact, and urges conduct in line with the natural laws of social evolution, it is the greatest help in our development. If it rests on false assumptions, forces into the mind illogical and contradictory deductions, and urges conduct which interferes with right progress, or which is quite useless, its tremendous power keeps us down instead of lifting us up.

To judge and measure religious doctrines, we must have some wider knowledge than that of the ancients. To criticize the basic assumptions of a religion, we must have in mind other assumptions, based on fact.

The assumptions underlying this study are these:

That humanity is an organic relationship of human beings;

That it is in process of evolution, social evolution;

That such social evolution is in line with natural law, and is to be greatly promoted by our conscious behavior, or greatly hindered and perverted;

That man is the only creature constructing his own environment, both physical and mental: he makes that which makes him;

That it is easily within our power to make this world such an environment as should conduce to the development of a noble race, rapidly and surely improving from generation to generation, and so naturally producing better conduct;

That our pitiful failures are due to an unnecessary ignorance, and to certain misconceptions, notably those of religion;

That the most widely entertained religious misconceptions rest on a morbid preoccupation with death and "another world";

That this is mainly due to the fact that they have been introduced and developed by one sex only, the male, in whose life as a hunter and fighter death was the impressive crisis;

That the female, the impressive crisis of whose life is birth, has an essentially different outlook, much more in line with social progress;

That a normal feminine influence in recasting our religious assumptions will do more than any other one thing to improve the world; and that no truth, in any religion, will be controverted by such natural development.

✳   ✳   ✳

In the range of sex-distinction the female is superior; she, more than the male, is the race type; but in human distinction the female of our species is at present markedly inferior to the male. She is retarded by thousands of years of restriction, is seldom his equal in those processes which maintain social life and conduce to its progress; and, even as a female, does not fully exercise her primal powers nor fulfill her primal duties.

Her human capacities are by nature equal to his, but they have atrophied through long suppression, and her great power as selector of the best male for race-improvement, has been abrogated by her economic dependence upon him. As a mother, her influence has been limited by isolation and pitifully lowered by her position as domestic servant.

The "feminist revolt" of the last century was mainly against pressing personal injustice, and the enthusiasm of woman's new freedom seems, so far, to point more toward a distinctly masculine "self-expression" than to a feminine sense of duty to the race.

It is by no means generally realized by women that their true sex purpose is race-improvement; that their influence upon religion should be to turn its sublime force to human betterment on earth; that they have it in their power swiftly and strongly to push forward this so long-neglected world.

The main line of race-improvement is through the child.

The human mother fails in her full duty to the child because of her unnatural position as servant to the man.

SOURCE: Charlotte Perkins Gilman, *His Religion and Hers: A Study of the Faith of Our Fathers and the Work of Our Mothers* (New York and London: Century, 1923), 5–9.

Humanism

1926

Curtis W. Reese (1887–1961), best remembered as a Unitarian humanist, started his professional life as a Baptist pastor, but the influence of Higher Criticism nudged his beliefs closer to those of Unitarianism, and he became the minister of a Unitarian church in Alton, Illinois, in 1913. He served as the president of the Western Unitarian Conference from 1919 to 1930. During this time, his beliefs became more concretely humanist in emphasis, and he helped to prepare the Humanist Manifesto of 1933; he also served as the first president of the American Humanist Association, which was founded in 1941. Reese characterized his humanism as religious humanism, in which a focus on human lives and this-worldly pursuits replaced the other-worldly, supernaturally centered approach of traditional religion. This selection from a 1926 paper elucidates his understanding of humanism as a more fully and honestly religious way of approaching all of human life. Further Reading: Charles H. Lyttle, Freedom Moves West: A History of the Western Unitarian Conference, 1852–1952 *(Boston: Beacon Press, 1952); Mason Olds,* American Religious Humanism, *rev. ed. (Minneapolis: Fellowship of Religious Humanists, 1996).*

— Emily Mace

A word is a symbol of reality. This is true whether the reality be a perceptual fact or conceptual theory. When reality changes, clear thinking requires that the old symbol be exchanged for another or that the change in content be clearly recorded. When a word symbolizes a movement with continuity of problem and of attempt at solution, the familiar symbol should be kept and its changed meaning recorded. Psychology is a case in point. Once psychology was the name of the science that dealt with the *soul*; later of the science that dealt with *mental faculties*; then of the science that dealt with *states* of *consciousness*; and now psychology is the name of the science that deals with *behavior*. The old symbol still holds. Much more should this be true when the symbol is weighted with sacred associations and memories. Religion is a symbol which not only has continuity of problem and of attempt at solution but which is also surrounded with the most hallowed associations and memories. Religion symbolizes the human quest to discover in the nature of man and the universe the kind of life that is inherently desirable, and to enlist in its behalf all instrumentalities, both human and cosmic, that are capable of assisting in its realization. This quest is man's religion. In early religions the quest took the form of attempts on the part of man to relate himself to those instrumentalities and values that seemed to have significance for the welfare of the group; and later it took the form of attempts to placate the personal gods in order to gain personal peace. While the forms of religion have undergone revolution, we shall retain the term "religion." My chief purpose, however, is not to justify the word but to record certain changes in its content and form.

The common denominator of the old religions is found in *man's response to super-human sources of fortune.* This belief in and relation to super-human sources of fortune is characteristic of the old religions. Without this psychological situation the old faiths cannot admit the religious validity of any human behavior. Hence the old religions have resulted in a servile psychological attitude.

This pathetic and tragic outcome of the old religions is now somewhat relieved by humanistic tendencies which are gradually growing everywhere. Modern thinkers are finding the content of religion in human worths and its cosmic significance in man's co-operation with and control of the processes of life to the end that human possibilities shall be completely and harmoniously realized. Humanism aims at the conscious experience of the fullness of life. It regards this as the aim and end of religion and of all social instrumentalities. In other words, humanism stands for the complete and permanent satisfactions of human life.

The object of the old religion is the superhuman unknown and the chief content of the old religion is the sentiment entertained toward the superhuman unknown. The object of humanism is *life*, and its chief content is *loyalty* to life. In the old religion right and wrong are defined in terms of conformity to standards extrinsic to human life; in humanism right and wrong are defined in terms of consequence to human life. The old religion is characterized by trust and receptivity; humanism, by aspiration and creativity.

Whatever theological significance is inferred from or attached to humanism, it is functional, tentative, secondary. The old religion judges man by his contribution to the gods; humanism judges the gods by their contribution to man. In the old religion theological beliefs are central and imperative; in humanism theological theories are types of "spiritual short hand." In the old religion a theological revolution is spiritual treason; in humanism a theological revolution is a change of mental attitude, a shifting of postulates, a minor part of the day's work.

According to the old view, religion without superhuman objects of faith is impossible. But if religion is the quest of man to discover and live the inherently desirable life, manifestly theological convictions and philosophies of the ultimate nature of the universe are not prerequisite to the religious life. Religion is not constituted of theology or philosophy or metaphysics—but it may use them as instruments in the enhancement of human life. Man may be utterly void of theology and yet be deeply religious. Religion is enhanced by various intellectual and aesthetic devices, such as philosophical theories and liturgical forms, but none of them is exclusively essential.

In the theocentric world of the pre-scientific days man wanted super powers or beings whom he could placate and so secure special agency. But science has discredited special agency. It has found the universe to be a self-operating system. It finds ordinary cosmic events and processes routine and impersonal, and other things cared for by highly specialized parts of nature such as man. It regards order and purpose as self existent. Reality is found, but its ultimate nature is not yet determined. Man's whole world outlook is vastly different from what it once was and it is still subject to change. Hence humanistic religion does not regard the acceptance of any philosophical or theological hypothesis as religiously necessary.

Yet, in order to make its committals effective in the realization of its goals, humanism needs a science of values. Such a science must be evolved through long experimentation. It must be founded on enlightened experience, true to basic desires, and attested by its fruitage in the complete and harmonious realization of human life.

Humanism regards all the normal human impulses as valid and worthful and it seeks the complete and harmonious realization of them all. There is no question of higher and lower impulses. None is mean or unclean. All are good and sacred. Humanism proclaims the democracy of the human impulses. Conflicts in the impulsive life are abnormalities due to misunderstanding and misuse of the impulses. The well-balanced, fully-developed, and intelligently controlled impulsive life is the full life. Of all the needs of the race, the greatest are for freedom from repression and oppression, and for committal to the fullest possible realization of life on the highest possible human plane.

Humanism is bound up with the full life. It is intimately concerned with all social instrumentalities; with education and politics, with science and art, with industries and homes. It seeks not only to interpret these but to guide them. It aims to direct all social instruments and powers to the ends of human life, and to create new instruments and powers of life. It regards the whole sweep of life—the sex life, the political life, the economic life—as within it province. It regards the proper world order as a religious order. The whole of life goes up or down together and none of it is foreign to the interest of religion. When the purpose of thought and conduct is human well-being, such thought and conduct is religious in character. *When thus motivated, consecration to science is religious consecration, works of art are religious works, governmental achievements are religious achievements, social relationships are religious relationships, and moral victories are religious victories.*

In its wider significance, understood as loyalty to life and reinforced with modern imagery, religion shall become man's supreme concern!

SOURCE: Curtis W. Reese, *Humanism* (Chicago: Open Court, 1926), 21–26.

JOHN DIETRICH

"Unitarianism and Humanism"

1927

Raised in the Reformed Church, John Hassler Dietrich (1878–1957) initially served a Reformed congregation in Pittsburgh, Pennsylvania. When he modernized the service and introduced a hymnbook written by a Unitarian, problems emerged, leading to his defrocking in 1911 for denial of central Christian doctrines. The American Unitarian Association then welcomed him into fellowship, and he served a Unitarian congregation in Spokane, Washington, for five years. In 1916, he accepted a call to the First Unitarian Society of Minneapolis, where he ultimately found his most successful ministry as an apostle of humanism through remarkably successful radio broadcasts of his sermons. This selection reveals Dietrich's humanism to be a faith in and responsible to men and women and their human lives, without taking up the question of the existence of God or requiring an atheistic perspective. It also underlines several reasons why Unitarianism was a likely place for a humanist perspective to flourish. Further Reading: Margaret Carleton Winston, This Circle of Earth: The Story of John H. Dietrich *(New York: G. P. Putnam's Sons, 1942).*

—Emily Mace

I must be brief in regard to the relationship between Unitarianism and Humanism in order to have time for some discussion of the fundamental tenets of this faith. In the first place, Unitarianism offered opportunity for the enunciation of Humanism by virtue of its underlying principle of spiritual freedom, by its insistence upon intellectual integrity rather than upon intellectual uniformity, by its offer of religious fellowship to every one of moral purpose without regard to his theological beliefs. But this is not the important thing. The real reason why Unitarianism was the natural soil for the growth of Humanism is the fact that Unitarianism was a revolt against orthodox Christianity in the interest of the worth and dignity of human nature and the sanctity of human life. The real origin of Unitarianism is to be found in the revolutionary interpretation of human nature which was taught by Channing and his colleagues. Previous to the revolt of Unitarianism the Christian church looked upon men as almost entirely worthless, of no more value than the worm which crawls in the dust. It was taught that man was conceived and born in sin, totally depraved, doomed to eternal torment, from which he could be saved, not by any merit of his own, but only by the saving grace of God. This horrible doctrine was preached in its crudest form in New England by Jonathan Edwards and his cohorts, and it was into this New England of a hundred years ago, with no loftier conception of human nature and human destiny than this, that there came the revolutionary ideas of Channing and other men of noble mind. "Every human being," said Channing in his discourse on Slavery, "has in him the germ of the idea of God; and to unfold this is the end of his existence. Every human being has in his breast the elements of that divine everlasting law—of duty; and to unfold, revere, obey this, is the very purpose for which life is given. Every human being has the idea of what is meant by truth. Every human being has affections, which may be purified and expanded into a sublime love." "Such," says Channing, "is our nature. These are the capacities which distinguish us from the animals. These are the things which make it possible for every man to be regarded as a being of infinite work and sanctity." And it was the pronouncement of this doctrine in contrast with the doctrine of human degradation as held by New England Calvinism that formed the basis of Unitarian thought.

It is only a step from this thought to another which forms the basis of Humanism; namely, that man not only is of worth but of supreme worth, that he is an end and not a means. In other words, Humanism is merely an expansion and a more rigorous application of the fundamental principle of Unitarianism. Indeed Channing announced this logical conclusion, but it has not been fully preached by the majority of Unitarians. Directly following the words which I have just quoted, he says, "Such a being was plainly made for an end in himself. He is a person, not a being. He is an end, not a mere instrument or means. He was made for his own virtue and happiness, and not of the virtue and happiness of another. It is to degrade him from his rank in the universe to make him a means and not an end." And this doctrine which Channing preached one hundred years ago is seized upon by certain followers of Channing today and made the basis of a religion.

* * *

Men and women, do you realize what this faith of ours means? It means that we, I mean humanity, are responsible for the present miserable condition of this world; it means that we are responsible for the millions of lives that were snuffed out in the great war; it means that we are responsible for the hundreds of thousands who are starving in Europe today; it means that we are responsible for the millions of people who suffer for the lack of employment at this time; it means that we are responsible for every undesirable feature of our civilization; and that we are responsible for the future condition of society. The life of humanity at least on this planet rests in our hands. We can choose the path that we will follow, and we can follow the path that we choose, if we really so desire. We can make this world what we will. We hold the keys to the future in our own hands. If there is ever to be a better order of human society it will depend upon us and upon no one else. Think of the awful responsibility this places upon our shoulders; and in the light of this responsibility how can we keep on dallying with petty manners in religion—reading bibles, mumbling prayers, throwing ourselves in the arms of Jesus.

This is the basis of the faith which we call Humanism, and this indeed is the religious need of the world, and I pray that our Unitarian churches shall ring not only with all the old-time enthusiasm of our fathers, but also with the modern-time spirit, which needs only their lofty devotion and willing sacrifice to fulfill the world's new sturdy saving summons, "Thou must do the justice that thou cravest." In the light of such a faith it becomes our supreme duty in this world to hold before the gaze of men the vision of a perfect social order, to preach the absolute necessity of the practice of human brotherhood, to hold aloft as the supreme object of our allegiance human life itself, and to turn the thoughts of men from the altars of the departed gods to the tasks which lie about them, and to help them realize that the destiny of human life on this planet rests in their hands; for, once we transfer men's efforts from seeking help from heaven, whence no help comes, to a firm and confident reliance upon themselves, the progress of humanity toward an era of peace and happiness is assured.

In fact, I am assured that there is no possible future for religion except as it broadens itself out into this Humanistic position. All real progress is brought about by the application of the spirit of Humanism, by a real and living faith in the power of man to achieve, and a consecrated devotion to the ends of human life. Every advance in freedom and self-development is a result of the application of this spirit; but in the past it has been applied by men of science and of industry, and not by religion. It is right that men of science and industry should be at the back of all efforts of progress; but religion should be there also, and should be the inspiring force; and religion would be there if it were the religion of Humanism.

SOURCE: John H. Dietrich, "Unitarianism and Humanism," in Curtis Reese, ed., *Humanist Sermons* (Chicago: Open Court, 1927), 100–102, 111–13.

"The Humanist Manifesto"

1933

The signers of the Humanist Manifesto of 1933 attempted to state in fifteen brief points what a humanistic religious perspective had to say about the major questions of humanity's origin, purpose, and place in the universe. It brought a thoroughly scientific and evolutionary perspective to humanity's origins and cultural development and recognized a religious but naturalistic dimension to the question of where humanity had come from. Initiated by Western Unitarian Conference secretary Raymond Bennett Bragg, the Manifesto elevated all of human endeavor to the plane of the religious. Of the thirty-four signers, fifteen were Unitarians, including eight ministers. Further Reading: Edwin H. Wilson, The Genesis of a Humanist Manifesto, *ed. Teresa Maciocha (Amherst, NY: Humanist Press, 1995), and William F. Schulz,* Making the Manifesto: the Birth of Religious Humanism *(Boston: Skinner House, 2002).*

—Emily Mace

The time has come for widespread recognition of the radical changes in religious beliefs throughout the modern world. The time is past for mere revision of traditional attitudes. Science and economic change have disrupted the old beliefs. Religions the world over are under the necessity of coming to terms with new conditions created by a vastly increased knowledge and experience. In every field of human activity, the vital movement is now in the direction of a candid and explicit humanism. In order that religious humanism may be better understood we, the undersigned, desire to make certain affirmations which we believe the facts of our contemporary life demonstrate.

There is great danger of a final, and we believe fatal, identification of the word religion with doctrines and methods which have lost their significance and which are powerless to solve the problem of human living in the Twentieth Century. Religions have always been means for realizing the highest values of life. Their end has been accomplished through the interpretation of the total environing situation (theology or world view), the sense of values resulting therefrom (goal or ideal), and the technique (cult), established for realizing the satisfactory life. A change in any of these factors results in alteration of the outward forms of religion. This fact explains the changefulness of religions through the centuries. But through all changes religion itself remains constant in its quest for abiding values, an inseparable feature of human life.

Today man's larger understanding of the universe, his scientific achievements, and deeper appreciation of brotherhood, have created a situation which requires a new statement of the means and purposes of religion. Such a vital, fearless, and frank religion capable of furnishing adequate social goals and personal satisfactions may appear to many people as a complete break with the past. While this age does owe a vast debt to the traditional religions, it is none the less obvious that any religion that can hope to be a synthesizing and dynamic force for today must be shaped for the needs of this age. To establish such a religion is a major necessity of the present. It is a responsibility which rests upon this generation. We therefore affirm the following:

FIRST: Religious humanists regard the universe as self-existing and not created.

SECOND: Humanism believes that man is part of nature and that he has emerged as a result of a continuous process.

THIRD: Holding an organic view of life, humanists find that the traditional dualism of mind and body must be rejected.

FOURTH: Humanism recognizes that man's religious culture and civilization, as clearly depicted by anthropology and history, are the product of a gradual development due to his interaction with his natural environment and with his social heritage. The individual born into a particular culture is largely molded by that culture.

FIFTH: Humanism asserts that the nature of the universe depicted by modern science makes unacceptable any supernatural or cosmic guarantees of human values. Obviously humanism does not deny the possibility of realities as yet undiscovered, but it does insist that the way to determine the existence and value of any and all realities is by means of intelligent inquiry and by the assessment of their relations to human needs. Religion must formulate its hopes and plans in the light of the scientific spirit and method.

SIXTH: We are convinced that the time has passed for theism, deism, modernism, and the several varieties of "new thought."

SEVENTH: Religion consists of those actions, purposes, and experiences which are humanly significant. Nothing human is alien to the religious. It includes labor, art, science, philosophy, love, friendship, recreation—all that is in its degree expressive of intelligently satisfying human living. The distinction between the sacred and the secular can no longer be maintained.

EIGHTH: Religious Humanism considers the complete realization of human personality to be the end of man's life and seeks its development and fulfillment in the here and now. This is the explanation of the humanist's social passion.

NINTH: In the place of the old attitudes involved in worship and prayer the humanist finds his religious emotions expressed in a heightened sense of personal life and in a cooperative effort to promote social well-being.

TENTH: It follows that there will be no uniquely religious emotions and attitudes of the kind hitherto associated with belief in the supernatural.

ELEVENTH: Man will learn to face the crises of life in terms of his knowledge of their naturalness and probability. Reasonable and manly attitudes will be fostered by education and supported by custom. We assume that humanism will take the path of social and mental hygiene and discourage sentimental and unreal hopes and wishful thinking.

TWELFTH: Believing that religion must work increasingly for joy in living, religious humanists aim to foster the creative in man and to encourage achievements that add to the satisfactions of life.

THIRTEENTH: Religious humanism maintains that all associations and institutions exist for the fulfillment of human life. The intelligent evaluation, transformation, control, and direction of such associations and institutions with a view to the enhancement of human life is the purpose and program of humanism. Certainly religious institutions, their ritualistic forms, ecclesiastical methods, and communal activities must be reconstituted as rapidly as experience allows, in order to function effectively in the modern world.

FOURTEENTH: The humanists are firmly convinced that existing acquisitive and profit-motivated society has shown itself to be inadequate and that a radical change in methods, controls, and motives must be instituted. A socialized and cooperative economic order must be established to the end that the equitable distribution of the means of life be possible. The goal of humanism is a free and universal society in which people voluntarily and intelligently cooperate for the common good. Humanists demand a shared life in a shared world.

FIFTEENTH AND LAST: We assert that humanism will: (a) affirm life rather than deny it; (b) seek to elicit the possibilities of life, not flee from them; and (c) endeavor to establish the conditions of a satisfactory life for all, not merely for the few. By this positive morale and intention humanism will be guided, and from this perspective and alignment the techniques and efforts of humanism will flow.

So stand the theses of religious humanism. Though we consider the religious forms and ideas of our fathers no longer adequate, the quest of the good life is still the central task for mankind. Man is at last becoming aware that he alone is responsible for the realization of the world of his dreams, that he has within himself the power for its achievement. He must set intelligence and will to the task.

(Signed)

J. A. C. Fagginger Auer—Parkman Professor of Church History and Theology, Harvard University; Professor of Church History, Tufts College.

E. Burdette Backus—Unitarian Minister.

Harry Elmer Barnes—General Editorial Department, Scripps-Howard Newspapers.

L. M. Birkhead—The Liberal Center, Kansas City, Missouri.

Raymond B. Bragg—Secretary, Western Unitarian Conference.

Edwin Arthur Burtt—Professor of Philosophy, Sage School of Philosophy, Cornell University.

Ernest Caldecott—Minister, First Unitarian Church, Los Angeles, California.

A. J. Carlson—Professor of Physiology, University of Chicago.

John Dewey—Columbia University.

Albert C. Dieffenbach—Formerly Editor of *The Christian Register*.

John H. Dietrich—Minister, First Unitarian Society, Minneapolis.

Bernard Fantus—Professor of Therapeutics, College of Medicine, University of Illinois.

William Floyd—Editor of *The Arbitrator*, New York City.

F. H. Hankins—Professor of Economics and Sociology, Smith College.

A. Eustace Haydon—Professor of History of Religions, University of Chicago.

Llewellyn Jones—Literary critic and author.

Robert Morss Lovett—Editor, *The New Republic*; Professor of English, University of Chicago.

Harold P. Marley—Minister, The Fellowship of Liberal Religion, Ann Arbor.

R. Lester Mondale—Minister, Unitarian Church, Evanston, Illinois.

Charles Francis Potter—Leader and Founder, the First Humanist Society of New York, Inc.

John Herman Randall, Jr.—Department of Philosophy, Columbia University.

Curtis W. Reese—Dean, Abraham Lincoln Center, Chicago.

Oliver L. Reiser—Associate Professor of Philosophy, University of Pittsburgh.

Roy Wood Sellars—Professor of Philosophy, University of Michigan.

Clinton Lee Scott—Minister, Universalist Church, Peoria, Illinois.

Maynard Shipley—President, The Science League of America.

W. *Frank Swift*—Director, Boston Ethical Society.

V. *T. Thayer*—Educational Director, Ethical Culture Schools.

Eldred C. Vanderlaan—Leader of the Free Fellowship, Berkeley, California.

Joseph Walker—Attorney, Boston, Massachusetts.

Jacob J. Weinstein—Rabbi; Advisor to Jewish Students, Columbia University.

Frank S. C. Wicks—All Souls Unitarian Church, Indianapolis.

David Rhys Williams—Minister, Unitarian Church, Rochester, New York.

Edwin H. Wilson—Managing Editor, *The New Humanist*, Chicago, Illinois; Minister, Third Unitarian Church, Chicago, Illinois.

SOURCE: "Humanist Manifesto I," available at americanhumanist.org/humanism/humanist _manifesto_I

"A Universalist Missionary to Japan 1925–1936"
1936

The Women's National Missionary Association sent numerous workers to the Japanese mission and to ecumenical service projects in Japan. Among them was Georgene E. Bowen (1898–1984), a European American woman who served for more than a decade at the Blackmer Home in Tokyo, which prepared impoverished girls for full participation in Japanese society. After returning to the United States, she worked at a settlement house in New York City and as an organizer of "Golden Age Clubs" for the elderly in Philadelphia. Bowen's memoir offers a glimpse of the missionary spirit in Universalism. Further Reading: Mary Agnes Hathaway, The Blackmer Home Girls *(Boston: Woman's National Missionary Association, 1927).*

—Dan McKanan

There had been much talk in the religious and political circles of the United States about world peace, and how to achieve it. I believed that I could help bring about that goal by being a friend and assisting people in Japan. My greatest interest had always been in people. And here I wanted to meet and learn to know them wherever in Japan they dwelt. I wanted to reach out beyond the Home and our Mission. Every opportunity I had I would spend with them.

* * *

Very early in my Japan experience—perhaps the first time I opened my mouth to sing—the doors to the Japanese and foreigners opened wide. Everywhere I was asked to sing or teach English songs. . . .

The Tokyo Y.W.C.A. asked me to teach a class of fifteen girls to sing the English songs. The Tokyo Union Church invited me to sing in some of their oratorios. One was the Messiah in which I sang the alto solo before an audience of 350 persons. By February 1926, I had two singing groups.

At the Blackmer Home I was not expected to do religious teaching, but I was well prepared to do it with materials that I collected in my courses at the School of Religious Education and Social Service [at Boston University]. I had religious pictures of Jesus' life, a collection of quotations, sacred music and Bible passages.

* * *

As I worked with Japanese girls and tried to help them, many things they did were puzzling. Why did they do them? There had to be a reason. They thought differently, but what did they think? They were as intelligent as American girls. What really made the difference? Gradually, I had to figure it out.

Why did they smile when there was nothing to smile about? (To conceal their worry or embarrassment.) Why did they not look me in the eyes when they spoke? (It would be rude to do so.) Why did they so often cover their mouths with their hand when they talked or ate? (They felt improper to show the inside of their mouths.) Why did they bow lower to men and to their elders, than they did to one another? (Because their status was inferior.) . . . Why did they so quickly accept a difficult situation without even trying to change it? (Because as women, they had no legal or social power to change things.) Why could they feel so free to be naked in a communal bath? (Because there was nothing to be ashamed of about the natural body.) Why did they shrink from kissing or being kissed—even the children? (Because they felt that kissing was a sexual act, not appropriately used in public or private.) Why don't girls and young women offer to take more responsibility even when they want something to be done? (They wait to be asked, hesitate, usually apologize, then go ahead and do their very best, but they also often lack the power to carry it through.) Why? (Because they have been trained to be retiring and self-effacing.) . . .

The twenty girls being sheltered and protected by the Blackmer Home must, therefore, be encouraged to think and to take responsibility. They must be prepared to take a stronger role in their lives, their homes and their communities. I tried to help them assume leadership at the Home and in the church, and to gain confidence in themselves. It was a challenge every day and every year while I labored in the Japan field.

SOURCE: Georgene E. Bowen, A Universalist Missionary to Japan 1925–1936 (Philadelphia, 1984), 8–9, 17–18.

Unitarians Face a New Age
1936

In 1934, the American Unitarian Association assigned its Commission of Appraisal the task of addressing the question of what role or function Unitarianism would have in the modern world. Commissioners included Frederick M. Eliot (Chairman), James Luther Adams, Samuel P. Capen (Consultant), Walter Pritchard Eaton, Eduard C. Lindeman, Frederic G. Melcher, James Bissett Pratt, and Aurelia Henry Reinhardt, with H. Paul Douglass as the Director of Studies. Published in 1936, the Commission's report attempted to address that question as well as make conclusions and recommendations. This excerpt comes from the commissioners' introduction to the report. In it, they pose the question of "whether or not Unitarianism has a function to perform in the modern world," with the assumption that it should be dissolved if not, suggesting the very real fear that liberal religion as found in Unitarianism had outlived its usefulness. The introduction offers telling commentary about what stood at the root of that fear, as well as a clear indication of the role they hoped liberal religion could continue to play.

—Emily Mace

The first question which the members of the Commission of Appraisal decided must be answered, if their enquiry was to have practical value, was whether the organized religious movement known as Unitarianism has any real function to perform in the modern world. If not, it would clearly be better to liquidate the present organizations and resources, for the mere continuation of any institution after it has ceased to meet a real need is wasteful, and for this to happen to an institution calling itself "liberal" would be a tragic irony of fate.

If this question is to be answered in the affirmative, it must be in different terms from those in which the function of Unitarianism was defined a hundred years ago—or fifty, or even twenty-five. The radical spirit of the founders and re-founders of Unitarianism may be the inspiration for our present effort to re-think and re-formulate the purposes of our movement; but some of the basic ideas and certainly the specific phrases used must be worked out in the light of the present situation and under the impact of forces in the modern world impinging upon all churches. What Channing, Emerson, Parker, Henry W. Bellows, and Thomas Starr King did for their generations must be done anew for ours, but their formulas will not serve to meet our needs.

The genius of the Unitarian movement has been its power to adapt the vocabulary and practices of a religion whose roots are sunk deep into the past to new knowledge, new conditions, and new situations. If this genius should fail us now, the time will have come to write "finis" to the story of Unitarianism.

Whatever may be the actual future of the name Unitarian, there can be little doubt of the need in the modern world for some organized expression of the liberal spirit in religion. In a time when revolution and chaos are everywhere threatening, when ideals are again forming an alliance with tyranny and dogmatism, when intellectual confusion and social discontent are blindly trying to fight their way out of situations where only the problem-solving temper of mind can be of real help, when a fresh birth of the nationalistic spirit is everywhere offering its spurious comfort to tired and discouraged people—in a time like ours there is imperative need for a religious fellowship that will bring order and hope and confidence to men of the liberal tradition.

The need is so great that it will in the long run create the instrumentalities for its own fulfillment. But there seems to us a possibility that among the existing agencies of religion there may already be some that can transform themselves into the new pattern that is required, and thus not only bridge the gap between the old order and the new but also make shorter the period of transition. If in the process such institutions should ultimately lose their identity and sacrifice their specific historical character, that would be a small price to pay for the privilege of rendering a great service.

For more than a hundred years the liberal churches of America have stood and fought for religious freedom, by which they have meant chiefly the right of each individual to think out his own religious beliefs and the right of each congregation to choose its own forms of worship and church polity. The struggle has been largely against the authority of creeds and ecclesiastical traditions, and the principal methods employed have been preaching and teaching, based upon faith in the power of human reason to work out all the problems of human life, provided it were liberated from ignorance, prejudice and dogmatism.

Today liberal churches find themselves facing a very different world, in which different conditions impose the necessity for a new formulation of basic purposes, principles, and methods. What is needed in the world of 1936 is an association of free churches that will stand and fight for the central philosophy and values of liberal religion, as set over against any philosophy that denies the spiritual nature of man, making him merely the product and plaything of a material universe in which only blind chance and ruthless force have sway.

Throughout the western world this basic philosophic issue is revealed, in the realm of practical affairs, as the issue between those who affirm and those who deny the possibility of so adapting the traditional democratic processes as to make them effectively applicable to the problems confronting modern society. It must be apparent to everyone that in their older forms these processes have failed to meet the test of such problems as have arisen in recent years in the economic and international fields. The identification of the philosophy of democracy with the laissez-faire policy in the economic field, for example, is no longer tenable, and has already done serious damage to the cause of democracy everywhere. In some countries, this has led to a complete rejection of the philosophy and practice of democracy, and with them the whole set of spiritual values which liberals for two centuries have cherished and sought to promote. Nor is this merely the result of war-weariness and despair, ready to acquiesce in the alluring promises and demands of ambitious dictators. It is much more the fruit of a slow process of disillusionment with the ineffective and half-hearted way in which the champions of democracy have sought to deal with the social and political problems of our time. Many intelligent and thoughtful students of history have come to the conclusion that democracy carries within itself the seeds of its own inevitable corruption and death. The tide is today strongly moving in the direction of arbitrary and absolute authority; and, if the democratic processes are to be saved from something very like obliteration, there must be prompt and vigorous action. It is high time for those who believe in democracy to take their stand and organize their forces aggressively.

In that struggle, religion has a part to play that may well be decisive; for without the support of religious principles and religious enthusiasm liberalism cannot hope to fight a long, hard campaign in any field. Political liberalism has suffered serious defeat whenever it lacked foundations of philosophic thought or the stamina of moral endurance which religion can supply. Social and economic liberalism have fallen into disrepute for the same reason. But religion can supply the basic ideas and the inexhaustible driving-force of emotion and will that are necessary to meet on equal terms the forces now arrayed against democracy, provided it be religion that is itself consistent with the principles of liberalism. Furthermore, unless history has no lessons at all to teach the present age, this power of religion will not be available on a large scale or over a prolonged period of time except through some form of organized life which is in harmony with its own essential character. Liberal religion must express itself through liberal churches.

*   *   *

Three questions will immediately force themselves upon our attention. (1) How far does the actual church under examination fall short of the ideal as outlined? (2) What must be done to bring it reasonably close to that ideal? (3) Is the expenditure of effort necessary to bring about that change justified by the promise of success?

SOURCE: *Unitarians Face a New Age: Findings and Recommendations of the Commission of Appraisal to the American Unitarian Association* (Boston: Commission of Appraisal, 1936), 3–5, 9.

"The Position and Credo of the Independent Church"

1939

Gregorio Aglipay (1860–1940), a Roman Catholic priest, and Isabelo de los Reyes, Sr. (1864–1938) were leaders in the Philippine Revolution that began in 1896. Inspired by the revolutionary martyr José Rizal, they believed that religious independence from Rome should accompany political independence from Spain. In 1902, the year the United States consolidated its control of the Philippines, they organized the Philippine Independent Church, with civilian governor William Howard Taft as its vice president. Taft, a leading Unitarian, supplied Aglipay and de los Reyes with Unitarian literature and connections to denominational leaders. Aglipay, in particular, became increasingly Unitarian in his theology. This statement, prepared by Bishop Isabelo de los Reyes, Jr., during former American Unitarian Association president Louis Cornish's visit to the Philippines, implied that Aglipay's views were widely shared. But shortly after Aglipay's death in 1940, Bishop de los Reyes began a process that culminated in the affiliation of the Philippine Independent Church with Anglicanism. Two splinter groups, the Independent Church of Filipino Christians and the Philippine Unitarian Church, carried on the Aglipayan tradition in a much-reduced form for some years. Further Reading: Francis H. Wise, "The History of the Philippine Independent Church (Iglesia Filipina Independiente)," MA thesis, University of the Philippines, March 1955.

— Dan McKanan

Isabelo de los Reyes, Jr., "The Position of the Independent Church"

The Independent Church of the Philippines has as its background centuries of theocratic despotism under Spain. All the best sons of the country wrote against the abuses of the Spanish friars. . . .

The execution of almost all these great Filipinos gave more power and prestige to their writing so that they became the gospels of our race. When United States' sovereignty brought the Philippines separation of Church and State, freedom of worship, and other blessings, our Independent Church was established as an expression of faith in the immortal teachings of our Heroes. Led by the influence of their writings, it has from its inception proclaimed religious liberalism. . . .

Our Church has retained from the Roman Catholic Church all that was found reasonable and harmless. The vestments and many of its magnificent ceremonies, that possess so great an appeal for the Filipinos and other artistic peoples, were retained, but with a rational interpretation. What is a myth to science must be a myth to us. The ritual is for the service of men, our prayers are translated into all the dialects. Rejecting all ecclesiasticism, we preserve the real teachings of Jesus: "Love to God and of our fellow beings." . . .

We accept the leadership of Jesus as the greatest Master of men, but we acknowledge him not as God but as a man, not exempted from certain frailties common to all humans. We maintain always that modern science must inspire our doctrines; hence since our establishment we have declared that through evolution man has become what he is today. We admit no miracles. We believe in God as the Mysterious Energy that keeps the Universe and that gives life and directs all beings. We always have maintained that the Bible has many interpolations and inaccuracies. Yet we consider the Bible as a holy book with many excellent lessons. We believe that all the scriptures of the world contain good. . . .

Isabelo de los Reyes, "The Seven Sacraments Used in the Independent Church"

The Independent Church considers the Sacraments as a collection of ritualistic prayers through which we ask God for special graces. We deny that these Sacraments have any intrinsic virtue. While the majority of Christian denominations use only two Sacraments . . . we of the Independent Church follow the Seven Sacraments established by the Council of Trent, but we eliminate all superstitious elements. . . .

We do not hold that Baptism cleanses us of original sin. We hold that Baptism is a visible profession of a faith in God and the teachings of Jesus. . . .

Communion we consider as a survival of the brotherly dinners that Jesus held with his poor disciples. . . . Although we keep the form of the Mass of the Roman Church in large measure, our service differs essentially. It is a memorial, and we deny that the bread and wine are offered as sacrifice. We deny transubstantiation. . . . .

"The Credo of the Independent Church"

I believe in one God, we praise His Holy Name, the Force which fills the Universe, as said the prophet Jeremiah; which fills the heavens and the earth; intelligent, eternal, supreme and mysterious; which gives life, directs, moves, and sustains all beings; which is the great soul of the universe, the beginning of all life and movement. Although His nature has not yet been completely manifested unto us, we try to apprehend it and to see in His marvelous works His power and His admirable wisdom. We hear in the depths of our conscience His most Holy voice, we experience His diligent and loving fatherhood in the providential satisfaction of our daily

95

needs. I believe that as God is the Supreme Being, He is also the Supreme Perfection. I believe that God made man to contribute with his virtues and activities to the general well-being and progress; and for this reason, we ought to be useful always and with our work we should seek for the satisfaction of our needs, think and work well, for God will recompense the good in this world, and will punish in this world bad intentions and deeds, but not with the absurd hell. The inexorable justice of God is perfected through His infinite compassion. I believe that the Eternal as my most loving Father protects me now, and will recognize me at my death, as a good father, full of pity, would recognize His son. As it has been proved by modern science, I shall not disappear forever but only be transformed. Amen.

SOURCE: Louis C. Cornish, *The Philippine Calling* (Philadelphia: Dorrance and Company, 1942), 78–82, 86–87.

VERNA HILLS

Martin and Judy in Their Two Little Houses

1939

The New Beacon Series of religious education curricula, developed under the supervision of Sophia Lyon Fahs (1876–1978), embodied humanist values and the child-centered pedagogy taught by John Dewey at Columbia's Teachers College. In her introduction to the curriculum for preschoolers, Fahs explained that the overarching goal was to cultivate the sense of wonder that Catholic writer Gilbert K. Chesterton had called the "beginning of the praise of God." Yet explicit reference to God was deliberately omitted on the grounds that "unverbalized experiences should come before religious language is used for describing them." Instead, Martin and Judy *featured ordinary experiences of children encountering the forces of nature, birth and death, sickness and shadow, creativity and choicemaking. Sophia Fahs explained the rationale for that choice in her 1952 book,* Today's Children and Yesterday's Heritage, *also excerpted in this volume. Further Reading: Roberta M. Nelson, ed.,* Claiming the Past, Shaping the Future: Four Eras in Liberal Religious Education, 1790–1999 *(Providence, RI: Liberal Religious Educators Association, 2006); Richard S. Gilbert,* Growing Up Absorbed: Religious Education among the Unitarian Universalists *(Bloomington, IN: iUniverse, 2014); Robert L'Hommedieu Miller, "The Educational Philosophy of the New Beacon Series in Religious Education," ThD thesis, Boston University, 1957; David B. Parke, "The Historical and Religious Antecedents of the New Beacon Series in Religious Education (1937)," PhD thesis, Boston University, 1965.*

— Dan McKanan

Two Little Houses

Once there were two little houses side by side. One little house was just as tall as the other little house. It was just as wide as the other little house. It was just as long as the other little house.

The two little houses had the same kind of porches. They had the same kind of chimneys. They had the same kind of windows. They had the same kind of doors. They had the same kind of yards.

The two little houses had the same kind of rooms. They had rooms to sleep in. They had rooms to eat in. They had kitchens. They had bathrooms. They had living-rooms. They had play-rooms.

The two little houses were both painted white.

When the sun was shining, it shone on both the little white houses.

When the wind was blowing, it blew on both the little white houses.

When the rain was raining, it rained on both the little white houses.

The little white houses were exactly alike. But the people who lived in the little white houses were not exactly alike.

Martin lived in one little white house. Martin's father and Martin's mother and Martin's big sister all lived there, too. So did Stubby, the dog.

Judy lived in the other little white house. Judy's father and Judy's mother and Judy's big brother all lived there, too. So did Judy's baby sister. So did Dusky, the cat.

Martin was a boy.

Judy was a girl.

Martin and Judy were friends.

Martin and Judy liked their little white houses. They liked their yards to play in. They liked each other.

*　*　*

Off to the Duck Pond

Judy and Martin and Martin's mother were going for a walk.

They were going for a walk to the pond.

They were going to see the ducks.

Up the hill they went, step, step, step.

Down the hill they went, run, run, run.

Over the wall they went, climb, climb, climb.

"We are almost there," said Martin. "Soon we shall see the pond."

"We are almost there," said Judy. "Soon we shall hear the ducks."

"Yes," said Martin's mother. "We are almost there. We will go up the path between the trees. We will go down the path beyond the trees. Then we will look for the pond."

Judy and Martin and Martin's mother walked on and on.

They went up the path between the trees.

They went down the path beyond the trees.

They looked for the pond.

They looked for the ducks.

Judy and Martin and Martin's mother looked and looked again.

They did not see any pond at all.

They did not see any ducks.

They saw just one big puddle of mud.

"What has happened to the pond?" asked Martin.

"What has happened to the ducks?" asked Judy.

Judy and Martin and Martin's mother looked and looked again.

"I did not think," said Martin's mother, "that the pond would be so dry. We have had many days of hot sunshine. We have had no rain. That is why the pond has grown smaller and smaller."

"But where are the ducks?" asked Martin.

"They have flown away to look for another pond," said Martin's mother.

"Will they come back?" asked Judy.

"We must wait and see. We must wait until it rains."

"Do you think it will rain today?" asked Martin.

Martin's mother looked up at the sky.

She saws that it was blue and bright.

She saw no clouds at all.

"No," said Martin's mother. "I don't think it will rain today."

Judy and Martin and Martin's mother turned around to go home.

They went up the path that led to the trees.

They went down the path between the trees.

Judy and Martin were wondering where the pond had gone.

Judy and Martin were wondering where the ducks had flown.

They were wishing that it would rain.

Over the wall they went, climb, climb, climb.

"Couldn't we make it rain?" asked Judy.

"No," said Martin's mother. "We could not make it rain."

Up the hill they went step, step, step.

"Couldn't Daddy make it rain?" asked Judy.

"No," said Martin's mother. "Daddies cannot make it rain."

"Can policemen make it rain?" asked Judy. "Can firemen make it rain?"

"No," said Martin's mother. "No person can make it rain."

Down the hill they went, run, run, run.

"Why can't we make it rain?" asked Martin.

"Because we cannot make clouds come. Because we cannot make the winds blow."

"When will it rain?" asked Judy.

"When the winds blow the clouds over our heads. When the clouds spread out over the sky. Then it will rain. But I don't know when that will be."

Judy and Martin and Martin's mother were coming near the two little white houses where they lived.

Martin's mother went into the house.

Martin and Judy walked up and down the yard.

They looked up at the sky.

They wished it would rain and fill the pond full.

They wished it would rain and the ducks would come back.

Judy and Martin looked up at the sky again.

They saw it was bright and blue.

They saw no clouds at all.

Judy and Martin knew that it would not rain that day.

SOURCE: Verna Hills, *Martin and Judy in Their Two Little Houses* (Boston: Beacon Press, 1939), 1–2, 9–12.

"Why Liberal?"

1939

James Luther Adams (1901–1994) was the pre-eminent Unitarian scholar during the middle decades of the twentieth century, serving successively on the faculties of Meadville Theological School (1936–1956), the University of Chicago Divinity School (1943–1956, as part of its Federated Theological Faculty), Harvard Divinity School (1956–1968), and Andover Newton Theological School (during his retirement). The child of a fundamentalist preacher, Adams embraced militant atheism as an undergraduate and was then steered to religious humanism by a professor who recognized the religious passion underlying his attacks on religion. Adams attended Harvard Divinity School, served pastorates in Salem and Wellesley Hills, Massachusetts, then began his academic career as a doctoral student at the University of Chicago and a professor at Meadville. From the beginning, he sought to revitalize liberal religion by separating it from the shallow optimism of the late nineteenth century. The new liberalism Adams envisaged was a self-critical, democratic faith, capable of resisting political totalitarianism, religious fundamentalism, and the salutary but overblown criticisms of such former liberals as Karl Barth and Reinhold Niebuhr. To promote this vision, Adams co-founded the Journal of Liberal Religion *and published this editorial in its second issue. Further Reading: George Kimmich Beach,* Transforming Liberalism: The Theology of James Luther Adams *(Boston: Skinner House, 2004); James Luther Adams,* Not without Dust and Heat: A Memoir *(Chicago: Exploration Press, 1995).*

— Dan McKanan

Some time ago I was visiting a philosopher in Germany whom we Americans consider to be one of the most distinguished representatives of what is left there of the liberal tradition, the tradition which claims such men as Harnack, Troeltsch, and Otto. During the course of our conversation I casually referred to my host as a liberal. He immediately demurred, saying, "Please do not call me a liberal. That word is taboo here. And besides, I am not a liberal." Certain allowances must, of course, be made for the fact that the word "liberal" has had a slightly different meaning among the Germans than among us. Yet, this man had just been speaking to me of his favorable interest in the International Association for Liberal Christianity and Religious Freedom.

It is not alone in Germany and among the Nazis that we find this contempt for the word "liberal." In America as well as in Germany the word has become a sort of whipping post for those who would give histrionic evidence of having achieved an alleged spiritual maturity. Some years ago two stalwart liberals, even John Bennett and Walter Marshall Horton, attracted wide attention by discussing, a little prematurely perhaps, what would come "after liberalism." Today it is difficult to find a magazine "in the vanguard" which does not contain some assertion (in a tone of finality) concerning the demise of liberalism.

If liberalism is dead, why should any of us be willing to exert ourselves on behalf of the liberal church? And is not a *Journal of Liberal Religion* at this late date merely a sign of "cultural lag"? . . .

For if liberalism is dead, then, we say: Long live liberalism. As will be seen, we would not venture to continue the paraphrase by asserting that liberalism can do no wrong. But we do affirm that the royal lineage is not dead and will not die. Having once got into the world, the liberal spirit will blow where it listeth. It may, along with the scientific spirit, be driven under ground but only in appearance. We remember that Christianity has from time to time been reported dead; and those who have wished to be a little more cautious have assured us that its days are numbered. In the nineteenth century when the idea of progress was glorified as the faith once for all delivered, we were told that "the religion of the future" would leave Christianity behind. Yet even today many people persist in avowing critical allegiance to Christianity. Indeed, there is irresistible evidence that the Christian religion is now waxing rather than waning.

*　*　*

Liberalism may, like Christianity, also have its apostolic age and acute secularization, its reformation and renaissance, its loss and (we should hope also) its recovery of proletarian interest. And as it passes through these or other phases, the question will ever be posed, What is the essence of liberalism? And so it is today.

In order to answer this question we must, of course, have the courage not to over-simplify. A vital liberalism has within it tensions, struggle, a dialectic if you will. Indeed, it will be the aim of this *Journal of Liberal Religion* to help make explicit and operative these necessary and salutary tensions. With a self-denying ordinance which disclaims finality or authoritativeness, we venture the following characterization of the essential elements of liberalism.

First, liberalism holds that nothing is complete, and thus nothing is exempt from criticism. Liberalism itself, as an actuality, is patient of this limitation. At best, even our symbols of communication are only referends and do not "capsule" reality. Stating this principle in religious terms, we may say that liberalism presupposes that revelation is continuous in word, in deed, and in nature, that it is not sealed, and that it points always beyond itself. Not only is significant novelty both possible and manifest, but also significance is itself inchoate and subject to inner tensions of peril and opportunity, of self-assertion and dependence.

Second, liberalism holds that "all relations between men ought ideally to rest on mutual free consent and not on coercion." Obviously, this principle cannot be advocated in any strict or absolute sense. . . . Education, for example, may be compulsory within the liberal state, if not in the liberal church. All responsible liberals recognize the necessity for restrictions on individual freedom. . . . This second principle, like the others, can be stated in religious terms in various ways. For the sake of brevity, we venture the statement familiar to religious liberals: All men are children of one Father. The implication intended here is that the liberal method of free inquiry is the *conditio sine qua non* of both the fullest apprehension of the divine and the preservation of the human dignity which comes from our being children of one Father.

Third, being an ethical procedure, that is, purporting to be significant for human behavior, liberalism involves the moral obligation to direct one's efforts towards the establishment of democratic community. A full definition of the term "community" need not be attempted here. It involves, of course, a common life which gives rise to the expression of the manifold, creative impulses of the human spirit, an expression which presupposes a cooperative life impelled by the motives of love and justice. . . . And this it is also which makes the role of the prophet central and indispensable in liberalism.

Fourth, liberalism holds that the resources (human and divine) which are available for the achievement of meaningful change justify an attitude of ultimate optimism. This does not necessarily involve immediate optimism. In religious terms this principle may be stated thus: The divine element in reality both demands and *supports* mutuality. Thus the ground of hope is in the prevenient and the actual grace of God.

We may now return to the previous question, Why liberal? And we answer: Because confidence in the principles of liberalism is the only effective resistant to ultimate skepticism and despair on the one side and to blasphemous claims to authority and suppressions of criticism on the other. These are the enemies of the human spirit whose dangers are threatening today. Therefore, it is at these points that the efforts of liberals must be concentrated. And of the two dangers it appears to us that totalitarianism is the lesser. To be sure, some authoritarians assert that the liberal who will not accept a single, divinely inspired book or a divinely instituted church or state is deluded by his *own* pride and conceit. But, from the liberal point of view, the most pretentious pride of all is that of the man who thinks himself capable of recognizing infallibility, for he must himself claim to be infallible in order to identify infallibility.

Far the more powerful and subtle enemy of liberalism, however, is scepticism. Authoritarianism, totalitarianism, fascism today grow for the most part out of a scepticism with regard to the actuality of truth and the possibility of man's finding it, a scepticism which also despairs of man's bettering the human condition. Thus the Barthian sceptic "takes the leap." Any one who knows the younger generation of Barthians in Europe knows that they are tired sceptics. The very violence of their assertiveness bespeaks an inner uncertainty and a compensation in the form of pseudo-certitude. There is nothing a jelly fish wants so much as a rock. Scepticism is the real foundation of their pretentious claims to divine authority, the avowed foundations being ingeniously supported by the superstructure.

But in the American scene the scepticism which yearns for authority is not the imminent danger. Not yet, at least. It is rather an indifference to moral values, a cynical anti-intellectualism, a sophisticated "failure of nerve." Honesty and courage are accounted expensive luxuries inimical to "good fellowship" and "good business." For evidence of this relaxing of morale we need not search far on any side. Many people are too weary even to feel moral indignation at the corruption of contemporary municipal politics, at the treatment of the Chinese by Japan, and at the "neutral" American policy which makes this treatment possible. We read with well-fed equanimity of the slaughterous "peace-loving" penetration of China and Austria and Czecho-Slovakia.

But in certain circles there is something more subtly destructive than this weakening of moral fibre. As already suggested, it manifests itself in religious groups as irrationalism. . . .

We see, therefore, that liberalism stands in a middle ground between two excesses, each of which is a threat to man's humanity. Thus it is a safeguard against those who on the one side appeal to an unconditioned heteronomous authority transcending all relativism and against those who on the other side say that thinking is a laryngeal itch twitching up from the unconscious and providing only an index of one's class and vested interests. In short, liberalism is the unrelenting critic of all who say that since thinking is an illusion, let us take what suits us.

It is this sort of skepticism which the (today admittedly sobered) confidence of liberalism must cure. If this confidence is unwarranted, then none of the escapes offered by the cultured despisers of religious liberalism will be able to save us, and even if they should be able to help in the effecting of this cure, it would be because they too in the end rely upon the same human nature and the same divine resources which have ben our help in ages past. It would be because they too share in the ultimate optimism of the liberal faith, an optimism which in our civilization is the heritage from Christianity.

SOURCE: James Luther Adams, "Why Liberal?" *Journal of Liberal Religion* 1/2 (Autumn 1939): 3–8.

AURELIA HENRY REINHARDT

"Education for Service in Democracy"

1940

Aurelia Henry Reinhardt (1877–1948), a nationally prominent educational leader, was the president of Mills College in Oakland, California, from 1916 to 1943. An active Unitarian, she served a brief interim ministry in Oakland, delivered the Ware lecture in 1932, and was chosen as the first female moderator of the American Unitarian Association in 1942. In this speech delivered for the Unitarian Radio Hour, she did not mention Unitarianism, but she did give voice both to Unitarianism's progressive educational philosophy then transforming religious education and to the wartime concern for strengthening democracy that she shared with Frederick May Eliot and James Luther Adams, with whom she served on the first Commission of Appraisal. She also expressed a philosophy of change somewhat similar to the process theology then being developed by Charles Hartshorne. Further Reading: George Hedley, Aurelia Henry Reinhardt: Portrait of a Whole Woman *(Oakland, CA: Mills College, 1961).*

—Dan McKanan

With such unselfish promise for improved public education as evidenced by the work of Horace Mann a hundred years ago, there should be less of mystery today about the directed growth of the individual which we call education, and about the application of the achievement of that individual growth to government which we call democracy. But we persist in making of both a mystery. Why should this be? Because both processes are *difficult.* Because both mean long concentration and consecration to the ends involved. Because both mean achievement of the individual applied to group results. Because the laziness, neglect, or failure of the individual lowers the progress, achievement, and success of the group. Because it is temporarily easier for one direct, competent person to make decisions and finish a task than for a variety of less competent persons to proceed. But true democratic education should greaten everyone.

❊　❊　❊

The *fear* of change, or the failure to see *life* in change, is an ancient fault. Humanity has so long clung to the notion of the absolute as the desirable and certain characteristic of man, that a century of scientific discovery proving the opposite has done little to qualify man's instinctive belief in its value to him. . . .

105

Only after faith in the ultimate value for man of the absolute and static had begun to fade could the idea of growth and democracy begin to emerge. Man glimpsed the gift of growth—seed to tree, babe to man. He glimpsed the gift of assistance to growth—the education of child toward manhood through life. And in that glimpse was the earnest of the vision which belongs to the youth of the world, the vision it must realize, the vision that must become, generation after generation, a living, changing, adjusting reality, and never the unachieved dream of senescence.

*　*　*

But this is 1940. We turn to our own time and country, our democracy achieved under a constitution a century and a half ago, our system of education chosen and proclaimed almost as early—a system which owes its development to many socially-minded Americans, a system of which we are highly critical despite its material achievements. For the United States has made it possible for a larger percentage of its people to have free schooling, a free choice of occupation, a larger daily wage, and more material comforts than any nation that has come into greatness.

It is nationally acknowledged that the results of our educational processes are inadequate. There is unemployment, social unrest, migration of population, poverty, crime. . . . What is important to this discussion is that these facts do not deny the validity of the democratic idea; they are a challenge to its better proof. . . .

The central faith holds that man can learn. Indeed, that he must learn, if he is to be a democratic citizen, is *imperative*. Putting aside fear of change that is healthy growth, and the desire for the absolute which does not belong to the life of finite man, American education can best serve our democracy in three ways. . . .

First, the school is child-centered, not teacher-centered, nor subject-centered. The child learns—learns how to learn, learns whether it is difficult or not, learns whether he likes every step or not, learns so that he grows in mind and body. If we say the school is child-centered, we are trying to make it clear that we want a whole and balanced person to emerge at every level of learning. . . .

Second. There has been and is today almost a desperate effort to "educate children for citizenship." . . . But other efforts must go side by side. Parents and teachers must themselves be good citizens, obey the laws, act with some respect toward government and its officials, otherwise all the textbooks in the world will not create good citizens. . . .

Third. American schools must develop a more adequate educational approach to vocational preparation. . . .

To sum up: education in a democracy, in our democracy, must use all the instruments of civilization, home, church, community, as well as school, for the adequate, suitable development of each child. This means that character and imagination, as well as heart and hand, are developed together.

Education in a democracy must consciously direct reading and observation, principle and practice to the happiness, the responsibilities, and the participation of group living. Government in a democracy is not "they," it is "us."

SOURCE: Aurelia Henry Reinhardt, "Education for Service in Democracy," no. 2 of the 1940–1941 series of the Unitarian Radio Hour sponsored by the American Unitarian Association. First broadcast November 17, 1940.

"Food for Babies in the Basses Pyrenees: Emergency Project, Summer, 1940"

1940

Social worker Martha Sharp (1905–1999) and her husband, Waitstill Sharp (1902–1983), pastor of the Unitarian Church of Wellesley Hills, Massachusetts, were the second and third Americans honored as "Righteous Among the Nations" by Yad Vashem, the Holocaust Martyrs' and Heroes' Remembrance Authority. They helped hundreds of refugees from Nazism escape to the United States and laid the foundation for the ongoing work of the Unitarian Service Committee. American Unitarian Association president Frederick May Eliot recruited the Sharps to go to Prague in February 1939 because the Unitarian congregation there had become a place of refuge for Jews and others fleeing the newly occupied Sudetenland. They were forced out after six months' service there, but returned to Europe in the early years of World War II as representatives of the newly formed Unitarian Service Committee. Based in Lisbon, Portugal, and Marseilles, France, the Sharps arranged for the safe departure of physicist Otto Meyerhof and novelists Heinrich Mann and Lion Feuchtwanger. They also circumvented restrictions on Jewish immigration (imposed both in Europe and in the United States) to bring many Jewish children safely to the United States. This report conveys the tragedy of the refugee experience and Martha Sharp's strategy for galvanizing solidarity among Unitarians. Further Reading: Susan Elisabeth Subak, Rescue & Flight: American Relief Workers Who Defied the Nazis *(Lincoln: University of Nebraska Press, 2010); Ken Burns and Artemis Joukowsky,* Defying the Nazis: The Sharps' War *(film, 2016).*

—Dan McKanan

From February 4th, 1939, until December 16th, 1940, a span of 22 months, I spent thirteen as a representative of American Unitarianism in Europe. This is a brief report of some of the work which I carried on as Commissioner of the Unitarian Service Committee from June to December 16th, 1940.

When we flew from New York on June 17th, Paris had just fallen, but Americans still cherished a desperate hope that France could not be defeated. We were sent to a France at war to help wherever the need seemed greatest.

We arrived in a Lisbon choked with refugees. . . . Thousands fleeing from France—Americans, Belgians, Dutch, French, Czechs, Poles, Austrians—arrived daily at the Spanish-Portuguese frontier. . . . They told unbelievable tales of crawling along roads by day and night, bombers overhead, accidents by the way. One man's wife was a direct hit as she ran into the woods, and her husband was unable to find even a piece of her dress afterwards. Children were lost from refugee trains streaking southwards pulling into tunnels when the enemy began to shell them. . . . It is estimated that ten million people were on the road from June 9th to 15th.

* * *

The worst conditions in non-occupied France today exist in the internment camps for foreigners. I visited Gurs, in the Basses Pyrenees, and St. Nicholas near Nîmes, where Germans, Austrians, Czechs, and Poles are placed. I have talked with inmates of all the others. They lie on straw mattresses in unheated windowless wooden barracks in freezing weather. If they are lucky they have a cotton blanket. Their food is barely enough to sustain life. Lack of fats and vegetables result in deficiency diseases—teeth loosen, hair falls out. Dysentery, typhus, and typhoid are readily transmitted through overcrowding, unsanitary conditions, and the rats and lice which infest the barracks. There are plenty of doctors but not enough medicines. Diabetics are without insulin. Children have no milk. Clothes are not sufficient. And amid all this agony there is nothing to do, no schools for the children, no books to read, no paper to write upon, and no materials to make clothing or utensils. Over 400 deaths occurred at Gurs in the month of November alone.

Many of these people can be emigrated to the United States or other countries, if someone who is free can find them, attend to their necessary papers, and get into touch with relatives and friends and consulates. Hundreds of the children could be brought to America to be placed with relatives or in foster homes. We were able to help with the emigration plans for many adults and children who otherwise would today be in these camps.

For those who are unable to leave the country it is possible to arrange their release from camp and their living as private citizens if a money guarantee is provided. We were able to take care of several cases of this kind pending emigration arrangements.

SOURCE: *Journey to Freedom: The First Chapter of Unitarian Service: Reports of Commissioners Waitstill and Martha Sharp*, 12–13, 20–21, Unitarian Universalist Service Committee, Administrative Records, ca. 1935–2006, Andover-Harvard Archives, bMS 16114/3(43), Andover-Harvard Theological Library, Harvard Divinity School, Cambridge, MA.

JAMES LUTHER ADAMS

"The Changing Reputation of Human Nature"

1941

*James Luther Adams's commitment to reformulating liberal religion intensi-
fied with the onset of World War II. He had spent a sabbatical year in 1935–
1936 in Germany, visiting religious leaders (including some Unitarians) both
who colluded with the Nazis and who participated in the underground opposition. Adams came to admire theologians Karl Barth and Paul Tillich, both
of whom found resources for opposition to Nazism in classical Christian theology. Adams did not fully embrace their theologies, but in this essay—first
delivered as the Berry Street lecture and then expanded for publication—he
turned to ancient Christian sources to rethink liberal attitudes about human
nature. He also drew on the essay by William Wallace Fenn that appears in
this anthology.*

—Dan McKanan

It would be wrong therefore to suppose that Dean Fenn's criticism stands alone
in the literature of liberalism or that his criticism is illiberal in spirit or consequence.
It is of the essence of liberalism to criticize itself. Moreover, among religious liberals there is and there has always been a considerable variety of opinion about human
nature as well as about many other matters. In other words, although religious liberals have been at one in espousing certain liberal principles, such as freedom of
inquiry and freedom of conscience, they have not all brought forth the same ideas in
their exercise of these freedoms. Thus we see that the liberal method or attitude is
one thing, the specific content of liberalism is another. Hence, the liberal doctrine
of man may change while the non-authoritarian method of liberalism remains in
fundamental respects the same. Indeed, if some particular doctrine of man—or of
God—held among liberals should be viewed as final in its form of expression and as
exempt from criticism or change, the principle of freedom in liberalism would
thereby be surrendered.

* * *

In the very process of assimilating the new knowledge of man that has resulted
from the application of modern scientific methods and that has accrued from view-
ing man in a changed historical situation, many people have been led to a new
appreciation of certain earlier estimates of human nature and the human situation.

We now turn our attention to a consideration of three of these basic rival conceptions. Our purpose in presenting these rival conceptions is not merely to provide an orientation for the consideration of the current changes in the reputation of human nature, but also to indicate the relative merits of these conceptions and to draw from such a study an indication of the changes needful in the older Liberal doctrine of man.

In the ancient Greek tradition we find two of these typical estimates of human nature and the human situation. The one view is associated with the classical philosophers; it is usually called the intellectualistic or rationalistic view, the Apollonian view. According to this view, reason is the masterful principle of creation, and thus the cosmos is a moving shadow of a world of eternal ideas, essences, or forms. Correspondingly, man's primary, distinguishing faculty is his reason, and through it he can release a vitality that will enable him to achieve control of himself and of the human situation by subjecting them to clearly envisaged forms. . . .

The other view of human nature in the Hellenic tradition interprets existence more in terms of vitality than of form, a vitality that is both creative and destructive, that imbues every form but that also eludes and bursts the bounds of every structure. It is associated with one of the major traditions in popular Greek religion, with certain pre-Socratic philosophers very close to this religious tradition, and in certain respects, with the great tragedians. It has usually been characterized as the Dionysian view. In recent decades this view and certain modern variations of it have been spoken of as "voluntarism."

In general, this view exalts the dynamic aspects of existence; therefore it conceives of man's proper goal as the fulfillment of the life-giving powers inherent in existence. But here the elements of struggle, contradiction, and tragedy rather than the element of harmony is emphasized.

* * *

In the light of what has been said, it should be clear that we cannot properly understand the third influential attitude toward man and existence—the Judeo-Christian view—if we interpret it as constituting a complete contrast with "the Greek view of life." It is true that there is little in common between the Jewish-and-early-Christian view and the Apollonian attitude. . . .

On the other hand, the Greek Dionysian view and the Judeo-Christian attitude bear a resemblance to each other in their possession of a "tragic sense of life" as well as in their emphasis upon the dynamic elements in the world and in human life. According to the Judeo-Christian view, God is a righteous will fulfilling his purpose in history; man and nature are fallen; man's natural will is at variance with the divine will, and man's sin and guilt and his conflict with the principalities and powers of this would are an inextricable part of human experience. Thus in both the Greek tragic view and the Jewish prophetic and primitive Christian outlook there is an

111

awareness of an ontologically as well as psychologically grounded tendency in man to rebellion, perversion, and self-destruction, and thus there is an assertion of the universal guilt of man. Moreover, in both views the attention is centered upon the dynamic, creative-destructive aspects of existence and upon the affective aspects of the human psyche.

Yet, there are also certain fundamental differences to be observed between the Judeo-Christian and the Greek "tragic" view. Two of these differences may be noted here. The first has to do with the ultimate valuation they place on existence.

The Judeo-Christian doctrine of creation involves the idea that in substance the world is good, for it is God's creation. Nothing in existence is absolutely anti-divine. . . .

The other major difference between the Judeo-Christian and the Dionysian view concerns their contrasting attitudes toward reason and morality. The Dionysian view was strongly characterized by "enthusiastic" irrationalism and amoralism, defects made familiar to most of us through the diatribes of Euripides against Dionysianism. The Judeo-Christian mentality in its formative period made no virtue of irrationalism and it strongly opposed amoralism.

*   *   *

The modern development of intellectualism must be understood as a reaction against these extreme forms of voluntarism. In large degree the Renaissance was a revolt against the obscurantism and authoritarianism of the Middle Ages and also against certain forms of earlier voluntarism, (though it must be added that the Renaissance was also voluntaristic in some respects). Likewise, intellectualism in later centuries represents a revolt against extreme forms of voluntarism found in orthodox Calvinism and Lutheranism.

Indeed, religious liberalism itself can be understood in its proper perspective only when interpreted as an aspect of this opposition. In religious liberalism the rationalistic view of human nature and of the human situation appeared as a revolt against the older forms of authoritarianism, a revolt in the name of the principles of freedom of mind and freedom of conscience. But concomitantly the liberal movement represented also a revolt against the Protestant dogma of the total depravity of human nature, that is, against a depraved, lopsided, rationalized form of the Christian doctrine of original sin. In short, it was a revolt against a voluntarism that had gone to seed.

The Unitarians and their predecessors were among those who were in the vanguard of this revolt against the pessimistic Reformation conception. In opposition to the Calvinist view, and in no small measure utilizing the dialectical powers inherited from Calvinism, the Unitarians asserted that man's possession of the faculty of reason gives him the dignity of a child of God; and they held that by means of this faculty man could eliminate the superstitions and unworthy accretions of the Christian tradition, and bring about both a fulfillment of the human spirit and a return to "pure Christianity."

The fruits of this struggle and of the great humanitarian impulse of the nineteenth century represent no mean cultural accomplishment. This fact can scarcely be over-emphasized. Moreover, contemporary Protestantism owes to religious liberalism the social emphasis that in the past century has been reintroduced into Protestant thought and action.

But, unfortunately, not all the fruits issuing from the new movement were actually intended or expected by its proponents. Nor was the movement able to maintain in the main body of its adherents the prophetic power of its early days. The new intellectualism, which in its early stages was powerfully dynamic, more and more moved in the direction of emphasizing again the cognitive aspects of human nature ("the theoretical attitude of distance") and of thus neglecting the affective side of human nature and "the attitude of decision." The influence of the scientific method, despite its value in other respects, played no small role in accelerating this tendency.

* * *

This faith and its supporting conception of the universe is what is generally referred to when the modern historian of culture speaks of Liberalism (with a capital L). It is against this type of Liberalism and its contemporary residues that much of the current criticism of religious liberalism is directed. In so far as it is valid this criticism does not involve a repudiation of the liberal ideal of liberating the human spirit from the bondage of economic, social, and ecclesiastical tyrannies.

* * *

History is the realm of both necessity and freedom. Man is fated as well as free. . . . Man is fated also to be free; he is compelled to make decisions. For he can transcend his situation and in some measure he can freely change it; he can even change himself. As a creative entity he can act to preserve or increase, destroy or pervert, mutuality,—though it must be remembered also that conditions over which he has little control may affect the results of his action. Thus man lives both in and above history. He is fatefully caught in history, both as an individual and as a member of a group, and he is also able to be creative in history.

Through the use of this creative freedom man expresses the highest form of vitality that existence permits. Indeed, since this creativity is a manifestation of a divinely given and a divinely renewing power, we say that man is created in the image of God, that is, he participates in the divine creativity. This and not reason alone is the basis for the liberal's faith in man, and no change in the reputation of human nature could involve a denial of this fact without also repudiating the very essence of the liberal doctrine of man.

Because of this freedom, human history not only exhibits a singularity that transcends all *a priori* conceptions of the intellect; it also provides a more complex and spiritual form of conflict than that to be found on the level of nature. For history is a theatre of conflicts in which the tensions between the will to mutuality and the will to power appear in their most subtle and perverse forms. In short, history is tragic. Let it be said immediately that this does not mean merely that men violate the moral code or disobey the law.

*　*　*

When we say that history is tragic, we mean that the perversions and failures in history are associated precisely with the highest creative powers of man and thus with this greatest achievements. One might call this the Oedipus motif is the sphere of history: nemesis is very often encountered almost simultaneously with the seemingly highest achievement. The very means and evidences of progress turn out again and again to be also the instruments of perversion or destruction. The national culture, for example, is the soil from which issue cherished treasures of a people, their language, their poetry, their music, their common social heritage. Yet nationalism is also one of the most destructive forces in the whole of human history. Progress in transportation has assisted tremendously in the raising of the standard of living: yet it has produced also a mobility in our cultural life which has brought in its train a new rootlessness and instability.

*　*　*

The older Liberalism underestimated the destructive possibilities of the contradictions in human nature and was thus unrealistic. It offered salvation through the "restraints of reason." But the "restraints of reason" are inadequate for entering the "war within the cave." Merely intellectual education is not enough. The world has many educated people who know how to reason, and they reason very well; but, curiously enough, many of them fail to examine the pre-established premises from which they reason, premises that turn out on examination to be anti-social, protective camouflages of power. Where a man's treasure is, there will his heart be also. And where his heart is, there will be his reason and his premises. The "theoretical attitude of distance" needs for its completion the existential "attitude of decision." St. Paul underlines this fact when he speaks of the foolishness of the wise. The element of conflict inherent in man and in man's relations with his fellows can, as St. Paul knew, be dealt with only by a regenerated will, a will committed to the principles of liberty and justice and love, a will prepared by a faith, a decision, a commitment sufficient to cope with the principalities and powers of the world.

*　*　*

This element of commitment, of change of heart, of decision, so much emphasized in the Gospels, has been neglected by religious liberalism, and that is the prime source of its enfeeblement. We liberals are largely an uncommitted and therefore a self-frustrating people. Our first task, then, is to restore to liberalism its own dynamic and its own prophetic genius. We need conversion within ourselves. Only by some such revolution can we be seized by a prophetic power that will enable us to proclaim both the judgment and the love of God. Only by some such conversion can we be possessed by a love that will not let us go. And when that has taken place, we shall know that it is not our wills alone that have acted; we shall know that the ever-living Creator and Re-creator has again been brooding over the face of the deep and out of the depths bringing forth new life.

SOURCE: James Luther Adams, "The Changing Reputation of Human Nature," *Journal of Liberal Religion* 4 (Autumn 1942 and Winter 1943), 63–66, 68–70, 72–74, 76, 140–42, 156–57, 160.

Songs Composed in Dresden Prison

1942

Between 1921 and 1941, Norbert Fabián Čapek (1870–1942) built the Unitar-
ian Church in Prague into the largest Unitarian congregation in the world,
with three thousand two hundred members. Inspired by the Hussite heritage
of his homeland, Čapek gravitated from Catholicism to the Baptist faith to
liberal Christianity, and then encountered Unitarianism at a 1910 meeting of
the International Association for Religious Freedom to which he was invited
by future Czech president Tomáš Masaryk. In exile during World War I, he
joined the Unitarian congregation in Orange, New Jersey, and then returned
to his newly independent nation to build Unitarianism there. Deeply com-
mitted to new rituals, he crafted a "Flower Communion" that was eventually
widely adopted by Unitarian Universalist congregations in the United States.
He also wrote hymns throughout his career, including three—"Mother Spirit,
Father Spirit," "View the Starry Realm," and "Color and Fragrance"—that
are included in Singing the Living Tradition. *A fervent opponent of Nazism,*
Čapek supported the early rescue work of the Unitarian Service Committee
and was killed in a Nazi prison camp in 1942. He wrote a final cluster of
hymns during his last days. Further Reading: Richard Henry, Norbert Fabián
Čapek: A Spiritual Journey *(Boston: Skinner House, 1999).*

—Dan McKanan

"*Among Children*"

Among children, among children,
Here is the fountain of youth:
Among children, among children,
The whole world is transfused in a rosy hue of joy.

Among children, the whole world 'round,
You cannot find one treacherous soul.
As in a crystal-clear stream
You can see all the way to the bottom.
Among children laughter bubbles brightly
Even from the tiniest reason for joy.
Hardly ever do you see a tear
But it changes at once into a smile.

Among children love sings its sweetest melody.
It runs from heart to heart
And chases away every hint of anger.

Among children, from their starry eyes
Hope shines into the world.
In their now quite weak muscles
Is growing the next harvest of great deeds.
Among children, whosoever shows them a good example,
Indeed, serves God far better than those
Who place sacrifices on the altars of cathedrals.

"In the Depths"

In the depths of my soul
There where lies the source of strength,
Where the divine and the human meet,
There, quiet your mind, quiet, quiet.

Outside let lightning reign,
Horrible darkness frighten the world.
But from the depths of your own soul
From that silence will rise again
God's flower.

Return to your self,
Rest in your self,
Live in the depths of your soul
Where the divine and the human meet.
Tune your heart to the eternal
And in the depths of your own soul
Your panting quiets down.
Where the divine and the human meet,
There is your refuge.

"Where Holy Enthusiasm Is"

When a holy enthusiasm seizes the heart
Your face lights up. You feel like a star singing.
Your very soul, hearing your song, is radiant.
It was, and it will be again.

With the sun on our brows,
Enthusiasm will bloom once more.
With paradise in our hearts
Clouds will disappear,
And the sun's rays bring the earth back to life.
The sun of your hope will shine again
Along the dangerous narrows of your life,
Bringing warmth and light
And the air of freedom, peace and happiness.
It was, and it will be again.

Courage will be astir in the air
And prompt you to action
To create warmth in harmony with the Highest
And Nearest Friend.
Success will attend you.
It was, and it will be again.

You would embrace the whole world,
Have peace touch every flower,
You would like to give yourself away completely to everybody,
Forgive everything, play host to everyone.
You would lift this earth to heaven.
It was, and it will be again.

SOURCE: Richard Henry, *Norbert Fabián Čapek: A Spiritual Journey* (Boston: Skinner House Books, 1999), 300–303.

FREDERICK MAY ELIOT
"Bring in the Candles"
1942

Frederick May Eliot (1889–1958) had deep Puritan and Unitarian roots. His ancestor John Eliot was famous as the "apostle to the Indians"; his grandfather William Greenleaf Eliot founded the First Unitarian Church of Saint Louis, the Western Unitarian Conference, and Washington University; and his mother's family linked him to abolitionist Samuel May, Jr., and to Louisa May Alcott. T. S. Eliot was a first cousin. Frederick May Eliot himself served Unity Church in Saint Paul, Minnesota, for twenty years, chaired the first Commission of Appraisal, and was elected president of the American Unitarian Association in 1937. This piece from the Christian Register *reflects his approach to wartime leadership. He was utterly committed to the Allied cause and equally committed to honoring the right of conscience for pacifist dissenters. Further Reading: Cynthia Grant Tucker,* No Silent Witness: The Eliot Parsonage Women and Their Unitarian World *(New York: Oxford University Press, 2010).*

— Dan McKanan

Today the churches of our Association stand together in full commitment to the overthrow of totalitarian power wherever it seeks to dominate free people or destroy the institutions of free nations, and in complete dedication to the establishment of a world order in which an enduring peace shall be possible. Together we are ready to pay whatever price may be exacted by the ideals of freedom and democracy, not only through the period of war but also through the period of reconstruction. Already this commitment has brought a deeper solidarity, which extends beyond this continent to include our brethren of the free spirit in every land.

*   *   *

But we shall look to our churches for more than the reinforcement of courage. There are other candles which we must bring in, whose light within the sanctuary of our churches may symbolize the principles of our free faith through the dark days that lie ahead, and give us strength to apply our religion with unfaltering devotion to the special needs of the present crisis.

There is the candle of humanitarian service, which has always shone with steady and reassuring flame upon the altar of our faith. In recent years, through the agency of the Unitarian Service Committee, this tradition has been given new meaning and wider scope.

*   *   *

Then there is the candle of human fellowship, deeper and more enduring than the forces that divide us by barriers of race, or creed, or nationality. It will not be easy to keep this flame burning, but it would be tragic to let it flicker out. Its light will remind us of our duty to maintain an inner sanctuary which no sudden panic of fear can destroy and no hatred invade or desecrate. With no lack of "firmness in the right, as God gives us to see the right," we must nevertheless strive to keep our hearts clean of hate and desire for vengeance.

Finally there is the candle of hope, of the great hope which has inspired and invigorated men's souls from that far distant day "when the first man stood God-conquered," the hope of Israel and of Christendom, of Isaiah and Jesus, once again made flesh in the dauntless souls who first dreamed our American dream and laid the good foundations for a new kind of society upon this new continent. That hope has met countless frustrations and setbacks and defeats, but it has never surrendered. . . .

The grounds of our hope lie in just these innate qualities and capacities of our common human nature, the "resources in us on which we have not drawn," the "unweariable endurance" of idealism. This is our gospel, in sunshine and in storm. We must proclaim that message now with greater confidence than ever before. "Bring in the candles!"

SOURCE: Frederick May Eliot, "Bring in the Candles," *Christian Register*, January 1942, 3.

Proposed and Final Applications for Membership in the Federal Council of Churches

1942

The Federal Council of Churches was the major ecumenical body for American Protestants in the first half of the twentieth century. In 1944 and again in 1946, the Universalist Church of America was denied membership in this body. UCA General Superintendent Robert Cummins (1897–1982), who also supported the full inclusion of humanists within the Universalist denomination, promoted FCC membership in order that Universalists might "join hands in good works" with Protestants, especially with the backdrop of World War II. The proposed application gave a detailed theological rationale for FCC membership, but the trustees ultimately chose to submit a much briefer statement. In the first vote, six of eighteen FCC member denominations supported admitting the Universalists: the Congregational Christians (predecessor to the United Church of Christ), Disciples of Christ, Friends, Seventh Day Baptists, Colored Methodist Episcopal Church, and African Methodist Episcopal Church. Those who voted against did so on the grounds that Universalists held an essentially Unitarian view of Christ.

—Dan McKanan

Proposed Application:

Voted that The Universalist Church of America make application for membership to the Federal Council of Churches of Christ in America and that the special committee which has had this matter in charge be continued to present that application and take all action with relation to it, and that in authorizing this action the Board of Trustees indicates its position in the matter of the application by adoption of the following statement, with such variations in form as the committee may see fit to make:

The primary motive that prompts this action is genuine sympathy with the avowed purpose of the Council "more fully to manifest the essential oneness of the Christian churches of America in Jesus Christ as their divine Lord and Savior, and to promote the spirit of fellowship, service and cooperation among them." That sense of oneness in Christ as the basis of Christian fellowship is thrown to the fore in the official declaration of the Universalist Church of America, as follows:

> The bond of fellowship in this Convention shall be a common purpose to do the will of God as Jesus revealed it and to cooperate in establishing the Kingdom for which he lived and died.

As we interpret the avowed purpose of the Federal Council, it sets up the ideal of unity in permitted and respected diversity. It disavows "authority to draw up a common creed or form of government or of worship." It would unite Christians in fellowship and service on the basis of their common loyalty to our common Master. We think of the Universalist Church as a branch of the Church Universal, whose catholic unity is centered in Jesus Christ. Our Universalist faith we regard as a means to the end of serving God whom he revealed and the kingdom he came to establish. To the degree that it does that it is of value to us and can be entitled to the respect of others.

We recognize of course that the phrase "divine Lord and Savior" means different things to different Christians. The differences however are as great among the members of churches now in the Federal Council as between them and Universalists generally. If our primary loyalty is to Christ, differences of theory concerning his personality need not separate but may enrich our common faith and experience.

The interest of Universalists in the ideal of the Federal Council is not one of theory only, or of present date. For a number of years they have been active in local and state councils and federations and in various branches of the Federal Council's work. Often they have been and are officials and leaders in such cooperative undertakings. A list of such participations is available if desired.

Another indication of desire to cooperate whenever the cause of Christian Unity can thus be furthered appears in the number of federated churches in which Universalists participate — 52 in all. Of these, 22 are Congregationalist-Universalist; 17 Unitarian-Universalist; and the others of various combinations, Methodist, Baptist, etc. Especially significant in this connection is the fact that the Universalist Church officially cooperated in inaugurating the Larger Parish movement in Maine, which was the first interdenominational enterprise of this sort in the United States.

If the Universalist Church should become a constituent member of the Federal Council, it would involve the forming of no new unfamiliar attitudes. It would be but carrying to logical conclusion of habits already established.

It is in this spirit that we are moved to apply for membership in the Federal Council. We should regard it as a privilege to add our testimony to the essential oneness of Christ of the Christian Church of America which the Council seeks to manifest and to cooperate more fully in the united Christian service carried on under the Council's auspices, at a time when such expressions of unity are so sorely needed.

Final Application:

The Universalist Church of America, through its Board of Trustees, as authorized by vote of the General Assembly at its session in September 1941, hereby applies for membership in the Federal Council of the Churches of Christ in America.

The motive that prompts this action is genuine sympathy with the objects of the Council as set forth in the Constitution. We should regard it as a privilege to add our testimony to the essential oneness in Christ of the Christian churches of America which the Council seeks to manifest and to cooperate more fully in united Christian service at a time when such expressions of unity are so sorely needed.

SOURCE: Robert Cummins, *Excluded: The Story of the Federal Council of Churches and the Universalists* (Boston: Unitarian Universalist Association, 1966), 14–16.

AMERICAN UNITARIAN YOUTH

"Political Resolution"

1945

The international fight against fascism brought the United States into alliance with the Soviet Union, and back home this allowed for widespread cooperation between political liberals and "radicals." Beginning in 1935, the Communist Party actively promoted Popular Front alliances on such issues as labor organizing, anti-racism, and anti-colonialism, and many Unitarians were enthusiastic participants. This postwar statement by the Unitarian youth organization epitomized the Popular Front worldview and reflected the influence of the Unitarian Director of Youth Work, Stephen H. Fritchman (1902–1981). Further Reading: Charles W. Eddis, Stephen Fritchman: The American Unitarians and Communism: A History with Documents *(Lulu. com, 2011).*

—Dan McKanan

We, the American Unitarian Youth, are proud of the victory of America, with her allies, over the armed forces of German Fascism, but we demand that the sacrifice of lives shall mean the extirpation of Fascism everywhere, and the extension of democracy; otherwise victory is empty.

As American youth and Unitarians we assume that the war against militaristic Japan will be vigorously prosecuted to a victorious close, without a negotiated peace allowing the Mikado and his reactionary supporters to remain in power. We believe that this goal can be more quickly and less bloodily achieved with a United China, and Asiatic peoples. We believe that labor will maintain its no-strike pledge for this victory, as it has done so well in the past, providing that an end is put to provocations by employers.

As American youth and as Unitarians, while we commend the splendid work done by the State Department in helping to form the United Nations' organization, we nevertheless condemn the tendencies in the American State Department that would destroy the fruits of victory: concretely, at the San Francisco Conference, the admission of Fascist Argentina, the refusal to grant independence to colonial peoples as proposed by the U.S.S.R. and the withholding of recognition from the World Labor Conference. We also condemn support to allied intervention against democratic forces in Belgium, Italy, Greece, and Trieste, the bolstering of the reactionary Kuomintang government faction of China with no aid to the anti-Fascist

"Communist" Chinese armies, and the repeated acts of our military government in Germany, discouraging democratic movements and perpetuating Naziism.

As American youth and Unitarians we call for the carrying out of the decisions made at the Crimea Conference, the legacy of our beloved Franklin Delano Roosevelt, whose death we deeply mourn. The American people must be on guard against being stampeded into distrust and hatred of our Soviet ally by sinister interests. We must grasp tightly the unity forged in war as the guarantee of the new United Nations' organization and the economic proposals of Bretton Woods. Other indispensable steps towards lasting peace must be taken: the punishment of Fascist war criminals guilty of atrocities, the breaking of relations with Fascist Spain and Argentina, the freedom of self-determination of nations, and the pursuance of all steps against imperialism, including independence for American colonies whose people desire it.

As American youth and as Unitarians we call upon all Americans to rally around President Truman in his every effort to solve the even greater problems of peace. We believe that the G.I. Bill of Rights must be followed and practiced regardless of race, creed or color . . . ; that a job for every worker and a guaranteed decent minimum standard of living must be provided by the government, if necessary, by widespread public works. . . .

As American youth and Unitarians we abhor anti-Semitism, Anti-Negroism, racism of all other sorts and red-baiting, and we demand the outlawing of the Fascist groups that spread these poisons. We ask for the continued elimination of discrimination in the armed forces, for the passage of the federal F.E.P.C. and anti-poll tax bills, and the outlawing of Jim Crow. We uphold the right of labor to organize and to bargain collectively, and condemn the extremely dangerous Ball-Burton-Hatch anti-labor bill now pending action.

SOURCE: "AUY Conference Political Resolution," *Christian Register*, September 1945, 347.

"The Threat of American Communists to the Liberal Church and Other Organizations"

1946

Popular Front alliances were abruptly disrupted by the onset of the Cold War. Though the aggressive anti-communism of Senator Joseph McCarthy is well known, socialists and pacifists also played a role. For more than a decade, they had been frustrated by the Communists' lack of commitment to democracy and their sometimes secretive attempts to control social justice organizations. In this privately circulated document, Homer A. Jack (1916–1993) gave voice to such concerns. The child of Jewish socialist parents, Jack was at the time of this writing both a Unitarian minister and executive secretary of the Chicago Council against Racial and Religious Discrimination. A cofounder of the Congress of Racial Equality, he went on to lead the National Committee for a Sane Nuclear Policy, the Social Responsibility Department of the UUA, and the World Conference of Religions for Peace.

—Dan McKanan

For decades, American churchmen have erred by refusing to cooperate and identify themselves with the significant secular social action movements of the nation. For this conservatism, the church has been roundly denounced and has lost prestige among a not inconsiderable number of liberals (or progressives). Recently, an increasing—if small—number of American churchmen have been erring in the other direction: of identifying themselves closely with certain secular social action movements which, while professing aims similar to those of prophetic religion, are really antithetical to it. Specifically, certain churchmen are cooperating very closely with American communists and communist-front or communist-dominated organizations. And the church, as a result of this cooperation, has continued to lose prestige in the eyes of these same liberals. . . .

Right at the beginning the author must frankly confess his bias. It may be reduced to several presuppositions. First, communism is not "red fascism" and although communism and fascism have certain superficial resemblances, they are fundamentally different. Second, communism is not the worst of all possible social and economic systems. . . . Third, Russian communism is solving certain essential problems (especially those of discrimination against minorities and economic exploitation) better than many of the western democracies. Fourth, American capitalism must learn to work with Russian communism. . . . And fifth . . . American communists have every right to operate in the United States as a recognized political party. . . .

Having said this, one must set down a corollary to the last proposition: namely, that American liberals have every right to analyze communist activity and oppose what they feel wrong with American communists and their various organizations.

* * *

It is estimated that there are less than 75,000 communist party members in the United States today. At no time is it believed that there were more than 100,000 enrolled members in this country. But why, then, the concern about communists? How can the relative handful of American communists be a threat to liberalism and liberal organizations including portions of the liberal church? The answer to this important question lies both in the zeal of communists and in their method of operation. A communist is not a one-hour-a-week member, as most churchmen are members of their organizations. . . .

Apart from their zeal, communists have exerted influence all out of proportion to their numbers by their method of operation: clandestine activity through all kinds of organizations. In order to make an impact on public opinion, communists try to take over existing organizations.

* * *

Religion may be, to communists, the opiate of the people, but like other drugs, it often is very useful. Thus American communists, though traditionally opposed to organized religion, have never been opposed to using the church. They have made several partially-successful attempts. First, they have tried to take control of certain unofficial denominational social action agencies. They have dominated the recent policies of the United Christian Council for Democracy . . . [and] the Methodist Federation for Social Service. . . . A third nucleus of communist-dominated activity through the church is the People's Institute of Applied Religion, directed by the Rev. Claude Williams. . . . A fourth area of attempted communist influence is through individual ministers who exert unusual control of denominational policy by virtue of their denominational positions.

* * *

Actual party members in strategic positions in society do not carry the hammer and sickle or even a party card. . . . The fellow-travelers (which A. Powell Davies in a recent sermon called the "travellers' aid") are of two principal types: those who know what they are doing and those who don't. The first knows very well what he is doing in supporting various communist-dominated movements and ideologies, although for various reasons he prefers not to become a member. The second type of fellow-traveler is the naïve liberal who is hypnotized by words like Democracy and Justice. . . .

But what is wrong with the communists, anyway? One might indicate two undemocratic characteristics which are closely allied: a slavish dependence on Soviet foreign policy and a cynical ethic which says that the end justifies the means.

* * *

But suppose the communists take over your favorite liberal organization? So what? Aren't they—despite their preoccupation with Russia and their questionable ethics—working for the same ends as the liberal, only with a lot more zeal? Hasn't the time come at least to examine some of these ends to see whether "we all are pretty much working for the same thing?" The liberal is working, at varying speeds, for world government, but the communist's aim is Big Three Unity a la Yalta and opposition to world federation. The liberal is working for the rights of labor, but the communist easily denied the right of labor to strike during the war against fascism. The liberal is working for the civil rights of all, but the communist denies the civil rights of those he defines as "the enemies of the people." . . . The liberal is working to end imperialism, first American and secondly wherever else he finds it. The communist is noisy about British and American imperialism, but no others. The liberal is working to end militarism, but the communist is silent about militarism except when it is expedient to launch a "peace mobilization."

* * *

But just how can individuals and organizations be identified as being communist? There is no infallible rule and one should always give the individual or organization under investigation the benefit of any doubt—where there is doubt. The most reliable way is perhaps to examine the records of the individual or group in question over a long period of time in relation to certain political issues or even personalities. . . . In each instance, a thinking individual might agree with the communist line on any issue and decidedly not be a communist, but when an individual or organization follows continuously the girations and nuances of the communist line, the resulting configuration spells communist or fellow-traveler. And there is always one final test: ask the individual or organization how he differs or has differed from the communist line. . . .

Liberals should—if possible—work only with those organizations which they know have a democratic orientation in fact as well as in name. Instead of cooperating with the National Negro Congress, liberal churchmen should cooperate with the National Association for the Advancement of Colored People. Instead of working with the American Youth for Democracy, liberal churchmen should work with the United States Student Assembly. Instead of supporting the Civil Rights Congress and its various satellites, the liberal churchmen should support the American Civil Liberties Union.

* * *

After saying all these things, one should affirm a sense of political proportion. Communism is no foreseeable threat to America. As Philip Murray told the recent CIO convention, a far greater threat than communism is "the boom or bust profiteering of the exploiters." The prime threat to America is fascism. It *can* happen here. The central problem of the next decade is, therefore, to build a liberal or progressive movement which will prevent American reaction and ultimately American fascism and which will establish increased democracy. This liberal movement, and its secular and religious constituents, will be smeared at every step—and called communist whether or not communists are actually in control.

SOURCE: Homer Jack, "The Threat of American Communists to the Liberal Church and Other Organizations," Homer Alexander Jack Papers, 1903–1967, Andover-Harvard Archives, bMS 01270, Andover-Harvard Theological Library, Harvard Divinity School, Cambridge, MA. Reprinted in Charles W. Eddis, *Stephen Fritchman: The American Unitarians and Communism: A History with Documents* (Lulu.com, 2011).

CLINTON LEE SCOTT

Parish Parables

1946

Clinton Lee Scott (1887–1985) was one of the most influential Universalist denominational leaders in the twentieth century. Ordained in 1914, he served congregations in Vermont, New York, Pennsylvania, California, Georgia, Illinois, Massachusetts, and Florida. An outspoken pacifist during World War I and the only Universalist to sign the Humanist Manifesto, Scott had sufficient pastoral sensitivity to earn the respect of ministerial colleagues and was chosen as superintendent of the Massachusetts and Connecticut Universalist Conventions. In that role, he recruited Unitarian humanist Kenneth Patton to revitalize Boston Universalism at the Charles Street Meeting House. He was also an early champion of consolidation with the Unitarians, and served on the UUA's first Board of Trustees. Scott's whimsical parables of parish ministry reveal both the informal, self-deprecating style of twentieth-century Universalism and its ongoing engagement with biblical themes and motifs. Further Reading: Clinton Lee Scott, Some Things Remembered (Boston: Church of the Larger Fellowship, 1976) and Clinton Lee Scott, Parish Parables (eBook reissue) (Boston: Skinner House Books, 2011).

—Dan McKanan

Of a Woman That Was Deaf

Now the Master was new to the Temple, having lately come to be the Master. And each Sabbath he looked and beheld a woman, small of stature, and of many years. And she was dressed in black raiment and did sit near the front in the Great Congregation. And the soul of the Master did greatly rejoice in her because of her faithfulness.

And it happened on a certain day that the woman spake unto him, saying, Sir, all my ancestors worshipped in this Temple and my fathers hath been its pillars, and the strength of its beams: therefore am I found here as often as the gates are opened, and it shall be thus as long as the Lord giveth me life: yet hear I not a word that thou speakest to the Great Congregation, for upon me is laid a great affliction; my ears hear not. Then did the Master answer her as if with a humble heart, yet in a manner to hide his vanity, and speaking in a loud voice that the deaf woman might hear him, saith, Peradventure thou misseth little when thou hearest not that which I speak to

130

the Great Congregation. And the woman answered him, saying, Even so hath it been told me by them that hear thee.

Of Him That Is Ordained

Now the Master of the Temple was bidden to a ceremony that was to ordain a young man, and send him forth to preach. And there were assembled them that were high in the counsel of the people, priests and Levites, and scribes who did interpret the Law, and pray, and did read words from the book of Moses. And they placed their hands upon the young man's head to ordain him, and to impart unto him their blessing.

And the Master of the Temple did approve of all this which was done according to custom. But thinketh he in his heart, How hardly can one man or many, even though they be priests, and Levites, and scribes, consecrate another: for it remaineth to every man to ordain himself to the high calling to which he is called. And thou, O young man, must oftentimes ordain thyself in the days that are before thee, when the burdens upon thee will be grievous, and the lamp upon the altar of thy spirit burneth low. For thou shalt stand along, and thy brethren will not be at thy side, and will not lay their hands upon thee with blessing.

SOURCE: Clinton Lee Scott, *Parish Parables* (Boston: Murray Press, 1946).

The Faith of an Unrepentant Liberal

1946

A. Powell Davies (1902–1957) was a mid-twentieth-century pastor and denominational leader whose ministry was characterized by a fierce commitment to justice and an evangelical zeal for the growth of Unitarianism. From the pulpit of All Souls Church in Washington, D.C., Davies fought McCarthyism, helped lead the desegregation of the city, and advocated for civilian control of atomic energy. His powerful preaching and compelling vision drew many to Unitarianism, allowing All Souls to plant five new congregations in the Washington suburbs. In The Faith of an Unrepentant Liberal, *adapted from his sermons, Davies offers a "plain restatement" of religion for the postwar world, "one that reckons candidly with what the modern age requires." The following selection reveals the power of both his vision and his oratory. Further Reading: George N. Marshall,* A. Powell Davies and His Times *(Boston: Skinner House, 1990); William O. Douglas, ed.,* The Mind and Faith of A. Powell Davies *(Garden City, NY: Doubleday, 1959).*

—Robert Hardies

Never was the need for faith as desperate as now; and never was it more essential that belief be genuine. We cannot face the future empty-hearted; we cannot face it with an untrue creed. . . .

In the age of opportunity and peril that confronts us, only disaster can be harvested from false beliefs. The religions of the creeds are obsolescent; they have no will to face reality; the basis of their claims expired with yesterday; to what is now required they are irrelevant; the authority of myth and miracle is over. Surely it should be clear at last that all the compromises of religion must be ended. The world is much too dangerous for anything but truth.

Only this can now avail us: that we leave the childhood of the race behind and come to spiritual maturity.

*   *   *

For too long, now, men have feared to be fully and altogether men. The time has come for liberation from their fears; the time to seek a nobler stature.

There is a religion that says Freedom! Freedom from ignorance and false belief. Freedom from spurious claims and bitter prejudices. Freedom to seek the truth, both old and new, and freedom to follow it. Freedom from the hates and greeds that divide mankind and spill the blood of every generation. Freedom for honest thought. Freedom for equal justice, freedom to seek the true, the good and the beautiful with minds unimpaired by cramping dogmas and spirits uncrippled by abject dependence. There is a religion that adds to Freedom, Universal Brotherhood!—a religion that says mankind is not divided—except by ignorance and prejudice and hate—that sees mankind as naturally one and waiting to be spiritually united; a religion which proclaims an end to creedal reservations and exclusions—and declares a brotherhood unbounded! a religion that knows that we shall never find the fullness of the wonder and the glory of life until we are tall enough in moral stature to deserve it; that we shall never have hearts big enough for the love we call the love of God until we have made them big enough for the world-wide love of man.

Only this faith in freedom linked with universal brotherhood can be enough to save the world and then rebuild it. All lesser faiths are dwindling and collapsing—or running for protection to brutality and tyranny. They will be swept away or ridden to their doom by fierce fanaticisms to which they yield in desperation. Only this faith, this free and universal faith, is now possible; only this faith is powerful. Only this faith can march with truth; only this faith can liberate us from the fear and ignorance of the past or set us free towards the future: the faith that begins in individual freedom of belief and goes out to the limitless, building throughout the world the Free and Universal Church.

I am an unrepentant liberal. If the gods of yesterday are dying, I am willing that they die. For there is a God who never dies, the one and only living God whose face is ever set towards tomorrow. And for those who follow where he leads, the winds of morning are already blowing, and however long the night may linger, the day of triumph is in sight.

SOURCE: A. Powell Davies, *The Faith of an Unrepentant Liberal* (Boston: Beacon Press, 1946), 3, 14–15.

"A Faith for Free Men"
1946

Throughout World War II, James Luther Adams (along with American Unitarian Association president Frederick May Eliot and other liberal leaders) sought to mobilize religious commitment on behalf of the war against fascism, while steering clear of the nationalistic prejudices that characterized the First World War. In this piece, Adams seeks to do so by reflecting on the theological concept of faith. The influence of his friend Paul Tillich, who redefined faith as "ultimate concern," is evident throughout, as is Adams's sympathy for the emerging movement against racial segregation.

—Dan McKanan

Human history is not the struggle between religion and irreligion; it is veritably a battle of faiths; a battle of the gods who claim men's allegiance.

Not long ago I heard a German exile tell a story of Nazi horror. As he reached the end of his story he became mute with revulsion and indignation. How could he speak with sufficient contempt of what the Gestapo had done to his friend? Painfully he groped for words, and then, speaking with revived fear of the Gestapo officers who had committed the murder in cold blood, he asked, "Are these men completely without awe, are they completely without faith?" Immediately he answered his own question: "There is," he said, "no such thing as a man completely without faith. What a demonic faith is the faith of the Nazis!" We can readily understand what he meant. The differences among men do not lie in the fact that some have faith and others do not. *They lie only in a difference of faith.* The Gestapo put its confidence in obedience to the Führer, in obedience to the call of "blood and soil." Its victim placed his confidence in something thicker than blood, in something stronger than death or fear of death. Whether or not this particular victim used the word "faith" or any other words from religious tradition, we do not know, but it is evident that he put his confidence in something more powerful and commanding than the Gestapo. It is possible that his was a faith for free men. In any event, such a faith did rise up against the Gestapo.

Fortunately, not many of us have had the experience of confronting Gestapo agents. We have liked to believe that we did not share *their* faith, yet we have all had some part in creating or appeasing Gestapos—and we could do it again. We have also had some part in stopping the Gestapo. In fact, the spirit, if not the brutality, of the Gestapo has to be stopped in ourselves every day, and we are not always success-ful, either because of our impotence or because of our lack of conviction. The faith of unfree men can raise its ugly head even in a "free" country.

Recently this fact was impressed upon me in an unforgettably vivid way. During the second World War it was at one time my task to lecture on the Nazi faith to a large group of American army officers who were preparing for service later in the occupation army in Germany. As I lectured I realized that together with a just resentment against the Nazis I was engendering in the students an orgy of self-righteousness. This self-righteousness, I decided, ought somehow to be checked. Otherwise, I might succeed only in strengthening the morale of a bumptious hundred-percent "Americanism," and that was not the faith we were supposed to be fighting for. Towards the end of the lecture I recapitulated the ideas of the Nazi "faith," stressing the Nazi belief in the superiority of the Teutons and the inferiority of other "races." I also reminded the officers of similar attitudes to be observed in America, not only among the lunatic and subversive groups but also among respect-able Americans in the army of democracy. Then I asked these army officers to pose one or two questions to be answered by each man in his own conscience. First: "Is there any essential difference between your attitude towards the Negro and the Jew, and the Nazi attitude toward other 'races,'—not a difference in brutality but a difference in basic philosophy?" "If there is an essential difference," I said, "then the American soldier might logically become a defender of the Four Freedoms, but if there is no essential difference between your race philosophy and that of the Nazis, a second question should be posed: 'What are you fighting for?'"

I blush when I think of some of the responses I received. I was immediately besieged with questions like these: "Do you think we should marry the 'nigger'?" "Aren't Negros a naturally indolent and dirty race?" "Haven't you been in business, and don't you know that every Jew is a kike?" Questions like these came back to me for over an hour. I simply repeated my question again and again: "How do you dis-tinguish between yourself and a Nazi?" Seldom have I witnessed such agony of spirit in a public place.

* * *

The question concerning faith is not, "Shall I be a man of faith?" The proper question is, rather, "Which faith is mine?" or, better, "Which faith should be mine?" for, whether a person craves prestige, wealth, security, or amusement, whether he lives for country, for science, for God or for plunder, he shows that he has faith, he shows that he puts his confidence in something.

* * *

As creatures fated to be free, as creatures who must make responsible decisions, what may we place our confidence in? What can we have faith in? What should we serve?

135

The first tenet of the free man's faith is that his ultimate dependence for his being and his freedom is upon a creative power and upon processes not of his own making. His ultimate faith is not in himself. He finds himself an historical being, a being living in nature and history, a being having freedom in nature and history. The forms that nature and history take possess a certain given, fateful character, and yet they are also fraught with meaningful possibilities.

* * *

The second tenet of the free man's faith is that the commanding, sustaining, transforming reality finds its richest focus in meaningful human history, in free, cooperative effort for the common good. In other words, this reality fulfills man's life only when men stand in right relation to each other. Man, the historical being, comes most fully to terms with this reality in the exercise of the freedom that works for justice in human community. Only what creates freedom in a community of justice is dependable. "Faith is the sister of justice." Only the society that gives every man the opportunity to share in the process whereby human potentiality is realizable, only the society that creates the social forms of freedom in a community of justice (where every man is given his due), only the freedom that respects the divine image and dignity in every man are dependable.

* * *

The third tenet of the free man's faith is that the achievement of freedom in community requires the power of organization and the organization of power. The free man will be an unfree man, he will be a victim of tyranny from within or from without, if his free faith does not assume *form*, in both word and deed. The commanding, transforming reality is a shaping power; it shapes one's beliefs about that reality, and when it works through men it shapes the community of justice and love. . . .

There can be no reliable faith for free men unless there are faith-ful men and women who form the faith into beliefs, who test and criticize the beliefs and who then transform and transmit the beliefs. This process of forming and transforming the beliefs of the free faith is a process of discussion; it is a co-operative endeavor in which men surrender to the commanding, transforming reality. The only way in which men can reliably form and transform beliefs is through the sharing of tradition and new insights and through the co-operative criticism and testing of tradition and insight. In other words, men must sincerely work with each other in order to give reliable form and expression to faith. This is the only way in which freedom *from* tyranny can be fulfilled in freedom *with* justice and truth.

SOURCE: James Luther Adams, "A Faith for Free Men," in Stephen H. Fritchman, ed., *Together We Advance* (Boston: Beacon Press, 1946), 47–50, 53, 56–67, 59–60.

"A Research on Church Extension and Maintenance Since 1900: A Progress Report" and "Unitarian Lay Groups"

1946

A crucial change in the growth activity of the Unitarian denomination occurred after World War II at the initiative of Lon Ray Call (1894–1985) and Munroe Husbands (1909–1984). Originally a Southern Baptist minister, Call later came to view himself as an evangelist for Unitarianism. In the words of UUA President Eugene Pickett, he "wanted everyone in America to have the chance to be a Unitarian." To this end, he recommended both an energetic program of church planting and the creation of a new category of lay-led fellowships in cities too small to support a church. At one point, in 1967, there were over four hundred Unitarian fellowships in addition to regular churches. Many of the more successful fellowships became churches with ordained ministers, but this was not the original goal. Call's two memos from 1946 identified some "surprises" about Unitarian church extension, proposed cities for church planting, and offered a blueprint for "Unitarian Lay Groups." Further Reading: Laile E. Bartlett, Bright Galaxy: Ten Years of Unitarian Fellowships *(Boston: Beacon Press, 1960), and Holley Ulbrich,* The Fellowship Movement: A Growth Strategy and Its Legacy *(Boston: Skinner House, 2008).*

—Avery (Pete) Guest

Surprise #1. Zeal in the establishment of new churches has weakened with the passing of the years. I have always assumed that there was a great deal of truth in the oft-repeated remark that, while Unitarians had very little missionary spirit before the turn of the century, since then we have been getting missionary-minded. Well, the record shows just the opposite.

* * *

Surprise #2. It is amazing how many of our churches have ceased to exist since 1900. The number is 254 (240 dead and 14 dormant). By "dead" is meant those that have actually been dropped from the Year Book. The actual dropping is usually years after the church has become dormant.

* * *

Surprise #3. No well founded policy of church extension is apparent since 1900. New churches have sprung up in random fashion in all kinds of places and under all kinds of circumstances.

*   *   *

Surprise #4. Over a million dollars have been spent since 1890 on churches that have not survived. No one could ever accuse us of being stingy in our missionary endeavor. Aside from every material assistance in helping churches purchase lots, erect buildings and keep them in repair, aid has been given through our department in subsidies for the payment of ministers' salaries.

*   *   *

Surprise #5. The shock of the great amount spent is alleviated by the knowledge that close to a million dollars has come to the Association from the members of these closed churches. It is natural that one would be almost nonplussed at the enormity of our futile missionary endeavors. Some people make a great outcry about it; but there have been gains that have largely offset the losses. Quite aside from the spiritual benefits that resulted from some of the churches that accomplished great good over many years, we can count the material returns to the Association when buildings have been sold, endowments assigned and bequests made.

*   *   *

Surprise #6. We are forced to conclude that with all our spending we did not spend enough. It appears from the record that to spend money on a new Unitarian church almost anywhere is a good financial risk. But quite apart from that, the record indicates that we have practiced a very poor economy as we have undertaken missionary ventures in place after place with extreme reluctance to back up our venture with our purse.

*   *   *

Surprise #7. *Some of the best cities in the country have been overlooked in Unitarian extension.* It is difficult to understand why we have started churches in so many extremely unpromising places and ignored the more fertile fields.

*   *   *

Manifestly, we need a technique for appraising towns and cities regardless of size. Population is not the most important factor. . . . Of course the presence of other liberal churches is a factor, but also to be considered are such things as the percentage of foreign born and negro, how people make their living, what they read and whether there is evidence of an urge to culture and higher education. Most of all we need to find out in all the cities of 50,000 or more what needs to be done religiously in that city and will likely not be done unless the Unitarians do it. With very inadequate information about them, I will list the 40 cities which in my judgment are now good fields for extension:

138

Arlington, Va., which has grown in 20 years from 16,000 to 57,000 and which has already some impetus from the people of the Washington church.

Asheville, N.C., which has grown from 28,000 in 1920 to well over 50,000, a year around resort and a good all around city where we would probably have had a church had our prosperous beginnings in 1930 not been nipped by one of the worst local financial disasters in the history of the nation.

Austin, Tex. The prosperous state capital and site of the university. A university enrollment of 18,000. The city has grown to 87,000 in 1940 from 34,000 in 1920. We have tried there twice but with "one candle power."

*   *   *

Unitarian Lay Groups

In the consideration of Unitarian lay groups we must remember that we have everything to gain and nothing to lose if the plan is well conceived and carried out. . . . The project can be the most successful thing the Unitarian Association has ever undertaken or it can be the most dismal failure. . . .

A Unitarian lay group is not a forum. It is not a discussion club. It is not a Sunday School. It is not a prayer meeting. It is not a social club and it is not a church. It is disappointing to find when the lay group idea is mentioned that so many confuse it with a plan to provide a very poor substitute for a church service, with a sermon at second hand to be read by someone present, and perhaps discussed a little, with perhaps an introduction from a Scripture reading and a concluding prayer. Among Unitarians such a plan would likely lead only to failure.

*   *   *

Of course the primary function of a Unitarian lay group is to provide spiritually satisfying meetings for religious liberals in lieu of a church in towns where in all probability religious liberalism is practically unknown. Unless we can do this and do it well we will fail. I am convinced, however, that we can do it so well that in many respects it will be as satisfying to the individual concerned as many a church service. I am also convinced that it will provide our Unitarian movement with strength enough to more than offset the waning virility of our churches.

SOURCE: Lon Ray Call, "A Research on Church Extension and Maintenance Since 1900: A Progress Report" and "Unitarian Lay Groups," American Unitarian Association, Department of Extension and Maintenance, Administrative Records, Andover-Harvard Archives, bMS 11049, Andover-Harvard Theological Library, Harvard Divinity School, Cambridge, MA.

EGBERT ETHELRED BROWN

"Why I Am What I Am"

c. 1947

Egbert Ethelred Brown (1875–1956) founded the Harlem Unitarian Church in 1920 and served it until his death in 1956. Born and raised in Jamaica, he was employed as an accountant until, following a mid-life crisis, he felt called to the Unitarian ministry. In 1912, after two years of preparation at Meadville Theological School he returned to Jamaica, but when the American Unitarian Association withdrew support for the mission he began anew in New York during the Harlem Renaissance. Among the church's founding members were prominent black Marxists and Socialists. In Harlem he served as chaplain for the African Blood Brotherhood, chair of the Jamaican Benevolent Association, president of the Jamaican Progressive League and vice president of the Federation of Jamaican Organizations. Notwithstanding, his relationship to the AUA was contentious from the beginning. AUA officials discouraged him from attending Meadville, then in 1929 withdrew his fellowship, refusing to reinstate it in 1931 when petitioned by a group, only to reverse course in 1935 under threat of a lawsuit. In 1939 his colleague in Brooklyn, John H. Lathrop, said "[He] carries the Unitarian flag with wide reaching influence ... [and] would be easily worth supporting if he had no Sunday night of his own." Further Reading: Mark D. Morrison-Reed, Black Pioneers in a White Denomination, *3rd ed. (Boston: Skinner House, 1994); Juan M. Floyd-Thomas,* The Origins of Black Humanism: Reverend Ethelred Brown and the Unitarian Church *(New York: Palgrave Macmillan, 2008).*

— Mark D. Morrison-Reed

It has been truly stated that what we have been makes us what we are.

*   *   *

But why did I ultimately chose to be a Unitarian minister? I have to go back once more to the long ago. There were two characteristics I had from childhood. I do not refer to them on account of boastfulness at all. In fact they are inherited traits for which I am thankful. I was an inquisitive youngster and also a truthful boy. I liked to ask questions. Some of you have heard me tell how I question my teacher in Scripture class one day when the lesson was the fall of Jericho. You remember the story. For six days the Israelites walked around Jericho each day and then on the seventh day they walked around seven times concluding the seventh round with a terrible shout—and then the walls fell flat. My innocent question was—Why was so much time wasted, why was not the wall shouted down on the first day?

* * *

Some of you have heard me tell how as a young man I left the Parish Church on Easter Sunday dissatisfied with the arithmetic of the Athanasian Creed, and how on that very day by a strange coincidence I was introduced to Unitarian literature which changed my whole theological attitude for all time. True there was an interim of 14 years when as organist of a Wesleyan Methodist Church I forgot all about theology in the practical services which I rendered in the words of Father Hall as a Minister of Music.

Then came 1907—the year of decision. Without tiring you with details which are not really relevant to our topic let me say that on a certain day in 1907 I received two letters from America,—the one from the Bishop of the African Methodist Episcopal Church practically accepting me as a candidate for the ministry of that church, the other from the President of the Meadville Theological School, accepting as a student in the school, but frankly informing me that there was no colored Unitarian churches in America, and that as at that time no white church in America was likely to accept a colored man as its minister, the school could hold out no prospect of assignment after my graduation. Both letters were replies to letters of mine. I wrote the application to the A.M.E. Bishop on the serious suggestion of the local minister in charge of the A.M.E. mission just started in Jamaica. I had no sooner posted the letter than all the old doubts and rejections of orthodoxy teachings faced me as well as the acceptable doctrines of Unitarian to which I was introduced when I severed my connection with the Episcopal Church. I did not know anything of the Unitarian set-up here; in fact I was not sure if there were any so I took a chance and wrote the very next day after posting my application to the Bishop, a letter addressed to any Unitarian minister in New York. It had last the Secretary of the Fellowship Committee who referred it to the President of the Meadville Theological School. And so on one day I got two replies. In the one case I could start almost at once well as soon after ordination could be arranged to be a minister of the A.M.E. Church, in the other course I had to take a special course of two years at Meadville with the understanding that nothing may happen at the end of the course.

As you imagine it was a serious hour in my life—a vital decision hung in the balance. I decided to face the situation alone. It was a fierce but a short struggle. I said to myself,—"Brown you need not be a minister at all, but if you do decide to enter the ministry, then you must enter the church wherein you can be absolutely honest—honest with your people and honest with yourself."

The same week I wrote the Bishop withdrawing my application, and I wrote the President of the Meadville Theological School, definitely asking to be booked as a

141

special student to enter the school in the fall of 1908. And that is how and why I am a Unitarian instead of a Methodist minister.

*   *   *

Why then am I a Unitarian minister. Because I could not be enchained by the creeds and traditions of the orthodox churches which I had long since intellectually and ethically outgrown. I wished freedom—freedom to be my own self—to express my self as myself and I believed then as I believe now that a minister of religion must first of all be absolutely loyal to Truth. And no other church grants its minister that freedom but the Unitarian Church. We alone of all churches have in the truest sense a free pulpit in a free church. I am a Unitarian minister because I believe in sharing with my people new truths as I discover them for myself. Orthodox churches claim that all truths—at least all necessary truths—have already been proclaimed. Unitarian churches on the other hand are dedicated to the progressive transformation and enrichment of individual and social life through religion, in accordance with advancing knowledge and the growing vision of mankind.

It is something of inestimable value to be a free minister in a free pulpit in a free church of free men, presenting and interpreting religion not according to exploded and discredited theories but in accordance with advancing knowledge and the growing vision of mankind.

I am a happy man—free and untrammelled—not tempted to adopt subterfuges and tricky arguments but provoked by the set-up and environment and demands of my church to be honest.

SOURCE: Egbert Ethelred Brown, "Why I Am What I Am," Egbert Ethelred Brown papers, Schomburg Center for Research in Black Culture, New York Public Library.

HENRY NELSON WIEMAN

"Neo-Orthodoxy and Contemporary Religious Reaction"

1947

Theologian and philosopher Henry Nelson Wieman (1884–1975) is generally regarded as the founder of "religious naturalism," a view that regards God as a natural process that is entirely knowable through empirical means. Educated at Harvard and ordained as a Presbyterian, Wieman was recruited to the faculty of the University of Chicago Divinity School because of his reputation as the first American to understand the work of Alfred North Whitehead, though his approach was less metaphysical than Whitehead's. Wieman was critical of earlier strands of liberal theology, which were prone to hubris and idolatry because they conflated "created good" with "creative good." But he was equally opposed to the neo-orthodoxy of Karl Barth and Reinhold Niebuhr, which presented biblical religion as the only antidote to idolatry. Two years after he contributed this essay to a Beacon Press volume of responses to neo-orthodoxy, Wieman joined a Unitarian congregation. Further Reading: W. Creighton Peden, The Life and Thought of Henry Nelson Wieman (1884–1975): An American Philosopher *(Lewiston, NY: Edwin Mellen Press, 2010).*

— Dan McKanan

Neo-Orthodoxy is a stage through which we had to pass to recover from a situation that might otherwise have been hopeless. It is like the fever of a diseased organism; it is a form of pathology, but if it does not continue too long or go too far it enables the organism to throw off the poison infecting it and thereby return to normal health. . . .

The poison that afflicted our religious life and brought forth the fever of Neo-Orthodoxy was the religious liberalism and fundamentalism that flourished during the first two decades of the twentieth century. These would have been fatal had they continued to dominate our thought and practice. Doubtless, along with Neo-Orthodoxy, they will always continue as minor ingredients in our collective religious life; neither a living organism nor a culture can ever get rid of its past. Furthermore, all in their proper time and place, these elements made a contribution to our religious devotion and understanding. But the time has now almost come when all these *must* relinquish that level of importance and control over religious life which they have held in the past. They "must," not in the sense that they automatically and inevitably will give way, but in the sense that we cannot carry through the great constructive effort of our time if we do not have a better religion to provide. . . .

Old-fashioned . . . religious liberalism tried to establish religion upon "religious experience." That is like trying to establish the family upon "love experience" without having particular and clearly distinguished individuals as the ones to love. "Love experience" not directed toward particular individuals will wreck the home; it is promiscuity. Religious liberalism of thirty years ago produced promiscuity in religious living by following religious experience rather than any definite and well-defined reality, clearly distinguishable from other entities, as the guide of life and recipient of devotion.

These liberals sometimes tried to set up the historical Jesus as the guide and object of devotion, but the historical Jesus is not a present living reality to which one can commit himself and from which derive the immediate religious experience they sought. One can experience immediately only his own interpretation of that historical figure, and this interpretation is many-times mediated down through history.

The promiscuity of religious experience when not controlled and directed by devotion to something well-defined and distinguished and assuredly known to be the present source of human good, is futile sentimentalism—when it is not deadly corruption. Therefore men had to escape from that kind of religious liberalism. Neo-Orthodoxy was the way out.

* * *

Neo-Orthodoxy asserts that God, and the supreme directives that come from God, can reach us in adequate form only by way of revelation. Revelation (so it teaches) is a disclosure or delivery into human life from a source that is super-historical, super-temporal, beyond the reach of human observation and human reason. This transcendent power is revealed by certain mighty acts which appear as events in history; but these events can carry genuine revelation to us only when they transform us and when a faith emanating from them awakens in us.

But how can we know that any selected events in history are truly the revelation of God? And how can we distinguish within those events the reality revealed? And how can we demonstrate that what we discriminate is, in truth, the creative and redemptive God? Neo-Orthodoxy can answer these questions only by saying that God-given faith and accepted myth alone can inform us. Human reason cannot inform us because human reason imposes on God the constructions of the human mind and so produces an idol. No observation or intellectual analysis of events now occurring in our lives can provide the answer to these questions because all such observations and analyses are corrupted by pride, envy and other perversions of sinful man. Also, the reality in question, being beyond time, cannot be identified with anything occurring in this world where alone such observations and analysis can operate. In sum, God's initiative, and the myths created in history by God's initiative, can alone guide us aright.

I am quite ready to agree that God's initiative, and the myths created in history by God's initiative, can alone guide us aright. But when and if they do guide us aright, they must guide us to something that can be known in truth to be the creative and redeeming God when the resources and methods of rational and observational inquiry have been developed in such a way as to be applicable to this problem.

According to the view of the present writer, the source of all things good is a kind of creative interchange between human individuals and groups, and between the organism and its environment. This creative interchange does not ordinarily enter human awareness, and for a very good reason. What creates any instance of conscious awareness must obviously be prior to the emergence of that awareness. Therefore, the awareness when it emerges can scarcely be conscious of what created it. The interchange creating our minds at any given moment is already past and done when the awareness, issuing from that interchange, begins to exist.

Hence, creative interchange, in its capacity of being creative of the appreciative mind and its appreciated world, could not be discovered until certain biological, psychological and social facts were brought to light and put together in such a way as to reveal this creative source of life. This putting together has been done in the last twenty-five years and more by such men as Charles Horton Cooley, George Herbert Mead, M. P. Follett, John Dewey, A. N. Whitehead, W. S. Plant and others.

Since the creative source of human mind and human value is hidden after the manner indicated, it was inevitable that men prior to its discovery should represent it mythically as beyond the reach of observation; some have even said, and still say, beyond the reach of the reason. Myths have represented it as a super personality, free of the limitations of space and time, beyond history and society, yet potently working in our world. So long as psychological, sociological, biological and biochemical research had not yet penetrated to the data required to yield knowledge of specific characters identifying and distinguishing this creative power in our midst, men could not voluntarily deal with it in any other way than by myth. Nevertheless, if observation is understood to include all that we can discover by analyzing the component parts of any perceptual event, then this creative power can be observed. . . .

Men will never outgrow the need of non-cognitive myths in dealing with the creative source of life and also in dealing with much else. We live now, and always will, with realities so intimately and pervasively involved in our existence and so complex in their nature that we cannot analyze and discriminate the structures we would need to comprehend in order to know them in respect to their specific natures. In dealing with such relatively unknown realities, we must have myths if any linguistic signs at all are needed to guide us. In time we may penetrate cognitively into the nature of existence beyond any known limit; but always there is something more to discover. Always we shall live with sustaining and creative events so intimately, invariably, and intricately wrought into our existence, that we cannot know them in their specific characters, even though we may know they are there. Myths do not specify or describe, but they adumbrate; they adumbrate what the human mind at the time cannot analyze or clearly discriminate. In that way they guide in areas where knowledge cannot go.

There comes a time, however, when myth in certain areas must give way to knowledge if we are to find our way and be saved from destruction. As human power increases through the development of technology, the equilibrium of conditions is disturbed which heretofore made it possible for creative interchange to work effectively in sustaining and enriching the good of human life. So long as this ancient equilibrium continued, ways of living under guidance of myth may have served well enough. But now when people live in great cities and nations, when the most diverse races and cultures are bound together by an intricate network of technological interdependence, and when people move about with the speed of sound, and communicate with the range and speed of lightning, new ways of ordering life must be discovered and established. Furthermore, these new ways must be fitted to release and serve the creative source of human good. But this requires more intellectual understanding of how this creative source works and what it demands of us, than was ever needed in other times. This makes it plain why myth can no longer be used in those areas where intellectual understanding and construction are required to meet demands for which myths were never fitted.

✳ ✳ ✳

We have tried to set forth what we understand to be the true nature and function of religious myth and have done so as a way of criticizing Neo-Orthodoxy. Neo-Orthodoxy has rendered a great service. It has given us a new and profounder appreciation of the importance of myth and of much else in our religious heritage. It has made us more keenly aware of the depths of evil in human life and the inability of man by his own effort alone to deliver himself or to create the better world and better life. But it cannot lead us religiously in the struggle to find a way through the present confusion in the direction of life's fulfillment. Its way of interpreting the ancient faith unfits it to meet the need and achieve the promise of our time. We must have more rational understanding of the creative sources of the appreciative life than any form of Neo-Orthodoxy will permit.

Liberal religion can appropriate to itself all the resources accessible to Neo-Orthodoxy and yet preserve freedom of inquiry and the searching tests of reason. It can serve the need of our time in this way if it will interpret the myths of Neo-Orthodoxy so as to be true to the best they have to offer and yet expose that best to the inquiring mind.

SOURCE: Henry N. Wieman, "Neo-Orthodoxy and Contemporary Religious Reaction," *Religious Liberals Reply* (Boston: Beacon Press, 1947), 4–13, 15.

"Americans Bearing Gifts"

UNITARIAN COMMISSION ON WORLD ORDER
"The Greek Crisis"
1947

Stephen Fritchman (1902–1981), a graduate of Union Seminary who was ordained a Methodist but soon switched his ministerial fellowship to Unitarianism, was appointed as American Unitarian Association Director of Youth Work in 1938 and as editor of the Christian Register *in 1942. Along with his Union Seminary mentor Harry Ward, Fritchman was a prominent clerical ally of the Communist-inspired Popular Front, and Communist perspectives were prominent in the pages of the* Register. *Facing criticism for this, AUA president Frederick May Eliot created an editorial advisory board, with which Fritchman awkwardly cooperated for several months. Fritchman was finally forced out after he attempted to publish this sharp denunciation of President Truman's policy in Greece, which denominational leaders replaced with a more equivocal statement prepared by the Unitarian Commission on World Order. Further Reading: Charles W. Eddis,* Stephen Fritchman: The American Unitarians and Communism: A History with Documents *(Lulu.com, 2011); Philip Zwerling,* Rituals of Repression: Anti-Communism and the Liberals *(Los Angeles: First Unitarian Church, 1985).*

—Dan McKanan

Americans Bearing Gifts

We strongly urge all Unitarians to read the official statement on Greece by the Unitarian World Order Commission to be found on page 184. It is a fine minimum statement of protest against President Truman's proposals for intervention in Greece and Turkey. From our own editorial sanctum we would point out that the issue of food relief is irrelevant since funds for this type of aid were voted for Greece and other European countries by our Government prior to the President's speech to Congress, and the proposed 400 million loan, it is now admitted, is almost entirely intended for military purposes. The issues are nakedly exposed to public view. Are we going to substitute Truman's two worlds for Franklin Roosevelt's and Wendell Willkie's one world? Are we going to support reactionary governments from Turkey to Korea if only they will fly the flag of anti-Soviet hatred? Are we going to call "Communist" every government that resolutely seeks reform and change for the welfare of its people? . . .

Are we, in the name of a world-wide crusade against Communism, going to make the name of America despised by every race and nation that has hopes for peace and security through the United Nations? Would not a fresh advance in democracy at home, a new attack on the problems of housing our people, controlling monopoly, and extending public education win us more friends around the planet at this hour . . . ?

A clear and practical plan, extremely specific in its proposals, was prepared by a United Nations commission in Greece, and it lay on the President's desk as he addressed Congress. It proposed roads and dams and farm equipment—not tanks and guns and military advisers. If the welfare of the Greek people were our State Department's true concern, instead of oil for the Navy, it would have welcomed the proposals of the United Nations FAO Commission instead of ignoring them. . . . Our occupation of bases in the Pacific, the continued presence of our military advisers and military equipment in China, the fortification of the frozen wastes of northern Canada—these things make our protests at Soviet "expansionism" less than impressive in the eyes of world citizens. Our honest differences with the Soviet Government can and must be worked out in the United Nations chambers if we want peace and prosperity for all people. . . .

America holds the key position in the question of world peace. Our government can determine whether the democratic will of free peoples is advanced or delayed, whether a few Americans desiring investments and foreign markets can betray our nation into steps leading to war, or whether we play our proper role in the United Nations. Whether our sons die on new battlefields is up to us.

"The Greek Crisis," a Statement by the Unitarian Commission on World Order, April 4

We sympathize deeply with the people of Greece who are suffering from food shortage, internal dissension and threat of external aggression. We believe that until a stable government is established, suffering from all three causes will continue.

We want to see the Greeks themselves establish a government to their liking. We do not believe the present government is such a government. Neither do we believe that a Communist government would be any more popular or effective. Any government maintained by outsider power in the long run is a threat to world peace.

We believe that alleviation of the present economic distress will make it easier to establish a more acceptable regime in Greece. We, therefore, urge prompt and generous aid in the shipment of food to that country.

On the other hand, we urge extreme caution in proceeding with financial and military aid to Greece. If it is believed desirable from the point of view of world peace to supply financial and military assistance, we urge that this be done in such a way as not justifiably to lay the United States open to the charge of endeavoring to perpetuate the present Greek government, of threatening the Soviet Union, or of by-passing the United Nations. We urge, therefore, that if such additional aid is extended, the United Nations be brought into the picture at the earliest possible moment in order that others may share our problem and responsibilities.

We urge that if similar aid is extended to Turkey similar steps be taken to bring the matter as speedily as possible within the jurisdiction of the United Nations.

SOURCE: Stephen Fritchman, "Americans Bearing Gifts," Melvin Arnold Papers, Andover-Harvard Archives, bMS 204/2, Andover-Harvard Theological Library, Harvard Divinity School, Cambridge, MA. "The Greek Crisis," *Christian Register*, May 1947, 181. Both items are reprinted in Charles W. Eddis, *Stephen Fritchman: The American Unitarians and Communism: A History with Documents* (Lulu.com, 2011).

FREDERICK MAY ELIOT

"The Message and Mission of Liberal Religion"

1947

During his five terms as president of the American Unitarian Association, Frederick May Eliot (1889–1958) achieved remarkable growth in both sheer numbers and social outreach. He energetically supported the fellowship movement, which led to the founding of hundreds of new congregations, and the Unitarian Service Committee, which worked tirelessly to rescue victims of the Holocaust. Perhaps no cause was dearer to Eliot's heart than liberal religious unity. In this sermon delivered at the 1947 General Conference of the AUA, Eliot articulated his vision for a "United Liberal Church of America." Further Reading: Carol R. Morris, "Frederick May Eliot, President of the American Unitarian Association (1937–1958)," Ph.D. dissertation, Boston University, 1970.

—Dan McKanan

The time for talk is over. The time for action has come. The God of Job speaks to our generation, interrupting our debates as to who caused the whirlwind and how it might be brought under control, speaking to us in rude terms of demanding not arguments but deeds, reminding us that we are required to answer to Him for what we do. His word comes with the tone of command. . . .

This voice is today heard wherever men are willing to stop chattering and listen. It speaks to all mankind. But tonight, in this great and beautiful church, it behooves us to ask ourselves what that voice means to us as Unitarians.

At first glance, the record of our Conference together might be misleading and discouraging. For three whole days—morning, afternoon and evening—we have been talking, discussing, arguing; and the nearest we have come to action has been to pass a set of resolutions! . . .

But appearances can be deceitful, and these three days have, in reality, demonstrated that we Unitarians are growing thoroughly impatient with "mere words and phrases." In recent years we have been doing more than talk. . . . We are, I believe, ready for definite plans and instructions and even commands—not handed down from any commanding officer, but suddenly coming to a sharp focus within the mind of the fellowship as a whole. . . . All that needs to be done is to make a simple and unified statement of what we propose to do next.

1. We propose to take the lead in creating a new federation of religious liberals on this American continent, from Hudson's Bay to the Canal Zone, which might be called "The United Liberal Church of America."

There are today three major bodies of organized religion in America—the Roman Catholic Church, the Federal Council of the Churches of Christ . . . and the less unified body of adherents to the Jewish faith. . . .

To these should be added a fourth—the United Liberal Church, as sharply set off from what Dr. Stanley Jones calls the "United Church of Christ," with its standard of admission the "Petrine Confession," as that church is from Roman Catholicism.

There are areas where all four bodies could cooperate, and within which close team-work should be developed; but this ought to be on the basis of mutual respect. The necessary first step is to build up the organized forces of religious liberalism into a united, effective body, that can deal on a self-respecting basis with the three orthodox bodies.

Such a united fellowship of religious liberals should include not only liberals with a Christian background but also Liberal Judaism and those liberals who find their most intimate spiritual ties in the Ethical Society and other organizations that have less concern with historic religious alignments. It should include all religious liberals, "of every name and sign," united in a common allegiance to freedom, faith, and fraternity, and in a common resolve to promote these values in a world that is at the moment far from sympathetic with them.

2. We propose to take a leading part in creating a world-wide federation of religious liberals, centering in the existing International Association (the I.A.R.F.) but extending much wider and greatly strengthening its organizational effectiveness.

Such a federation must be frankly and vigorously "more than Christian." It must acknowledge that all forms of high religion are brothers, working together with mutual regard untainted by any thought of spiritual superiority; recognizing that the basic faith of all is identical in essentials, and rejoicing in the added richness that comes through variety in non-essentials. . . .

3. We propose to give united and sacrificial support to a world-wide program of humanitarian service, without regard to race, nationality, politics, color, or creed, on the basis of the magnificent record of the Unitarian Service Committee, and in full co-operation with all other agencies that share our humanitarian purposes.

✳   ✳   ✳

The flaming chalice is our symbol and pride. We do not propose to limit the area of its beneficent influence by our pettiness or niggardliness or Laodicean indifference.

4. We propose to mobilize the full energy and resources of religious liberalism for the defense and extension of the democratic way of life, in a world where the

151

forces of tyranny are exploiting the present discouragement of many people with the indifference and timidity of the democratic nations, in order to enslave the minds, bodies, and souls of men.

We must insist, with far greater urgency and persuasiveness than ever before, that religion is the basis of democracy, and that only liberal religion can provide the inspiration and reinforcement that will keep believers in democracy always alert to the dangers that threaten the values of individual personality which are the essence of both democracy and religion. . . .

5. We propose to renew, with humble but resolute hearts, the spiritual dynamic of our free faith, knowing that freedom without consecration is only another form of slavery, and that reverence for that which deserves reverence, both in our heritage from the past and in our experience of the present, is a duty that can be neglected only at the peril of our souls and at the price of any long-term usefulness. . . .

The cure is a new birth among liberals of the power of the spirit, which will not come about by accident or by grace, but as the fruit of a fresh determination to give priority in personal and corporate living to the abiding realities of spiritual energy and the quiet confidence of deep-rooted spiritual faith.

These five things we propose to do. On all of them we have in recent years made at least a beginning; but we propose to undertake them with far deeper dedication and in a united spirit of endeavor, confident that they are of real importance not for ourselves alone but for mankind. We propose to swing into action now, to have done with words that darken counsel and divide our forces and weaken our united will. We propose to shake off the dust of futile controversies, to harbor no grudges, to rise above all petty and self-seeking ambitions, to forgive and forget whatever offenses may have been given or received, to widen the horizon of our vision and imagination and sympathy, and to walk with one another as befits a society of friends and a brotherhood of faith.

SOURCE: Frederick May Eliot, "The Message and Mission of Liberal Religion," *Christian Register*, November 1947, 423–24, 436.

The Liberal Woman of Today
1948

The General Alliance of Unitarian Women, originally known as the Women's Auxiliary Conference, was founded in 1880. Like its Universalist counterpart, it was a national organization with strong chapters in many congregations—indeed, many congregations owed their founding and their financial stability to the organizing work of the Alliance. For its first half-century, the Alliance mostly focused on its founding mission, which was to raise funds for religious work at the local, national, and international levels. In 1947 the Alliance elected Margot (Isrel) Pieksen (1894–1986) of Saint Louis as its president. Passionate about social justice and international peace, she created the Alliance's first Commission on Minorities and worked hard to assure members that the Alliance would not be dominated by influence from Boston. This pamphlet, created by women from twenty-two cities, reflects Pieksen's broadening vision for the Alliance. In addition to the passages included here, it offered reflections on the role of the liberal woman in her church, her community, and her world. Further Reading: Sara Comins, In Unbroken Line: History of the Alliance, 1880–1955 *(Boston: General Alliance of Unitarian and Other Liberal Christian Women, 1955).*

—Dan McKanan

Introduction—The liberal woman of today is a complex creature—a product of the chaotic, fast moving age in which she lives. The intricacies in the world challenge her way of thought and her way of life. The world is at her doorstep more insistently than ever before. All the peoples of the earth are her neighbors and their problems are those of her own family.

* * *

The Liberal Woman's Religion and Philosophy—The liberal woman is religious, knowing that spiritual values are fundamental to happy homes and a healthy society. Her actions and words tell many things about her—both are matters of record and can be collected and studied. But there is a far more vital facet of personality which concerns the inner resources of her being, that which we might call her personal philosophy.

Unfettered by orthodox tenets or established forms of political or religious philosophy, the religion of the liberal woman of today is responsible and honest. As the result of her thinking it makes her a sympathetic person guided by intelligence and not emotionalism. This free religion satisfies her spiritual needs and in its energizing powers she finds happiness and satisfaction. But at the same time, she realizes that being a liberal gives her a freedom which may become license without maturity and faith.

The liberal woman believes in intellectual liberty and freedom of thought for all people. . . .

Her religion is based on belief in the Fatherhood of God and the Brotherhood of Man. She has a conviction that the Creative Source of all life is God, that all people are a part of that life and can receive strength and guidance from it. . . .

This religious liberal has studied her own religious heritage. . . .

The liberal woman of today is actively conscious of the liberal influence that was the source of our American institutions and of our national history. . . .

The religious liberal assumes the responsibility of a free religion. She knows that part of the responsibility to create a good society rests with her. No longer for her does a personal Deity intervene to save humankind from the fruits of its folly. Neither does a divine priesthood, or even a group of good wise men, hold the controls which will bring peace to the earth.

In all her activities the liberal woman strives to apply the principles of democracy and affirm her opposition to authoritarian methods. She realizes that liberalism, like peace, is something for which one must work constantly. . . .

Love is at the center of her life. The religious liberal, much more than ever before, works to break down the divisive barriers of race, creed, caste, and color, and bring about the true brotherhood of man. The world becomes her country; every child her responsibility; all uplifting influences to her church. To her, religion is a way of life to be lived here and now.

*　*　*

The Liberal Woman in Her Family—Love is the cornerstone of the home. The liberal churchwoman wants to realize her dream of an ideal home where family living becomes a fine art.

As a homemaker and mother she tries to put into operation the principles of democratic living. She respects the individual feelings and beliefs of the individual members of her family, humbly recognizing that she does not necessarily have the final answer. . . .

In order to teach her children the principles of liberalism which she believes, she must demonstrate them herself and make application of similar standards desirable to her children. . . .

The liberal woman understands herself. She considers and accepts the limitations of her physical energy, just as she learns to estimate her own capabilities and to avoid petty and trivial things that dissipate her time and energy. The mechanics of homemaking she learns to handle easily. In her vigilance for the physical and psychological well-being of her family, she does not lose sight of the fact that she has a responsibility for keeping a balanced view of life.

But home duties do not shut out the world. The liberal woman will be conscious of the importance of the family in the community, and will not think of her family as an isolated and independent unit. Her God looks alike upon all His children, and it follows that she makes no distinction of race, creed or color and sees to it that her family is a broadminded unit of society. . . . She knows that her child will not be secure until every child, everywhere in the world whatever race, or color, or nationality, is equally privileged.

The Liberal Woman in Employment—Actions are the fruits of philosophy of life. . . . A strong and direct influence of this Unitarian philosophy upon society is made by the liberal woman engaged in business, industry and the professions.

The Unitarian woman in the field of business and industry represents *liberal religion at work.* Her faith in equality and her urge to raise the standard of living bring the direct influence of liberal religion into office and factory.

In her work the religious liberal is ready to go forward in new situations and to reject old routines. She does not tacitly accept the status quo; but through democratic methods she endeavors to improve conditions.

She is keenly aware of her bond with all other human beings, regardless of their race, creed, or color, and tries in her personal life to be true to herself and to her heritage of the spiritual values of Truth, Brotherhood, and Service . . .

The principles of free religion are also felt directly through the influence of the liberal woman in the fields of education, law, medicine, social work, government, and research.

The role of the liberal woman in education, for example, cannot be overemphasized. . . . Faith in the sacredness of personality makes the educator insist upon the kind of education which will provide for the development of the talents of *every* child.

It is from this group of employed Unitarian women that we find many of our crusaders—those women who believe so strongly in the fundamental principles of truth, justice, and world brotherhood that they devote their lives to the causes which contribute to the progress of man.

SOURCE: *The Liberal Woman of Today* (Boston: General Alliance of Unitarian Women's Unitarian Extension Committee, 1948).

A. POWELL DAVIES

America's Real Religion

1949

Born into British Methodism, A. Powell Davies (1902–1957) embraced his adopted country (the United States) and faith (Unitarianism) with the zeal of a convert. In America's Real Religion, Davies argues that the same religious faith that inspired American democracy can now unite a world bitterly divided by war and ideology.

— Robert Hardies

Because democracy exalts freedom, not dogma, it can be world-uniting. The attempt to unite the world upon the basis of dogma, whether political, religious, or any other kind, is sure to fail. Dogma divides. It is dogma that is dividing the world now: communist dogma, authoritarian religious dogma. They can only deepen the world's divisions at the same time that they are lowering the level of civilization. Democracy, however, which converts the war-to-the-death of dogma into the peaceful conflict of opinion can provide the world with unity.

But if it is to do this, we must understand much better what democracy is, *spiritually*. Without its spiritual content, democracy as a system will be emptied of what gives it substance and will collapse. What, then, in spiritual terms, is the definition of democracy? Most simply stated, democracy is the social and political expression of the religious principle that all men are brothers and mankind a family; democracy is *brotherhood: brotherhood unrestricted by nation, race or creed.*

* * *

This is what was meant when it was written that all men are endowed by their Creator with the same inalienable rights: the rights to life, liberty and the pursuit of happiness. It was what was meant when Jefferson swore on the altar of God, "eternal hostility to every form of tyranny over the mind of man." And it was what he meant when he said that he accepted the moral teachings of Jesus but not the miracles and creeds. It was also what Lincoln meant when he said much the same thing, adding that the true significance of Jesus was "a spirit in the life." For that is what the moral teachings of Jesus had pointed to: the brotherhood of free men, freely following the higher law of conscience as it was revealed to them by the spirit of God within them.

No lesser faith than this can possibly unite the world—or even maintain the unity of the American people themselves. No sectarian faith can do so. It is useless—as well as being an evidence of spiritual pride and a sort of Christian

156

imperialism—to pretend that the world will all become ecclesiastically Christian. Or that America will. . . .

The world will never unite behind a Christian creed, or any other creed. Hindus, Mohammedans, Confucians, Taoists—they will no more accept the Christian dogmas or the spiritual supremacy of the Christian church than a modern-minded American will. But they will accept the religion of Thomas Jefferson and William Ellery Channing. They will accept the religion of Abraham Lincoln. The will accept the religion of the American reformers, the American heretics, and the New World poets.

* * *

The time for this religion has arrived. It has arrived not only in America but everywhere. For America's real religion is the world's real religion. The only religion that can save us and heal our dissensions and build a world of justice and liberty and peace. It has had, down to now, its greatest opportunity in America—but its insurgency is universal. It is not American at last—not merely American. It is as large as humanity. But it is in the New World in the day of its ascendancy and leadership that first of all it must become supreme: the New World to which it was given when the earth's most privileged nation was being founded.

For the faith upon which democracy is based—the faith *within* democracy—is neither local nor ephemeral: it is the victory of truth over superstition, of liberty over servitude, of the universal over the provincial, of ennoblement over debasement, of brotherhood over exclusiveness, of the God of light over the gods of shadows, of love over fear. It is the higher religion which has always struggled with the lower: the religion, and the only one, that can lead the stricken world of the present into a happier, more hopeful future.

SOURCE: A. Powell Davies, *America's Real Religion* (Boston: Beacon Press, 1949), 9, 79–82.

JAMES LUTHER ADAMS

"Theological Bases of Social Action"

1950–1951

Like his friend Paul Tillich, Adams regarded the tendency to separate love from power as one of the flaws of the old liberalism. In this selection, Adams grounded his social ethic in an understanding of divine power that anticipated some of the themes of liberation theology and the Black Power movement of the late 1960s. Written during the ascendancy of religious humanism, the essay also challenged Unitarians to engage continually with the resources of Christian theology. Further Reading: Gary Dorrien, Social Ethics in the Making: Interpreting an American Tradition *(Malden, MA: Wiley-Blackwell, 2008), 324–34.*

—Dan McKanan

The decisive element in social action is the exercise of power, and the character of social action is determined by the character of power expressed. Power has always a double character: first, as the expression of God's law and love; second, as the exercise of man's freedom. To understand power as God's law and love is to understand it as Being; to understand it as man's freedom is to understand it as his response to the possibilities of being, a response which is both individual and institutional. All response is therefore social action in the broad sense. Here we shall be concerned with social action in this broad sense and also in the narrower sense of group action for the achievement of consensus with respect to the shaping of social policy. Both of these types of social action are expressions of necessity as well as of freedom. The expression of power in the dimensions of both freedom and necessity must be understood by the Christian in terms of its theological bases. The definition of the theological bases of social action must be achieved in terms of the ultimate purposes and resources of human life; it must be achieved equally in terms of the threats to the fulfillment of these purposes. Taken together, God's law and man's freedom operate for the creation of community or, through God's wrath, for its destruction. According to the Judeo-Christian view of God's law and love, it is the destiny of men to love and to be loved; there is an interdependence of spiritual destinies; this is the "plan of salvation." All response on the part of men to God's law and love is social action in the broad sense, whether the response furthers community or perverts and destroys it.

Much social thought has misunderstood or ignored the dual character of power as God's law and man's response. The misunderstanding has come out of exclusive preoccupation with the dimension of man's freedom and the ignoring of the dimension of God's law. It is not enough to say with Henry Adams that "power is poison," or with Jacob Burkhardt that "power is by its nature evil, whoever wields it." The power that is law understood as God's is not in itself evil; it is the ground for the possibility of man's exercise of power for good or evil. Acton's assertion that "power tends to corrupt, and absolute power corrupts absolutely" is true as he understood it, namely, as applying only to man's freedom, the social-political dimension. Power can be understood to corrupt absolutely only when the social-political power is sundered from its theological ground, God's law and love. . . .

The idea of power is in no way alien to religion. Religion cannot be adequately described without one's employing the conception of power; likewise, power cannot be properly described without one's employing religious concepts. Power is both the basic category of being and the basic category of social action. The crucial question for both religion and social action is the question concerning the nature and interrelation of divine power and human powers. All social action is therefore explicitly or implicitly grounded in a theology, and all theology implies a fundamental conception of social action. Politics, therefore, must consider the theology of power as much as theology must consider the politics of power. When power is not considered in its proper theological character but only in its political, it becomes demonic or empty, separated from its end. . . .

"All power is of one kind," says Emerson, "a sharing in the nature of the world." We may take this to mean that all power is of one kind in the sense that all power is capacity or ability possessed or exercised within the context of existence as it is "given." One is reminded here of Plato's laconic remark, "And I hold that the definition of Being is simply power." Plato understands power as creative, as the condition and limit of man's social existence. For Plato this definition considers power as primarily law; it is transmuted in the Stoic and the Christian tradition as God's law, *Logos*. Here power is not understood differently from what is stressed in the typical modern generic definition, wherein it is simply the capacity to exercise influence. The modern definition is true so far as it goes. But it is true only with respect to the power of freedom, the power to influence others, the power to control one's own behavior (freedom). Plato observes in the *Sophist* that power is present equally in the capacity *to be influenced*. Power exhibits duality, but it is one in this duality: There is no adequate conception of power as freedom except as it is simultaneously conceived of as law and except as it is viewed in a context of interaction ultimately grounded in the divine power of being (with its possibilities in terms of free and also ambiguous response).

God is not to be understood merely as a rigid lawgiver, nor man merely in terms of freedom. As there is a dialectic between the two primary terms of power—man's freedom and God's law—there is also a dialectic within each term. Plato suggests that power is twofold: it is both active and passive. In the Christian view the active and passive powers, in both God and man, are dialectically related. God is creative, redemptive power, active power. But God takes satisfaction in man's free obedience; in this respect he is influenced by man's behavior. Man possesses creative freedom to influence himself and others; this is active power. But he is also influenced by participating in God's power, that is, by being affected by God's law and love and by other people's behavior. This is passive power. Where mutuality of influence appears, both active and passive power operate; and, ideally, coercive power is employed primarily for the maintenance of mutuality.

* * *

Divine Power in Primitive Religion. Explicit religion involves the belief that there are divine powers with which man must enter into relations for the maintenance or fulfillment of meaningful existence. (We must omit here the discussion of the question whether the divine power may properly be conceived to be *a* being alongside other beings.) There is no notion of God, even among primitive peoples, in which deity is not power, or does not have power.

One of the most widespread primitive conceptions of power (which may or may not be associated with deity) is the idea of Mana, a mysterious impersonal force which can be in anything and which makes that thing strikingly effective.

* * *

Prophetic Conceptions of Divine Power. For a Christian theology of social action the definitive conception of divine power is set forth in the New Testament—the conception of power (*dynamis*) as forgiving, healing love working toward the fulfillment of the divine purpose of history. The law of grace is sovereign. This conception is a far cry from the primitive idea of Mana and from the powers on which primitive or "civilized" tribalism lives. Between the primitive conceptions and the New Testament conception there stands more than a millennium of religious experience. This period of history is very familiar territory to the reader precisely because its ideas have been decisive for Judeo-Christian theologies of social action. Despite its familiarity, however, we may, perhaps with some warrant, view it in the light of our concern with a theology of power as the basis for a theology of social action.

* * *

The prophetic conception of the divine power was shaped, then, in the stress of power politics; conversely, the conception of power politics was shaped under the stress of a new vision of the divine power. To the degree that the conception of divine power changed its character, Israel reacted differently to subjugation, indeed transcended it, and found a new meaning in it. The divine power was not only ethicized.

It was also interiorized; it was interpreted as operating in the most intimate aspects of psychic experience and of divine-human fellowship. Both God and men were now seen to be bound together not only in the realm of politics but also in the inner life. This remarkable interiorization of piety represents the translation of the conception of divine power into a new dimension: it represents also a deeper conception of the conjugation of the active and passive powers. . . .

Since the present brief essay aims primarily to be a constructive statement rather than a historical one, we shall not try to express the Hebrew prophetic outlook exclusively in its own vocabulary. Rather, we shall try to present it in a way that readily lends itself to an appreciation of its perennial relevance for a theology of power.

(1) The power that is worthy of confidence is the Creator of the world and man. . . . Being as such is good; it is of God. Good is possible only within being. God offers the possibility of good. The doctrine of *Imago dei* is an application of this view to the doctrine of man. Man in freedom participates in this divine law and creativity. Recasting this affirmation in terms of a theology of power, we may say that to exist is to possess, or to participate in, the divine power of being; it is to be the beneficiary of the divine power which is the ground of order and meaning.

This means that the prophetic view renounces any radical asceticism in the face of the material order. It rejects the cynic's notion that all power is evil. . . .

Yet, the Judeo-Christian doctrine of creation asserts also that the divine power is not to be identified with the world or with any part of it. It is never capsuled anywhere in the world, not in a "superior" race or nation, not in a religious tradition, not in religious ceremony, not even in the prophet's word. The attempt to capsule the divine power is the attempt to control and manipulate it, to become sovereign over it; the attempt is blasphemous. . . .

(2) The power that is worthy of confidence, the power that alone is reliable, has a world-historical purpose, the achievement of righteousness and fellowship through the loving obedience of its creatures. As an ethical, historical religion prophetism is not mystical in so far as mysticism is interpreted as a flight above the temporal world into timeless communion with eternity. . . .

(3) The power that is reliable in history places an obligation to righteousness upon the whole community of the faithful as a community, though to be sure the fulfillment is in God's own time. The response to the divine power is responsibility. The covenant of God is with the community and the individual members of it; it imposes responsibility upon community and individual for the character of the community and especially for concern with the needy and the oppressed. Religious institutions, cultus, political and economic institutions must serve God's righteous purpose. There is no enclave that is exempt from his sovereignty.

(4) The power that is reliable and sovereign in history offers itself as the basis of a fellowship of *persons*. Before working on the visible, outer side of history it

generates the inner side of history and community; it manifests itself in the responsive, creative, healing powers of justice and love, of tenderness, forgiveness, and mercy. These qualities are not merely human devices. They are the capacities and feelings that express the fullness of the divine power. . . .

The theological bases of social action cannot properly offer a blueprint for social action. The attempt to make a blueprint and to give it a divine sanction always runs the danger of issuing in idolatrous legalism. Yet the relevance of any theology of social action can become clear only when one discerns the demands that it makes upon social action and organization. Right attitudes are never sufficient alone. They must find embodiment in social institutions.

✻ ✻ ✻

Conceptions of the Divine Power in the New Testament. The reference to Jesus' figure about the seed (employed by Jesus in parables that have metaphysical as well as moral depth) assists us to observe the way in which he continued, extended, and deepened the prophetic conceptions of the community-forming power of God. In his conceptions of Love and Law he emphasized, as did the prophets, the divine yearning and initiative for intimacy of fellowship between God and man and between men. But, going beyond their eschatological hopes (which we have had to leave out of our explicit discussion), he stressed the idea that the kingdom of God has already "broken in." . . .

We should notice here another important difference. In his conception of the Kingdom of God, Jesus shared with the prophets, as we have indicated, the desire for intimacy of fellowship. In many respects his mentality and that of his immediate disciples was similar to that of the prophets in the sense that it was conditioned by agrarian protest against urbanization. "The gospel," says F. C. Grant "is, in fact, the greatest agrarian protest in all history." But the prophets do not appear to have formed continuing intimate groups in which their theology of power, their theology of fellowship, could find application. The Christians *did* form a social organization in which the power of the spirit, the power of love, could find organizational embodiment. Moreover, in the conception of the Body of Christ they found a new ontological basis for the working of the divine power that was in Jesus, namely, the *koinonia*, a group living a common life with Jesus Christ as its head and informing power. Participation in a believing fellowship became the soil for the working of the divine power. Again, we observe that the divine and human powers were interpreted as both active and passive; moreover, the noncoercive aspects of power were greatly stressed. The New Testament ethic is an ethic of abundance.

✻ ✻ ✻

Power and Social Action in the Democratic Society. The attitude of responsibility appropriate for achieving consensus toward the end of shaping social policy in modern democratic society is better represented by the nineteenth-century British

162

theologian, William Whewell: "Every citizen who thus possesses by law a share of political power, *is* one of the powers that be. . . ." Although the fellowship of the *koinonia* is perhaps possible only in the church itself, the vocation it places upon the Christian in the world must presuppose the ongoing attempt to make its conception of the divine power applicable outside the *koinonia* as well as within it, in the latent as well as in the manifest church. The theological and ethical principles of Christian social action which are appropriate for the church are ultimately the criteria for judging and transforming society. The Christian looks for a society in which all men may be treated as persons potentially responsive to God's redemptive purpose for history. And in working for it, he must perforce use that kind of fellowship today called the voluntary association, where within the church and outside it consensus is formed and social action is undertaken.

SOURCE: James Luther Adams, "Theological Bases of Social Action," *Journal of Religious Thought* 8 (Autumn/Winter 1950–1951): 6–8, 10–11, 13–17, 19–21.

SOPHIA LYON FAHS

Today's Children and Yesterday's Heritage

1952

From 1937 to 1961 Sophia Lyon Fahs (1876–1978) was the curriculum editor for religious education at the American Unitarian Association. Drawing on the pedagogical theories of John Dewey, she moved the American Unitarian Association away from its use of an indoctrinating, content-centered education toward more child-centered pedagogies. While earlier curricula had been Bible-focused, hers emphasized science, world religions, and a contemporary context. Her book, Today's Children and Yesterday's Heritage, *was her major contribution to this effort and the foundation of the New Beacon Series. Fahs used poetry and conversations with children to provide examples of how her philosophy impacted the lives of the children, the teachers, and the overall programs of religious education in Unitarian and Universalist congregations in the 1950s. Her educational philosophy and theology are still evident in current Unitarian Universalist faith development for children, youth, and adults sixty years later, notably the Tapestry of Faith curricula. Further Reading: Sophia Lyon Fahs and Elizabeth Manwell,* Consider the Children: How They Grow *(Boston: Beacon Press, 1940); Richard S. Gilbert,* In the Middle of a Journey: Readings in Unitarian Universalist Faith Development *(Bloomington, IN: iUniverse, 2013).*

—Elizabeth M. Strong

A superficial review of modern life often gives the impression that religion is an unimportant concern. It is casually remarked that what one believes matters little; all that is important is how one lives. The history of civilization, however, is one long witness to the power of religious beliefs in affecting mankind's behavior. . . .

Because of religious beliefs men have gone to war. They have sacrificed physical comforts, health and home in order to promulgate their faith in foreign lands among those whose beliefs were different from their own. . . . No one can understand the history of any people at any period who does not understand its religion.

Religious beliefs have gathered such importance that most people now equate *being religious* with *believing.*

* * *

So-called "religious liberals" have sometimes been disparaged because it has been said that they think it does not matter much what one believes. They seem to spend so much of their vital enthusiasms in protesting against those beliefs which they regard as false—it is sometimes said—that they have left their people without any constructive faith. Because such groups have not required a statement of belief for acceptance in their societies, it has been assumed that what their members individually believe is after all of small consequence. In fact, this criticism has sometimes been justified. Some liberal societies have avoided public discussions of their differing beliefs. Indeed, freedom in belief presents a serious problem to those to whom religious beliefs are important. Can our religious beliefs continue to be of vital concern to us while at the same time we try to cultivate tolerance of opposing beliefs and appreciation of a variety of points of view? Can it matter to the individual which beliefs he holds, while at the same time he feels no concern for what his neighbors and friends believe? A refusal to delve beneath or behind activities and deeds in order to recognize the ideas, the thinking, the beliefs that motivate those activities surely is superficial. How can worth-while doing and living come without worth-while thinking and believing? . . .

If, then, religious beliefs are regarded as being of such great significance by large numbers of adults in our society, at how early an age are children influenced by the beliefs of their parents? . . . How much freedom shall they be given to choose between the alternatives which the presence of different sects and religions suggest? Shall we continue to segregate our children in our different denominational and sectarian camps in order to assure ourselves that at least our own kin will accept our own special inheritance of faith? Or does a culture in which multiple religious systems are actively present require a radically different approach to the religious nurture of youth from the usual way of propaganda?

* * *

From the point of view of this study, one's religious "belief" or one's "religion" is the "gestalt" of all his smaller specific beliefs. One's faith is the philosophy of life that gathers up into one emotional whole—and sometimes, although rarely, into a reasoned whole—all the specific beliefs one holds about many kinds of things in many areas of life.

For example, one of the most important of man's beliefs is what he thinks of himself. . . . Few, however, think of belief in oneself as a religious belief. Yet it is like the main stem out of which the body of one's faith must grow. And what a person believes about himself depends on what he believes about his mother and his father, his brothers and his sisters. And what he believes about these persons in his intimate family influences what he believes about his neighbors and others in his larger world. . . . All these in time become linked with what he believes about Negroes and whites, about Communists and Democrats, about rich and poor, about the strong and the weak, about what is good and what is bad. All these and unnumbered other beliefs go into the caldron of experience, together with ideas of God, prayer, the Bible, Jesus, Moses and eternity. It is quite impossible to separate these beliefs into

165

two kinds, secular and religious. To the extent that any one of these beliefs affects the quality of the "gestalt" or total configuration of belief, it is religious.

What then is it that is most significant about the total pattern of one's religion? Surely it is not its conformity to Christianity or Judaism, its likeness to Buddhism or Mohammedanism. Its significance must be found at a deeper level where universal truth and universal human need are found.

* * *

One morning Margaret was swinging in the church school playground, pushing the swing higher and higher. So confident was she that she did not even hold onto the rope as she was swinging. "Margaret," called the teacher in charge, "you had better hold onto the ropes or you will fall." But Margaret called back, "O no, I don't need to hold the ropes. I am not afraid to go high, high, high! Jesus will not let me fall." The amazed teacher repeated her warning, but the child gleefully repeated her song: "Jesus will not let me fall."

In a few minutes the child did fall. . . .

It was fortunate that Margaret's experience did not result in any real physical injury. It is more difficult to measure the impact of the emotional shock she felt when she discovered that the basis on which she had built her courage was false to reality. There was no Jesus available to do for her what she had been led to believe he could do.

* * *

Eight-year-old Jimmie fortunately had quite a different experience. For a long time he had felt frustrated because for some vague reason he had not learned to read. His slowness was so marked in contrast to the skill of the other children in his class that Jimmie felt disgraced. His teacher finally decided to give him special attention for a while. She worked with him alone on one specific bit of reading until he felt confident of himself. Then he was given an opportunity to read this small section in a public program given by the class. Jimmie did so well in this instance that the other children recognized his achievement and complimented him. "Why, you can read well!" . . . The boy's feeling of personal worth grew rapidly.

That night before going to bed, he was saying his prayer as usual. "Now I lay me down to sleep. Bless Papa and Mama and Auntie." He stopped. Usually he went on to say, ". . . and help Jimmie to be a good boy." His mother waited. . . . Finally the words came from Jimmie himself. "Help me." But then he stopped, and lifted himself from his knees. "I guess I won't say that tonight. Jimmie has done pretty good all by himself today."

During that memorable day, Jimmie had discovered a new feeling about himself, and this discovery led him to change his belief about prayer and his conception of his relationship to God. He also found a new meaning in the words "being good" over which he could really be pleased. This discovery changed Jimmie's whole pattern of emotional need. This new belief was neither Presbyterian nor Episcopalian. It was neither Unitarian nor Catholic. No teacher had taught the boy his new belief. He had found it for himself, and in this experience his selfhood had expanded and his hopes had been energized. Jimmie's changed belief in himself was a religious experience.

* * *

The religious beliefs which an individual makes his own undoubtedly influence his character development. But of even more profound influence than the beliefs themselves are the *ways* through which beliefs are acquired. It is here that the really vital issue is joined between the major divergent groups in religious education.

In one group religion is considered as something *given* to an individual by an authority other than himself, by an authority coming from the past—from revelation, from an inspired book, from a divine person, or from a divinely ordained church. . . .

The other group holds a less common and sharply different conception of religious development. For them beliefs regarding the universe and man's destiny in it should be the products of maturing emotional experiences, meditation and critical thought, and not assumptions with which to begin. Religion is, therefore, not a heritage which the child has a God-given right to receive, not something to be imparted to him by a teacher or a group. Rather it is regarded as a vital and healthy result of his own creative thought and feeling and experience as he responds to life in all its fullness.

* * *

How much difference does it make *how* a child comes by his beliefs? Is the *how* as significant as the *what*? Suppose a child is led to feel that he ought to believe what he hears because the Bible tells him so; or suppose he is encouraged to question the standards of long ago and the ways people used to think of God, asking why they felt as they did and why today some people feel and think differently: how much difference will these two ways of dealing with ideas and practices make in the child's personality development? . . .

The results of a recent extensive piece of research . . . are enlightening. . . . 120 [children] were chosen for detailed study. One half of this smaller group were chosen because they were found to be extremely prejudiced against those who differed from them. The other half were chosen because they were the children who showed the smallest number of such prejudices. . . .

It was found that the children in the more prejudiced group had been educated for the most part in home, school and church by authoritarian methods; while the other group had been nurtured in what the author of the study characterizes as a "liberal" manner. Their parents had been more permissive, democratic and flexible in their controls and had given their children more responsibility in the forming of their ideas and beliefs.

The children who had been accustomed to authoritarian controls were already becoming authoritarian in their attitudes toward others. Having been obliged to accept conformity for themselves, they demanded it of others also. . . . and they tended to condemn those whose ways were different. . . .

On the other hand, the group of children who had lived in "liberal" homes . . . were found to be more tolerant of differences and more able to maintain an "equalitarian and individualized approach to people" of different types. They took "internal values" more seriously than "external appearances." . . . They were "more oriented toward love and less toward power."

*   *   *

How can a little child begin to be religious naturally without being instructed in the religious beliefs of his parents? At how early an age are these natural steps taken? . . .

While many religious leaders have assumed that they knew by dogma the nature of the newborn baby, modern psychologists and pediatricians have been studying babies and small children in order to find out what they are actually like. . . .

A young baby is an emotionally dynamic person, already strongly motivated to struggle for what is most important to his development. A new baby is not a creature who can be easily influenced or molded into a pattern other than that which he himself desires. A baby's emotions are all-absorbing and a more decisive factor of or against his health and growth than any other of the usual variables in his physical care. . . .

What is the most dominant and important of all the young baby's emotional needs? The psychologists and pediatricians seem agreed that it is the need for love; and being loved is the first step toward learning to trust and then how to love in return.

*   *   *

Whether his religion later on will be wholesome and broad in its sympathies will depend, therefore, not only on the reasonableness and clarity of the ideas taught him, but much more on the degree to which he has, in his early childhood, learned to love and to develop a general trust in life. In short, this emotional pattern of personality that has become quite clearly defined by the end of the first year, and even more clearly defined by the end of the second year, is probably the most significant element that will ever influence his religious growth.

*   *   *

Now let us look at a young child's curiosity or urge to learn the truth—another value which all high religions have cherished. This urge becomes clearly apparent when young children have learned to talk well enough to ask questions about things. . . .

*   *   *

A few years ago some of us felt keenly the need to experiment with a more natural way of religious education by starting with children's own experiences, and then moving along with them according to the natural sequence of their own growing.

*   *   *

When, therefore, we were given the opportunity to prepare stories for use by preschool children which might help to encourage this natural process of religious development, we had a basis for selecting the types of experiences to portray. We were not interested simply in entertaining children. . . . The choices for the episodes grew out of the study we had made of the kinds of experiences that had been found to be especially provocative of wonder and thought. . . .

1. Experiences are told in which the two story-children, Martin and Judy, face the great forces or universal phenomena of nature, such as the wind, the rain, the snow, the sun and moon.

2. Experiences are related in which the contrast between animate and inanimate things becomes apparent. . . .

3. Experiences with birth, such as seeing newborn kittens, the hatching of chickens, or watching a newborn baby, dramatize the mystery of life.

4. Experiences with death are also included for a child's first close experience with death is necessarily a challenge. . . .

6. Some of the narratives present the children playing with their shadows. Young children are universally fascinated and sometimes made afraid by their shadows. . . .

8. A number of the stories were written to portray the child's feelings of social relatedness to others. . . . These are germinal experiences from which the larger feelings of human brotherhood grow. . . .

11. Experiences are narrated in which choices have to be made. . . .

12. Finally . . . Martin and Judy, the two story-children, are found puzzling over thoughts of God, and taking their first steps in prayer. Such thinking of God is brought about by the children's own wonderings, and praying is presented in a way that can have some meaning for the young child. . . .

Our purpose in preparing these stories was to accent certain significant experiences in a child's natural religious growth by putting them into the stories of two imaginary children. If the children who hear these stories can identify their own feelings with those of Martin and Judy, the significance of their own experiences may be increased in them.

*   *   *

When children become older, the heritage from the past and the rituals and ceremonies that live in the society to which the children belong will inevitably influence them. . . . They will wish to examine the Bible records. First of all, however, children need to have many opportunities to learn and notice for themselves. . . .

They need to discover that "people have learned all of what we know about God by seeing for themselves what is in his world." . . .

Because an understanding of the religious heritage from the past is important for the older child, we shall examine . . . our Judeo-Christian heritage as it has been embodied in "the Bible."

*　*　*

The old Bible of Christian and Jewish orthodoxy is looked upon as the true revelation of God's purpose on behalf of humanity. Beginning with the creation of the world and ending with the creation of a new heaven and a new earth, it is one continued story from Genesis through Revelation.

*　*　*

Should this old story be the core of Christian religious education today? Should it be taught as a whole? If not, what should be omitted? How much revision can be made in this "divinely revealed story" of man's destiny and still have the truth in it preserved? What are the values in this old tradition for us today? How much of it can we believe? Does it express our faith?

*　*　*

The Bible newly interpreted, as a result of our new knowledge, is shown to be a collection of records of human experiences. It is about people. It tells us what they were like and how they believed about God and their world, and how these beliefs affected their living. In short, whereas the old Bible is thought of as divine, the new Bible is human.

*　*　*

To study the new Bible one must be prepared to examine different beliefs and practices and codes of ethics. There is no one message of truth pervading the entire collection of writings.

*　*　*

From these long years of persistent delving into the Gospels and into other contemporary reports, which tell of conditions in the Near East during the period when Jesus lived, scholars are now presenting an impressive picture of a dynamic and creative religious teacher. They are finding a man who not only had an outlook on life and religion markedly different from that of the Pharisaic leaders of his generation, but one who had a point of view that was in profound contrast to the religious assumptions of the churches that now worship him. In the new Bible of human experience there walks a new Jesus—not a divinity desiring worship, but a man who can be understood, honored, and in deep ways followed.

*　*　*

Children in our Western culture need to be vividly exposed both to the old Story of Salvation and to some portions of the Bible as reinterpreted by modern scholarship. Without knowing the Story of Salvation in its old and unexpurgated form, no

170

one can fully appreciate the power and persistence of certain basic assumptions that permeate our Western ways of living and feeling. . . . Moreover, if one is unaware of the kinds of treasures that may be mingled with the gathered dust of the ages he may, in his ignorant digging, destroy much that is of high worth.

※　※　※

Teaching "the Bible" to children, then, can no longer be looked upon as a simple task, that of spreading intelligence regarding a series of more or less interesting Bible stories. Nor can the present generation of youth be content merely to know the Old Story of Salvation, and the meaning of its emotional and intellectual penetration into the life of the Western world. They will need also the corrective that can come only through some understanding of the true history of the Hebrew people in contrast to the theologically biased conception of God in history as portrayed in the Old Story of Salvation. . . .

Naturally when the uniqueness of the Bible has been removed and it becomes an ancient historical source from which to glean an understanding of the experiences of one national group, children will ask: Why then should we not learn of other peoples also? Were the Hebrews the only religious people of ancient times? Why should we not learn of other great religious teachers as well as Moses and Jesus? Thus the door is wide open, leading into a study of the universal experiences of mankind in building religious faith and practice. This means that this generation of youth will be asking for more than both Bibles—the old Bible and the reinterpreted Bible. . . . As humanity seeks one common human brotherhood, embracing all religious cultures, and differing religious beliefs are exchanged freely and sympathetically, we may discover the great ways in which we are all alike.

※　※　※

No matter how adequate the materials put on the printed page may be, the intimate and most vital responsibility rests with the group leader. The name "group leader" is here used in preference to "teacher" in order to clear away the impression that the function of such a person is to give instruction, to pass on knowledge, to affirm beliefs, to preach principles or to proclaim a message. . . .

Leadership means providing the setting and the warmth of atmosphere that will encourage intelligent and hearty fellowship and a sympathetic outreach of interest.

Leadership means being an imaginative artist, learning ways of awakening interest in new fields of knowledge and experience. It means being creative oneself in one's own thinking, and expecting the same of the children. . . .

Leadership means being well informed and interested in the subject matter to be investigated. It means being able to turn facts stated on the printed page into human experience. . . .

Leadership means being able being able to respond sensitively to children's moods. . . .

Leadership means learning the techniques of group discussion and guidance. . . .

Leadership means learning how to help children to review their experiences through original drama and role-playing, through free art expression and through discussion. . . .

Leadership means psychologically sitting on the floor with the children sharing in the blame for failures as well as in the celebrations of achievements. . . .

Leadership means learning when to give one's own opinions frankly and when to restrain oneself. . . .

Leadership means learning to enjoy living with children, learning to love oneself and one's opportunities with them. Leadership means learning to love especially the child whose attitudes are the most unlovely of all.

* * *

What Shall Children Study?

All that quickens sympathetic imagining,
that awakens sensitivity to other's feelings,
all that enriches and enlarges understanding of the world;
all that strengthens courage,
that adds to the love of living;
all that leads to developing skills
needed for democratic participations—
all these put together are the curriculum
through which children learn.

SOURCE: Sophia Lyon Fahs, *Today's Children and Yesterday's Heritage: A Philosophy of Creative Religious Development* (Boston: Beacon Press, 1952), 3, 5–9, 11–13, 15–16, 22–24, 31–33, 46–47, 51, 53–58, 62, 75–77, 82, 94, 96–97, 156–58, 176.

Constitutions of American Unitarian Youth and Liberal Religious Youth

1953

After World War II, denominational consolidation was a serious consideration. In 1947, the Unitarians passed a resolution supporting an exploration of merger. A joint AUA-UCA Commission on Union was created in 1949, but it bore fruit only in terms of shared religious education programming. Financial pressures necessitated difficult cuts. Amidst conflicts with President Eliot regarding authority over the AUA youth director, a 1950 budget crisis required discontinuing that position. The UCA employed only one religious educator, Alice Harrison, who served youth aged twelve to twenty-five and was highly regarded. In this atmosphere, visionary American Unitarian Youth and Universalist Youth Fellowship leaders created a joint convention in 1951. Leon Hopper was the key architect of the 1950–1952 merger process. He would later become a minister, serve as Executive Director of Liberal Religious Youth, and receive the Award for Distinguished Service to Unitarian Universalism. Post-war youth culture was changing and influencing the merger. Note the different tone in the "Purposes" of LRY compared to AUY. Youth leaders were younger but more self-aware. Creating Liberal Religious Youth made financial sense. However, it heightened the tension between youth autonomy and adult staff leadership for programs serving youth. Further Reading: Wayne B. Arnason and Rebecca Scott, We Would Be One: A History of Unitarian Universalist Youth Movements *(Boston: Skinner House, 2005); "Freedom to Question: Voices from a Century-Plus Tradition of UU Youth Groups," freedomtoquestion.org*

—Wayne Arnason

Constitution and By-Laws of American Unitarian Youth

ARTICLE II. Purposes

Section I. The purposes for which this corporation is formed are as follows:

1. To help young people discover and develop the ideals and practices of the Unitarian Church, and to encourage total participation and active loyalty in church life, interpreting liberal religion as personal experience, group worship and fellowship.

2. To help young people find opportunities for constructive citizenship through cooperation with all who seek to build at home and abroad a classless and just world community free of racial, religious, or national discriminations.
3. To broaden the scope of personal religion through active participation in the cultural, intellectual, and social life of today.
4. To state the views of Unitarian youth on issues of vital importance.
5. To assist youth to build strong personal character through the achievement of the above purposes.

Constitution and By-Laws of Liberal Religious Youth

ARTICLE II. Purposes

Section 1. The preamble of and the purposes for which this Corporation is formed are:

To SEEK understanding of ourselves, of our fellow man, and of our world. We seek meaning in our existence, understanding of our responsibility toward our fellow man, and knowledge of our relationship to our world.

To CHOOSE the approach of liberal religion: freedom and responsibility of belief, the use of reason, readiness to accept new ideas, and respect for the dignity of all mankind.

To FORM the Liberal Religious Youth, dedicating ourselves to this search and this approach, to help young people

1. to deal creatively and imaginatively with religion as the quality and spirit of living.
2. to realize the scope and nature of a working democracy, its privileges and responsibilities.
3. to find fellowship of others with like mind or approach.
4. to gain a reasonable and durable faith through personal and group experiences, worship, and service.

To PLEDGE, as members of the Liberal Religious Youth, and on the basis of our convictions, to strive for the achievement of a just and peaceful world community.

SOURCE: "Constitution and By-Laws of American Unitarian Youth," "Constitution and By-Laws of Liberal Religious Youth," Liberal Religious Youth, Director/Executive Director, Administrative Records, AUY and UYF, Andover-Harvard Archives, bMS 10035, Andover-Harvard Theological Library, Harvard Divinity School, Cambridge, MA.

JOINT MERGER COMMISSION
Information Manual
1958

The process of consolidating the Universalist Church of America and the American Unitarian Association began in earnest with the creation of a Joint Merger Commission in 1956. This was the culmination of a courtship that was almost as old as the two denominations themselves. Earlier impulses toward union had led to the joint publication of Hymns of the Spirit *in 1937 and to the practice of holding joint biennial conferences. At the first such conference in 1953, the Council of Liberal Churches was established, bringing together the denominations' educational and public relations work. A year later, the youth organizations united as Liberal Religious Youth. Under the leadership of William B. Rice (1905–1970), the Joint Merger Commission designed a series of plebiscites to ensure that all congregations were democratically represented in the final decision and prepared this study guide to ensure that their votes were fully informed. Along with a vast body of institutional data, this study guide highlighted the leading arguments for and against merger. Further Reading: Warren R. Ross,* The Premise and the Promise: The Story of the Unitarian Universalist Association *(Boston: Skinner House, 2001).*

—Dan McKanan

Why is all of the present attention being paid to merger? Is it as significant and important as it is made out to be? What does merger mean? Is merger a clear yes or no question? These questions need answers as preliminaries to the main consideration.

Some Whys

The first and basic why has already become clear. It is no accident that for one hundred years various rapprochements between the two denominations have been made. There is an affinity between them of which there is a growing awareness. The differences which separate become of decreasing importance, the likenesses of point of view, purpose, organization and operation increase in significance. Such feelings have become so strong and have been accentuated by merger activities and especially the creation and operation of the Council of Liberal Churches to an extent that some individuals and churches have already taken it for granted that merger has been accomplished.

A second why is to be found in the strong tendency toward merger in all possible areas of current American life. It has been found by experience that the competition of many small units frustrates the attainment of goals, is costly, duplicates unnecessarily organization, equipment and personnel, and consequently is less efficient and effective. The ecclesiastical realm cannot escape the influence of this current thinking. . . .

A third reason is common to all national organizations and is especially pressing in those made up of independent and self-sufficient local units. It is the constant questioning of the economy, efficiency and function of the national organization. . . .

There is a fourth reason of which many deeply religious and serious minded people are increasingly sensitive. In a world demanding considerable social and religious conformity within several large patterns of orthodoxy, it is obvious, that by their very natures, religious beliefs and professions, Unitarians and Universalists would be very aware of the existence of each other as individuals, churches, and national movements and would gravitate towards each other in one or more respects. . . . A kind of merger or approach-to-merger has been occurring albeit without national institutional sanctions and blessings. There is evidence that each national office has been having a problem in maintaining strict denominational-sectarian lines in the face of this "coming-togetherness" at lower levels. . . .

A fifth reason is closely related to the fourth. Much time and effort have hitherto, as well as currently, gone into wrestling with the question of Unitarian-Universalist relations. In general, it is quite clear that both denominations wish to dispose of the question, one way or another as there is much to be done. Today liberal religion appears to be on the threshold of a new era, a new life where it seems imperative that the sooner this question is resolved the better. . . .

What Is Merger

The word merger does not have the same meaning for everyone. To some, it means a form of federal union of the two denominations, to others it means a complete, functional merger resulting in a new denomination. To still others it means the continuance of one of the denominations with the other dropping all its denominational apparatus and its churches simply becoming members of the continuing denomination. . . . The recommendations of the Joint Interim Commission which were approved by the Unitarian General Conference in August, 1955, included the following:

> We conceive merger to mean the establishment of one corporation
> which will perform for Universalists, Unitarians (and possibly others) all
> the functions now performed for them by the Universalist Church of

America, the American Unitarian Association and the Council of Liberal Churches. . . .

Liberal Religion in North America

Liberalism as a way of thinking and behaving throughout the ages has been closely related to the dynamics of all societies. Pressures are always towards conformity and the acceptance and preservation of the status-quo. It is the insight, understanding and faith of liberals which form the growing edges of any society and bring about the renaissances and reformations, and generate the enlightenment of any period in history, thus playing a great role and making a very significant contribution in freeing men's minds. No better illustration exists than that of the United States, where liberalism from its very beginnings has played a monumental role in all the important avenues of life and activity. Liberal religionists have long pointed with pride to the forward-looking leaders in American history who have been related to the liberal churches. There is no denying the fact that throughout their history, the Unitarian and Universalist Churches have had a considerable role in inspiring and sustaining the liberal currents of thought and action so basically important in American society.

The United States has recently been in an extended reactionary period manifested by the resurgence of traditional orthodoxy, the astounding growth of a variety of literalist religious sects, the federal investigations into a very narrowly defined "loyalty," witch hunting, the widespread growth of suspicion and thinking in terms of guilt by association, the reemphasis on absolutism in ethics and authoritarianism to the point where freedom has been in jeopardy and liberalism has taken cover. Pendulums swing and as the current swing is away from reaction, a virile, aggressive influence is needed to generate a resurgent liberalism and keep strong the basic attitudes of freedom.

※ ※ ※

Advantages of Merger

1. A new liberal religious denomination would have more strength at the local level and its members as congregations and as individuals through greater impact of programs at the grass roots would be in a better competitive position regarding the social, economic and ideological manifestations of surrounding orthodox religions.
2. Sectarianism is inherent in each present denomination and this is inherently exclusive, consequently, a merger would be advantageous because it would lessen or eliminate to a large degree present manifestations of sectarianism.

※ ※ ※

12. The present Uni-Uni churches, the CLC, and other forms of cooperation indicate the Unitarians and Universalists have found rapprochement to varying degrees.

13. If merger does not come about, and assuming that cooperation continues to grow at the local and regional levels, the respective denominations may find themselves in embarrassing positions.

*   *   *

20. Both names — Unitarian and Universalist — have sectarian connotations largely in doctrinal terms, therefore it would be an advantage if some name could be devised for a new denomination which would more nearly indicate the real meaning of liberal religion.

21. All denominations lose churches from time to time, including Unitarians and Universalists; likewise all denominations have marginal churches including the A.U.A. and the U.C.A., and while it is true that there are more marginal Universalist than Unitarian churches, there are not as many such churches in the U.C.A. as is commonly supposed; a merger would force reassessment of all churches with the likelihood that it would bring a new interest and renewed strength to a significant number of such churches, thus avoiding the loss to liberal religion of some present churches.

*   *   *

The Disadvantages of Merger

The disadvantages of merger include:

1. Some of the present ministers and laymen in both denominations would face a period of readjustment and may find it difficult to align themselves with a new system that requires de-emphasizing or possibly eliminating denominational identities which mean a great deal to them and the modification of the working relationships, sanctions and more that have been painstakingly built up in each present denomination.

2. Building new traditions, new over-all identities, reshaping loyalties, replacing the two national and the several State Convention organizations and their administrations with a new system, plus realigning social structure coupled with loss of current identity, will for a period produce confusion and possibly some obstructions due to reluctance to give up present organizations, meanings and purposes and may handicap merger in addition to each denomination losing the progress it could be making.

8. The total respective denominational resources, not including local church property, are significant in amounts yet they are disproportionate; this condition

178

may be regarded as a serious disadvantage by some persons in both present denominations.

9. It is conceivable that national office public relations program makers would have difficulty in securing agreement on what the new denomination stands for either ideationally or message-wise, thus creating a time gap in promotion initiative, causing a slow down, or rather, not as much gain as might be expected, at least for a time.

SOURCE: Joint Commission on Merger of the American Unitarian Association and the Universalist Church of America, *An Information Manual for the Use of Unitarian and Universalist Churches, Societies and Fellowships in Considering the Question of Merger or Alternatives to Merger* (Wellesley Hills, MA: The Commission, 1958), 7–9, 74–79.

ALBERT Q. PERRY

"The Uniqueness of Universalism"
1958

Though support for merger was strong among Universalists and Unitarians, their denominational magazines took care to present both sides of the debate. The most articulate Universalist critic of merger was Albert Q. Perry (1915–2001), a Maine native and Tufts-educated minister who served the First Universalist Society of Cincinnati from 1952 to 1961. (Interestingly, that congregation merged with a New Thought church early in Perry's ministry.) From Perry's perspective, Universalism was the bearer of an inclusive, love-centered theology that was unlikely to survive a merger with the more elitist Unitarians. This piece, published early in the merger process, helped establish him as a leader of the opposition.

—Dan McKanan

Universalism is a great and significant religious movement which has been represented occasionally by a segment of the church or by a denominational movement of numerical size and influence comparable to its importance. Self-evidently, this is not the case today. . . .

One thing that is certain is that institutionalized Universalism has been shrinking in size for about a century. From 1750 until 1860, the movement grew with great rapidity. From 1835 until 1859, it about doubled in size.

* * *

Had we maintained the rate of growth in the first century of our existence during the second, all of the United States would now be Universalist.

There are many possible explanations of this shrinkage in numbers and vitality, but it cannot be blamed entirely upon the fact that competing churches have adapted their message so as to separate us from potential membership or upon the fact that secular interests have absorbed energies which once went into the support of inclusive religion. Both of these things have happened, but the real difficulty is that Universalism started out to be and prospered as a result of being a unique religion, the nature of which is all but forgotten today.

* * *

First, it should be recognized that Universalism is a religion and not a political platform, sociological project or psychological experiment. Universalism does not make sense unless one believes certain things about the purposefulness of creation, the direction of the cosmic process, the nature of man, and the destiny of the human spirit. An inclusive optimism may result from a wide variety of convictions and be described with many different words, but it is the product of answering peculiarly religious questions.

There are political, sociological and psychological implications which naturally flow from Universalist religious ideas, but these are of secondary importance and not necessarily within the realm of doctrinaire *liberalism*. More often than not, Universalists will logically concern themselves with peace before justice, with human values rather than institutionalized society, with tolerance rather than right, and with individual fulfillment rather than social change.

The Universalist logically thinks of freedom as something ordained by God rather than as something established by law. Therefore, he seeks to develop the ability to exercise his inner freedom more often than he enters into the political arena to influence its institutions. . . .

An objective study of our history reveals the kind of inconsistencies which result from an overemphasis upon some specific goal or program. On my desk, as I write this, is a copy of *The Dew Drop*, published in January 1845, in Taunton, Massachusetts. This publication resulted from early Universalist enthusiasm for prohibition and was edited by Universalists, but it expressed its feelings in most un-Universalist descriptions of saloons which were pictured as containing the gates to hell and of "rum-sellers" who were accused of being associates of Satan. In more modern times, Universalist enthusiasm for equal rights has resulted in equally un-Universalist condemnations of "White Supremacists."

Next, I would point out that Universalism is, by its nature, a majority rather than a minority faith. This may be an unrealized ideal, but the kind of attitudes which will perpetuate the organization of a thin splinter of people are not sustained by our belief in the supreme worth of every human personality.

* * *

People sense the real nature of a church more accurately than even its ministers. Universalism still makes its greatest appeal to "majority-minded" folk. Prospects, when faced by a choice between two avowedly *liberal* churches, choose Universalism only if they are seeking a more inclusive, tolerant and deeply religious movement than institutionally-minded sects. However, because our membership has little logical justification for thinking of a particular institution as important, they will not fight to keep control of a church when it is swinging from one extreme to another. A church, for our membership, is not an arena for the fulfillment of a thirst for power. *Universalists will quickly drift away from and disassociate themselves from a church which has becomes the instrument for the expression of a disciplined or defined minority.*

Finally, we need to notice that Universalism is not naturally a religion of reason. Our faith is founded upon the most completely emotional base of any sect and it makes sense only when related to such a foundation. We believe in love; cosmic love as the creative force and human divine love as the law of life. This conclusion is sustained by an exercise of faith, as a result of an intuitive analysis of experience, or by a reverent interpretation of man's scriptural inheritance. It is but rarely the product of sensory evidence, reason or logic.

Early Universalism was a middle-to-lower class, farmer and immigrant movement. It flourished among those with educational limitations or, at least, with no intellectual pretensions.

*   *   *

We are able to serve educated people comparatively well, but not because we are an intellectual movement or think that the discovery of truth is of supreme importance. Intellectuals may marry for other reasons than to get a companion with whom to discuss nuclear physics, and they may also recognize the value of association with an inclusive religion.

However, those who do evaluate life in terms of intellectual standards are often dissatisfied in our churches. They find it difficult to accept as an equal or friend the fellow member whom they consider inferior, stupid or wrong. If an intellectually oriented group or minister comes into a dominant position in a Universalist church, many other members may soon leave. They may not be able to explain why, other than that they feel uncomfortable or criticized. Perhaps they sense the inconsistency of a presumably inclusive church classifying people on the basis of intellectual qualifications. . . .

There is no reason today why a person with a college education and professional degree may not successfully minister to most Universalist churches if he understands that *the innate and historic mission of the church is to inspire love rather than to dispense truth.* . . . Educational qualifications for ordination ought to be dropped that we may also have leaders emotionally equipped to serve groups and in areas where Universalism is unknown, but where a doctrine of love would be well received.

There are implications in this study which obviously relate to the current discussion about possible denominational merger with Unitarians. It may be that after a clarification of the logical nature of Universalism, most would feel that it should not be promoted in the modern age. Many Universalists already sense a dissatisfaction with inclusive religion and this may help them to understand their feelings. Merger could provide an opportunity for a complete and final break with rejected traditions. Many Universalists can see in merger an opportunity for transferring their loyalty and devotion to the organizational patterns and traditions of Unitarianism, and would experience a kind of emotional relief as a result of abandoning principles and implications contrary to their convictions.

Unitarianism is a great movement which I sincerely respect and which I recognize as having done a considerable amount for this nation and Western European civilization. . . . In recent years, it has rediscovered its logical nature and sufficiently reorganized that it might appeal to the new aristocracy of the twentieth century.

Unitarianism has its weaknesses, most of which are far better understood by its membership than by Universalist observers. There is considerable evidence that a significant portion of that denomination sincerely admires the concept of inclusiveness and desires the confidence which may be built upon a reverence for cosmic love and a respect for human nature. Some Unitarians are hoping that merger with Universalism will result in a deepening of what has often been a synthetic and superficial faith and in a broadening of an accepted minority status.

It should be recognized that we cannot achieve in merger both the intellectual integrity of Unitarianism and the emotional security of Universalism: both the efficiency of Unitarianism in appealing to the selected minorities and the ability of Universalism to influence the total religious climate. At least, we should be aware of the predictable results of merger, depending upon which tradition gains supremacy.

*   *   *

Despite a similarity in names and birthplaces and superficial emphases, Unitarianism and Universalism are fundamentally unlike and it is doubtful if the traditions of both can survive a merger. What we really need is a reshuffle, but this is not a predictable solution. In all probability, the best for which we can hope is that discussions of merger will help to clarify a general awareness of our dissimilarity *and to produce a willingness on the part of each to be what it really is. If so, Universalism can face the future with confidence.* It is a unique church with a mission which corresponds to the needs of an age which has more knowledge than it can safely use, which is threatened by conflicts which must be reconciled, and which is seeking a religion which does not contain a built-in obsolescence.

SOURCE: Albert Q. Perry, "The Uniqueness of Universalism," *Universalist Leader*, October 1958, 232–35.

GORDON McKEEMAN

"The Place of Hosea Ballou in Present-Day Universalism"

1959

Albert Perry's worry that Universalism's unique theology might be endangered by merger was shared even by individuals who favored merger. In this reflection, also published in the Universalist Leader, *Gordon McKeeman (1920–2013) identified "ultimate confidence" as the "hallmark of Universalism" and called for its ongoing cultivation. Educated at Salem State College and Tufts University, McKeeman was a founding member and lifetime "Abbot" of the Humiliati, a Universalist renewal movement that blended Clarence Skinner's progressive vision with an appreciation of Christian liturgical and monastic traditions. He served several Massachusetts congregations early in his career, including Saint Paul's Church of Palmer, Massachusetts, where he was the minister in 1959.*

—Dan McKanan

Present-day Universalism is the product of two primary influences. The first is its historic position in the spectrum of Christian theology. Obviously, this position is pre-Ballou. . . . Universalism's primary characteristic was "ultimate confidence." In Origen, our greatly revered and little-known Church father, this ultimate confidence took the form of the doctrine of salvation of the Devil. . . . Eighteenth-century Universalism was another expression of this "ultimate confidence."

* * *

So the primitive Universalism of the pre-Ballou Universalists expressed in the language of the prevailing faith of its time the principal characteristic of Universalism, "ultimate confidence." Into this setting came Hosea Ballou.

When Hosea Ballou finally left the Baptists and entered the Universalist fold, his theology was not at all distinguishable from that of his contemporaries in his newfound faith. . . . In one particular . . . Ballou never changed his theology. He always held to the major characteristic of Universalism, its ultimate confidence. In common with Universalists of his day, he held to *cosmic love as a metaphysic and human love as an ethic.* What did change in Ballou was his method of approach to religion from his original premise. It has been pointed out recently, notably by Ernest Cassara of Tufts, that Ballou apparently fell under the influence of one of New England's famous sons, the deist, Green Mountain boy, Ethan Allen. To quote from Dr.

Cassara's monograph, *Hosea Ballou and the Rise of American Religious Liberalism.* "Allen's book, *Reason the only Oracle of Man,* taught Hosea to examine everything by the light of reason. Ballou was an eminently reasonable person; but his inherited reverence for the Bible had kept him from questioning Christian doctrine too closely. He learned from Allen that Reason is a gift from God. As such, it cannot be incompatible with Scripture."

Subsequent to this encounter between Hosea Ballou and the thought of Ethan Allen, Ballou worked his way through to a new position in theology. He began with the same premise that had always held dominance among Universalists, the love and sovereignty of God, that is, "ultimate confidence." But he rejected the Calvinist doctrines of Atonement, Predestination, Particular Redemption, Total Depravity, Effectual Calling, Final Perseverance. In its place, he erected a theology which placed emphasis on the goodness of man's intention (or God's intention in man) and the final inevitability of God's triumph over man's errors, aberrations and ignorance. . . .

To summarize then, the importance of Ballou to Universalism was this: he took the earlier, half-realized, intuitive insight of Universalism, its "ultimate confidence," and set it upon more adequate foundations than the Biblical proof texts of his predecessors (and his contemporaries). Once Ballou became convinced that Reason was as much God's gift as the Bible, he used reason without restriction and summoned Biblical texts only as supportive evidence of the rightness of conclusions he had already arrived at by reason. . . .

Let it here be said, however, that Ballou placed his emphasis on the doctrine and not on the method. He neither defended nor glorified the method, nor exalted it to the status of a religion. It was for him *a tool* for the defense of the doctrine of Universalism. . . .

What shall we say, then, of present-day Universalism in the light of this analysis? . . .

There are not many Murray Universalists left. In one sense, this is a tribute to the magnetism of Ballou's interpretation of Universalism. . . .

There are other varieties of Universalism, among them that which still seeks to foster the inclusiveness of Universalism. Its advocates think of Universalism as the full Christian gospel, the completion and correction of Christianity's error of limitarianism. . . .

And there are those who have adopted half of Ballou, his rational approach, but have neglected or rejected that "ultimate confidence" which made Ballou a Universalist. These Universalists (or liberals, for such they are) compare the methods of Universalism and Unitarianism and find no distinction between the two. And, as regards the predominant method, they are probably correct. They point out, proudly and accurately, that Ballou was an early advocate of all that Unitarianism preached;

but neglect to suggest what was also true, that Ballou in his "ultimate confidence" went further than most Unitarians are willing to go.

These who have chosen the method and tool of Ballou might do well to remember that there are those among the Universalists who, if it comes to issue as to whether to embrace the message or the method, will gladly choose the message. . . .

While this is not a discourse on the role of reason in religion, I do want to point out that rationalism, by itself, arguing from no point of reference or departure save our fragmentary knowledge of the world (outer and inner) ends in confusion and contradiction. The Unitarians currently have this situation, wherein using reason as the only oracle of man (to adopt Ethan Allen's title) they have Christian Unitarianism, humanism, ethical culturism, and both Christian and atheistic existentialism struggling to become predominant. And to the extent that Universalism has imbibed the method above, it, too, is involved in a similar question.

Then, there are those among us who feel vague stirrings of discontent in the current situation. To merge or not to merge, that is the question. These, and some days I am one of them, cannot quite place the finger upon the source of difficulty. Let us try to put it into a syllogism. Liberalism and Universalism are compatible. Ballou exhibits this to us. But they are not identical. It may be possible, unlike the situation as between love and marriage, to have the one without the other. Liberalism and Unitarianism are also compatible. Whether or not they are identical, I cannot say. My guess is that they are, but I would stake little on this guess. . . .

The presumption is, that if you put these two Churches together, you will get a liberal church in which the method of discovering truth will be the binding force and the central core. Conclusions, if any, i.e. the faith, will then be sacrificed upon the altar of a common method. . . .

If this is what we want, we can have it; but Universalism as it was, the institutional expression of ultimate confidence, can disappear in the process. . . .

My plea is that we use Ballou, all of him. . . . "Ultimate confidence" . . . is the hallmark of Universalism as I see it, enabling us to include peoples of vastly different points of view within our church and our concern, without demanding conformity to creed, cult, culture or method; to look with appreciation and understanding upon the formulations and efforts of all religions, Christian and otherwise, considering all to be the products of good intention, emerging out of deep human need; to insist that there is always hope, never final despair, absolute alienation or damnation; to value rational and non-rational approaches to Universalism.

In an era of paralyzing fear and crippling anxiety, this religious point of view is to me of crucial importance.

SOURCE: Gordon B. McKeeman, "The Place of Hosea Ballou in Present-Day Universalism," *Universalist Leader*, March 1959, 59–61.

IRVING R. MURRAY
"A Case for Merger"
1959

Irving R. Murray (1915–1992) served as minister of the First Unitarian Church of Pittsburgh from 1944 to 1961, after which he served both First Unitarian of Baltimore and First Unitarian of Toledo. A talented preacher, Murray effectively bridged divisions between humanists and theists, energetically promoted social action, and achieved significant membership growth. As a strong champion of a merger of Unitarians and Universalists, he was invited to debate the topic with the minister of All Souls in New York City, Walter Donald Kring. It was thus natural for the Unitarian Register *to feature the views of both men. Further Reading: Kathleen R. Parker,* Here We Have Gathered: The Story of Unitarian Universalism in Western Pennsylvania, 1808–2008 *(Pittsburgh: Ohio Meadville District of UUA, 2010).*

— Dan McKanan

It is unrealistic sectarianism to postulate the progress of Unitarianism onward and upward forever on the basis of two decades of good fortune.

Of course we have an able leadership and faithful workers in Unitarian advance. Many have labored long and hard to bring about a 50 per cent increase in Unitarian membership in the last twenty-odd years. Their success, on the other hand, has been more a product of historical forces beyond their or our control than, in our devotion and/or pride, we are wont to recognize.

Unitarianism is an urban movement, with great appeal to thoughtful men and women, especially to those with some scientific orientation. Never in all history has there been as great an increase in the number of young men and women going to college, in the number of people employed in scientific research, and most especially in the millions moving from rural to urban areas as has occurred in our time. In consequence, our Pittsburgh Unitarian church, for example, *had* to grow. It would have taken extraordinary skill to prevent its growth. A young engineer coming to Pittsburgh to work at one of the Westinghouse atomic power installations was almost certain to choose our church if he had any inclination towards religious liberalism. The odds were perhaps 1,000,000 to 1 against his driving thirty-some miles to rural Smithton to attend the nearest Universalist Church. . . .

Neither we nor the Universalists caused America's phenomenal urbanization, which has brought leadership as well as manpower to us, while taking them away from the Universalists.

When the opponents of merger argue that we Unitarians should exploit to the full our precious wave of the future and let the Universalists go do whatever they like, the neglect the realistic facts of our historic situation.

Fact 1: a riplet of luck is not a wave of the future.

Fact 2: our Unitarian capital, in round figures $12.5 millions, is not adequate for the work we have to do.

The Universalist capital, $5.5 millions, is wholly inadequate.

Neither group has enough. But put their capital together—eliminate the wasteful duplication of effort that today all too often prevails—and both together might have, for example, enough capital to underwrite for the first time in their history a really effective continental public relations program.

* * *

In the twenty-odd years just past, McCarthyism, neo-orthodoxy, and Billy Graham have, all unintentionally, served our cause. They have made freedom-loving men and women aware of needs that, in urban, industrial communities, we alone were prepared to supply.

In the decades ahead, we cannot count on continuing help from our enemies, and we must expect tomorrow's demands to exceed our capacities, Unitarian and Universalist alike. . . .

We Unitarians and Universalists have enough in common to make merger possible and enough of difference to make it fruitful. The differences must not be exaggerated.

Every variety of liberal theology is found in both our denominations. It may be said, nevertheless, that the Universalists know something more of piety, of the emotional components of religion, and of the rural or small-town way of life than we do. Many of them will bring slightly different values to our common deliberations. If we identify the difference with the rabid Universalist sectarianism we have sometimes had to contend with in the Council of Liberal Churches, we shall make the same mistake the Universalists might make if they were to identify as the quintessence of Unitarianism the stiff-necked pride we sometimes exhibit at Joint Biennials when the talk turns to Unitarian advance. . . .

The merger corporation should not be conceived, however, as Unitarian and Universalist only. The commission errs, I think, in not making it plain in the manual that many individual Jewish and Christian congregations (not national bodies) will wish to join the new corporation if a self-respecting basis for membership is provided. . . . If that is done, I should expect the Unitarian and Universalist churches together to be outnumbered by the others in fifty, to one hundred years. The new corporation should, at the end of a century, be an association of *three or four thousand* congregations united to advance liberal religion on this continent—on this planet! . . .

The question before us is both subtler than some of the argument would suggest and simpler. It is not a matter to be settled by metaphors from marriage, nor by mere notions as to the value of a name or the fabulous promises of our Unitarian wave of the future. It is, on the other hand, as simple a matter as the arithmetic of a corporation engaged in a continental enterprise. . . .

Above all, we must recognize that only by uniting *all* the resources of liberal religion on this continent can we hope to build from yesterday's good fortune to tomorrow's disciplined, sober, steady advance.

SOURCE: Irving R. Murray, "A Case for Merger," *Unitarian Register*, March 1959, 6, 30.

"A Case against Merger"
1959

Walter Donald Kring (1916–1999) began his career at the First Unitarian Church of Worcester, Massachusetts, and served as minister of All Souls Unitarian Church in New York City from 1955 to 1978. An eloquent champion of the Christian wing of Unitarianism, Kring was deeply devoted to the legacy of Henry Whitney Bellows and wrote both a biography of Bellows and a multi-volume history of All Souls. (His research on Bellows also led him to publish a book on Bellows's noted parishioner, Herman Melville.) At the time he wrote this essay, Kring was also serving as the secretary of the American Unitarian Association.

—Dan McKanan

At the outset, I should make it clear that I am speaking in opposition to merger as a personal conviction. I am not speaking as the unpaid secretary of the American Unitarian Association or as the minister of the Unitarian Church of All Souls of New York City. I do not know how my own church will vote on this matter. . . .

I believe that I am speaking for a great number of persons, Unitarians and Universalists, who want continued and increased co-operation between our two church bodies but who do not believe that these mutual interests will best be furthered by organic merger of the two denominations. Some of us feel that the energies of the liberal religious movement in America will be dissipated and retarded by merger. . . .

There are two main reasons why merger rather than other more important considerations are in the focus of Unitarian and Universalist circles today. The first is that to the "man in the street," it seems appropriate on first glance that churches should unite. Our two churches are so similar; they have common backgrounds and ideals. Yet it does not follow that both would necessarily profit from merger. I think that in this case, this first intuition or "hunch" should be more carefully considered. . . .

The second reason merger is so much in the limelight is that the Joint Interim Commission, which was appointed by the board of directors to report at the Detroit Biennial Conference in 1956, took the attitude that after one year of experimentation, the Andover Plan of merger of three departments into the Council of Liberal Churches had failed.

* * *

I also am sorry that this complication of discussion and a series of votes on merger should come at this particular time in our denominational history. In the period of our greatest growth, it seems that we should be concentrating on realization of growth rather than discussion of a question which may hamper rather than strengthen growth.

* * *

From the churches' point of view, I deplore this requirement that we study merger completely. You are as aware as I that never will any considerable group of Unitarians feel that any subject has been discussed adequately. This is a problem of a highly literate and vocal group. To follow the discussion patterns outlined in the report of the Joint Merger Commission (and it is probably correct if this matter is really to be discussed adequately) would require most of the energies of most of the people of most of the churches for the next two years. . . .

The Joint Merger Commission manual gives many arguments for and against merger. Most of those arguments for merger are, in my estimation, arguments against it. . . .

Second, it is called to our attention in the manual that 60 per cent of the Universalist churches are in communities of less than 10,000 population, while approximately 60 per cent of the Unitarian churches are in communities of more than 25,000 population. The great mass of Universalists come from the smaller towns; the great mass of Unitarians from the larger cities. That is given as an argument for merger.

Do you really strengthen a church by trying to mix people with widely different backgrounds, or do you simply confuse your efforts? It might make us more cosmopolitan, but my own experience is that the new Unitarians are very cosmopolitan. Is merging of these two diverse groups really an advantage to both, or do you merely set up a new set of problems, such as regionalism and sectionalism?

Third, the commission's report states that both denominations have growing edges in common. But if we are very honest about this, the Unitarian church has been growing rapidly in the past few years, whereas the Universalist church has just stopped a rapid decline, if present trends are maintained. . . .

Fourth, the commission suggests that one of the advantages of merger is that there are differences of ideology and theology within the Unitarian and Universalist churches. There certainly is a considerable variety of theological and social opinion within both churches. But I think that those of us who are Unitarians ought to remind ourselves that there are enough differences within our own Unitarian ranks at the present moment so that we have approached the danger point on several occasions in the last decade.

* * *

Now I come to what I believe is the crux of the matter—the change of name. The commission reports this as an advantage. I am not convinced that a change to the hyphenated name Universalist-Unitarian, or to any name, would be an advantage. It is difficult enough to explain to new people what it means to be a Unitarian. How much longer would it take to explain Unitarian-Universalist?

The commission then suggests a name, "The Liberal Church Association of America." I am not certain whether the "Liberal" refers to the organization of the association or to the kind of churches associated.

✻ ✻ ✻

There is also another possibility which many people do not consider. . . . The very fact that some people wish to scrap the name Unitarian will make some of our more traditional, larger, and more conservative churches maintain their own independence. They may decide that the name Unitarian means more than any new name. There may then be a "Continuing Unitarian Church," and thus our efforts have been divided rather than co-ordinated with all of this planning. How many churches are we willing to lose in the process of merger?

The great emphasis in merger seems to be upon de-emphasizing the Unitarian name. Many of us, particularly in the larger cities, are discovering that this is just the name which is bringing people to our doors and to our church schools. We are not ready to trade in the old name, which has such historic and traditional connotations and still says something positive about what we believe, for a name that will put us with the "queer" religions on the church page. . . .

The important issue is this: will merger benefit the Unitarian and Universalist causes better than continued co-operation and a completely understandable working together?

My own conviction is that it will do more harm than good to each of us. I say this after mature consideration of the many factors involved. The more merger is discussed, the more I believe we are "wasting our substance on riotous discussion," and the more I find reasons unearthed which to me make merger a secondary matter and one which is not an advantage at the present time.

SOURCE: Walter Donald Kring, "A Case against Merger," *Unitarian Register*, March 1959, 7, 31.

"A Minister's Wife Has Rights"

1959

Despite the early acceptance of women's ordination in both Universalism and Unitarianism, the number of ordained women declined in the first half of the twentieth century and women's voices were scarcely heard in the national debate over merger. But this piece from the Universalist Leader *suggests some of the latent discontent that would soon give rise to a new wave of feminist activism.*

— Dan McKanan

During the fifteen years that I have been married to a minister, I have always wondered, as I am sure all ministers' wives have, what is expected of me by the parish and by my husband, and why it is expected. Am I a strange creature that the church and community can use in any way they see fit, or am I just another human being with a few ideas of my own who would like to live as other human beings live in modern society?

Parishes vary in their needs and expectations, of course, but it has been my experience in most of them that we have served for them to feel free to ask anything and everything of me. In fact, sometimes I haven't even been asked, but just put on committees because they felt that I should be doing something for them.

I think I had been a minister's wife for about two weeks when one of the ladies informed me it was my *duty* to attend all meetings and serve in every way necessary. I can remember that I was quite incensed about this. It didn't stop here, though. Every parish since then has practiced the same methods of using me.

In one parish, my time was occupied almost entirely by serving on supper committees, attending women's organizations, and choir practices, either at the church or at the parsonage. Whenever they needed an organist, or a committee member, or officer for an organization, or a place to entertain, they never bothered to look further for people to supply these posts than to me.

Our home was the same thing all over again. It was used for everything. People came and went as they pleased. It was a common thing to come home and find people using the telephone, playing the piano, or having choir practice, or even making themselves a cup of coffee in the kitchen. Our home was just a place to eat and sleep. My children were on public display at all times and so were we. There was just no such thing as privacy. To protest would have been useless. People had always used the parsonage this way when other ministers had been there, so naturally it was the expected thing.

Then we come to what is expected of us by our husbands. How many times do ministers say, "Of course, come to the house for your meeting, my wife will be glad to serve refreshments. You need an extra Sunday School teacher? My wife will do this. . . ."

In one parish, where we spent eight years, all of these things happened; yet I never felt that my efforts were appreciated, either by the church or my husband. I think that when they decided they were tired of him as minister of their church, I was secretly quite pleased. I was fed up to the ears with churches in general. I felt that if they were all like this, I wasn't interested in being a minister's wife.

After being out of church work for two years and having a chance to live like a normal human being again, things began to look a little better. When my husband decided to go back into the ministry, I had made up my mind about a few things.

*   *   *

For the last three and a half years, we have lived on this basis. When we first moved in, the ladies' group that had always met at the parsonage for their weekly meetings came to see if they could still do this. We told them, no; that it was our home, and we felt sure they could find some other place to meet. It was quite a hard blow for them to take, but they managed to find regular meeting places. Since that time, I have been asked to attend meetings, but I haven't done so. They accept this, but tell me that if I should like to come, they would like to have me. My husband never puts me on committees or entertains without asking me what my plans are first. I have worked outside the home for three years and enjoyed doing this. I'll never be afraid to stand up for my rights again.

SOURCE: "A Minister's Wife Has Rights," *Universalist Leader*, May 1959, 121–22.

Constitution of the Unitarian Universalist Association

1959

In August 1959, after congregations voted in a plebiscite to continue the process, the Joint Merger Commission published a "blue book," entitled The Plan to Consolidate, *that included a proposed constitution and bylaws for the new denomination. By this time, they had agreed that "Unitarian Universalist Association," rather than the "Liberal Church" as favored by Frederick May Eliot, would best honor the deep heritage of the two traditions. They had also agreed that a "consolidation," rather than merger, was the best strategy for avoiding legal challenges. In October, the two denominations held a joint assembly in Syracuse, New York. The two groups of delegates were asked to vote separately on the constitution. The most challenging section proved to be the second item in the list of principles. The Commission had proposed a vague reference to "the great prophets and teachers of humanity," which was initially approved by the Universalists. The Unitarians, on the other hand, passed an amendment to delete the item, then narrowly defeated an amendment that would have restored the original wording along with an additional reference to "our Judeo-Christian tradition." Well past midnight, both groups of delegates finally approved a compromise that simply changed the word "our" to "the," achieving a degree of distance from Christianity that was acceptable, if not ideal, to the majority. The delegates then voted approval by 518 to 43 among the Unitarians and 238 to 33 among the Universalists. A second plebiscite of congregations achieved a 90-percent participation rate and overwhelming support for consolidation, after which the deal was sealed in a second joint assembly in Boston in 1960. Further Reading: Warren R. Ross,* The Premise and the Promise: The Story of the Unitarian Universalist Association *(Boston: Skinner House, 2001); David B. Parke, "What Happened at Syracuse?"* Journal of Unitarian Universalist History 35 (2011–2012): 50–74.*

— Dan McKanan

ARTICLE I

Name

The name of this organization shall be Unitarian Universalist Association.

ARTICLE II

Purposes and Objectives

Section 1. The Unitarian Universalist Association is an incorporated organization which by consolidation has succeeded to the charter powers of the American Unitarian Association, incorporated in 1847, and the Universalist Church of America, incorporated in 1866, by virtue of legislation enacted by The Commonwealth of Massachusetts and the State of New York, respectively.

The Unitarian Universalist Association is empowered to, and shall devote its resources to and exercise its corporate powers for, religious, educational and charitable purposes. It is further empowered: to solicit and receive funds separately or with others to support its work; to make appropriations to carry on its work including appropriations to its associate members and to other organizations to enable them to assist the Unitarian Universalist Association in carrying on its work; and without limitation as to amount, to receive, hold, manage, invest and reinvest and distribute any real and personal property for the foregoing purposes.

Section 2. In accordance with these corporate purposes, the members of the Unitarian Universalist Association, dedicated to the principles of a free faith, unite in seeking:

(1) To strengthen one another in a free and disciplined search for truth as the foundation of our religious fellowship;

(2) To cherish and spread the universal truths taught by the great prophets and teachers of humanity in every age and tradition, immemorially summarized in the Judeo-Christian heritage as love to God and love to man;
[Original: (2) To cherish and spread the universal truths taught by the great prophets and teachers of humanity in every age and tradition, immemorially summarized in their essence as love to God and love to man;]

(3) To affirm, defend and promote the supreme worth of every human personality, the dignity of man, and the use of the democratic method in human relationships;

(4) To implement our vision of one world by striving for a world community founded on ideals of brotherhood, justice and peace;

(5) To serve the needs of member churches and fellowships, to organize new churches and fellowships, and to extend and strengthen liberal religion;

(6) To encourage cooperation with men of good will in every land.

Section 3. The Unitarian Universalist Association hereby declares and affirms the independence and autonomy of local churches, fellowships and associate members; and nothing in this Constitution or in the By-Laws of the Association shall be deemed to infringe upon the congregational polity of churches and fellowships, nor upon the exercise of direct control by their memberships of associate member organizations, nor upon the individual freedom of belief which is inherent in the Universalist and Unitarian heritages. No minister shall be required to subscribe to any particular interpretation of religion, or to any particular religious belief or creed to obtain and hold Fellowship with the Unitarian Universalist Association.

ARTICLE III

Membership

Section 1. All churches and fellowships which are members of the American Unitarian Association and all churches and fellowships which are members of or in full fellowship with The Universalist Church of America on the effective date of this Constitution shall be members of the Unitarian Universalist Association.

Section 2. Those individuals who, on the effective date of this Constitution, were Life Members of the American Unitarian Association and were so constituted on or before May 1, 1925, shall be Life Members of the Unitarian Universalist Association and shall have all the rights and privileges of membership, including the right to vote at meetings of the Association. Those individuals who, on the effective date of this Constitution, have served as Presidents of The Universalist Church of America shall be Life Members of the Unitarian Universalist Association and shall have all the rights and privileges of membership, including the right to vote at meetings of the Association.

Section 3. A church or fellowship may become a member of the Association upon acceptance by the Board of Trustees of the Association of a written application for membership stating that it subscribes to the purposes and objectives of the Association and pledges itself to support the Association.

Section 4. Any church or fellowship which is a member shall have the right through delegates to vote at meetings of the Association, during the fiscal year in which it becomes a member and thereafter, provided such church or fellowship has met the following conditions in the next preceding fiscal year:

(1) Made a financial contribution to the Association.
(2) Conducted regular religious services.
(3) Maintained a regularly constituted organization with adequate records of membership, with elected officers and with provisions for annual meetings of members.

(4) Furnished the Association with required reports on church statistics and activities.

Churches and fellowships which do not comply with these requirements in one fiscal year shall not have their delegates accredited in the next fiscal year nor until the beginning of the fiscal year next following their compliance therewith. The Board of Trustees shall have the duty of determining compliance or non-compliance with these requirements and it shall make rules to carry out the intent of this Section.

Section 5. The Board of Trustees may admit to associate membership any other organization the purposes and programs of which, in the Board's judgment and discretion, are auxiliary to and support the purposes and objectives of the Association, upon a written application from such organization stating that it subscribes to the purposes and objectives of the Association and pledging itself to support the Association. Such membership shall continue so long as in the Board's judgment and discretion such organization's purposes and programs continue to be auxiliary to and in support of the purposes and objectives or the Association. Each associate member, through delegates, shall have the right to vote at each meeting of the Association during the fiscal year in which it becomes an associate member and thereafter provided such associate member has made a financial contribution to the Association in the next preceding fiscal year.

ARTICLE IV

Conduct of the Association's Affairs

Section 1. Delegates and individuals having the right to vote shall constitute the General Assembly of the Association. The General Assembly shall be the overall policy making body for carrying out the purposes and objectives of the Association and shall direct and control its affairs. The Board of Trustees shall conduct the affairs of the Association and, subject to the provisions of its Constitution and By-Laws, shall carry out the policies and directives of the General Assembly and shall have the usual powers of corporate directors as provided by law. The Officers of the Association, including those elected by the General Assembly and those appointed by the Board, shall be subject to the direction and control of the Board and shall have all the usual powers of such officers as provided by law.

Section 2. The responsibility for investment of funds of the Association is vested in the Board which may from time to time delegate these powers to its Investment Committee, but no such delegation shall relieve the board of its overall responsibility in this respect.

Section 3. The Association, as of the effective date of this Constitution, hereby assumes all financial obligations and debts of the American Unitarian Association and the Universalist Church of America and agrees to pay and discharge the same. Funds and assets held prior to said effective date for the benefit of any church, fellowship or organization by either the American Unitarian Association or The Universalist Church of America shall be held by the Unitarian Universalist Association upon the same conditions and obligations, so far as required by law. If, after the effective date of this Constitution, the Association shall consolidate, merge with, or become the successor of any organization (other than the American Unitarian Association or The Universalist Church of America) which holds funds or assets for the benefit of any church, fellowship or organization, any such assets and funds thus acquired by the Association shall be held under the same conditions and obligations, so far as required by law. Unless subject to specific restrictions, such funds or assets may be invested in the General Investment Fund of the Association.

Section 4. The Association shall raise capital and operating funds to carry out its purposes and objectives and also may raise capital and operating funds for the use of its associate members and others as provided in Article II, Section 1.

ARTICLE V

Regions

Section 1. In order to provide for the services and work which can best be accomplished through regional organizations, the Association shall support areas of regional responsibility to be known as Regions, the same to be established in such number and with such geographical location as the General Assembly, following consultation with authorized representatives of the churches and fellowships concerned, shall from time to time determine. Recognizing that prior to the formation of the Association, Conferences and Councils of Unitarian churches and fellowships, and State Conventions of Universalist churches and fellowships had been created by groups of churches and fellowships and vested with certain duties and powers, independent in whole or in part from the jurisdiction of the American Unitarian Association or The Universalist Church of America, respectively, and recognizing that the Boards and Officers of these units and their successors can continue to contribute a major part of the direction and operation of regional services and work, and recognizing also that the development of the pattern of the cooperation of these Conferences, Councils and Conventions with the Association will not be necessarily contemporaneous or in identical form, such Regions shall make use of a system of having regional organization based on the principle of local autonomy, consistent with the promotion of the welfare and interests of the Association as a whole and of its member churches and fellowships.

ARTICLE VI

The Ministry

Section 1. Ministers having Ministerial Fellowship with the American Unitarian Association or The Universalist Church of America on the effective date of this Constitution shall thereby have Ministerial Fellowship with the Unitarian Universalist Association. Other ministers may be admitted to Ministerial Fellowship upon filing an application with the Association and meeting its requirements as set forth in its By-Laws and rules made pursuant thereto. The Association recognizes and affirms that member churches alone have the right to call and ordain their ministers. The Association alone shall have the right to grant Ministerial Fellowship with the Association.

Section 2. The Association shall establish and maintain a pension system for ministers having full Ministerial Fellowship with the Association. Ministers who, on the effective date of this Constitution, have pension rights and benefits theretofore conferred by the American Unitarian Association or The Universalist Church of America shall not have those rights or benefits abridged without their written consent insofar as the same are at that time vested rights and benefits which constitute legal obligations.

ARTICLE VII

Financial Services to Churches and Fellowships

Section 1. The Association may receive funds and other assets for investment and custody and hold the same for the benefit of member churches, fellowships and other organizations subject in each instance to the approval of the Board of Trustees. The Board shall establish rules to carry out the intent of this Section and such rules shall include the right of withdrawal of such funds and assets on reasonable notice.

ARTICLE VIII

Seal

The Association shall have a corporate seal which shall be in such form as the Board of Trustees shall approve.

ARTICLE IX

Rules Under This Constitution

Rules made under the authority of this Constitution shall take effect upon adoption but may be amended or repealed by vote of the General Assembly.

ARTICLE X

Amendments

This Constitution may be amended or repealed by the General Assembly at a regular meeting of the Association at which a quorum is present if two-thirds of those present and voting so order, but the General Assembly shall act on any proposed amendment or repeal only when the same has been submitted in accordance with the By-Laws and read at the previous regular meeting.

SOURCE: Joint Merger Commission, *The Plan to Consolidate The American Unitarian Association and The Universalist Church of America* (Wellesley Hills, MA: The Commission, 1959).

"Questions About Jesus"
1960

Though he had earlier expressed some reservations about merger, in this piece Gordon McKeeman came out in strong support of the decisions reached at Syracuse, including the statement of principles. "We have not voted Jesus out," McKeeman declared, because a broader "spirit of inclusiveness reflects the spirit of Jesus." In the wake of consolidation, McKeeman was called as minister of the Unitarian Universalist Church of Akron, Ohio, which he served for twenty-two years, and as president of the historically Unitarian Starr King School for the Ministry, which he led from 1983 to 1988.

—Dan McKanan

The accounts that have appeared in the newspapers of the convention of The Universalist Church of America, and its joint biennial conference with the American Unitarian Association have caused confusion and more than a little apprehension in some quarters; and I can understand the apprehension and the confusion.

In order to clarify the issues that are involved, it seems necessary to take a brief look at our history as a church.

Universalism, in a modern sense, began when men began to take exception to some of Christianity's cherished doctrines. . . . Universalism began by assuming that God is love and if God be love, He will surely never condemn any of his children to an eternal suffering in hell. This was the beginning of Universalism.

The critics of Universalism replied that this would sever the nerve of moral effort. If everyone eventually goes to heaven anyway, they ask, what is the motivation for living a good, upright, moral life? . . .

As time went on, they discovered that these claims, which they had made against Universalists, were not true. Far from being immoral, Universalists were in the forefront of practically every advance on the social scene. In prison reform, in anti-slavery measures, in the fight for women's rights, in the founding of the Red Cross, and in countless other ways, Universalists proved by their lives that the things the orthodox had said about them were simply not true. After a while the controversy abated and friendly relations grew between Universalists and other churches; differences were minimized and similarities emphasized and in time there came an era of good feeling. Many Universalists thought that the work of the Universalist Church was done and that it would be wise for us to merge with some church similar to ours; preferably, most of them thought, the Congregational Church.

Then, in 1944, the Universalists applied for membership in the Federal Council of Churches (now called the National Council of Churches) and the application was rejected. It was rejected on the grounds that Universalists were not Christian, since they did not believe that Jesus Christ was the only begotten son of God. This was the only test of a Christian; if he believed this, he was a Christian; if he didn't, then he couldn't be. This was a blow to most Universalists who had always considered themselves Christian, if of a somewhat peculiar stripe. They were shocked and surprised that the majority of Christians had, by definition, excluded them from Christianity.

What to do about it was the problem that faced Universalists. There were two general trends. The first was to insist that the definition of Christianity which was proposed by the Federal Council of Churches was altogether too narrow; that it dealt with a religion *about* Jesus and ignored any reference to the religion which Jesus himself professed and practiced, which he summarized as "Thou shalt love the Lord they God with all thy heart and with all thy soul and with all thy mind and with all thy strength and thou shalt love thy neighbor as thyself." . . .

Others took a somewhat different approach. They pointed out that the things Jesus taught about love to God and love to man were not exclusively Christian; that these insights into religion were shared, not only by the Jews, but also by most of the other major religious groups in the world; that these truths of Jesus were universal truths; that they were found in most of the world's religious traditions. So we began to find a new and promising mission for our ancient and honored name. *Universalists* began to mean believers in universal truths, believers in universal salvation, believers in a universal outlook. We began to develop symbols to express our faith. The universal truths taught by Jesus and revered by Universalists, whether *called* Christians or not, were symbolized by the circle within which was put the cross to indicate that these truths have come to us through the medium of Christianity, its wisdom, its insights, its symbolism.

*   *   *

Now to address myself to some specific issues raised by the news stories and by what was done at Syracuse. Let me make it crystal clear—*we have not voted Jesus out.* Surely the life of a man so great as this cannot be expunged from the record of humanity or from the tradition of a church by a motion or a show of hands. We shall continue in whatever manner and by whatever means we desire and deem appropriate to find inspiration in the life of Jesus, wisdom in his teachings and the call to consecration in his death. We shall do this with the understanding and acceptance of our brothers in Universalist and Unitarian churches, whether they agree with us or not; for we are guaranteed freedom of belief and practice, and we can be Christians (in our own meaning of that term) so long as we dare to cherish the term for ourselves.

*   *   *

As I said before, we have not voted Jesus out, nor could we, nor do we wish to; nor have we abandoned our heritage. You cannot simply drop a heritage by a show of hands. Our heritage is a part of us as much as the multiplication table and the alphabet are a part of us. We have been nurtured in it and inspired by it and challenged to live up to it. The National Council may define us out of Christianity, but it cannot exclude us from the riches, the depths of wisdom and insight which are contained within Christianity. We can take and use or violate and abuse our heritage, but we cannot simply drop it. It is ours irrevocably. *Our* heritage includes an insistence upon greater breadth, greater understanding, greater generosity of spirit. So long as we continue these things, we shall be true to our heritage *and* to the heritage of Jesus, whether we name him by name or not. Surely no formula of words can make us do this; no omission of words can prevent it if we will it to be so. Most of all, the standard by which we judge religions and their adherents is the standard which Jesus used—"By their fruits ye shall know them."

SOURCE: Gordon McKeeman, "Questions About Jesus," *Universalist Leader*, January 1960, 7–9.

ALBERT Q. PERRY

"Decisions and Implications"

1960

In this piece, merger opponent Albert Q. Perry interpreted the Syracuse deci-
sions for his congregation and for the readers of the Universalist Leader. *Soon*
thereafter, he resigned from the ministry of his Cincinnati congregation. He
devoted the next few years to civil rights activism, then ran for Congress on
a platform of opposition to the Vietnam War. He then returned to the minis-
try, serving Unitarian Universalist churches in Rhode Island, New York, and
Maine. He retired as minister of the Universalist Church in Eastport, Maine,
in 1990.

—Dan McKanan

After a great deal of discussion and a few slight changes, the proposed Constitution
and Bylaws for what would be called "The Unitarian Universalist Association" were
approved and referred to the churches for a vote this winter. If approved by that vote,
they will be formally ratified by a special General Assembly to be held next May and
what, to all intents and purposes, will be a new denomination, will take the place of
the two old, historic ones. I do not now have the time to discuss the very long and
involved document which was approved, but I would mention a few items which I
considered significant and symptomatic.

First, in the document and perhaps first in importance was the formal statement
of purpose or purposes for which this denomination would be established.

✻   ✻   ✻

Presumably, this statement of purpose was intended to be a compromise
between the traditional statements of the Universalist and Unitarian denominations,
and probably we had no right to expect more than a compromise. However, it must
be noted that entirely omitted was the optimistic emphasis which, to my way of
thinking, was our most significant and valuable characteristic. In place of the affirmation which proclaimed that love was divine or that God was love, and that this
force was "unconquerable," we have an exhortation to love God and man whatever
we expect the results to be. In place of an affirmation that good will and sacrificial
service will progressively overcome all evil, we are urged to co-operate with those
who have good will toward us. This, I would proclaim as *the least idealistic statement*
ever made by any organized religious movement. The only conclusions that one can

reach is that these statements are not compromises but a complete and abject surrender of a great and creative faith.

I will not now go into all the debate which was precipitated by the failure to mention Jesus by name or to specifically recognize that we have our roots in the Judeo-Christian tradition. It did not appear in the original draft and many objected to its omission. Although a meaningless compromise was worked out, the real problem was not resolved, and that is the relationship of liberal religion to our spiritual inheritance. Personally, I always expect adolescents to be somewhat ashamed of their parents. This is a natural part of growing up and gaining experience in independence. People of emotional maturity, even though they continue to differ greatly from their parents, make peace with their past and have faith in their personal accomplishments, even as they recognize their rootage in a continuing process of growth. I do not consider myself as narrow-minded nor as extremely conservative, but I do not want to be a part of an adolescent church. I believe that we, as a church, ought to conform to the kind of maturity which we recognize as essential for individuals. If we have not done this in this statement of purpose—and I am not sure that we have—there is a real danger that liberal religion will become a superficial movement.

* * *

At the moment, I see little chance of reversing the trend toward consolidation and re-establishing the Universalist denomination as a separate, close-knit movement. Possibly, this plan could be defeated in the coming plebiscite, but I think that many churches have so completely transferred their loyalties that the result of an effort to separate now would be a fragmentation of our denomination. I am not saying that people should not vote as their consciences dictate, and I will not be disturbed if we fail to ratify this plan; but I believe that the plan will be ratified and that there is almost no alternative to ratification.

Furthermore, I see little possibility of our remaining outside the new denomination even if we should happen to disapprove of it in some aspects. . . .

I would say that in this looser and less inspiring movement, I anticipate the need for our local church to be far more specific about its nature and mission than it has previously bothered to be. I regret this loss of breadth and flexibility, but it will make possible the kind of aggressiveness which has recently been a characteristic of Unitarianism. Previously, we have been satisfied merely to identify ourselves as Universalist and this really meant something very positive and pertinent to our times, even though interpreted very broadly. In the future, if we do not wish to drift into negativism or nothingness, we shall have to establish and keep up-to-date a definition of the particular kind of liberalism for which we exist. At the very least, we shall have to incorporate our Avowal of Faith, or some acceptable alternative to it, in our

Constitution so that when it is used in a worship service, it may express more than the whim of a minister.

Finally, although I regret many things that have happened, I am not pessimistic about the future of our church.

SOURCE: Albert Q. Perry, "Decisions and Implications," *Universalist Leader*, January 1960, 10–13.

"Frankly Speaking"

1960

Dana McLean Greeley (1908–1986) was the child of a family with deep Unitarian roots. Ordained in 1932, he served congregations in Lincoln, Massachusetts, and Concord, New Hampshire, and was then called at age twenty-seven to succeed former AUA president Samuel Atkins Eliot as minister of Boston's Arlington Street Church. He proved a worthy successor to William Ellery Channing, both in his liberal Christian faith and in his deep civic engagement. In 1958 he was elected as the final president of the American Unitarian Association, succeeding the recently deceased Frederick May Eliot. Greeley's monthly column in the Unitarian Register *was entitled "Frankly Speaking," and in it he gave voice to his enthusiasm and vision for the new denomination—enthusiasm that would continue during his two terms as UUA president. Further Reading: Dana McLean Greeley, 25 Beacon Street: And Other Recollections (Boston: Beacon Press, 1971).*

—Dan McKanan

If Unitarianism and Universalism, as a result of the plebiscite that ends this month, are destined to merge in America, we shall witness the confluence of two streams of faith that belong to each other as much as the Mississippi and the Missouri or the Ganges and the Brahmaputra rivers; and the duration and the depth of their flowing together will make their separate origins seem brief and shallow in retrospect. Arius, of Alexandria, at the Council of Nicaea in 325 A.D. argued that Jesus was different from, and less than, God, and is sometimes recognized as the first Christian defender or prophet of Unitarianism. Origen, perhaps the greatest and most distinguished theologian of the ancient church, in the same city of Alexandria proclaimed the universal restoration of all men, and could be cited in this sense as the first Universalist.

But Unitarianism and Universalism as we know them are the products of modern times and more particularly of the late eighteenth and early nineteenth centuries. William Ellery Channing, the father and foremost leader of Unitarianism in the Western world, preached in Boston from 1803 until 1842, and persistently reiterated what he called his "one sublime idea," the dignity of human nature, from which grew the "flowering of New England" and much of the fruit of liberal religion on the entire continent. Edwin Booth, church historian and biographer, and Howard

Thurman, chaplain of Boston University, sat in my living room recently telling me, as supposedly objective critics, that the liberating, affirmative mission of Unitarianism, on the basis of Channing's "idea," is only begun. Hosea Ballou, the greatest man in the Universalist church, preached in the same city of Boston from 1817 until 1852. He attacked the doctrine of the trinity, and asserted the moral sovereignty as well as the infinite love of God. "His logic was as simple as the talk of a child, yet strong as the tread of a giant." It is time for the rebirth of the movement to which he gave his life, and for the proclamation again of a childlike but gigantic logic in the realm of religion for the rank and file of mankind. Some few years ago the churches of Channing and Ballou joined forces. I see no reason why their denominations cannot consolidate to present a united front to the world.

A half a century ago there were twice as many Universalist churches in America as there were Unitarian churches, although they were smaller in membership. Today there are more Unitarian churches and fellowships than there are Universalist societies; Unitarianism represents a larger constituency. But looking at the two denominations today, which may presently merge with one another, one thinks of Alaska, which is smaller than the forty-eight states, but which Leonard Hunting, our Portland, Oregon, geographer, tells me has a longer coast-line, than the other forty-eight states put together, from the Pacific to the Gulf of Mexico to the northern Atlantic. Perhaps Universalism's limits are vaster even than Unitarianism's. But this is unimportant, if the two together, like the United Sates and Alaska, can face the future with a single witness for the cause of democracy in religion, and for the advancement of religion as democracy is enhanced in the lives and the society of men.

Unitarianism means the dignity of man as against tyranny and totalitarianism in all their forms; and it is coterminous with the principles of freedom and reason in religion and in the whole of life. Universalism means the salvation of all men, and that there can be no isolated redemption or well-being or special privilege for some while others suffer or are condemned; and it is coterminous with the concept of the integrity of nature and the cosmos, and the goodness of God and of life. Together Unitarianism and Universalism will constitute a faith for the future, a faith for the mind and for the heart, a faith in the quest for the truth, and in the establishment of the kingdom of righteousness and peace upon the earth.

SOURCE: Dana McLean Greeley, "Frankly Speaking," *Unitarian Register*, March 1960, 31.

WALTER DONALD KRING

"We Ought to Be"

1960

Despite his reservations about consolidation and about the new statement of principles, Walter Donald Kring led his congregation, All Souls in New York City, into active participation in the Unitarian Universalist Association. This sermon presents his rationale.

— Dan McKanan

The Unitarian denomination (or its successor, the Unitarian Universalist Association, if the present merger plans are voted) rests basically upon the primacy and validity of individual belief. The present American Unitarian Association is a group of churches deriving what little authority it has from its constituent churches. I believe that this association or any new association should be not a superchurch, but an association of churches which can do things in common better than separately. Such an association must have some statement of purposes in order to organize. . . .

The statement of purposes finally adopted at the Joint Biennial Conference in Syracuse, New York, is admittedly a compromise:

> *"To cherish and spread the universal truths taught by the great prophets and teachers of humanity in every age and tradition, and immemorially summarized in the Judeo-Christian heritage as 'love to God and love to man.'"*

This does not say all that some of us would like to say, but it says enough to enable us to have a national organization. In no sense are these words authoritative tests or creeds.

The Unitarian Church of All Souls in New York City has a covenant or bond of union: "In the freedom of the truth and in the spirit of Jesus we unite for the worship of God and the service of man."

* * *

When we look at the larger picture of our denomination in the United States and Canada, we do not find such unanimity. This is natural; and it is not just the Unitarian church which has important difference of opinion within its ranks.

There is serious discussion in our midst as to whether Unitarianism is a sect within Christianity or whether Unitarianism now represents a new kind of universal religion which goes "beyond Christianity." This is the kind of discussion that would rip most church bodies apart and would be prevented at all odds by church leaders who wished to create a good public image. Unitarians speak the truth as they see the truth, which in today's conformist society often seems dangerous. My personal conviction is that this discussion is constructive, even though sometimes we air our differences in public.

A large segment of our denomination believes that Unitarianism best performs its function in the historical tradition in which it arose, as a sect of the Christian religion. . . .

As a Christian sect, we naturally look to the spiritual founder of Christianity for special inspiration. Unitarians never have had much sympathy with the theological thinking of the Apostle Paul, the actual founder of the Christian religion. Hence, the phrase in the statement of purposes adopted at Syracuse, "the Judeo-Christian heritage," is not really the best description for those who believe that Unitarianism is and should continue to be a sect within Christendom. The statement which All Souls proposed seems much better to me:

> "To cherish and spread the universal truths taught by Jesus and the other great prophets in every age and tradition, and prophetically expressed in the Judeo-Christian tradition as love to God and love to man."

We feel far more kinship with the ethical ideals of Jesus than with what we term "the Judeo-Christian heritage." . . .

Another point of view has grown up among Unitarians. It received early emphasis in Transcendentalism with Ralph Waldo Emerson. It was a vision of a universal intuitive faith which claimed to be "beyond Christianity." . . .

The tendency to consider Unitarianism as a new universalism has several motivations. One is the desire for a religion in which persons other than Christians may join without becoming Christians. Another is the desire of certain groups to use the Unitarian church with its historical roots for purposes which are largely propagandist in nature. The desire to form the church into a social action group in various fields of social and political endeavor is one of earnest souls who wish to use a prominent, if small, church for their own purposes. Many of these sincere people wish this church to be a "universal church."

There also is a sincere motivation to move away from Christian sectarianism.

*   *   *

I have great sympathy with their aims. Those of us who wish the Unitarian religion to remain as a sect of Christianity deplore the cultural and intellectual smugness of Christianity. We also want Unitarian Christianity to be aware of and interested in the teachings of the prophets of every age and every land. I must say, however, that

I deplore the attempt to take the Unitarian religion out of the Christian tradition. We belong to the great tradition of Christianity which always has had divergencies within it.

If I properly understand modern Protestant biblical scholarship, it is evolving a concept of the historical Jesus very much like the concept of Jesus which Unitarians have had for years. Yet, just as this change is taking place in orthodox scholarship, the world religionists wish to go off and play a different kind of a theological drama. I, for one, prefer to remain within Christianity and have a "homecoming" celebration for the orthodox!

There is room within the Unitarian denomination for both those who believe in the Unitarian religion as a Christian sect and those who wish to go beyond this and form some world religion. I believe that there is room because within the Unitarian ranks we can discuss these matters creatively. I am not at all certain that the way to discuss them is when we are confused with such an issue as the merger of two denominations. Certainly, the pressure of making decisions about statements of purpose is not the best atmosphere for such discussion. Within the next decade the Unitarian denomination (or the Unitarian Universalist denomination) can fill a constructive role for religious people over the world by exploring this question: does a religion function best by trying to change within a tradition or by separating itself from a tradition and going it alone as a new world religion?

* * *

It behooves all of us as we seek for the truth not to deprave ourselves by belittling the motives of those who disagree with us or by withholding our support because things do not go exactly our own way. Nothing ever has been accomplished by withdrawing. This kind of discussion will make our denomination more the denomination it ought to be, provided our motives and our ideals are right.

SOURCE: Walter Donald Kring, "We Ought to Be," *Unitarian Register*, April 1960, 3–5.

DONALD S. HARRINGTON
"We Are That Faith!"
1960

The consolidation of the American Unitarian Association and the Unitarian Church of America was completed in a joint assembly held in Boston in the summer of 1960. After the final vote, delegates gathered for a celebratory worship service at Symphony Hall, with Donald S. Harrington (1914–2005) preaching. Eleven years earlier, Harrington had succeeded John Haynes Holmes as minister of Community Church of New York, which he guided toward closer ties to the Unitarian and now Unitarian Universalist denominations. He also served on the final board of the American Unitarian Association and the inaugural board of the Unitarian Universalist Association.

—Dan McKanan

There is a mysterious magic in milestones, as in the first quavering cry of a new born babe. . . .

We stand tonight at such a milestone, one which is partly a birth, partly a commencement, partly a kind of marriage, and which involves also a degree of death, an end of things which have been precious to us and of institutions with which we have been lovingly familiar.

We have achieved a union which is the result of more than a hundred years of striving, and which now, at last, when the time is fully ripe, has come to completion. It is our tremendous potential, born of the world's response to our new relevance, caused by this new world's need for a religion which is dynamic instead of static, unitive instead of divisive, universalistic instead of particularistic, history-making rather than history-bound, that has made this Unitarian-Universalist merger necessary and inevitable.

As long as we were organizationally quiescent, there was little need for us to merge. The moment we began our great modern expansion, continued separation became intolerable. We needed each other's strength and experience and each other's complementary city and country constituencies. We needed to consolidate our resources, to use wisely every ounce of influence in every minister, layman, and available dollar. We needed to be able to present a united face in the communities across the land in which Unitarian and Universalist fellowships were appearing. We needed to mobilize our combined resources for a long-neglected great world task, as the same combination of forces which sparked our advance on this continent began to appear everywhere on earth.

*   *   *

We need now to pause a moment to look back over the way that we have come.

*   *   *

Today's Unitarian Universalism, as I like to call it, developed out of the body of historic Christianity. It was the persistence of the influence of Essenic Judaism, with its emphasis on righteousness above ritual, into the Christian era, which appeared in the Arianism of the early Christian church. This very-close-to-the-Jewish form of Christianity was stamped out by the Roman emperor, Constantine, but re-emerged during the Renaissance and Reformation in Europe, and erupted spontaneously in established churches of America.

Originally, Unitarianism and Universalism were based upon doctrinal dissent within the orthodox Christian around the middle of the eighteenth century in the church. The Unitarians denied the validity of the doctrine of the trinity and affirmed the unity of God. The Universalists denied the doctrines of predestination and damnation and affirmed the ultimate salvation of all souls and the unqualified goodness of God.

John Murray of the Universalists and William Ellery Channing of the Unitarians were the chief spokesmen for these dissenters and heretics. . . .

History records the emergence of the liberal spirit in most of the world's great faiths. This spirit insists that religion shall serve man, not man religion, that what is required of man is not elaborate theological belief or ritual of one kind or another, but to do justly, love mercy, and walk humbly with God. This spirit derives not so much from the teachings of the great faiths as from human nature, which insists upon freedom. It appeared in Judaism in the prophets and in Jesus' effort to return Judaism to the simple essence of prophetic Hebrew ethics. It appeared in Christianity as Arminianism, Socinianism, Unitarianism, Universalism, and the Hicksite Quaker movement. It appeared in Hinduism first as Buddhism and later in the Vedanta and the Brahmo Samaj, and in later orthodox Buddhism as the mystical movement of Zen.

All of the world's great faiths have two emphases, often contradictory, the particularistic and the universalistic. The particularistic is usually a mythological construct and represents its exclusive claim on truth through divine revelation. In Christianity, it is the doctrine of the incarnation of God in Christ upon which the salvation of all mankind hangs. In Judaism, it is the concept of the covenant, of God's having chosen one holy people to mediate his salvation in the world.

The universalistic emphasis expresses itself in teachings concerning the great spiritual, ethical, and social relationships. In this area, the great faiths reinforce each

214

other. Dealing with essentially the same human nature and the same human situations, the come to surprisingly similar conclusions.

Our forefathers in Unitarianism and Universalism moved quickly away from particularism into emphasis upon the universals of method and spirit. The great leaders were Hosea Ballou and Ralph Waldo Emerson. Hosea Ballou made Universalism theologically unitarian, but he went beyond that, insisting upon a spirit of toleration and mutual acceptance in religious fellowship. . . .

But the greatest prophet of the universality of religion, truth, and life was Ralph Waldo Emerson, the sage of Concord. He saw that this common ground of faith in human nature and the human situation was what was really important.

* * *

It is sometimes said in criticism of the concept of universal religion that it is a synthetic, by which the critic means an artificial patching together of the supposedly best parts of existing religions, which, it is claimed, is an utterly futile venture. Emerson knew quite well that all the existing great religions were synthetic in precisely this sense.

Christianity is a synthesis constructed upon the base of Jesus' simple, ethical Judaism, plus the vivid Jewish Messianic hope, and containing elements of Zoroastrian dualistic imagery, Greek philosophy, Mithraic ritual and Roman and Norse terminology. Organic synthesis is the religious method that history records. Emerson's quest for universality in religion was simply carrying forward into our own day the method unashamedly employed by past generations.

His discovery of the universality of inspiration did not lead Emerson to reject the teachings and example of Jesus. It excited and inspired him as it also can us, to find the same sublime thoughts in the teachings of great men of widely separate times and places. It led him to dare to believe that the same inspiration lay as a personal potential in every man alive and to look for it to speak again, and yet again, in modern times.

By 1867, Francis Ellingwood Abbott and Willard [sic] Potter [William James Potter] were trying to organize the Free Religious Association, "based on individual freedom of belief, the scientific study of religion and the conviction that a single universal spirit underlay all historic faiths." They failed in 1867, as did subsequent efforts, but the vision of universal religion slowly gathered strength and substance as the years went by. More and more men moved over to support it, culminating with the great leaders of our day. Clarence Skinner and Clinton Scott, Minot J. Savage, A. Powell Davies, and John Haynes Holmes. . . .

This is the story, in brief, of how Unitarianism and Universalism, fired and reformed by Emerson's vision of universal religion and Ballou's spirit of universal good will, have come to the place where we finally have joined forces. We are the children of the Judeo-Christian heritage. We affirm with gratitude and joy the

215

universal truths taught by Jesus and embraced by Christianity. We affirm equally the universal truths taught by the great Jewish prophets and embraced by Judaism, plus the universal truths taught by all the other faiths and philosophies, Oriental, African, or Occidental, and by modern science. We are not less than Christian, but more!

What we have seen emerging in Unitarian-Universalism in this century is nothing less than a new synthesis, the coalescence of a new consensus, a new world faith, formulated by and fitted for this great, new world age. It is taking its place beside the Big Three religious groups on this continent, the Catholics, Protestants, and Jews. Its counterparts are beginning to appear in other cultures, within the bodies of the Oriental orthodoxies. It speaks to the needs and condition of the modern, world-minded man, and it is spreading across the earth like the living tide of green grass in the spring.

It has given a new and broader meaning to the old theological labels, "Unitarian" and "Universalist." Unitarian now stands not only for the oneness of God, but it affirms the unitary nature of the universe and everything in it as the single sacred reality whose physical and spiritual laws set the bounds of our being, within whose meaning and ultimate purpose our little lives find their significance.

Universalism has grown beyond the idea of universal salvation to embrace the concept of the universality of truth. It has come to stand for the seeking out and stressing of the great universals which can lead sorely-divided men into the great unities. It desires the one universal spirit of compassionate and all-redeeming love, which has the power to inspire, judge, encourage, and ultimately gather man's separate and warring tribes into one world fellowship of the free.

Looking forward, I see the need for us to prepare ourselves to absorb the shock of the incredible growth which will accompany our newly-won relevance. Millions upon millions of persons have been drifting away from the world's historic faiths, disillusioned and dispirited at being compelled to subscribe to ancient myths for religious truth. Many thousands have married across faith lines and are looking for a faith by which to live in dignity and freedom for the welfare of all men. We can be, we *are* that faith!

It is an awesome challenge to make more meaningful the freedom which is our fountain-force.

* * *

In America, the Negro, so long subject, finally has raised his head, and now with burning, yearning eyes, asks us, "Be we brothers? Yes or no?" Our swelling response must be, "Yes, brother, yes!" We must show it in daring deeds, not easy words.

To the south of us, the other Americas, still, by and large, stand uncertainly in rags and poverty like a slum shack in a palace garden. We must learn how truly to help our neighbors to help themselves.

From Africa and Asia come unending anguished cries. The young nations there face impossible problems, with underdevelopment, unemployment, ravaged resources, and exploding populations. They face a bloody, savage rage of tribal hate unless we now can help them massively to set themselves constructively to the development of their resources and the federal union of their lands.

In the West, as all across the world, men worship idols their own hands have made and wave themselves more tightly into the webs of things. We need to summon them back from the suicide superhighway of merely having to the beauteous summit trail of being!

The nations snarl and growl and brandish blasphemy and threaten time itself. Speaking in God's name for all the little peoples' hopes and dreams, we need to call them now and, if necessary, to command that, foolish quarrels set aside, they shall disarm and build together one world community of the free under world law, to make the United Nations the heart and mind and voice of a united world.

This is the vision, the challenge, the opportunity. These are the tasks that wait the coming of the great, uniting new world faith. May we, Unitarians and Universalists and men and women of good will everywhere, strive with all our might to make our lives, our churches and fellowships, and our new Unitarian Universalist Association the vehicles of this vision!

SOURCE: Donald S. Harrington, "We Are That Faith!" *Unitarian Register*, Mid-Summer 1960, 3–6.

WILLIAM B. RICE AND DANA McLEAN GREELEY
"Nominees for President, U.U.A."
1961

One of the first tasks of the new denomination was to elect its founding president. UCA General Superintendent Philip Giles believed that neither he nor AUA president Dana McLean Greeley should run, but Greeley disagreed. The UCA board then insisted that Joint Merger Commission chair William B. Rice be nominated as well. Rice and Greeley both held dual ministerial fellowship but had served only Unitarian congregations as minister. The election thus featured two friends with competing visions for the presidency: Would it be the relatively weak office envisioned by the Joint Merger Commission or the charismatic leadership role that, Greeley believed, had allowed the AUA to achieve dramatic growth under Frederick May Eliot? The 1961 General Assembly delegates opted for the latter choice, but the debate would be replayed during the Greeley administration and in many subsequent elections. Further Reading: Warren R. Ross, The Premise and the Promise: The Story of the Unitarian Universalist Association *(Boston: Skinner House, 2001).*

—Dan McKanan

William B. Rice

On January 11, I was asked by the Board of the A.U.A. and the U.C.A to be one of the two candidates for the President of the U.U.A. when it begins next May. I accepted because I am deeply concerned about the new Association and feel that I can bring to its service the quality of experience and understanding which will help to create the kind of consolidated organization which churches and fellowships expect. I further believe that I appreciate the fears which opponents to merger held, and that I am sufficiently sensitive to their problems to see to it that in the months ahead reasonable doubts can be allayed.

The heritage of both denominations is part of my background. As a child, I attended a Universalist church school, and as a young man I was active in Unitarian youth work. I was educated at Tufts College and Tufts School of Religion and I have served in various denominational posts for thirty-five years. I have full fellowship with both A.U.A. and U.C.A.

During the past five years as Chairman of the Joint Merger Commission, it has been my good fortune to share in intensive studies of the traditions, the plans, and

218

the organization of both denominations, and the financial, administrative, and policy structures presently existing. Few have ever had the fullness of this unique opportunity or have had the benefit of the training and discipline which this experience has produced. I am therefore prepared to face the problems of the new organization without a special commitment to either of the former groups. I am jealous for its future.

Your Merger Commission placed great trust in the democratic process, and we should be willing to do so in the new denomination. Basic policy should not be entrusted to the staff or the Board, but to the Assembly, in which all have a voice. The President and the Board should present major policy matters well before the meeting of the Assembly and should feel themselves not only guided but bound by Assembly decisions, as the Assembly in turn should represent the informed opinions of the churches and regions.

We are faced with great problems in finances. Primarily, can we provide an adequate budget for an expanding liberalism? Recent mistakes in fiscal policy and fund raising have resulted from an undemocratic approach to the problem. In the future, if the budgetary needs are presented fully and openly to the Assembly, and are supported, one is *led* to believe that fair quotas will be accepted and met, and no dire emergencies can be expected. Parenthetically, we believe that a sound and factual analysis of present fund raising attempts should be presented to both present denominations in a simple and open form. Thus we would enter into our next stage of growth with a sober appraisal of the facts, and would be able to prepare a reasonable budget, devoid of guesswork, designed to fit our resources and our needs.

I would endeavor to place administration and finance in the hands of sound and capable executives and would expect that their policies and actions would be open to the scrutiny of the Assembly at the Annual Meetings, and that proper reports would be sent out before the Meetings.

We are living in a climate of paradox. In it there are great opportunities for a genuinely liberal religious movement. There are thousands awaiting the challenge of a faith which appeals to them as reasonable and heroically visionary. We have no doubt that if we approach these potential liberals with a truly effective missionary zeal, our program will be well received and our strength and numbers will grow.

Conversely, the same climate has produced a fear of outspoken and honest liberal religion. This has subjected us to attack from without, and to some anxious concern within. It behooves us, therefore, to re-examine our life, to make certain that there are great and common loyalties and agreements within us which are more real and significant than those issues on which we appear to differ. This calls for a sober reappraisal of the principles of religious liberalism and their application to our common life, so that we may be more profoundly united and challenged than we have been in the past century.

I would not have accepted this nomination had I not believed that those chosen to administer our common efforts might, by a sound and honest application of the principles of democracy, and by an impassioned loyalty to a profound religious liberalism, share with you in creating a new denomination which in its time might have as great and good an effect on its own life and the life of the world as our Unitarian and Universalist churches have in their proud histories.

Dana McLean Greeley

About a month ago the chairman of the Joint Nominating Committee, a Universalist, came to me and asked if my name could be presented to the two Boards as the single nominee for the President of the new Unitarian Universalist Association. I explored with him some of the relevant questions concerning the days ahead. He assured me that the Nominating Committee was presenting my name because I was its considered choice, and not because I was president of the Unitarian Association. Convinced of a generous spirit of confidence on the part of these representatives of both denominations, I accepted. I felt doubly honored because I have advocated merger vigorously for a generation, and labored for it in every way.

As is now known, our two boards met, and did not act in concert on the recommendation of their Nominating Committee. The Directors of the American Unitarian Association were sturdy in their support of the recommendation. The Universalist Board of Trustees insisted that it could not accept an incumbent, and presented the name of William B. Rice, a colleague and minister of our Wellesley Hills Unitarian Society, and one, like myself, who has had secondary Universalist fellowship for many years. In order to make any common report possible, the two Boards finally agreed to present both candidates. I concurred with the thought that a contested election, in addition to giving the people a choice, would provide in some ways a better chance to clarify the great opportunities confronting us.

I might ask my friends of both denominations to let me stand on my record, which is well known among Unitarians, and hardly less known among Universalists. Naturally, I feel better equipped at present than I could have been three years ago to cope with the tasks at hand. But you want to know more of the future than of the past.

I pledge my ability and my energy to the acceleration of our present remarkable growth: the further enlistment of high-caliber and devoted lay leadership; improved ministerial recruitment, training and placement procedures; and overall provision for our ministers; and the continued increase of our financial strength to implement our programs.

What else will be among my aims and aspirations? First, we must conclude the act of consolidation. We will soon be one, and our discussions of unity will be supplanted by the fact of unity. With you, I welcome this great day in the history of liberal religion.

Second, we must strengthen the continental nature of our movement without sacrificing one precious portion of local autonomy or regional initiative. Admittedly this is not easy; the path of freedom lies close to that of contentiousness. But we must, we will, find our way. And we will do it without succumbing to "bureaucratic convenience." With further progress by our newly-instituted Office of Information Services the task will be easier. When interested Unitarians and Universalists are well informed, they make intelligent and reasonable decisions.

Third, we are still committed to the essential role our new association must play in the search for peace. We are producing new materials needed for a study of this most critical problem of our generation. Even now plans are being laid for a continental ministers' seminar on arms control to be held at an early date. When C.P. Snow and Harrison Brown suggest that we may be the last adult generation on this earth, isolation from the work of nuclear control and disarmament becomes unthinkable.

Fourth, we have now established and will further support the six Study Commissions on the Free Church in a Changing World. These Unitarian Universalist Commissions reflect a deep concern for developing the relationships of our religion to the cultural values of our civilization. These commissions, with a brilliant strength in leadership will bring us closer to the affirmative guidelines we need for action.

Unitarians have now pledged more than $2,900,000 toward the furtherance of these and other programs, which will become more essential as we merge and grow.

I see a new day emerging in which we shall be less conscious of our Unitarian Universalist labels: one in which we can spread our message far beyond the old boundaries.

G. K. Chesterton suggested that if we had more visionaries among our statesmen, we might get something really practical done. How we need them in religion! We must develop mutual respect and positive good will for creative conversations among the widely divergent groups in our free denomination. That diversity is the ground for our growth in ideas. We have been moving toward more adequate and imaginative services for our members, churches and fellowships. While some would encourage us to delay that we might consolidate our strength, I believe more firmly than ever that this is not the time for institutional or religious conservation. Daring does not preclude sound financing and efficient organization, but we must develop a program commensurate with our purposes. Toward the fulfillment of these high aims I offer my whole-hearted strength.

SOURCE: "Nominees for President, U.U.A.," *Universalist Leader*, March 1961, 64–65.

Resolutions Adopted by Unitarian Universalist Association

1961

The first general assembly of the Unitarian Universalist Association elected Dana McLean Greeley as president and adopted "general resolutions" on contemporary social issues ranging from African decolonization to domestic desegregation to Medicare, which had first been proposed in the final weeks of the Eisenhower administration. The practice of issuing social statements was inherited from both predecessor denominations and can be traced back as far as the recommendations attached to the 1790 Universalist Articles of Faith. But this practice was not without controversy: Unitarians had debated the usefulness of resolutions throughout the 1950s, and in 1962 the UUA General Assembly tabled a proposed bylaw change that would have limited them to three per year. We have included the full set of 1961 resolutions as a baseline for comparison with subsequent social statements.

—Dan McKanan

MIGRATORY WORKERS

WHEREAS: Migratory workers are the most disadvantaged group in our population with below-minimum wages, sub-standard health and housing, and restricted opportunities for their children; and

WHEREAS: Protections of social legislation established for the benefit of industrial workers are non-existent for migratory workers, and such non-existence constitutes special discrimination against the agricultural worker and his family;

THEREFORE BE IT RESOLVED: That the Unitarian Universalist Association send letters to Senator Harrison Williams Jr., the Secretary of Labor, the Secretary of Agriculture and to the President's Committee on Migratory Labor, urging them to recommend to Congress passage and vigorous enforcement of the legislative program that has been drawn up by the Senate Sub-Committee on Migratory Labor which will accomplish the following:

    (a)   Provide for an agricultural minimum wage (Resolution S. 1122)
    (b)   Prohibit agricultural child labor (S. 1123)
    (c)   Provide for the education of migrant children (S. 1124)

(d) Provide for the education of migrant adults (S. 1125)

(e) Require the registration of agricultural labor contractors (S. 1126)

(f) Assist in the providing of housing for domestic farm labor (S. 1127)

(g) Make the provisions of the National Labor Relations Act applicable to agriculture (S. 1128)

(h) Provide for the stabilization of the farm work force (S. 1129)

(i) Supply improved health service for migrant families (S. 1130)

(j) Supply improved welfare services for migrant children (S. 1131)

(k) Establish a Citizen's Council on Migratory Labor (S. 1132)

VOTE: For—385; Against—15

MENTAL HEALTH

WHEREAS: Every second hospital bed in the United States is occupied by a mentally ill person with most public mental hospitals caring for 1,000 to 14,000 patients; and

WHEREAS: Medical knowledge has developed to the degree that many of the mentally ill could, with proper individual care, be returned to live useful lives in society;

THEREFORE BE IT RESOLVED: That the churches and fellowships of the Unitarian Universalist Association study their own communities to determine whether facilities and budgets are adequate for the care of mental patients within their own communities, such facilities to include psychiatric units in general hospitals, "halfway houses" for discharged mental patients, vocational and counseling services, and special classes in the public school system for emotionally disturbed and mentally retarded children;

BE IT ALSO RESOLVED: That member churches and fellowships strive to inform themselves in this field in order to give compassionate understanding towards the mentally ill as family, friends, or employers and to assist through direct volunteer service in appropriate places; and

BE IT FURTHER RESOLVED: That Unitarians and Universalists accept positions of leadership in their communities where they can influence public opinion and government agencies so that the financial and medical needs of the mentally ill may be met.

PASSED UNANIMOUSLY

CAPITAL PUNISHMENT

WHEREAS: Respect for the value of every human life must be incorporated into our laws if it is to be observed by our people; and

WHEREAS: Modern justice should concern itself with rehabilitation not retribution; and

WHEREAS: It has not been proved that fear of capital punishment is a deterrent to crime; and

WHEREAS: Human judgments are not infallible, and no penalty should be used which cannot be revoked in case of error; and

WHEREAS: Capital punishment has not always been used impartially among all economic and racial groups in America;

THEREFORE BE IT RESOLVED: That the Unitarian Universalist Association urges its churches and fellowships in the United States and Canada to exert all reasonable efforts towards the elimination of capital punishment; and

BE IT FURTHER RESOLVED: That copies of this resolution be sent to the Governors of all states in which capital punishment has not yet been eliminated, and to the Canadian Minister of Justice.

PUBLIC SCHOOL INTEGRATION

WHEREAS: Denial of equal opportunities for education on account of race or color continues to be widespread seven years after the Supreme Court's unanimous declaration that the Constitution forbids it; and

WHEREAS: Such disregard for the supreme law of the land presents a moral crisis no less than that resulting from the violation of human rights involved;

THEREFORE BE IT RESOLVED: That the Unitarian Universalist Association commends the President of the United States for public statements already made and urges his continued appropriate action to clarify the moral issues and to enlist active public support for their resolution by prompt integration of the public schools at all levels; and

BE IT FURTHER RESOLVED: That this assembly call upon the Federal Courts to implement the Supreme Court decision with speed and firmness.

VOTE: For—475; Against—34

FREEDOM OF RESIDENCE

BE IT RESOLVED: That the Unitarian Universalist Association urges its churches and fellowships to:

1. Call upon their individual members to make all housing, urban and suburban, new or old, which they control as owners, dealers, brokers, builders, or mortgagors available to any qualified person, without regard to race, color, creed or national origin.
2. Call upon all real estate dealers, brokers, and mortgagors to do the same.
3. Request their city and state legislators to repeal all existing laws requiring racial segregation and to urge the adoption of local and state laws prohibiting discrimination in housing.
4. Stimulate, encourage, and participate in educational programs, meetings, and other activities sponsored by both governmental and voluntary agencies and designed to promote equality of opportunity in housing.

ABOLITION OF THE HOUSE UN-AMERICAN ACTIVITIES COMMITTEE AND THE SENATE INTERNAL SECURITY SUB-COMMITTEE

WHEREAS: The House Un-American Activities Committee and the Senate Internal Security Sub-Committee have failed to accomplish the purposes for which they were established; and

WHEREAS: Over the years of their existence, the effect of these committees has too often been only to harass people who held unpopular opinions; and

WHEREAS: The cause of National Security has been used by these committees as an excuse to call into question long-standing individual freedoms granted under the Constitution of the United States;

THEREFORE BE IT RESOLVED: That the Unitarian Universalist Association

1. Recommends to the Congress the abolition of these two committees and
2. Urge all Unitarians and Universalists to call upon their representatives in the Senate and House of Representatives to vote against further appropriations for these committees.

VOTE: For—485; Against—43

DISARMAMENT AND TEST BAN TREATY

WHEREAS: The settlement of international conflicts by war is inconsistent with our commitments under the charter of the United Nations and the prolongation of present tensions threatens mankind with annihilation; and

WHEREAS: Weapons of mass destruction are inconsistent with our moral and religious principles; and

WHEREAS: The testing of nuclear weapons threatens mankind with disease and early death, and future generations with hereditary defects; and

WHEREAS: The continued production of armaments diverts energy and wealth from present human needs and postpones the rich future now within Man's grasp;

THEREFORE BE IT RESOLVED: That the Unitarian Universalist Association affirms its belief in total universal disarmament under controls and urges, as an initial step, that the United States Government proceed with sincere, conscientious and continuing negotiations for a treaty to effectively ban the development and testing of nuclear weapons.

AFRICA

WHEREAS: 1960 was the "Year of Africa" in that 17 new states became independent, 14 of which were admitted to the United Nations; and

WHEREAS: In other areas of Africa, notably Algeria, S. W. Africa, the Rhodesias, Mozambique and Angola, Africans are denied self-government and other basic human rights; and

WHEREAS: The newly-independent African states are greatly in need of technical and economic assistance;

THEREFORE BE IT RESOLVED: That the Unitarian Universalist Association urges:

1. That the governments of Canada and the United States tender substantial technique and economic assistance to the newly-independent African nations, to be channeled through the United Nations, and
2. That unrelenting pressure be applied to these governments to press for the political and economic freedom of those areas under colonial rule, and
3. That the newly-freed peoples of Africa, both as individuals and as nations, be accorded esteem and courtesy commensurate with the vital role they are playing in international affairs, and

4. That copies of this resolution be forwarded to the appropriate officials of the United States, Canada, the United Nations, and the newly-formed countries of Africa.

AID TO PUBLIC EDUCATION

WHEREAS: Unitarians and Universalists have historically and continuously supported our great public school system, we reaffirm our pride in our public schools and stand staunchly against any public funds through loans or grants being given to parochial or church-related schools as being unconstitutional and in violation of the long-established principle of the separation of church and state, and support the Administration bill for Federal Aid to Education.

DESEGREGATION

RESOLVED: The Unitarian Universalist Association, in its First Assembly, reaffirming its devotion to the ideal of human liberty and brotherhood, extends its firm and continuous support to its member churches and fellowships in their efforts to express this in the present drive to desegregate our public schools.

CUBA

BE IT RESOLVED: That in this troubled period of national self-examination and conflict of thought about future United States policy on Cuba, the Unitarian Universalist Association go on record as being opposed to United States military intervention, direct or indirect, in Cuba, but rather urges that any action that may be deemed necessary with respect to Cuba be sought through the Organization of American States and/or the United Nations.

VOTE: For—343; Against—70

source: "Resolutions Adopted by Unitarian Universalist Association," *Unitarian Universalist Register-Leader*, Midsummer 1961, 32–33.

DOROTHY SPOERL

"Is Our Religious Education Religious?"

1961

Dorothy Tilden Spoerl (1906–1999), a born Universalist who was ordained in 1929, was a curriculum editor for the Council of Liberal Churches and, from 1955 to 1960, editor for the New Beacon Series of the Unitarian Universalist Association. She also served churches in both Massachusetts and Vermont as a director of religious education and minister and taught at American International College and Starr King School for the Ministry. This essay was republished as a widely circulated pamphlet.

—Elizabeth M. Strong

One of the questions most often asked in our denomination is: What is religious about our religious education? To answer it, one needs to pose himself a few questions: Do you believe that religion motivates the things you do? Do you have a basically religious frame of reference, through which your values operate and through which they come to fruition in the sundry actions you perform? Most importantly, does the fact that you are a religious liberal make a difference in your behavior in personal relationships, community responsibilities, and world vision? In other words, before anyone can say whether the education he is giving his children is religious, he must decide what religion is for him.

If we accept John Dewey's statement that "religion is a quality of experience" (and thus avoid the theological definitions), the yardstick by which we measure our education becomes the actions which it motivates. If we believe, and I think most people do, that education is the process by which we share our cultural heritage, personal values, and hopes and dreams with the coming generation, religious education becomes the process by which we transmit the best that we envisage in terms that can be translated into action. The question thus resolves itself to: What factors in our society relate to the process of religious education?

Ours is a competitive society, holding out for itself the ideal of co-operation. The two do not work together, yet we train our children to compete and urge them to co-operate. From the time they are infants, we push and urge them to achievement, not merely their best, but to match (or preferably outstrip) that of their peers. We rear them in a society in which status symbols predominate, measuring too many things by monetary value and too few in spiritual terms. We strive not for perfection in science, but rather for a science that will consummate its achievements *before* the Russians. Such are the attitudes, basically, of an irreligious society.

Our religious education becomes religious if we are strengthening the remaining shreds of co-operative behavior in our children. It is religious if we are teaching them that to be different is not to be wrong. It is religious if we are teaching them that things are done for the sake of the value they have for all people.

Ours rapidly is becoming a passive society which "takes in" and "accepts" what is presented. Hours spent before a television set are having serious effect on our children because they are losing the habit of active participation both in play and thought. Television programs, teaching machines—so much of our society is based on built-in answers, prefabricated kits, numbered oil paintings!

Our religious education will become religious when we give our children opportunities for active participation in the life of home, church, and community. There is no place in our kind of religious education for predigested materials. Learning to make choices between possible answers so that one knows which is *his* answer makes for real religious education.

Many in our society are bowing before a new false god: Science. Perhaps more than any other, this question is asked of the Department of Education: "Why, when the science teaching of today is so superlative, do we still teach science in the church school?" Science can be taught in many ways, and far too often our children emerge with the view that science has the ultimate answers. Seldom in our schools does a teacher go on from the facts to the awe and wonder which those facts hold.

Our religious education is religious if it can teach science as a method, as a way of attacking a problem, a means of searching answers to the unknown. It becomes successful if we are helping children to face the unknown with curiosity rather than fear and to thrill to the struggle of the scientist.

There is a growing authoritarianism in our society, in the demands of those who would have education be more "basic," in the attempts of those who would revitalize the House Un-American Activities Committee, in the over-organized recreation and extracurricular activities of our children.

Our religious education is religious when it is the quiet searching together of teacher and children, more in the sense of the students of Abelard than in that of the test-happy students struggling for college entrance requirements. To learn the attitudes of a Jesus, a Gandhi, a Schweitzer is to begin to believe that all life is sacred.

We do not need to worry about the education we are giving our children, or be concerned about the propriety of using the adjective *religious* to describe it, if we have the faith—and the strength to implement that faith in action—in man, in the world, and in the everlasting potential of the future.

SOURCE: Dorothy Spoerl, "Is Our Religious Education Religious?" *Unitarian Register and Universalist Leader*, Midsummer 1961, 17.

Churchwoman. . . . or Churchmouse?

1962

The Unitarian and Universalist women's groups began working together soon after consolidation. As this pamphlet illustrates, they were almost immediately caught up in the new feminist consciousness. A year before Betty Friedan published The Feminine Mystique, *Unitarian Universalist women were encouraging one another to play a more assertive role in church and society, recasting the role of the church women's group as women's empowerment.*

— Dan McKanan

What do we mean, church woman . . . or church mouse [ellipsis in original]?

Quite simple! . . . The "Churchwoman" is the whole person interested in growth, study, leadership, and service; and the "mouse" is the one who is content to sit by while others build their lives to rich and enduring fulfillment.

The role of the "churchwoman" in America has historically been an important one. In no area of concern has the "hand-that-rocks-the-cradle" been such a guiding force as in the development of the liberal way of religion. With the development of the Unitarian Universalist philosophy and the growth of our denominational structure in America, women have found a place to help and be helped. Here in direct contrast to general social custom, the men of the group have welcomed the assistance, guidance, yes, even the leadership of women. The part played by the mother, housewife and homemaker in supporting her denomination as a foundation of faith for a growing family is a familiar one.

But to many women this is only a partial answer. Women of all ages, married, single, widowed, or divorced, all want different things from their church, and here, as elsewhere, the individual often feels lost or helpless unless she can communicate her thoughts to others.

Where, then, can a churchmouse best evolve into a Churchwoman?

Where indeed but in a liberal churchwomen's group. Of course, churches of almost all faiths have women's groups of some nature, but in the Unitarian Universalist churches, free-thinking women are free to shape their own activities. Even in the liberal church, however, *the voice of a group is often heard louder and clearer than the voices of individuals* and, because of a shared religious philosophy, often local groups together speak with a strong voice.

SOURCE: *Churchwoman. . . . or Churchmouse?* pamphlet published by Pacific Southwest District Unitarian Universalist Association for Alliance of Unitarian Women and Association of Universalist Women, 1962.

JAMES LUTHER ADAMS

"The Indispensable Discipline
of Social Responsibility"

1962

James Luther Adams spent much of his lifetime reflecting on the difference between democracy and totalitarianism, and he came to believe that voluntary associations—including, but not limited to, free churches—were indispensable to any democratic regime. This piece, first delivered at the University of Padua when Adams was in Italy as a Protestant observer at the Second Vatican Council, expresses that conviction against the backdrop of his experience in Nazi Germany thirty years earlier.

—Dan McKanan

In 1927 in the city of Nuremberg, six years before the National Socialists came into power, I was watching a Sunday parade on the occasion of the annual mass rally of the Nazis. Thousands of youth, as a sign of their vigor and patriotism, had walked from various parts of Germany to attend the mass meeting of the Party. As I watched the parade which lasted for four hours and which was punctuated by trumpet and drum corps made up of hundreds of Nazis, I asked some people on the sidelines to explain to me the meaning of the swastika that decorated many of the banners. Before very long I found myself engaged in a heated argument. Suddenly someone seized me from behind and pulled me by the elbows out of the group with which I was arguing. In the firm grip of someone whom I could barely see I was forced through the crowd and propelled down a side street and up into a dead-end alley. As this happened I assure you my palpitation rose quite perceptibly. I was beginning to feel Nazism existentially. At the end of the alley my uninvited host swung me around quickly, and he shouted at me in German, "You fool. Don't you know? In Germany today when you are watching a parade, you either keep your mouth shut or you get your head bashed in." I thought he was going to bash it in right there. But then his face changed into a friendly smile, and he said, "If you had continued that argument for five minutes longer, those fellows would have beaten you up." "Why did you decide to help me?" I asked. He replied, "I am an anti-Nazi. As I saw you there, getting into trouble, I thought of the times when in New York City as a sailor of the German merchant marine I received a wonderful hospitality. And I said to myself, "Here is your chance to repay that hospitality." So I grabbed you, and here we are. I am inviting you home to Sunday dinner."

This man turned out to be an unemployed worker. His home was a tenement apartment in the slums. To reach it, we climbed three flights up a staircase that was falling apart, and he ushered me into a barren room where his wife and three small children greeted their unexpected American guest in astonishment. We had the Sunday meal together, a dinner of greasy dumplings and of small beer drunk from a common jug. Within a period of two hours I learned vividly of the economic distress out of which Nazism was born. From this trade-union worker I learned also that one organization after the other that refused to bow to the Nazis was being threatened with compulsion. The totalitarian process had begun. Freedom of association was being abolished. "You keep your mouth shut, and you conform, or you get your head bashed in." A decade later in Germany I was to see at first hand the belated resistance of the churches to this attack upon freedom of speech and freedom of association.

At this juncture I had to confront a rather embarrassing question. I had to ask myself, "What in your typical behavior as an American citizen have you done that would help to prevent the rise of authoritarian government in your own country? What disciplines of democracy (except voting) have you habitually undertaken with other people which could serve in any way directly to affect public policy?" More bluntly stated: I asked myself, "What precisely is the difference between *you* and a political idiot?"

Immediately after the Second World War the Swiss theologian Karl Barth made a speaking tour in Germany, and in his talks he stressed the idea that every conscientious German citizen should now participate actively in voluntary associations committed to the task of making democracy work. I do not know whether Karl Barth as a professor in Germany practiced his own preaching when Nazism was on the rise. But in giving his admonition to the Germans after the war, he pointed to a characteristic feature of any democratic society, namely, freedom of association.

Every totalitarian theory rejects just this freedom. Indeed, the rejection of freedom of association, the rejection of the freedom to form groups that attempt democratically to affect public policy, can serve as the beginning of a definition of totalitarianism. We are familiar with the fulminations against freedom of association by Hobbes and Rousseau. Hobbes the totalitarian warns against "the great number of corporations which are as it were many lesser commonwealths in the body of a greater, like worms in the entrails of a natural man." The late Senator Joseph McCarthy worked in the spirit of Hobbes when he tried to smother freedom of association.

As against Hobbes the theorists of democracy have asserted that only through the exercise of freedom of association can consent of the governed become effective; only through the exercise of freedom of association can the citizen in a democracy participate in the process that gives shape to public opinion and to public policy. For this reason we may speak of the voluntary association as a distinctive and indispensable institution of democratic society.

*   *   *

Any healthy democratic society is a multi-group society. One finds in it business corporations, religious associations, trade unions, educational associations, recreational, philanthropic, protective and political associations, and innumerable social clubs. These associations are, or claim to be, voluntary; they presuppose freedom on the part of the individual to be or not to be a member, to join or withdraw, or to consort with others to form a new association. By way of contrast the state and the family, for example, are as associations involuntary, and in some countries the church also is virtually involuntary. Every person willy-nilly belongs to a particular state and to a particular family. It is not a matter of choice whether he will belong to these two associations. In this sense they are involuntary. There are other associations, to be sure, which it is difficult to classify under either category, voluntary or involuntary. Taken together, these associations, involuntary and voluntary, represent the institutional articulation of the pluralistic society.

The appearance of the voluntary association in Western society did not come without a struggle. The initial demand for voluntary association came from the churches of the left wing of the Reformation. These churches insisted that religion, in order to be a matter of choice, must be free from state control. Therefore they demanded the separation of church and state. This struggle for freedom of religious association continued for over two centuries. It was accompanied or followed by a struggle for freedom of economic association, for freedom to establish political parties, for freedom of workers to form unions, and for freedom to institute reforms in society. . . .

The voluntary association at its best offers an institutional framework within which the give and take of discussion may be promoted, an institutional framework within which a given consensus may be brought under criticism and be subjected to change. It offers a means for bringing a variety of perspectives into interplay. It offers the means of breaking through old social structures in order to meet new needs. It is a means of dispersing power, in the sense that power is the capacity to participate in making social decisions. It is the training ground of the skills that are required for stable social existence in a democracy. In short, the voluntary association is a means for the institutionalizing of *gradual* revolution.

*   *   *

The sinfulness of man expresses itself, then, in the indifference of the average citizen who is so impotent, so idiotic in the Greek sense, as not to exercise his freedom of association for the sake of the general welfare and for the sake of becoming a responsible self.

233

Ernst Troeltsch has made a distinction that is of prime significance here. He distinguishes between what he calls subjective and objective virtues. Subjective virtues are virtues that can be exhibited in immediate person-to-person relations. Objective virtues require an institution for their expression. Thus, from the larger human perspective we can say that the isolated good man is a chimera. There is no such thing as a good man as such. There is only the good father or the good mother, the good physician or the good plumber, the good churchman, the good citizen. The good man of the subjective virtues, to be sure, provides the personal integrity of the individual. Without it the viable society is not possible. But from the point of view of the *institutional* commonwealth the merely good individual is good for nothing. Moreover, the narrow range of responsibility of the man who confines attention merely to his family and his job serves to dehumanize him. This narrowness of range and of responsibility is neatly symbolized in an epitaph reported from a cemetery tombstone in Scotland:

Here lies John MacDonald
Born a man
Died a grocer

At the outset I spoke of the experience in pre-Nazi Germany when a man told me, "you either keep your mouth shut, or you get your head bashed in." In the democratic society the non-participating citizen bashes his own head in. The living democratic society requires the disciplines of discussion and common action for the determination of policy. The differences between men are determined by the quality and direction of their participation. In this sense we may understand the New Testament word, "By their fruits shall you know them"; but to this word we should add the admonition, By their groups shall you know them.

SOURCE: James Luther Adams, "The Indispensable Discipline of Social Responsibility," *Journal of the Liberal Ministry* 6 (Spring 1966): 80–83, 86.

ANGUS MACLEAN

"The Method Is the Message"

1962

Angus Hector MacLean (1892–1969) was raised a Presbyterian but later
became an ordained Universalist minister. He was a professor of religious
education and dean at St. Lawrence University Theological School from 1928
to 1960. During this time he prepared ministers to engage in and value reli-
gious education, leading many of them to be certified as religious educators
when they were ordained to the ministry. His books, The Wind in Both Ears
and The New Era in Religious Education, *served as foundational texts for*
Unitarian Universalists in the second half of the twentieth century. Further
Reading: Roberta M. Nelson, ed., Claiming the Past, Shaping the Future:
Four Eras in Liberal Religious Education, 1790–1999 *(Providence: LREDA/*
Blackstone Editions, 2006); Richard S. Gilbert, In the Midst of a Journey:
Readings in Unitarian Universalist Faith Development *(Bloomington, IN:*
iUniverse, 2013).

—Elizabeth M. Strong

This is a restatement of the main contention in an address given before the Universalist Sabbath School Union of Greater Boston at its centennial dinner meeting held
in Arlington Street Church, October 29, 1951.

* * *

I claim here simply that the effective method of teaching values is itself the
living exercise of such values. . . .

The contention that method can have value content, curriculum content, if
you like, should be of special interest to a faith that has abandoned creedal finalities
and moralistic fixities and judgments in favor of what is called "Openness." If this
openness be emptiness, we haven't even a myth to cherish. . . .

Openness seems like a requirement of human nature. Man cannot seem to
contend with reality without recognition of the limitations of his powers of discernment in one way or another. . . . This necessity rests in the nature of human perception and in the uniqueness of individual experience as well as in the nature of truth
itself.

* * *

So, I argue, openness in religion as in all fields of experience, is required by the
nature of things. . . .

But what is this openness? Something to be welcomed or an inescapable some-thing to be feared? Does it mean that we liberals despairing of historic doctrines walk without truth, and face the coming years without historic ties? . . . Man . . . needs historic roots. . . . Man will just not go on without something that carries from today to tomorrow. He'll go back to old certainties and absurdities first. What I am saying, is that unless this openness is itself a life-giving kind of content we are as badly off as we ever were.

The issue is a serious one for us, for one of the big words in our openended faith is *confidence*. Upon what can confidence rest? . . . There is an expanding body of truth, of course, but would anyone dare say any of it would never need reformulation? *There are methods of ascertaining truth that are truths themselves*, and are among the most important truths in the world. And may not this be even more true in religion?

※　※　※

The great body of our common faith is made up of such insights, and not one of them tells us that Heaven is up or down, or so many cubits this way or that; they do not say that God is three "persons" or one, and is or is not, nor do they say when the world was created or what happened when we shall shuffle off this mortal coil. They are wise ways of living, laden with the victories and defeats of the human spirit throughout the centuries. In the broad sense of the word, they are principles of method. They suggest what I have in mind; namely, that attitudes and procedures that have caught up the best fruits of human experience can be seen for what they are, the central stabilizing factors in our faith, as indeed in many faiths.

※　※　※

Let me say again, that although we have difficulty in being certain about the nature of man or God, or in even finding grounds for hope for peace of the world, we *have* discovered assured ways of addressing ourselves to life, and these should be recognized as being at the very heart of our religion, and of our religious education efforts. . . .

I have labored so far over the message of the church because I believe the appro-priate methodology is implicit in that message. I have really been hinting at teaching relationships necessary between persons as they face the mysteries of life and death. To teach the great learnings of humanity; that love is the greatest thing in the world; that justice for all in the long run serves all best; that whenever goodwill rises to dominate the councils of men, they are drawn together, and that they are separated by suspicion and fear and greed and domination; that man's nature requires freedom for growth and that without it he degenerates or fails to develop his powers; that man can find his own way with serenity of spirit and leave others to do the same without breach of fellowship; that we can accept wisdom from any time or culture and have fellowship with people who differ from us. The business of communicating such values becomes, in a contingent sense, as important as the values themselves, and if

236

one pursues this business far enough he will find out that the living of values and their communications are inseparable. . . .

Such values as we are concerned with cannot be communicated except as they are set in operation, given life, in the human relations in which teachers and taught are involved, that they cannot be, that they have no existence except as forms of human relations. Love exists only when someone is loved. Freedom exists when relations worthy of that name govern communication and action between persons. Such values are communicated only when "live," if I may borrow and somewhat distort a TV term. This is why I have so often said that a faith which is so largely a faith of dynamic ethical and intellectual values, should make method the heart of the curriculum.

It should be obvious that when I speak of method I have not in mind a bag of tricks by which we hope to transfer something from one mind to another. In a teaching situation . . . values always become active, that is, some kinds of values. These are the ones that tend to be communicated. . . .

How often we have said that the home is a most powerful teaching agency in so far as basic value patterns are concerned! This power roots in the fact that the values expressed between the stove and the sink, the nursery and the bath, and between the soup and the nuts, are the ones that are absorbed by the young as ways of living. . . .

Look at a school situation in which children are guided in the study of the Declaration of Independence and the Constitution of the USA . . . and at the same time, are never permitted to question a teacher's statements or offer an opinion. . . . What happens to the effort to teach democracy? . . . Whether the teaching be good or bad it carries the values inherent in the teacher-student relations be they acknowledged or not. . . .

Along with direct experience comes appreciation, reflection, inquiry, insight, imaginative play, and devotion. And these require words, concepts, ideas, principles, etc., to help identify, evaluate, and simplify experiences to make their fruits more available for meeting new experiences. Words are so important that we should have little capacity for thought, for moral self-direction without them. Knowledge and ideas and insights enrich and illumine experiences, skills implement them, and devotion ties them together and elevates them to the level at which a reaction to such a simple things as a flower may involve Heaven and earth and all the mysteries, joys, and tragedies in which one is personally involved. . . .

I am interested in a process through which the learner directly experiences value, and as a result is in a better position to learn and use words and concepts. I am also interested in a process that makes assets rather than liabilities of the child's restless energy, his activism, his consuming curiosity, his love of fun, his tendency to dramatize life, his constructive impulses. The child's nature is in harmony with the process by which "live" values are communicated.

I am interested also in a process by which attempted teaching and learning are not in conflict. . . . Such conflict is born of the failure to live the values with children which we wish them to acquire. So I am interested in the kind of teaching situation that uses a child's learning energies. Such a situation will permit a significant percentage of time for work with hands, for talk, and free movement whenever any or all of these are called for by the task in hand. It will be a place in which teacher and child can respond to each other in value terms; where one can think freely, where the teacher loves his or her charges and exercises patience and understanding; where much is expected, and life exciting; where a teacher confronts realities, ranging from the grassfrog or angleworm to the mysteries of time and eternity, along with the child; where a wisdom-communicating relationship exists.

A father was confronted by his five-year old son with the question, "If God made everything, who made God?" So he asks me what answer to give him. My answer was for the father. I told him that the verbal answer he might give would probably have little significance, but that taking advantage of the relationship the question offered for facing life's mysteries together was the only effective answer. . . .

It was with all this in mind that I so often urged the greater and wiser use of arts and crafts and enterprises of all sorts in the teaching of religion. I fully appreciate the psychological value of creative play and free expression, but what I always had mostly in mind was the natural human setting for living the values we talk about. . . .

The subject matter may be what you please at any time . . . but since our methods communicate the values implicit in them, such matters as love, the ability to reason, the experience and appreciation of freedom, mutual tolerance and understanding, justice, etc. must be taught by being used all the time in all the classes and all the courses. If anything was ever worthy of being called the "core curriculum" this is.

SOURCE: Angus MacLean, *The Method Is the Message* (Boston: Unitarian Universalist Association Department of Education, 1962), 5–9, 11–15.

General Resolution Commending
Pope John XXIII's Encyclical
"Peace on Earth"
1963

In October 1962, the recently elected Pope John XXIII opened the Second Vatican Council, promising an updating of Catholic practice in dialogue with the modern world. Unitarian Universalists were forced to rethink the long-standing assumption that "American freedom" was incompatible with "Catholic power," as Paul Blanshard had put it in the first of a series of books published by Beacon Press between 1949 and 1973. This resolution highlighted John XXIII's final encyclical, which harmonized with Unitarian Universalist positions on nuclear nonproliferation and on the goal of world community.

—Dan McKanan

WHEREAS, the Encyclical of His Holiness, Pope John XXIII, entitled "Peace on Earth" issued on April 11, 1963, and concerned with "establishing universal peace in truth, justice, charity, and liberty," is a wise and noble utterance and is directed not only to the faithful of the Roman Catholic Church, but to all men of goodwill; and

WHEREAS, this Encyclical calls for the development through the United Nations of a "public authority of the world community" . . . "having world-wide power and endowed with the proper means for the efficacious pursuit of its objective which is the universal good in concrete form" and which "must tackle and solve problems of economic, social, political, and cultural character which are posed by the universal common good," a public authority "inspired by sincere and real impartiality" whose "purpose is to create, on a world basis, an environment in which the public authorities of each political community, its citizens and intermediate associations, can carry out their tasks, fulfill their duties and exercise their rights with greater security"; and

WHEREAS, such an organized common peace with liberty and justice for all, in a world community united under law, through the development of the United Nations, has long been a declared objective of the Unitarian Universalist Association, its antecedent organizations, and its member churches and fellowships; now

THEREFORE BE IT RESOLVED: That the Unitarian Universalist Association gathered in General Assembly in May, 1963, rejoices with His Holiness, Pope John XXIII, with the members of the Roman Catholic Church, and with all men of good-will everywhere of every race, nation, or faith, in this great statement of the imperative requirement of this age and hour, and pledges itself, and calls upon its member churches and fellowships, to work diligently and tirelessly for such organized world peace with justice under law through the United Nations until the day comes when it shall have been attained.

SOURCE: Unitarian Universalist Social Justice Statements, uua.org/statements/commending -pope-john-xxiiis-encyclical-peace-earth

General Resolution on the Commission on Religion and Race
1963

Throughout the 1960s, Unitarian Universalist General Assemblies issued resolutions in support of the civil rights movement. The 1961 resolutions on public school integration, open housing, and desegregation were followed by a broader 1962 statement on civil rights. Then, in 1963, the General Assembly institutionalized this commitment by creating a Commission on Religion and Race. The following year saw a resolution endorsing a "Freedom Fund" to garner support for the Commission. The National Council of Churches, of which the UUA was not a member, had recently created a body with the same name, and both commissions sought to make the economic and organizational resources of the churches available to the movement. The Commission's work prepared the way for the massive Unitarian Universalist presence in Selma in 1965 and for the gatherings at which Unitarian Universalists began to grapple with the Black Power movement. Further Reading: James F. Findlay, Church People in the Struggle: The National Council of Churches and the Black Freedom Movement, 1950–1970 *(New York: Oxford University Press, 1993).*

—Dan McKanan

WHEREAS, the Unitarian and Universalist movements have historically affirmed the supreme worth of every human personality, the dignity of man, the use of the democratic method in human relationships, and the ideals of brotherhood, justice and peace; and

WHEREAS, refusal to welcome persons into membership in any of our churches or fellowships because of race, color or national origin would contradict our historical testimony and the declared constitutional purposes of our Association;

THEREFORE BE IT RESOLVED: That all member congregations of the Unitarian Universalist Association be charged to declare and practice their faith in the dignity and worth of every person and that all member congregations of our denominations are hereby strongly urged to welcome into their membership and full participation persons without regard to race, color, or national origin; and

BE IT FURTHER RESOLVED: That, to implement the declared constitutional purposes of our Association:

1. The President, with the concurrence of the Board of Trustees, be instructed to appoint a Commission on Religion and Race, composed of at least seven members, whose duty shall be to explore, develop, stimulate and implement programs and actions to promote the complete integration of Negroes and other minority persons into our congregations, denominational life, ministry and into the community;
2. This Commission be adequately financed within the budget of our Association; and
3. The report of the action and future program of the Commission be conveyed to the 1964 General Assembly; and

BE IT FURTHER RESOLVED: That all groups applying for membership in the Association be informed by the Board of Trustees of the Unitarian Universalist Association before being accepted into membership of the Unitarian Universalist Association on the stated policy of the Association, which welcomes all qualified persons, regardless of race, color, or place of national origin, into the membership of the churches, fellowships and organization.

SOURCE: Unitarian Universalist Social Justice Statements, uua.org/statements/commission-religion-and-race

General Resolution on Reform
of Abortion Statutes
1963

*This resolution was the first in a long series of denominational statements
related to reproductive freedom and justice. Abortion had been criminalized
in the United States since around 1880, but women continued to seek illegal
and often unsafe abortions throughout the twentieth century. In the early
1960s, advocates of more permissive laws generally stressed the dangers of
back-alley abortions and the professional prerogatives of doctors—arguments
that are central to this statement. An explicitly feminist case for abortion
rights was articulated by "Jane," an underground abortion service launched
by the Chicago Women's Liberation Union in 1963. Religious support for
abortion rights centered on the Clergy Consultation Service, a network of
ministers who helped women obtain safe abortions. The General Assembly
expressed its support for such activities in 1969 and explicitly endorsed the*
Roe v. Wade *decision in 1973. Further Reading: Megan Powers, ed., Ameri-*
can Social Movements: The Abortion Rights Movement *(San Diego, CA:
Greenhaven Press, 2005).*

—Dan McKanan

WHEREAS, we as Unitarian Universalists are deeply concerned for dignity and
rights of human beings; and

WHEREAS, the laws which narrowly circumscribe or completely prohibit termination of pregnancy by qualified medical practitioners are an affront to human life and
dignity; and

WHEREAS, these statutes drive many women in the United States and Canada to
seek illegal abortions with increased risk of death, while others must travel to distant
lands for lawful relief;

BE IT THEREFORE RESOLVED: That the Unitarian Universalist Association
support enactment of a uniform statute making abortion legal if:

1. There would be grave impairment of the physical or mental health of the
   mother;
2. The child would be born with a serious physical or mental defect;

3. Pregnancy resulted from rape or incest;
4. There exists some other compelling reason—physical, psychological, mental, spiritual, or economic.

SOURCE: Unitarian Universalist Social Justice Statements, uua.org/statements/reform-abortion-statutes

KENNETH L. PATTON

A Religion for One World: Art and Symbols for a Universal Religion

1964

*In 1949, Kenneth Leo Patton (1911–1994) launched a pilot project in Boston
to revitalize Universalism. At the invitation of Clinton Lee Scott and the Massachusetts Universalist Convention, he set out to serve religious liberals there
who were hungry for a faith that was bold, broad, and engaging. An artist by
temperament and a prophet by calling, Patton had already brought a creative humanist voice to the First Unitarian Church in Madison, Wisconsin. In
Boston he became a leading proponent of a "new Universalism." He and
pioneering congregants offered a fresh model of ministry to liberal religionists
at large, creating a temple at the Charles Street Meeting House for "a religion for one world." The Meeting House and its minister were not without
controversy. Patton's prickly personality was a liability and many colleagues
did not appreciate the new thing being created on Charles Street. After fifteen
years at the Meeting House, Patton went on to serve the Unitarian Society of
Ridgewood, New Jersey, until his retirement in 1986. The venture on Charles
Street shuttered in the 1970s, but the experiment left an indelible imprint
on Unitarian Universalism. Further Reading: Maryell Cleary, ed.,* A Bold
Experiment: The Charles Street Universalist Meeting House *(Chicago:
Meadville Lombard Theological School Press, 2002).*

— Shari Woodbury

Today a universal and international world religion is no more an impossibility than
is the United Nations in the political world. It will have small beginnings, but those
beginnings are already starting to emerge. It will be the work of the liberals of various cultures, for internationalism and universalism are liberal sentiments and disciplines. Orthodox and conservative religions are isolationist, or else rely upon religious
imperialism and colonialism. Liberalism, like science, is tolerant and inclusive in its
outreach. It seeks to receive teaching, not to proselytize. It seeks to join, not to conquer and submerge others.

* * *

An increasing number of people are dissatisfied with any religion or world view
that establishes one tradition as supreme. In the West they have disassociated themselves from Christianity. They do not deny that Christianity possesses many virtues,

but they no longer wish to be named Christians or to be limited to Christian beliefs. They call themselves liberals and "universalists." . . .

The major argument within the [Unitarian Universalist] Association centers on whether Unitarian Universalism shall be a world religion or the liberal wing of Protestant Christianity. The "universalists" desire a fellowship that will include liberals who have developed from Confucian, Hindu, Taoist, Buddhist, Shinto, and Islamic religious backgrounds, even as we have come out of Christian and Jewish traditions. None of these people would seek to identify themselves with the religion they had outgrown, the religion whose dogmatism and provincialism they had repudiated. They would declare themselves to be members of a universal and world religion which included the religious ideals and traditions of all peoples.

*   *   *

The experiments at the Charles Street Meeting House, Unitarian Universalist, in Boston, Massachusetts, attempt to combine the art, literature, idealism, philosophies, music, and symbolism of all the world's religions into a religion for one world. Although we are ill educated and naïve, our intentions are creative and honest. In an experimental venture we become educated as we proceed.

*   *   *

Those who believed in and worked in the League of Nations, and those associated with its successor, the United Nations, are the pioneers of a new kind of human loyalty, loyalty to the race as a whole. Their idealism and commitment to the goal of world unity, world law, and world brotherhood increase one's faith that humanity can grow into such character and imagination as will be needed. If these comparatively few people can respond with an idealism that is nothing short of religious, then potentially all men can rise one day to attain the reality in the concept of "one world—one humanity."

*   *   *

Some of us, quite aware that we are adding new dimensions to an old name and movement, believe that the name Universalism must expand to include these new "universals," such as universal brotherhood, universal peace, universal welfare, universal health, universal freedom, universal security, universal science and understanding. We are committed to "the truth known and to be known," and therefore we feel no hesitancy in demanding that the basic ideals and concepts of Universalism grow. . . . No loyalty and denominationalism of another day can be allowed to bar us from the loyalties and identities that our own age requires of us, and these cannot be less than world-wide.

*   *   *

The answer to the question "Does religion need symbols?" can be given dogmatically. Religion cannot operate without symbols. The question is not whether we use symbols but what kinds of symbols we will employ.

246

We should have reached an age of enlightenment in the twentieth century where ancient tribal taboos no longer inflict their prejudices upon us. But this is not the case, for even those who call themselves "liberals" still react with violent aversion to the use of symbols as such. They are simply one form of communication, a form of language, and they are good or bad only in terms of whether or not their usage is enlightened or corrupt.

Those of us who dwell in the open, non-supernatural world of naturalism will mistrust any symbolism that leans toward the occult. We will want symbols that have clear and definite denotata, even as we desire definite and determinable realities to lie behind our words and rhetoric. But we should not confuse the necessity of ridding symbols of their superstitious overlay with eliminating symbols themselves. . . .

The Charles Street Meeting House in Boston . . . has universal symbols, such as the atom, the nebula, the earth, and the circle, but also includes the basic symbols of all the major human religions of all ages and places.

We have assembled sixty-five symbols from the various world religions, and additional symbols relating to the various activities, concepts, and ideals of man and the processes of nature. Likewise the collection of religious art from the many cultures of the race, ancient and modern—although within these collections are hundreds of different symbolisms—comprises one single symbol: a symbol of one world. The entire auditorium, with all its symbols and artistic decorations, is a symbol of oneness, of one nature, one world, one fellowship of life, one human race, one human culture, and one human religion. . . . Underlying all the various sciences is the presumption of the basic unity of science. Even so, on a religious level, a universal religion must find a way to effectively symbolize the unity that prevails within all the diversity of the cultures, arts, ethical systems, and religious institutions of humanity. The temple, in all its detail, must have the ultimate integrity of a single symbol. . . .

Liberal religionists lack appreciation of the aesthetic necessities in the development and motivation of human groups. Although their beliefs are highly principled and intelligent, they do not attract or stir any large numbers of people because they have not discovered and exploited their effective symbolism. Ideas and ideals need to be caught up in, to be enlarged and glorified in, symbols, rituals, and songs. The translations and restatements of ideals need not distort and sentimentalize them. The finest poetic images do not caricature the object or emotion portrayed, but enlighten and clarify it, enabling it to be discerned in a transparent and lucid reality. Thus seen, it carries an immediacy and solidity of impact that no intellectual abstraction ever possesses.

The great and conclusive issues in our struggle for survival in the atomic age are root and stock a matter of symbols. They are a matter of supplying the minds of men with the concepts and reasons why there must be a gathering of the nations. They are a matter of providing the symbols for the focusing of emotions and loyalties and dreams upon the image of one human family.

Social action consists not only of good deeds and the espousing of reformist causes. Social action is participation in the very construction of society and entails concerns with elaborating the symbols whereby society thinks, feels, and is moved to act.

* * *

Upon being introduced to the Meeting House project in collecting and integrating the art and symbols of the world religions, people have asked, "But isn't this eclectic?" The question seems to imply that something eclectic is superficial and less "real" emotionally and intellectually than the integral cultural practice of an ethnic group. The answer is no. We believe that the religions and cultures of humanity are one interrelated structure. Their uniting identities are more pervasive and enduring than their differences. . . .

The paths of the earth's peoples cross and recross as they travel over the same plot of earth. For a million years men have been in constant interrelation and intermixture. The restless migration of the peoples, their trade, travel, and conquest, have brought about a continual inbreeding of language, mores, institutions, inventions, arts, and personality traits. Even where there has been comparatively extended isolation, as with the Australian aborigines and the Indians of the Americas, it has been only a matter of degree, not an absolute. The most extravagant variations known due to such isolation are not sufficient to alter the judgment of the anthropologists on the essential unity of human culture.

In gathering together in one setting the symbols, art, music, literature, and moral wisdom of the family of man, we are not trying to paste together inherently unrelated ideas and histories. We do not have to *join* these together, because they are one continuous fabric. We are merely tracing the existing connections of a structure that never has been destroyed. We do not call it eclecticism when a doctor examines the liver, heart, lungs, blood, stomach, and intestines in order to determine our state of health. They are all part of one organism, and the health of one depends upon the health of all. Even so, in history, culture, and religion mankind is one organism. The analogy cannot be carried too far, but we cannot appreciate the symbolism of our own group without knowing the symbolism of the entire human group. We cannot understand our own tongue without knowledge of the great network of tongues that comprise human speech. To explore the traditions of neighboring cultures is to explore our own culture, since they have grown with it in the same great matrix of human history. . . .

Man's cultural differences would be inherently creative and fertile, were we to allow them to freely mix and stimulate each other. It is only man's fear and habitual stupidities and antagonisms that create dangers out of the cultural divergences that exist.

* * *

A religion suitable for the dimensions and needs of one world will be the most difficult and notable religion humanity has yet devised. There have been suggestions of a universal religion in the tribal and cultural religions of the past. Confucius acclaimed all the men of the four seas as his brothers. The Jews affirmed that God had made of one people all nations. But even the verbalism of universal brotherhood and love has been rare, and too often it has been couched in the terms of a universal missionary enterprise to convert all humanity to the one true faith.

* * *

A clue to an answer is found in the fact that there are a few people who do seem to have concern, affection, and conscience regarding the whole of humanity. Such scope of religious devotion has been attributed to Jesus, Gandhi, and Schweitzer, and it is undoubtedly a characteristic of other people less well known. If these persons can think, feel, and behave, then we know that this universality is a potentiality of human nature, at least in its highest development. And religious idealism should be the apex of our striving as human beings, not some level of mediocrity.

* * *

Here is a task, of moral, aesthetic, sociological, and philosophical inventiveness: to create and apply the symbols needed, and through education and association to build in people that enlargement, those attitudes, that "posture of mentality," that will enable them to have compassion for all mankind, without which universal religion is but idealistic twaddle, true "globaloney." . . .

Only when the mystic finds in his culture such universal symbols, such universal attitudes and convictions, will his mystical experience support and enwrap these ideals. Our mystical intuitions and sense of reality work intimately with our intellectual understanding and convictions. They work in and through the symbols, concepts, thought patterns, even prejudices of the culture within which they arise and develop. . . .

There is only one weaving. Thought and science are the warp, and the emotions and mysticism are the woof, and together they weave a cloak to cover the shivering of humanity's alarm. . . .

Can we create the windows, paintings, sculptures, chalices, the songs, anthems, meditations, the shapes of assembly, the styles of group behavior and organization, that will declare our membership in humanity, our kinship to all living creatures, and our at-home-ness in the universe? . . .

If we do, a new generation of religious mystics will arise, whose mystic vision will be the single family of man, living in the wide and sun-warmed world, husband-men of the one large farm of the world, citizens of the commonwealth of man. And these mystics will find in themselves a fire, a vision, that will lighten their own minds and imaginations, and they will touch unto like fire all those upon whom their words fall, all those upon whom the doves of their compassion alight. Men will move in freedom amidst their dreams. Slowly their dreams will take shape upon the earth, and paths of further growth will be opened, and another and yet another vision of morality and splendor and strength will spring up in awakened minds and hearts.

SOURCE: Kenneth L. Patton, A *Religion for One World: Art and Symbols for a Universal Religion* (Boston: Beacon Press, 1964), 1–4, 21–22, 56–58, 61–62, 65–66, 68, 70–72, 158–59, 165–66.

General Resolution on Vietnam
1964

United States military involvement in Vietnam began in 1950 and intensi-
fied after an American destroyer battled North Vietnamese ships in the Gulf
of Tonkin in 1964, which prompted Congress to authorize the deployment
of ground troops. Beginning in that year, General Assemblies issued nearly
annual statements on the war, expressing at first concern and eventually
adamant opposition. In 1968, the General Assembly called for an uncondi-
tional end to bombing and a "speedy and complete withdrawal" of troops. In
1969 it called for an end to the draft, and in 1970 it condemned war crimes in
Vietnam and the expansion of the war into Laos and Cambodia. Further
Reading: Who Spoke Up? American Protest against the War in Vietnam,
1963–1975 *(Holt, Rinehart and Winston, 1985); Charles DeBenedetti, An*
American Ordeal: The Antiwar Movement of the Vietnam Era *(Syracuse,*
NY: Syracuse University Press, 1990).

—Dan McKanan

WHEREAS, the political and military situation in South Vietnam is steadily deteri-
orating; and

WHEREAS, the danger of enlargement of the present war into a multi-national
conflict is ominously increasing; and

WHEREAS, the intent of the Geneva Conference of 1954 was to neutralize the
whole Indochinese peninsula;

THEREFORE BE IT RESOLVED: That we urge the United States government to
reconsider its policy in Vietnam and to explore solutions other than military; and

BE IT FURTHER RESOLVED: That we urge the United States government to
express its wish to participate in a reconvened Geneva Conference to consider the
demilitarization and neutralization, under international guarantees, of Cambodia,
Laos, and Vietnam.

SOURCE: Unitarian Universalist Social Justice Statements, uua.org/statements/Vietnam

MARTIN LUTHER KING, JR.

"A Witness to the Truth"

1965

The voting rights movement in rural Selma, Alabama, began in January 1965. On February 18, African-American activist Jimmie Lee Jackson was shot by a state trooper. He died a week later, and Martin Luther King, Jr., responded by calling on the leaders of predominantly white denominations to join in a protest march from Selma to Montgomery. Forty Unitarian Universalist ministers were among the 450 religious leaders who answered the call and participated in the march that was violently turned back at the Edmund Pettus Bridge on March 9. Later that night, Unitarian Universalist ministers James Reeb, Clark Olsen, and Orloff Miller, all of them white, were assaulted by segregationists. Reeb died from his injuries, and King delivered this eulogy at Selma's Brown Chapel on March 15, as hundreds more Unitarian Universalists streamed to Selma. On March 25, protesters reached the state capital in Montgomery, and that evening another white Unitarian Universalist, Viola Liuzzo, was murdered as she prepared to drive marchers home. Further Reading: Mark D. Morrison-Reed, The Selma Awakening: How the Civil Rights Movement Tested and Changed Unitarian Universalism *(Boston: Skinner House, 2014); David J. Garrow,* Protest at Selma: Martin Luther King, Jr., and the Voting Rights Act of 1965 *(New Haven, CT: Yale University Press, 1978).*

—Dan McKanan

And, if he should die,
Take his body and cut it into little stars.
He will make the face of heaven so fine
That all the world will be in love with night.

These beautiful words from Shakespeare's *Romeo and Juliet* so eloquently describe the radiant life of James Reeb. He entered the stage of history just thirty-eight years ago, and in the brief years that he was privileged to act on this mortal stage, he played his part exceedingly well. James Reeb was martyred in the Judeo-Christian faith that all men are brothers. His death was a result of a sensitive religious spirit. His crime was that he dared to live his faith; he placed himself alongside the disinherited black brethren of this community.

The world is aroused over the murder of James Reeb, for he symbolizes the forces of goodwill in our nation. He demonstrated the conscience of the nation. He was an attorney for the defense of the innocent in the court of world opinion. He was a witness to the truth that men of different races and classes might live, eat, and work together as brothers.

James Reeb could not be accused of being only concerned about justice for Negroes away from home. He and his family live in Roxbury, Massachusetts, a predominantly Negro community. [They] devoted their lives to aiding families in low-income housing areas. Again, we must ask the question: Why must good men die for doing good? "O Jerusalem, why did you murder the prophets and persecute those who come to preach your salvation?" So the Reverend James Reeb has something to say to all of us in his death.

Naturally, we are compelled to ask the question, *Who* killed James Reeb? The answer is simple and rather limited when we think of the *who*. He was murdered by a few sick, demented, and misguided men who have the strange notion that you express dissent through murder. There is another haunting, poignant, desperate question we are forced to ask this afternoon, that I asked a few days ago as we funeralized James Jackson. It is the question, *What* killed James Reeb? When we move from the who to the what, the blame is wide and the responsibility grows.

James Reeb was murdered by the indifference of every minister of the gospel who has remained silent behind the safe security of stained-glass windows. He was murdered by the irrelevancy of a church that will stand amid social evil and serve as a taillight rather than a headlight, an echo rather than a voice. He was murdered by the irresponsibility of every politician who has moved down the path of demagoguery, who has fed his constituents the stale bread of hatred and the spoiled meat of racism. He was murdered by the brutality of every sheriff and law enforcement agent who practices lawlessness in the name of law. He was murdered by the timidity of a federal government that can spend millions of dollars a day to keep troops in South Vietnam yet cannot protect the lives of its own citizens seeking constitutional rights. Yes, he was even murdered by the cowardice of every Negro who tacitly accepts the evil of the system of segregation, who stands on the sidelines in the midst of a mighty struggle for justice.

So in his death, James Reeb says something to each of us, black and white alike— says that we must substitute courage for caution, says to us that we must be concerned not merely about who murdered him but about the system, the way of life, the philosophy which produced the murder. His death says to us that we must work passionately, unrelentingly, to make the American dream a reality, so he did not die in vain.

* * *

One day the history of this great period of social change will be written in all of its completeness. On that bright day our nation will recognize its real heroes. They will be thousands of dedicated men and women with a noble sense of purpose that enables them to face fury and hostile mobs with the agonizing loneliness that characterizes the life of the pioneers. They will be faceless, anonymous, relentless, young people, black and white, who have temporarily left behind the towers of learning to storm the barricades of violence. They will be old, oppressed, battered Negro women, symbolized in a seventy-two-year-old Negro woman in Montgomery, Alabama, who rose up with a sense of dignity, and with the people who decided not to ride the segregated buses, who responded with ungrammatical profundity to one who inquired about her weariness, "My feets is tired, but my soul is rested." They will be ministers of the gospel, priests, rabbis, and nuns, who are willing to march for freedom, to go to jail for conscience's sake. One day the South will know from these dedicated children of God courageously protesting segregation, they were in reality standing up for the best in the American dream, standing up with the most sacred values in our Judeo-Christian heritage, thereby carrying our whole nation back to those great wells of democracy which were dug deep by the Founding Fathers in the formulation of the Constitution and the Declaration of Independence. When this glorious story is written, the name of James Reeb will stand as a shining example of manhood at its best.

SOURCE: *Witnessing for the Truth: Martin Luther King, Jr., Unitarian Universalism, and Beacon Press* (Boston: Beacon Press, 2014), 11–13, 15.

LON RAY CALL

"Fellowships: Yesterday, Today and Tomorrow—With the Accent on Yesterday"

1967

Two decades after launching the Unitarian fellowship movement, Lon Ray Call reflected on what he saw as the fellowships' contribution to a revitalized denomination.

—Avery (Pete) Guest

It has been said by way of endorsement of fellowships that they are creative, and indeed they are. I recall that Emerson yearned for a church to come which he said would be "without shawms or psaltery or sackbut" but which he prophesied "will have science for symbol and illustration, and fast enough gather beauty, music, picture, poetry." He must have been dreaming about fellowships. I have served as visiting preacher for many a fellowship and have never yet been handed a shawm, or a psaltery or even a sackbut. And I have seen an amazing development of what at least passes for beauty, passes for music, pictures and poetry, and I have encountered a lot of scientific orientation. Emerson, alas, should be living, at this hour.

It has been said that fellowships help strengthen in religious ways people who are naturally shy. . . . Men and women who in their wildest moments never dreamed of preaching a sermon find themselves doing just that. . . .

Furthermore, not only have the modest ones been brought forward but there have been many instances when exceptionally able laymen have been catapulted into positions of leadership not only at the local level but throughout the denomination. The matching of great talent to the crying need for leadership has happily been a major result of the fellowship movement.

It has been said that fellowships avoid the stigma that often attaches to a church as a personality cult, and indeed they do tend to foster a revolutionary spirit of anti-clericalism. And although I am a clergyman, I sometimes think the anti-clerical layman may have a point: from the highest motives a clergyman may become so attached to the cause his church stands for, or even to the church itself, he will identify himself so completely with it that he will come to see in its success a reflection of himself.

* * *

I am not here subjectively to defend anti-clericalism. I don't like it. But objectively I am convinced of three things, namely: 1) that the fellowships which are able to do so . . . will become churches and give us wider scope than we have ever enjoyed; 2) that our fellowships are proving that religious groups can get along without ministers, as they will have to do if our UU movement continues to grow as it is now growing; and 3) that as fellowships increase the role of the minister increases also. I have heard no ministerial complaint that we ministers are having less and less to do in our own professional fields of activity.

It has also been said of the fellowships that they are not representative of a well-integrated and well-unified religious denomination: in short, that we are not a movement but a conglomeration. I do not know how great may be the variety but we differ much more widely in fellowships than we have ever differed in our churches, great as that has been.

SOURCE: *Take a Giant Step: Two Decades of the Fellowships* (Boston: Unitarian Universalist Association, 1967), 5–13.

CHARLES HARTSHORNE

A Natural Theology for Our Time
1967

Charles Hartshorne (1897–2000), with Unitarian and Unitarian Universalist affiliation in later life, is best known for what he called "neo-classical theism," positing a naturalistic God-concept that would be logically coherent and free from the traditional, "mistaken" understandings of omnipotence, omniscience, and immutability that rendered older ideas of God scientifically and rationally untenable. Influenced by the process/relational metaphysics of Alfred North Whitehead but pursuing a somewhat independent course, Hartshorne was especially concerned to establish the "worshipful perfection" of a self-surpassing God whose power was supremely relational and persuasive. He affirmed particular debt to the proto-unitarian Polish Brethren theologians Fausto Sozzini and Jan Crell, who, in the early 1600s, were among the earliest to insist on God's temporality and mutability as a necessary concomitant of human free will. Further Reading: Charles Hartshorne, The Divine Relativity: A Social Conception of God *(New Haven, CT: Yale University Press, 1948); Charles Hartshorne,* Omnipotence and Other Theological Mistakes *(Albany: State University of New York Press, 1984).*

— Jay Atkinson

What is a philosopher to mean by "God"—assuming he uses the word? There are three ways of reaching an answer to this question. One is to ask theologians. But there are important disagreements among theologians as to the connotations of the central religious term, and these disagreements have if anything increased during the past century or two. Thus we cannot find an answer to the terminological question in this way. A second approach is the following. If the philosopher's system or method leads him to formulate a conception having at least some analogy with the central operative idea in the practices, not simply in the theological theories, of one or more of the high religions, he may call his conception by the religious name. If the analogy is weak he may with some justice be accused of misusing the word. Spinoza has been called "God-intoxicated" and also "atheist." There is a fairly strong case for both descriptions. But this, in my view, constitutes an objection of some force to Spinoza's system. It seems odd to think that an idea so essentially religious should be so mistakenly conceived by all the great religions concerned with it as the religious idea must be if Spinoza is correct. Contrariwise, it is an argument in favor

257

of a philosophy if it can make more religious sense out of the theistic view than other philosophies have been able to do.

A further consideration is the following. Basic ideas derive somehow from direct experience or intuition, life as concretely lived. Moreover, it is demonstrable from almost any classical conception of God that he cannot be known in any merely indirect way, by inference only, but must somehow be present in all experience. No theist can without qualification deny the universal "immanence" of God. Even Aquinas did not do this. And if God is in *all* things, he is in our experiences and also in what we experience, and thus is in some fashion a universal datum of experience. But then it seems reasonable to suppose that religion, whatever else it may be, is the cultivation of this aspect of experience. Hence what it says about "God" deserves to be taken seriously, at least so far as the meaning of the term is concerned. The burden of justification is upon those who would use the word in a drastically non-religious sense. So our first question is, what is the religious sense?

In theistic religions God is the One Who is Worshipped. This is in some sort a definition. We have, therefore, only to find out what worship is to know the proper use of the name "God." This is the third approach to the definitional problem. But here, too, a difficulty arises. Are there not many sorts of worship—noble, ignoble, primitive, sophisticated, superstitious, relatively enlightened, idolatrous . . . what you will [ellipsis in original]? And does not divinity take on a different apparent character with each form of worship? Spinoza claimed to have the noblest and most enlightened form of worship, the "intellectual love of God"; hence to require him to refrain from using the word because other, perhaps less enlightened, people worship differently may be to rule against enlightenment and in favor of vulgar superstition. Moreover, the mere fact that many, or even most, people (at least in certain cultures) have worshipped God in a certain way is nothing but a contingent empirical fact. Should we allow our view concerning the essential nature of the eternal deity to depend upon any such facts? All classical meanings treat God as in some sense eternal. How can there be valid inference from a mere temporal fact to truth about eternal things? Much less could counting noses determine such truth. . . .

To obtain a broad perspective we may remind ourselves that subrational animals, below the level of language, can scarcely be thought to worship, unless in some radically deficient sense. Only man, among this earth's inhabitants, is a "religious animal." This suggests that consciousness, in the sense requiring language (or else, if God is conscious, something superior to language), is part of the definition of worship. To worship is to do something consciously. To do what? That which all sentient individuals must do, at least unconsciously, so far as they are sane and not in at least a mild neurosis or psychosis. Worship is the *integrating* of all one's thoughts and purposes, all valuations and meanings, all perceptions and conceptions. A sentient creature feels and acts as one, its sensations and strivings are all *its* sensations

258

and strivings. So are its thoughts, if it has them. Thus one element of worship is present without worship, unity of response. The added element is consciousness: worship is a consciously unitary response to life. It lifts to the level of explicit awareness the integrity of an individual responding to reality. Or, worship is individual wholeness flooded with consciousness. This is the ideal toward which actual worship may tend.

If this account is correct, worship is in principle the opposite of a primitive phenomenon. The more consciousness, the more completely the ideal of worship can be realized. Those who pride themselves on transcending worship may only be falling back to a more primitive level. Of course, as many are fond of reminding us, one can live without worship. Why not, since the lower animals do so? And we are all animals; the animal way is partly open to us still.

However, there are two possible theories of worship, the theistic and the nontheistic. According to the former, the conscious wholeness of the individual is correlative to an inclusive wholeness in the world of which the individual is aware, and this wholeness is deity. According to the nontheistic view, either there is no inclusive wholeness, or if there is one, it is not what religions have meant by deity. Perhaps it is just The Unknown, or Nature as a Great Mystery, not to be thought of as conscious, or as an individual in principle superior to all others. Perhaps it is even Humanity. Or (more reasonably) it is all sentient creatures.

My view I shall put bluntly. It is the lower animals for whom the Whole must be simply Unknown, sheer Mystery, and their own species practically all that has value. The difference between agnostics (or "humanists") and the nonspeaking creatures is that, whereas the mere animal simply *has* integrity, the agnostic feels the need and possibility of raising integrity to the conscious level, but does not quite know how to do so. Thus he is in some degree in conflict with himself. However, animal innocence is there to fall back upon.

God is the wholeness of the world, correlative to the wholeness of every sound individual dealing with the world. Note that this has no peculiar connection with the human race, "father-images," the parental function, or anything of the sort. Any sentient individual in any world experiences and acts as one: the question is if its total environment is not therewith experienced as, in some profoundly analogous sense, one. An individual (other than God) is only a fragment of reality, not the whole; but is *all* individuality (in other than the trivial sense in which a junk pile, say, is an "individual" junk pile) similarly fragmentary? Or is the cosmic or all-inclusive whole also an integrated individual, the sole non-fragmentary individual?

Note, too, that our question is definitely not the question, "Are all wholes or individuals 'finite,' 'limited'?" For it is at best a leap in the dark to assert the nonfinitude of our *total* environment (or "all with which we have to do"—as W. E. Hocking puts it). This totality is vastly more than, and includes, ourselves; but it may for all that be finite in certain respects. Indeed, it must be so! Fragmentariness, not finitude, sets the problem of worship. Here countless theologians long ago made an initial mistake for which the full price has yet to be paid: they began the idolatrous worship of "the infinite." Cosmic wholeness, not infinity, is the essential concept. Infinity comes in if and only if—or in whatever sense and only that sense—we should view the whole as infinite. And this is to be determined by inquiry, not take for granted.

The reader may feel that we have not followed our own injunction to look to the religions for the meaning of "God." Is "cosmic wholeness" a religious conception? My reply is, by fairly clear and direct implication, yes, it is such a conception. I shall now try to show this. Three religions, if no more, Judaism, Christianity, and Islam would, I think, agree with the conception of worship embodied in: "Thou shalt love the Lord thy God with all they heart and with all thy mind and with all thy soul and with all thy strength." I ask, how more plainly could the idea of wholeness of individual response be stated in simple, generally intelligible language? The word "all" reiterated four times in one sentence means, I take it, what it says. It does not mean, *nearly* all—or, all *important*—responses, or aspects of personality. Simply every response, every aspect, must be a way of loving God. That the God correlative to this integrity of response is Himself "One" or individual is also a Jewish-Christian-Islamic tenet, at least apart from the subtleties of the Trinity, which are surely not *intended* to contradict the divine wholeness or integrity.

SOURCE: Charles Hartshorne, A *Natural Theology for Our Time* (LaSalle, IL: Open Court, 1967), 1–8.

WILLIAM G. SINKFORD

"Questionnaire on Sex and Sexual Relations"
1967

William G. Sinkford (1946–) was a member of the First Unitarian Church of Cincinnati's Liberal Religious Youth (LRY) group. He was elected continental president of Liberal Religious Youth for his sophomore year at Harvard University in 1965–1966. (After a career in business, he entered the ministry and served as president of the Unitarian Universalist Association from 2001 to 2009.) Sinkford served as LRY president during a time marked by a national concern that the sexual experiences and values of youth were changing in a more libertarian direction. Sinkford drafted and data-coded the "Sinkford Sex Survey" in order to obtain information from UU youth to reliably inform this discussion. It was distributed through the monthly packet sent to youth leaders and became the basis of his senior thesis at Harvard.

—Wayne Arnason

Dear LRYers,

This year one of the most important areas that LRY has been investigating has been relationships between boys and girls, and masculinity and femininity. What does it mean to be a boy? A girl? How do boys and girls relate to one another? How does sex figure in this? At their March meetings, the LRY Executive Committee authorized me to proceed with a study of sex and sexual relationships among LRYers. The questionnaire which follows is the major part of the study.

The directions on the questionnaire are simple and direct. I realize that answering some of the questions may be difficult. If you have real difficulty answering a question, go ahead and answer it as best you can and express your qualifications in the margin. I will look at the qualifications as well as just the answers.

The questionnaire is designed for people from 14 to 19 years old. There are questions and issues in it that you may not have any experience with. Some of them may apply primarily to people older than you are. I hope you won't be put off by either the language or the issues. Answer the questions based on your own experience—however great or little that may be. Be frank and honest—the questionnaire is completely anonymous; I will never see a name on a questionnaire. The success of the study depends on your accurate reporting of your feelings and experience.

Take your time. It will probably take you about 45 minutes or 50 minutes to complete the questionnaire. If you want to make a number of comments about the issues or the questions themselves, feel free. These can be very helpful. A questionnaire like this can tend to be simple minded, asking for yes-and-no type answers where they are not possible. Your comments can clarify and deepen my understanding of what you mean.

One final note about language: The terms sex and sexual are used frequently throughout the questionnaire. They are intended to refer to a broad range of activity and not to one particular activity.

The results of the questionnaire will be analyzed and hopefully can provide significant data for Continental Conference this summer and future program development. Those groups who take the questionnaire will receive a report of the results.

Thank you very much for your cooperation.

We would be one . . .

Bill Sinkford

SOURCE: *Questionnaire on Sex and Sexual Relations* (Boston: Liberal Religious Youth, 1967).

"The Black Caucus Report"

1967

The ongoing injustice and inequities experienced by African Americans fomented explosive conditions in America's urban ghettos. In the wake of the riots that were erupting across the nation the UUA Commission on Religion and Race sponsored the Emergency Conference on the Unitarian Universalist Response to the Black Rebellion on October 6–8, 1967, in New York City. There were about 140 in attendance, of whom 37 were African-American UUs; of these, 30 broke off from the planned agenda and formed a black caucus. What follows is excerpted from that caucus's report. After being hotly debated it was affirmed by over two-thirds of the conference participants. The debate was not about its content but rather about the caucus's demand that the conference endorse and submit it in toto to the UUA Board of Trustees. When the Board balked at accepting all of the caucus's proposals and, instead, restructured the Commission of Religion and Race and revised its mandate, the caucus and its white supporters began organizing to take the caucus's case to the 1968 General Assembly. There the delegates rejected the administration proposal and accepted the establishment of the Black Affairs Council (BAC), its funding, and program. Further Reading: Victor Carpenter, Long Challenge: The Empowerment Controversy (1967–1977) *(Chicago: Meadville Lombard Theological School Press, 2003);* Empowerment: One Denomination's Quest for Racial Justice, 1967–1982 *(Boston: Unitarian Universalist Association, 1984); Mark D. Morrison-Reed, ed.,* Darkening the Doorways: Black Trailblazers and Missed Opportunities in Unitarian Universalism *(Boston: Skinner House, 2011).*

— Mark D. Morrison-Reed

Preamble: The New Black Revolution

The New Black Revolution is an awakening of the black man to the fact that he is a man. He cannot and will not endure the shackles of prejudice any longer. Prejudice, the progeny of slavery, propagated by history and perpetuated by the white man in his daily thoughts and deeds has so permeated his heart and mind that neither love nor reason reaches the root cause, *his own moral decadence*, which has rot-gutted his soul and paralyzed his mind.

The black man likewise has been affected by the effect of history and the white man's thoughts and deeds by virtue of having been reared in the white man's culture and inculcated consciously or subconsciously with the white man's values.

He is now unloosing the shackles of such values with an awareness of his own black values, and his own black worth, not because he is black, but because *he is*. . . .

The Black Revolution is a clash between the awareness of dignity and the societal servitude imposed by a history of disabled morally decadent whites.

Recognizing that "love" has not and cannot work, because a rot-gutted soul cannot pull itself up by its own bootstraps; recognizing that reason cannot work, since reason ultimately is the slave of the *total being*, therefore other force must be applied with sufficient impact to overcome.

There is no power greater than a man's self respect. Therein lies the meaning of the Black Revolution.

Recommendations of the Denominational Affairs Committee of the Black Caucus

The denominational affairs committee of the black caucus calls upon the Unitarian [Universalist] Association to commit itself to the following:

1. To concur in the establishment of a Black Affairs Council to implement the specific recommendations of the Black Caucus, and to insure a vehicle to express the interests, feelings and aspirations of Black Unitarian-Universalists for power within the denomination, that makes their presence more visible and facilitates their greater contribution to the life of the denomination, and the whole society. . . .

a. The Black Affairs Council will assume the role of an affiliate agency. . . . The Board of the Black Affairs Council will consist of Unitarian-Universalists with a clear majority of blacks. The Board will be appointed by a joint committee of the Unitarian-Universalist Association Board and the Black Caucus.

b. The specific nature of the above Council will be determined by a re-convening of the Black Caucus, plus other Black Unitarian Universalist members. . . .

2. To take immediate steps to include black Unitarian-Universalists on the following committees and boards with the concurrence of the black caucus: Unitarian Universalist Executive Staff, The Board of Trustees, Finance Committee, Business Committee, Program Committee, Nominating Committee, Ministerial Fellowship Committee. . . .

3. To take immediate steps to increase the number of official black representatives to the Unitarian-Universalist General Assemblies by a financial subsidy.

4. To establish a subsidy for black Unitarian Universalist ministers in fellowship in order to allow adequate time for black ministers to seek and obtain Unitarian Universalist pulpits.

5. That the Unitarian-Universalist Department of Education initiate a program to recruit, train and subsidize black Religious Education Directors and to relate effectively their talents to church school programs.

6. To establish within an appropriate predominately black theological school, a professorial chair, to assist in the education and recruitment of potential black Unitarian-Universalist ministers.

7. That the Unitarian-Universalist Association Board of Trustees urgently request Beacon Press to seek out and publish black authors and poets, and to cooperate with C.O.R.E.'s existing publishing program, and that the Department of Curriculum Development produce and distribute materials on black history, and the black builders of America.

8. That the Unitarian-Universalist Association determine to make a real financial commitment to black people by:

a. immediately making sufficient funds available for the reconvening of the black caucus, and

b. to make available from Unitarian-Universalist Association unrestricted endowment funds of $250,000 a year, for the next four years.

SOURCE: Emergency Conference on the Unitarian Universalist Response to the Black Rebellion, "The Black Caucus Report," Unitarian Universalist Association, Black Empowerment Controversy Records, 1968–1979, Andover-Harvard Archives, bMS 531/5, Andover-Harvard Theological Library, Harvard Divinity School, Cambridge, MA.

Business Resolution on Investment Policy
1967

The Unitarian Universalist Association took an initial step toward the practice of socially responsible investing with this business resolution passed at the 1967 General Assembly. In this case, the goal was to promote racially integrated housing. A year later, the General Assembly directed the Investment Committee to create a subcommittee for social responsibility, again with a focus on open housing. In 1972, the General Assembly passed a similar business resolution emphasizing the anti-apartheid struggle in South Africa, setting in motion the process that culminated in the UUA's divestment from companies doing business in South Africa in 1985. By that time, a broad commitment to social responsibility characterized the UUA's investment practices and those of many member congregations.

—Dan McKanan

The Sixth General Assembly of the Unitarian Universalist Association:

REQUESTS the Board of Trustees of the Association, with the aid of the Department of Social Responsibility, to exercise the power represented by the Association's ownership of common stock as an effective instrument for promoting social justice by combating discriminatory business practices;

REQUESTS the Board of Trustees of the Association and member societies to consider devoting, consistent with other program needs, a portion of their unrestricted funds, in relatively small amounts where this is legally necessary, to enterprises having clearly stated policies and practices of non-discrimination, including those which provide genuinely integrated housing in previously segregated areas, provided local legal requirements are complied with;

REQUESTS the member societies to ask their individual members to do likewise; and

REQUESTS the Association to compile and keep active a list of enterprises genuinely working towards integrated housing in previously segregated areas and to make such list available upon request to member societies.

SOURCE: Unitarian Universalist Social Justice Statements, uua.org/statements/investment-policy

JACK MENDELSOHN

"The Church and the Draft Resisters"

1967

Jack Mendelsohn (1918–2012) was a prominent Unitarian Universalist minister and a civil rights and anti-war activist. His book Being Liberal in an Illiberal Age *was one of the most widely circulated articulations of Unitarian Universalism in the late twentieth century. He also wrote a biography of William Ellery Channing. While he was serving as the senior minister of Arlington Street Church, on October 16, 1967, the congregation held an interfaith worship service during which more than three hundred draft cards were collected. At the service, some of the young men present burned their cards, sparking a controversy within the congregation. The collection and destruction of the cards violated federal law, and five of those present were subsequently indicted for conspiracy to resist the draft. They were convicted, but their conviction was overturned on appeal a year later. At its 1968 General Assembly, the Unitarian Universalist Association passed a general resolution that expressed respect for nonviolent resistance and urged congregations to offer "symbolic sanctuary" and make their facilities available for "services of resistance in the tradition of the one held at Arlington Street." Further Reading: Jessica Mitford,* The Trial of Dr. Spock, the Rev. William Sloane Coffin, Jr., Michael Ferber, Mitchell Goodman, and Marcus Raskin *(New York: Knopf, 1969); Michael S. Foley,* The War Machine: Draft Resistance During the Vietnam War *(Chapel Hill: University of North Carolina Press, 2003).*

—Colin Bossen

A hue and cry has arisen over the sixty young men who burned their draft cards in the chancel of Arlington Street Church. No matter that 280 young men took the more solemn and perilous step of turning in their draft cards for transmittal to the Justice Department. No matter that much of the hubbub was irrational and uninformed. The love and honesty human beings owe to one another require that the question be dealt with lovingly and honestly.

It may come as surprising news to some that I react very negatively to the burning of draft cards. It is too flamboyant for my taste, too theatrical, too self-indulgent. Anyone who thinks I encouraged it is wrong. But that is beside the point. I did not forbid it, and under similar circumstances I would not again. What happened here on Monday, October 16, was conceived, organized and implemented by a remarkable group of students and seminarians who, in the most serious and open-eyed manner are relinquishing their draft immunity and inviting arrest in order to disavow the American war in Vietnam. The integrity and moral depth of the young leaders of this Resistance are extraordinary. I told them how I felt about draft card burning, and they listened. But in the end they listened more to their responsibilities as democratic leaders, which is as it should be. The overwhelming majority of the Resisters neither burned their draft cards nor encouraged others to do so, but they recognized that the moral outrage felt by a minority of their fellows drove that minority to the extreme gesture of card burning, and they made orderly, respectful provision for it. . . .

There is not really much more to be said to those who are enraged, lacerated or confounded by the draft card burning. Time and continuing dialogue will clarify perspectives. Meanwhile, there is an inevitable polarization of feeling, as illustrated by two letters which reached me. They represent remarkably well the contradictory reality with which we are dealing. The writers of these letters have similar cultural backgrounds and enjoy similar economic and social status. The first says: "Dear Dr. Mendelsohn: I have no further interest in supporting the Arlington Street Church when you as the leader have, apparently permitted and encouraged the burning of draft cards on the altar. It is unforgiveable in my estimation. I think you will find many old friends feel the same way. I am not writing this on the spur of the moment but only after many conversations, trying to prove to myself that I was wrong. Please remove my name from mailings."

This correspondent, as you now know, is right in assuming that I permitted the draft card burning, but is wrong in assuming that I encouraged it. Among the many conversations which he refers to, there was not one with me. I hope there will be, however, and I will seek it. The second letter goes as follows: "Dear Reverend Mendelsohn: I attended the service in your church on Monday, October 16. I am one of the people who hasn't been in church in years. I don't know whether I can express the feeling that I have that at that time, in that place something happened that was sacred in any sense of the word. The hymns, the prayers, the responsive readings, the speakers and most of all, the restrained courage of the young men resisting the draft contributed to an event that I shall never forget. Thank you for so much."

I appreciate but take no personal pride in the gratitude of this correspondent. It is the policy of our church to place in my hands final decisions about public assemblies to take place here. . . . Most such decisions require little soul-searching, and no real sweat. In one sense this one didn't either. . . .

But in another sense this was a very tough decision because I was so keenly and personally aware of what was involved. . . . One does not lightly commit an institution to lend the prestige of its facilities and senior clergyman to the launching of a premeditated, long-range program of civil disobedience.

First I had to determine whether or not I could commit myself to such a program. I decided I could. Then, after consultation, I had to judge whether or not this church could constructively incorporate into its ongoing life the tension, controversy and stress inevitably to come. No other church was available. It was this one or none. There were many sympathetic Clergymen. At least a hundred participated in the service here. But none had an established milieu capable of sustaining such use of their premises.

For me, it came down to this. I had to decide that either this church could bear the pressure and grow stronger because of it, or that it could not, in which case it would have been necessary, in light of my own convictions, to support the students but resign my post here. . . .

Civil disobedience is a harsh, ghastly, contaminating business. It is morally credible only when there is irredeemable disillusionment with the lawful processes of protest and dissent. Because I hover so tremblingly close to this point, I can appreciate what it means to the young to be prepared to accept the ruination of their careers, ridicule, harassment, imprisonment, death. Sadly, it seems to matter little that some of those who are now most outraged by this present group of civil disobeyers would not be here at all except for the civil disobedience of their ancestors. Or that this nation would not exist but for the civil disobedience of its founding fathers. Or that the abolition of our vile system of slavery was spurred by civil disobedience. Or that the voting franchise for women was fueled by civil disobedience. . . .

Given the total spectrum of possibility within which this nation might end its Vietnamese escalation and slaughter short of nuclear holocaust, given the stark reality that none of the protests, none of the appeals to conscience . . . has reversed the escalation, or the slaughter, or the vaulting toward worldwide nuclear war, how can any sober person wonder that there are those whose moral revulsion has come at last to civil disobedience?

Has anything short of it worked? The answer is an agonized no. . . .

Will civil disobedience make the kind of impact needed? Will it so shock the nation that a drastic shift in our policy will occur? Frankly, I don't know. I rather doubt it.

Why then undertake it? . . .

When an issue of this magnitude is joined, when there are those who, having exhausted without effect every lawful means of opposing the monstrous crimes being committed in their name by their government, who cannot accept silence or inaction, and choose instead the Gethsemane of civil disobedience, how is the church to respond?

That was the question posed to this church. You know how it was answered last Monday. But the continuing answer, the one that really counts, is yours.

SOURCE: "The Church and the Draft Resisters" by Jack Mendelsohn, sermon delivered at Arlington Street Church in Boston, Massachusetts, on October 22, 1967, Arlington Street Church Archives.

HAYWARD HENRY

"The Caucus Story"
1968

Among the demands made by the Black Caucus, formed during the Emergency
Conference, was the convening of a gathering exclusively for African-American
Unitarian Universalists. With the financial support of the Commission on
Religion and Race, this took place in Chicago from February 23 to February
25. At the opening plenary, Hayward Henry Jr. (later known as Mtangulizi
Sanyika), a former activist with the Student Nonviolent Coordinating
Committee, graduate student in microbiology, board member of the Second
Unitarian Church of Boston, and chair of the Black Caucus Steering Com-
mittee, addressed the conference. During that weekend the Black Unitarian
Universalist Caucus (BUUC) was founded and Henry was elected its National
Chairman. Further Reading: Peniel E. Joseph, Waiting 'Til the Midnight
Hour: A Narrative History of Black Power in America *(New York: Henry*
Holt, 2006).

—Mark D. Morrison-Reed

There is nothing more tragic than an institution or nation which sleeps through
a revolution. Let there be no mistake about it. There is going on in this country a
revolution, a black revolution, and you may choose whatever way you would to
define it, but we are in it, we are part of it. Our presence here tonight is witness
to that fact.

Who would have thought but one year ago that black Unitarian Universalists
would have dared to form into a caucus from which whites were excluded. But the
peculiarity about the revolution we are experiencing is that great institutions, including our own church, find themselves "hung up." They don't know what to do. "What
do you want?" "What is this all about?" "Why do you exclude me?" "Why are the
brothers burning?"

*   *   *

So, when you talk about integration in the church and integration in the society, you're not being honest. It does not exist. And let me further say about the
whole concept here, that as long as a black man is forced into a white institutional
situation in which his total psyche must be absorbed into the white psyche, he
becomes destroyed. That is a form of chaotic self surrender. That is what our society

has insisted upon—that integration always be this one-way street, where black people, by definition, must integrate into something white.

I want all of you to understand something. There is nothing inherently wrong, evil or inferior about black people existing among themselves in any form they choose. It only becomes an evil when I destroy the right of another man to be human, and when that man destroys my right to be human. That is where the evil exists. There are a whole host of existing black organizations—beautiful organizations—which have done much in our own history. And, certainly, I don't think that they are inferior, in any sense of the word—our fraternal organizations being a prime example.

Some of us talk about a new kind of relationship. Let us talk about a new kind of social strategy. Let us talk about defining a new issue for ourselves within the church and for black people in the larger society. We must destroy once and for all the idea that power is something exclusively experienced by whites, that it is a mysterious phenomenon that black people have no business being concerned about.

Our collective experience as a nation of people within this nation has been that of being powerless and social change only comes through the intelligent application of power, not through the negation of power. And don't tell me anything about love and reason negating the usage of that power. It does not negate the use of power, rather, it defines how it should be used.

That is a lesson the white man ought to think about. And we black men must be courageous enough to tell that story endlessly, that power is the vehicle through which we obtain change. It is not the vehicle through which we destroy change, and we blacks have the right to obtain the kind of power through which we can define our community, ourselves, our institutions, and build and grow and develop into that which is great, glorious and wonderful for all black people.

＊　＊　＊

We are saying to whites, you must deal with the fact that ours is a racist society, that power is in the hands of whites and that black communities all over this country are not controlled within those communities but outside of those communities. That has to be dealt with. That has to be coped with. And for all those who want to be involved, we call upon them to join us in this kind of involvement, for once to speak to the true problems of the society.

We come here, many of us, disagreeing, and we come here from many places and many backgrounds. We've come here with many reflections and ideas about what the black caucus is. We've come here not knowing what black power is about. We've come here not understanding what is going on in the church, or the society. We come here as individuals, we shall leave here as a community—one way or the other. For those who don't want to join us in this effort, all we ask is that you not obstruct us. You have the right to your opinion. We want you to have the right to your freedom. But we also want you to carefully understand what we are saying and look at those realities so that when we leave here, we leave here as black men, as a black community.

SOURCE: Hayward Henry, "The Caucus Story," *Caucus*, May 1968, 4–5, 7, Unitarian Universalist Association, Black Empowerment Controversy Records, 1968–1979, Andover-Harvard Archives, bMS 531/5, Andover-Harvard Theological Library, Harvard Divinity School, Cambridge, MA.

"Questions and Answers on the Black Affairs Council"

1968

In November 1967, Supporters of Black Unitarians for Radical Reform (SOBURR) was organized by white members of Unitarian Universalist societies in the greater Los Angeles area. It sent a letter to all Unitarian Universalist congregations asking them to support the Black Affairs Council (BAC) and protest the UUA Board's decision not to fully endorse BAC's demands. That March two ministers in the Philadelphia area proposed the formation of a continental organization. The aim of "For Full Recognition and Funding of the Black Affairs Council" (FULLBAC) was to marshal white support for BAC at the upcoming General Assembly. On April 4, the first meeting between the BAC and FULLBAC steering committees was interrupted by news of the assassination of Martin Luther King, Jr.

—Mark D. Morrison-Reed

Q. *What is the Black Affairs Council?*

A. The Black Affairs Council (BAC) is a committee of nine persons serving as a coordinating agency for Unitarian Universalist efforts in the fields of race relations and Black empowerment.

✻   ✻   ✻

Q. *Is BAC separatist?*

A. No. BAC has applied for affiliate status with the UUA. Furthermore, the delegates to the national conference of the Black Unitarian Universalist Caucus in Chicago in February 1968 voted overwhelmingly against the creation of an independent Black Unitarian Universalist Church.

Q. *Is the demand for a Black Affairs Council extremist?*

A. No. This is a request by Black people to make their own choices, their own decisions, and their own value system. As stated by James Luther Adams, it is "a movement of people who are no longer ashamed to be Blacks and who are expressing a sense of self-worth." It is a "thrust in the name of human dignity" for which white men should be grateful "even though we cannot take credit for it."

Q. Is BAC undemocratic?

A. No. Democracy requires self-determination. Self-determination requires power. Power requires organization. BAC is a means toward the end of fuller participation by our Black members in national and denominational life. Not less democracy, but more democracy will result from the full exercise of the genius of our Black members.

SOURCE: FULLBAC, "Questions and Answers on the Black Affairs Council," *Caucus*, May 1968, 8, Unitarian Universalist Association, Black Empowerment Controversy Records, 1968–1979, Andover-Harvard Archives, bMS 531/5, Andover-Harvard Theological Library, Harvard Divinity School, Cambridge, MA.

JOSEPH L. FISHER

"Guest Editorial"

1968

Joseph L. Fisher (1914–1992) served as the moderator of the UUA from 1964 to 1977. Known for his graciousness and fairness, Fisher began his tenure when Marshall Dimock's combative relationship with UUA president Dana McLean Greeley led Dimock to resign. Fisher, who was white, continued serving through the tumult around Black Power and stepped down after he was elected to the U.S. House of Representatives, where he served from 1975 to 1980. This editorial appeared in the issue of the Register-Leader *that appeared just before the May 1968 General Assembly in Cleveland.*

—Mark D. Morrison-Reed

A caucus has been established in our denomination made of exclusively of black Unitarian Universalists, intelligent, sincere, and courageous men and women from various parts of the country who are groping to find a way toward a better life soon for all Negroes in this country, and thus for all citizens. They have chosen the method of a separate but parallel organization within which a program for alleviating race problems in the denomination and in the country is to be developed. The Black Caucus has formed a Black Affairs Council to be spearhead of its work. Although their program is by no means entirely clear, it appears to include recognition of the Black Affairs Council by the UUA as an affiliated agency, dissolution of the denomination's Commission on Religion and Race, co-operation with white radicals in examining problems of white racism, more emphasis on the ministry in the inner city, financial aid to black ministerial candidates, an investigation of the assassination of Malcolm X, and ample funds from the Association to begin the program. The General Assembly, which will convene May 23 in Cleveland, will undoubtedly be confronted with the demands of the UU Black Power group and will have to respond in one way or another. . . .

My concern as moderator of the Association, is that this thrust of the more militant blacks and their white supporters be received by the body of the denomination with sympathy for the genuine grievances that lie behind it, tolerance of any abrasiveness in the tactics chosen, and encouragement of the aspiration for respect and decent treatment of all people. At the same time I trust the denomination will hold firmly to its historic devotion to racial justice in an inclusive society, and to its belief in "the supreme worth of every human personality, the dignity of man, and the use of the democratic method in human relationships." In brief, our task, as always, is to deal honorably and constructively with the challenge at hand.

I believe the actions of the Board of Trustees in March . . . will set us in motion toward dealing with the race problems in our midst, and in the country as a whole, more purposefully and vigorously than we have ever done before. If it is not precisely all that this group or that one would want, I hope nevertheless that all will want to close ranks in support of this program, or some improved version of it. We have neither the time nor the energy to waste in internal feuding, nor will the urgency of the problems permit it.

SOURCE: Joseph L. Fisher, "Guest Editorial," *Unitarian Universalist Register-Leader*, May 1968, 2.

HAYWARD HENRY

"The Black Caucus: Toward a New Unitarian Universalism"

1968

By the time of Dr. King's assassination, an edition of the Register-Leader *that would address the issues raised by the emergence of the Black Unitarian Universalist Caucus was in the process of being written and edited. Joseph Fisher's editorial introduced that May 1968 edition and was followed by ten articles, among which was one written by Hayward Henry, Jr., and another by Kenneth B. Clark.*

—Mark D. Morrison-Reed

Rigid social systems which are unable to accommodate conflict within their structure are subject to further conflict. If the system is more flexible and encourages conflict, it survives because it is able to adjust to the new balance of power which conflict produces. Our denomination is beset with such a conflict. A Black Unitarian Universalist Caucus (BUUC) has emerged. It insists that an inter-racial Black-controlled agency, the Black Affairs Council (BAC), be officially established and funded ($250,000 per year for four years) by the denomination to attack societal and denominational racism. BAC would attempt to harness Black UU expertise to advance institutions and approaches which may be expected to generate unity and power for Black people. It would further attempt, where possible, to strategically deploy the enormous economic, professional, and intellectual power of the entire denomination to this end and to humanize White institutions. There exists denominational precedent for funding an affiliate of the UUA without controlling its program and personnel; however there exists no precedent for Black people stating their dissatisfaction with feeble UUA attempts to deal with race relations and for subsequently demanding the right to control and direct future activities in this area. Thus, a major issue is Black Power versus White Power. It is this shifting balance of *power* which has made it impossible for institutional bureaucrats to creatively respond to the issue of UUA irrelevancy to which BUUC addresses itself.

We as UUs assert our belief in the "brotherhood of men," but we've lacked an aggressive strategy and serious organization which could vigorously attack the causes of institutional racism. Many individuals and churches are to be commended for their efforts. However, such efforts do not at all reflect "total denominational commitment." The UUA, as most institutions, is a peculiar species of animal. It would be all too typical of us to expect the classical Pavlovian responses to institutional change, *i.e.*, reform an existing structure, hand-pick its decision makers, control its budget and thus its program, and buy off dissident leadership by appointment to the reformed structure. Racist America has great skill in this manipulative pacification which it historically employs to silence Black Radicalism; but to witness this phenomenon in the UU church is a shocking revelation of sententious hypocrisy. Yet upon the recommendation of the UUA administration, the UUA Board agreed to, and participated in, such chicanery. At its March meeting, it welcomed BAC as an affiliate with no recommendation for funding, and simultaneously reorganized the former Commission on Religion and Race into a UU Commission for Action on Race, with a proposed $300,000 budget of which, if so disposed, it could give BAC a few crumbs if we are good boys. The Commission decision makers were promptly hand-picked, with three leaders of the Caucus represented. Its consultants were named in traditional UU fashion. The majority of those designated were inevitably UUA types — conventional on race relations. Its program bears a superficial resemblance to that of the Black Caucus, which can only be suggestive of a pernicious intellectual imperialism.

* * *

BUUC considers it an affront to be told that White UUs were in Selma and Montgomery when in fact most UUs did not show up until a White man was killed. A Black man died two weeks earlier and the number of White UUs in Selma were countable on the fingers — racism, even in death. Why even go to Selma to fight Jim Clark while Black ministers in the church are denied full-time pulpits? Only two Black ministers out of about fifteen have even held a full-time head ministership. Even the top UUA bureaucrats acknowledge this racism. We pontificate about "racial inclusiveness" but apparently we don't mean inclusiveness at seats of power. To this day, only one dark face occupies a decision-making role in the UUA hierarchy — Vice Moderator Wade McCree. There are no Blacks on the UUA board except he; no Blacks on the nominating committee, finance committee, committee on appraisal, planning committee, fellowship committee, or investment committee. In other UUA departments, the same pattern in repeated. The departments of extension, ministry, religious education, curriculum development, and publications are conspicuous for their absence of Black people. Are these examples of integration and racial inclusiveness? BUUC does not see in the Religious Education curriculum a "Black Builders of America" program. Afro-American history abounds with significant achievements which have shaped American and world history which should be communicated by the denomination to all local churches. Our sin of omission is the expression of unconscious racism of the soft-core variety. BAC could begin to correct this condition. Beacon Press, our publishing house, is notable for its contributions to social dialogue. However, it is yet to undertake a major publishing program dealing with emergent radicalism in Black thinking. BUUC would welcome such an effort through its Black Affairs Council (BAC). Perhaps what is more tragic about the variety of experience which UUism purports to offer is its lack of concrete expression of Blackness as a liturgical form, as a form of worship. Most Black UUs are from the religious background of Black Protestantism which expresses the range of human emotion through dance, song, and rhythm. An institution which supposedly welcomes Black participation should provide the opportunity to validate this expression much as we do for Eastern worship forms. In short, the denomination chronically deprives Blacks and Whites of Blackness as a valid form.

If the above is what our denomination regards as "integration," then we need no more of it. Let us cease this sententious hypocrisy. No one wishes to answer the charge for malintegration in the church or society, or to offer constructive solutions. That is why a Caucus exists in our own church as well as in the Methodist, Baptist, Episcopal, Presbyterian, and Congregational churches. The only alternative to this kind of White deception and hypocrisy is the institutionalization of the collective voice of Black people throughout the society.

Our denomination is at a standstill. We are not growing, expanding, or progressing; rather, atrophy and blight have set in. BAC might be our last chance to be Unitarian Universalists, our last chance as a denomination to reinfuse ourselves with meaning and relevance, our last chance to build and advance our noble ideals. But it offers us more than an opportunity to speak to Black needs, for Whites will never be free of exploitation and racism until Blacks are free. White UUs will never be free until Black UUs are free and self-determined, for ours is a common destiny. BACs created everywhere might be America's last chance to peacefully correct the gross imbalance in goods, resources, and power. As concerned parties, let us become liberal conservatives and radical liberals, for the issue has been drawn, the dream exposed as fraud, the possibility to be human given a polite detour. Black people are the stern challenge to the cherished ideals of Justice (political and economic), Freedom (self-determination), Equality (worth of personality), and Peace (that men can nonviolently resolve their differences). To the extent that UUs and White Americans resist, avoid, and further deny, Blacks will continue to rebel and become true separatists. The struggle is against institutional Whiteness, not individual Whites. It is against social distortion, and against reformist nonsense. In time of moral and social crisis, let it not be said that we repudiated our history and slept through a revolution.

SOURCE: Hayward Henry, "The Black Caucus: Toward a New Unitarian Universalism," *Unitarian Universalist Register-Leader*, May 1968, 13, 16.

KENNETH CLARK

"Racism for the UUA?"

1968

Immediately after the Emergency Conference on the Black Rebellion, Homer Jack, the Director of the UUA Department of Social Responsibility, consulted with Dr. Kenneth B. Clark. The following is from the response Clark sent to the UUA Board. Clark, a well-known and respected child psychologist, served with his wife, Mamie, also a psychologist, as an expert witness in Briggs v. Elliot, *a school desegregation case that was the first of five combined into* Brown v. Board of Education of Topeka. *In 1954, that case brought an end to legal school segregation. In 1955, Beacon Press published Clark's seminal work,* Prejudice and Your Child. *Clark, a member of the Community Church of New York, was one of three high-profile African Americans who wrote articles in opposition to BAC. The other two were Cornelius McDougald, an influential Harlem lawyer who chaired the Board of the Community Church of New York and the UUA Commission on Religion and Race, and the Honorable Wade H. McCree, Jr., the first African-American judge in the Sixth Circuit Court of Appeals and vice moderator of the UUA Board of Trustees.*

—Mark D. Morrison-Reed

The most important first step for me is to make perfectly clear my own position on matters of race relations in America. It would be dishonest for me to pretend that I do not have firm value positions on this matter. Anyone who knows me and knows of my work knows that I am committed to a struggle for a racially integrated American society. I believe that racial segregation in its subtle or flagrant forms is dehumanizing to both Negroes and whites. I believe that racially segregated communities perpetuate intolerable forms of social pathology. I believe that racial segregation and discrimination in employment are pivotal in perpetuating the total pattern of family instability, dependency and neglect of human beings, particularly of Negro children.

Given these beliefs, which are backed by evidence, reason, and morality, I am unable to accept any ideology, plans, or programs which I believe directly or indirectly contribute to the perpetuation and intensification of any form of racial segregation in American life.

My study of the Black Power movement and my reading and analysis of the materials which are related to the Emergency Conference on the Unitarian Universalist Response to the Black Rebellion led me to the conclusion that the demands made by the Black Caucus are specific manifestations of a new racist thrust. The method of the Black Caucus, the rationale, and its specific suggestions and demands make clear the fact that a certain group of Negroes have come to the conclusion that racial integration in significant areas of American society, including the church, is an impossible goal. In rejecting this goal, they are explicitly and implicitly now asking for a racially separatist system. . . .

It has been argued that one should be more attentive and responsive to the racist demands of the Black Power movement because this is necessary to build a racial pride and dignity which must precede serious racial justice in America. I do not accept this. . . First, a similar argument could be offered in support of the racism of white segregationists. One could accept even the most cruel and flagrant manifestation of white supremacy as essential to building the dignity and pride of otherwise deprived and insecure whites. Second, I do not believe that any genuine pride in race or nationality can be built upon the realities of racial desegregation, the realities of economic deprivation, the realities of criminally inferior and racially segregated education, the realities of the total pattern of pathology inherent in racially segregated housing. Genuine pride and dignity for whites and Negroes can come only when an affluent society such as ours makes available the necessary financial and intellectual resources to bring about the massive social and economic changes essential for social justice. We have the resources; so far we have lacked only the commitment. And third, I personally question the validity of pride based on color of skin, whether it be white or black. Such a pride seems to me at best tenuous and at worst destructive of the potential of a human being to develop a more fundamental basis for pride and dignity.

* * *

While I can understand the depth of frustration out of which the Black Power movement comes, and understand also the fact that the masses of Negro people justifiably are revolted by verbal civil rights "victories," tokenism, and the pervasive moral hypocrisy which perpetuates dehumanizing American racism, I am personally convinced that the Black Power and Black Caucus method of reacting to these realities is self-defeating in that it tends to intensify rather than to remedy this violent disease of American racism.

Integration or Separatism?

Given this perspective, the question arises whether I can play a constructive role in helping the UUA deal with this problem as it is presented to it by the Black Caucus form of confrontation. . . . I would suggest that the first step in any attempt at rational discussion and constructive resolution of the problem posed to the Association would be for the Board of Directors of the UUA to re-examine its own value positions and goals on the matter of the American racial problem. I cannot in good conscience ask that the UUA accept my values and goals and reject those of the Black Caucus. I can only assert that the reactions of the Board of Directors to the specific demands will certainly reflect the fundamental position of the Board on matters of race. If the UUA and its Board of Directors are committed to the goals of an integrated America, an America in which the fact or the fiction of race becomes irrelevant in the enjoyment of the rights of American citizens, then it would seem to me that it could not be logical to attempt to obtain those goals by intensifying race and by making it the relevant factor in seeking to obtain the goals of racial democracy.

If, on the other hand, Unitarian Universalists are ambivalent, and are prepared to abandon or to postpone indefinitely the difficult struggle for the attainment of an integrated America, then it would seem consistent to entertain seriously the inherently racist demands of the Black Caucus. . . .

I am not suggesting that this is easy. Reason and unswerving adherence to moral and democratic goals are particularly difficult to maintain when they are being emotionally attacked, particularly when there appears some justification for their rejection. But it is precisely at those times when these values and goals must be most vigorously defended if they are to be preserved . . . [ellipsis in original].

It may be that the deep sense of guilt and racial ambivalence on the part of rational liberal whites in America, and probably the deeper sense of frustration, anger, and bitterness on the part of a growing number of Negroes contribute to the irrelevance of those voices which continue to ask for unswerving allegiance to reason, morality, and human dignity.

I cannot accept with equanimity a call for racial separatism coming from human beings with dark skins any more than I can tolerate such calls coming from human beings with lighter skins. Both groups of human beings to me reflect the pathos, the despair, the anguish of unfulfilled lives. It is no more just to acquiesce to the demands of the one than to those of the other—particularly when they are the same in effect. Justice can be served only by remaking our society so that it realistically fulfills the requirements for dignity for all human beings. This demands that Negroes, whites, and all others join forces, speak together, work together, argue with one another, and fight the formidable forces of irrationality and immorality as allies.

SOURCE: Kenneth B. Clark, "Racism for the UUA?" *Unitarian Universalist Register-Leader,* May 1968, 11–12.

Resolution

1968

The 1968 General Assembly of the Unitarian Universalist Association took place in Cleveland, Ohio, on May 24–29. The Ware Lecture was delivered by the Honorable Carl B. Stokes, the first African American elected mayor of a major U.S. city. The meeting drew 1,350 delegates. This attendance was 28 percent higher than the 1967 General Assembly and 39 percent higher than the one in 1966. In addition to voting on a Business Resolution to support the Black Affairs Council, the delegates adopted general resolutions calling for a halt to the bombing of North and South Vietnam, supporting abortion rights, urging the termination of the anti-ballistic missile program, and endorsing the Poor People's Campaign.

—Mark D. Morrison-Reed

On Sunday afternoon the Assembly debated and took action on items of business having to do with the Black Affairs Council, the Black Unitarian Universalist Caucus and Black and White Alternative. First, acting as a Committee of the Whole, the Assembly debated proposals by Black Affairs Council and Black and White Alternative and recommendations submitted by the Board of Trustees. After long debate it became evident that the Assembly as a Committee of the Whole would not reach any agreement under this informal procedure. Thereupon the Moderator acting in accordance with the Rules of Procedure dissolved the Committee of the Whole and the Assembly reconvened in regular session. A motion was immediately made and seconded to adopt the resolution set forth below. A delegate then moved to close debate and this motion was carried, thereby preventing the introduction of any motion to amend or to substitute a different resolution. The question was put and by a vote of 836 to 327 the following resolution was adopted:

BE IT RESOLVED:

1. That the Unitarian Universalist Association Board of Trustees and Administration recognize and finance a Black Affairs Council which will serve to suggest and implement programs to improve the conditions of black Unitarian Universalists and black people in America.

2. That the Black Affairs Council be accorded associate or affiliate membership status with the Association, similar to that now maintained by the Unitarian Universalist Women's Federation, the Laymen's League (Unitarian Universalist) and the Unitarian Universalist Service Committee, Inc.

3. That the Unitarian Universalist Association contribute annually for four years, for the support of the Black Affairs Council, a total of $250,000. This annual contribution should be made in the following manner:

(1) $150,000 should be contributed to the Black Affairs Council no later than July 1, 1968.

(2) The remaining $100,000 will be raised by the Unitarian Universalist Association with the cooperation of the Black Unitarian Universalist Caucus during the eight month period beginning July 1, 1968. In the event that the fund raising effort is unsatisfactory, the Unitarian Universalist Association would make up the deficit. This process will be continued throughout the four year period beginning July 1, 1968.

SOURCE: "Seventh General Assembly of Unitarian Universalist Association," Unitarian Universalist Association, Black Empowerment Controversy Records, 1968–1979, Andover-Harvard Archives, bMS 531 Andover-Harvard Theological Library, Harvard Divinity School, Cambridge, MA.

UNITARIAN-UNIVERSALISTS FOR BLACK AND WHITE ACTION

Constitution

1968

Shortly before the Cleveland General Assembly a group that was originally named Black and White Alternative (BAWA) was organized by Donald S. Harrington and Cornelius McDougald. Harrington was the senior minister and McDougald the chair of Community Church of New York, the UUA's most thoroughly integrated congregation. BAWA drew support from those distressed by BAC's demands, confrontational style, and rejection of integration as a goal. The majority of the African-American members of the First Unitarian Church of Berkeley were opposed to BAC and sent Betty Bobo Seiden to General Assembly to represent them. She became BAWA's secretary while Glover Barnes, an African-American medical researcher from Buffalo, NY, and Max Gaebler, a white minister serving the First Unitarian Society of Madison, WI, were elected co-chairs. At its June meeting, the UUA board unanimously approved BAWA's application to become an official UUA-affiliate organization.

—Mark D. Morrison-Reed

ARTICLE I

Purposes

To create a racially inclusive church and denomination in an unsegregated society whose benefits and privileges are open to all of its citizens. To pursue a program of action for equality within the association and within society at large. To foster cooperation among people of all races and to avoid racial separatism.

ARTICLE II

Objectives

The specific and immediate objectives of the organization will be set forth in the By-Laws.

ARTICLE III

Membership

Membership shall be available to persons who support the purposes and objectives of the organization. Voting membership shall be available only to Unitarian-Universalists. Participating membership shall be available to any other person. Additional requirements of membership including dues may be provided in the By-Laws.

ARTICLE IV

Officers and Executive Committee

The officers shall consist of two co-chairmen, a secretary and a treasurer to be elected by majority vote of the members at the Annual Meeting. They shall serve two-year terms with the secretary and treasurer being elected in alternate years.

SOURCE: Constitution of Unitarian-Universalists for Black and White Action, Unitarian Universalist Association, Black Empowerment Controversy Records, 1968–1979, Andover-Harvard Archives, bMS 531/2, Andover-Harvard Theological Library, Harvard Divinity School, Cambridge, MA.

Constitution

1969

The Second Annual meeting of BUUC was held in Detroit and attended by 165 delegates and observers. On the agenda for that meeting, in addition to the adoption of a constitution, was accepting BAC's first annual report, developing election procedures for BUUC and BAC, and deciding what role they would play in the 1969 UUA presidential election.

—Mark D. Morrison-Reed

PREAMBLE

We, a fellowship of Black Humanists, do covenant together out of our collective Black experience for the conscious development of Black community in order to actualize the potentiality we have inherently developed by virtue of the history we have experienced and the history we are yet to enjoy as a unique people. From a glorious past anchored firmly in the African womb of human existence, to a tumultuous presence rooted deeply in America's especially perverse racism, we have learned that *man's continued inhumanity to man* will not and must not ever be tolerated. Thus, we commit ourselves to the complete destruction of white racism, white imperialism and white colonialism in any form as inherent evils to human ends.

Believing that there has been a systematic conspiracy against all people of Black African descent, we do dogmatically proclaim that all such persons are legitimate members of the oppressed community. Therefore, we dedicate ourselves to the total liberation of our people, employing whatever means are appropriate to the situation. In particular, we see as urgent the creation of *alternative constellations of power* and the design of *new Black institutions* for the systematic realization and enjoyment of our liberation. In this task, we shall not be diverted, nor shall we be compromised; we shall not grow weary, nor shall we slumber. We shall carry forth relentlessly the *revolutionary torch of Black fire,* and we shall have Peace, Power, and Glory forever. In Black Love: In Black Fellowship: In Black Community—KNOW US OF BUUC BY THESE COMMITMENTS.

Article I—Name

The name of this organization shall be the "Black Unitarian Universalist Caucus (BUUC)."

Article II—Objectives

The objectives of BUUC are:

1. To provide Black Unitarian Universalists (UUs) with a vehicle for discovering each other and the beauty of our blackness as expressed in our history, culture, and life style.
2. To make Black UUs more visible and to facilitate their greater contribution to the life of the whole society.
3. To build cooperative relationships with other Black-oriented organizations around programs and public issues affecting Blacks.
4. To sensitize non-blacks to the need for unity, power, and self-determination for Black people and other oppressed peoples.
5. To creatively engage, analyze, and support programs and organizations which lead to the empowerment, unity, and self-determination of Black people.
6. To serve as a critic of the institutions of the society, focusing attention on such areas of urgent concern as the racism built into their use of influence, wealth, program, education, liturgy, and administration.

Article III—Membership

Section 1. Membership shall be limited to those Blacks who subscribe to the purpose and objectives of BUUC and who have demonstrated concern for the collective well-being of Black people.

Section 2. A local caucus is defined as five or more Black persons who have formally organized around BUUC objectives and whose composition satisfies the requirements of this Constitution. No church or fellowship shall have more than one caucus. No person shall belong to more than one caucus or join a caucus outside his immediate geographic area, if a caucus exists in that region.

                                *   *   *

Article V—Election of the Black Affairs Council

A. Composition of the Black Affairs Council (BAC): Eligibility of BUUC members for election to BAC shall be restricted to those in good standing with national and local BUUC for at least 18 months. The Black Affairs Council shall be 11 in total number and composed of the following categories and numbers in each category:
    1. Five regions shall exist for the purpose of insuring broad geographic representation on BAC from the BUUC constituency, and each region shall have one representative on BAC, making a total of five members from the category of regional representation.

2. Two seats shall be reserved for Black sisters to insure their participation in BAC. This does not preclude their serving as regional representatives, nor does their serving as regional representatives reduce the total number of two for this category.
3. Three seats shall be reserved on BAC for non-Blacks with a demonstrated history of concern for Black people's survival and self-determination.
4. The National Chairman of BUUC shall serve on BAC automatically to insure input into BAC from the BUUC Steering Committee.

B. Method of Nomination:
1. Regional representatives (five) to be nominated by regional caucuses. Additional nominations may be presented from the floor with the following stipulation: that delegates can only nominate regional representatives from their own respective region.
2. Two sisters shall be nominated by the Nominating Committee with additional nominations being proper from the floor.
3. Three non-Blacks shall be nominated by the Nominating Committee with additional nominations being proper from the floor.
4. National Chairman (one): no nominating action necessary since this position is automatic and defined elsewhere.

C. Method of Election: All members of BAC with the exception of the seat reserved for the National Chairman must be elected by a majority vote of the constituency of BUUC at its national meeting.

D. Term of Office: All BAC members except the BUUC National Chairman shall serve a term of one year but may be re-elected annually for an indefinite number of terms.

E. Replacement: Should a voluntary vacancy or vacancies occur between annual elections, the BUUC Steering Committee is empowered to name replacements for the remainder of the term. Such replacements shall follow the characteristics of the category in which the vacancy occurs. There shall be no alternates on the Black Affairs Council.

SOURCE: Constitution of the Black Unitarian Universalist Caucus, Unitarian Universalist Association, Black Empowerment Controversy Records, 1968–1979, Andover-Harvard Archives, bMS 531/5, Andover-Harvard Theological Library, Harvard Divinity School, Cambridge, MA.

"BUUC Position on the Funding of BAWA"
1969

On January 31, a letter protesting the imposition of mandatory UUA dues was circulated. It included the signatures of both BAC and BAWA support-ers. The UUA's financial situation was dire. A $694,000 deficit was projected if the Board did not make deep cuts to the budget. Subsequently, among $92,500 in cuts recommended by the UUA Finance Committee was $50,000 from BAC's $250,000 allocation. The administration recommended that BAC's funding not be reduced and the motion was defeated 7–5. Another motion added $50,000 to the budget for BAWA. The administration did not support the motion, which nonetheless passed 13–5. BUUC swiftly responded to the Board's recommendation.

—Mark D. Morrison-Reed

The recent UUA Board recommendation to the General Assembly that BAWA be funded for $50,000 must be resoundingly defeated. Such a recommendation is not only insulting and demoralizing to the progressive forces of our denomination but also counter-productive for the major thrust of the activities and concerns of the Black Affairs Council.

Last year's General Assembly had a clear choice between BAC and BAWA. The General Assembly chose to recognize and fund BAC only; however, the Board, at its June, 1968, meeting, disregarded the expressed will of the people and granted BAWA affiliate status. This year it has chosen to go one step further and to recommend funding for BAWA. We wonder what the next step will be.

We consider it basically unjust and unfair to recognize a group whose explicit purpose is to create an alternative to Black empowerment, especially, since BUUC took its case to the people for nine months prior to the General Assembly. Such was not the case for BAWA; therefore, there is no justification for the Board's action except the admitted political desire to pacify the opposition. Under some political circumstances, this *might* be understandable; however, in a "revolutionary age" in which the people have spoken, it is incomprehensible and absurd. No amount of rhetoric about "liberal pluralism" can justify this action. To recognize and fund BAWA is, in fact, to repudiate the choice of the people and to further subject the majority of the Black constituents of the denomination to the subtle but vicious perpetuation of white racism.

We would rather reject any funding at all than to accept funding with the condition that those hell-bent on destroying Black self-determination must be funded likewise.

SOURCE: "BUUC Position on the Funding of BAWA," Unitarian Universalist Association, Black Empowerment Controversy Records, 1968–1979, Andover-Harvard Archives, bMS 531/5, Andover-Harvard Theological Library, Harvard Divinity School, Cambridge, MA.

HOMER JACK

"Keeping the Backlash Liberal"

1969

Homer A. Jack (1916–1993), director of the UUA Department of Social Respon-sibility, was a long-time peace and civil rights activist. In 1942, Jack became a founding member of the Congress on Racial Equality (CORE). He was among the first Freedom Riders in 1947 and the first white Northerners to go to Montgomery in support of the Bus Boycott. He also attended Ghana's independence celebration in 1957 and accompanied Dr. King's body from Memphis to Atlanta in 1968. In May 1969, preaching at the First Unitarian Society of Wilmington, Delaware, Jack offered his appraisal of the dilemma faced by the UUA.

—Mark D. Morrison-Reed

The climate of denomination and nation is the beginning of our discussion. We live in a world in multiple revolutions, in a nation with several rebellions which could become revolutions, and in a denomination—to put it mildly—in turmoil if not rebellion. The world revolutions are well known: social, economic, political (inde-pendence), atomic, space, technological. The U.S. rebellion is not only Black; it is generational. The denominational ferment is the result of the impact on us of Amer-ican society, the imminent departure of the Dana McLean Greely regime from our denominational life, a vigorous campaign by eight candidates for the Association presidency, severe financial difficulties, and the beginning of a serious fragmenta-tion of our movement by special denominational interests.

The Kerner Report on Civil Disorders issued more than a year ago stated that "our nation is moving toward two societies, one Black, one white—separate and unequal." That is one unmistakable trend in American society and also in our Uni-tarian Universalist denomination which is a kind of microcosm of our society—only more white, more upper middle-class, more educated, and more suburban. But racial separation today is not the only current major trend. One can also assert that perhaps more today than at least in the recent past, and to paraphrase the Kerner Report, our society and denomination are moving toward two societies, one liberal, one radical—separating if not yet separated.

✻　✻　✻

The New Left has arisen, in society and denomination, because of the need for rapid social change in all of our institutions: voluntary and governmental, local, national, worldwide. The institutions of the past are plainly not fulfilling present personal and social demands. One does not have to be a member of SDS or FULLBAC to accept the thesis that the arteries of our institutions are hopelessly clogged. Thus, all kinds of institutional changes must be made: the structure of the United Nations, the relations between nations, the role of the Pentagon, municipal/county relations, teaching at the universities, the role of the local church, the function of the religious denomination, etc. Norman Cousins recently wrote in the *Sunday Review*: "The biggest problem lies not in change itself but in the absence of enough awareness that change is necessary."

✳ ✳ ✳

We liberals must consider carefully the demands of the New Left on our institutions, whether local, regional, or national. None is ultimately "non-negotiable," and we should not be diverted by such labels or even tactics. We should consider the demands of the New Left and put them at least to the test of fact and of reason. These are not the sole tests, but they are among the tests. If, then, the demands of the New Left do make sense we should not be afraid to say, "Yes." We listened, as a denomination a year ago, to the demands of the Black Unitarian Universalist Caucus, and 72% of our General Assembly delegates agreed to fund the Unitarian Universalist Black Affairs Council.

We liberals, in considering carefully the demands of the New Left, must also not be afraid to say, "No." . . . We whites over thirty should not be so drenched with guilt that we capitulate at every turn to Blacks or youth. When we do, we are guilty of the worst form of paternalism. Often we act the patsies—the spineless creatures—our critics say we are. FULLBAC appeared until recently to assume that role by automatically endorsing every proposal of the Black Caucus. We whites should, on the contrary, be every bit as candid as the Blacks; we old liberals should be every bit as outspoken as the New Left. No group has a monopoly on telling it like it is! We should, in the end, vote for what we feel is right, not what is expedient, and on occasion that could mean voting in the negative.

We liberals, in church and denomination, must insist upon community. President Robert C. Kimball of Starr King School for the Ministry in a recent discussion at our denominational Continental Study Conference on Social Action courageously suggested that the Black Affairs Council has not maintained community—in our Unitarian Universalist denomination. It seemingly has hardly tired. We should insist upon dealing as a family with goals, priorities, and budgets. There are, in our wide—if small—church family, admittedly special interests, special priorities, even special compensatory treatment for Blacks, if not outright "reparations." But no group, no budget, not even that of the Black Affairs Council, should be sacrosanct. And no pressures, no threats, should force us as a denomination to do something which we democratically feel should not be done. The recent action of the UUA Board to allocate $250,000 to the Black Affairs Council and also $50,000 to Black and White Action (BAWA) lies almost within this surrealistic arena: a refusal to face the financial discipline of community.

We liberals, in church and denomination, must insist upon pluralism. The denominational umbrella must be big enough to include the New Left as well as the old reactionaries. Hayward Henry and Senator Roman Hruska are both Unitarian Universalists! We Unitarian Universalists do not know how to ex-communicate, and we should never try to find out how to do so. But there may again come a time when groups to the extreme left or extreme right might themselves feel uncomfortable to remain with us. That is their decision. But their going still would be our loss and our regret more perhaps than theirs.

SOURCE: Homer A. Jack, "Keeping the Backlash Liberal," Unitarian Universalist Association, Black Empowerment Controversy Records, 1968–1979, Andover-Harvard Archives, bMS 531/6, Andover-Harvard Theological Library, Harvard Divinity School, Cambridge, MA.

"The Youth Agenda"

1969

Larry Ladd's career as a national UUA volunteer leader began with his presidency of Liberal Religious Youth (LRY) in 1968–1969. Raised in a small-town New England church, with a short haircut and an intellectual demeanor, Ladd was an unlikely and welcome LRY president during a year when the social and political movements in the wider culture were driving UUA adults and their youth organization apart. LRY's adult executive director, Richard Kossow, had announced he would resign at the end of Ladd's term. Inspired by the black empowerment philosophy and organizing strategy of the Black Affairs Council, which LRY strongly supported, Ladd's executive committee shaped a Youth Agenda for the 1969 General Assembly, demanding $100,000 in funding for youth and young adult programs along with independent authority to manage it. This sermon announced the Youth Agenda to the larger movement. While the financial issues surrounding the demands of the Youth Agenda were resolved before the 1969 General Assembly began, it would take ten years before professional staff were again hired to work with UUA youth programs. Ladd disappeared from UUA involvement during his young adulthood, becoming a university administrator and higher education consultant. In 1997, when Ladd was budget director at Harvard University, he was encouraged to become involved in UU leadership once again by running for financial advisor of the UUA. He served in that role for three different terms over twelve years, as well as in other volunteer positions.

—Wayne Arnason

A time bomb is ticking in our world today. And with each succeeding tick, the moment of ultimate destruction approaches. The bomb was built by men who used power to degrade, exploit, and oppress other men, the fuel is the accumulated rage of those who have been oppressed, and the fuse is the empty promises of liberalism. The riots in the cities, the rebellions on the campuses and in the high schools, a war in Vietnam and the revolutions in the Third World are all part of the steady ticking of the bomb.

Time is running out. Either the bomb will explode destroying a corrupt world or a new era of human liberation will emerge. These are the only choices we have.

The time bomb is a testament to our burning need for justice and to the failure of the liberal process. Liberalism has failed because it has promised much while its lack of action perpetuated the conditions that created the bomb. It has tolerated the intolerable. During the liberal era, men were free to kill, free to exploit, free to manipulate. That kind of freedom has created the sick society in which we live.

We have tried the liberal way, heard the rhetoric and waited patiently. But the ticking is getting too loud.

The new era is struggling to be born. The victims of the former age are getting their heads together and planning their course of action. We will have what is rightfully ours: control over our own affairs and no arbitrary power over us that we have not sanctioned. People shall be recognized as people—shall live as free human begins be they black, yellow, or young.

We were born into a world that is against us; that treats us as things rather than as people. Now is the time to awaken America's conscience to what it is doing to its children.

It has often been said that growing up is a process of "finding oneself." On the contrary, growing up in our society is much more a process of defending oneself against a system determined to convince us of our worthlessness and shape us in its own image. In the past our defenses have failed, as is demonstrated by the empty robots that inhabit America. We as youth have been denied all human rights and responsibilities until we leave Never-Never Land and approach the Kingdom at 21 years of age. By then we are good niggers who know our place and are unable to handle either freedom or responsibility.

Our schools are youth ghettos training us to fit into existing culture rather than educating us to be individual men and women. . . .

Our churches join the partnership in repression. The youth group is usually kept at a safe distance from the rest of the church. No one pays much attention to us unless we do something judged wrong by adult standards, at which point we are brought into the fold for quick corrective measures. We are denied use of buildings or financial resources if we move off the chosen path. And when we do participate on church boards and committees, it is as tokens who are not to be taken seriously. We are not regarded as people, but as nuisances.

* * *

Our religious beliefs are the building blocks of the new age of liberation. As the institution that embodies those beliefs, we must become the vanguard of the forces leading the way to that era. If we hesitate now, we will be left behind and die with the old. We now face the most difficult challenge of all: learning to practice what we preach. For the generation gap is inconsequential in contrast to the glaring gap between what Unitarian Universalists say and do.

Youth and Blacks are the leaders of the effort to put our movement in the forefront by putting our principles into practice. And it is at this point that we, as the youth of the movement, must come alive!

I assert that I am a man, not a thing, a pet, or a slave. I will no longer tolerate being treated as such.

The keynote of the youth liberation movement is youth self-determination and empowerment. We are demanding the personal liberties and responsibilities inherent in our humanity. We demand the right to determine our own life-styles without adult intimidation. We now must be accepted for what we are—there shall be no more "holier than thou" judgments—no more arbitrary power over our values whether those values are expressed by our politics, sexual attitudes, or anything else. If adults cannot go beyond these and see us as persons, then dialogue is impossible. Finally, we are demanding that our church join us in our struggle for liberation.

We do not pretend to represent a majority of the young, or even necessarily a majority of LRY or SRL, for your first task will be to repair the damage done to this majority.

Our agenda is long, but we must be totally committed to it now—for time is running out and too many people are being destroyed.

✳ ✳ ✳

Our youth liberation movement is very threatening, for it will touch every person in his own home. And adults will feel especially threatened by the youthful idealism and individualism that they have repressed in themselves.

We may be "out of order," but we insist upon a new order and will settle for nothing less. We may be out of place, in a world we did not shape, but we are determined to shape it for our own lives. For while we are oppressed by institutions, we are possessed of vision. . . .

Ready or not, here we come!

SOURCE: Larry Ladd, "The Youth Agenda," provided by the author.

"UUA Budget Recommendations"
1969

The eighth General Assembly of the UUA was held in July in Boston. Its 1,785 delegates represented the highest attendance at a General Assembly up to that point and for many years to come. It was a tumultuous General Assembly dominated by the election of a new UUA president and a rebellion that became known as "The Walkout." First, BUUC members and their allies commandeered the microphones until their motion was addressed. After the Assembly voted against changing the agenda to consider the budget, BUUC members walked out. Subsequently BUUC supporters, who later called themselves the "Moral Caucus," marched out and gathered at the Arlington Street Church. The Annual Report of the British General Assembly of Unitarians described the meeting as "lively and at times explosive." The following day, after hours of negotiation, BUUC members and allies returned to the meeting and the resolution was taken up and passed, as were their other demands.

—Mark D. Morrison-Reed

Dr. Raymond C. Hopkins, Executive Vice President, reviewed for the Assembly the 1969–70 budget of the Association. The General Assembly recommended to the new Board of Trustees the following actions relative to the 1969–70 budget:

That this General Assembly goes on record as funding either Black and White Action (BAWA) or Black Affairs Council (BAC) but not both.

(Adopted by a vote of 798 to 737.)

That the General Assembly accept the action of the Board of Trustees of the UUA on the refunding of the Black Affairs Council.

That the Eighth Annual Meeting of the Unitarian Universalist Association strongly recommends to the Board of Trustees of the UUA that; 1) The cuts in financial aid to theological schools reflected in the proposed budget for 1969–70 be restored and; 2) Scholarship funds for theological students be increased from $25,000 to $70,000, to reflect the increased number of students and the higher cost of living.

The General Assembly urges the Board of Trustees to appropriate $50,000 for the empowerment of the Chicano community in the United States in their struggle for human dignity and economic security in both agricultural and urban pursuits.

That the General Assembly recommend to the Board of Trustees to reinstitute the budget cut in the United Nations office.

That the religious education of children be given a higher priority in the Association's budget so that it may move ahead vigorously and rapidly in religious education curriculum research, field services and personnel recruitment and training.

That this General Assembly recommends to the Board of Trustees of the UUA that a much higher priority be given to the work of the Canadian Unitarian Council in the annual budget allocation.

The General Assembly most strongly urges the Board of Trustees to move as rapidly as possible and in any event, not later than the fiscal year 1970–71, to a balanced budget for the Association based on realistic projections of expected income.

SOURCE: "Eighth General Assembly of the Unitarian Universalist Association," *Unitarian Universalist Association 1970 Directory* (Boston: Unitarian Universalist Association, 1970), 175–76.

GLOVER BARNES

"The Case for Integrated Unitarianism"
1969

*In 1969, the First Unitarian Society of Cleveland began a process of discern-
ment about whether to give its building to the local BUUC. In the lead-up to
a vote, both Hayward Henry and Glover W. Barnes (1923–2009) preached to
the congregation. Raised in Alabama, Barnes was a microbiologist, a member
of the First Unitarian Church of Buffalo, and BAWA co-chair. When Barnes
delivered the following sermon to the congregation on October 12, BUUC
members walked out. On November 2, after four votes, those present voted to
give the property to BUUC. That vote was contested in court. Opponents of
the plan eventually lost their court case, and on March 1, 1970, the building
and $35,000 were transferred to BUUC.*

—Mark D. Morrison-Reed

To put it bluntly, I am here to tell you what I, as a Black Integrationist Unitarian
would recommend, in practical and philosophical terms, to a congregation of religious liberals who—being mostly white—are being pressured to leave a black community. We are told that we cannot worship together, we are told that white people
are no longer relevant. We are told that *Negroes* are no longer relevant. We are told
that *colored people* are no longer relevant. We are told that *Black individuals* are no
longer relevant. It is only a *"Collectivist of Blackness"* that is relevant.

What garbage!

I am told that I must change White masters for Black Masters. I did not come to
this movement to do that. I came to this movement to free you and to free myself.
This is the only way in this society that we are going to be able to look one another
in the eye and celebrate ourselves. Before any of you decide on this matter finally, I
hope your minds are still open to a consideration of alternatives that are not necessarily couched in inflaming rhetoric of the counter-revolution which offers to take
us back in time despite the insistence on the part of proponents of this counter-
revolution that we should turn our back on history. You see, history is nevertheless
born in upon us.

❊   ❊   ❊

There is no substitute in this multi-racial society for true integration. You can
dilly-dally, you can avoid, you can retreat, you can rationalize, and I'm going to

continue to look you in the eye, and celebrate in you my blackness, and you had better celebrate in me your whiteness because we do it together or we all die.

*   *   *

I am an integrationist because I know what this society needs. I can't say that I speak for all or even some Black people. I do believe that there are those who share my beliefs. When I came to this movement, I didn't come to this movement to be white, perish the thought! I didn't need a psychiatrist; I celebrated my blackness, that is why I came to this movement. You see, if I celebrate my blackness I cannot deny your whiteness because I have no need to deny your whiteness. I don't need to deny my blackness, therefore I will not deny your blackness.

We are a nation of men. We have our laws, and we are and obey—and celebrate—and reject—and remove—and rejuvenate—and regenerate law,—but—*we relate to one another as men.*

*   *   *

Basically the problem is that true integration has never really been tried. What we call integration was not really integration. It was desegregation. It was palliative. How many Black people do you have in this congregation? You don't even know. Why don't you use your resources? Is it too much for you to go and count Black faces, Black heads? It's not too much for me—start counting here now—"Hi Brother," there's one there. "Hi Sister." I can count! Make a realistic assessment of your resources. Find out what your people really want. Find out what the problems are in this community. Forget about yourselves for a moment, would you, please, for the sake of the human revolution.

Do you know what happened when they tried to maintain a separatist system in the South? They went broke. Do you realize the reason we always cried poor in the South was because we were trying to maintain two separate societies? Today, in the South, *they are getting smart.* And what is happening to us in the North? We think it's time to retrogress. Somebody throws a brick, a real one or one of rhetoric, and we are ready to run.

Didn't you know there were going to be brickbats? When you joined this movement what did you expect? Comfort? Prestige? Status? Forget it! The human revolution is not concerned with these things. The human revolution is concerned about the integrity of the relationship between Black men, White men, Yellow men, and Red men and all the other men of the earth. We all seek to be free. It can only be done together.

SOURCE: Glover W. Barnes, "The Case for Integrated Unitarianism," Unitarian Universalist Association, Black Empowerment Controversy Records, 1968–1979, Andover-Harvard Archives, bMS 531/6, Andover-Harvard Theological Library, Harvard Divinity School, Cambridge, MA.

NIKKYO NIWANO

Honzon: The Object of Worship
of Rissho Kosei-kai
1969

Nikkyo Niwano (1906–1999) founded Rissho Kosei-kai, an association of lay Buddhists with a special devotion to the Lotus Sutra, in Japan in 1938. In the aftermath of the Second World War, Niwano became deeply committed to activism against nuclear weapons and to interfaith dialogue. He attended the Second Vatican Council in 1965 and the twentieth World Congress of the International Association for Religious Freedom (IARF) in 1969. (He later served as the IARF's first non-Western president.) Niwano met Dana McLean Greeley in 1968, when Greeley was touring Asia in search of partners for an interreligious peace organization. Two years later, they cofounded the World Conference of Religions for Peace, an international network closely aligned with the United Nations. With a current membership of approximately 1.2 million households, Rissho Kosei-kai has been one of Unitarian Universalist's most steadfast partners in interfaith dialogue. Niwano's book on the statue of the Buddha that is the "object of worship" for Rissho Kosei-kai began by describing his vision for the role of religion in the modern world. Further Reading: Jaquelin Stone, "Nichiren's Activist Heirs: Soka Gakkai, Rissho Koseikai, Nipponzan Myohoji," in Christopher Queen, et al., eds., Action Dharma: New Studies in Engaged Buddhism *(London: RoutledgeCurzon, 2003), 63–94.*

—Dan McKanan

In modern society man lives with various problems born from endless human desires. There are the problems of food, clothes and shelter indispensable to everyday human life, the problems of human relationships at home and in society, and finally the problems of international relations and world peace.

When we look back at human history, we find that many efforts have been made by man for the purpose of solving these problems. It can be said that politics, business and science, each in its field, have contributed to the solution of these human problems. . . .

But all advancement of the sciences cannot solve all human problems. Since man is a living being, the inevitable problems of birth, age, disease and death, and the ultimate problems of the purpose and way of life will remain unsettled.

Furthermore, politics, science and all other branches of human civilization which should exist for the good of man, sometimes deprive man of his freedom, oppress and throw him down into a profound unrest.

The fear of a nuclear war is a conspicuous example. There are many examples of this kind in past history. Even now all modern people feel a great unrest, but we should not repeat such mistakes in our age when we have this powerful nuclear energy at hand.

Therefore, if politics, science and other branches of civilization which man possesses should truly contribute to human happiness, a fundamental wisdom is necessary as their common base. . . .

This means that religion should

first, teach the fundamental way to solve the various problems and desires occurring in daily life;

second, teach the fundamental guiding principles and wisdom of human life which are the common base of politics, science and other branches of civilization, in order to have them contribute to true human happiness;

third, give the fundamental solution to the ultimate problems of birth, age, disease, death and others which no man can avoid;

fourth, give an ultimate solution concerning the purpose or mental attitude with which man should live such as, "For what purpose does man live?" and "How should man live?";

fifth, teach the way that enables man to exert the fullest ability and make the best contribution in order to become perfect as an individual and to establish peace of society.

SOURCE: Nikkyo Niwano, *Honzon: The Object of Worship of Rissho Kosei-kai*, trans. Chido Takeda and Wilhelm Schiffer (Tokyo: Rissho Kosei-Kai, 1969), 5–8.

General Resolution on Survival and Population Control

1970

This detailed statement on environmental issues was approved by the Unitarian Universalist General Assembly just a few months after the first celebration of Earth Day in April 1970. It built on a 1962 resolution on "Population," which presented birth control and family planning as the antidote to "uncontrolled and unplanned population growth," as well as a 1966 resolution supporting the Clean Air Act and other recent environmental legislation. But this was the denomination's first statement highlighting the broader religious implications of the "ecological crisis."

—Dan McKanan

WHEREAS, two hundred scientists from fifty different countries meeting in Paris in the fall of 1968 under the auspices of the United Nations Economic Social and Cultural Organization came to the conclusion that within a period of approximately twenty years the life process on earth will be seriously threatened if not in fact dead unless major changes are made immediately; and

WHEREAS, U Thant has repeatedly warned the nations of the world that fundamental political, economic and environmental changes must be made very quickly if we are to forestall an irreversible destructive course within ten years; and

WHEREAS, we recognize that the "ecological crisis" is not just around the corner; it is here now. An estimated four million people a year—over ten thousand a day—starve to death. Millions more die from conditions caused or aggravated by environmental decay. One half of the world's people are either malnourished or undernourished. Population continues to mount at an explosive rate, creating drains on already diminishing resources. Slums, poverty, and war testify to the fact that man has not learned that he is dependent on a limited life system; and

WHEREAS, we are convinced that man's survival as a species is imperiled by his mushrooming technology and by his excessive breeding rate;

THEREFORE BE IT RESOLVED: That the Unitarian Universalist Association:

1. Recognize that many distinguished ecologists believe that environmental problems are not ultimately solvable by mere science or technology. A new religious emphasis is needed which includes a deep reverence for the diversity of life and understands people's dependence upon the planet's life system. Such an awareness would lead to a new life style which is balanced ecologically;

2. Encourage the leaders of the great religions of the world to send delegates or observers to Stockholm, to the United Nations 1972 Conference on the human environment;

3. Use its present resources in such a way that Unitarian and Universalist Churches and Fellowships increase their ecological understanding and undertake appropriate action by:

   a. giving emphasis to environmental matters in the UU world;
   b. developing materials and curricula on the religious aspect of ecology;
   c. urging Beacon Press to publish pertinent books when possible;
   d. calling upon our UUA representatives in Ottawa, Washington DC and the United Nations to support legislation of resolution on environmental change;
   e. encouraging each society to participate in local environmental action programs;

4. Urge the members to restrict themselves and their own future family planning to no more than two children per family except by adoption;

5. Support the right of each individual to limit his family size through freely available contraceptive materials, abortions, and sterilization, and publicize the availability of these materials;

6. Work with the Unitarian Universalist Service Committee and other groups or agencies who are working toward worldwide population control.

BE IT FURTHER RESOLVED: That the UUA:

1. Recognize Canada's efforts to prevent pollution of the Arctic; and
2. Support Canada's legislation creating a 100-mile offshore pollutional control jurisdiction zone around Canada's North coast and Arctic islands;
3. Notify the United States government and the Canadian government of the UUA's endorsement of Canada's pollution control legislation.

SOURCE: Unitarian Universalist Social Justice Statements, uua.org/statements/unitarian-universalist-statement-survival-and-population-control

General Resolution on Equal Rights and Opportunities for Women

1970

Despite its repeated affirmation of support for abortion rights, the Unitarian Universalist General Assembly did not pass any broader resolutions addressing women's rights until 1970. In that year the delegates joined a growing movement to revive the Equal Rights Amendment, which had been first proposed by Alice Paul in 1923. The National Organization for Women, which had been organized in 1966, began picketing the Senate for hearings on the amendment in February 1970. It was passed by the House of Representatives in 1971 and by the Senate in 1972, and was then ratified by thirty-five states, three short of the number needed for a constitutional amendment to be enacted. Further Reading: Ann Braude, "A Religious Feminist—Who Can Find Her?: Historiographical Challenges from the National Organization for Women," Journal of Religion 84 (October 2004): 555–72; Sara Evans, Personal Politics: The Roots of Women's Liberation in the Civil Rights Movement and the New Left (New York: Vintage Press, 1980).

—Dan McKanan

RECOGNIZING: That women have minority status in terms of employment opportunities, legal rights, the educational system, political power, and positions of influence in religious bodies;

AWARE: That woman tend to react to their cultural image by limiting their aspirations and by forming low evaluations of their own capabilities;

OBSERVING: That profound changes are occurring in our society affecting the role of women and men, including trends toward smaller families, increased education for women, and the growing number of women in employment;

BELIEVING: That critical social problems require the full use of educated, trained womanpower in responsible positions;

BE IT RESOLVED: That the 1970 General Assembly:

1. Urges special concern for improving the image, aspirations, and opportunities of women so that they may work together with men toward creating a more fully

human society for both; and to that end changes are called for in the education and counseling of girls and boys to ensure this kind of equality;

2. Asks for greater efforts to prevent discrimination against women in employment and to encourage the utilization of women in significant levels in business, education, and government;

3. Calls upon the United States and Provinces of Canada to enact fair employment legislation prohibiting discrimination on account of sex where such laws do not now exist;

4. Requests that a special effort be made in the Unitarian Universalist Association, its churches and fellowships, to place greater numbers of qualified young and mature women in policy-making positions, and to secure equal opportunities and pay for women in the ministry, religious education, and administration;

5. Calls upon the United States Congress to pass the Equal Rights Amendment without delay and supports its ratification by the states.

SOURCE: General Resolution on Equal Rights and Opportunities for Women, uua.org/statements/equal-rights-and-opportunities-women

General Resolution on Discrimination against Homosexuals and Bisexuals

1970

The gay liberation movement is often dated to the Stonewall riots of 1969, when patrons of the Stonewall Inn in New York City took to the streets rather than accept continuing harassment by the police. A foundation for activism had been laid earlier by the "homophile" organizations of the 1950s and by religious organizations such as the Council on Religion and the Homosexual (founded in 1964) and the Metropolitan Community Church (founded in 1968). Many individual Unitarian Universalists supported the budding movement; as early as 1957 and 1958, Unitarian ministers Ernest Pipes and Harry Scholefield began performing weddings for same-sex couples. This resolution was the first expression of denominational opposition to discrimination based on sexual orientation. Further Reading: Jeff Wilson, "'Which One of You Is the Bride?' Unitarian Universalism and Same-Sex Marriage in North America, 1957–1972," Journal of Unitarian Universalist History 35 (2011/2012): 156–72; *Lillian Faderman,* The Gay Revolution: The Story of the Struggle *(New York: Simon & Schuster, 2015).*

—Dan McKanan

RECOGNIZING THAT:

1. A significant minority in this country are either homosexual or bisexual in their feelings and/or behavior;
2. Homosexuality has been the target of severe discrimination by society and in particular by the police and other arms of government;
3. A growing number of authorities on the subject now see homosexuality as an inevitable sociological phenomenon and not as a mental illness;
4. There are Unitarian Universalists, clergy and laity, who are homosexuals or bisexuals;

THEREFORE BE IT RESOLVED: That the 1970 General Assembly of the Unitarian Universalist Association:

1. Urges all peoples immediately to bring an end to all discrimination against homosexuals, homosexuality, bisexuals, and bisexuality, with specific immediate attention to the following issues:

    a.   private consensual behavior between persons over the age of consent shall be the business only of those persons and not subject to legal regulations;

    b.   a person's sexual orientation or practice shall not be a factor in the granting or renewing of federal security clearance, visas, and the granting of citizenship or employment;

2.   Calls upon the UUA and its member churches, fellowships, and organizations immediately to end all discrimination against homosexuals in employment practices, expending special effort to assist homosexuals to find employment in our midst consistent with their abilities and desires;

3.   Urges all churches and fellowships, in keeping with changing social patterns, to initiate meaningful programs of sex education aimed at providing more open and healthier understanding of sexuality in all parts of the United States and Canada, and with the particular aim to end all discrimination against homosexuals and bisexuals.

SOURCE: General Resolution on Discrimination against Homosexuals and Bisexuals, uua.org/statements/discrimination-against-homosexuals-and-bisexuals

"Statement of Disaffiliation of the Black Affairs Council, Inc., from the Unitarian Universalist Association"

1970

Robert N. West was elected UUA president at the 1969 Boston General Assembly. Upon taking office, West discovered that the UUA faced a terrible financial situation. The UUA, and the AUA before it, had routinely run budget deficits in excess of 12 percent; now the unrestricted funds were depleted and there was an outstanding bank demand note for $450,000. At the 1969 General Assembly, the delegates had added more money for districts, theological schools, and Chicano empowerment to a budget that was already unbalanced. To reach a balanced budget as urged by the Assembly, $1 million had to be cut from a $2,600,000 budget. The UUA Board of Directors, rather than the Assembly, bears primary fiduciary responsibility for the UUA. One of many measures the Board took to balance the budget was to vote to affirm its commitment to allocating $1 million to the Black Affairs Council, but to reduce the annual remittance to $200,000, to be disbursed over five years instead of four. Furthermore, if the Annual Program Fund exceeded its goal, the first $50,000 would go to BAC. This change led BAC to disaffiliate from the UUA.

—Mark D. Morrison-Reed

On Saturday, January 24, 1970, the Board of Directors of the Unitarian Universalist Association (UUA) voted *not to reverse* an earlier decision it had made to cut its current allocation to the Black Affairs Council (BAC) by $50,000. Furthermore, the UUA Board recorded its intent to extend the balance of the $1 million commitment to BAC over a five-year period rather than the four-year period we originally agreed on in 1968.

Most Uni-Uni's are well aware by now that the question of BAC funding has been subjected to more scrutiny and wide-based decision-making (it was the prime issue in two General Assemblies) than any program this denomination has considered. We feel that the People have made known their collective will on this issue: that the Black Affairs Council should receive $250,000 per year for a four-year period, and that this is but a pittance of what is owed. The two votes at the General

Assemblies of 1968 and 1969 said very clearly that Unitarian Universalists, responding positively, wished the Black Agenda to be the top U-U priority and meant to commit themselves to that action with dependable financial support.

It must be understood, however, that the majority of this denomination's hierarchy—the UUA Board of Directors—have never favored the existence and funding of BAC. They put the question of BAC affiliation and funding before the General Assembly, it's true, but they also acted at *the same time* to affiliate another organization and even attempted to fund it. It is safe to conjecture that had it not been for THE PEOPLE of this denomination, BAC affiliation and funding would never have been realized. The Board's response to BAC has been comparable to the response that white institutions normally give to Blackamericans—racist and reactionary. . . .

Blackamerican Uni-Uni's have put as much time and energy as we can afford into a process that has led simply to our being "the last hired and the first fired." We must now move beyond the recalcitrance of the UUA Board and take our case to the People.

We feel that the majority of white Uni-Uni's want to see the BAC program continue. In refusing to accept the conditions established by the UUA Board, we feel that most Uni-Uni's will be inspired by our *integrity* in that we did not allow *the People's will* to be violated after it had been expressed by two General Assemblies.

Many people have asked why we cannot be "good sports" and take our lumps along with the other programs that were cut. We feel that a program that has been as meticulously debated over two and one-half years, as has the BAC program, cannot be placed in the same category as other denominational programs. Further, we do not agree with those persons throughout the land who would relegate this nation's racial problems to some obscure position on the list of national priorities. We still see racial inequities as the number one problem of the United States, ecological imbalances notwithstanding.

The fact that the UUA is spending 1.6 million dollars in the current fiscal year (in addition to BAC's allocation) shows clearly that money was available, but the decision-makers obviously lacked an unequivocal commitment to black empowerment through BAC. It is hard to understand why the Board could not have "frozen" the $250,000 due BAC and pared the remaining budgetary items accordingly.

BAC is the major social outreach program of the UUA affecting large numbers of non-Unitarian Universalists. It deals with the most crucial social issues in America today and is thus uniquely translating the Unitarian Universalist rhetoric of "brotherhood and humanity" into concrete form. . . .

BAC is the most viable program the denomination has, and its imaginative structure and style make it a model that other denominations have already begun to follow for relating to the Blackamerican community. Therefore, we *now appeal to all who recognize the necessity for the program's continuance and growth to back our efforts by funneling financial support directly to the Black Affairs Council, instead of through the UUA Annual Fund.*

SINCE WE WISH TO DO THIS AND SINCE AFFILIATE AGENCIES OF THE UUA ARE NOT PERMITTED TO RAISE FUNDS INDEPENDENTLY, WE MUST ANNOUNCE THE DISAFFILIATION OF THE BLACK AFFAIRS COUNCIL, INCORPORATED, FROM THE UUA.

There are a number of relevant points that our supporters must remember about this disaffiliation:

(1) Disaffiliation of BAC from the UUA should not affect the participation of Blackamerican Unitarian Universalists at the local church level;

(2) Disaffiliation does NOT mean that BAC is no longer a Unitarian Universalist program, but like the Unitarian Universalist Service Committee, *it is simply not a program of the UUA.* In its new status, BAC will be more dependent than ever upon the denomination's individual members.

(3) Disaffiliation does not mean that Black Unitarian Universalists have given up on the institution of the Unitarian Universalism. Unitarian Universalists have gone further than most predominantly-white institutions in developing *new institutional responses* to Blackamericans, only to have that progress systematically negated by a monolithic Board of Directors that is not responsive to the will of the People. Black Unitarian Universalists feel that the main work of developing a positive response in this institution *is yet before us.*

(4) Disaffiliation means that BAC must raise $50,000 to make up the amount that was cut from its budget in the current fiscal year. In that the 1968 General Assembly had made its $1 million commitment to our *four-year* program, indigenous groups are looking to us for continued support based on that commitment, especially since it is viewed as a partial reparational settlement of the capital owed to Blackamericans.

It must be clearly understood that when we speak of fund-raising and of the current year's goal of $50,000, we are referring to BAC's operating budget. It is through this budget that we support hard-core organizing projects across the country as well as BAC's administrative operation.

In addition, we have our economic development program which will be conducted through the sale of *BAC BONDS*. This is an *investment* program for churches, fellowships and individuals and should not be confused with the appeal for *donations* to the operating budget.

Disaffiliation will NOT affect our investment program. We have already begun carrying that to the People and will continue to do so.

(5) In 1967 and again in 1968, BAC proponents were told that, as an affiliate of the UUA, the Black Affairs Council could not engage in independent fund-

raising activity. In 1969, when we witnessed another affiliate was involved in its own independent fund-raising, we inquired about the propriety of such fund-raising activity, only to be given an ambiguous ruling: that *funded* affiliates (BAC) could not be involved in fund-raising, but non-funded affiliates (BAWA) could. We consider this ruling to be a good example of institutional game-playing with a racist motivation.

(6) There is a historical precedent for the action we are taking: Some years ago, the Unitarian Universalist Service Committee (UUSC) also disaffiliated from the UUA. . . .

(7) It must also be clearly understood that we will not attend the business sessions of the 1970 General Assembly. We refuse to spend time and energy in a process which subverts the will of the People, and until it is decided whether this institution will operate through the will of the People rather than a select hierarchy, we abstain. The General Assembly now becomes the business of the white agenda.

Despite the considerable difficulty, the double-standard treatment, the unresponsiveness and the curious insensitivity we have experienced from the UUA Board, we feel that we have not allowed its actions to diminish the positive support the BAC program has received from U-U individuals and from individual churches and fellowships of this denomination. We need and intend to expand upon that support, and by this method raise the capital owed to our People.

POWER TO THE PEOPLE AT LAST!

SOURCE: "Statement of Disaffiliation of the Black Affairs Council, Inc., from the Unitarian Universalist Association," Unitarian Universalist Association, Black Empowerment Controversy Records, 1968–1979, Andover-Harvard Archives, bMS 531/1, Andover-Harvard Theological Library, Harvard Divinity School, Cambridge, MA.

DERYCK CALDERWOOD

About Your Sexuality

1971, 1973

deryck calderwood (1923–1986), wrote About Your Sexuality *(AYS) just before becoming the founding director of the first graduate program in human sexuality education at New York University. calderwood, who wrote his name in lowercase, was a consultant for the Sex Information and Education Council of the United States (SIECUS) when he co-led the 1967 Fall Conference of the Liberal Religious Educators Association (LREDA) on the subject of sexuality. This was a fraught topic for congregations and parents alike in the midst of the 1960s Sexual Revolution, and the conference sparked the idea of a new curriculum that would reach most young people before the onset of sexual activity, embodying the best of psychology and biology, progressive morality, and educational theory. calderwood developed the program with a team of ten professionals. SIECUS later gave calderwood's program a critical review, questioning AYS's use of explicit educational filmstrips. During the twenty-nine years of AYS's use in our congregations, the explicit filmstrips depicting masturbation, heterosexual lovemaking, and homosexual lovemaking remained its most controversial elements. AYS also broke new ground as perhaps the only sexuality education program that affirmed birth control, challenged gender norms, and recognized homosexuality and bisexuality as natural. In response to the 1970 UUA General Assembly's directive, AYS was quickly revised, with a 1973 edition including far more education about "Homosexual Life Styles." AYS firmly established Unitarian Universalism as a leader in sexuality education for young people, a role it continues to play with* Our Whole Lives. *Further Reading: Sarah Gibb Millspaugh, "In Context: A Study of the* About Your Sexuality *Curriculum and Its Times,"* Religious Humanism *42/1 (Fall 2011): 3–29; Robert Nelson West,* Crisis and Change: My Years as President of the Unitarian Universalist Association, 1969–1977 *(Boston: Skinner House, 2007), 53–54.*

— Sarah Gibb Millspaugh

What Is About Your Sexuality

About Your Sexuality is a pioneering educational program to improve the quality of education for human sexuality for junior high young people. (It can also be an important educational experience for older teen-agers and adults.) Beginning with the questions which the young people themselves bring to the program, the materials of *About Your Sexuality* are designed to help young people explore, according to their interest, the facts, feelings, attitudes, and values they must take into consideration in order to understand their own sexuality and to be responsible decision-makers in this area of their lives.

* * *

The reader may be so much in agreement with the possible opportunities provided by *About Your Sexuality* . . . that he may be unaware of the potentially controversial nature of the program. He may even feel he has read similar statements of intent for other programs of education for human sexuality and conclude that this program is similar to others he has seen or even used.

This Program Is Different

Unlike most sex education materials–

. . . it represents an openness and honesty with young people to which some in our society would object;

. . . . it offers young people an opportunity to inquire into and clarify attitudes toward expressions of human sexuality, including those, such as homosexuality, which are not usually discussed openly and honestly;

. . . . it portrays visually and explicitly various expressions of human sexuality, such as lovemaking, masturbation, same-sex and homosexual behavior;

. . . it offers junior high young people an opportunity to obtain and discuss accurate information under proper educational auspices about aspects of human sexuality.

Because *About Your Sexuality* represents a breakthrough in sex education materials, it is important to give careful attention to building among the members of your organization an understanding of the purpose of and need for this program and to developing informed support for its use. . . .

Why Was About Your Sexuality Created?

The importance and need for effective sex education are widely recognized. The report of the President's commission on obscenity and pornography observes that "the very foundation of our society rests upon healthy sexual attitudes grounded in appropriate accurate sexual information." (*The Report of the Commission on Obscenity and Pornography* [New York, Bantam, 1970]). The commission also noted that:

> A large majority of sex educators and counselors are of the opinion that most adolescents are interested in explicit sexual materials, and that this interest is a product of natural curiosity about sex. They also feel that if

adolescents had access to adequate information regarding sex, through appropriate sex education, their interest in pornography would be reduced.

The commission recommended that "a massive sex education effort be launched" and stated that a program embodying the characteristics formulated by the commission would provide a "powerful, positive approach to the problems of obscenity and pornography."

*   *   *

The responsible social institutions—home, school, and church—continue to maintain silence concerning sex. As a result, peers, pornography, and the popular press serve as the available sources of sex information for adolescents today. If we are going to change such an untenable situation, the socializing institutions of our society will need to take the initiative in establishing programs for youth which provide them the opportunity for learning what they want and need to know about human sexuality in a totally honest educational experience guided by well-prepared teachers. Such programs will need to make use of imaginative educational materials and methods which actively involve youth in the learning process. Only then will youth develop an understanding of their human sexuality and integrate it into their total personality development. *About Your Sexuality* is such a program.

*   *   *

Why Is Explicit Visual and Other Multimedia Material Used in About Your Sexuality?

Today's youth are visually oriented. They have become accustomed to photographic presentations of everything from fetal life to space exploration. Visual aids have become an integral part of the formal educational process in every subject except sexuality. The absence of explicit visual presentations in most sex education materials is the "norm," despite the fact that young people often have access behind the scenes to pornographic materials, and are exposed to sexual materials in settings that give them a distorted perception about human sexuality.

Moreover, without explicit visuals it is extremely difficult for teachers to give young people accurate information in an understandable fashion and to answer the questions that young people have about their sexuality. Experience during early stages of the field test revealed that diagrammatic representations, as opposed to actual photographs, did not provide the young people with the information they wanted and needed. When the diagrammatic representations were replaced by explicit visuals, the teachers were able to communicate more effectively with the students.

*   *   *

Homosexual Life Styles (1973)

Objectives

To point out that homosexuality, bisexuality and heterosexuality are all forms of sexual expression. Any one of these may be a valid form of sexual expression for some people.

To help students understand that a significant minority of our population live gay life styles, and to help students accept these styles as viable life patterns for gay men and women.

To help young people with homosexual feelings realize that they are not alone and that others, past and present, share their feelings.

To point out that affectionate, loving, satisfying relationships can be and are experienced by persons who live homosexual, bisexual and heterosexual life styles.

To emphasize that society discriminates severely against gay people; that this discrimination violates the commitment to equal justice for all; and that gay people, like other minorities, are organizing to overcome this discrimination.

To help students understand that a person becomes aware of his or her sexual orientation through a variety of life experiences. An individual does not deliberately choose his or her sexual feelings, whether homosexual, bisexual, or heterosexual. Individuals can choose the ways they express their sexual feelings.

To help young people relate positively to peers, relatives and other individuals who may be homosexual.

※ ※ ※

A Word to the Teacher

There is probably no area of sexual behavior where objective fact is more clouded by myth, misunderstanding, fear, and guilt. To avoid communicating attitudes and responses based on the myths of an earlier generation, the resource reading *must* be done. It is vital to be aware that some members of your class may be experiencing feelings of affection and love for someone of their own sex and may be wondering if they are gay. They may even be involved in homosexual behavior. A condescending look at "what those people do" is not appropriate. Some of "those people" are us.

SOURCE: deryck calderwood, "Introductory Notes" and "Homosexual Life Styles," *About Your Sexuality*, rev. ed. (Boston: Beacon Press, 1973).

"Introduction," *The Pentagon Papers*

1971

Senator Mike Gravel (1930–) represented Alaska in the United States Senate from 1969 to 1981. Raised in the Catholic Church, Gravel moved to Alaska in 1956 and joined the Anchorage Unitarian Universalist Fellowship soon thereafter. In 1971, the former Defense Department staffer Daniel Ellsberg began leaking secret documents related to the Vietnam War to the New York Times, *but their publication was blocked by federal injunction. After being refused by more prominent legislators, Ellsberg persuaded Gravel to read the documents at a subcommittee hearing that he chaired and to place them in the Congressional Record. After publication in the* Times *resumed, Gravel arranged for Beacon Press (which is owned by the Unitarian Universalist Association) to publish a comprehensive, four-volume edition of what were by then known as the Pentagon Papers. This resulted in an FBI investigation of Beacon Press and solidified Beacon's reputation as a publisher fully committed to the free and responsible search for truth and meaning. Further Reading: Daniel Ellsberg,* Secrets: A Memoir of Vietnam and the Pentagon Papers *(New York: Viking Press, 2002).*

—Dan McKanan

These are agonizing times for America. This nation has been torn apart by a war that has seared its conscience. We have spent lives and wealth without limit in pursuit of an unworthy goal, preserving our own power and prestige while laying waste the unfortunate lands of Southeast Asia.

✳   ✳   ✳

Free and informed public debate is the source of our strength. Remove it and our democratic institutions become a sham. Perceiving this, our forefathers included with our Constitution a Bill of Rights guaranteeing the maximum competition in the marketplace of ideas, and insuring the widest opportunity for the active and full participation of an enlightened electorate.

The American people have never agreed that the performance of their elected officials should be immune from public discussion and review. They have never failed to support their government and its policies, once they were convinced of the rightness of those policies. But they should not be expected to offer their support merely on the word of a President and his close advisors. To adopt that position, as many do today, is to demonstrate a basic mistrust in the collective wisdom of the people and a frightening lack of confidence in our form of government.

* * *

For it is the leaders who have been found lacking, not the people. It is the leaders who have systematically misled, misunderstood, and most of all, ignored the people in pursuit of a reckless foreign policy which the people never sanctioned. Separated from the public by a wall of secrecy and by their own desires for power, they failed to heed the voice of the people, who saw instinctively that America's vital interests were not involved in Southeast Asia. Nor could they bring themselves to recognize the knowledge and insight of that large number of private citizens who foresaw the eventual failure of their plans. As we now know, they were able even to ignore the frequently accurate forecasts of the government's own intelligence analysts.

The barriers of secrecy have allowed the national security apparatus to evolve a rigid orthodoxy which excludes those who question the accepted dogma. The result has been a failure to reexamine the postulates underlying our policy, or to give serious attention to alternatives which might avoid the kinds of disastrous choices that have been made in the past decade.

Nothing in recent history has so served to illuminate the damaging effects of secrecy as has the release of the Pentagon Papers, the Defense Department's history of American decisionmaking on Vietnam. This study is a remarkable work, commissioned by the men who were responsible for our Vietnam planning but who, by 1967, had come to see that our policy was bankrupt. The study was thus a unique attempt, by the Administration that had developed the policy, to look at its foundations and to see what had gone wrong.

* * *

However, the public has not had access to this study. Newspapers in possession of the documents have published excerpts from them and have prepared their own summary of the study's findings. In doing this, they have performed a valuable public service. But every American is entitled to examine the study in full and to digest for himself the lessons it contains. The people must know the full story of their government's actions over the past twenty years, to ensure that never again will this great nation be led into waging a war through ignorance and deception.

It is for this reason that I determined, when I came into possession of this material, that it must be made available to the American public. For the tragic history it reveals must now be known. The terrible truth is that the Papers do not support our public statements. The Papers do not support our good intentions. The Papers prove that, from the beginning, the war has been an American war, serving only to perpetuate American military power in Asia. Peace has never been on the American agenda for Southeast Asia.

But now there is a great awakening in our land. There is a yearning for peace, and a realization that we need never have gone to war. There is a yearning for a more free and open society, and the emerging recognition of repression of people's lives, of their right to know, and of their right to determine their nation's future. And there is a yearning for the kind of mutual trust between those who govern and those who are governed that has been so lacking in the past.

If ever there was a time for change, it is now. It is in this spirit that I hope the past, as revealed in the Pentagon Papers, will help us make a new beginning, toward that better America which we all seek.

SOURCE: Mike Gravel, "Introduction," in *The Pentagon Papers: The Defense Department History of United States Decisionmaking on Vietnam: The Senator Gravel Edition* (Boston: Beacon Press, 1971), 1:ix–xii.

The Invisible Minority: The Homosexuals in Our Society

1972

In the early 1970s, the UUA Department of Education and Social Concern developed The Invisible Minority, *an adult education curriculum consisting of a three-part filmstrip with accompanying LP audio, to help educate congregants about the challenges faced by the gay and lesbian community and to promote the universal human dignity of all people regardless of sexual orientation. The filmstrip, created by photographer Wasyl Srkodzinsky and Dr. deryck calderwood, consultant in human sexuality, consists of interviews and photographs of gay people from around the United States who speak to their diverse experiences of being gay in the 1970s, as well as interviews with activists and academics. The three segments, approximately twenty minutes each in length, are entitled: "The Changing View of Homosexuality," "Understanding the Homosexual," and "Questions and Answers Concerning the Homosexual Way of Life." In 1973* The National Council of Family Relations *awarded* The Invisible Minority *with First Place for Best Filmstrip/Record Educational Program.*

—Natalie Malter

Part I—The Changing View of Homosexuality

Narrator: People. Young people. Older people. People from every faith. Of every race and culture. People from small towns. And big cities. People from all walks of life. People just like those you see and mingle with every day. Ordinary people. But these people have one thing in common: they all belong to the same minority group. The characteristic of this minority group is not something you can see. It's an invisible characteristic that cannot be seen even by others who share it. These are the people who find their basic love and sexual satisfaction primarily with members of their own sex. These are the people we label homosexual in our society. They are the invisible minority.

Oscar Wilde, writing in Victorian times, called homosexuality "the love that dare not speak its name." Until a few years ago this taboo of silence continued to exist. Homosexuality was not considered a proper subject for discussion. The silence concerning this minority group caused their problems to go unrecognized by society.

These are the doors to the headquarters of one of the oldest homosexual organizations in the United States. ONE, located in Los Angeles, like similar pioneer organizations across the country has been working quietly for years to obtain equal rights for the homosexual.

Mr. W. Dorr Legg: My name is W. Dorr Legg, and I am Education Director of ONE, Inc., in Los Angeles. ONE was founded on October 15th, 1952, at a meeting in my home. I have been active with it ever since that time. The structure of the corporation has several divisions. It has an Education Division, which is engaged in the serious academic- and college-level study of male and female homosexuality. Then we have publications: *ONE Magazine*, which is primarily literary in its orientation. Then comes a division which some of our people feel is one of our most important if not the most important, and that is Social Service. During the year since we have been founded more than five thousand men and women have come to us for personal counseling.

Narrator: A recent lecture at ONE provides an example of the dramatic changes in society's attitudes that are taking place today. Rev. Tom Maurer, a speaker from the National Sex and Drug Forum, announces the release of the National Institute of Mental Health's final report of the Task Force on Homosexuality.

Rev. Tom Maurer: I can't tell you how much this thrills my guts. To know that a branch of the federal government actually has a task force that has released a report such as this one. Really, honest, thirty years ago no one could ever have convinced me that I would live to the day when our government would be at this point, and the National Institute of Mental Health is committed to changing the scene in America and its practices and attitudes toward homosexuality.

Narrator: In Washington, DC, Dr. Frank Kameny is the President and Founder of the Mattachine Society there, and the first candidate for Congress to openly campaign as a homosexual citizen. Dr. Kameny emphasizes the significance of the report.

Dr. Frank Kameny: This is the first time that an official American governmental report has come out proposing that a whole body of discriminatory laws and policies be modified or dropped. Public attitudes toward homosexuality are changing very, very rapidly, and one of the most important aspects of that change is the fact that the subject can be talked about now, whereas as little as three or four years ago, it couldn't be. Nowadays, of course, you have newspaper articles, magazine articles on it, radio and television discussion of it at great length. The word can be used in a rather matter of course fashion.

* * *

Dr. Frank Kameny: Now obviously when the wraps are first taken off of a subject you're going to have it approached with a certain amount of distortion and a certain amount of sensationalism, and this you're getting. It's a novelty. It's something new, and so we'll have to go through a phase. Now meanwhile of course, besides familiarizing the general public with the topic so it can be talked about and people can be made aware of it, this is having a very, very profound effect on the homosexual himself, which is critically important. A new militancy is developing in the homosexual community. People are getting fed up with and sick and tired of the old covertness and hiding in closets and the double life and the mask and the camouflage and the disguise and are coming out in the open. You have groups like the Gay Liberation Front and other organizations who are beginning to demonstrate publicly when things are done that they don't like.

*   *   *

Narrator: Traditional religious attitudes have made it difficult for many homosexuals to reconcile their sexual orientation with the teachings of their church. In the past, homosexuals have felt excluded from openly participating in church services and religious activities. Today, they can meet in churches organized by and for homosexuals.

Rev. Troy Perry: My name is Rev. Troy D. Perry. I'm the pastor of Metropolitan Community Church in Los Angeles. Our church helps the homosexual to help himself. The breakdown of the church body is about seventy percent male homosexual, fifteen percent lesbian, and fifteen percent heterosexuals who just happen to like our mode of worship. MCC is an independent congregational church. We are probably the largest homophile religious organization in the world. At MCC we believe that the homosexual should have every right that heterosexuals do and one of those rights is the right to marry. We perform wedding services for two guys or two girls, as well as for a male and a female. We perform heterosexual marriages, but we do perform the other type, because we feel like marriage after all is just receiving a blessing from the church. While it's not legal in the state of California yet, it is legal, we feel like, in the sight of God.

*   *   *

Part III—

Question: What needs to be done in our society to improve conditions for homosexuals? What are homosexuals asking for?

Narrator: The homophile organizations have developed a listing of the basic rights they seek, as follows: the right to have unbiased laws, equal law enforcement and equal justice before the courts, the right to work without fear of discharge in private industry and for local, state, and federal government, the right to serve one's

323

country in the armed forces, and the right to veteran's benefits upon discharge from the service, the right to peacefully assemble in public places, the right to live without fear.

Barbara Gittings: I look forward to a time when your sexual orientation—be it homosexual, heterosexual—will be no more important than the color of your eyes, let's say.

Jack Nichols: Both Loge and I are very strong integrationists. We'd like to see the homosexual community and the heterosexual community merge so that instead of there being two different, separate camps of sexuality, that there will be only one world of people rather than homosexuals and heterosexuals.

Kipper Revere: I think that the society that all of us would like to see is just everybody being able to freely love whomever they chose. Just to be able to say "I love you" no matter who you are, male or female, and for that to be good because love is good, and not to have somehow love of some sort being bad. I think this is the sort of society that all of us sort of dream of and hope for and are working towards.

SOURCE: *The Invisible Minority: The Homosexuals in Our Society* (Boston: Unitarian Universalist Association, 1972); available at uua.org/re/tapestry/adults/resistance/workshop15/182932 .shtml

WILLIAM R. JONES

Is God a White Racist?
A Preamble to Black Theology

1973

William R. Jones (1933–2012) was the leading black humanist scholar of his generation. Educated at Howard, Harvard, and Brown Universities, he was ordained in 1958 and briefly served as assistant minister and director of religious education at First Unitarian in Providence, Rhode Island, before embarking on his academic career. He taught at Yale and then at Florida State, where he was the founding director of the African-American Studies Program. Is God a White Racist? *offered a humanist response to the "black theology" crafted by theological supporters of the Black Power movement, most notably James Cone. Jones argued that Cone and the others were right to make black liberation the criterion for theology, but wrong to insist that the omnipotent God of the Christian scriptures was on the side of black liberation. In a world characterized by chronic black suffering, he held, only steadfast human action could bring liberation. Further Reading: Anthony B. Pinn, ed.,* By These Hands: A Documentary History of African American Humanism *(New York: New York University Press, 2001).*

—Dan McKanan

Because of the novelty of the concept of divine racism, it is beneficial to describe its essential features by examining some concrete examples in which the concept is highly visible. Thomas Gossett's interpretation of sections of the *Rig Veda*, the Hindu scriptures of ancient India, and I. A. Newby's analysis of "religious racism" provide the desired specimens.

In Gossett's interpretation, Indra, the God of the Aryans, is described as "blowing away with supernatural might from earth and from the heavens the black skin which Indra hates." The account further reports how Indra "slew the flat-nosed barbarians," the dark people called Anasahs. Finally, after Indra conquers the land of the Anasahs for His worshipers, He commands that the Anasahs are to be "flayed of [their] black skin."

Proposition one. The first distinctive trait of divine racism to be noted is its appeal to a "two-category system"; it presupposes a basic division of mankind into an "in" group and an "out" group. In addition, this fundamental division is supported, initiated, or sanctioned by God Himself. God has special concern for the "in" group, and it receives His sustaining aid and grace. By contrast He is indifferent or hostile to the "out" group. In sum, God does not value all men equally; consequently He treats them differently. And this difference is not accidental but central to His will and purpose.

Proposition two. In the context of divine racism, the two-category system is correlated with an imbalance of suffering; the "out" group suffers more than the rest of the population. In the account from the *Rig Veda* we know that God has less affection for the Anasahs, because they suffer far more than the Aryans. The Anasahs are the vanquished, not the victor.

Proposition three. Implicit in the concept of divine racism is a third principle: God is responsible for the imbalance of suffering that differentiates the "in" and the "out" groups. Indra is the major warrior on the field of battle bringing about the Anasahs' defeat. Thus honor, praise, and thanksgiving are addressed to Him for His might acts in slaying "the flat-nosed barbarians." Perhaps, however, the concept of divine racism is defined too narrowly if it must be God's own hand that flays the ethnic outcasts. For my purpose I would emphasize only that the imbalance of suffering must express God's will or purpose, thus allowing that men or angels, for instance, could be the actual instrument and executioners of the divine plan.

Proposition four. God's favor or disfavor is correlated with the racial or ethnic identity of the group in question. God's wrath and hostility are directed toward the very features that characterize a particular racial or ethnic community. As the account from the *Rig Veda* concludes, Indra hated their blackness.

Proposition five. Newby's analysis of religious racism—"the idea that racial inequality is the work and will of God"—describes another essential feature of divine racism: God must be a member of the "in" group. In the context of this study, God must be white.

❊   ❊   ❊

To speak of divine racism is to raise questions about God's equal love and concern for all men. It is to suggest that He is for some but not for others, or at least not for all equally. It asks whether there is a demonic streak in the divine nature. The charge of divine racism, in the final analysis, is a frontal challenge to the claim of God's benevolence for all.

No doubt the phrase "divine racism" falls on the ear with contradictory import; it is akin to speaking of a married bachelor or a square circle. This is so, precisely because the concept of God's benevolence is being attacked. The case is the same with any God talk that hints at a demonic God. Only by picturing God as a supernatural Dr. Jekyll and Mr. Hyde can space be found for a malevolent deity. Clearly, in the context of Western monotheism, benevolence is as essential to the definition of God as is His existence. Hence there is an instinctive tendency to make God and goodness interchangeable terms and an inclination to make either man or some

326

other creature, e.g. the devil, the ultimate cause of evil. One point is unmistakable in the framework of the Judaeo-Christian tradition: we can establish the legitimacy and irreducibility of the category of divine racism only by a frontal attack on the concept of God's *intrinsic* goodness.

The quickest and most effective way to execute this attack is to show that events are multievidential; specifically the materials and events that have traditionally been interpreted as evidence of divine benevolence can just as easily support the opposite conclusion, of divine malevolence.

* * *

The divine suffering at Golgotha yields a possible interpretation of divine hostility. A similar conclusion can be drawn from any instance of human suffering; it, too, is multievidential. Any given occurrence of human suffering harmonizes equally well with antithetical positions, divine favor or disfavor, God's grace or God's curse. Consequently, in the face of human suffering, whatever its character, we must entertain the possibility that it is an expression of divine hostility. Moreover, if it is allowed that the general category of human suffering raises the possibility of a demonic deity, then the particular category of black suffering—and this is the crucial point for the argument—at least suggests the possibility of divine racism, a particular form of hostility.

* * *

I have attempted thus far to show that the multievidentiality of suffering, in part, forces consideration of the question, Is God a white racist? At this juncture it is necessary to enlarge the complex of categories that generates the issue of divine racism. The concept of ethnic suffering, the correlate of divine racism, will be our immediate focus.

Four essential features constitute ethnic suffering: (a) maldistribution, (b) negative quality, (c) enormity, and (d) non-catastrophic character. By accenting the ethnic factor I wish to call attention to that suffering which is maldistributed; it is not spread, as it were, more or less randomly and impartially over the total human race. Rather, it is concentrated in a particular ethnic group. My concern in utilizing the concept of ethnic suffering is to accentuate the fact that black suffering is balanced by white non-suffering instead of white suffering. Consequently, black suffering in particular and ethnic suffering in general raise the issue of the scandal of particularity. . . .

If we differentiate between positive and negative suffering, ethnic suffering in my stipulate definition would be a subclass of negative suffering. It describes a suffering without essential value for man's salvation or well-being. It leads away from, rather than toward, one's highest good. In contrast, certain advocates of types of asceticism, for instance, would regard suffering positively, as something to be actively pursued.

A third feature of ethnic suffering is its enormity, and here the reference is to several things: There is the factor of numbers, but numbers in relation to the total class, i.e., the number of suffering Jews or blacks in comparison with the total number of Jews or blacks. The factor of numbers raises the issue of divine racism at the point where the level of suffering and death makes the interpretation of genocide feasible.

Enormity also designates suffering unto death. Ethnic suffering reduces the life expectancy or anticipates the immediate death of the individual. The importance of this feature is that it nullifies various explanations of suffering and thereby narrows the spectrum of possible theodicies. Suffering unto death, for instance, negates any interpretation of pedagogical suffering; i.e., we learn from a burn to avoid fire. This makes little sense if the learning method destroys the learner. Suffering as a form of testing is also contradicted if the amount and severity of the suffering are incommensurate with the alleged purpose. It is for this reason that Rabbi Richard Rubenstein, for instance, denies that the horror of the suffering of Jews at Auschwitz could ever be likened to the testing of Job.

The final feature to be discussed is the non-catastrophic aspect. Ethnic suffering does not strike quickly and then leave after a short and terrible siege. Instead, it extends over long historical eras. It strikes not only the father but the son, the grandson, and the great-grandson. In short, non-catastrophic suffering is transgenerational.

When these aspects of ethnic suffering are connected, one is not tempted to account for their presence on the grounds of the operation of indifferent and impersonal laws of nature. Rather, one is more inclined to explain its causal nexus in terms of purpose and consequently person. This, too, is but a short step to seeing God as perhaps that person.

It is my contention that the peculiarities of black suffering make the *question* of divine racism imperative; it is not my position that the special character of black suffering *answers* the question. What I do affirm is that black theology, precisely because of the prominence of ethnic suffering in the black experience, cannot operate as if the goodness of God for all mankind were a theological axiom.

SOURCE: William R. Jones, *Is God a White Racist? A Preamble to Black Theology* (Garden City, NY: Anchor Books, 1973), 3–4, 6–7, 9, 20–22.

RICHARD NASH

"How Are Unitarian Universalist Gays Discriminated Against?"

1973

At the 1971 General Assembly in Washington, D.C., Richard Nash and Elgin Blair co-founded the Gay Caucus, later known as Interweave Continental. The Gay Caucus worked diligently to end discrimination against gay people in Unitarian Universalist churches, distributing educational materials at General Assembly and printing a monthly newsletter, addressing the unique challenges faced by gay Unitarian Universalists. As an openly gay minister, Nash faced significant bigotry, and in 1971, soon after the founding of the Gay Caucus, he was arrested by the Los Angeles Police Department on falsified prostitution charges. Throughout the duration of his court case, which lasted two years, Nash wrote prolifically about his personal experiences and the experiences of other gay Unitarian Universalists, advocating tirelessly for equality and justice. Nash wrote the following article in the midst of his trial, and it was published in the March 1973 edition of the Gay Caucus Newsletter. *The charges against him were dismissed on July 13, 1973, but his continued writing and work with the Gay Caucus throughout the 1970s demonstrates that the gay, lesbian, and bisexual community faced discrimination even within a liberal religious association. Further Reading: Mark Oppenheimer,* Knocking on Heaven's Door: American Religion in the Age of Counterculture *(New Haven, CT: Yale University Press, 2003).*

—Natalie Malter

Discrimination against gay people in Unitarian Universalist churches and fellowships is not everywhere the same, either in kind or degree. While I know of specific examples of each of the forms to be discussed here, I can not claim that every form is present in all societies. Where somebody can point to exceptions, I will be happy. The discrimination which gay people experience, however, is the rule rather than the exception. For purposes of this discussion, I'll deal with our discrimination under five headings.

1. *When the way we are treated is based upon myths.* There is a widespread fallacy, believed even by educated people and often especially by educated people, that to be gay is to be sick or symptomatic of sickness. This notion is particularly prevalent

in our denomination, where older views of sin are denied or soft-pedaled and where another basis is needed to justify peoples' prejudices. Sometimes, even when the sickness theory is rejected, the position is maintained that, given the current level of oppression by society against gay people, it is preferable that gays be encouraged to change or that everything be done to discourage young people from developing this life style as their own. Careful scientific research as well as the experience of liberated gay people challenges these concepts. I do not claim that all scientists are in agreement; they are not. But, when you compare, for example, the work of Evelyn Hooker, whose results contradict the sickness theory, with that of Irving Bieber, who supports the sickness theory, it is clear that the person whose technique is scientifically faulty is Mr. Bieber.

* * *

2. *When the services of the church or fellowship are not equally available to us.* In some instances now ministers will perform ceremonies to celebrate our love relationships as they do with non-gay couples. But, too often we are still refused this service of the church. Sometimes the refusal is justified in terms of the minister's own bias, but in other cases, where he is prepared to do it, he uses the unreadiness of the people in the church as the excuse. In rare instances gay people are beginning to socialize together—such as dance together—at church functions, but I think nobody would disagree that this is mostly taboo. When something like this is discussed, the reaction usually is, "I wouldn't want my children to be exposed to that." Obviously we do not feel as welcome as others to church functions when we cannot feel as free to be ourselves.

* * *

3. *When our uniqueness is not represented.* All minority people are at a disadvantage in social institutions where the needs and cultural assumptions of majority people are taken for granted and are used as the basis for planning activities. I have seen no UU society where the holidays and the heroes of the gay community are celebrated. I doubt that most UUs even know we have our own holidays and heroes. We also have a cultural tradition which has expanded rapidly in the last few years which I do not see reflected in what happens in our churches and fellowships. I don't hear the gay works of Shakespeare, Whitman, and the other great writers or the more contemporary writing of Altman, Fisher, Abbott, or Martin and Lyon. People aren't generally aware of what's happening in the gay community because of the intense media blackout on events and developments there. Is this not all the more reason for the churches in our tradition to pay attention?

* * *

4. *When we are asked to be sexual neuters.* A double standard is often used by non-gay people. They will say to us that what we do in the privacy of our bedroom is our business and acceptable to them, SO LONG AS WE DO NOT PARADE IT IN

PUBLIC. The fact that they give free expression to their heterosexuality in public is ignored. They can hold hands, but we can't. They can kiss, but we can't. Their sexual conquests can be discussed, but ours can't. The joys and sorrows of their relationships can be shared, but ours can't. Nobody is expected to keep his/her sexuality so separate from the rest of his/her life are we are.

Even the church asks us to leave our sexuality at the door when we enter. Usually heterosexuals are not aware how explicitly their sexuality is a part of what happens in the church, because their orientation is taken so much for granted. Marriage and childbirth are celebrated there. Love is often discussed in a non-sexual context, but when its sexual implications are illustrated, it's always heterosexual. The family is the basic unit of the church. People are either married (heterosexually) or single. A heterosexual couple would be one pledging unit. A gay couple would be two pledging units. Suppose the non-churched husband of a member died. It is likely the minister would officiate at a service, which would be seen as helpful to the wife. Suppose the non-churched lover of a gay person died. Is it likely there would be a similar service?

* * *

5. *When we are made to suffer for other's prejudices.* I was told, face to face by a Unitarian minister, "I don't want homosexuals to feel welcome here. I'm trying to attract young married couples, and if gay people come in any numbers, the couples will not." His logic was not even sound, but accepting that there could be the relationship he was suggesting, I asked, "Why will the couples not come? Is it because gay people are so bad? Or is it that the heterosexuals have some hangups?" He had to agree it was they who had the problem. And, I wondered why we were the ones he wanted to make suffer.

As a minister I am often invited to fill pulpits on Sundays. Often I get letters from societies which do not know me personally, inviting me to speak. When I respond telling them that I'd like to speak out of my experience in Gay Liberation, I seldom hear again from them. Not even an excuse. It is easy, when a group of people are in the minority and have been silenced as long as we have, to make us suffer for the hangups of others. However, this makes it no less excusable or detrimental to everybody involved.

Gay people are hopeful that non-gay UU's will understand the discrimination we face in our societies, that they will recognize that it is not in the best interest of either of us, and that plans will be mounted to counteract it.

SOURCE: Richard Nash, "How Are Unitarian Universalist Gays Discriminated Against?" *UU Gay Caucus Newsletter*, March 1973, 3–5, Unitarian Universalist Association Office of Lesbian and Gay Concerns, 1972–1999, Andover-Harvard Archive, bMS 1309/1, Andover-Harvard Theological Library, Harvard Divinity School, Cambridge, MA.

Resolution for the Creation of
an Office of Gay Affairs

1973

Although this was not the first resolution pertaining to gay rights passed at a General Assembly, the Resolution for the Creation of an Office of Gay Affairs represented a significant victory for gay rights advocates within the UUA. The campaign to create the Office was led by Richard Nash and his colleagues in the Gay Caucus, who believed firmly that in order for the UUA to follow through on its 1970 anti-discrimination resolution, it needed to cre-ate an office specifically designed to prevent discrimination in the UUA and in society at large. Once funding sources were established in 1975, Arlie Scott became the first director of the department, which came to be known as the Office for Gay Concerns. In the decades since its founding, the name of the Office of Gay Concerns has changed to reflect its growing commitments, and today it is known as Lesbian, Gay, Bisexual, Transgender, and Queer (LGBTQ) Ministries, a department of Multicultural Ministries at the UUA.

—Natalie Malter

WHEREAS, it is among the purposes of the Unitarian Universalist Association to affirm, defend and promote the supreme worth of every human personality; and

WHEREAS, the 1970 General Assembly passed a resolution urging all peoples immediately to bring an end to all discrimination against homosexuals, homosexual-ity, bisexuals and bisexuality; and

WHEREAS, the Association since then has established no mechanism by which this resolution might be implemented within our churches, fellowships and denomina-tionally related organizations; and

WHEREAS, second class status keeps all oppressed minorities disabled and robs everyone of their potential contributions;

NOW THEREFORE BE IT RESOLVED: That the 1973 General Assembly urges the Board of Trustees of the UUA to create at the denominational headquarters an Office on Gay Affairs. The Office shall be staffed by gay people and it shall have the full benefit of the experience, talent and status of the UUA in developing sources of funding outside the denominational budget. Would such sources be unavailable, the UUA will not be further responsible for funding the Office.

BE IT FURTHER RESOLVED: That the functions of the Office be a resource to the denomination at all levels in all matters pertaining to gay people and the gay community. The office shall initially make a 30-day study of the immediate needs of gay Unitarian Universalists and ways of developing an outreach into the gay community. Results of the study shall be distributed to all churches, fellowships and denominationally-related bodies with recommendations for implementation.

SOURCE: uua.org/statements/creation-office-gay-affairs

ROBERT NELSON WEST
"A Matter of Priorities"
1974

UUA President Robert West's editorial, "A Matter of Priorities," published in the Unitarian Universalist World *on November 15, 1974, demonstrates the controversy over establishing an Office of Gay Concerns in the UUA. Although the 1973 resolution successfully established such an office, it was passed without any clear source of funding, leaving the future of the office uncertain. As reflected in his writing, West was wary of establishing a separate Office of Gay Concerns with its own funding, because he believed that it was beyond the UUA's financial scope and responsibilities. As a result of this debate over funding, both the 1974 and 1975 General Assemblies passed resolutions in support of UUA funding for the Office of Gay Concerns. Thus, at the time this article was written, funding had already been allocated to the Office and implemented by the Board of Trustees. However, West had received significant criticism from the Gay Caucus and other allies for his reticence to establish and fund the office, and in his editorial, he asserts that his resistance did not reflect prejudice but rather differing views on the priorities of the UUA. Further Reading: Robert Nelson West,* Crisis and Change: My Years as President of the Unitarian Universalist Association, 1969–1977 *(Boston: Skinner House, 2007).*

—Natalie Malter

The 1974 UUA General Assembly voted 376–311 to urge the UUA Board of Trustees to establish a UUA Office of Gay Concerns as part of UUA headquarters by allocating $38,500 from the Grants Section of this year's budget, the funds to be obtained by eliminating the Research Program and reducing the amount for Publicity and Radio-Television. On October 12 the UUA Board of Trustees voted 12–11 to establish the Office.

My clear recommendation to the UUA Board in both October, 1973 and October, 1974 was that the Office not be established as part of UUA headquarters. I believe that the establishment of such a UUA office is a distortion of our priorities. We have a wide range of social concerns and denominational needs. To establish such an office with a full-time professional staff person, full-time secretary, travel expenses, and program money for one particular cause constitutes a distortion of priorities and a disproportionate utilization of resources. The two people will be

334

added to the UUA Department of Education and Social Concern, which under the Department Director at 25 Beacon Street currently has one professional staff person devoting less than full time to working on the entire range of social concerns with a part-time secretary.

I continue to support UUA efforts to eliminate discrimination and prejudice against gay people and to promote understanding and equality. First as parish minister and then as UUA President I have initiated and encouraged such efforts. The UUA has followed a responsible course in this area of concern. Examples are the UUA sex education kit "About Your Sexuality," the award-winning unit "The Invisible Minority," and activities of the Department of Ministry and the Administration.

The central issue in this matter is not prejudice and discrimination against gay people. The central issue is priorities among programs which serve our member congregations and address many pressing problems and needs.

As President I am subject to the direction and control of the UUA Board and, just as I developed a model for the Office, I am proceeding to establish it as voted by the Board.

I urge the next General Assembly to consider priorities in the whole range of Unitarian Universalist concerns.

SOURCE: Robert Nelson West, "A Matter of Priorities," *Unitarian Universalist World*, November 15, 1974, page 1.

MARJORIE NEWLIN LEAMING

"Women in the Unitarian Universalist Ministry"

1974

In 1967, after completing her Bachelor of Divinity at Meadville Lombard Theological School at the University of Chicago, Marjorie Newlin Leaming (1915–2010) became one of the first women ordained into Unitarian Universalist ministry. She served as the minister of education at the Unitarian Community Church of Santa Monica from 1966 to 1968, before moving to the Unitarian Universalist Church of Santa Paula, California, as the senior minister in 1969. When she was called to Santa Paula, fewer than forty women were ordained as Unitarian Universalist ministers, and Leaming was one of the only women ministers to have her own pulpit. In addition to her role as a minister, Leaming was actively involved in various UUA organizations, helping to found the Ministerial Sisterhood Unitarian Universalist in 1974, where she advocated on behalf of equality for women ministers. As a member of the Unitarian Universalist Ministers Association's Executive Board, she conducted the following survey of women in ministry in 1974. While Leaming refrains from naming the twenty women ministers who responded to her survey, their answers to her questions about gender discrimination in the UUA, particularly in relationship to salary and marital status, provide insight into the unique challenges faced by women in ministry in the 1970s. Further Reading: Mark Chaves, Ordaining Women: Culture and Conflict in Religious Organizations *(Cambridge, MA: Harvard University Press, 1997).*

—Natalie Malter

I. At the Crossroads

The most sacred domain of maleness has been the ministry. For thousands of years one sex has dominated the religious hierarchies to the virtual exclusion of half the human race. Little cracks in the fortress have appeared from time to time, but for the first time in history the crack is widening. Women in unprecedented numbers are seeking careers in the ministry and are demanding to be taken seriously.

—Rev. Polly Laughland

The question confronting the Unitarian Universalist denomination is, what will be our response to women seeking careers in our ministry? What will be the response of the ministers themselves, both male and female, the Department of Ministry, and the churches? We seem to be at a paradoxical time, a time when we are going both ways at once. Even a non-response is a response that will have a great deal of influence on the future of our movement.

One woman minister wrote to me, "We have no choice but to encourage, support, and welcome whatever new or additional realities we can muster to strengthen and enrich our collective religious life. Besides, our problem-solving insights need all the help they can get!" In answer to her self-asked question, "Do you think many women are anxious to make these contributions—in other words, do you think women are waiting breathlessly in the wings of the church to do this?" she says, "No, they're busy making their contributions elsewhere, usually with less hardship, more acceptance, fewer frustrations, greater rewards."

The point is that because women are so frustrated trying to get into the parish ministry, they are abandoning the church and going elsewhere, leaving the church high and dry and devoid of the positive influence for good that they can bring. Mary Lou Thompson . . . also makes this point. She says, "Among the factors devitalizing the modern church may be an exodus of women who have become alienated by the language and the fact of patriarchal religion. If this should leave behind mostly women whose sensitivities have not been affected by the women's movement, it will ensure the continuation of male dominance in the religious world, but the church will be standing outside the mainstream of a social revolution that will have profound effects on all aspects of living. . . ."

II. The Dialogue Begins

Some people may not like what I have to say in this paper; there are some things about it that I don't even like myself. First I want to say that although I am trying to be objective, I know in my interpretation of the various responses I have had to this project I have not avoided my own subjectivity. I have included some things and I have left out others. I have edited. I am an avowed feminist. I am sorry if I offend some of my colleagues who so graciously responded to my request for information and who may feel betrayed by what I'm saying. I've thought about this a lot, and have not been able to come up with a way to avoid it except by not distributing the paper. I have for the most part refrained from using names, hoping this will help. And second, I am not by any means proclaiming that this is the final word on women in the UU ministry. . . .

III. The Call for Testimony

On March 8, 1974, I sent a letter to 34 women ordained to the Unitarian Universalist ministry as listed in the 1974 *Directory*. I tried to include all ordained women, but I have since found that I omitted at least two, and there may be a few more.

※   ※   ※

I received replies from 19 women; I also have responded; so this paper is based on 20 responses.

* * *

IV. Does Prejudice Against Women Ministers Really Exist?

I find that Unitarian Universalists have an especial problem with women in the ministry. As liberals who are calm, reasonable and (always—heaven forbid!) rational, it is difficult for those who feel upset by the sight of a woman in the pulpit officiating in a senior minister role to admit the feeling to themselves. Where a person with another orientation might easily say: a woman shouldn't do that—or I don't feel comfortable with her—or it really upsets me to see her officiating at a wedding, it is, it seems, hard for UUs to admit that they are afflicted with the same kinds of irrational yet real prejudices and perceptions as any other form of humanity. And, if they can't say it themselves, it is impossible to get it out in the open.

—Rev. Jane Raible

The letters I received raise several issues, but the most significant centers around prejudice. Does prejudice against women ministers exist? Some think it does; others do not, or at least feel they have not experienced problems in this area themselves. Taking all the letters into consideration, it seems apparent that there is a difference in the level of consciousness between older and younger women regarding their oppression, just as there is in the general population. In other words, there is a generation gap; however, there are feminists and antifeminists on both sides with some in the middle; I happen to be an older woman who is a feminist.

By prejudice I mean the simple feeling of wishing *she* weren't there because a man could do it better. Just because she is a woman she is prejudged as incapable to function in the role of minister. Even when she is given the opportunity to minister and does perform satisfactorily in every way and as competently and as effectively as a man, she may still be prejudged as incapable because of the psychological predispositions and blinders of the person doing the evaluating, the judging.

* * *

I'll close this section with one more point, which may not be the most crucial but it is bothersome. She says, "Finally, a funny thing—what do I wear in the pulpit? Why should that be a problem—or anything beyond my own decision . . . [ellipsis in original]? But in the beginning of my ministry, I found that it really bothered some of the older people. What should I wear—was it too short—too open—too loose—too tight?"

V. Salaries

There are approximately 23 women in UU theological schools at the present time and more are expected to enter in the fall. I have heard that half the entering class this fall at Andover-Newton will be women. I understand that they are headed for the parish ministry. The big question is, can they find churches when they graduate? The bigger question is, will they depress the salary scale? Since women seem to be able and for the most part are willing to get along on less money than men, the answer seems obvious.

* * *

Salaries are always a complicated issue. Now I want to get out my feelings about the matter from a different angle. . . . I went through an interesting experience last fall at a ministers retreat. We were talking about salaries, and I said I had not had an increase in mine since I came to Santa Paula; for one thing the church could not increase its budget as we were already deficit funding. . . . I was saying I was more concerned about the future of the church and saving it than I was about the financial index of my success as a minister.

For another thing I could care less about my salary because I didn't need any more money as I had some income from another source. The other ministers there, all male of course, seemed to get upset by this, and one of them was quite indignant that I was subsidizing the church and doing an injustice to other minister who could not afford to do this. I began to feel quite guilty about being a scab, and the suggestion was made that I *could* go into a part time ministry.

I came home from that meeting very upset, so upset that I finally had a long talk with the Chairperson of the Ministerial Advisory Committee about it. I was actually ready to go on a part time basis for the honor of my male colleagues, even though the last thing in the world I wanted was to be a part time minister. After talking with the Chairperson about it, I could see that my congregation was going to feel equally if not even more upset at the prospect of my going on part time because it would be a set back to them; that they had failed or at least hadn't made any real progress. So then I went into a feeling of depression over whether to resign or not—that might be the only solution to my guilt. . . .

I did not go on part time and I did not resign. But when the budget committee later met to set the new budget, I suggested that I be given a raise, and they considered a $2,000 increase, knowing that it was totally impossible. We finally agreed on $500 since that was a much more realistic figure. It has solved the problem for the time being. Anyway, I no longer feel so much like a scab, but I am still wondering if I should.

This is an old labor relations problem. I've always been on the side of labor and opposed to exploitation by management, and I've though that scabs were scum. Yet when I find myself caught in this thing, I wonder at the complexity of scabbing. Is it never justified? I think one of the big problems of the future that the UUMA will have to face is "women as scabs." We might as well begin by calling it that ourselves because the men will anyway. By admitting it, perhaps we will be better enabled to deal with our guilt.

If a minister actually cares more about saving and strengthening a church than she does about her salary, should she not serve that church for whatever they can afford to pay her? . . . Sometimes we women are so grateful for having a church to minister to at all that we are willing to work for less than they can afford to pay, and we also have all our culturally inculcated doubts about whether we really deserve to get paid at all. Some way we have to get all these things in balance.

✻ ✻ ✻

IX. Ministerial Settlement

One of my primary reasons for wanting to write this paper is in connection with the prejudice that comes up at the time of settlement of a minister in a church.

One person who is currently looking for a church says, "There is a lot of token-ism around. I was finally fellowshipped, but my first go at that was very sexist . . . [ellipsis in original]. There are a great many fine women attempting to enter the ministry. I'm not at all sure how they'll make out as far as jobs are concerned . . . [ellipsis in original]. I think that there are unique features in being a woman and I think the churches need what we have to offer in this day and age with the general societal unrest, etc. I hope some church realizes that soon as I'm anxious to get employed. I really love the parish ministry—all parts of it."

Another writes, "I feel that I am being supported in my search for a church by the Department of Ministry. This, I believe, is mainly due to the fact that about half the UU ministerial students are now women . . . [ellipsis in original]. My guess is that the climate of opinion has changed sufficiently so that pulpit committees will carefully consider a woman minister now: *Calling* one is another matter!"

Another writes, "I'd like to give Dave Pohl a big hand for his assistance. He has been unfailingly helpful, willing to send my name out to churches—sometimes to churches that I thought were way over my head." Since writing that, she has been settled.

✻ ✻ ✻

X. What Can the UUMA Do for Women in the Ministry?

One respondent doubts that men ministers will do much if anything for women ministers unless particular women or groups of women press for the changes they want. She says, "If it happens by our ministers association—mostly men—being asked or nudged to be well-intentioned and to manipulate or intervene for more

340

women in our ministry, it's tokenism—and who wants or needs to be a token? Or it's paternalism—and you know where that's brought us!"

*   *   *

I believe that the UUMA can do something to convince women of this fact if by no other way than raising their own male consciousness of the truth of it, and I also believe the UUMA has a moral responsibility to do something about these many absurdities put forth in this paper that confront women in the UU ministry.

SOURCE: Marjorie Newlin Leaming, "Women in the Unitarian Universalist Ministry," Unitarian Universalist Association, Women and Religion Committee Records, 1976–1981, Andover-Harvard Archive, bMS1022/3, Andover-Harvard Theological Library, Harvard Divinity School, Cambridge, MA.

BETTY BOBO SEIDEN

"Sojourner Truth to Shirley Chisholm"

1974

A Unitarian Universalist laywoman, Betty Bobo Seiden (1929–) is a member of the First Unitarian Church of Oakland, California, and has served on the Board of Trustees of Meadville Lombard Theological School in addition to the UUA Ministerial Fellowship Committee. Deeply committed to the quest for racial justice in the UUA and the broader society, and one of the black critics of the Black Affairs Council, Seiden served as the secretary of Black and White Action. The following essay by Seiden, originally presented at a seminar on feminism, explores some of her concerns with regard to racial equality and the second-wave feminist movement, which was often dominated by white women's voices. In her eloquent writing, Seiden draws comparisons between the first-wave feminist and abolitionist movements of the nineteenth century, advocating for the importance of intersectionality across liberation movements.

—Natalie Malter

I am delighted to participate in a seminar on the feminist movement because I see our major problem in today's world as being not one of technology and space exploration but of understanding human beings and meeting human needs so any attempt to raise our consciousness about this human experience that we all share is a good thing. I was surprised to get a call requesting that I speak. Being quite absorbed in my responsibilities as teacher-in-charge of an educational program for pregnant high school girls, the question came immediately to mind, has there been any change in either the number of teenage pregnancies or in the career expectations of our students in the past few years? Planned Parenthood has been working hard on Prevention Programs through rap sessions. Surveys among college graduates show more serious career plans. The answer followed close upon the question—there has been no change. But that is to be expected. The militancy of most movements, The Feminist Movement, The Black Liberation Movement, The Indian Movement and The Gay Liberation Movement leaves many people unmoved and unaffected. Most potential beneficiaries of any liberation movement are more threatened and embarrassed by the extreme actions that seem necessitated by public apathy than they are inspired by the promise of enlarged opportunities. For example, when I mentioned to our school nurse that I might attend a conference on the Feminist Movement she asked "why do they burn their bras?" She went on to say "I've always been liberated. I don't need to be liberated." That led me to ask then "Why didn't you become a doctor instead of a nurse?" She was taken aback to realize that it would have been easier to raise her family had she been she been a doctor. Despite the long history of the Feminist Movement most women still avoid fields of business, math, science and law. They are expected to become secretaries instead of lawyers, hygienists instead of dentists, nurses instead of doctors, and teachers instead of architects. To be fair to women however, we should point out that most men also avoid the rigors of professional responsibility and decision-making. There are many more men wasted on Skid Row than women. We would be deceiving ourselves too if we believed that men actually make the decisions that affect our lives. You may have heard about the man who claimed his wife made all the small, unimportant decisions like where the family would live and who their friends would be while he made all the big, important decisions like whether President Nixon should be impeached. I suspect many members of Congress vote as their wives suggest.

*　*　*

It is often pointed out that the Feminist Movement is a white, middle class movement and certainly it was when John Stuart Mill stood in the House of Commons in 1867 to propose an amendment to the reform bill enfranchising women. And it is still a fairly accurate description today. Who else has the *time* to be involved? Color and class have much less to do with it than education and leisure. A few educated women were the first to challenge the position of women and their traditional roles of wife and mother. If the choice is between managing the home and taking a menial and monotonous job there's a much more challenging satisfaction in home management. Any movement requires time and energy whether one has the secure leisure of being in a position of not having to work for a living or whether one suffers the enforced leisure of being denied access to the job market. In 19th century America middle class women came together to realize their inequality when they formed abolitionist groups in the north and west. They were not without support from some slaves who had escaped their servitude. . . . Frances Gage . . . give[s] an account of one such former slave [Sojourner Truth]: . . .

"At her first word there was a profound hush, she spoke in deep tones, which though not loud, reached every ear in the house, and away through the throng at the doors and windows. 'Well, children, where there is so much racket there must be something out of kilter . . . [ellipsis in original]. What's all this talking about? That man over there said that women need to be helped into carriages and lifted over ditches and to have the best place everywhere. Nobody ever helps me into carriages or over mud puddles or gives me the best place.' And raising herself to her full height and her voice to a pitch like rolling thunder she asked: 'And ain't I a Woman? Look at me! Look at my arm!' (And she bared her right arm to the shoulder showing her

343

tremendous muscular power.) 'I have ploughed and planted and gathered into barns and no man could head me!'

"'And ain't I a woman? I would work as much and eat as much as a man when I could get it—and bear the lash as well! And ain't I a woman? I have borne 13 children and seen them most all sold off to slavery and when I cried out with my mother's grief none but Jesus heard me! And ain't I a woman? Then they talk about this thing in the head, what they call it? (Intellect, whispered someone near) that's it, honey. What's that got to do with woman's rights. If my cup won't hold but a pint and yours holds a quart, wouldn't you be mean not to let me have my little half measure full?' And she pointed her significant finger and sent a keen glance at the minister who had made the argument. The cheering was loud and long. 'Then that little man in black there, he say women can't have as much rights as men because Christ wasn't a woman. Where did your Christ come from?' Rolling thunder couldn't have stilled that crowd as did those deep wonderful tones, as she stood there with outstretched arms and eyes of fire. Raising her voice still louder she repeated, 'Where did your Christ come from? From God and a woman! Man had nothing to do with Him.'

"She ended by asserting, 'If the first woman God ever made was strong enough to turn the world upside down all alone these women together (and she glanced her eye over the platform) ought to be able to turn it back and get it right side up again! And now they are asking to do it, the men better let them.' Long continued cheering greeted this. Amid roars of applause she returned to her corner, leaving more than one of us with streaming eyes and hearts beating with gratitude. She had taken us up in her strong arms and carried us safely over the slough of difficulty turning the whole tide in our favor."

The suffragettes however, both here and in England, watched the working man get the vote, the former slave get the vote, the recent immigrant get the vote—all men, of course. And they felt humiliated to the point of wishing to deny their argument for equal rights.

Many of them fought the 14th and 15th amendments because those amendments failed to include women in the rights of citizens to vote. There was something prophetic in Sojourner Truth's words because it was at the end of World War I when women had taken over so many of the jobs formerly held by men that the right to vote was finally won.

From Sojourner Truth's day to this, one important difference has persisted between the Afro-American sub-culture and the general American culture. This is the amount of job discrimination, especially against males. . . . Although more jobs have opened up in the last few years than were dreamed of only 20 years ago, it is still a fact that unemployment among males in the black community is more than twice that of the white community. . . . The result has been that a much higher proportion of women have held jobs. . . . There is a large number of working women in the black community—mothers, grandmothers, and single women—many of them professional, but most of them at the bottom of the pay scale. It is shameful that the plumber who comes in to repair your toilet can make $50 an hour after hours and on weekends (25 dollars), he also has paid vacations, a health plan and retirement benefits while the lady who comes in to clean your bathroom gets $2 an hour, no paid vacation, no health plan and what happens to her when she retires? . . .

The justification for the wage difference is supposed to be that women are only supplementing the family income, but the facts are that 60% of the women working are single, divorced, widowed or have husbands who would have to support their family on incomes less than $7000. More than one out of five households is headed by a woman, one out of three in the Afro-American community, and the median income of those families is less than half the median for families headed by men. These are the reasons why the Feminist Movement should *not* be only a white middle class movement. Any such tyranny works against the public good. Because we have all been acculturated to believe that men must be the breadwinner, take care of his family, be a good provider, etc. Afro-American women have been more concerned about their sons and husbands being able to fulfill that manly role. What my students want out of life is a husband with a good job, and that fact is not likely to change. . . .

From Sojourner Truth to Shirley Chisholm the road has been long, rough and sparsely traveled. A few doors have opened a crack and too few have attempted to enter. At this historical time it seems important for the Feminist Movement to do two things:

1. Encourage and listen to the voices of dissent and apathy.
2. Unite in a common cause. . . .

Any change for the betterment of humankind requires more than cooperation, fellowship and coalitions. An ideal society requires unification of all toward a common purpose. Any one's movement then can become everyone's movement—not just Gays for Gay Lib, Blacks for Black Lib, Women for Women's Lib but Humans for Human Liberation. If we were not so ethnocentric we could look at some other societies, both past and present where the inequities and the violence that exist today were/are not so prevalent. In Sweden, for example, the whole country is *committed* to equality of opportunity. Boys take homemaking, girls take shop and the school texts do not reflect the rigid sex roles that we are accustomed to. In the Soviet Union education is free to everybody and not just for either those who *can* pay or those who cannot. In China young people are selected to be educated to serve their people by their ability and dedication. Congress' move yesterday to equalize public school education facilities and curriculum may be a move in the right direction. Right now we are all competing like rival siblings. Affirmative action programs open the doors

345

for some while they close the doors to others. It's not fair. We can close our eyes to sex, race, age and income and open the doors to ability and interest. That *is* fair because our goal is *good* doctors and *dedicated* lawyers, be they male, female, black, white, brown, yellow, red, pink, poor, gifted, or gay. If we can ever see ourselves as part of one human family we can save the world.

SOURCE: Betty Bobo Seiden, "Sojourner Truth to Shirley Chisholm," Unitarian Universalist Sankofa Special Collection, Meadville Lombard Theological School, Chicago, meadville .edu/uploads/files/63.pdf. Seiden adapted her account of Sojourner Truth's speech from Frances D. Gage, "Sojourner Truth," in Elizabeth Cady Stanton, Susan B. Anthony, and Matilda Joslyn Gage, eds., *History of Woman Suffrage* (New York: Fowler and Wells, 1881), 1:116–17.

General Resolution for the Right to Abortion

1975

At the 1975 General Assembly in Minneapolis, Minnesota, delegates voted in support of the General Resolution for the Right to Abortion, advocating for the importance of reproductive justice and a woman's right to choose. Over a period of thirty years, ten different General Assembly resolutions were passed pertaining to reproductive rights, beginning in 1963 with the Resolution on Reform of Abortion Statutes. The 1963 resolution reflects a more conservative stance on women's reproductive rights, supporting abortion in specific cases of the physical health of the mother, rape, and incest. Ten years later, in the wake of Roe v. Wade *(1973), another brief resolution was passed in support of the Supreme Court decision. However, the 1975 Resolution for the Right to Abortion is the earliest comprehensive resolution on reproductive rights, and it reflects more contemporary, progressive language about a woman's right to choose. This resolution was particularly significant following* Roe v. Wade, *which ignited the national debate over abortion in the United States.*

—Natalie Malter

WHEREAS, every female should be accorded the right to decide whether or not she should bear a child;

WHEREAS, contraceptive methods are not perfect and do not absolutely protect against pregnancy; and

WHEREAS, abortion can be a relatively simple and safe way to terminate a pregnancy;

THEREFORE BE IT RESOLVED: That the delegates at the 1975 General Assembly of the Unitarian Universalist Association reaffirm the right of any female of any age or marital or economical status to have an abortion at her own request upon medical/social consultation of her own choosing; and urge all Unitarian Universalists in the United States to resist through their elected representatives the efforts now under way by some members of the Congress of the United States and state legislatures to curtail that right by means of constitutional amendment or other means;

AND BE IT FURTHER RESOLVED: That we urge all Unitarian Universalists and all Unitarian Universalist societies in Canada through the Canadian Unitarian Council to strive for making these rights available in Canada;

AND BE IT FURTHER RESOLVED: That the General Assembly deplores the legal persecution by the Canadian authorities of Dr. Henry Morgenthaler for his courageous fight for the abortion rights of Canadian women and his willingness to assist them in exercising those rights. . . . The General Assembly commends the Canadian Unitarian Council for its support of Dr. Morgenthaler and requests the CUC to convey the concern of the General Assembly to the Prime Minister of Canada and the Prime Minister of Quebec, and to request the Prime Minister of Canada to procure for Dr. Morgenthaler a royal pardon.

SOURCE: Unitarian Universalist Social Justice Statements, uua.org/statements/right-abortion

Business Resolution on
Women and Religion

1977

In the earliest years of the Unitarian Universalist Association, fewer than forty women were ordained in the ministry, and of those women, only a select few served churches as senior ministers. As the second-wave feminist movement gained momentum in the United States in the 1960s and 1970s, more UU women began to attend seminary and enter the ordination process. However, many Unitarian Universalist women were aware that while numbers of women in ministry continued to increase, patriarchal language, liturgy, and theology continued to pervade the Association. A committed group of radical feminist laywomen, led by Lucile Schuck Longview (1911–2010) of First Parish in Lexington, Massachusetts, campaigned actively for an Association-wide commitment to gender equality, advocating for a deeper transformation of patriarchal consciousness in UU churches. At the 1977 General Assembly in Ithaca, New York, the Resolution on Women and Religion passed unanimously. The passing of this resolution marked a significant denominational shift toward gender equality, contributing to increased numbers of women pursuing UU ministry and catalyzing efforts to revise the UUA Principles. Further Reading: Alice Echols, Daring to Be Bad: Radical Feminism in America 1967–1975 *(Minneapolis: University of Minnesota Press, 1989).*

—Natalie Malter

WHEREAS, a principle of the Unitarian Universalist Association is to "affirm, defend, and promote the supreme worth and dignity of every human personality, and the use of the democratic method in human relationships"; and

WHEREAS, great strides have been taken to affirm this principle within our denomination; and

WHEREAS, some models of human relationships arising from religious myths, historical materials, and other teachings still create and perpetuate attitudes that cause women everywhere to be overlooked and undervalued; and

WHEREAS, children, youth and adults internalize and act on these cultural models, thereby tending to limit their sense of self-worth and dignity;

THEREFORE BE IT RESOLVED: That the 1977 General Assembly of the Unitarian Universalist Association calls upon all Unitarian Universalists to examine carefully their own religious beliefs and the extent to which these beliefs influence sex-role stereotypes within their own families; and

BE IT FURTHER RESOLVED: That the General Assembly urges the Board of Trustees of the Unitarian Universalist Association to encourage the Unitarian Universalist Association administrative officers and staff, the religious leaders within societies, the Unitarian Universalist theological schools, the directors of related organizations, and the planners of seminars and conferences, to make every effort to: (a) put traditional assumptions and language in perspective, and (b) avoid sexist assumptions and language in the future.

BE IT FURTHER RESOLVED: That the General Assembly urges the President of the Unitarian Universalist Association to send copies of this resolution to other denominations examining sexism inherent in religious literature and institutions and to the International Association of Liberal Religious Women and the IARF; and

BE IT FURTHER RESOLVED: That the General Assembly requests the Unitarian Universalist Association to: (a) join with those who are encouraging others in the society to examine the relationship between religious and cultural attitudes toward women, and (b) to send a representative and resource materials to associations appropriate to furthering the above goals; and

BE IT FURTHER RESOLVED: The General Assembly requests the President of the UUA to report annually on progress in implementing this resolution.

SOURCE: Unitarian Universalist Social Justice Statements, www.uua.org/statements/women-and-religion

LESLIE ARDEN WESTBROOK

"Grailville '79—To Extend Support to All of the Women of the Church"

1979

Following the passage of the groundbreaking Resolution on Women and Religion in 1977, Leslie Arden Westbrook was hired by the UUA to act as the Minister for Women and Religion. Her task was to oversee several initiatives including the Women and Religion Committee and the Affirmative Action Program Advisory Committee, which worked to advocate for gender equality in the UUA, especially for women ministers. The continental gathering of seventy-two Unitarian Universalists at the Grailville retreat center in Loveland, Ohio, on Memorial Day weekend in 1979 was organized to consider ways to implement the commitments of the 1977 resolution, including eliminating sexist language and stereotypes from UU worship and ministerial settlement. Over the course of the weekend, religious professionals and laywomen alike discussed the challenges of eradicating sexism in the UUA, with workshops and discussions on topics ranging from Goddess worship to gender equality in seminaries. The gathering at Grailville also provided women leaders the opportunity to discuss the problem of sexist language and provided impetus for the revision of the UUA Principles and Purposes in 1985. This article was published in the Unitarian Universalist World *to share the experience at Grailville with the larger Association.*

—Natalie Malter

Seventy-two religious leaders committed to the health and growth of the Unitarian movement and to the task of erasing sexism within our denomination met at Grailville, a spiritual retreat center outside of Cincinnati, Ohio, over the 1979 Memorial Day Weekend. The conference, called "Beyond This Time," was the first such continental effort sponsored by the UUA Office of the President to explore the religious roots of sexism and to begin to examine the ways men and women in the denomination overlook and undervalue women.

The UUA is the only religious organization that has formally acknowledged a direct and destructive relationship between religious beliefs and attitudes toward women. We are groundbreakers in the larger religious community, as we begin the process of examining our own religious beliefs and how they stimulate and nurture sexual discrimination in every aspect of our lives.

Participants at the UUA Continental Women and Religion Conference came from twenty-one UUA districts. The group included more than ten ordained Unitarian Universalist women ministers and more than ten religious educators, as well as theologians, students, and others active in leadership roles in their societies.

The active involvement and support of the UU Women's Federation, Liberal Religious Education Directors Association (LREDA), and the UU Women Ministers Association (Ms. UU) insured a broad base of support for the effort.

Workshops and celebrations ran from 9 a.m. to 11 p.m. each day. Among the topics of concern were: who we are as religious women; a theology of culture; non-sexist literature in religious education; strategizing for implementation of the resolution in the UUA districts; the Goddess throughout history; how to organize around an issue; how to develop women's worship services; UU principles and whether they bespeak the experience and need of religious women; and women and religion—where we want to be in five years.

Original music, verse and slide presentations were a feature of the weekend.

Members of the UUA Women and Religion Planning Committee are Carol Brody, Billie H. Drew, Lynn Lyle, Rosemary Matson, Carolyn McDade, Joan Mendelsohn, Denise Tracy, Jean Zoerheide and Leslie Westbrook, UUA Minister for Women and Religion.

Women and Religion activity at GA/79 continued to be strong, visible and positive. The Women's Room, located in a dormitory lounge, was a gathering place for people who browsed through the literature, bought a Women and Religion T-shirt, drank coffee or tea, looked at the display of pictures taken at Grailville and posters of our foremothers and just visited.

Each night 40 to 50 women gathered for Idea Generating Sessions that began at 10 p.m. and went on . . . and on [ellipsis in original]. Ideas on theology, worship, history, scholarship, education and communication were developed that will be helpful in planning the Women and Religion Convocation in Albuquerque in 1980 immediately prior to GA/80.

SOURCE: Leslie Arden Westbrook, "Grailville '79—To Extend Support to All of the Women of the Church," *Unitarian Universalist World*, September 15, 1979, 7.

"Principles of the Unitarian Faith"
1979

The Unitarian Union of North East India is the denominational body for the Unitarians of the Khasi and Jaintia Hills and other locations in North East India. This list of principles was approved by the Union's Board on February 10, 1979, at Nongkrem, and again on October 9, 1988, at Madan Laban, Shillong. The opening affirmation of God as both Father and Mother reflects a distinctive dimension of Hajom Kissor Singh's theology. Combining the traditional Khasi understanding of God as having both male and female attributes with Jesus' affirmation of God as Father, Singh referred to God as "Father-Mother" in his influential hymns. This document was translated from Khasi to English in 1999 by D. K. B. Mukhim, working with John Rex.

—Dan McKanan

We believe—

1. In ONE GOD who is FATHER and MOTHER of all our humankind and in the brotherhood/sisterhood of us all.
2. In the forgiveness and in the love of GOD.
3. That man is not a wretched and failed creature, but is a son of GOD, and that man keeps progressing in good and respectful life.
4. In eternal life and progress of the soul.
5. That Jesus was a Great Teacher (not God, but "Son of God" as all humans are children of God); and in the two main commandments: "To love God and to love fellow humans."
6. In the great Leaders of other Religions too. (With the understanding that God expresses His own truth in other Prophets or Religious Leaders as He did in Jesus.)
7. That the Bible is the writing of God-searching people which has truths in it, and at the same time, because it was written by people from memories or legends, it also contains errors in it. Therefore, we accept the truths that we find in it, and reject those things that are untrue present in it.
8. That the books of other Religions are also good and helpful to us towards better knowledge about God.
9. In the salvation by deeds, for Jesus said, "Not everyone who says to me, 'Lord, Lord,' will enter the kingdom of heaven, but only the one who does the will of

my Father in heaven." (Matthew 7:21) This shows that salvation chiefly depends on doing the will of God. James too shows that faith without action will not deliver a man; he says, "As the body without soul is dead, so also faith without action is dead."

10. In the power of thought and reasoning for thought and reason are one of the blessings that God has given people to make use of, and we find only through thought and reason that we can separate untruth from that which is true.

11. In freedom to find out truth by ourselves. We consider our sacred duty is to open our hearts to accept truths from anywhere we can find, either from Religion or Science, and to give the right to a man to multiply those truths according to his own righteous conscience.

12. In Righteousness/Justice, in equality and in compassion to help and to support each other.

13. In a continuous search for peace in our community, country and the whole world.

14. In respecting and valuing our environment, (that is, not to be careless towards plants, animals, birds, fish, etc.).

15. In positive acceptance of one another and in encouraging each other to progress upwards in spiritual life.

SOURCE: John Rex, "Khasi Unitarians of North East India: A Presentation to the Harper's Ferry Ministerial Study Group," November 1999, 20–21.

Report of the UUA Affirmative Action Program Advisory Committee
1980

In response to the passage of the 1977 Resolution on Women and Religion, the UUA Affirmative Action Program Advisory Committee was founded to promote the involvement of women in ministry and religious leadership positions. The report, published in 1980, explores the specific challenges faced by women ministers and women seminarians through responses to questionnaires distributed to ministers and seminarians in 1978 and 1979. The findings of this report suggest that while the UUA was ahead of other religious organizations in gender equality, women ministers continued to face discrimination, especially with regard to fair compensation and larger church positions. Additionally, while the seminarians surveyed believed that the UUA was relatively unbiased with regard to gender, they did experience unique challenges in field education placement and Clinical Pastoral Education programs.

—Natalie Malter

In 1977 a revolutionary resolution entitled WOMEN AND RELIGION was passed unanimously by delegates to the UUA General Assembly meeting in Ithaca, New York. The resolution created little discussion among delegates at the time of its passage. It would have engendered more discussion if it had been accurately subtitled, "A recommendation to explore the religious roots of sexism within our denomination."

In response to the resolution, a three year program was launched by the UUA in June of 1978. A Minister for Women and Religion was appointed by the President to develop programs to implement the resolution. The task of the Office for Women and Religion was to begin to eradicate sexism within our denomination. As a result of the recommendations of nine task forces which worked during 1977–78, the two major foci of the three year program were to be:

(1) To develop educational and programmatic materials in the area of women and religion and prepare UU leadership to use these materials in the fellowships, churches and districts: and

(2) To focus on leadership within the denomination to determine how religious beliefs cause us to overlook and undervalue women in leadership roles.

The UUA Affirmative Action Program Advisory Committee was appointed with the special task of developing an affirmative action program for women ministers and women theological students within the denomination.

* * *

During 1979, the Affirmative Action Program Advisory Committee sent a questionnaire to all individuals preparing for the UU ministry. Responses were received from over 50% of those questioned. . . .

Forty-five respondents were enrolled in one of the three designated UU schools: Harvard Divinity School, Meadville/Lombard and Starr King School for the Ministry. The remaining 45 were in non-UU schools or independent study programs. The majority of the male respondents were enrolled in a UU school, with a greater percentage of female respondents studying in non-UU schools. In the Boston area, most of the students at Harvard are men, while the reverse is true at Andover-Newton Theological School.

* * *

In choosing a theological school, women saw vocational counseling, geographical location and family concerns as somewhat more important than did men. Most of the respondents saw a need for their school to change in its treatment of issues relating to women and religion and suggested some methods of improvement. Although the majority of students had positive field work experiences, a number of women reported negative experiences during CPE. As anticipated, most respondents saw parish ministry as their future goal. Both groups also considered other options, with a slightly higher percentage of women noting non-parish goals. The bulk of women, and many men, saw their future as related to gender and/or family concerns. Most respondents saw the role of the UUA thus far as positive. No indications of perceived sexism or differences between male and female responses in the role of the UUA were noted. Both men and women pinpointed specific future action the UUA might take, with women more heavily interested in UUA involvement in their career plans.

* * *

To begin assessing the role of women clergy in the Unitarian Universalist Association, the Committee used a questionnaire answered by thirty-five settled women ministers, the bulk of settled women ministers in our denomination, in the fall of 1978 and winter of 1979.

The women ranged widely in age: six were below age 30; eight were 30–39; thirteen were 40–49; and, eight were 50 or older. Seventy-four percent of the women who responded felt that they had problems and concerns unique to them as women in the liberal religious ministry. Ninety-four percent stated that they had experiences that were directly affected by their gender, both positively and negatively. A total of eighty-three percent had not approached a church for settlement that would not

356

consider a woman minister. However, in describing the settlement process, sixty percent of the women did so in negative terms. Although few women had encountered overt rejection in the settlement process, many felt that their gender remained an issue in their ministry. Many respondents urged that the denomination take steps to correct any inequities faced by women in the ministry.

In order to gauge the positions held by women in our ministry a number of factors were analyzed and cross tabulated. These factors included age, years in the ministry, position, church size and salary. It has been argued that the use of these factors does not fully measure "success" within the ministry. In fact, it was recognized by the Committee that many other factors such as personal satisfaction, congregational strength and family growth are also important factors in any determination of a "successful" ministry.

※ ※ ※

Of the thirty-five respondents, fifteen had been active in the ministry for five or more years while the remaining twenty had been settled for less than five years. Fifty-two percent of the full-time, settled women ministers in the Unitarian Universalist Association had been active in their ministry for five or more years. Both older and younger women were included among the full-time clergy with five or more years of experience. Although the influx of women into the Unitarian Universalist ministry and theological schools has been cited as a reason for problems with settling women clergy, there are now some women with substantial years of service in our ministry. It would appear that there are women in our ministry with sufficient pastoral experience to assume the pulpits of some of our larger churches. However, this has rarely happened.

A substantial number of our women clergy, both full and part-time, serve as senior ministers. Twenty-six respondents were senior ministers and only eight were non-senior ministers. The non-senior category includes assistant or associate ministers and those co-ministers who did not consider themselves to be in the senior position. The senior position seems to be independent of a woman's length of pastoral experience. The data suggest that women often begin their ministry as senior ministers. This may be due, in part, to the fact that we have few churches large enough to accommodate more than one minister on the staff.

Few of our women clergy work in these large churches, either as senior or non-senior clergy. . . . Four respondents work full-time in churches with three hundred or more members, as non-senior clergy, while three work in such churches as part-time, non-senior ministers. Only three women ministers work in churches with over three hundred members on a full-time, senior basis. . . .

When church size and years of ministry are cross tabulated, it is evident that years in ministry does not necessarily bring a large church for our women clergy. Five women who have been in the ministry for more than five years serve churches with fewer than 200 members. It is not known, however, whether women are actively choosing smaller churches for family or other personal considerations. The data indicate that there are few women clergy serving larger churches.

Since data on church size served by women clergy is mitigated by the preponderance of small churches within the Unitarian Universalist Association, the salaries of women clergy may be more useful to consider. . . .

Forty-four percent of the full-time women clergy make below $15,000 per year. All part-time clergy who reported their income stated that it was below $15,000 per year. Only four full-time women clergy make $20,000 or more. There are ten full-time women ministers who have served in the liberal ministry for more than five years who make less than $20,000; half of those women receive salaries of less than $15,000 per year. At the time that this data was collected, the average salary for all Unitarian Universalist clergy was reported as $20,000. Since the bulk of the clergy are men, we can assume that the average salary for male clergy at this time was approximately $20,000 per year. Only four women ministers reached this average salary figure. Eleven women who are senior ministers receive less than $15,000 per year in salary. Despite the fact that the bulk of women ministers are in positions of seniority, their salaries remain low and the congregations they serve are, on the whole, smaller societies.

Conclusions

In the ability to settle women in their first parish, the Unitarian Universalist Association is ahead of many other denominations. The Unitarian Universalist Association and the Ministerial Settlement Office, as well as individual congregations, have reason for self-satisfaction. However, the task of affirmative action for women remains. . . .

Unfortunately, the present questionnaire did not enable us to judge each individual's circumstances or concerns. It seems clear that issues such as family plans, personal growth, and personal measures or feelings of success are important factors and may be deserving of further consideration. Many women seem to choose to stay in their present position for significant personal reasons. It is not the intent of this analysis to judge the worth or success of any woman or man within the Unitarian Universalist ministry. Nor do we make the case that these data are the only measure of success. Clearly, other factors are important.

The data available do indicate two areas of focus of affirmative action for women:

(1) Second settlement, with the possibility of a larger church and higher salary level, and

(2) Salary packages.

An important consideration in the second settlement is whether women feel free to pursue a second level settlement. If not, are these limitations personally imposed or the result of an unwillingness on the part of congregations to consider women clergy? The paucity of women ministers in larger congregations is not solely the result of limited pastoral experience. It is the belief of the Committee that both self-selection (the decision of women to stay where they are) and resistance to women in the ministry are factors in the lack of women ministers in larger second level churches. To address these issues, the Committee feels that it is important to implement educational programs for church Search Committees, Ministerial Settlement Representatives, and church communities. Equally important is a need to approach the issue of self-selection among women clergy, ensuring that women are making their choices freely with self awareness and a belief in their own potential.

The question of salaries received by women clergy is now clearly a problem. . . . It is generally true in the larger society that women receive lower salaries than their male counterparts. It is to be hoped that the Unitarian Universalist Association will place itself in the vanguard, ensuring sufficient salaries for its women ministers.

The task before us is a difficult one. Our problems and dilemmas in affirmative action for women are more nebulous than in the past. We are called not only to settle women clergy in Unitarian Universalist churches, but to ensure, as much as we are able, that they can move into larger churches if they so choose and that they receive not only positions of seniority but adequate pay for the work they do. Even if women chose to work in smaller societies, we need to ensure that their salary level is adequate.

As a beginning, the Affirmative Action Program Advisory Committee has developed a series of settlement designs which we believe will assist in the acceptance, settlement and support of women clergy within the denomination. We hope that these plans are the beginning of a continuing dialogue, a search to make what is already good, even better.

SOURCE: Report of the UUA Affirmative Action Program Advisory Committee, Unitarian Universalist Association, Women and Religion Committee Records, 1976–1981, Andover-Harvard Archive, bMS1022/5, Andover-Harvard Theological Library, Harvard Divinity School, Cambridge, MA.

LUCILE SCHUCK LONGVIEW
AND CAROLYN McDADE

"Coming Home Like Rivers to the Sea: A Women's Ritual"

1980

Originally designed as a worship service for the Women and Religion Conti-
nental Convocation of Unitarian Universalists in East Lansing, Michigan,
in 1980, "The Water Ritual" has become a common ingathering service in
Unitarian Universalist churches throughout the United States. Often incor-
rectly referred to as "Water Communion," the ceremony takes place in many
churches at the end of the summer and consists of people bringing water from
a place that is meaningful to them, naming that water, and then pouring it
into a common vessel. In some churches the water is saved for child dedication
ceremonies. As originally created by Carolyn McDade (1935–) and Lucile
Schuck Longview (1911–2010), both prominent feminists, the ritual was a
feminist service with an emphasis on water as a metaphor for life, birth, and
women's empowerment. Each participant was meant to take some of the com-
ingled water home with them. Further Reading: Teresa Berger, ed., Dissident
Daughters: Feminist Liturgies in Global Context (*Louisville, KY: Westmin-*
ster John Knox Press, 2002).

—Natalie Malter

We were beginning to reach for new and inclusive symbols and rituals that speak
to us of our connectedness to one another, to the totality of life, and to our place on
this planet. We moved in an intuitive response to the potential of water as a symbol
of women's spirituality.

We were working together to create a worship service for the November 1980
"Women and Religion" continental convocation of Unitarian Universalists, to be
held in East Lansing, Michigan. The universality of water as a symbol emerged as
we worked on what became the service now known as "Coming Home Like Rivers
to the Sea." As we worked to shape the service our awareness increased of water's
presence and deep meaning in all our lives.

The water ceremony became the central part of a religious service that broke
with tradition in significant ways. It was created by lay women, women who had long
been silent in the pews. The ritual space was also made sacred by the women themselves. We gathered to worship in a way authentic and liberating to us, not as in a

church but in a semicircle around a large common earthen bowl. It was a ritual of women's being connected by a universal symbol, water, a ritual of women being connected to the totality of life.

The vital parts of the ceremony are the bringing of waters, the sharing of their meaning, the experiencing of the intermingled waters by the group, and the taking of the waters from the ritual. The ceremony flows from what the participants bring to it. Each brings a container of water that has special meaning to her. She shares with the group why this water is significant to her and what it symbolizes in her life. The water ceremony names water as a symbol close to us as women that is reflective of and enabling to our daily lives. The ceremony releases from us an expression in words of what is vital, rooted and connected to us. In small gatherings each woman can bring water and speak of its meaning to her. In large groups such as the one at East Lansing a number of women are invited in advance to bring water and participate in the ritual on behalf of us all.

When the water has been mingled, it is then experienced in some way by the women gathered together. We have subsequently been in small groups who circled the bowl, putting our hands in it; we have witnessed the water passed around the circle as women used it to heal one another. We have seen ceremonies spontaneously shaped in the moment or carefully planned, each portion reflected upon. During or after the service there should be an opportunity for those gathered to take a small portion of the water to be carried away. The collected and mingled water thus journeys on into individual lives and often flows into a common bowl at other water ceremonies. As the ritual is continued, water deepens in meaning for us, just as water deepens during its long and winding journey to the sea.

"Sometimes I Feel Like a Motherless Child"
> Sometimes I feel like a motherless child . . .
>> a long way from home, a long way from home.
> Sometimes I feel like I've never been heard . . .
>> a long way from home, a long way from home.
> Sometimes I feel like I've never been seen . . .
>> a long way from home, a long way from home.
> Sometimes I feel like the day has come . . .
>> and I am coming home, and I am coming home. [ellipses in original]
>>> —TRADITIONAL SPIRITUAL, ADAPTED

The Centering

Religions in recent times have been about the empowerment of men. Women have been lost, unseen and unheard. We gather to lift up our woman identity, our self-understanding. We come with our yearning to find her who acknowledges our birth and our presence, who nurtures life and spirit. It is she who is ourselves—she who, upon meeting, we recognized and need no introduction. It is she who gives birth to all we are and can be—to ideas, thoughts, words and songs—to foggy shaped long-ings and to fiery rage and to all-encompassing love. She is the center inside ourselves which is our truest truth, our primary honesty—that being, tender, insistent, and passionate toward survival and wholeness. We give birth to her as she gives birth to us, as we give birth to one another.

Making our way like rivers from places distant and near, we come together to give shape to a new spirituality. For there is no theology that calls women to strength rather than to support the strength of others; that calls women to action rather than to passivity; that calls women to full expression rather than to meek acceptance.

Recognizing that, we see we must question every box, every definition, every assignment from an authority outside our own be-ings so that we can create and re-create *for ourselves* the rituals and symbols that give meaning to us. So we come together to question. To hear. To share. To speak. To inspire. And to celebrate through new rituals, knowing that our energy and our love are transforming.

Celebrating now our connectedness, we choose water as our symbol of our empowerment. As rivers in cycle release their waters and regain new beginnings, so do we cycle. For us as women these beginnings are powerful, but not easy. But still we come to create and to celebrate and to live by the only spirituality worthy of our devotion—a spirituality that uplifts, empowers and connects.

The Meaning of the Waters: "Water Song"

Listen, Sister, listen,
Listen to the waters
calling us like rivers
to run our truest paths to sea—
from high hill and lowland valley,
and remote areas of our inner be-ings,
in rushing fury, white-foamed and swift,
at times quieting
to hold the colored leaf,
settling in cracks and breaking dams,
tides waxing and waning to answer
the moon,
blood running,
rain falling,
tears
dropping,

the heart beating upstream,
the earth pulling down,
rising in vapor,
falling
in rain,
soaking the roots.

Birth waters holding the babe,
wetting the canal,
signaling the birth
Water—the mirror giving us back
to ourselves,
our images, our beauty,
our strength,
bodies and faces double-lined
with waves and years.

Water, you fall—there is poetry,
you run, there is music,
you rise, there is dance,
sweeping, swirling, spinning, running,
settling, rushing,
quieting,
rising,
misting,
fog-thick and ice-formed,
thawing, dripping, enlivening
the dry root,
juice of the flower, wine of the fruit,
drop by drop and ocean full,
one water around one earth,
dashing the shore,
soothing the sand,
leaving, returning, together,
apart,
distinct
collective,
Source of Life,
the great recycler,
carver of rocks, writer of canyons, shaper of earth.

Water, you come from the early whispers of my beginnings,
on and on,
intimate of every generation and all to come.
The great equalizer,
morning tea, evening broth,
I know you waters.
We've met some time before.
Why do I know you so well?
You run over my body and I am at home,
you fall on my naked face and I feel
welcomed
from a long journey.
You of a thousand stories, a million
years,
spiraling through formless time,
you of the endless flow,
blood rhythmic, red, mindful
of the moon.

O, but waters, I know,
how I know
and will never forget
you are blood spilled,
blood of the girl-child terrorized
who never had a chance
against the man
entrusted with
her care;
blood of the victor's rape,
and rape
and rape again,
he the returning hero,
honored, medaled,
showered with paper
rain;
blood of the back rooms,
women anguished, near death,
in a world too moral to share the front.
Yes, you are like me, waters,

time upon time caught, channeled, used,
without rights or consultation,
receptacle,
receiver of wastes,
assigned to clean the mess,
or hide it, or
hold it,
exploited, bearer of life they call their own,
confined, owned, fought over,
lost, won,
feared, disregarded, unseen,
unheard,
motherless
in a world that milks the breast,
shuns the blood and terrorizes
the womb,
damming the creative flow for its own sake
while calling itself humane.

Water, I yearn for you in some place
deeper than hope.
surer than faith.
some place I only know must be
the source of love.
I strain my ears to hear you, Beloved Sister,
beloved one of my earth,
you in my veins.

As I hear, I shall never lose
your call from rising cloud to running stream,
from feather frost to the deep
and holding sea.
I hear you call—
you call to me gently,
strongly,
clear-depthed, you say
"O, Sister, Beloved One,
come home,
come
home."

The Bringing of the Waters

At the first water ceremony in East Lansing we asked women coming from distant points to bring water. From a stream near East Lansing Linda Pinti came with water, saying: "I took my bucket and went out to the Grand River. As I gathered water I watched the river: moving, flowing, changing, I was reminded of an image in depth-psychology which tells us that each of us, each of our beings, is like a well; if you dig down deep enough into the well of our beings, you will hit the ground water that we all share. The ground water which flows between and among us connects us to each other and to the 'All That Is.'"

"For me the gathering of water is a symbol of the essence and meaning of [women's gathering.] It is a tapping into the collective ground water that flows among us: the collective energy of the goddess, the liberating transforming power which is in each of our sisters and in the sister within our brothers."

There was water from the Rio Grande River in the desert near Albuquerque that another woman brought, but her words were for that moment only and never written down. Edith Fletcher came with water from a mountain lake in New York State. She said: "This water comes from a spring-fed pond on the summit of a foot-hill of the Taconic Range in upstate New York. To me it symbolizes the essence of the place where I find renewal—renewal of my physical well-being by swimming in it, canoeing, rowing, sailing on it, exploring fish and insect and plant life in it; renewal of intimacy with my children, grandchildren, and friends who share my love of this place; renewal of my pleasure and wonder in the natural world of forest and fields. This water symbolizes the sustenance and replenishing of those qualities I find good in myself."

* * *

Coming Home to Our Women's Identity

As our ears become attuned to hearing our inner voices, and the voices of one another, so also do we hear the call of our sisters from far beyond. What spirals in, also spirals out, and beyond space and time. Thus we hear the anguished words and the more anguished silences of women around the earth and through time. We know that our sisterhood extends beyond our land and that we must teach beyond clans and nationalism, beyond languages and cultures, beyond institutions, beyond religions—to our sisters, living hand to living hand, eye to eye, thought to thought, with our compassion for one another, our love of this earth, our very love of life itself, creating bonds between us.

We must lift up in our culture women's significant strengths, insights and under-standing, our ways of coping and thinking. We must enter now and shape our world toward one of compassion and a new justice that dares to see and to feel and to respond, toward human concern for life and affirmation of life, toward joyfulness

366

and celebration, toward relationships of love, respect and mutual concern—toward cooperation, connectedness and responsiveness. We bring the inclusiveness of the cycles and the spheres. In our way of understanding life, we name a new meaning.

Such a promise demands that we keep our identity as women.

We cannot fall back to the false assumptions of the faiths of the past, to the biased assumptions that have failed our half, the female half, of the world. We can no longer embrace the patriarchal assumptions underlying traditional faiths. All religions keep women invisible, hide our issues, turn our energy and our loyalty toward concerns which, though labeled "human concerns," consistently lift the priorities of males above all else.

No vision, no world view, has the ability to sustain a just and caring society without a feminist perspective—a perspective that seeks the empowerment of women as well as men. Women must be the ones to promote that perspective, for we are the unbounded ones in crucial ways. We have an outsider understanding and we need to draw on that knowledge. We do not have the bonds with the power of domination that men have been acculturated to hold and to cherish.

Ours can be an enabling power.

We must *come home*—come home to our self-understanding.

Let us embrace our woman-identity!

Taking the Waters for Women's Empowerment

We take these birthing waters *to name our empowerment*, to name our strength to be ourselves, and to name our ability to rise up and to move forth.

We take these birthing waters *to call forth our power of questioning*, our powers to doubt, our powers to examine every definition and every authority outside ourselves.

We take these amniotic waters *to name our imagination and creativity*, our power to unveil our thinking and to create new visions.

We take these waters, symbolic of our becoming, *to name the reclaiming of our energy and loyalty*, to signify that we put ourselves—the thoughts of our mind and the work of our hands—to what we most deeply value.

We take these waters, symbolic of a new genesis, *to name our love*: of this earth, of our connectedness with people everywhere, and of our devotion to life itself.

At East Lansing five women took of the waters in a symbolic way for all of us, because we were so many. Then we were told that, if we wished to take some of the waters home with us, we should find a way to do so. "Look among the items you brought," we were told, "the lotions, the creams, the perfumes. Those containers carry the veils we wear—the reminders of our inadequacies. Empty one of those containers. Take with you this symbol of our becoming. Take some of the birthing waters."

We must lift up life-giving symbols and keep them before us as symbols of our women's identity, symbols of our empowerment, our questioning, our imagination and creativity, our energy and loyalty, our nurturing and love. We must have our own reminders that we have put aside those other symbols of exclusion and domination, those symbols which have diminished us and now lead to the destruction of our planet.

✻   ✻   ✻

Sharing of the Waters

As water changes form and moves in a life-giving cycle, so this water ceremony must move, be in process, change, be in motion. It needs always to be reflective of and integral to the time and place of the people creating it.

In reading or using this service we think it is important to notice that the water ceremony was woven into a worship service. Creating that service has had its own value for us in what it gave to us. It brought us together for many hours of sharing and conversation, analyzing, planning, creating, clarifying. It called us to articulation, to pulling foggy-shaped thoughts into words. We each spoke and listened. We wrote down one another's words. We spoke them back with added meaning. It was a bonding and empowering experience for us, and we commend this sort of experience to you.

We hope our sisters continue to reach for the depth and inclusiveness of symbols that speak to women and that draw upon our daily experiences. We need symbols with enabling power that connect us with what we most deeply value and which empower our expression of this in our lives.

SOURCE: Carolyn McDade and Lucile Longview, "Coming Home Like Rivers to the Sea: A Women's Ritual," in Elizabeth Dodson Gray, ed., *Sacred Dimensions of Women's Experience* (Wellesley, MA: Roundtable Press, 1988), 124–30, 131–34.

"O = E A P, or If I Can't Have Everything, How Much Can I Have?"

1980

At the 1977 General Assembly in Ithaca, New York, Sandra Mitchell Caron (1935–1999) became the first woman moderator of the UUA, serving with Paul Carnes, the newly elected UUA president. Caron became a Unitarian Universalist when she joined the Unitarian Church of All Souls in New York City as a young adult. In addition to her term as moderator from 1977 to 1985, Caron served as board chair of the Clara Barton Camp for Girls with Diabetes, and she had a successful career as an attorney, working in corporate real estate and for the New York State Departments of Commerce and Transportation. In the 1985 UUA Presidential election, Caron ran unsuccessfully against William Schulz, becoming the first woman to run for the UUA Presidency. Caron presented the following sermon as a guest speaker at the Unitarian Church of Arlington in Arlington, Virginia, several years into her term as moderator. The sermon was part of a larger service, which addressed the changing roles of women in church and society at large.

— Natalie Malter

A week or two ago my solitary lunch at the World Trade Center was enlivened by the conversation of two young women at the next table. (I really couldn't help hearing — my elbow was in their soup.)

They were twenty-five-ish, beautiful, with the clear skin and the lush, slightly soft-edged figures that seem to characterize takers of "the Pill." And they were bright. I gathered that they had recently finished law school and from the lack of anguish in their conversation, must have received that best of all December mail, notice from the New York Court of Appeals that they had passed the bar exam. One, as it turned out, was married, while the other was semi-detached, if I may use a real estate term.

They discussed their jobs for a while, the unmated one still pondering the law-firm-versus-corporation-versus-government choice and what each of those choices would mean in terms of life style and years of commitment. The other, seemingly on the verge of giving full commitment to her job, was held back only by the fact that her husband was considering a two-year assignment elsewhere — an "elsewhere" that they would not consider settling in permanently. Friends were advising her that this temporary exile would be a good time to have her children, but she considered two years an awkward time period—not quite long enough to have two children, and too long to waste. Her friend congratulated her on at least having settled two major questions: what form of law she wanted to practice and the identity of the principals in the child-bearing venture, while she herself had settled neither. The two firmly agreed that one must have settled such matters and passed certain major guide-posts by the age of thirty or the prognosis for any meaningful achievement was very poor.

Good grief, I thought over my Charlotte Russe cake, how very different their lives had been from my first twenty-five years!

Like most women born in this country in 1935, my growing up was a ramshackle non-structure. In my case this was compounded by the fact that I was born in a part of the country where it was generally believed that if one went to Wednesday night prayer meeting and church on Sunday morning the Lord would provide. (Presumably if one also went on Sunday night, He would provide *abundantly*.) Planning, which was often equated with scheming to get ahead of one's fellowman or to get rich ("easier for a camel to get through the eye of the needle"), was probably un-Christian and, until Pearl Harbor, unpatriotic. Still further, most social workers would have called as a "multi-problem family." (There were four of us and it seemed to me we were each a problem.) Our attitude was that if we made it through this moment's crisis with our skins, we were hallelujah-lucky and this was no time to tempt fate by worrying about the next one. It was generally assumed from the time I was five or so that I was going to be a writer—an impression that I did nothing to dispel inasmuch as I had nothing better to replace it with. You didn't have to plan to be a writer, of course, it was a "gift." The fact that I hated to write had nothing to do with the case—I had, after all been inordinately fond of first Peter Rabbit and then Annabel Lee, hadn't I? Who ever heard of someone growing up to be a reader? Ergo, I must be intended to write. . . .

When an adult friend persuaded my high school to graduate me at the end of my junior year, it troubled me not a whit. Even starting college at sixteen, I was certain to perish before I had to make any major decision, and there was certainly no pressure to chart a course. Even if the cause was different, my lack of focus was entirely typical of the female Class of '55. There was one difference in our procedure: while the others waited for the football captain to "take them away from all this," I, with my peculiar conviction that I would not pass that way again, tried to take every course in the university. What mattered to me was not grades, which would be of limited utility in the next world, but the sheer delight of sampling the great smorgasbord of subjects. It was a glorious, and nearly fatal, gluttony.

When nineteen came and went, and I did not, there I was adrift on the open sea of life. . . .

Soon—almost overnight it seemed to me—women were being told they could have everything. Letty Pogrebin, Caroline Bird and others said it, and seemed to demonstrate it. This was what my father had said in the beginning and suddenly it seemed that he was right after all. It was not a linear promise, but everything at once, work, husband, babies: love, achievement, renown. Just as the *small* child had been told, "If you try hard enough, you can have anything you want," the woman was hearing, "If you try hard enough you can have *everything* you want." In the first instance, not having lived long enough to understand gravity, I tried to jump over the moon like the cow in the nursery rhyme; this time I merely reached for it.

Now, after twenty years of living this century's women's movement, I think I am beginning to grasp the equation of femaleness. I would postulate that outcome equals effort times ability times planning. The amazing thing to me—even now— about the conversation between my unknown young sisters is how much more they know about each factor in the equation than my generation did—but still far too little for the journey they will make.

Obviously self-knowledge is a *sine qua non*. Without clear-eyed assessment of one's energy quotient and abilities, planning is either fatuous hope or unwarranted despair. Yet who will help us quantify these? Modern science with its precise calibration and psychology with all its insight falter when asked to gauge which of us, given both abilities, can nurture the child *and* create the novel without putting the head in the oven. What is the level of energy and organization at which one can have one-third of everything? . . . two thirds [ellipsis in original]?

Knowledge of self must include knowledge of our bodies, but even now, with all our control and sophistication, who among us knows how many years we have in which to have our children, or how many years at all for that matter? The young women of a few short generations ago assumed they had from puberty to menopause to have children. Today's young women ponder statistics of birth defects after age thirty-five, and after forty, and expect amniocentesis to warn them of impending tragedy. Yet none can know with precision how long fertility will last, nor can the healthiest of us depend on a trouble-free gestation. Our science attempts to conquer death. Can it also penetrate the unknowns of life? Our bodies, ourselves—yes indeed, and how much more we need to know!

No corporation could make a market plan, no high command could plot a skirmish, let alone a war, and expect to be successful with so little data. Yet our young women must try it every day.

As I watch my baby daughter, I wish her energy and ability, time and determination, and most particularly self-knowledge. Perhaps in the stillness born of her confidence, she will hear her inner clock. Perhaps she will move gently, surely, to the sweet, strong music of her own song, its tempo clear in her inner ear. Perhaps she will have everything—at least everything worth having.

SOURCE: *Bread and Roses: A Sermon Presented by the Worship Committee . . . with a Special Contribution by Sandra Mitchell Caron* (Arlington, VA: Unitarian Church of Arlington, 1980).

CAROLYN McDADE

"Spirit of Life"

1981

In addition to her work as a teacher, social justice activist, and feminist, Carolyn McDade is known as one of the most prolific and talented composers of music used in Unitarian Universalist churches today. A singer-songwriter, McDade recognized the power of music as an instrument of social change and has harnessed that energy in all of her work, some of which is included in the Unitarian Universalist hymnal Singing the Living Tradition. *Her deeply held belief in women's equality inspired much of her music, which reflects her feminist views. The best known of all of her songs, "Spirit of Life" has become a weekly doxology in many Unitarian Universalist congregations. Although the hymn is only six lines long, its transformative power and ability to speak to people across different spiritual traditions has made it one of the most beloved songs in Unitarian Universalist churches. Further Reading: Kimberly French, "Carolyn McDade's Spirit of Life," carolynmcdademusic.com/uu2007article.pdf*

—Natalie Malter

Spirit of Life, come unto me.
Sing in my heart all the stirrings of compassion.
Blow in the wind, rise in the sea;
Move in the hand, giving life the shape of justice.
Roots hold me close; wings set me free;
Spirit of Life, come to me, come to me.

SOURCE: Carolyn McDade, "Spirit of Life," #123, *Singing the Living Tradition* (Boston: Beacon Press, 1993).

CAROLYN OWEN-TOWLE
"Abortion: An Agonizing Moral Choice"
1982

Carolyn Owen-Towle was ordained as a Unitarian Universalist minister in 1978, the year following the passage of the Business Resolution on Women and Religion, at a time when the number of women in Unitarian Universalist ministry was just beginning to expand rapidly. Along with her husband and fellow Unitarian Universalist minister, Tom Owen-Towle, Carolyn co-pastored the First Unitarian Church of San Diego from 1978 to 2002. In addition to her work as a minister and activist, Carolyn served as the president of the Ministerial Sisterhood Unitarian Universalist from 1979 to 1982, as a board member of Planned Parenthood in San Diego from 1979 to 1982, as the first woman president of the Unitarian Universalist Service Committee from 1983 to 1985, and as the first woman president of the Unitarian Universalist Ministers Association from 1987 to 1989. In 1993 she ran and lost against John Buehrens in the UUA presidential election. She preached her sermon "Abortion: An Agonizing Moral Choice" on January 10, 1982, at her congregation in San Diego. Written at the beginning of her career, it reflects the contentious nature of the national debate about abortion ten years after the Supreme Court's Roe v. Wade *decision. In her sermon, Owen-Towle explores the various arguments about reproductive rights in the United States, providing historical context for the debate and ultimately asserting the importance of protecting a woman's right to choose.*

—Natalie Malter

A number of years ago I remember arguing, perhaps in hindsight, glibly about a woman's right to decide what to do with her own body—about her right to seek abortion upon demand. The conversations, and I had several, were with a professor of Religion, a Catholic, at the University of Iowa. I was as passionate in my defense of women's rights as he was in his protective stance toward the unborn child. Yet, I remember experiencing uneasiness in my so-called certainty. My newfound feminist self was quick to insist upon women's rights. I had not, however, deeply thought this issue through.

A number of years later, with some growth, thought and counseling experience, I am unwilling to acknowledge anything simple or clear about the subject. In the intervening time I have, for one thing, incorporated a deeper appreciation for ambiguity as being central to all important life and death questions. If there is any subject in which shades of gray predominate, it has to be that of abortion. This is a complex issue on which reasonable persons disagree. And it is of importance enough to a Unitarian Universalist's basic moral approach to life to be seriously considered. It is of importance even if it cannot fully be understood by anyone who has not found herself in this decision-making place.

In 1973 the Supreme Court decision in Roe vs. Wade destatutized abortion insuring the right of a woman within certain limitations to make her own moral decision regarding abortion. Yet even after such legalization, abortion remains one of the most controversial and complex issues. This decision spawned the right-to-life movement. Currently Sen. Orrin Hatch (fitting name) has opened hearings on constitutional amendments on abortion. His aim is to reverse Roe vs. Wade by removing abortion from the realm of private moral decision-making and placing every aspect of abortion squarely in the political arena. The Hatch Amendment is the first step in an elaborate long-term strategy to end abortions.

* * *

Moving beyond politics for a moment, let us look at some of the ethical moral issues involved. First the stakes are enormously high in this issue. If advocates of the right and responsibility to have an abortion are correct, the woman who is required to bear a child against her will is having forced upon her enormous economic and psychological burdens. On the other hand if those who see abortion as a moral outrage are correct, the act is among the worst forms of taking human life—the willful destruction of an innocent, helpless person.

Many different issues are involved. One is the question of who ought to decide when an abortion is acceptable, whether legally or ethically. . . .

Another issue is that of rights—rights of the woman vs. rights of the unborn fetus. Now a right, ethically speaking, is something to which one is thought to have a morally justified claim. . . .

What of the moral status of a fetus? . . . One cannot logically offer a strictly biological argument for the status of the fetus. One can, however, claim that some biological event, such as conception, or implantation, or the beginning of breathing is a factor that ought to be given moral significance.

* * *

Throughout history there have been varying stands on abortion ranging from total prohibition to relative indifference. Augustine saw every sexual act as intrinsically evil redeemed only by a good intention, mainly that of procreation. While we are shocked today by that view, I can remember my own Mother saying, self mockingly, that as a child she was convinced that her parents only did THAT the four times it was necessary to have four children. Ah, the holdovers of good old Victorianism.

374

Did you know that Aristotle advocated the view that the fetus did not actually receive a spiritual or human soul until forty days after conception for the male and eighty days for the female. I can't even comment on that. This view was known as 'infusion' and was apparently held as well by Thomas Aquinas. It wasn't until the 17th century that Roman Catholics came to believe that infusion of the soul takes place at conception. Up until the 16th century abortions were apparently tolerated because there were doubts as to the precise point at which human life begins. But in response to the Reformation and as counter influence to worldly trends, the Pope placed stringent restraints upon all practices, including abortion.

But, you see, at precisely this point in time a group of people began to emerge whose principles eventually came to be the basis of a new humanism and a new understanding of the nature of moral life. The emphasis was no longer on human virtues or on the church as a basis for ethics, but on the responsible decisions that every individual must make in the light of her/his best understanding of faith. Some of these were Christians and the more radical of these were Unitarians.

Now Luther still had trouble resolving his own conflicts with the flesh. For him procreation remained the most justifiable consequence for sexual intercourse. Good old Calvin was somewhat positive in his espousal that the sexual act was "undefiled, honorable and holy, because it is a pure institution of God." Although he did not emphasize the enjoyments of sex, he did reject the proposition that the act itself was a source of sin.

Wouldn't they have been scandalized to realize that it has become at least the Western world's greatest, most delightful avocation?

A growing emphasis upon marriage as a fellowship contributed, in time, to a shifting of rank order in the purpose of sexual intercourse. The needs of the personal came to be first, while procreation moved to second place. It became easier to see abortion as a moral option after procreation ceased to be the primary function of marriage.

Unitarian Universalists and many Protestants have long placed emphasis upon the privacy of personal conscience in matters of morals, even when the exercise of conscience is in conflict with a social policy that is believed to be good for the majority.

* * *

Abortion is deeply a women's issue. My Grandmother once said that she had a life long feeling of being violated as a woman in that she could not control reproduction. She loved her husband and she loved her children, but she was talking about being a victim—a victim of circumstance who could not have control over her life in this sense. Even with the advent of birth control, if women are forced to give birth they will again lose their recently won autonomy as human beings. They will be subjugated. They will become less valued than a fertilized egg. This historic victim-ization has killed people's love for sex, for closeness, and it has spawned resentment. It has put unwanted children in jeopardy. Men simply cannot know that sense of helplessness in the same way.

Abortion is as well an issue of humanity—for no segment of it may be forced to act against its conscience and will without dehumanizing another. Each individual who believes in the right and responsibility of personal privacy and choice must actively defend that right for others. We live in a pluralistic society. Individual deci-sion must not be constrained by any one group's dogma or value system.

* * *

In conclusion, the very fact that parenthood is so fundamentally important a matter demands that it arise only out of the personal freedom to make moral deci-sions. It is theologically and ethically responsible to affirm that when all the related human values are taken into account, for some a decision to have an abortion may be the most appropriate, even redemptive choice a person can make.

As a Unitarian Universalist I believe that freedom, responsibility and privacy are inalienable personal rights. Therefore, I must go to the barricades to uphold those rights. And I will. This is an issue for which I will march. No longer with a glib assur-ance that the individual decisions will ever be easy, but with the conviction that the right to choice is sacred and must be upheld.

SOURCE: Carolyn Owen-Towle, *Abortion: An Agonizing Moral Choice* (San Diego, CA: First Unitarian Church, 1982).

Common Ground: Coming of Age, A Report of the 1982 UUA Youth Assembly

1982

Liberal Religious Youth (LRY) was founded in 1954 when the American Unitarian Youth and the Universalist Youth Federation merged. LRYers developed the philosophy of youth autonomy, the belief that an organization of youth should be run by youth. In 1969, LRY ceased to employ adult staff. Tensions between it and the UUA mounted. In the early 1980s, the UUA cut funding to LRY and pressured LRY's leadership to dissolve the organization and create a youth organization with greater adult supervision, and Young Religious Unitarian Universalists (YRUU) was the result. YRUU was developed at two conferences: Common Ground (1981) and Common Ground: Coming of Age (1982). Further Reading: Wayne B. Arnason and Rebecca Scott, We Would Be One: A History of Unitarian Universalist Youth Movements *(Boston: Skinner House, 2005).*

—Colin Bossen

Worship

There was a sense during Common Ground: Coming of Age that the whole week was one worship service, one long liturgical process. Even (especially) our business sessions were begun, refreshed, and ended by song, by holding hands and hugging, by affirming again and again that we remembered we were one, even when we seemed most fragmented.

*   *   *

Midweek during the Assembly, the LRY Board of Directors presented its "Last Board Meeting" as a worship event. "The LRY Service meant the most to me. It started off as a zany (I guess normal) LRY Board meeting. It slowly got more serious as all members shared what LRY had meant to them. It showed what I call 'the true spirit of LRY.' As youth we are silly sometimes, but when it gets down to it, we're willing to do anything for what we believe in."

*   *   *

What's In a Name? by Wayne Arnason

"Liberal Religious" became the appropriate substitute words for "Unitarian" or "Universalist" or both. At different times during the history of LRY, the meaning of

377

the words in the name was explored. LRY'ers asked themselves whether "liberal" was a word that really described them, politically or religiously. Successive generations of youth at conferences and local meetings had programs on "The R in LRY," seeking to articulate what was religious about their youth group within a church which had so few of the usual "identifying characteristics" of mainstream religions.

* * *

"Young Religious Unitarian Universalists" clearly designates our youth organization as a part of our church, and this reaffirms the recommendations and the sentiment of the first Common Ground Youth Assembly. Yet it retains two of the words and initials from "Liberal Religious Youth." . . . It is striking that the word this group of young people wanted to retain in their name was the word "Religious," a word that was a constant focus of questioning, discussion, and debate in the old name. Even though it really doesn't fit, even though it makes you wonder whether there are any "young *secular* Unitarian Universalists," . . . our youth organization wants to live with the word "Religious," to grapple with it, understand it, and make it into a word that describes who we are as Unitarian Universalists.

* * *

Appendix B: The Last Will and Testament of Liberal Religious Youth

We the undersigned, being the last Board of Directors of Liberal Religious Youth, and also being of sound mind and body, do hereby leave the following assets of Liberal Religious Youth to Young Religious Unitarian Universalists:

The many hours of love, dedication, planning, and typing that I and many others have put into bringing locals together and opening communications on the continental level.

Wintergreen lifesavers—which show phosphorous sparks when crunched in the dark.

The freedom of expression and belief that has previously been fostered by the uniqueness and diversity of our liberal youth group. . . .

Faith that youth in general *can* and *will* take responsibilities for their own bodies and emotions and will act with respect and discretion on the wishes of the community of youth. . . .

I leave all forms of pagan worship: howling at the moon, group ohms, and singing by starlight. . . .

I leave warm fuzzies, frisbees, foofing, Joe Taco, Suzy Creamcheese, bad puns, the retardos, and love.

I leave love, respect for one another, a shoulder to cry on, dedicated advisors, and a dash of cosmic to hold it all together. . . .

The U.U. youth I have met who are not affiliated with LRY, they too are great people, and so I am optimistic for the future of the combined groups. . . .

378

I leave, while we also keep, being we are *all* part of the new youth group, so, we share with the new youth group the love we have experienced and shared with each other throughout the years.

SOURCE: *Common Ground: Coming of Age, A Report of the 1982 UUA Youth Assembly, Submitted to the Unitarian Universalist Association and Its Board of Trustees by the UUA Continental Youth Adult Committee, September, 1982* (Boston: Unitarian Universalist Association, 1982), 8, 20–21, 26–27.

Business Resolution on Gay and Lesbian Services of Union

1984

At the 1984 General Assembly in Columbus, Ohio, delegates passed the following resolution, affirming the ministerial decision to perform same-gender services of union. Although such services did not have all of the social and legal benefits of marriage, many saw the support of gay and lesbian services of union as an important milestone in the LGTBQ movement within the UUA. The resolution was passed fourteen years after the first UUA resolution pertaining to LGBTQ equality banned discrimination against "homosexuals and bisexuals" in the church and society at large. It reflects the growing momentum of the LGBTQ equality movement in the UUA. Further Reading: Jeff Wilson, "'Fear, Trembling, and Joy': Unitarian Universalism and Same-Sex Marriage in the U.S. and Canada, 1973–1984," Journal of Unitarian Universalist History 36 (2012/13): 84–111.

—Natalie Malter

WHEREAS, the Unitarian Universalist Association has repeatedly taken stands to affirm the rights of gay and lesbian persons over the past decade; and

WHEREAS, legal marriages are currently denied gay and lesbian couples by state and provincial governments of North America; and

WHEREAS, freedom of the pulpit is a historic tradition in Unitarian Universalist societies;

BE IT RESOLVED: That the 1984 General Assembly of the Unitarian Universalist Association:

1. Affirms the growing practice of some of its ministers of conducting services of union of gay and lesbian couples and urges member societies to support their ministers in this important aspect of our movement's ministry to the gay and lesbian community; and

2. Requests that the Department of Ministerial and Congregational Services:
   a. distribute this information to Unitarian Universalist religious professionals and member societies;

b. develop printed material for ministers to assist them in planning and conducting services of union for gay and lesbian couples;

c. develop a pamphlet intended for laypersons which describes services of union for gay and lesbian couples and is distributed to member societies.

SOURCE: Unitarian Universalist Social Justice Statements, uua.org/statements/gay-and -lesbian-services-union

"The Principles and Purposes"
1985

The original statement of Principles and Purposes of the Unitarian Universalist Association was drafted as part of the proposed bylaws in 1959 at a conference in Syracuse, New York, where the two denominations met to adopt a "Plan for Consolidation," which was finalized two years later. With the rise of the second-wave feminist movement and the passage of the 1977 Resolution on Women and Religion, members of the UUA became increasingly critical of the sexism of the original Principles and Purposes. Conversations about reforming them occurred at gatherings of women around the country, including at the 1979 Grailville conference in Ohio, where Lucile Schuck Longview sponsored a workshop entitled "Do UUA Principles Affirm Women as They Affirm Men?" The first version of revised Principles and Purposes was presented at General Assembly in 1981, and a special committee was created to study the issue. The committee spent several years debating the issue before arriving at a final proposal. Since UUA bylaw amendments require two votes to pass, the revised Principles and Purposes were voted on and passed at the 1984 and 1985 General Assemblies and include the seven Principles and five Sources that exist today. The sixth Source, celebrating the power of earth-centered traditions, was added ten years later at the 1995 General Assembly.

—Natalie Malter

Seven Principles:

1. The inherent worth and dignity of every person;
2. Justice, equity and compassion in human relations;
3. Acceptance of one another and encouragement to spiritual growth in our congregations;
4. A free and responsible search for truth and meaning;
5. The right of conscience and the use of the democratic process within our congregations and in society at large;
6. The goal of world community with peace, liberty, and justice for all;
7. Respect for the interdependent web of all existence of which we are a part.

Six Sources:

1. Direct experience of that transcending mystery and wonder, affirmed in all cultures, which moves us to a renewal of the spirit and an openness to the forces which create and uphold life;

2. Words and deeds of prophetic women and men which challenge us to confront powers and structures of evil with justice, compassion, and the transforming power of love;

3. Wisdom from the world's religions which inspires us in our ethical and spiritual life;

4. Jewish and Christian teachings which call us to respond to God's love by loving our neighbors as ourselves;

5. Humanist teachings which counsel us to heed the guidance of reason and the results of science, and warn us against idolatries of the mind and spirit;

6. Spiritual teachings of Earth-centered traditions which celebrate the sacred circle of life and instruct us to live in harmony with the rhythms of nature. [Added in an amendment in 1995]

SOURCE: "What We Believe," uua.org/beliefs/what-we-believe

General Resolution Opposing
AIDS Discrimination
1986

At the height of the HIV/AIDS crisis in the 1980s, the Unitarian Universalist Association passed a resolution opposing discrimination against those living with HIV/AIDS. The resolution was passed in part in response to a ruling by the Department of Justice in the same year that having AIDS was legal grounds for dismissal from work. Following the passage of the resolution at General Assembly, the UUA added an anti-discrimination clause to its employment policies. The UUA, like all communities in the United States, was personally confronted with the tragedy of the epidemic, especially following the loss of Mark Mosher DeWolfe (1953–1988), a UU minister from Ontario, Canada, who died of AIDS at the age of thirty-five. The 1989 General Assembly passed another resolution in support of finding a cure for the disease. Further Reading: Randy Shilts, And the Band Played On: Politics, People, and the AIDS Epidemic, *20th-Anniversary Edition (New York: St. Martin's Griffin, 2007).*

—Natalie Malter

BECAUSE, the member congregations of the Unitarian Universalist Association covenant to affirm the inherent worth and dignity of every person, and to promote justice, equity and compassion in human relations; and

BECAUSE, we are members of the interdependent web of existence and therefore responsible for one another and for the society in which we live; and

WHEREAS, on Friday, June 20, 1986, the US Department of Justice, Office of Legal Counsel, concluded that an employer's fear of the spread of AIDS, whether reasonable or not, constitutes grounds for dismissal; and

WHEREAS, this opinion is clearly contrary to the spirit of Section 504 of the Rehabilitation Act of 1973 and the September 1985 ruling of the US Court of Appeals for the 11th Circuit; and

WHEREAS, the Center for Disease Control and other experts and researchers working with AIDS have repeatedly and emphatically stated that the HTLV-III/LAV/HIV virus cannot be transmitted by casual contact; and

WHEREAS, there have been no documented cases of AIDS transmitted to co-workers, health care workers, family or friends in routine contact with persons with AIDS or persons tested positive for the HTLV-III/LAV/HIV antibodies; and

WHEREAS, the Justice Department opinion is a gross violation of civil rights and could apply to as many as two million Americans who currently would test positive for the HTLV-III/LAV/HIV antibodies;

THEREFORE BE IT RESOLVED: That the 1986 General Assembly of the Unitarian Universalist Association opposes discrimination based on AIDS, the fear of AIDS, or the presence of the HTLV-III/LAV/HIV antibodies; and

BE IT FURTHER RESOLVED: That a copy of this resolution be sent immediately to the President of the United States, the US Attorney General, and all members of Congress; and

BE IT FURTHER RESOLVED: That UUA Canadian societies study the parallels in Canada, and take action in a manner consonant with the intent of this resolution; and

BE IT FURTHER RESOLVED: That the UUA, its member societies and affiliate organizations be urged to promote programs which provide education about the cause of AIDS, how AIDS is transmitted, the real risks of casual contact and which generally increase community awareness about AIDS; and

BE IT FINALLY RESOLVED: That the UUA, its member societies and affiliate organizations be urged to support such action as will ensure the civil rights of persons with AIDS and those who test positive to the HTLV-III/LAV/HIV antibodies.

SOURCE: Unitarian Universalist Social Justice Statements, uua.org/statements/opposing-aids-discrimination

SHIRLEY ANN RANCK

Cakes for the Queen of Heaven
1986

Shirley Ann Ranck served many Unitarian Universalist congregations in the course of her thirty years of active ministry, primarily in interim positions. However, Ranck is best known for her development of the adult Religious Education curriculum, Cakes for the Queen of Heaven, *published in 1986. Inspired by the 1977* Women and Religion *resolution as well as a goddess worship conference, Ranck developed the curriculum, at the request of Leslie Arden Westbrook, to help adult women recognize the sacrality of the feminine by exploring the early forms of goddess worship in a variety of different cultures. The title for the curriculum comes from a passage in the Book of Jeremiah in the Hebrew Bible in which Jeremiah writes, "The women knead dough to make cakes to the Queen of Heaven" (Jer. 7:18). In a 2006 interview at General Assembly, Ranck estimated that approximately eight hundred congregations have used the curriculum since it was first published in 1986. Further Reading: Naomi R. Goldenberg,* Changing of the Gods: Feminism and the End of Traditional Religion *(Boston: Beacon Press, 1979); Carol P. Christ,* Rebirth of the Goddess: Finding Meaning in Feminist Spirituality *(New York: Routledge, 1997).*

—Natalie Malter

"Women have no past, no history and no religion," wrote Simone de Beauvoir in 1949. Today we know that women definitely have a rich past, an illustrious history, and a great variety of religious experience. We have been unaware of our female history because for the past twenty or more centuries the major world religions have expressed primarily male experience and views of the world and have ignored or suppressed female experience. Women have been here all along, of course, and now that we have women historians, archaeologists, and theologians, our enormous contributions to human culture and religion are being recognized.

Women within the traditions of Judaism and Christianity are discovering strong biblical women, pointing out biblical passages where the divine is imaged as female, and finding feminist attitudes in the teachings of Jesus. These women are now demanding that the love and justice proclaimed by these traditions be applied to women.

Other women are looking to the prepatriarchal religions of the ancient world in their search for female roots. Before the advent of the major world religions as we know them, and for a long time after their birth, human beings practiced other religions for many centuries. We have often dismissed these religions as primitive, amoral, and of little interest to us. In recent years, however, archaeological and anthropological findings have stimulated a new interest in and respect for the earlier religions of humankind. Women have been particularly interested to learn that that these ancient religions revolved around a powerful Goddess who was expected to assure the health and prosperity of the people and of the earth. What would it have been like to grow up in a world where God was a woman?

Other women claim that the Goddess religion never really died but came down to us in the form of witchcraft. Witchcraft?! Yes! We have been let to have the utmost contempt for the alleged superstitious devil worship of witchcraft, but this attitude reflects the male bias of the religions that took over. It is not an accurate description of contemporary witchcraft. So covens are forming and women are rediscovering and seriously studying the centuries-old female lore.

Unitarian Universalists are in a unique position to develop a truly creative feminist thealogy. We have roots in the biblical tradition of course, but since the turn of the century most of us have come to perceive that tradition as only one among many avenues to spiritual enlightenment. To put it another way, we take pluralism seriously. Our sanctuaries make use of the symbols of many religions, and our ministers draw inspiration from many sacred and secular texts. We are under no obligation to make the Bible or any other writings authoritative for the community of faith. Our faith is in our human freedom to choose what we find of value in any religious or secular writings. Of course, until recently, almost all these resources were just as mired in patriarchal assumptions as the biblical material. But we do have that freedom.

The question facing Unitarian Universalist feminists is whether or not that freedom can be exercised to include women's religious history. We have long had religious education materials about the insights of Ahknaten and the Buddha as well as of Moses and Jesus. Are we now open to acquiring an understanding of the many thousands of years of human history, from ice age artists to the closing of the last Goddess temples at the end of the Roman Empire when the chief deity was female? Are we ready to include in the Christian tradition the newly discovered Gnostic gospels, which are full of female imagery and point to more powerful positions for women in the early Christian churches than is evident in New Testament writings?

Unitarian Universalism As a Mystic Religion

To claim such freedom of choice means that we must look to no authority but that of our own experience. Ours is in many ways a "mystic" religion, in the sense that theologian Ernst Troeltsch used the term. Each person is forced back on her personal experience with the divine as the final authority for what is loving and just. The divine is usually experienced as immanent in oneself and in the natural world, and enlightenment is usually felt as a harmony with the process of nature. Troeltsch assumed that such religion was too individual and personal, too indifferent to society to have any impact on the world or to attract large numbers of people. He concluded, however, that mystic religion was the only kind possible for modern people in a pluralistic society.

What is missing from Troeltsch's description of mystic religion is the way in which harmony within oneself and in relation to the natural world often puts one in direct conflict with the social order. It is no accident that the arch-mystic and nature lover Henry David Thoreau wrote a tract on civil disobedience and went to jail for refusing to pay taxes because they would be used to support a war. It is no accident that his essay influenced another arch-mystic in India whose nonviolent expression of his convictions caused momentous political changes. More recently we have seen not only individual leaders but literate masses of oppressed people demanding the love and justice they have been told are the ideals of Christianity and other world religions. They have discovered that no outside authority or deity will relieve their oppression, that they must articulate their own convictions as to what is just. Is this a form of mystic religion? I suggest that *mystic* today has come to mean being fully aware of one's life situation and taking responsibility for altering it if it is not in line with the values one derives from that very personal experience of harmony within the self. It is this definition that I have in mind when I say that Unitarian Universalism is a mystic religion.

For women, especially, to tap the power of authentic selfhood is to be painfully aware of the myriad ways in which society works against the expression of female experience. To express that experience is to be in conflict with almost everything in society—language, the legal system, the government, the economy, the structure of the family, and the symbolism of most world religions, all of which were designed to express and enhance the experience of males.

Religions and Their Symbols

Unitarian Universalists are open to the use of a variety of religious myths and symbols because they believe that the truth expressed by any one symbol is partial. It seems to me that this is an important principle for women. The Western symbols in use over the past twenty or more centuries express a partial truth about the world— that of Western male experience. It is an important first step toward a more complete truth for women to dig into history and hold up to light the symbols of female divinity and power. We cannot integrate male and female symbols if we have not first examined the female symbols.

Here I make the assumption that religions and their symbols change. Naomi Goldenberg's book is aptly titled *Changing of the Gods*. The deities have changed before and they are changing now. We need no longer rely on questionable nineteenth-century scholarship for evidence that in vast areas of the ancient world female deities reigned supreme for thousands of years, and only later were they superseded by male deities. The archaeological discoveries of the past twenty to thirty years provide overwhelming documentation in the form of thousands of Goddess images and figurines, elaborate temples devoted to Ishtar and other powerful goddesses, and sacred writings never before available to us. A theme running through much of the ancient mythology from a variety of cultures is the contest for power between the Goddess and her ever more powerful son-lover. In all these myths she is ultimately either destroyed in a grand battle or tricked into giving up her power to the male. This shift in divine power occurred gradually, over many centuries, and during early historical times most cultures had both male and female deities, with varying amounts of power. Archaeologist Raphael Patai has suggested that the Israelites were no exception and that for many centuries Yahweh had a powerful female consort.

The idea that gods and religions change is not a new one. Many years ago Harry Emerson Fosdick traced what he perceived to be the changes in Yahweh's characteristics, which occur as we move from earliest biblical sources to later ones. He suggested that Yahweh is at first a tribal deity who travels from place to place with his people. Only later does he develop the quality of omnipresence. He is at first a jealous and vengeful deity, only later acquiring the attributes of mercy and love. Ernst Troeltsch pointed out that a crucial part of any religion is the world view that supports and is supported by it. He traced the changes in world view that made medieval Christianity a strikingly different religion from that of the early church in the days of the Roman Empire and from the ascetic Protestantism of later times. Troeltsch concluded that the world view of ascetic Protestantism was not adequate for the twentieth century and that a new world view would mean a new formulation of religion.

A Shift from Outer to Inner

We need to be aware of the world view that is emerging in this latter part of the twentieth century and the radical changes that are occurring in our concept of divinity. We are trying to come of age as human beings, to give up our childish dependence on a parental deity enthroned in a supernatural realm. But it is not enough to pronounce the patriarchal god dead. We are still faced with the ultimate questions about life and death and meaningful existence. Naomi Goldberg suggests that what is happening is the internalization of religion, the awareness of an immanent god or goddess within each of us, and an inner spiritual journey toward value and meaning as adults. Such a transformation of religion from outer to inner makes each of us responsible for our values; it is mystic religion. It requires us to become fully aware of our personal and social situation and to articulate that experience. It gives validity to female as well as male experience. It challenges us to alter society whenever it fails to support harmony within the self, among selves, and in relation to nature.

If women really articulate the realities of their experience, they call into question the very symbolism of Judaism, Christianity, and other world religions, where that symbolism is overwhelmingly male. This is a difficult task because we have taken that male symbolism for granted and have been raised to believe it is the only symbolism that ever existed. Here is where knowing of the existence of powerful as well as nurturing female images of the divine in the ancient world is so important. We cannot revive uncritically religions whose world view was so different from ours. But we need to know that they existed and that for thousands of years both men and women found the worship of female divinity meaningful. Whatever we may call the religions of the future, if they take women seriously they cannot perpetuate exclusively male symbols.

A Shift from Supernatural to Natural

Feminist thealogy, like Unitarian Universalism, rejects the idea that nature is fallen and sinful. Instead, we perceive humans as part of a natural world that has within it the potential for both good and evil. We are not automatically good or bad. We do not reject a realistic assessment of the human potential for good and evil, but we do reject a negative prejudging of the situation based on belief in a "higher" supernatural realm. We assert our limited but quite real freedom to discern and to choose the good. This assertion is based on a twentieth-century scientific world view that encompasses constant change and startling novelty and therefore the possibility of freedom.

As creatures of the natural world, we participate—in an inner, more conscious way—in the same power that resides in all of nature. To the extent that feminist thealogy perceives the divine as "out there" as well as within, it is identified with the natural world and not with a supernatural realm. Such a concept of the divine as immanent implies a rejection of the distortions of human civilization that result from childish dependence on the supernatural. Being in harmony with the Goddess of the natural world does not, for example, give one power over anyone or anything. The fear that feminist goddess imagery is a demand for female dominance over men is based on a concept of divinity most Unitarian Universalists have long rejected, a concept of the divine as supernatural, as "over against" the natural world rather than immanent in it. To be in harmony with that kind of supernatural deity is indeed to demand "dominance over." But feminist thealogy identifies the divine with the natural world and seeks power in harmony rather than in dominance.

390

What About Judaism and Christianity?

Although Judaism and Christianity are considered by many Unitarian Universalists to be but two among many source of inspiration, they are nevertheless the traditions within which most of us were raised. However liberal or unorthodox our theological interpretations, many of us have strong emotional ties to either Judaism or Christianity. Many women, therefore, seek ways to reinterpret or transform it so that it will be meaningful to contemporary feminists, both women and men. Elizabeth Cady Stanton pointed out many years ago, "So long as tens of thousands of Bibles are printed every year, and circulated over the whole habitable globe, and the masses in all English-speaking nations revere it as the word of God, it is vain to belittle its influence. The sentimental feelings we all have for those things we were educated to believe sacred, do not readily yield to pure reason." She gathered a committee of learned women, and they produced a commentary on every biblical passage that mentions women. Stanton dryly remarked, "As all such passages combined form but one-tenth of the Scriptures, the undertaking will not be so laborious as, at the first thought, one would imagine."

Today some feminist theologians insist that male scholars and clergy down through the centuries have misinterpreted and distorted the message of the biblical tradition which proclaims justice and love for all persons, male and female. The god of the Bible was at times described with female images; there were female prophets and judges; Jesus treated women with the same dignity that he did men; in the early Christian church women preached and taught and shared all responsibilities equally with men; and Paul at his best proclaimed that "in Christ there is neither male nor female." Church history is being reexamined to discover the contributions of strong women, and the writings of female mystics are being read with new interest. For women who wish to maintain their commitment to the biblical tradition there are many new approaches.

One of the most exciting discoveries in recent years has been a large collection of ancient manuscripts buried in Upper Egypt by Early Christians. These writings included a number of gospels, versions of Jesus' life and work written by very early Gnostic Christians and never before available to us. Elaine Pagels, who has analyzed a large number of these writings, points out that Gnostic Christians used many female images to refer to the divine, and that women had far more power and responsibility in their churches than in those that became orthodox. Another phenomenon of interest to Unitarian Universalists is that the organization of Gnostic churches appears to have been nonhierarchical and nonauthoritarian. These ancient texts give strong support to the notion that the suppression of women in the Christian Church as we have known it occurred for political reasons and is a distortion of Christianity as it was known to many in the early churches.

This seminar does not attempt to cover female religious history worldwide. There is a wealth of goddess material rooted in Africa, the Far East, and among the original peoples of the Americas. It should all be available to us. We must remember, however, that women constitute one-half of the world's population and our religious heritage cannot be contained in one short seminar.

As women we have a right to know all of our female religious roots, from ancient goddesses to witchcraft to strong women in the biblical tradition. It is up to us to relate that history to our own experience as women in the modern world and to demand that our roots and our experience be taken seriously as a basis for new non-sexist theologies. The following program is an attempt to begin that process.

SOURCE: Shirley Ann Ranck, *Cakes for the Queen of Heaven Kit: A Ten-Session Adult Seminar in Feminist Thealogy* (Boston: Unitarian Universalist Association, 1986), 9–13.

JACQUI JAMES
"Affirming Beauty in Darkness"
1988

In addition to her work as a Director of Religious Education and her activism in the anti-oppression, anti-racism movement in the 1980s in the Unitarian Universalist Association, Jacqui James (1937–) served as director of worship resources and affirmative action officer for the UUA. As evidenced in this sermon preached at the UUA Chapel on March 8, 1988, James was a remarkable advocate for racial justice in the UUA, especially calling attention to the ways in which racist language continued to pervade UU worship and organizational practices. In her writing she encourages Unitarian Universalists to consider the ways in which their hymns employ metaphors about "light" as positive and "dark" as negative, which privileges white people over people of color. At the time she preached "Affirming Beauty in Darkness," James was serving as the UUA staff representative on the Hymnbook Resources Commission, a commission responsible for developing a collection of hymns and readings for UU worship. Published several years after James's sermon, Sing-ing the Living Tradition (1993), one of the official hymnbooks of the UUA, represents James's legacy with its emphasis on anti-racist, anti-oppressive lan-guage and its celebration of multiculturalism.

—Natalie Malter

Is there no beauty in darkness?
I ask this question.
— Frederick W. Wilson

The question [raised] in this poem by Fred Wilson is not a rhetorical one. Our cul-ture and our language reinforce the exclusion and devaluing of persons of color. In our culture, white has come to represent all that is pure and good, it has become "superior." White is associated with the heavenly, the clean, the innocent. At the same time, our language portrays a generally negative usage of the word black, asso-ciating it with sin, evil, wicked, gloomy, depressing. Ascribing negative and positive values, respectively to the colors black and white enhances the institutionalization of this country's racist values . . . [ellipsis in original].

Blacklist
Blackmail

Black Mark
Black Magic
Black Market
Black Mass
Black Monday
Black Hearted
Black Plague
Black Mood

Good guys wear white, bad guys wear black; we fear black cats; we talk about the Dark Continent. However, it's okay to tell a white lie; lily-white hands are coveted, it's great to be pure as the driven snow; clouds are white and dolls, angels and brides wear white. The color white is associated with purity, the color black with impurity. Devil's food cake is chocolate; angel's food cake is white!

We shape language, and we are shaped by language. Our use of light and dark language and imagery shapes our attitudes about persons of color and inflicts constant psychological damage on the entire society by the use of connotations that have racist implications. Our thoughtless use of the terms white and black, dark and light, assume dimensions of overt racial significance. If we are ever to be free of racism, we must understand the many ways that racism is manifested in our society, and that language is one of them.

There is a common misconception that racism in America no longer exists; that it ended sometime in the late 60's or early 70's. Let's be clear about one thing. Racism is as alive today as it was 20 years ago, though it is often manifested in more subtle ways. America is a racist culture; it has been one since it was first colonized by Europeans. Racism continues to be a core value and practice of American culture and life. "The problem of the twentieth century is the problem of the colorline—the relation of the darker to the lighter races," wrote W. E. B. DuBois in *The Souls of Black Folk*, published in 1903. The problem of the colorline is still with us as we approach the end of the 20th century.

Twenty years ago, the Kerner Commission issued a report which warned, "Our nation is moving toward two societies, one black, one white—separate but unequal." Last week a group of specialists on race and urban affairs, some of whom worked on the Kerner Commission, reported that the problems seen then still persist. While strides have been made in some areas of race relations, the plight of the poor, inner-city blacks, they concluded, is more dismal now than it was 20 years ago. . . .

We like to think that the sports arena is one place where we have attained equality and an absence of racism. However . . . [one study] found that the announcers of National Football League games on the three major television networks, subjected black athletes to more negative comments about their talents, abilities and motivation. . . . It seems that the bias against black even extends to those wearing black uniforms. . . .

Language not only influences how white people view persons of color, it also influences how black people see themselves. These unremitting negative racial associations have a subliminal effect, in the same ways that the sole use of man and mankind to indicate dual-sex humanity distort the vision after a time. Researchers have found that two-thirds of the black children participating in a recent study prefer white dolls. . . .

It is time for our language to reflect the beauty of both black and white. It is time for our language to fashion new mirrors to reflect positive images of all people. Then, perhaps we can help to grow persons to know their own worth within themselves.

My mother and I have been discussing grandparents and great-grandparents a lot lately. Remembering her grandmother, she writes me, "I am certain that Grandma never considered herself prejudiced, but consider: I was the darkest of the grandchildren, the youngest and her favorite, whether because I spent so much time with her or because she pitied me, I don't know. But she called me her 'Brown Sugar' and often said, 'Poor, Brown Sugar Child, all your mother did for you was to give you a nose and a little hair.'" My own beloved grandmother, whom I never thought had a prejudiced bone in her body, when faced with the stillbirth of her only son's child said, "It's all for the best." I thought she meant because my aunt and uncle were both nearing forty and the marriage seemed to be in trouble. My mother tells me, no, she was afraid the child would be dark like my uncle's wife. I don't think either of these foremothers of mine was operating out of prejudice, but rather out of the knowledge that in this culture, white is perceived as good and black is not!

What does all this have to [do] with religion and UUism in particular? Our Principles and Purposes speak of "the inherent worth and dignity of every person" and "Justice, equity and compassion in human relations" and of "The goal of world community with peace, liberty and justice for all." Our language as a religious people must constantly reaffirm the equal worth and beauty of all people. As the Hymnbook Resources Commission looks at our current hymnbooks, we see that UUs have a problem here.

Our theological language in general and especially our hymns use light and dark as metaphors for good and bad. The preference for white/light is obvious. The opposition to black/dark is equally obvious. We present only the positive images of light and white are presented in our religious language. Likewise only the negative images of black/dark are used.

Some examples from *Hymns for the Celebration of Life* make this abundantly clear:

In the darkness drear
Too long the darkened way we've trod
Turn our darkness into day
I saw the powers of darkness put to flight
On shadowed thresholds dark with fear
And dawn become the morning, the darkness put to flight
Praise ye, daughters and sons of light
Ring out the darkness of the land, ring in the light that is to be
O'er white expanses, sparkling pure the radiant morns unfold

Is there no beauty in darkness?

Our hymnbooks contain no negative images of light/white. Our hymnody reflects a bias toward light/white and a bias against black/dark. We've become stuck in a single interpretation of the rich symbolism of dark and light. . . .

Mark Belletini writes, "The impulse toward inclusive language is rooted in a religious ground. It is a discipline of consciousness-raising that claims by redefinition the vision of Universalism. Such consciousness roots our actions in the richest soil of our UU heritage." This is a discipline which each of us is capable of undertaking. . . .

It is vital that we acknowledge that there are negative connotations to white. It can be soft, vulnerable, pallid, and ashen. Light can be blinding, bleaching, enervating. We must acknowledge that darkness has a redemptive character, that in darkness there is power and beauty. It is the place that nurtured and protected us before our birth. Welcome darkness, don't be afraid of it or deny it. Darkness brings relief from the blinding sun, from scorching heat, from exhausting labor. Night signals permission to rest, to be with our loved ones, to conceive new life, to search our hearts, to remember our dreams. The dark of winter is a time of hibernation for both plants and animals; seeds grow in the dark, fertile earth.

The words black and dark don't need to be destroyed or ignored, only balanced and reclaimed in their *wholeness*. The words white and light don't need to be destroyed or ignored, only balanced and reclaimed in *their* wholeness. Imagine a world that had only light—or a world which had only dark. We could not exist in either. Imagine, if you can, a world where everyone looked and acted just the same. We need to revalue both light and dark, they are both necessary to our continued survival.

SOURCE: Jacqui James, "Affirming Beauty in Darkness," Unitarian Universalist Sankofa Special Collection, Meadville Lombard Theological School, Chicago, meadville.edu/uploads/files/95.pdf

"Proclamation of the Society for the Larger Ministry"

1988

Unitarian and Universalist ministers have always worked alongside lay-people in ministries of justice and service to the larger society. This impulse was part of the Puritan tradition of concern for the "common wealth" and found institutional form in Joseph Tuckerman's ministry-at-large (now the Unitarian Universalist Urban Ministry) and, a century later, in the Unitarian and Universalist Service Committees. Olympia Brown and James Reeb were just two among many well-known ministers who pursued Unitarian Universalist values in organizations not directly affiliated with Unitarianism or Universalism. Beginning around 1981, ministers who felt called to what came to be known as community ministry began advocating for formal recognition by the Unitarian Universalist Association. This proclamation was prepared at the second national conference of the Society for the Larger Ministry (SLM), held at Meadville Lombard Theological School in November 1988, and it is now recognized as the founding document of the SLM's successor, the Unitarian Universalist Society for Community Ministries. It affirmed a definition of community ministry that included both ordained and lay ministers. Three years later, the 1991 General Assembly of the UUA approved a bylaw amendment directing the Ministerial Fellowship Committee to recognize community ministry as fully equal to parish ministry and the ministry of religious education. Though this three-track system was abolished in 2005, community ministry remains a large and growing component of Unitarian Universalist ministry as a whole. Further Reading: Kathleen R. Parker, "'Let It Rise On Wings'—Community Ministry Achieves Formal Standing," in Dorothy May Emerson and Anita Farber-Robertson, eds., Called to Community: New Directions in Unitarian Universalist Ministry *(Boston: Unitarian Universalist Society for Community Ministry, 2013), 61–90; Kathleen R. Parker,* Sacred Service in Civic Space: Three Hundred Years of Community Ministry in Unitarian Universalism *(Chicago: Meadville Lombard Press, 2007).*

—Dan McKanan

We, as people living in a world that is both dying and seeking to be reborn, who are shaken to our very roots by the massiveness and depth of planetary and human suffering, are empowered by a driving passion to bear witness to that suffering, participate in its transformation, and affirm the inherent glory of life.

Therefore, we do covenant together:

- To respond to these cries of pain, to our own brokenness, and to awaken the healing spirit of hope.
- To engage in a broad spectrum of ministries through and with Unitarian Universalist congregations, with the larger community, and increasingly, in a global context.
- To celebrate the diversity of life within our elemental interconnectedness.
- To challenge one another as individuals and as members of institutions to identify, analyze, and act upon the basic causes of human hurt and separation.

Thus empowered, we join hands with the community of faith in acknowledging the larger ministry which addresses our common vision. We call upon our denomination to recognize a variety of lay and ordained ministries as embodiments of the Unitarian Universalist principle and purpose. All of our creative ministries including academic, administrative, aesthetic, AIDS, campus, camp and conference centers, chaplaincies, community-focused, environmental, gay/lesbian/bisexual, healing, legal, men-focused, music, parish, pastoral counseling, pastoral psychotherapy, peace, religious education, social justice, women focused, young adult and ministries not yet envisioned . . . are valid, necessary, and life affirming [ellipsis in original].

Such compassionate, liberating, prophetic ministries are at the very heart of our religious tradition.

SOURCE: "Proclamation of the Society for the Larger Ministry," in Dorothy May Emerson and Anita Farber-Robertson, eds., *Called to Community: New Directions in Unitarian Universalist Ministry* (Boston: Unitarian Universalist Society for Community Ministry, 2013), vi.

Report and Recommendations of the Common Vision Planning Committee
1989

The Common Vision Planning Committee was established by the Unitarian Universalist Association in 1987 to investigate the views of Unitarian Universalists toward gay, lesbian, and bisexual people in their churches. In spite of the nearly twenty years of vocal support in favor of gay, lesbian, and bisexual rights, the results of the report demonstrated that Unitarian Universalists still faced many challenges when it came to prejudice and inclusion in congregations. As a result of the report's findings, the Common Vision Planning Committee, chaired by Lesley Rebecca Phillips, recommended that the UUA establish a Welcoming Congregations program, and a business resolution was passed at the 1989 General Assembly in support of establishing the program. In 1990, the first edition of the Welcoming Congregations Handbook *was published with resources and teaching materials to help congregations become more open and affirming of people of all sexual orientations. As of 2010, it was estimated that 650 UU congregations were officially recognized by the UUA as Welcoming Congregations, making the UU Welcoming Congregations program one of the most successful such programs in any denomination. Further Reading: "Welcoming Congregations," uua.org/lgbtq/welcoming/program*
> —Natalie Malter

RECOMMENDATIONS.
Mission and goal statements, below, crafted by the Common Vision Planning Committee, are proposed for adoption:

I. A *Mission Statement* for a unified and integral Unitarian Universalist effort toward gay, lesbian and bisexual inclusion and outreach.
The Unitarian Universalist mission regarding lesbian, gay, and bisexual persons is to affirm and support the living and celebrating of the affectional and sexual truths of lesbian, gay, and bisexual persons, through whose combined vision, spiritual growth and healing strength a future may be realized in which all persons can live with wholeness and integrity.

II. *Goal Statements* **for a unified and integral Unitarian Universalist effort toward gay, lesbian and bisexual inclusion and outreach.**

1. Preserve, honor and celebrate the rich and unique experiences of gay, lesbian and bisexual culture as a source of truth and knowledge.
2. Prophetically voice opposition to homophobia within the Unitarian Universalist community.
3. Bear witness to the world of larger possibilities for justice, inclusion, and the inherent worth and dignity of all.
4. Design inclusive programs to affirm and promote the worth and dignity of every gay, lesbian and bisexual person.
5. Minister to families of gay, lesbian and bisexual people.
6. Achieve equal opportunity in ministerial settlement, employment and congregational leadership.
7. With the Unitarian Universalist Association, bring our Unitarian Universalist institutions into harmony with the Principles and Purposes of the Association.

III. *Goal Statements* **for the Office of Lesbian and Gay Concerns (OLGC).**

1. Develop, implement and administer the Welcoming Congregation Program.
2. Educate, advocate and liaison with UUA departments, districts and congregations.
3. Coordinate the activities of the various UUA departments and programs in regard to gay, lesbian and bisexual people.
4. Raise and interpret to the Unitarian Universalist Association issues relating to gay, lesbian and bisexual people.
5. Provide appropriate services to Unitarian Universalists for Lesbian and Gay Concerns (UULGC).
6. Represent the Unitarian Universalist Association in the larger gay, lesbian and bisexual community, together with Unitarian Universalists for Lesbian and Gay Concerns (UULGC).
7. Provide information and referrals.

IV. *Goal Statements* **proposed for the Membership Organization, Unitarian Universalists for Lesbian and Gay Concerns (UULGC).**

The Planning Committee proposes to UULGC the following Goal Statements, to be adopted and prioritized by a vote of the membership.

1. Create a climate of support, care and affirmation for gay, lesbian and bisexual people and their families.
2. Increase visibility of gay, lesbian and bisexual people within our community of faith.
3. Foster gay, lesbian and bisexual spirituality.

4. Organize, encourage and support district and local groups.
5. Provide communication with members and chapters.
6. Represent together with the Office of Lesbian and Gay concerns (OLGC) a liberal religious presence within the gay, lesbian and bisexual community.

* * *

The Welcoming Congregation Program

The Welcoming Congregation program, below, is proposed by the Common Vision Planning Committee for adoption:

Preamble.

Whereas, the fear of same-sex love deeply embedded in our culture and religious traditions persists also in our Association, and

Whereas, the present situation demands education and action, and the will to live our Principles and Purposes:

Be it therefore resolved that the Common Vision Planning Committee urges the implementation of an Association-wide effort, as described below, to be called the Welcoming Congregation Program.

Definition.

1. A Welcoming Congregation is inclusive and expressive of the concerns of gay, lesbian and bisexual persons at every level of congregational life in worship and program, welcoming not only their presence but the unique gifts and particularities of their lives as well.
   a. A Welcoming Congregation does not assume that everyone is heterosexual. Vocabulary of worship reflects this perception.
   b. Lesbian, gay and bisexual life issues are fairly represented in Religious Education (RE).
2. The by-laws and other official documents of a Welcoming Congregation include an affirmation and non-discrimination clause affecting all dimensions of congregational life, including membership, hiring practices and calling of ministry.
3. A Welcoming Congregation has programming that takes into account gay, lesbian and bisexual life issues in these areas:
   a. Worship that celebrates the diversity of its people by inclusivity, language and content.
   b. Religious education, social and other programs of the congregation: Gay, lesbian and bisexual experience will be incorporated fully throughout all programs. No longer will heterosexuality be assumed.

4. The Welcoming Congregation does outreach into the gay, lesbian and bisexual communities both by advertising in gay, lesbian and bisexual press and by supporting actively other gay, lesbian and bisexual affirmative groups.

5. A Welcoming Congregation offers Congregational and ministerial support for same-gender services of union, memorial services, and celebrations of an ever expanding and growing definition of family on an equal basis.

6. A Welcoming Congregation celebrates the lives of all people and welcomes same-sex couples, recognizing their committed relationships; and equally affirms all displays of caring and affection.

7. A Welcoming Congregation seeks to nurture ongoing dialogue between gay, lesbian, bisexual and heterosexuals, and to create deeper trust and sharing.

8. A Welcoming Congregation encourages the presence of a Unitarian Universalist for Lesbian and Gay Concerns chapter (UULGC).

9. A Welcoming Congregation observes and celebrates gay, lesbian and bisexual pride as part of its regular celebratory cycle (most gay, lesbian and bisexual communities celebrate this in June).

10. A Welcoming Congregation, as an advocate for gay, lesbian and bisexual people, attends to legislative developments and works to promote justice, freedom and equality in the larger society. It speaks out when the rights and dignity of gay, lesbian and bisexual people are at stake.

11. A Welcoming Congregation celebrates the lives of all people and their ways of expressing their love for each other.

Behavioral Objectives.

What follows is a list of measurable criteria for recognition as a Welcoming Congregation.

1. A society will establish a Welcoming Congregation committee and monitor the implementation of these goals.

2. A Welcoming Congregation's by-laws and other official documents will include an affirmative, non-discrimination clause to include membership, hiring practices and calling of ministry.

3. Inclusive language and content will be a regular part of worship service. All worship coordinators and speakers will receive guidelines on this practice. The Welcoming Congregation committee will be responsible for monitoring this process.

4. The Minister, Religious Education Minister or Director, or where appropriate, the President or Chair of a society, will participate in a training seminar concerning a Welcoming Congregation.

5. A homophobia workshop will occur in a congregation. A quorum of the membership as defined by the society by-laws and a simple majority of the governing

board will constitute the minimum attendance requirement to qualify for a Welcoming Congregation status.

6. The Welcoming Congregation will work with the religious education department of a society to see that gay, lesbian and bisexual life issues are incorporated into all aspects of religious education.

7. During the teaching of *About Your Sexuality* (AYS), the full curriculum will be used. All possible orientations will be affirmed.

8. Advertising will be placed in the local gay, lesbian and bisexual press and/or other media with specific outreach to the gay, lesbian and bisexual community.

9. Contact will be made with local gay, lesbian and bisexual groups to increase outreach, offer support and promote dialogue and interaction.

10. Use of sanctuary and service of minister (where applicable) will be made available for rites of passages (same-sex unions, celebrations, dedication of the lives of gay, lesbian and bisexual people).

11. Follow-up opportunities for discussion following the homophobia workshop at various forums will occur during the church year.

12. A congregation will provide free church space for local society members who request such to begin a Unitarian Universalist for Lesbian and Gay Concerns (UULGC) chapter.

13. A celebration of gay, lesbian and bisexual pride will occur during a church year and will be documented in a society's newsletter.

14. A society will take visible, documentable action to help create justice, freedom and equality for gay, lesbian and bisexual people in the larger society.

15. Society information and programming will reflect the requested status of any individual as the individual sees appropriate (lesbian and gay couples will be recognized in directors and other information as they desire).

*   *   *

ADDENDA TO THE REPORT.

7. Survey.

The first-phase survey generated a picture of where UUs are now relative to gay/lesbian/bisexual inclusion. . . .

This report represents those among the first 2,362 responses who identified themselves as heterosexual. . . .

About 14 percent of the respondents were gay, lesbian, or bisexual; 86 percent identified themselves as heterosexual. The 14 percent of the responses coming from gay/lesbian/bisexual persons are *not* figured into the statistics you're about to read. Had they been included in this preliminary report, the results would have come out somewhat more favorably on the matter of full inclusion. . . .

Questions 13–15 asked respondents to identify possible strengths or weaknesses in the UUA ministry with gay, lesbian, and bisexual persons. . . .

Strengths listed on *question 13* included: outreach 45%; visibility 34%; providing a place to meet 59%; leadership 27%; fulfillment of UUA principles 54%; supportiveness 70%. Weakness listed on *question 14* included: UULGC is little known 46%; goals are not clear 48%; UUs fail to affirm gay, lesbian and bisexual people 11%; limited acceptance 16%; attract too many gay, lesbian and bisexual people 11%; resolutions not implemented 11%; goals not shared by individual congregations 27%. . . .

Question 16 asked respondents to agree or disagree with the statement, "I would have a difficult time voting for an openly gay, lesbian or bisexual ministerial candidate for my congregation."

UUs were split. There are large groups *strongly* agreeing and *strongly* disagreeing, but slightly more disagree. There are large groups agreeing and disagreeing, but slightly more agree.

A later question poses the statement, "I would have a difficult time accepting an openly gay, lesbian or bisexual person as a ministerial candidate for my congregation."

More respondents felt they could *accept* an openly gay ministerial candidate (*question #20*) than could *vote for* one (*question #16*). But the pattern of responses to both questions is similar. . . .

"I worry that we will become a 'gay church'," *question #22*, shows most respondents disagreeing. But there's a correlation between those agreeing with questions 16 and 20 and this question. Some of those who, in answer to 16 and 20, didn't want a g/l/b minister, expressed the fear of becoming a 'gay church' or of hindering church growth while professing no personal discomfort with a gay minister.

Question #32, "I think my church or minister should offer ceremonies of union to gay, lesbian or bisexual couples," brought evidence of broad acceptance. Those disagreeing tended toward the view that marriage was pretty much out of date and that sexual minorities shouldn't seek to adopt such a custom. Some objected out a traditional view of marriage, which institution they felt was being distorted by services of union. . . .

On #23, "Gays, lesbians and bisexuals are fully integrated in my congregation," responses were fairly evenly spread with a slight tilt toward neutrality. Some thought there were no such members in their congregation.

Question #24 says, "I feel uncomfortable around gays, lesbians, and bisexuals," and a vast majority disagreed or were neutral. Those who agreed tended to agree strongly, sometimes by extending the line to the left or with more than one checkmark. . . .

Has the AIDS crisis "confused the issues surrounding gays, lesbians, or bisexuals in my congregation" (*question #30*)? The majority said No, or were neutral. A few said that, rather than confusing issues, AIDS has clarified them, since homosexuality is unnatural or a moral evil.

Do "gays, lesbians and bisexuals represent just another special interest group in the UUA" (*question #31*)? Yes, said a majority, and many wrote that there are entirely too many special interest groups in the UUA at present.

On *question #33*, "I think gays, lesbians, bisexuals and heterosexuals can benefit from knowing more about each others' lives," there was broad agreement. This question elicited the largest majority in the survey.

SOURCE: "Report and Recommendations of the Common Vision Planning Committee to the Board of Trustees Unitarian Universalist Association," January 1989, Unitarian Universalist Association Office of Lesbian and Gay Concerns, 1972–1999, Andover-Harvard Archive, bMS 1309/5, Andover-Harvard Theological Library, Harvard Divinity School, Cambridge, MA.

"Some Day"
1991

Margaret Williams Braxton was a music therapist and Unitarian Univer-salist laywoman who contributed significantly to the Association with her leadership from the 1960s to the 1990s. Prior to moving to Boston, where she worked as an educational consultant to the UUA Department of Education and Social Concern from 1970 to 1975, Braxton served as director of religious education at All Souls Church Unitarian in Washington, D.C., from 1966 to 1970. She also served on the Administrative Board of the Unitarian Univer-salist Women's Federation in the 1970s, at the time when the Resolution on Women and Religion was passed, and in 1976 she was awarded an honorary doctorate from the Starr King School for the Ministry. In addition to her work as a music therapist and educator, Braxton was also a musician and pub-lished poet whose work drew on her black cultural heritage. Her poem "Some Day" is commonly used in Unitarian Universalist worship services.

—Natalie Malter

Once upon a time I was
Now I am
Some day I will become

Once there was
And now there is
Soon there will be
And some day there surely shall be

Once upon a time we were
Now we are
And some day (Hallelujah!) we shall surely become

Amen
Amen

SOURCE: Mark D. Morrison-Reed and Jacqui James, eds., *Been in the Storm So Long* (Boston: Skinner House, 1991).

"Introduction" to *Cries of the Spirit*

1991

Marilyn Sewell was one of the first women senior ministers of a large church (550 or more members) when she answered her first call to the First Unitarian Church of Portland, Oregon, in 1992, where she served until 2009. Within her first year of ministry, Sewell led a church campaign against anti-LGBTQ ballot measures in Oregon, famously wrapping the downtown building of First Unitarian Church in red ribbons and publically declaring the church a hate-free zone. As a result of her advocacy for human rights and her visionary leadership, the already-large church grew by 40 percent within her first year. Published the year before beginning her ministry in Portland, Cries of the Spirit, *Sewell's anthology of women's poetry, illustrates the growing emphasis on poetry as a part of worship and liturgy in Unitarian Universalist services and explores the connection between poetry and the feminist movement. Further Reading: Cindy Cumfer,* Toward the Beloved Community: The First Unitarian Church of Portland, Oregon, 1865–2015 *(Portland, OR: The First Unitarian Church of Portland, 2015); Marilyn Sewell,* Raw Faith: Following the Thread *(Portland, OR: Fuller Press, 2014).*

—Natalie Malter

Not long ago I discovered that I have no language. Not just me personally, of course, but women. Women have no language.

That discovery shook me deeply. It explained perhaps why I often have this sense of muteness, this pulling back from known words and patterns of language, this doubling back and redoubling upon myself. But where am I to find a voice? The cultural/lingual patterns were laid in place, solidly, years before I even came into this world, were they not?

All writers must be creators, but women writers must create twice: we must re-create our materials—the very words and word-patterns of our medium—and at the same time we must create our individual pieces of writing. We have no ready-made system, no vocabulary in place, no easy syntax, no context of allusion, no given subject matter to embrace us and call us forth.

Where can we begin? Perhaps with the silences, the monumental silences: the multitude of feelings and understandings that we have discounted as not real because there has arisen no word, no phrase, no pattern of thinking to legitimate our experience. To remain in these silences is to be alone. There is no way to connect flesh with flesh, no way to perceive, to preserve, to *know*. So we fumble with words, playing with them, caressing them, trying to tease out meaning. We work as if our lives were at stake. As if *life* were at stake. And we would be right in supposing so.

*   *   *

For women, the sacred seems to be rooted in experience, rather than in institution—in the body and in nature, not in culture. Institutional language narrows and constrains, but experience elbows its way out, to a broader place. Poetry is its natural vehicle. Who can order the Holy? It is like a rain forest, dripping, lush, fecund, wild. We enter its abundance at our peril, for here we are called to the wholeness for which we long, but which requires all we are and can hope to be.

*   *   *

A revolution has started, there's no doubt about it. And what will happen if the masculine world order, built on language, continues to be challenged and shaken? "Then all the stories would have to be told differently," writes Hélène Cixous, "the future would be incalculable, the historical forces would, will, change hand, bodies, another thinking as yet not thinkable, will transform the functioning of all society."

Can we not envision a world in which both men and women honor the flesh, refusing to separate it from spirit, cherishing the earthly as holy stuff? Can we not envision a time when caring for and nurturing both the earth and one another become more important than dominating and conquering? Can we not look forward to the day when we regard all living things as part of the creative matrix, from which we cannot divorce ourselves and survive?

I am not a separatist: I do not conceive of men, or a particular man, as the enemy. But the entrenched system of patriarchy is death-dealing, and in contrast to the stench of decay all about, women choose to write of life. I see it everywhere I turn in their work. I suppose the reverse of Professor Higgins' question haunts me: "Why can't a man be more like a woman?" Not that it is our job to save him—but all who are privileged and burdened to live just now do have some responsibility for creating a world that is safer and saner and more just than the one we have. What better way to do it than with words, holy words.

SOURCE: Marilyn Sewell, *Cries of the Spirit* (Boston: Beacon Press, 1991), 1, 3, 16.

"Give Thanks"

1992

Kim K. Crawford Harvie was raised in Concord, Massachusetts, educated at Middlebury College and Harvard Divinity School, and ordained to the Unitarian Universalist ministry in 1984. As minister of the Universalist Meeting House in Provincetown, Massachusetts, from 1985 to 1989, she built deep relationships with that community during the height of the AIDS crisis. In 1989, she was called as the senior minister of Arlington Street Church, becoming the first woman and the first lesbian to lead a Unitarian Universalist congregation in Boston. In 2004, Crawford Harvie performed the first legally recognized same-sex marriage in a church in the United States. This homily, preached at Arlington Street in 1992, draws on her experiences in Provincetown.

—Dan McKanan

I'm thinking of Dennis.

I saw him on the last afternoon he was coherent. I asked him what I should preach about on Sunday. It was not easy for him to speak, but he did, without hesitation. *Don't hate*, he told me. *No time.*

Facing death, life—the preciousness of life—is clearer.

I'm thinking of Paul.

Paul was a big, blonde, boyish Midwesterner with the energy and exuberance of a Labrador Retriever. On his own initiative, with his Baptist heart, Paul recruited new church members by inviting groups of six friends at a time to Sunday brunch in his home. The hitch was that the invitation started with the church service from 11–12; if you planned to eat, you had to meet Paul in his pew. He was shameless; he was charming.

I'm remembering one particular late summer Sunday afternoon. The last wedding party of the day was being photographed on the sunny front lawn of the church under a cloudless sky. Paul popped in and said, "My boat's at the pier—Let's go!"

I could see the Kaposi's sarcoma erupting on his left calf. I was exhausted, but I went.

Paul motored way, way out into the bay, until the leaning steeple of the church took its place in Provincetown's silhouette on the horizon. He threw the anchor and we sat there, in silence. From a distance, the dying and death, loss and grieving all took their place. Then Paul said to me, "Listen. Even if it kills every single one of us, even if there is no one left to tell the stories, it matters that we care for each other in all this madness. It matters that, even in the face of death, we love each other well."

Within the year, Paul spoke his last words, which were later inscribed on his gravestone: *Speak from your heart.*

It matters.

I'm thinking of Patrick.

It was before he'd cut his hair. It was chestnut, long and thick, pulled back in a ponytail. His chiseled face was beautiful; I loved to look at him. I looked whenever I could; Patrick was sick—very sick.

The only decent hospitals were in Boston, a hundred miles away. Looking back, now, I see that we shouldn't have bothered with them; there was nothing anyone could do. But we were the first generation living without smallpox; doctors were gods. Of course we went to the hospital when something was wrong—especially, drastically wrong, as it so often was in people living with AIDS.

Sometimes that drive was daunting, but not that night; I was with Patrick, and I wanted it to last forever. He had lived in Tucson, and before he had helped found the Tucson AIDS Project, before he was so busy with the business of the dying—and then dying, himself—he had loved the desert and the canyons of the southwest. Now, when we backpack into the Grand Canyon each summer, I pin a red ribbon to my pack—for Patrick, and for all of them who are gone.

He rode shotgun in my little red Volkswagen, with the seat tipped all the way back into a deep recline. I opened the roof; he loved the stars, which were brilliant in a perfect, black dome. The air was warm. Copland's "Appalachian Spring" played on the tape deck.

He was so still. His eyes were closed, and his face was drained of all color. I thought, "Patrick is dying. He may die before we even make it to the hospital."

And then he spoke.

"It doesn't get any better than this."

That was all: *It doesn't get any better than this.*

He had spoken quietly, but I felt as if I had been shouted awake. For a moment, all my hurtling into the future without him, all my fear and rage and grief, were shattered by his simple words. Sometimes—lots of times—it is more than enough to be alive, with all that life proffers in one single, shining moment.

I try this on as a touchstone, in moments of reprieve, at the eye of the storm, or after the storm is over. No one leaves without leaving a gift:

No time to hate.
It matters that we love each other well.
It doesn't get any better than this.

Give thanks.

SOURCE: Kim K. Crawford Harvie, "Give Thanks," reprinted by permission of the author.

MARILYN SEWELL
"What Women Really Want"
1993

"What Women Really Want," preached at the First Unitarian Church of Portland, Oregon, on March 7, 1993, is one of the only sermons directly pertaining to gender that Sewell preached in her tenure in Portland. Early women ministers often found preaching on women's rights to be a challenging task in the face of congregational pressure to avoid drawing attention to one's gender. Most Sundays the act of simply standing in the pulpit and preaching as the senior minister of a large church, sharing a woman's voice and perspective, was radical enough. However, this sermon provides insight into some of the unique challenges faced by women in ministry in the late twentieth century.

—Natalie Malter

Growing up as I did in the South, all the usual gender role messages for girls were delivered to me, only more so. I made two mistakes in adolescence that I knew would never be forgiven by the boys in my high school—I was tall, taller than most of them, and I was smart, smarter than most of them, even in math. I tried to take the role of the Southern belle but was a dismal failure. Ruffles and bows never looked right on me, since I was almost six feet tall.

The message I kept getting from the culture all around me was "get small." Even as an adult. Even from my own mother. I remember our last conversation before her death, some 12 years ago, not long after my divorce. She was unhappy that I was in school for yet another degree. She said, "Why do you keep going to school? I don't care what the libbers say—a man has to feel dominant. If you keep getting these degrees, you'll never find a man." (What can I say? She was right!) About a month later, she died. She went to her grave never understanding my love of books and study. I know she loved me, but she thought I was pretty weird.

Then there was the man who told me after a relationship of many years, "When I first met you, I thought you were a fragile flower. And now you're more like a tree. It's hard to love a tree." There it is again—"get small," be a fragile flower, if you want to be a real woman, if you want to be loved by a man. Maybe that's part of why I came to Portland—I heard you love trees up here.

"What Women Really Want"—a presumptuous title, for I know I cannot really speak for all women, and my own experience colors all that I will say. In this

412

congregation are women of all ages, women who are wealthy and women who are out of work, lesbian and straight women, single women and married women, mothers and those who have never give birth, women who have chosen traditional paths and those who are changemakers. And yet there are commonalities, and I hope those will emerge, at least in part, in my remarks today.

First of all, as a woman, I want to feel safe—and I don't. After a board meeting last week, and unkempt man followed me into the staff parking lot and spoke to me as I was about to back out. He said he wanted to know if he could leave his motorcycle there. I said, "Well, you can't," and began driving out. He approached my car again as I reached the garage door, and I whipped the car out, almost bumping him as I did. He might have been perfectly innocent, but I didn't want to take any chances. I felt vulnerable. Women are.

One in four women is sexually assaulted in her lifetime—and usually not by a stereotypical criminal. Domestic violence is the single largest cause of injury to women in the United States. There was a picture of a man named Lust, interestingly enough, on the front page of the *Oregonian* last Thursday. He is accused of killing two women, his former fiancée and his former wife. The single most common occasion for female homicide is an argument with a man.

And it's not just the men at the bottom of the economic heap who are violent toward women. In one recent survey, 51 percent of college men said they would rape if they could get away with it. Domestic violence occurs in all social classes. The question we must ask, says Gloria Steinem, is not why women can't escape male violence, but why men do it. Is there something about the way women are denigrated in this society that gives men permission to rape and batter and kill? As a woman, I would like to feel safe, and I do not.

As a woman, I want our political leaders to pass laws that make women and children and families a priority. In the last presidential election, we heard a lot about "family values." I'll say it loud and clear: I'm for family values. I want prenatal care for every pregnant woman. I want to be sure that babies and young children get the nutrition they need—which they don't always, when 20 percent of children are living in poverty. I want quality child care when both parents have to be in the workplace. I want a Headstart program that will serve all eligible children, not just a fraction of them. I would like medical research and treatment programs to pay more attention to women's diseases like breast cancer, instead of their present unbalanced focusing on ailments more characteristic to men.

As a woman, I would like to receive equal pay for equal work. Although a number of women have been spotlighted recently as they moved into prominent positions in business or political life, it is a fact that 80 percent of women are still relegated to the "pink-collar ghetto"—they are low-paid clerical workers or sales clerks. Women make 75 cents to every dollar men make, and a man with only a high school diploma makes a thousand dollars a year more than a woman with a four-year college education. In almost every field, men received higher wages than do women in comparable positions. That's true in ministry, for example. The other day I was talking to a senior minister in another denomination about his experience in hiring an associate minister. He said the church chose a man, but the man wanted his own house instead of living in the parsonage and he wanted this and he wanted that, so the church decided they couldn't afford a man and would have to settle for a woman. Fortunately, the woman has turned out to be an excellent minister—and for less money. Even in our own denomination, I'm sorry to say, women ministers of comparable experience get paid less than men.

As a woman in relationship, I would want to share equally in nurturing and caring. We know that in dual-career families, the wife generally does a much greater part of the domestic work. We sometimes fall into these patterns without thinking— we have learned our roles well. In my second year of marriage, I became pregnant and continued teaching full-time. I was also doing all the laundry, shopping, cooking, and cleaning. My husband *did* take out the garbage. Finally I became too exhausted to continue this routine, and I told my husband, "You'll have to help." But it wouldn't have occurred to either of us that this household work belonged to us both, equally. He was helping me with *my* work—even though we were both working full-time outside the home.

As a woman it was important for me to establish an identity aside and apart from my relationship with a man. Although this may sound simple and understandable, it is not always easy to do. Witness the brouhaha around the First Lady's deciding to call herself by her full name, Hillary Rodham Clinton. She's threatening so many people with just that little gesture. Why? Because she's claiming herself, and that is still a radical act in this culture.

*   *   *

As a woman, I would like to be judged on my own merits as a human being and not seen as inferior because I am female. I had a lot of new learning as a divorced woman—until then I didn't understand that sexism existed, for I had been so steeped in it, I couldn't see it. When I couldn't get a credit card without my husband's name, though our credit was impeccable, I began to understand. Then there was the day I applied for a communications position at IBM. I had two master's degrees by then, as I remember. They said they had no current openings but offered me a job as a secretary. As a minister, I visited ten different churches before choosing the First Unitarian Church of Portland. In almost all the interviews at these various churches, I was asked, "Do you think as a woman you can minister to men?" I invariably thought it a strange question. When have women *not* ministered to men? I knew that no male applicants would ever be asked, "As a man, do you think you could minister to women?" And I knew that some people questioned, "Is she tough enough?"

because they hadn't learned that softness and strength can be combined in the same person.

*   *   *

What does a woman want? In *Women Who Run with the Wolves*, Clarissa Estes gives this answer: a partner who will help her "find her true names, . . . to apprehend and comprehend the numinous substance from which she is made, . . . to stay with it And to sing out her names over her. It will make her eyes shine. It will make his eyes shine" [ellipses in original].

SO BE IT. AMEN.

SOURCE: Marilyn Sewell, *Wanting Wholeness, Being Broken: A Book of Sermons* (Portland, OR: Fuller Press, 1998), 62–66, 69.

MARJORIE BOWENS-WHEATLEY

"Kwanzaa, Cornrows, and Confusion:
The Dilemma of Cultural Racism
and Misappropriation"

1995

Marjorie Bowens-Wheatley (1949–2006) was among the earliest black women to be ordained to ministry in the Unitarian Universalist Association when she received her ordination in 1994. Prior to becoming a minister, she had a successful career in public television, worked as the director of public affairs for the Unitarian Universalist Service Committee, and served as the program officer of the Veatch Program at the Unitarian Universalist Society of Shelter Rock on Long Island, New York. Following her ordination in 1994, Bowens-Wheatley served congregations in New York, Texas, and Florida and worked as the adult programs director at the UUA. She was a founder of the African American Unitarian Universalist Ministry (AAUUM). Additionally, from 1993 to 1999 she worked on the Commission on Appraisal for the UUA. In this 1995 essay Bowens-Wheatley challenges her fellow Unitarian Universalists to consider the ways in which the predominantly white UUA misappropriates religious traditions from other cultures. In doing so, she insightfully calls attention to the unconscious racism that pervades Unitarian Universalist communities and belies even the best intentions in anti-oppression work.

—Natalie Malter

A feeling of discomfort has been welling up in my soul in spite of our recent efforts (including significant anti-racism training) to move toward greater racial, ethnic and cultural diversity. I have encountered several situations in which well-intentioned Unitarian Universalists of European American heritage have sought to "lift up" the cultural roots and experiences of people of color. Many of these have been done with varying degrees of disrespect and what is, no doubt, non-conscious racism. . . .

This is part of an ongoing conversation I have had with myself, and occasionally with others, for several years. In a way, we are all feeling our way through a new minefield. I hope that expanding the conversation will help us to delve into a dimension of race relations that is sensitive, difficult, and important. This essay focuses on three aspects of culture: (a) racism and other forms of cultural bigotry, (b) developing greater sensitivity in how we honor the heritage, traditions, and work of racial, ethnic, and religious minority groups, and (c) the threat of cultural genocide and the

416

need for cultural preservation. In these few pages we cannot capture the full scope of cultural racism, let alone analyze it. My purpose is simply to bring the issue to our attention as a religious movement, with the goal of opening up a dialogue between persons of European American heritage and those whose ancestry and heritage is in Asia, Africa, Latin America, the Caribbean and Pacific Islands.

Undoing the social and cultural constructs that have led to racism is, for me, a theological task. It is a transcendent experience—one step toward breaking down the barriers that divide us from each other, from all creation, and from the Great Spirit of Life that some of us call God. It is taking one step toward building a *beloved community*.

Racism is a prejudgment based on race, coupled with the power to affirm that prejudice. It is the exercise of power and the presumption of the privilege to establish and proclaim one race, history, identity, and experience as superior to all other groups. As such, racism is systemic. It saturates every part of our social system economically, politically, and culturally. Racism, including enculturated or cultural racism, imposes the power of one group to institutionalize its values and norms over all other groups. In the United States there is a limited acknowledgment of institutional racism, but cultural racism is often minimized or overlooked. Cultural racism finds its roots in the legacy of White supremacy and in placing more value in imagination than in history or facts. Toni Morrison's book, *Playing in the Dark*, is a literary critique of one form of cultural racism that focuses on the White imagination. One of the most widespread assumptions of White supremacy within the system of free enterprise is that the images, symbols, rituals, practices, and/or religious expressions of any culture can be freely appropriated by another, with or without permission. Cultural racism carries with it an all-pervasive set of assumptions, a deeply rooted taken-for-grantedness that affirms the bastardization (including commercialization) of a culture by placing its cultural productions on the auction block, so to speak.

Power of the Dominant Culture

The power of the White majority to decide what is valued as "normal" or acceptable, and to impart subtle and often unconscious messages about what is "right" and what is not, is especially critical when we consider children. Kenneth Clark found that, by the age of three or four, children develop opinions about their own racial groups based on socially prevailing ideas and other expressions from the dominant culture—in spite of the fact that the child may have had no direct experience with another racial, ethnic or cultural group.

Much of the critical writing on multiculturalism in education is really about intellectual racism as a specific form of cultural racism, but it has not been so named. Leonore Tiefer's article, "Intellectual Racism," is one of the few that begins to name the issue, but the challenge of cultural racism is multi-layered. Tiefer points to the necessity for European Americans to read the writings of people of color "widely and deeply" and to examine "ideas and models for their roles in perpetuating racial hierarchies." If we are to improve race relations within the Unitarian Universalist Association and in the country at large, it is also necessary to examine a multitude of values, norms and assumptions of mainstream culture just as partners in a business enterprise would examine the values, norms, and assumptions of a foreign culture in which they were seeking to do business.

Language is one of these assumptions, and it is a primary construct of racism that shapes cultural norms. I recall the exercise undertaken by Malcolm X in the early 1960s, in which he investigated the words "black" and "white" in the dictionary. Thirty years later, we still find "black" too often associated with negatives and evil, and "white" with goodness and purity. Assigning terms like: "nude" to nylon stockings or "flesh" to Band-Aids or crayons, for example, is based on Caucasian skin tones as the norm.

*   *   *

In spite of the tremendous power of language to influence cultural norms, the attempt to discuss linguistics in terms of race (or gender and sexual orientation) seems to spark a lightning rod. Too often, linguistic challenges are dismissed as "pandering to political correctness." Cultural racism is not about political correctness; it is about who gets to define language and establish and sustain cultural norms. It is about who gets to sit at the table and set agendas. It is about the need and the right to claim one's full humanity instead of accepting disrespect and varying degrees of dehumanization from others. It is about racist patriarchal supremacy. It is about power and freedom and justice.

Cultural Appropriation

There is probably no such thing as a pure religion or a pure culture. To some extent, we all appropriate culture. Since time immemorial, religions have borrowed from each other. Judaism was shaped in part by encounters of the ancient Hebrews with the Sumerians, the Babylonians, and the Egyptians. Similarly, Christianity is rooted in the Jewish tradition, Islam begins with both the Jewish and Christian traditions, and so on. In these modern times, with international tourism and media connecting people throughout the world, there is now a greater opportunity for cultural misunderstanding and misrepresentation, and hence, the concern about misappropriation and cultural preservation of indigenous cultures.

How can cultural appropriation be defined? First, it is most often a form of racial or religious prejudice, or in the most general terms, cultural appropriation is a form of plagiarism. It is consciously or unconsciously seeking to emulate concepts, beliefs or rituals that are foreign to a particular framework, individual or collective.

418

It is incorporating language, cultural expressions, forms, lifestyles, rituals or practices, about which there is little basis for direct knowledge, experience or authenticity, into one's being. It is also the superficial appreciation of a culture without regard to its deeper meaning. And finally, cultural appropriation is acting in ways that belie understanding or respect for the historical, social and spiritual context out of which particular traditions and cultural expressions were born.

The second principle of Kwanzaa, *kujichagulia* (or self-determination), provides a framework from which to examine cultural misappropriation as one dimension of cultural racism. From a political standpoint, self-determination means that people have the right to determine how they will be governed. Dr. Ron Karenga, who gave birth to this ritual, says that self-determination is the right "to define ourselves, name ourselves, create for ourselves, and speak for ourselves instead of being defined, named, created and spoken for by others." I would extend the definition further to say that self-determination is a basic human right. In a Unitarian Universalist context, it also means the right to interpret one's culture and theology.

It has been argued that Unitarian Universalism, particularly our approach to religious education, represents a "creative integration of cultures," with an acknowledgment that the new creation is just that—*new*. Such a critique raises important questions, among them these:

- How does "creative integration" of cultures honor and respect the root culture that sparked the development of the new? Is the *new* simply a cheap imitation?
- Who are the teachers and transmitters of racial, cultural and religious identity? Can or should such traditions be taught or transmitted only by a "native" of that tradition? If not, what is the standard of measurement by which authenticity should be measured?
- What is the source of racial or cultural identity? Is racial and cultural identity reserved only for those whose birth, history, or religious experience is firmly rooted in that culture? Or can one acquire an authentic identity from outside one's own culture of origin?
- What is appropriate and what is inappropriate cultural "borrowing?"
- What is the motivation for cultural borrowing? What is being sought, and why?
- How can cultural traditions that are not our own be honored, respected, appreciated, affirmed, and respectfully shared?

Instead of providing answers, I offer several scenarios to consider, around which discussions can be framed about the implications of cultural appropriation.

Cultural appropriation is problematic, in part, because it is rooted in the existing system of White power and privilege, and is based on the assumption that indiscriminate intercultural borrowing, transfers, or outright stealing are okay. . . .

If a sports team misappropriates a name that is a clear negative reference to Native Americans, for example, "Redskins," it is as disrespectful as referring to an African American by the "N" word. If a North American manufacturer offers a new line of clothing inspired by patterns, styles, or fabrics created by the Andean people, it is plagiarism to name the new line "Andean." If a European American woman believes that the cowrie shell is reminiscent of female genitalia, it is dishonest to place it within a West African context if that interpretation bears no relationship to that culture.

I do accept that many of the goals of those who support cross-cultural borrowing, as far as I can discern, are completely honorable. Often the motivation is simply appreciation for some element of a culture. In fact, sometimes the goal is to honor diversity and serve as a means to help break down barriers. In general, I do not believe there is an intention of malice or ill-will. However, naiveté seems to characterize the actions of many who find themselves in a delicate place relative to intercultural relations. At other times, as Deloria suggests, the motive is less clear, or more self-serving. Regardless of motive, when cultural borrowing becomes cultural racism, the result is often disrespectful and can be painful to those whose cultural expression was borrowed.

As Unitarian Universalists, we are indeed unique in our approach to embracing other religions in worship, programming and religious education. We intentionally seek to learn about world religions and to share other cultural rituals and traditions. We lack depth, however, in our understanding of the historical, racial, cultural and religious context, as well as sensitivity to these contexts. At worst, our approach is assimilationist, a combination of voyeurism and thievery, which in effect, seems to say: from the distance of time and space, we have permission to take a myopic look at whatever culture we choose, and to beg, borrow or steal whatever we like, and make it our own.

* * *

The celebration of Kwanzaa in our congregations presents a similar, yet different, concern. Although many of the principles of Kwanzaa are rooted in what I believe can become universal values, Kwanzaa is unique and particular to the experience of *African Americans*. Indeed, it was born out of the experience of struggle and redemption. It is a remembrance of how African Americans have been beaten down throughout centuries, and the ritual is designed to lift *their* spirits: "to define *ourselves*, name *ourselves*, create for *ourselves*, speak for *ourselves*," and so on. . . . Kwanzaa's reference to "*ourselves*" (African Americans) becomes irrelevant if the pronoun refers to anyone and everyone present. For this reason, congregational celebrations of Kwanzaa need to be rethought. A radical position would be that Kwanzaa should be celebrated only by African Americans. A more liberal position would say that Kwanzaa cannot be celebrated authentically without African

Americans leading the ritual, and that Whites who wish to participate as an act of solidarity can honor African Americans by substituting the word "yourselves" for "*ourselves*." In either case, it needs to be stated clearly that Kwanzaa's historical context is the suffering of *African American* people, and that the ritual is designed to affirm their commitment to self-renewal, self-reliance, self-determination, and self-redemption.

Though I have found ways to reconcile some of my own conflicts about this sensitive subject, I acknowledge that it is extremely complex. It is a tough issue. Just as we have assumed that we honor Judaism by celebrating Jewish holidays in a Unitarian Universalist setting, we have made the same assumption about Divali, Ramadan, Kwanzaa, and special holidays and holy days of other traditions. As an American of African heritage, I have participated in many Seder meals and have felt perfectly comfortable doing so *when invited*. What has been uppermost in my mind in such settings is that, in spite of the common experience of oppression of both Jews and African Americans, Passover is a *Jewish* story. Therefore, I look to Jewish people for guidance and for leadership of such a celebration. . . .

Freedom and Rights

The dimensions of cultural appropriation are further complicated by questions of freedom and rights. Who is to say what practices cross the line between appropriation and misappropriation? . . .

From my perspective, there is nothing inappropriate about a Kenyan wearing an Indian silk blouse or a Guatemalan woven belt, or a German wearing a shirt with a Mandarin collar or a Ghanaian Kente stole. These cultural creations are beautiful and have practical value. For a person of European American heritage, however to wear clothing reminiscent of a particular indigenous culture in an attempt to *be* African or Native American is typical of the *wannabe* syndrome—the notion that a particular racial or cultural group can actually become another ethnic or cultural group simply by learning the rituals and dressing the part. This syndrome expresses itself as cultural arrogance and misappropriation as well as internalized oppression.

✳   ✳   ✳

Justice-Making in Cross-Cultural Relationships

What can we, as Unitarian Universalists seeking to become an anti-racist, multicultural religious movement, do to keep justice-making at the center of our practice vis-à-vis cross-cultural relationships in worship, programming and religious education? Most importantly, there is a need for greater dialogue and engagement between European Americans and people of color as well as with those in and out of our congregations who practice many world religions. In addition to questions already raised, it may also be time to consider more tough questions:

- How can the dominant thinking about history be transformed from an emphasis on self-interest and conquest to new learnings and appreciation of different cultures?
- How can a culture maintain its meaning and authenticity if its traditions are thrust into the public arena—the free marketplace of ideas?
- Does diversity mean that we all join in celebrating many different traditions, or does it mean that we honor the need and the right of each culture to affirm and celebrate its own heritage and traditions, while maintaining the option of inviting others to join in as participant-observers?
- How do we support and affirm group identity and at the same time respect individual rights?
- How do we navigate cultural borders and boundaries in worship, programming, and religious education?
- Is there a line that can be drawn to say that it is okay to cross X boundary, but not Y boundary? Who decides?

Consensus on the above questions will be difficult. Certainly, there is no list of right or wrong answers, and it may be that these questions have no answers at all. Facing the reality of cultural racism and cultural misappropriation will be spiritually challenging for many Unitarian Universalists, because it calls for a willingness to engage in some difficult relearnings accompanied by an awareness of the need for a deeper degree of personal humility. . . .

Do these starting points mean that Unitarian Universalists should not embrace or participate in different cultural or religious traditions? No. It simply means that we need to think more deeply about how to embrace other traditions, how to honor and respect the cultural and religious contexts out of which they were born and continue to live. Reconciliation is a religious task, but it has a political dimension. It requires moving beyond first steps to completely dismantle the institutional and cultural practices that have sustained the power of one group over another in determining cultural norms, equal opportunity, equitable laws, and policies of governance.

How we respond to racism, in all its forms, is fundamentally rooted in how we answer larger ethical, religious, and political questions. What does it really mean to respect the inherent worth and dignity of every person in terms of their culture or religion? How is that principle made manifest in our approach to religious education, programming, worship, and even our personal lives? Will you continue to borrow pieces of my culture simply because you like it, or will you stand in solidarity with me against oppression? As a religious community, a community of justice and hope, if we are to err, let it be on the side of caution. Let it be in our dialogue rather than in our action. Let it be on the side of equality and justice.

Upholding European American ideas, values, and assumptions as the norm are as much a part of sustaining racism as segregation, scapegoating, or the lack of equal opportunity. Dismantling racism begins with saying that we can no longer do business as usual.

SOURCE: Marjorie Bowens-Wheatley, "Cornrows, Kwanzaa and Confusion: The Dilemma of Cultural Racism and Misappropriation," *Bridges to the Future: From Assimilation to Pluralism* (Fall 1995): 7–19. Published by the Liberal Religious Educators Association (lreda.org).

ELLEN K. CAMPBELL
"The International Council of Unitarians and Universalists: Its Founding Meeting"
1995

When the International Council of Unitarians and Universalists (ICUU) was founded, most of its member groups had relatively long histories. They differed in form and theology, but all of them had some established governance structure, a theological perspective, and a history and tradition of religious practice. Until 1995, these national or regional bodies were for the most part independent of each other, and there was no clear path for new groups of Unitarians or Unitarian Universalists to receive assistance in development. Impetus toward forming a worldwide organization began in 1987 after the British General Assembly passed a resolution that endorsed the exploration of this possibility. By and large the conversations took place at the annual meetings of the UUA, General Assembly of Unitarian and Free Christian Churches (GAUFCC), Canadian Unitarian Council (CUC), and International Association for Religious Freedom (IARF). In 1992, a World Unitarian Summit held in Budapest, Hungary, was attended by leaders of most of the major groups. The attendees wavered at creating a new organization but did establish a steering committee and agree to meet again. Subsequently, at the urging of a new UUA administration, a conference was held in Essex, Massachusetts, in March 1995, with representatives from the Canadian Unitarian Council; Czech Unitarian Association; Unitarian Universalist Church of the Philippines; Unitarian Universalist Association of Sri Lanka; Australia/New Zealand Unitarian Association; The Unitarian Church in Romania; Free Protestant Unitarian Church, South Africa; British General Assembly of Unitarian and Free Christian Churches, United Kingdom; Unitarische Kirkesamfund, Denmark; European Fellowships; Deutscher Unitarierbund, Germany; Unitarian Universalist Fellowship of Saint Petersburg, Russia; and Unitarian Universalist Association in attendance. Delegates from the Unitarian Universalists of Pakistan; Unitarian Church of Hungary; Unitarian Brotherhood Church, Nigeria; and Unitarian Union of North East India were unable to attend because of visa or health challenges. Further Reading: Mark Morrison-Reed, Ménage à Trois: The UUA, GAUFCC and IARF and the Birth of the ICUU.

—Mark D. Morrison-Reed

The meetings began on Wednesday night with the opportunity for all participants to share something of their own experience and reasons for coming. Some themes recurred: the desire for connection with others with similar beliefs and values in other parts of the world, a sense of isolation as Unitarians and Universalists, the opportunity to learn from others, past ties with Unitarians or Universalists in other places. Some of the group had been part of this religious community for their entire lives; others had come to it very recently. The group began, in this initial getting-acquainted and the worship which followed, to become a community.

The next morning began with a keynote address by the Rev. John Buehrens. He spoke of looking for a "right relationship" with Unitarians and Universalists around the world. Recognizing the differences we brought from our various religious and cultural communities he suggested that we should be focusing not on our creed but on our covenant with each other. . . .

Larry Peers of the Extension Office of the UUA was the facilitator of the initial working session, to explore a series of questions: What have we in common? What are our differences? Do we want a world organization? To do what? What are our goals?

It began with a brief presentation on each group represented: size; general characteristics of Unitarianism and/or Universalism different from other religious groups in the country; characteristics of membership; ministry; governance; financing. The exercise highlighted the wide divergence in some areas. In size, there was a range from Denmark, with thirty members, to the USA with 200,000. The German group, established just after World War II, had determined that it would not have clergy or other professional leadership; the Transylvanian church is organized with a fairly traditional church government under a Bishop. But it also illustrated some commonalities: commitment to freedom of conscience and the democratic process, and to free association.

In small groups participants considered their vision for a potential world body, thinking ahead a decade to 2005. Having shared their visions, the groups began to develop a set of purposes for the organization. The first formulation of the purposes was as follows:

- to affirm the worldwide Unitarian and Universalist faith
- to facilitate mutual support among member organisations,
- to promote our ideals and principles around the world,
- to provide models of liberal religious response to the human condition which uphold our common values.

Jeff Teagle and Herman Boerma facilitated sessions to develop a constitution. Working from a draft constitution which had been circulated in advance, the group suggested areas which needed to be added, developed further, or which might cause difficulty. Small groups worked on specific sections of the document. While much of this work was technical, three areas required more intensive discussion. The first was the need for a Preamble, more clearly affirming our common identity. The Preamble developed and adopted was as follows:

We, the member groups of the International Council of Unitarians and Universalists, affirming our beliefs in religious community based on:

- liberty of conscience and individual thought in matters of faith,
- the inherent worth and dignity of every person,
- justice and compassion in human relations,
- responsible stewardship of the earth's living system,
- and our commitment to democratic principles

The second area of concern was the numbers of delegates to which member groups would be entitled in future meetings. The draft constitution proposed that each group with more than 1000 members would have two votes, and those groups with fewer than 1000 members would have one. An alternate proposal was made that each group of whatever size would have one vote. After considerable discussion, agreement was reached on a proposal to give two votes to groups with more than three thousand members.

The third potential problem arose as the group developing the Preamble reviewed the Purposes which had been developed. One member felt that his group would not accept the Constitution without some reference to God, and proposed an addition, "to serve God and the human community." A second member of that small group proposed instead "Service to our religious ideals." They brought these alternatives to the larger body. The whole group recognized quickly that given the wide variation in belief within and between the religious traditions represented, this could be a divisive and difficult area. There was an extensive discussion of alternative wordings which might be satisfactory to the members of our various groups, and about eight were proposed. A voting formula was suggested whereby delegates indicated which of the proposals would be acceptable to their group, and identified one which was the most acceptable. To the group's surprise and pleasure, while a number of the possibilities were acceptable to people, there was strong consensus for one, and the following purpose was added to the original list:

- To serve the Infinite Spirit of Life and the human community by strengthening the worldwide Unitarian and Universalist faith.

❊　❊　❊

Delegates from the Czech Republic reported on a tragic schism within their church. After the "Velvet Revolution" in Czechoslovakia, the church in Prague called a minister, Vladimir Strejček, with support from the UUA and the IARF. Rev. Strejček had an authoritarian view of church governance, and he and the Prague congregation soon clashed over the management of the church's property and funds. After several episodes of conflict, he called a meeting of the minority of the Central Committee of the Czech Unitarian Association in June 1993. . . . They extended Rev. Strejček's authority to include management of administration and finances of the national general secretariat. They obtained recognition by the Czech government as the legal representative of Czech Unitarians. The legitimate leadership of the Czech church had lost control of their building and funds. Efforts to effect a reconciliation had proved unsuccessful. . . .

The meeting considered action to respond to the Czech situation. Discussions began with the hope that ICUU might break the impasse. A resolution calling on both sides to come together with our representatives was presented, but the group clearly did not feel comfortable with it. Support for a stronger resolution came particularly from the Philippine delegates, reflecting their own experience with religious persecution and undemocratic activity. In the end, the Council unanimously adopted a resolution which formally recognized the delegation at the meeting as the legitimate leadership of the Czech Unitarian Association, and called upon the other group "to relinquish all claims to the titles, offices, property and financial resources of the Czech Unitarian Association . . . together with all claim to be the representatives of the Czech Unitarian Association in the Czech Republic or in the worldwide Unitarian and Universalist movement."

This document was to be sent to the Czech government bodies which have responsibility for religious matters as well as to the affected groups.

✻　✻　✻

Perhaps most important were the worship services which had been developed by the Planning Committee. Each service included elements from the various countries and groups represented: music, reflection, readings. There were many special moments. Árpád Szabó's reading of the passage from St. Paul, "We are all one body;" singing together the South African hymn, "Grant Us the Grace to Be: United, Strong and Free," the "sharing circle" in which each person reflected on the day gone by—every participant will have memories of them.

Most significant was the closing service, in which the delegations pledged support on behalf of their own member groups to this fledgling body. A sermon by David Usher, who had made the original motion to establish such a body at the 1987 British General Assembly, reflected on the purposes and promise of this fledgling organization. Herman Boerma, in "The Home Planet," a meditation based on astronauts' reflections on seeing the earth from space, brought to the group a sense of the wonders of the universe and the unity of Earth. As the service ended, the group was connected by a depth of community which is rarely experienced.

Why was this meeting so successful? There would seem to be some major contributing factors:

- No one in attendance was seeking to enlarge a power base or to dominate the group. The delegates and others were there to achieve the goal of establishing a working network between the national bodies they represented, not to enhance those bodies or themselves.
- No one came with the idea that their particular perspective on Unitarian or Universalist religion was more "true" or "authentic" than any other. The purpose of the meeting was to find what the group had in common, not to identify or argue about their differences.
- There was a balance between vision and reality. Many of the "visioning" ideas were inspiring and challenging, but the group recognized that it needed to walk toward those goals, rather than run, if it was to make a successful start.

Perhaps the most effective way to close this chronicle of a significant moment in our religious history is with the final Preamble and Purposes from the Constitution of the International Council of Unitarians and Universalists:

We, the member groups of the International Council of Unitarians and Universalists, affirming our belief in religious community based on:

- liberty of conscience and individual thought in matters of faith,
- the inherent worth and dignity of every person,
- justice and compassion in human relations,
- responsible stewardship of the earth's living system,
- and our commitment to democratic principles,

declare our purposes to be:

- to serve the Infinite Spirit of Life and the human community by strengthening the worldwide Unitarian and Universalist faith,
- to affirm the variety and richness of our living traditions,
- to facilitate mutual support among member organisations,
- to promote our ideals and principles around the world,
- to provide models of liberal religious response to the human condition which uphold our common values.

SOURCE: Ellen K. Campbell, "The International Council of Unitarians and Universalists: Its Founding Meeting," July 1995, corrected and revised 2016. Reprinted by permission of the author.

JAMES ISHMAEL FORD
"An Invitation to Western Buddhists"
1996

James Ishmael Ford (1948–) was the first person ordained in both the Buddhist and Unitarian Universalist traditions. This helped him to bring these communities into conversation at a time when American Buddhism was transitioning from a counterculture to a subculture, while Unitarian Universalism was experiencing rapid diversification of styles and religious orientations within the movement. Raised Baptist in California, Ford became involved with Zen Buddhism in the 1960s. Later, he began attending UU churches, receiving ordination in 1991. Ford served as president of the Unitarian Universalist Buddhist Fellowship and as a minister for several UU churches, and he became minister emeritus of the First Unitarian Church of Providence after his retirement in 2015. He also founded Boundless Way Zen, a lineage with centers in the Northeast and, more recently, in California. He has written several books, including This Very Moment: A Brief Introduction to Buddhism and Zen for Unitarian Universalists *(Boston: Skinner House, 1996) and* If You're Lucky, Your Heart Will Break *(Boston: Wisdom Publications, 2012). Further Reading: Wayne Arnason and Sam Trumbore,* Buddhist Voices in Unitarian Universalism *(Boston: Skinner House, 2013).*

—Jeff Wilson

I've heard this conversation before. In many Dharma groups people with children ask how they can raise their children Buddhist? Unfortunately, the response they get is rarely satisfactory. However, what surprises me most is how often the response turns out to be a referral—quite frequently to a Unitarian Universalist church.

✳ ✳ ✳

To best understand contemporary Unitarian Universalism . . . the image I've generally found most helpful is to suggest Unitarian Universalism is a liberal religious movement that has one foot within Christianity and the other outside. And, this is very important, sometime during this century the weight shifted to the outer foot.

Today, as a radically non-creedal body, individual Unitarian Universalists hold many different theological opinions. One may be a Christian, a Jew, an atheist, even a neo-pagan, while still being considered a "good" UU. One may even be a Buddhist, and ever more frequently this is becoming the case. . . .

It is my impression that possibly as many as ten percent of UUs consider themselves Buddhist—or at the very least, seriously influenced by Buddhism. And, I feel, the percentage is possibly even higher among the clergy.

*   *   *

A place at the table has been prepared for Western Buddhists. I hope we will choose to join in. I find there are many reasons to consider doing this, and I hope we will think about them.

For Western Buddhists the first gain we get from joining Unitarian Universalist churches is obvious . . . religious education for our children.

Today few Western Buddhist centers are able to assist in providing competent or consistent religious education for our kids. The reasons for this are numerous. And, for good reasons or bad, it is not generally going to be possible to raise Western Buddhist children in currently structured Western Dharma centers. . . .

This is not to say that Unitarian Universalist societies are now places where one can raise Buddhist children without a great deal of conscious effort on the part of the parents. For instance, there are currently no explicitly Buddhist curricula available.

But. The existing curricula are very interesting, emphasizing the development of good self-esteem, critical thinking skills, and respect for the world's faiths. . . .

What is needed are Western Buddhist parents who will join UU societies and who will teach and begin to develop the curricula—for both children and for adults. There are great possibilities here for anyone willing to do the work. . . .

And there are things other than religious education going on, as well. Increasingly, Western Buddhists who join UU societies are establishing meditation groups within their churches. This is helpful for the individuals involved, providing a place for these groups to meet. And, it is helpful for the larger UU community—which . . . is seeking forms of practical spirituality that can heal the humanist/spiritual rift.

UU Buddhists may be of immense help here. . . . Buddhist meditation groups of nearly every type seem to have a place within UU churches. In fact, bringing Buddhist practices into the life of Unitarian Universalism may well be the greatest gift we can bring with us should we decide to come into these churches. . . .

Now, this UU/Buddhist connection is very much a two-way street. Besides providing the frame for a Buddhist religious education experience for our children, and places to engage our own spiritual practices; Unitarian Universalism offers interesting challenges to Western Buddhists. UUs have been in the forefront of ordaining women, as well as gays and lesbians to the clergy. Unitarian Universalists are deeply concerned with how human beings live lives engaged in the community. . . .

I certainly feel these are serious questions Western Buddhists need to be addressing. Within UU societies one encounters a forum to engage those concerns of manifestation, of real life in the real world. . . .

430

I find in reflecting on those questions, and seeking the depths of clear responses, we Western Buddhists may well discover ourselves transformed into something deeper and truer than we likely could be before joining as Unitarian Universalists. It is hard to be smug, or to sit on one's laurels, when asked "how can you possibly believe that?" Or, "Do you want to join in the death penalty protest?" Each of these questions may become koan for us, opening the way of deepest intimacy.

There are other areas of possible profit, as well. I know how important it has been for me to engage the spiritual questions of my religious heritage. I was raised a Baptist, and I owe a great deal to the faith of my childhood. At the same time there is no way I can return to a Baptist church.

But, within Unitarian Universalism, I can honestly pursue the meaning of my spiritual upbringing within the context of my adult faith. This is a precious gift that Unitarian Universalism has given me. . . . So, while I certainly understand it may not be the best choice for everyone, I feel quite a few Western Buddhists can find much of value in joining UU societies.

SOURCE: James Ishmael Ford, "An Invitation to Western Buddhists," uubf.org/wp/invitation

Resolution of Immediate Witness
in Support of the Right to Marry
for Same-Sex Couples
1996

The passage of this resolution in support of marriage equality represented the culmination of twenty-six years of Unitarian Universalist Association resolutions, campaigning, and outreach on behalf of LGBTQ rights. John Buehrens, UUA president at the time, was a significant proponent of the right to marry, and during a session at the General Assembly in Indianapolis in 1996, Buehrens invited all those couples that were unable to have their love legally recognized to stand on stage with him. Following this powerful act of witness and the ensuing debate over the issue, the Resolution of Immediate Witness passed, making the Unitarian Universalist Association the first religious organization in the United States to openly support marriage equality. It would not be for another eight years that the right to marry would be recognized at the state level in United States — first in Massachusetts — not coincidentally home of the UUA and many UU advocates for LGBTQ rights.

—Natalie Malter

Because Unitarian Universalists affirm the inherent worth and dignity of every person; and

Because marriage is held in honor among the blessings of life; and

WHEREAS many states, the Congress, and the President of the United States are acting to void the recognition of same-sex marriages and to deny "full faith and credit" to such marriages formalized in Hawaii or any other state;

WHEREAS debate about legally recognized marriage to same-sex couples has focused on the objections of certain religious communities, while the Unitarian Universalist Association has adopted numerous resolutions over the last twenty-six years supporting equal rights for gay, lesbian, bisexual, and transgendered persons, including support of Ceremonies of Union between members of the same sex; and

WHEREAS the Unitarian Universalist Association Board of Trustees and the Unitarian Universalist Ministers Association have voted their support for the right to marry for same-sex couples;

THEREFORE be it resolved that the 1996 General Assembly of the Unitarian Universalist Association adopts a position in support of legal recognition for marriage between members of the same sex;

BE IT further resolved that the 1996 General Assembly urges the Unitarian Universalist Association to make this position known through the media; and

BE IT finally resolved that the 1996 General Assembly of the Unitarian Universalist Association urges the member congregations to proclaim the worth of marriage between any two committed persons and to make this position known in their home communities.

SOURCE: Unitarian Universalist Social Justice Statements, uua.org/statements/support-right-marry-same-sex-couples

Business Resolution Toward an Anti-Racist Unitarian Universalist Association

1997

The Unitarian Universalist Association was born in 1961 at a time when courageous leaders of the Civil Rights movement were beginning to challenge the crisis of racial injustice in the United States. In the 1960s, many Unitarian Universalists joined as allies in the Civil Rights movement, with ministers and laypeople alike participating in the March on Washington and the march in Selma, Alabama, where UU minister James Reeb and UU laywoman Viola Liuzzo were killed. However, in spite of the desire for racial justice that pervaded many UU communities, at the end of the 1960s the UUA struggled in its ally-ship with the rise of the Empowerment Controversy and the debate over whether or not to fund a Black Affairs Council in the UUA. It was not until the 1980s that the conversation around racial justice came to the fore again due to the work of ministers, scholars, and activists such as Mark Morrison Reed, who published Black Pioneers in a White Denomination *in 1980. In 1992 a Resolution of Immediate Witness in Support of Racial and Cultural Diversity in Unitarian Universalism was passed at General Assembly, and the UUA subsequently began to examine more seriously its own institutional role in both perpetuating and dismantling racism. The 1997 resolution was based in a report by the UUA entitled "Journey Toward Wholeness—The Next Step: From Racial and Cultural Diversity to Anti-Oppression and Anti-Racist Multiculturalism," which explored the ways in which racism persisted in UU communities. The resolution acknowledges and commits to challenging racism on an individual and systemic level. Further Reading: Leslie Takahashi Morris, Chip Roush, and Leon Spencer,* The Arc of the Universe Is Long: Unitarian Universalists, Anti-Racism, and the Journey from Calgary *(Boston: Skinner House, 2009).*

—Natalie Malter

WHEREAS the 1996 General Assembly resolved that all congregations, districts, organizations, and professional and lay leaders participate in a reflection-action process throughout the 1996–97 church year using the Congregational Reflection and Action Process Guide and the Anti-Racism Assessment; and

WHEREAS our Unitarian Universalist principles call us to affirm and promote "justice, equity, and compassion in human relations" and "the goal of world community"; and

WHEREAS our history as Unitarian Universalists includes evidence of both great commitment and individual achievement in the struggle for racial justice as well as the failure of our Unitarian Universalist institutions to respond fully to the call for justice; and

WHEREAS racism and its effects, including economic injustice, are embedded in all social institutions as well as in ourselves and will not be eradicated without deliberate engagement in analysis and action; and

WHEREAS because of the impact of racism on all people, and the interconnection among oppressions, we realize we need to make an institutional commitment to end racism; and

WHEREAS the social, economic, and ecological health of our planet is imperiled by the deepening divisions in our world caused by inequitable and unjust distribution of power and resources; and

WHEREAS we are called yet again by our commitment to faith in action to pursue this anti-racist, multi-cultural initiative in the spirit of justice, compassion, and community;

THEREFORE BE IT RESOLVED that the 1997 General Assembly urges Unitarian Universalists to examine carefully their own conscious and unconscious racism as participants in a racist society, and the effect that racism has on all our lives, regardless of color.

BE IT FURTHER RESOLVED that the General Assembly urges the Unitarian Universalist Association, its congregations, and community organizations to develop an ongoing process for the comprehensive institutionalization of anti-racism and multi-culturalism, understanding that whether or not a group becomes multi-racial, there is always the opportunity to become anti-racist. Early steps toward anti-racism might include using curricula such as *Journey Toward Wholeness* for all age groups, forming racial justice committees, and conducting anti-racism workshops.

BE IT FURTHER RESOLVED that the General Assembly urges all Unitarian Universalist leaders, including ministers, religious educators, leaders of associate and affiliate organizations, governing boards, Unitarian Universalist Association staff, theological schools, and future General Assemblies to engage in ongoing anti-racism training, to examine basic assumptions, structures, and functions, and, in response to what is learned, to develop action plans.

BE IT FURTHER RESOLVED that Unitarian Universalists are encouraged to enter into relationships of sustained engagement with all people of color with a goal of opening up authentic dialogue that may include, but is not limited to, race and racism. Such dialogue should also include how to appropriately honor and affirm the cultural traditions of all people of color.

BE IT FURTHER RESOLVED that the General Assembly requests that the UUA Board of Trustees establish a committee to monitor and assess our transformation as an anti-racist, multi-cultural institution, and that the Board of Trustees shall report annually to the General Assembly specifically on the programs and resources dedicated to assisting our congregations in carrying out the objectives of this resolution.

BE IT FINALLY RESOLVED that in order to transform the racist institutions of our world, the General Assembly urges the Unitarian Universalist Association and all its parts to establish relationships with other international and interfaith organizations that are working to dismantle racism.

SOURCE: Unitarian Universalist Social Justice Statements, www.uua.org/statements/toward-anti-racist-unitarian-universalist-association

DENISE DAVIDOFF

"Preface" to *A Chosen Faith*
1998

Denise Taft Davidoff (1932–) is known for her active lay leadership in the
Unitarian Universalist Association since its beginning in the 1960s. While
she is best known for working as moderator of the UUA from 1993 until 2001
with former President John Buehrens, she also served the UUA in a variety of
other positions. Davidoff led the Unitarian Universalist Women's Federation
as president in the early 1980s, lending her expert leadership to the movement
to revise the gendered language of the Principles and Purposes. In addition
she has held positions on the Ministerial Fellowship Committee, the board
of the Church of the Larger Fellowship, and the board of Meadville Lom-
bard Theological School, and outside of the UUA, she had a successful career
as the founder of her own marketing firm. In her "Preface" to A Chosen Faith,
a collection of introductory essays to Unitarian Universalism, Davidoff pro-
vides insight into her own spiritual journey from Judaism to Unitarian Uni-
versalism, which represents the multi-faith backgrounds of many Unitarian
Universalists.

—Natalie Malter

My husband, Jerry, and I discovered the Unitarian Universalist church in Westport,
Connecticut, in the winter of 1960. We liked the people. We liked the Sunday morning worship in the Saugatuck School auditorium. We liked the potluck suppers. We
loved the minister, Arnold Westwood. Even three-year-old Douglass liked the place.
It seemed like a perfect fit.

Sounds easy, you say. But it wasn't. Signing the membership book in a Unitarian church was scary beyond belief for me even to contemplate. How would I tell
my parents I was rejecting the faith of my forefathers? (Yes, fore*fathers*! Remember,
this was 1960.) I don't just mean my Jewish grandfathers Louis Taft and Harry Zuck-
erman, who had emigrated from the Ukraine in the late nineteenth century. I mean
those *other* forefathers: Abraham, Isaac, and Jacob. How would I tell my aunts and
uncles and cousins? How would I tell my in-laws? How would I tell our friends, particularly those in the Temple Israel community in our town?

And *what* would I tell them? Who had a vocabulary in the early sixties to express
the stifling bonds of patriarchy I felt in the synagogue? How could I express feelings
of exclusion and put-down I later came to know as feminist? How to explain how

good that simple English language liturgy and those guilt-free, up-lifting sermons felt in the ears and, increasingly, in the heart? Emerson and Channing and Parker were names mentioned in courses I'd taken in American cultural history at Vassar. But join a *church*? (In my family, if you went to a church, you were a Christian. Many still don't believe me when I tell them that, while some Unitarian Universalists are Christians, many others claim other commitments and traditions.) Leave the family? Deal with Dad's wrath, Mom's tears, and my brother's bewilderment? Was I crazy?

Yes, it was scary. And it took me six and a half years to sign that book. By that time, I was teaching in the Sunday School, serving on committees, canvassing for the pledge drive, and reveling in the beautiful contemporary building we had built on Lyons Plains Road. But even then, all those years later, I still couldn't articulate this newfound faith of mine. The journey to articulation would take much longer than I could ever have imagined. To be truthful, it continues to this day.

Most of us who are active Unitarian Universalists don't know anything close to "enough" about our faith. We often don't understand where the Unitarian Universalist Association came from and, as a result, we cannot have a vision of where we might go. . . .

I delight to see that Unitarian Universalists are moving into the interfaith world, forging and joining coalitions to fight for the rights of others, to engage the radical religious right in the political arena, to stand for and seek ways to institutionalize antiracism. We do this work because our religious faith demands it of us. We do this work with others because we recognize that we are too small to do it effectively by ourselves. We do this work because we want people to know that Unitarian Universalists prefer to fight against the world's oppressions with other people of faith.

SOURCE: Denise Davidoff, "Preface," in John A. Buehrens and Forrest Church, *A Chosen Faith: An Introduction to Unitarian Universalism*, rev. ed. (Boston: Beacon Press, 1998), xv–xvii.

"Beyond Religious Tolerance: The Challenges of Interfaith Cooperation Begin with Us"

1999

In the 1990s the Unitarian Universalist Association embarked on a new approach to social justice statements. Every other year, the General Assembly selected a topic of broad interest, and the Association embarked on a four-year process of study and reflection at the local and national levels, culminating in the creation of a "Statement of Conscience" that would be deeply informed by Unitarian Universalist principles and oriented to concrete action by congregations as well as the Association. (General Assemblies continued to approve "Actions of Immediate Witness" on more specific and time-sensitive issues.) The first Statement of Conscience called Unitarian Universalists to a transformative practice of interfaith dialogue.

—Dan McKanan

We live in a global village that brings people of diverse economic, cultural, and religious backgrounds into close and interdependent contact. The resulting challenges are immense. They defy traditional efforts to ensure socio-economic fairness. While we hear the plea for a more just society in the teachings of many faiths, intolerance towards people of other faiths inhibits cooperative efforts.

The commitment of Unitarian Universalism to religious tolerance dates back to the first guarantee of religious freedom in Europe, issued in 1568 by the Transylvanian King John Sigismund, a Unitarian. Today, we accept others' rights to their own religious beliefs. However, our acceptance does not extend to tolerance of actions flowing from those beliefs that violate individual human rights and dignity. Acceptance thrives only where mutual respect exists, understanding is encouraged, and dialogue is nurtured among people of different faiths and philosophical traditions.

Contemporary Unitarian Universalism is a pluralistic faith, drawing its strength from its openness to many different sources. While religious interdependence is an integral characteristic of our living tradition, we are not immune to religious intolerance. There is still hard work to be done within our ranks to ensure that Unitarian Universalists with different theological and philosophical beliefs feel equally at home in our congregations. We need to grow beyond the stereotypes, symbols, and semantic barriers that divide Unitarian Universalists from one another.

We try to advance our Unitarian Universalist principles through our social justice agenda. We try to bring about mutual understanding, appreciation, and respect among people of faith—all people of faith. Recognizing shared values may help us avoid either accepting the intolerable or unquestioningly embracing interfaith cooperation. We want to foster cooperation among people of faith as a way of discovering shared values. These shared values may become a workable base on which to build a better world.

Interfaith cooperation sets a high standard of thought, feeling, and action for each individual and for each community that by its nature goes beyond the boundaries of self. It invites us to reach beyond ourselves into the world to confront fear, ignorance, and hatred wherever we find them. It also invites us to reach deep within ourselves to assess our own prejudices. This work begins with living our principles, thereby modeling what is possible in the broader community.

Therefore we are called to:

Educate Ourselves. Let us commit ourselves to increasing our own and our children's understanding and appreciation of other faith traditions. Let us search for deeper meanings and shared values that underlie our common humanity. Let us come to know who we are in a world of many different beliefs. Let us use our long-standing commitment to liberal education to overcome fear, ignorance, and hatred.

Honor Our Internal Religious Pluralism. Within our congregations, let us come to understand that the identity of our evolving faith is rooted in the free expression of our varied religious beliefs and deepest yearnings. Let us celebrate our differences as contributing to our creativity and to the unique fabric of our Unitarian Universalist heritage.

Converse with Other Faith Communities. Let us find the courage to explore through dialogue the values and goals we share with others. Let us listen to others carefully, avoid premature judgments, and speak only for ourselves. Let us speak out about who we are and be sure we are heard. Let us build from our conversations a network for collective action. Let us become involved as individuals, as congregations, and as a faith community in cooperative interfaith activities.

Participate in Interfaith Service Projects. Let us recognize and encourage those among us who reach out beyond themselves to take part, as Unitarian Universalists, in cooperative interfaith service projects and who embody our principles in their involvement.

Work for Social Justice. Social justice work, in addition to its intrinsic merit, can bring faith communities together and provide opportunities for personal transformation. Through the discovery of mutual interests, let us help build personal and institutional alliances that open channels of communication for further cooperative work.

Celebrate Diversity. Let us go beyond tolerance to build mutual understanding with respect, appreciation, and love for people whose religious traditions, symbols, and beliefs may differ from our own.

The Unitarian Universalist Association dedicates itself to the challenges of interfaith cooperation and calls upon its member congregations and individual Unitarian Universalists, within the dictates of conscience, to accept these challenges. May our commitment to building a better world begin with ourselves as we work with others to make the world awaited a world attained.

SOURCE: Unitarian Universalist Social Justice Statements, www.uua.org/statements/beyond -religious-tolerance-challenges-interfaith-cooperation-begin-us

Constitution and Bylaws of the Unitarian Universalist Church of the Philippines, Inc.

1999

The Unitarian Universalist Church of the Philippines, which has no direct connection to the Philippine Independent Church or its successors, was established on the island of Negros at the initiative of Toribio Quimada. Quimada had discovered Universalism in 1951 when, as a recently ordained member of an evangelical denomination called the Iglesia Universal de Cristo, *he wrote to a Universalist congregation in Wisconsin seeking educational resources. He was soon preaching universal salvation and other liberal doctrines, leading to his excommunication from* Iglesia Universal de Cristo *and to financial support from the Universalist Church in America. Quimada's ministry also had a social dimension, as he advocated for the land rights of small farmers like himself. That activism might have led to his murder in 1988. One month later, the Unitarian Universalist Church of the Philippines was accepted as a member congregation of the Unitarian Universalist Association (though it was actually a network of congregations). Soon thereafter, the UUA reaffirmed its prior policy of encouraging Unitarian and Universalist groups outside the United States to create autonomous institutions. The Constitution and Bylaws were first approved in 1996 and frequently amended at subsequent annual assemblies. Here we present the 1996 version of the Principles and Purposes, along with a mission statement that had been added by 1999. Further Reading: Fredric John Muir,* Maglipay Universalist: The Unitarian Universalist Church of the Philippines *(self-published, 2001).*

— Dan McKanan

UUCP Mission Statement: We believe in a loving God and a just, helpful and caring community. We affirm to promote the welfare of the environment and support for a just and economic, social and spiritual connection that will lead to build an open mind for a holistic life. We affirm to uphold an equal and peaceful relationship to every person and to every religion because we are here as One Big Family.

✳   ✳   ✳

Article III

Principles & Purposes

Section 1. Principles

We, the members of the Unitarian Universalist Church of the Philippines, Inc., covenant to affirm and promote:

1. There is only one God who is the God of Love (amended in 2008 to read, "There is God" and in 2015 to read, "There is one God, the God of Love");
2. The inherent worth and dignity of every person;
3. Human relation must be dealt with justice, equality, and compassion;
4. Accept and encourage each other's spiritual growth;
5. The rights of conscience and the use of democratic process in any undertakings;
6. A free and responsible search for truth and meaning;
7. To build a world community with peace, liberty, and justice for all;
8. The respect of the interdependent web of all existence of which we are a part. . . .

Section 2. Purposes

The Unitarian Universalist Church of the Philippines, Inc., shall devote its resources and exercise its corporate powers for religious, educational, and humanitarian purposes. The Church shall help its members uplift their economic lives; strengthen their relationships with one another and to the One whom they pay deep homage. It shall encourage her members to express freely their beliefs, opinions, and views, to use the democratic process in every undertaking, and to work for a better world to live, with peace, liberty, and justice for all, with respect of all existence of which we are a part.

SOURCE: Fredric John Muir, *Maglipay Universalist: The Unitarian Universalist Church of the Philippines* (self-published, 2001), 98–99.

REBECCA ANN PARKER

Proverbs of Ashes

2001

Rebecca Ann Parker (1953–) is a theologian, minister, and educator who served as president of Starr King School for the Ministry from 1989 to 2014. A United Methodist in dual fellowship with the Unitarian Universalist Association, Parker's theological work is strongly influenced by Unitarian, Universalist, feminist, and process theological contributions to Christian thought. This selection, from the first of two books Parker co-authored with Rita Nakashima Brock, describes the way her understanding of Jesus' death changed during her ministry at a Methodist congregation in Seattle. Further Reading: Rita Nakashima Brock and Rebecca Ann Parker, Saving Paradise: How Christianity Traded Love of This World for Crucifixion and Empire *(Boston: Beacon Press, 2008).*

—Robert Hardies

At the center of Western Christianity is the story of the cross, which claims God the Father required the death of his Son to save the world. We believe this theological claim sanctions violence. We seek a different theological vision.

✳　✳　✳

In the Bible, prophets and teachers repeatedly contend with their religion's failures and false claims. Job railed against the pious teachings of his day as he struggled with devastating loss and illness. The teachings of his friends reinforced his suffering. "Your maxims are proverbs of ashes!" he protested. . . . Our religious heritage gives us the imperative to confront it when it fails to foster life or advocate for justice.

✳　✳　✳

Sometimes we live for a long time with a certain belief, like the belief it is best to never speak about pain and abuse in our lives. We hold fast to our belief and live by it. But then something challenges this belief. We see it may not be the best way to live. We defend our old belief, fearing that if we let go of it our life will fall apart. But then we find we can't hold on. Life has asked us to let go. So we let go. We relinquish the way we have held our life together, the ideas that have guided us. It feels like falling, or dying. We are angry, frightened, resentful. But we discover that by letting go we have opened ourselves to something better. Grace comes to us. . . .

Life takes some of us to this place whether we want to go there or not. Our father beats us. We are raped walking home from school. We are drafted into the army and watch our best buddy blown to pieces in front of us. We are traumatized. We enter into the dark night—anguished that human violence can be this enormous. From this spiritual death, we struggle to find life.

* * *

What happens when violent realities are transubstantiated into spiritual teachings?

You've heard it or said it yourself. A mother loses her son to suicide. In an effort to comfort her you say. "God has a purpose in this. He sends pain to make us strong. You may not feel it now, but you will learn to give thanks for this experience, because through it, God will strengthen your faith."

These words take the grieving mother away from the reality of her lost child. Tragedy is renamed a spiritual trial, designed by God for the mother's edification. God becomes the sender of torture, who injures us then comforts us—a perverse love.

* * *

The mysticism of the cross teaches that violence is God's way of transforming people and communities into greater spiritual well-being. It clouds the realities of human violence in a haze of spiritual glory. . . .

We have to face pain more squarely. When grief and loss come to us, we cannot comfort ourselves by saying God is testing us or offering us a blessing that we don't yet understand. We have to face the pain without this divine sanction.

We have to learn to grieve full out and face forward, without covering over the realities of human cruelty and violence.

The dark night of the soul is this difficult. It is a night without comfort, without shield, without warmth.

* * *

Hadley Basque invited me to lunch. He'd been listening to my sermons and wanted to respond. . . .

"I was a prisoner of war during the Korean War," he began. "I was in the camp for two years. The winters were the hardest part. In North Korea the winters are very cold. It snows. The ground freezes. We had to sleep in drafty barracks on thin boards with one thin blanket. In winter, the guards would make charcoal fires in these barracks. They stood around the fires, warming themselves, in front of us. If you wanted to, you could take your blanket and go sleep by the fire.

"You could always tell the prisoners who had given up hope. They would go sleep by the fire. It was warmer there. You could make it through the night without shaking from the cold. But being warmed that way lowered your resistance. The

445

ones who slept by the fire would get sick, pneumonia or flu, or God knows what. They'd last for a while, but they wouldn't make it. They would die.

"Those of us who survived—we were the ones who never went to sleep by the fire." . . .

I had told the congregation we had to stop sleeping by the fire. My objection to every theology of the cross was that it mystified violence and offered dangerously false comfort. The restless concern, the fire in my bones, was to face violence in the world more squarely. Theology cloaked violence and taught people to endure it. Christianity's denial of violence appalled me.

You couldn't look at Jesus on the cross and see there, as the old liturgy said, "one perfect sacrifice for the sins of the whole world." You couldn't see the face of love. You couldn't see a model for an interior psychological process of dying and rising. You couldn't see pain inflicted by God for the spiritual edification of believers. All these ways of seeing Jesus on the cross ended up sanctifying violence against women and children, valorizing suffering and pain, or denying loss. You couldn't look on the man of sorrows and give thanks to God without ending up a partner in a thousand crimes.

The actual historical event of Jesus' crucifixion was neither sweet nor saving. . . .

The Romans suppressed resistance by terrorizing the local population. Crucifixion was their most brutal form of capital punishment. It took place in full public view, to teach a lesson through terror. . . . Jesus died a violent death, preceded by the torture of flogging, which was meant to score the flesh so deeply that the victim bled to death on the cross. . . .

His absence was acutely felt. Many of his followers dispersed, anguished and afraid. A few women remained to tend the body and see to his burial. They grieved deeply. . . .

⁂ ⁂ ⁂

The days of Lent were drawing us closer to Good Friday. I began preparations for the Good Friday services at the church. The choir was rehearsing to sing Gesualdo's setting of "O Vos Omnes" from the book of Lamentations. . . .

The anthem was a call to witness and to mourn. This is what we needed to do. We needed to face the man of sorrows, without softening the anguish with proverbs of ashes. His suffering was not unique. Is there any sorrow like his sorrow? Yes. Everywhere. Too often.

We designed a simple service for Good Friday, using the old Tenebrae service, the service of darkness. We set a candelabra with seven candles in the sanctuary. It was evening, and the church was lit with candlelight alone.

Passages from the gospels, telling of Jesus' crucifixion were read. The passages told of betrayal, abandonment, humiliation, torture, a cry of utter anguish, and a

446

surrender, finally, to death. Gradually, we extinguished candles. As each scripture passage was read, another light on the candelabra was snuffed. We interspersed readings of the gospel with other texts of terror from more recent crucifixions, public and private: the Holocaust, the death of a child from battering, the rape and murder of women in our community, the killing fields of Cambodia, the death of species from environmental destruction.

We said no prayers of thanks for Jesus' loving sacrifice; offered no praise to God for divine grace and mercy; made no promises to offer ourselves for sacrifice, taking up our cross and following Jesus. The music held sorrow and lamentation. We joined our voices with the anguished prophet Jeremiah:

> O that my head were a spring of water,
> And my eyes a fountain of tears,
> So that I might weep day and night
> For the slain of my poor people! —JEREMIAH 9:1

A darkness without fire or light descended on us. The old tradition keeps one candle burning, hiding it behind the altar, to symbolize hidden hope. Does any spark of kindness, or life, or divine presence, or holy breath, remain in the Golgothas of this world? We extinguished the last candle. We went together into the night. Without words. Away from the fire.

SOURCE: Rita Nakashima Brock and Rebecca Ann Parker, *Proverbs of Ashes: Violence, Redemptive Suffering, and the Search for What Saves Us* (Beacon Press, 2001), 8–9, 42–45, 47–50.

ELEK REZI

"Transylvanian Unitarian Theology at the Dawn of the New Century"

2001

Elek Rezi is professor of Unitarian Systematic Theology at the Protestant Theological Institute of Cluj-Napoca, also known as Kolozsvar, and has served on the Executive Committee of the International Council of Unitarians and Universalists (ICUU). He gave this address at a Theological Symposium sponsored by the ICUU in Prague, Czech Republic. Expressing optimism about the future, he reaffirmed the Transylvanian Unitarians' staunch commitment to liberal Christianity and offered a glimpse into his church's social and theological vision.

—Dan McKanan

Which is then the best way of Unitarianism at the dawn of the new century? On this answer, as on every other topic, Unitarians are divided. . . .

We do not know which is the best way for Unitarianism all over the world, but in Transylvania if we have to choose would prefer to remain on the "Christian side"; moreover on this side we entered into the new century, and on this side we would like to continue further on, of course improving our theology with new ideas (instead of a human-centered religion—a life-centered religion).

* * *

A life-centered orientation is the future of Unitarianism. Instead of dogmas and creeds we should emphasize the value of life, and prove an action-oriented faith. We welcome new knowledge of every kind, combat superstition and ignorance, foster the spread of wisdom and understanding, and seek always to weave a web of human brotherhood the world over, with the threads of love, truth and sincerity. Unitarianism, at its best is, "religion-in-life," an expression of the divine possibilities of life here and now—and further.

The respect of human rights was and will be a very serious Unitarian standpoint. . . .

Religious freedom and tolerance are our great heritage from the past. As you know, at the Diet of Torda (1568) religious freedom and tolerance was proclaimed for the first time in Europe. . . .

Humankind is standing face to face with *environmental crisis*. In our modern time people have tended to think of humanity as distinct from the nature. The traditional Transylvanian Unitarian view, however has been that humans are part of, and in communion with nature. Now more than ever is time for us to teach people to live in harmony with nature. . . .

Unitarianism has always maintained *a commitment to social service work.* . . .

After the main challenges of the new millennium I would like to summarize shortly some major theological principles of Unitarianism in Transylvania. First of all, Unitarianism in Transylvania theologically is entirely *Christian,* as I mentioned before. . . .

We consider that the one *purpose of real religion* is not to prepare people for another life, but to inspire them to live this life as it ought to be lived. . . .

We believe in the existence of *ONE GOD.* This statement is based on Jesus' teaching. . . . Transylvanian Unitarians do not believe in the Trinity of God; God is one, both in essence and person. But above all, God is LOVE. . . .

We believe that *human beings* are the noblest creation of God. God has blessed them with certain talents, virtues, and values. These are:

Faith, which keeps us in relationship with God, and which is the fundamental aspect of peace in our hearts.

Reason, which is the ability to gather knowledge, to think and to form opinions about God, ourselves, our neighbors and the world (universe).

Conscience, which is the spiritual talent which guides our actions, and encourages us for good, but restrains us from evil.

Free will, which is that spiritual gift by which we can make choices in our life, but which requires our responsibility.

Love, which is the most precious of the values that we have. It works in us to three directions: Love to God, Love to human beings and Love to world or universe. We think that the purpose of our life is this: with Love of God and neighbors, with free will and unselfish duty we must create happiness for all creatures on the Earth.

We believe that *Jesus* was a real human being. The Gospels do not teach that Jesus was God. His humanity is shown in his life. We consider that he was one of the best children and prophet of God. His teachings are more important than all ideas and dogmas about his life. . . .

The Bible is held in great reverence as a source of truth and a guide to human beings. To us it is an inspiration, from which we continue to draw ethical and spiritual encouragement. The Bible is accepted not blindly (*sola scriptura*), but under the guidance of reason and conscience.

The Church, according to our understanding, is a purely human institution. . . .

449

We have a great hope of a future existence (life eternal), but we stop short of expressing any definite knowledge concerning the *what* or the *where* of such existence.

SOURCE: Elek Rezi, "Transylvanian Unitarian Theology at the Dawn of the New Century," in Andrew M. Hill, Jill K. McAllister, and Clifford M. Reed, eds., A *Global Conversation: Unitarian/Universalism at the Dawn of the 21st Century* (Prague, Czech Republic: International Council of Unitarians and Universalists, 2002), 59–60, 63–68.

PEARL GREEN MARBANIANG

"Unitarianism in North East India at the Dawn of the Twenty-First Century"

2001

This address was delivered by Pearl Green Marbaniang—a college teacher and church visitor for the Unitarian Union of North East India as well as a member of the Executive Committee of the International Council of Unitarians and Universalists—at the Prague symposium. Marbaniang began by recounting the history of the Unitarian Union, then offered this overview of Unitarian faith. Subsequent sections of the address touched on Jesus, the Bible, human nature, life and death, and the relationship between Unitarianism and traditional Khasi spirituality.

—Dan McKanan

The Liberal Faith as held by the Unitarians is the only form of religion suited to the monotheistic ideas of the Khasi people, and calculated to raise their moral and spiritual conceptions. The object is to disseminate the religion of love and worship of the one true God and the love and service of man among the Khasi people, and to give them the benefit of civilization.

Refreshingly free from excessive emotionalism, elaborate rituals and complex theology, Khasi Unitarianism preaches the ideals similar to the universal aspects of Hinduism enshrined in the Vedanta, the Upanishads and the Gita. After the example of the *Brahmo Samaj*, Unitarianism is non-sectarian and non-idolatrous. . . .

The main doctrines of belief of Unitarians are: the oneness of God, the brotherhood of humankind, the leadership of all saints and sages of all times and salvation by character. It is a movement predominantly characterized by three leading principles. They are: complete mental freedom in religion rather than bondage to creeds or confessions; the unrestricted use of reason in religion rather than reliance upon external authority or past traditions, and generous tolerance of differing religious views and usages rather than on insistence upon uniformity in doctrines, worship or polity.

In short, Freedom, Reason, and Tolerance are the three salient characteristics on which Unitarianism rests and which prop it up as a force to reckon with today.

* * *

Unitarians can therefore be described as a "spiritual and scriptural" since the scriptures of all religions do not deny or reject but rather recognize the ultimate

451

truth of the unity of God. Religion, like science, can be explorative and experimental. This approach was suggested by Jesus of Nazareth two thousand years ago, "You have heard it said by them of old time . . . But I say unto you. . . ." (Matthew 5:21–22). And again, "Why even of yourselves judge you not what is right" (Luke 12:57). We believe humans are mature and intelligent enough to decide for themselves what is good.

*   *   *

God, in his kindness, has bestowed upon man the power to choose. Man took upon himself to create his own conception of God. Christians call him Jesus; Hindus, Bhawan; Muslims, Allah; Sikhs call out Ishwar; the Hebrews, Yahweh; and the Khasis, U Blei. But these different names refer to the same and only God. Therefore, it logically follows that all religions are equal in the eyes of God and that though different religions take different paths, yet they lead to the same almighty God. We cannot accept the claim of superiority, of one religion over another. While Unitarians affirm that each religion has its own great merits, all have their loopholes as well; but, at the same time, the object and goal of all religions is to merge unconsciously to that one and only universal God.

Let it be very clearly stated: Unitarians have no desire to criticize another person's religion, or to ridicule any one's deeply-held beliefs about God, Christ, immortality or other matters. It would be biased, misleading, bad manners and poor Unitarianism.

*   *   *

Nature is not a mere chance-collection of events or a mere jumble of accidents, but an orderly affair. Celestial bodies move regularly in their orbit, seeds grow into trees regularly, the four seasons succeed one another in order. Though we do not see the stars by the day, yet they do exist. Though we do not see the sun on a cloudy day, yet it exists. Even so, though we cannot see God with our physical eyes, yet God does exist.

SOURCE: Pearl Green Marbaniang, "Unitarianism in North East India at the Dawn of the Twenty-First Century," in Andrew M. Hill, Jill K. McAllister, and Clifford M. Reed, eds., *A Global Conversation: Unitarian/Universalism at the Dawn of the 21st Century* (Prague, Czech Republic: International Council of Unitarians and Universalists, 2002), 132–37.

452

"The Language of Faith"

2003

William G. Sinkford (1946–) served as president of the Unitarian Universalist Association from 2001 to 2009. As a teenager, he was an active member of the First Unitarian Church of Cincinnati, Ohio, and national president of Liberal Religious Youth. He pursued a business career until 1992, when he entered Starr King School for the Ministry. After ordination in 1995, he served on the UUA staff until his election as the first African-American president of a traditionally white denomination. After completing his service as denominational president, he was called as senior minister of the First Unitarian Church of Portland, Oregon. Sinkford's presidential tenure was marked by energetic public witness and, as this selection demonstrates, a concern to deepen Unitarian Universalist spirituality. He preached "The Language of Faith" in Fort Worth, Texas, engendering a denominational debate about ways to deepen religious language while honoring the theological diversity of Unitarian Universalism.

—Dan McKanan

I believe that Unitarian Universalism is growing up. It's growing out of a cranky and contentious adolescence into a more confident maturity in which we can not only claim our Good News, the value we have found in this free faith, but also begin to offer that Good News to the world outside these beautiful sanctuary walls. There is a new willingness on our part to come in from the margins. . . .

So I went and reread the Principles and Purposes. I know, I know . . . I'm supposed to know them by heart [ellipsis in original]. But as I reread them, I realized that we have in our Principles an affirmation of our faith that uses *not one single piece of religious language*. Not even one word that would be considered traditionally religious. And that is a wonderment to me; I wonder whether this kind of language can adequately capture who we are and what we're about.

Our Principles and Purposes date to the merger of the Unitarian and Universalist movements in 1961, when the effort to find wording acceptable to all—Unitarian, Universalist, Humanist, and Theist—nearly derailed the whole process.

The current revision of our Principles and Purposes dates back to 1984. It deals with the thorny question of whether or not to mention God or the Judeo-Christian tradition by leaving them out of the principles entirely, but including them in the section on the *sources* from which our living tradition draws. It was here that we placed reference to "Jewish and Christian teachings, which call us to respond to God's love by loving our neighbors as ourselves," as well as "Humanist teachings, which counsel us to heed the guidance of reason and the results of science, and warn against idolatries of the mind and spirit." And even that compromise went too far for those in our movement who feared "creeping creedalism," and not far enough for those who would have preferred more explicitly religious language.

Given the differences of opinion that needed to be bridged in one document, it's really not surprising that the wording adopted completely avoided anything that smacked of traditional religious language. The Principles and Purposes have become an integral part of our denominational life. Many of our congregations print them on their orders of service. They open our hymnal. They hang in our vestibules. Many of us carry them in our wallets.

They serve us well as a covenant, holding out a vision of a more just world to which we all aspire despite our differences, and articulating our promise to walk together toward making that vision a reality, whatever our theology. They frame a broad ethic, but not a theology. They contain no hint of the holy.

*   *   *

Our resistance to religious language gets reflected, I think, in the struggle that so many of us have in trying to find ways to say who we are, to define Unitarian Universalism. I always encourage people to work on their "elevator speech." Imagine you're on the sixth floor and you're going to the lobby and somebody asks you, "What's a Unitarian Universalist?" What do you say? You've got about forty-five seconds. Here's my current answer: "The Unitarian side of our family tree tells us that there is only one God, one Spirit of Life, one Power of Love. The Universalist side tells us that God is a loving God, condemning none of us, and valuing the spark of divinity that is in every human being. So Unitarian Universalism: one God, no one left behind."

As with every elevator speech, mine is a work in process. It says where I am right now; and it doesn't say anything at all about where you are.

Many Unitarian Universalists, I know, are bothered by the use of the word *God.* I understand that. When I came to Unitarian Universalism I was an ardent, some might even say a rabid, Humanist. If you had told me as a teenager that at age fifty-six I would be an ordained minister, using religious language in this pulpit, and have a prayer life that centered on thankfulness and gratefulness to God, I would have laughed out loud. The Humanist tradition was mine for a long time.

But we don't have this all permanently figured out at any discrete moment in time. In my case, it was direct experience of something I hadn't counted on—the kind of "direct experience of transcending mystery and wonder," which we also affirm as a source of our faith tradition—that changed my mind. It happened in the

454

midst of a crisis. My son Billy, then fifteen years old, had overdosed on drugs, and it was unclear whether he would live. As I sat with him in the hospital, I found myself praying. First the selfish prayers for forgiveness . . . for the time not made, for the too many trips, for the many things unsaid, and sadly, for a few things said that should never have passed my lips [ellipsis in original]. But as the night darkened, I finally found the pure prayer. The prayer that asked only that my son would live. And late in the evening, I felt the hands of a loving universe reaching out—the hands of God, the Spirit of Life. The name was unimportant. I knew that those hands would be there to hold me whatever the morning brought. And I knew, though I cannot tell you how, that those hands were holding my son as well. I knew that I did not have to walk that path alone, that there is a love that has never broken faith with us and never will.

My son survived. But the experience stayed with me. That is my experience, and my vocabulary for that experience. "Religious language" doesn't have to mean "God talk." I'm not suggesting that Unitarian Universalism return to traditional Christian language. But I do feel that we need some language that would allow us to capture the possibility of reverence, to name the holy, to talk about human agency in theological terms—the ability of humans to shape and frame our world guided by what we find to be of ultimate importance.

* * *

My growing belief is that, as a religious community and as individuals, we may be secure enough, mature enough to find a language of reverence, a language that can acknowledge the presence of the holy in our lives.

Perhaps we are ready. Perhaps this faith we love is ready to stop calling itself a movement, and call itself a religion.

Religion: to bind up that which has been sundered. To make connections in a world that would isolate us. To engage in the real journey toward wholeness.

Who knows? Perhaps we're ready.

So may it be.

Amen.

SOURCE: William G. Sinkford, "The Language of Faith," in Dean Grodzins, ed., A *Language of Reverence* (Chicago: Meadville Lombard Press, 2004), 1–5, 7.

"Images for Our Lives"

2003

Laurel Hallman was ordained in 1981 in the wake of the passage of the 1977
Women and Religion resolution, as the number of women in Unitarian Uni-
versalist ministry began to increase substantially. Her first call in UU minis-
try was to serve the Unitarian Universalist Church of Bloomington, Indiana,
where she was the minister from 1981 to 1987. In 1987, Hallman became one
of the first women senior ministers of a large church when she was called to
the First Unitarian Church of Dallas, Texas. In the course of her twenty-one-
year ministry in Dallas, Hallman served in a variety of denominational lead-
ership positions, from membership on the Ministerial Fellowship Committee
to the Unitarian Universalist Ministers Association's Whose Are We project.
In the election for the UUA presidency in 2009, Hallman became the fourth
woman candidate since 1985 to run for the senior leadership position and
lose. In her 2003 Berry Street essay, "Images for Our Lives," Hallman echoes
the call of former UUA President William Sinkford to embrace "a language
of reverence" and to encourage a mature Unitarian Universalist spirituality.

— Natalie Malter

I want to talk about imagination. About *religious* imagination, to be more specific. I
want to say that we are in a crisis of language, (and I believe that we are), because we
have forgotten what religious imagination is and does. The purpose of my essay
today will be to remind us of the importance of religious imagination in all our varied ministries. . . .

But first, let me go back to 1971.

I was 28 years old, home with my then one-year-old toddler. (I had been a
teacher and a curriculum consultant in my short career in education prior to that.)
I was asked by Roy Phillips, who was the new Minister at Unity Church-Unitarian
in St. Paul, Minnesota, where I was a member, to join a committee he was forming
to rewrite the Sunday School curriculum. He was gathering a group of members,
mostly teachers, to talk about what was needed. Mary Anderson, who is here today
as my guest, was a member of that group of seven. She is Lebanese, was raised a
Muslim, is a devoted UU and helped us broaden our perspective significantly in
those days, which now seem so long ago. Roy said that there was a felt need being
expressed in the congregation for a religious education that centered on traditional

religious themes—an education that would help the children to know themselves as religious people. Would I help?

Needing a project with some challenge in those days, I said, "Yes." It is to a large degree why I stand before you today.

Because you can ask a person what they believe, and they may tell you something halfway interesting. But if you ask them what should be taught to their children, you quickly get down to basics. We were about the gritty and difficult duty of deciding what would be taught our children, and how and why.

The curriculum was called *Images for Our Lives.*

That work, which took up four years of our lives, was long ago and far away. But I bring it up because I learned two important points that apply to what I want to say today.

The first was our decision always to look for the "religious existential dimension" of the story we were teaching, whether the story was from the Judeo-Christian tradition (as we called it in those days), or from our own Unitarian Universalist Tradition, or from Other World Religions. (We gave each of those categories 12 weeks a year.)

* * *

I'm not sure where that phrase came from. It wasn't tied to Existentialism *per se.* Roy says he used the dictionary definition at first: "grounded in existence or the experience of existence." But after much discussion we decided that the "Religious Existential Dimension" of each story was to be the center of our work. We would try to find the part of each story which would allow the children to "take the story as an image of their own experience of life."

* * *

That is why we called it "Images for our Lives." Every story we presented, whether Noah or Emerson or Kisogatami, was considered in its Religious Existential Dimension. As an image of existence, with imagination, with the recall of an image with which our children could associate their life experiences.

* * *

I recently spoke to our Adult Sunday School Class in Dallas on the topic "Why I am not a Theist." They packed the room to hear what I had to say, because of course they thought I was. Why did they think I was a Theist? Because I use the word God. Because I pray in the midst of the worship service. I was embarrassed a bit myself, to find that I had failed to make the distinction that the use of metaphors and poetry and scripture has to do with religious imagination, and not with one theological category or another. We had a lively and productive discussion that day, as I spoke, as I am today, about religious language, and how it communicates the depths of experience, and that it isn't always what it seems.

* * *

So if words don't stand still, if they are subject, over time to misplaced concreteness. If they don't necessarily represent one theology or another. If they are inadequate, even when they serve political and psychological purposes, even when they give us some meaning and purpose—. If words need to point to the depths of lived experience, (the religious existential dimension of life). If we live more deeply than we can think. If we are currently in a crisis of language (which I believe we are). If we are truly to minister in the fields of human need, what will save us from ourselves?

My answer is Poetry. . . .

By poetry I mean words and phrases, even whole narrative stories that point beyond themselves to the depth of human experience. I believe that poetry is scripture. I believe that scripture is poetry. I believe that poetry is the way deep truth is transmitted person to person and generation to generation. I believe that when Emily Dickinson said, "Tell the truth/but tell it slant" she was speaking of metaphorical truth, the poetic truth that nourishes the heart, and opens the mind, and communicates to the depths. By poetry I mean the products of the religious imagination.

First, let me say that I am keenly aware that there are many products of the imagination that are not centered in words. So if poetry seems an extraordinarily limited focus for all the possibilities of metaphorical truth that can communicate the depth—I will admit it is. But again, I want to remember where I am, and who we are, and what we do week after week after week. I know there are many different ministries represented here—and I hope you'll bear with me if I narrow my scope and talk about words and their uses between and among us, acknowledging that the music and art and even the silences of the soul are more profound than I could speak today. . . .

Consider these few lines as representative of Philip Booth's wonderful poem, *First Lesson*, about teaching his daughter to swim:

> Lie back, daughter, let your head
> be tipped back in the cup of my hand.
> . . . lie back, and the sea will hold you.

The entire poem has not one traditional religious word in it, as you will see if you read it whole. And yet it associates to deep realities beyond itself and across generations of human experience.

For a time I thought this would be enough. There are certainly enough images and stories out there to take us to the heights and depths of human experience without having to bother with traditional religious language. . . . Surely there is enough spoken and written in the literature of humankind to be able to speak to human experience without having to evoke a God, or think about Prayer, or use any of the words that have specifically religious associative meanings—those meanings that are so encumbered as to be almost impossible to use. Or so it seemed to me at the time.

First Lesson should be enough.

But then I heard a simple explanation about a Russian Orthodox Icon. The Priest explained that the value given the icon was in its ability to teach the people who sat with it. "They didn't analyze it. It taught them," he said. ("Not very American," he added.) . . . That simple explanation changed how I thought about the traditional words of Western religion. I couldn't drop them. They had evoked too much for too many people, over too long a time, and I needed to stay connected to the human struggles, the human understandings they represented, if only to inform my own. . . .

Who was I, to drop these words which had meant so much to our very own spiritual ancestors, as well as generations of human seekers, even if the associations might be complex. And perhaps the word "God" wasn't as dead as I had thought.

* * *

What we need to do then, is to break open these concretized words, to juxtapose them with words that create cognitive dissonance. For it is in the spaces between the juxtaposition that new associations are created.

The first inkling I had of that was when we began to use the pronoun "She"— "God/She." People laughed nervously, when they heard those words for the first time. You might not have been there—but it is true. People laughed. It was so strange. So odd.

The idea that metaphors which have suffered "misplaced concreteness" can be brought to life by simply juxtaposing them in surprising ways, is almost too simple. . . .

Remember, we're talking about the religious existential dimension of life, not definitions. We're talking about the products of the imagination here. We're pointing, not positing.

* * *

I was fortunate that when I went to Dallas that prayer was already part of the service. Slowly, I introduced relational words. Slowly I directed the prayer to "God of many names, and mystery beyond all our naming . . ." [ellipsis in original]. Slowly I began to ask for help and comfort and wisdom and strength. Slowly I began to name individuals who needed our prayer, and with whom we were celebrating. I gave thanks for new babies, and grieved over lost loved ones—naming Fathers and Mothers, and Sisters and Brothers who had died. I prayed our inadequacy to face the pain of our days.

459

This is not a rational posit to a responding deity. It is not a posture of groveling. It is an expression of our yearning, our grief, our gratitude. It has become an expression of our congregation as a whole. . . .

I was lucky enough to inherit from Bob Raible's ministry in the Dallas church, the closing to the prayer, which I commend to you. . . . People have said that they wept when they first heard the words:

We pray in the names of all those, known and unknown, present and absent, remembered and forgotten. We pray in the names of all the helpers of humankind.

This is language that opens up rather than shutting off.

This is language that points beyond rather than positing definitions.

This is language that connects us with the yearning of humankind, of all sorts and kinds, rather than setting us apart as literal in our rejection, closed in our disdain, set apart in our determination to reject language that will not imagine anything beyond what we see and know.

✳ ✳ ✳

We not only need to invite poets into the rooms of our hearts, but we need to invite our spiritual ancestors as well. They are raising a hand or two, wanting to be heard. If we say, "We'll listen but don't use any words that have become solidified in the meantime, no matter how fulsome they were for you"—we will have cut ourselves off, not only from our spiritual DNA, but from one part of the conversation that we desperately need to have.

Our President has called us to a language of reverence. We need a language of reverence. We need a language of forgiveness. We need a language of reconciliation. A language of hope. A language that gives voice to despair. To name a few. That language for centuries, and in countless cultures has been metaphorical, it has pointed beyond itself to something much deeper than it could name. It is our turn to keep such language alive, hold it to our hearts, and speak to the depths of those who so desperately need our good word.

SOURCE: Laurel Hallman, "Images for Our Lives," Berry Street Essay, delivered during Ministers' Days at the UU General Assembly, June 26, 2003, www.uuma.org/page/berrystreetessays

"Humanist Manifesto III: Humanism and Its Aspirations"

2003

The American Humanist Association issued this third version of the Human-
ist Manifesto in 2003, publicizing the fact that twenty-two Nobel laureates
(all in the physical sciences) had signed it. Unitarian Universalists were less
well represented among the signatories than Unitarians had been for the
original manifesto, with just nine of seventy-one "notable signers" indicating
a Unitarian Universalist affiliation. The text was deliberately shorter than its
predecessors, placing less emphasis on socioeconomic policies and more on
ecological interdependence. The seven core aspirations might be compared
with the seven Principles of the Unitarian Universalist Association.

—Dan McKanan

Humanism is a progressive philosophy of life that, without supernaturalism, affirms our ability and responsibility to lead ethical lives of personal fulfillment that aspire to the greater good of humanity.

The lifestance of Humanism—guided by reason, inspired by compassion, and informed by experience—encourages us to live life well and fully. It evolved through the ages and continues to develop through the efforts of thoughtful people who recognize that values and ideals, however carefully wrought, are subject to change as our knowledge and understandings advance.

This document is part of an ongoing effort to manifest in clear and positive terms the conceptual boundaries of Humanism, not what we must believe but a consensus of what we do believe. It is in this sense that we affirm the following:

Knowledge of the world is derived by observation, experimentation, and rational analysis. Humanists find that science is the best method for determining this knowledge as well as for solving problems and developing beneficial technologies. We also recognize the value of new departures in thought, the arts, and inner experience—each subject to analysis by critical intelligence.

Humans are an integral part of nature, the result of unguided evolutionary change. Humanists recognize nature as self-existing. We accept our life as all and enough, distinguishing things as they are from things as we might wish or imagine them to be. We welcome the challenges of the future, and are drawn to and undaunted by the yet to be known.

Ethical values are derived from human need and interest as tested by experience. Humanists ground values in human welfare shaped by human circumstances, interests, and concerns and extended to the global ecosystem and beyond. We are committed to treating each person as having inherent worth and dignity, and to making informed choices in a context of freedom consonant with responsibility.

Life's fulfillment emerges from individual participation in the service of humane ideals. We aim for our fullest possible development and animate our lives with a deep sense of purpose, finding wonder and awe in the joys and beauties of human existence, its challenges and tragedies, and even in the inevitability and finality of death. Humanists rely on the rich heritage of human culture and the life-stance of Humanism to provide comfort in times of want and encouragement in times of plenty.

Humans are social by nature and find meaning in relationships. Humanists long for and strive toward a world of mutual care and concern, free of cruelty and its consequences, where differences are resolved cooperatively without resorting to violence. The joining of individuality with interdependence enriches our lives, encourages us to enrich the lives of others, and inspires hope of attaining peace, justice, and opportunity for all.

Working to benefit society maximizes individual happiness. Progressive cultures have worked to free humanity from the brutalities of mere survival and to reduce suffering, improve society, and develop global community. We seek to minimize the inequities of circumstance and ability, and we support a just distribution of nature's resources and the fruits of human effort so that as many as possible can enjoy a good life.

Humanists are concerned for the well being of all, are committed to diversity, and respect those of differing yet humane views. We work to uphold the equal enjoyment of human rights and civil liberties in an open, secular society and maintain it is a civic duty to participate in the democratic process and a planetary duty to protect nature's integrity, diversity, and beauty in a secure, sustainable manner.

Thus engaged in the flow of life, we aspire to this vision with the informed conviction that humanity has the ability to progress toward its highest ideals. The responsibility for our lives and the kind of world in which we live is ours and ours alone.

SOURCE: "Humanism and Its Aspirations: Humanist Manifesto III, a successor to the Humanist Manifesto of 1933," www.americanhumanist.org/humanism/humanist_manifesto_iii

ROSEMARY BRAY McNATT

"The Problem of Theology in the Work of Anti-Racism: A Meditation"

2003

Rosemary Bray McNatt served as the senior minister of the Fourth Universalist Society of New York for thirteen years prior to becoming the first black woman president of Starr King School for the Ministry in 2014. In addition to her work as a congregational minister and seminary president, McNatt has served on the UUA Board of Trustees, the Committee of Urban Concerns and Ministry, and the UUA Panel on Theological Education, while also teaching UU history and polity courses at Union Theological Seminary and Yale Divinity School. Before entering the Unitarian Universalist ministry, McNatt had a successful career as an editor and author, editing for a variety of prominent publications including the New York Times Book Review. *She published her memoir,* Unafraid of the Dark, *in 1999. This essay was published as a chapter in* Soul Work: Anti-racist Theologies in Dialogue. *In her writing, McNatt shares her powerful conversation with Coretta Scott King and reflects insightfully on the promise and failures of the UUA to become a racially integrated religious movement.*

—Natalie Malter

Several years ago, in the middle of my seminary education, my literary agent called with an intriguing proposition. "Would I be willing to be considered as co-writer of Coretta Scott King's autobiography?" she wanted to know. I was one of several people being considered but the book's prospective editor was said to be partial to me. I was more than willing to talk about it, and a meeting between Mrs. King and myself was arranged at the editor's office.

I didn't make the final cut of writers under consideration, but that is not why I tell this story. During an hour of wide-ranging conversation, I mentioned to Mrs. King that I was in seminary to become a Unitarian Universalist minister. What frankly surprised me was the look she gave me, one of respect and delight.

"Oh, I went to Unitarian churches for years, even before I met Martin," she told me, explaining that she had been, since college, a member of the Women's International League for Peace and Freedom, which was popular among Unitarian Universalists. "And Martin and I went to Unitarian churches when we were in Boston."

463

What surprised and saddened me most was what she said next, and though I am paraphrasing, the gist of it was this: "We gave a lot of thought to becoming Unitarian at one time, but Martin and I realized we could never build a mass movement of black people if we were Unitarian."

It was a statement that pierced my heart and troubled my mind, both then and now. I considered what this religious movement would be like if Dr. King had chosen differently, had decided to cast his lot with our faith instead of returning to his roots as an African American Christian. And what troubled me most was my realization that our liberal religious movement would have utterly neutralized the greatest American theologian of the twentieth century. Certainly, his race would have been the primary barrier. In a religious movement engaged until the 1970s in the active discouragement of people of color wishing to join its ministerial ranks, Dr. King might have found his personal struggles to serve Unitarian Universalism at least as daunting as the Montgomery Bus Boycott.

But even if race had disappeared as an issue, Dr. King might have found the barrier of theology insurmountable. Though from the very start of his theological training he revealed a decided bent toward liberal religion, by the time his faith had been tried by the Civil Rights movement Dr. King had said no to the sunny optimism of liberal faith, an optimism frankly untested in the heat of the battle for liberty and dignity for African Americans.

*   *   *

Might Martin Luther King have one day joined a list of great Unitarian Universalists? Might his image have ended up on a tee shirt or banner at General Assembly? Would he one day have been enshrined in a religious education module? Perhaps no one with the power of Martin Luther King would have lived life in complete obscurity. But for him to have answered the call to a liberal religious faith, a faith that clearly resonated with him since his earliest days of graduate studies, would have meant a fatal separation from the sources of his power: a faith in a suffering God who stood with suffering people despite their mistakes and failures, and covenantal love between himself and oppressed African Americans, the people who grounded his passion for justice but did not restrict it solely to themselves.

The notion of the self-perfectibility of human beings was an inadequate theology in the face of the sustained hatred and embodied evil of the segregationist South. Yet Dr. King retained his faith in the great potential for goodness in humanity, his faith in the possibilities of human nature that Unitarians and Universalists would lift up as a corollary to our free faith. But it was reason and experience that revealed as much to Dr. King about humanity as about divinity, and what he thought and learned taught him the importance of both.

*   *   *

Do we really understand that in pursuit of this goal of an anti-racist association, we are risking more than we realize? Do we realize that we are risking being informed by varieties of religious experience not entertained in our churches for decades, if ever? Are we prepared to know what it is that informs the survival strategies used by people often on the margins? Are we prepared to accept that even among people of color at comfortable economic levels—as opposed to those poor, uneducated people who don't know any better than to praise God—there may be not only a theological but a cultural understanding of the divine that travels with them into our sanctuaries?

Sometimes a person's experience is informed by structural oppression. Sometimes, it's just life itself that has weighed on them. But there are many people who have found help and hope and strength from a source greater than themselves in order to endure what has often seemed unendurable. Do we risk their sharing with us how they have survived? What if they tell us, "God brought me through"? Do we dare to make room for them to share and to celebrate, to witness to what they have seen and felt and intimately know?

What if our liberal religious brother Dr. King had come to one of our congregations on that dark night during the movement after being bombarded with threats on his life and the lives of his family? What if he had said, not to God, but to one of us, that he couldn't go on anymore, that he was afraid? What if he had said, as he did say to God, "I am here taking a stand for what I believe is right. But now I am afraid. The people are looking to me for leadership, and if I stand before them without strength and courage, they too will falter. I am at the end of my powers. I have nothing left. I've come to the point where I can't face it alone"?

Might members of our congregations have prayed for him, or with him? Or would he have been consoled with words like these from [Charles Francis] Potter:

> If man habitually leans upon God when the going is hard, and expects God's help when he meets a difficulty, he loses the strength of character which is gained by the extra effort in emergencies. . . . And when, at a time of crisis, man does pray and depend on God, and help does come, does that prove that the help came from God? Too often, man thanks God for what man has done. [ellipsis in original]

In the end, Dr. King chose to forego the liberal religious enterprise and lean on the God who promised never to leave or to forsake him, even in death. Yet many of us who believe in the work have not left this movement. Many of us, in the free and responsible search for truth and meaning, have found our way back to belief in God after a long sojourn elsewhere. Many of us who grew up in the black church, and many others who can say that the black church grew up in them, have followed our varied paths to the doors of liberal faith. Are we here to provide interior decoration for our congregations, here to do spiritual domestic work on behalf of those wounded by God, by racism, by white privilege, or by the circumstances of their own lives? Can we who are called to serve as religious leaders discern when we are doing ministry and when we are doing minstrelsy? Might our own wounds stand in the way of clarity? Will there ever be a time when we can authentically be who we are, believe what we believe, speak our own truth, sing our own song—and be with one another?

The work of becoming an anti-racist religious movement is not an adventure in which I am willing to participate under false pretenses. I want it all: for us to anti-racist, religious, and a movement. I respect that the theological stance of others will differ from my own. But I am as hungry to be freed from the narrowness of our religious assumptions as I am to be released from the wary dance we engage in around race, class, and gender. I am as eager to see my congregants—and my ministerial colleagues—emerge from their massive blindness to the last thirty years of theology as I am to see what we might do in a religious community in which praxis is a given. I nurse a secret wish that one Sunday, my Pentecostal mother might wander into a Unitarian Universalist congregation and stay for services even if I'm not in the pulpit. Above all, I am praying for the transformation of the religious movement I love so much—and hoping for just one day when I won't have to explain why I might choose to pray.

SOURCE: Rosemary Bray McNatt, "The Problem of Theology in the Work of Anti-racism: A Meditation," in *Soul Work: Anti-racist Theologies in Dialogue*, ed. Marjorie Bowens-Wheatley and Nancy Palmer Jones (Boston: Skinner House, 2003), 27–33.

Goodridge et al. v. Massachusetts Department of Public Health

2004

In April 2001 seven lesbian and gay couples, led by Unitarian Universalists Hillary and Julie Goodridge, filed a case against the Massachusetts Department of Public Health for denying them access to marriage licenses. In the initial verdict issued on May 7, 2002, the Superior Court of Massachusetts rejected the plaintiffs' charge of discrimination, and subsequently the Goodridges and their fellow plaintiffs appealed the verdict to the Massachusetts Supreme Judicial Court. In a 4–3 decision announced on November 18, 2003, the Massachusetts Supreme Judicial Court found the restriction of marriage to couples of different genders violated the equality and liberty provisions of the Constitution of the Commonwealth of Massachusetts. The decision was upheld in the opinions issued by the justices of the Massachusetts Supreme Judicial Court on February 4, 2004, making Massachusetts the first state in the United States of America to legalize same-gender marriage. In the following years, Unitarian Universalists helped advance the cause of marriage equality throughout the United States, and in 2014 when Oregon legalized same-gender marriage, one of the plaintiff couples in the case, Lisa Chickadonz and Christine Tanner, were Unitarian Universalists and longtime members of the First Unitarian Church of Portland.

—Natalie Malter

Marriage is a vital social institution. The exclusive commitment of two individuals to each other nurtures love and mutual support; it brings stability to our society. For those who choose to marry, and for their children, marriage provides an abundance of legal, financial, and social benefits. In return it imposes weighty legal, financial, and social obligations. The question before us is whether, consistent with the Massachusetts Constitution, the Commonwealth may deny the protections, benefits, and obligations conferred by civil marriage to two individuals of the same sex who wish to marry. We conclude that it may not. The Massachusetts Constitution affirms the dignity and equality of all individuals. It forbids the creation of second-class citizens. In reaching our conclusion we have given full deference to the arguments made by the Commonwealth. But it has failed to identify any constitutionally adequate reason for denying civil marriage to same-sex couples.

We are mindful that our decision marks a change in the history of our marriage law. Many people hold deep-seated religious, moral, and ethical convictions that marriage should be limited to the union of one man and one woman, and that homosexual conduct is immoral. Many hold equally strong religious, moral, and ethical convictions that same-sex couples are entitled to be married, and that homosexual persons should be treated no differently than their heterosexual neighbors. Neither view answers the question before us. Our concern is with the Massachusetts Constitution as a charter of governance for every person properly within its reach. . . .

The Massachusetts Constitution is, if anything, more protective of individual liberty and equality than the Federal Constitution; it may demand broader protection for fundamental rights; and it is less tolerant of government intrusion into the protected spheres of private life.

Barred access to the protections, benefits, and obligations of civil marriage, a person who enters into an intimate, exclusive union with another of the same sex is arbitrarily deprived of membership in one of our community's most rewarding and cherished institutions. That exclusion is incompatible with the constitutional principles of respect for individual autonomy and equality under law.

The plaintiffs are fourteen individuals from five Massachusetts counties. As of April 11, 2001, the date they filed their complaint, the plaintiffs Gloria Bailey, sixty years old, and Linda Davies, fifty-five years old, had been in a committed relationship for thirty years; the plaintiffs Maureen Brodoff, forty-nine years old, and Ellen Wade, fifty-two years old, had been in a committed relationship for twenty years and lived with their twelve year old daughter; the plaintiffs Hillary Goodridge, forty-four years old, and Julie Goodridge, forty-three years old, had been in a committed relationship for thirteen years and lived with their five year old daughter. . . .

The plaintiffs include business executives, lawyers, an investment banker, educators, therapists, and a computer engineer. Many are active in church, community, and school groups. They have employed such legal means as are available to them—for example, joint adoption, powers of attorney, and joint ownership of real property—to secure aspects of their relationships. Each plaintiff attests a desire to marry his or her partner in order to affirm publicly their commitment to each other and to secure the legal protections and benefits afforded to married couples and their children.

* * *

The larger question is whether, as the department claims, government action that bars same-sex couples from civil marriage constitutes a legitimate exercise of the State's authority to regulate conduct, or whether, as the plaintiffs claim, this categorical marriage exclusion violates the Massachusetts Constitution. We have recognized the long-standing statutory understanding, derived from the common law, that "marriage" means the lawful union of a woman and a man. But that history cannot and does not foreclose the constitutional question. The plaintiffs' claim that the marriage restriction violates the Massachusetts Constitution can be analyzed in two ways. Does it offend the Constitution's guarantees of equality before the law? Or do the liberty and due process provisions of the Massachusetts Constitution secure the plaintiffs' right to marry their chosen partner?

*　*　*

For decades, indeed centuries, in much of this country (including Massachusetts) no lawful marriage was possible between white and black Americans. That long history availed not when the Supreme Court of California held in 1948 that a legislative prohibition against interracial marriage violated the due process and equality guarantees of the Fourteenth Amendment, *Perez v. Sharp*, 32 Cal.2d 711, 728 (1948), or when, nineteen years later, the United States Supreme Court also held that a statutory bar to interracial marriage violated the Fourteenth Amendment, *Loving v. Virginia*, 388 U.S. 1 (1967). As both *Perez* and *Loving* make clear, the right to marry means little if it does not include the right to marry the person of one's choice, subject to appropriate government restrictions in the interests of public health, safety, and welfare. . . . In this case, as in *Perez* and *Loving*, a statute deprives individuals of access to an institution of fundamental legal, personal, and social significance—the institution of marriage—because of a single trait: skin color in *Perez* and *Loving*, sexual orientation here. As it did in *Perez* and *Loving*, history must yield to a more fully developed understanding of the invidious quality of the discrimination.

*　*　*

The department has had more than ample opportunity to articulate a constitutionally adequate justification for limiting civil marriage to opposite-sex unions. It has failed to do so. The department has offered purported justifications for the civil marriage restriction that are starkly at odds with the comprehensive network of vigorous, gender-neutral laws promoting stable families and the best interests of children. It has failed to identify any relevant characteristic that would justify shutting the door to civil marriage to a person who wishes to marry someone of the same sex.

The marriage ban works a deep and scarring hardship on a very real segment of the community for no rational reason. The absence of any reasonable relationship between, on the one hand, an absolute disqualification of same-sex couples who wish to enter into civil marriage and, on the other, protection of public health, safety, or general welfare, suggests that the marriage restriction is rooted in persistent prejudices against persons who are (or who are believed to be) homosexual. . . . Limiting the protections, benefits, and obligations of civil marriage to opposite-sex couples violates the basic premises of individual liberty and equality under law protected by the Massachusetts Constitution.

SOURCE: *Goodridge et al. v. Department of Public Health*, 798 N.E.2d 941 (Mass. 2003), available online at masscases.com/cases/sjc/440/440mass309.html

JASON SHELTON

"Standing on the Side of Love"

2004

Jason Shelton (1972–) is one of the leading Unitarian Universalist hymn-writers and composers active in the twenty-first century. He serves as associate minister for music at the First Unitarian Universalist Church in Nashville, Tennessee, and was part of the task force that edited Singing the Journey: A Supplement to Singing the Living Tradition. *He was inspired to write "Standing on the Side of Love" by a conversation in which he heard UUA president Bill Sinkford tell a reporter that Unitarian Universalists "stand on the side of love" when it comes to marriage. Almost immediately, the hymn began to be used as a rallying cry by Unitarian Universalists working for marriage equality for lesbian, gay, bisexual, transgender, and queer persons. In the wake of the 2008 mass shooting at Tennessee Valley Unitarian Universalist Church in Knoxville, Tennessee, the UUA launched a formal advocacy campaign that used the "standing on the side of love" slogan to promote "the goal of harnessing love's power to challenge exclusion, oppression, and violence based on sexual orientation, gender identity, immigration status, race, religion, or any other identity." The campaign's clear message and bright yellow T-shirts made Unitarian Universalists more visible in work for marriage equality, immigrant rights, and other social justice causes. Some pointed out, however, that "Standing on the Side of Love" marginalizes persons whose disabilities prevent them from physical standing; in response, Shelton began a public process to change the title of his hymn.*

— Dan McKanan

The promise of the Spirit:
Faith, hope and love abide.
And so every soul is blessed and made whole;
The truth in our hearts is our guide.

Chorus:
We are standing on the side of love, [New version: We are answering the call of
   love,]
Hands joined together as hearts beat as one.
Emboldened by faith
we dare to proclaim
We are standing on the side of love. [We are answering the call of love.]

Sometimes we build a barrier
to keep love tightly bound.
Corrupted by fear,
unwilling to hear,
Denying the beauty we've found.

Chorus

A bright new day is dawning
when love will not divide.
Reflections of grace
in every embrace,
Fulfilling the vision divine.

Chorus

We are standing on the side of love. [We are answering the call of love.]

SOURCE: Jason Shelton, "Standing on the Side of Love," in *Singing the Journey: A Supplement to Singing the Living Tradition* (Boston: Unitarian Universalist Association, 2005), #1014. Copyright Yelton Rhodes Music, yrmusic.org

SHARON D. WELCH

After Empire

2004

Sharon D. Welch (1952–) began her teaching career at Harvard Divinity School, where Unitarian Universalists helped her realize that she, too, was a Unitarian Universalist. She taught at the University of Missouri from 1991 to 2007, where she chaired the Department of Religious Studies, and was appointed provost of Meadville Lombard Theological School in 2007. In her extensive writing on theological ethics, she has continued religious liberalism's constructive debate with Reinhold Niebuhr's Christian realism and, more recently, built bridges connecting religious humanism to feminist, liberationist, and deconstructionist theologies. She has also challenged Unitarian Universalists to move beyond the pacifist–just war debate by focusing on the common work of peacekeeping, peacemaking, and peacebuilding. In this passage, she explains how it is possible to acknowledge the amorality of religion while remaining passionately committed to the work of justice. Further Reading: Sharon D. Welch, A Feminist Ethic of Risk, *rev. ed. (Minneapolis: Fortress Press, 1990); Sharon D. Welch,* Real Peace, Real Security: The Challenges of Global Citizenship *(Minneapolis: Fortress Press, 2008).*

—Dan McKanan

To take seriously the religiously sanctioned exercise of violence leads us to question the relationship between religion and ethics and to reexamine our understanding of the divine, or of spirit, itself.

* * *

I once claimed that the cause of justice was better served if, rather than focus on God as the source of "right relations," we saw divinity as being "right relations," thus construing divinity as a quality of relations, an adverb rather than a noun. At that time I limited divinity to "right" relations, a move similar to that of other liberal and liberation theologians who describe God as the force of creativity and justice. Now I see creativity and intense relatedness as themselves amoral, and the task of giving them moral expression as socially and culturally mediated.

In describing what this means for a positive although intrinsically ambiguous appreciation of spirituality, I emphasize an ironic spirituality that holds the paradox of being founded by that which is amoral, contingent, and malleable. I speak for those who find the Barthian and Derridean escape untenable, whether expressed as

472

the idea that your encounter with the divine is religious and a projection, while we have received a revelation that has shattered even the pretensions of our Protestant religion and natural theology (Barth), or that your vision of justice is an idolatrous concrete messianism, while ours, in its radical openness and its "universal longing and restlessness," is free from the projections that create religious violence, coercion and fanaticism (Derrida).

*　*　*

It is important to realize that not one of these variants of religious experience (*ours included*), not one of these construals of the divine or divinities or spiritualities inevitably and reliably leads to ethical action. The construal of divinity as wholly other, as the excess of possibility, the not-yet that destabilizes all concrete messianism, can be found in prophetic denunciations of social injustice as well as in the cultured despair of the middle and upper classes and our withdrawal from political engagement. There is nothing that inevitably and irrevocably grounds our desire for justice. Justice, in all its forms, is our work, our creation, our unfinished task. . . .

I am not saying the religious is *immoral*. . . . Rather, the language of freedom and openness to others, the language of love and justice, coheres with the ecstasy and claim of the religious as easily as but *no more easily than* the language of exclusion and self-righteousness.

Another form of construing the sacred, found in feminist theology, process theology, and some African and African American theologies, is also instructive. Here the sacred is perceived as creativity itself. Let us think, though, about creativity. Creativity itself is amoral, as easily expressed in the operations of global capitalism, in the production of music videos and Web sites, and in the design and use of deadly weapons as it is in works of justice. Furthermore, creativity is fed by powerful connections with actually available human and natural resources. The work of scientists in Los Alamos constructing the first atomic weapons, for example, was a vivid manifestation of the power of human connection and creativity. . . . It may well be that the reason pacifist and prophetic movements are relatively weak in the face of military expansion and global capitalism is that *we are less creative* than they, because we, from our vantage point in the ideal, are less connected than they to the human and natural resources of the world around us. If we ground our prophetic social critique in the *tout autre*, in an ideal outside, we might then lack the creativity that comes from working with the resources that are here now. Injustice flourishes because those who love justice are singularly lacking in creativity, content to denounce the structures we see causing harm, inept in producing other forms of art, other economic structures, other political systems.

The experience of creativity and of intense forms of connection is simply this: the crucial synthesis of the energies of people from the past, within the present, and even in the future. We may be energized, but that does not mean our theological and political analyses are true or our ethics and political strategies are just. It is disconcerting to acknowledge that our ecstasy in connection, whether political or conceptual, is simply the energy of connection, an energy that may be used in amoral, immoral, or moral ways. We want the power we experience in connection and the affirmation we encounter in being seen or being loved to affirm the rightness of our choices, actions, beliefs, and desires. While these may be affirmations of our being, they do not affirm how we frame and express that being.

*   *   *

What brings us back to "the courage of living" is a matter of alchemy and desire. I see the religious not in terms of right beliefs and sure foundations, but as responses to amoral powers that can be given self-critically moral purposes. There are alchemical processes that have turned the bare bones of ontotheology into fierce, compassionate, and sustained movements for justice. We can do the same.

SOURCE: Sharon D. Welch, *After Empire: The Art and Ethos of Enduring Peace* (Minneapolis: Fortress Press, 2004), 14, 16–20, 22.

"Criminal Justice and Prison Reform"

2005

Unitarian Universalist concern with criminal justice policy dates back to Charles and John Murray Spear's ministry with ex-prisoners in the early nineteenth century, or even to the anguished response to the execution of Michael Servetus in 1553. The Unitarian Universalist Association issued a general resolution condemning capital punishment at its first General Assembly, and in 2005 it responded to rapidly increasing rates of incarceration with this Statement of Conscience.

—Dan McKanan

As Unitarian Universalists, we are committed to affirming the inherent goodness and worth of each of us. As Americans, we take pride in our constitutional promise of liberty, equality, and justice for all, including those who have violated the law. Yet the incarceration rate in the United States is five- to tenfold that of other nations, even those without such a constitutional promise. Our corrections system is increasingly rife with inequitable sentencing, longer terms of detention, racial and ethnic profiling, and deplorable jail and prison conditions and treatment. The magnitude of injustice and inequity in this system stands in stark contrast to the values that our nation—and our faith—proclaim. We are compelled to witness this dissonance between what America proclaims for criminal justice and what America practices. We offer an alternative moral vision of a justice system that operates in harmonious accord with our values as a community of faith. This vision includes the presumption of innocence, fair judicial proceedings, the merciful restoration of those who have broken the law, the renunciation of torture and other abusive practices, and a fundamental commitment to the dignity and humane treatment of everyone in our society, including prisoners. . . .

Although Americans take great pride in the freedoms we espouse, the American prison system violates basic human rights in many ways. The Universal Declaration of Human Rights, which the United States endorsed in 1948, states in Article 5, "No one shall be subjected to torture or to cruel, inhuman or degrading treatment or punishment." American correctional practice often subjects inmates to abusive treatment, such as torture and rape, and neglects basic human needs such as health care and nutrition. . . .

The American penchant for retribution squanders opportunities for redemption, rehabilitation, and restoration of the individual offender. Failures in the criminal justice system have created a disenfranchised, stigmatized class who are predominantly from lower-income backgrounds, poorly educated, or from racial and ethnic minorities. The punishment for crime is often simply separation from society, and the sentence one serves is the punishment. In our penal system, punishment often continues even after those convicted have completed their sentence. They are often stripped of voting rights, denied social services, and barred from many professions. If convicted of a drug crime, they become ineligible for federal student loans to attend college. Our criminal justice system makes it exceedingly difficult for anyone to reintegrate into society. People returning to their communities find that they lack opportunity, skills, and social services to fully function in society and hold down jobs, maintain families, or participate in their communities. Therefore, an unacceptable percentage of those released from our prisons and jails recidivate.

Not all prisoners who enter the system leave. One of the most shameful aspects of our current criminal justice system is the death penalty. Many countries have abandoned the practice of capital punishment. Studies fail to demonstrate that the death penalty actually deters crime. While the United States Supreme Court has ruled against the execution of juvenile offenders, the death penalty is still legal in the United States. Experience shows that judges and juries wrongly convict defendants. Given the number of death row inmates released on account of innocence, it is highly likely that we have executed innocent people and will do so again in the future unless we abolish the death penalty. . . .

The first two Principles of Unitarian Universalism address the inherent worth and dignity of every person and justice, equity, and compassion in human relations. Consistent with these fundamental principles, a new corrections policy must place a primary emphasis on community alternatives.

Community alternatives should be developed in the context of redemptive, rehabilitative, and restorative justice. Redemptive justice recognizes justice as relational. Its purpose is to restore wholeness and rightness in the social order and in the disposition of the offender, not to exact revenge. Rehabilitative justice is a process of education, socialization, and empowerment of the person to the status whereby she or he may be able to contribute constructively and appreciably to society. Restorative justice is a process whereby the offender can reconcile with the victim through appropriate restitution, community service, and healing measures. . . .

Separation from society may well be appropriate punishment for many crimes, but society's responsibility does not end there. A corrections system driven by compassionate justice would prepare offenders for successful reentry into society. An overwhelming majority of those who are incarcerated return to their communities, yet only a small percentage receive meaningful rehabilitative programming while in prison. In the reformed system, they will receive substantial rehabilitative services, including mental health treatment, educational programs, and vocational training during incarceration and employment and transitional housing once released. Redemption, rehabilitation, and restoration are not only humanely forgiving of those who have fallen off the main societal track; they are more effective and less costly in addressing the criminal justice needs of our whole society. . . .

Congregational Actions

- Form a study group within the congregation to learn about the local jail and state prison system, its budget, recidivism rates, rehabilitation programs (inside and outside the facilities), and opportunities for volunteers.
- Network and collaborate with existing community outreach programs and advocacy groups for prisoners and their families.
- Establish Unitarian Universalist prison ministries and encourage volunteers from the congregation to go into prisons and get involved with and/or begin peer-counseling and mentoring programs.
- Address re-entry issues by engaging in supportive work with formerly incarcerated individuals to reduce recidivism and increase success in the probation and parole system.
- Reach out and support congregational members who are personally affected by the criminal justice system.

Advocacy Goals

- Legislation that strengthens gun control, ends the so-called "War on Drugs," disallows mandatory minimum sentencing, provides for fair, equitable, anti-racist sentencing, and abolishes the death penalty.
- Reforms of the judicial system to establish drug courts that prescribe treatment rather than imprisonment, provide affordable and competent counsel for all defendants, and empower citizen review boards.
- Effective alternatives to incarceration such as arbitration, restorative justice programs, community service, in-house arrest, and mental health and substance abuse treatment.
- Dismantling of the for-profit prison industry.
- A publicly funded and managed system of correctional facilities accredited by the National Commission on Correctional Health Care and by the American Correctional Association, ensuring that children and youth in custody are separated from adults in the penal system, providing appropriate facilities and services for prisoners with mental health and other health concerns, addressing the unique medical and psychological needs of female prisoners, stopping

prisoner rape, and abolishing cruel detention and interrogation methods and the use of isolation for prolonged periods of time.

- Termination of the relocation of prisoners out-of-state or out-of-country.
- Support for families and family life by assigning prisoners to facilities near their homes, by providing facilities that are conducive to comfortable family visits, by maintaining parental rights as appropriate, and by allowing prison mothers to raise their infants.
- Universal access to rehabilitation, education, and job training programs and restorative and recovery programs for non-religious as well as for religious prisoners.
- A probation and parole system empowered and enabled to correct the excesses of past mandatory sentencing requirements, provide compassionate reprieves for the terminally ill and aged, support former prisoners as they reenter society, and allow for individual evaluation of technical parole violations.
- Elimination of post-prison restrictions on civil rights and civil liberties, including voting rights.

Through ongoing congregational education, advocacy, and action, we can make good on our Unitarian Universalist heritage and our American promise to be both compassionate and just to all in our society. Through our diligence and perseverance in realizing this promise, we can live the core values of our country and extend the values of our faith to the benefit of others.

SOURCE: Unitarian Universalist Social Justice Statements, www.uua.org/statements/criminal -justice-and-prison-reform

REBECCA ANN PARKER

"Choose to Bless the World" and "Benediction"
2006

In her twenty-five year tenure as president of Starr King School for the Minis-
try, Rebecca Ann Parker (1953–) shaped the theology of an entire generation
of Unitarian Universalist ministers. The following selections are responses to
the work of Unitarian process philosopher Charles Hartshorne. "Choose to
Bless the World" is adapted from Parker's contribution to a 1997 festschrift for
Hartshorne on his hundredth birthday. "Benediction" was written in response
to a charge Hartshorne once gave Parker: "Be a blessing to the world." The
poem appeared for many years in the catalogue of Starr King School for the
Ministry and has been adapted for liturgical use in Unitarian Universalist
congregations. Both selections are excerpted from Parker's essay collection
Blessing the World *from Skinner House Books. Further Reading: John A.*
Buehrens *and Rebecca Ann Parker,* A House for Hope: The Promise of Progressive Religion for the Twenty-First Century *(Boston: Beacon Press, 2010).*

                           —Robert Hardies

I first met the process theologian Charles Hartshorne when I was a graduate student at the Claremont School of Theology. I was assigned to help Charles's wife, Dorothy, catalogue his papers. Each spring break, I would travel to the Hartshornes' home to spend some time working with Dorothy and Charles. This was my introduction to their world and way of life, and it was an important part of my education in process thought.

One afternoon, Charles and I took a break from our cataloging to go bird watching. That is when I discovered that Charles did not drive. Thinking of my own grandfather who was deeply distressed when his failing reflexes resulted in the loss of his driver's license, I sympathetically asked the eighty-year-old Charles, "When did you have to give up driving?" He paused to think for a minute and, completing his mental calculations, said, "I'd say about forty-three years ago." He saw my surprise and explained, "I could see the environmental damage that would result from too many automobiles and resolved to use public transportation or walk."

Years later I was at an academic conference in which process thought was being roundly criticized. The enthusiastic attacker was detailing the failings of process theologians; they were heady and abstract and gave no attention to practical ethics or social justice. I asked if the critic drove a car. His argument couldn't stand up in the face of Hartshorne's relinquishment of the automobile.

While this may seems a small detail in the life of a great philosopher, the story of Charles and his automobile illustrates what I see as the gifts of process theology. Process theology helps us heal a philosophical dualism that does violence to the world, and it empowers human beings to be responsible moral agents who, with God, co-create a more just, beautiful, and sustainable world.

We live in a culture in which there is a long philosophical history that devalues the world and denies its real presence. The group suicide of the Heaven's Gate cult in San Diego is symptomatic of our culture's philosophic presuppositions. To these cult members, the body was a vehicle for a nonmaterial soul, and the death of the body was considered insignificant in the career of a soul that would travel beyond this earthly life to another world.

Though it is rarely portrayed so vividly, the philosophical view that splits mind and body, spirit and earth, into two separable realities—one valuable, the other unimportant—is pervasive in our culture. . . .

There is a history to this dualistic thinking. When Descartes said, "I think therefore I am," his revelation articulated an emerging worldview that, as it evolved, led to a greater and greater split between mind and matter. . . .

In this philosophical development the world itself—that which is tasted, touched, felt, seen, and heard, that which is *other* than the perceiver—has become distant, devalued, and nearly invisible. . . .

*   *   *

To ignore the world as an actual place is to imagine it empty of value, except for that which we bestow upon it. As the world recedes into obscurity, only the subject is bathed in the light of reality. This is the legacy of the Enlightenment. While it gave us the important gift of self-critical awareness, the Enlightenment also contributed to a construction of the self as master of the world. The knower paints meaning and value onto the world. The knower is active, even aggressive; the world is passive, a blank canvas.

This is not just a lesson in the history of ideas; it is a description of how we actually behave. In our debates over how to manage old-growth forests, we discuss the different values the forest has to competing subjects and interests, but we do not ascribe to the forest any intrinsic value, power, or presence. Once the earth has disappeared from our minds, its relentless exploitation is easy and its careful stewardship difficult. We can be comfortable consuming its resources because we are the bestowers of value; the resources themselves are without meaning. We matter. Earth doesn't.

*   *   *

Process metaphysics conceived afresh the basic character of reality. Instead of aggregates of atoms that are bits of matter, process thought conceives of the world as aggregates of little bits of activity. Each activity is a discreet entity that becomes

480

and passes away in the blink of an eye. Its existence is a moment of feeling. What is felt is every other entity in the universe as it flows into just that momentary point on the space-time continuum.

Picture the universe like Indra's net, an image from Hinduism. Indra's net is an interconnected web of countless strands, and at every intersection there is a jewel drop of water that reflects the whole. Process philosophy sees the universe as the plentitude of these jewel drops, each holding the whole in precisely the way the whole is reflected at that point of intersection.

* * *

The universe is emerging every moment, by the action of countless creators, co-creating in response to one another. The creators range in complexity and depth, from the simplest series of quarks that manifests an alternating pulse in an atomic dance, to a moment in the interstices of your brain when all the actual occasions that comprise your body spark as conscious awareness, to a moment within the fullness of the whole universe when everything is held together in such utter completeness that the moment deserves the name God.

This worldview, in which God, quarks, and a moment of your conscious awareness are all examples of the same process, variations of the same fundamental act of being/becoming, goes beyond the dualism of the Western philosophical tradition. In doing so, it opens up fresh possibilities for imagining God and our relationship to the world.

To the atheist who says, "I do not believe in God," the philosopher says, "Tell me about the God you don't believe in." The God that process theology doesn't believe in is the old God of dualistic philosophy, whose perfection is imagined as pure spirit, unsullied by the world, untouched by change, without feeling, unmoved, all-controlling, and all-knowing. The God that process theology believes in, as developed, for example, in Hartshorne's Divine Relativity, is a creator among creators, not different in kind from every other being. God is not all-knowing, because God cannot know how each moment of subjective immediacy—each dewdrop on Indra's net—will self-determine until the moment has crystallized. God is not all-powerful, because each moment is the agent of its own final crystallization.

God is supreme not in knowing everything but in receiving everything, not in controlling everything but in imagining everything. God is supreme in feeling, supreme in responsiveness. God is the subjective moment that holds the whole together with the greatest love and the cosmic embrace that tenderly welcomes all. Not the "unmoved mover" imagined by Aristotle but the being most moved by the world. Supreme in compassionate receptivity, God is also supreme in imagining what could be: an inexhaustible source of fresh possibility. Whitehead calls God "the poet of the world," whose power is like that of an artist. It is the power to inspire, persuade, and lure. In process thought, God's love is a compassionate, embracing

481

love that receives everything. It is also an erotic, enticing love that lures. But God is not an all-determining creator. Each creature is self-creating in relationship with all other creatures, including God, so we are co-creators with the Divine. We make God, as much as God makes us.

* * *

When "we know ourselves to be made from this earth" (Susan Griffin), we do not look to life beyond the grave as a place of liberation or greater meaning. We look to this life—this world—as the locus of the sacred, and ourselves as part of it. We do not see the world as a blank screen onto which we project whatever values please us, and we do not presume that we can cut down the old-growth forest and that the only loss will be to us. We will be more likely to give up our automobiles, because the earth is not our possession to abuse and discard as we please but has value in and of itself. We understand ourselves to be part of a plenitude of being, all of which is endowed with creativity and subjectivity, each part of which is intimately connected to, influenced by, and influencing all others.

When Charles Hartshorne gave up driving his car, he was acting from a perspective of critical examination of cultural assumptions and an analysis of how these assumptions would have consequences for future generations. He acted not just for himself but also out of social concern. He acted as if he were a part of a world: a world of extended social relations, a world that had intrinsic value and not just value for him. He took an action not just because it pleased him personally but also because it made a positive contribution toward all life, not only human life but also the lives of the red-winged blackbirds and the ruby finches.

We need a revolution, a conversion. The old dominant worldview says that we are self-interested individuals, unconnected and unconcerned with one another. It says that we are the determiners of value in a world that is empty of value, apart from that which we project upon it. It says that the purpose of life is to serve ourselves and compete with our neighbors, and it adds that such competition is the given nature of things. It institutionalizes these beliefs in economic theories and systems that dominate our days.

Process thought presents another way. We are not inherently self-interested individuals. We are connected to one another, and caring for others is fundamental to our existence. To deny this is to go against the character of reality. The purpose of life is not our own well-being in isolation from all others. We are subjects, the locus of intrinsic value, but this value is always fleeting and always relational. Our well-being enters into the well-being of others, adding a measure of health or joy. Our actions matter to us and also to all the world. We live both for ourselves and for one another, in a balance that is given in the nature of things.

The purpose of life, then, is to discover the joy or well-being that simultaneously pleases us and blesses our neighbor. Every act we commit is a contribution to

482

the world; the question is whether our actions will be a blessing or a curse. The basic question of life is not, "What do I want?" but rather, "What do I want to give?" . . .

On a spring evening, two of us were walking with Charles during a conference on process theology and aesthetics. We paused along the way noticing the plants, the birds, the sweet spring air. At the threshold where we would part, Charles turned around, took our hands in his, looked us squarely in the eye, and said, "Be a blessing to the world."

One is rarely given such a direct instruction, and it went straight to our hearts. When all is said and done in my life, I hope that I will have been faithful to this charge.

Benediction

Your gifts
whatever you discover them to be
can be used to bless or curse the world.
The mind's power,
    The strength of the hands,
        The reaches of the heart,
the gift of speaking, listening, imagining, seeing, waiting.
Any of these can serve to feed the hungry,
    bind up wounds,
    welcome the stranger
    praise what is sacred,
    do the work of justice
        or offer love.
Any of these can draw down the prison door
    hoard bread,
    abandon the poor,
    obscure what is holy,
    comply with injustice
        or withhold love.

You must answer this question:
What will you do with your gifts?
Choose to bless the world.

The choice to bless the world is more than an act of will
    a moving forward into the world
with the intention to do good.
It is an act of recognition,
    a confession of surprise,
    a grateful acknowledgment

that in the midst of a broken world
unspeakable beauty, grace and mystery abide.
There is an embrace of kindness,
that encompasses all life,
even yours.
And while there is injustice,
    anesthetization, or evil
there moves
a holy disturbance,
a benevolent rage,
a revolutionary love
protesting, urging, insisting
that which is sacred will not be defiled.
Those who bless the world live their life
as a gesture of thanks
for this beauty
and this rage.

The choice to bless the world
can take you into solitude
    to search for the sources
    of power and grace;
    native wisdom, healing, and liberation.
More, the choice will draw you into community,
    the endeavor shared,
    the heritage passed on,
    the companionship of struggle,
the importance of keeping faith,
the life of ritual and praise,
    the comfort of human friendship,
    the company of earth
    its chorus of life
    welcoming you.
    None of us alone can save the world.
Together—that is another possibility,
waiting.

SOURCE: Rebecca Ann Parker, *Blessing the World: What Can Save Us Now*, ed. Robert Hardies (Boston: Skinner House, 2006), 151–54, 156, 158–61, 163–65.

WILLIAM F. SCHULZ

"What Torture's Taught Me"

2006

William F. Schulz (1949–) was the fifth president of the Unitarian Univer-
salist Association, serving from 1985 to 1993. After his presidency, he served
as Executive Director of Amnesty International USA from 1994 to 2006, and
then as president and chief executive officer of the Unitarian Universalist
Service Committee. At the conclusion of his service to Amnesty International,
he was invited to deliver the annual Berry Street lecture. He took the opportu-
nity to deliver this searching and challenging reflection on Unitarian Univer-
salism's first Principle. Further Reading: William F. Schulz, What Torture
Taught Me: And Other Reflections on Justice and Theology *(Boston: Skin-*
ner House, 2013).

—Dan McKanan

There is a smell to refugee camps which, once you have inhaled it, you never
forget—a smell of goat dung and human waste; of sweat and tears and unstaunched
menstrual blood; but also a smell of desperation that gives way to sagging shoulders
and the decay of the human soul. For a body can be clothed in the raiment of fear or
stalked daily by death for only so long before the soul—whatever makes the human
animal "human"—begins to collapse upon itself as surely as the shoulders do. . . .

Of those things that I have seen nothing has had a deeper impact on me than
my exposure to torture—to both victims of torture and perpetrators of it and, not
incidentally, to all of us in between. So I want to talk with you this afternoon about
torture. . . .

It was not until 1754—only 252 years ago—that Prussia (now Germany) became,
ironically enough in light of subsequent history, the first country to abolish the use
of torture altogether. For about 150 years, torture went out of vogue—at least as an
official instrument of government policy. But in the twentieth century it began to
raise its ugly head again. And this time there was an important difference: for whereas
in ancient Greece and medieval Europe torture had been used to determine truth or
convict someone of a crime, in the twentieth century torture became an instrument
of pleasure, a means of intimidating political opponents, a way to inflict pain on
another person for the sheer sadistic joy of it.

The reason Abu Ghraib struck Americans like a thunderbolt is not because
prisoners were being tortured—some 63% of Americans say that torture is acceptable

485

at least occasionally when, for example, information about the location of a ticking bomb in a high density neighborhood must be procured quickly. . . . The reason Americans turned ashen at Abu Ghraib was because even the staunchest defender of the use of torture as a means of extracting information could not pretend that forcing naked prisoners to form a pyramid or to masturbate for the cameras or to be tethered to a leash like a dog had any purpose other than sheer humiliation.

*　*　*

Practices such as these have no rational purpose at all; they are designed solely to strip another of his or her humanity. If anything deserves to be called unadulterated evil, this does. I tell you about it not to shock you but to ask you to consider a question that has haunted me the last twelve years—is what I say from the pulpit about the world around us, about the nature of God and humanity, about the dynamics of human relationships—is what I preach to the people sufficient to encompass a world in which such coarseness and brutality exists? Or, to put it another way, if a member of my congregation or my listening audience had herself been a victim of such terror, would she find my words, my faith, my theology, naïve and pallid or authentic and satisfying?

I know of course that few Unitarian Universalists have been subjected to torture but far more people in our congregations than we know have been raped or abused and even those who have not have to live in a world, cope with a world, feel at home in a world in which such practices flourish. I find it a helpful exercise to use torture as a plumbline test of the adequacy of my worldview and sophistication of my sermonizing. I remember a cartoon from years ago in which the wayside pulpits of an Episcopal church and a Unitarian Universalist church were both visible on a street corner. It was Easter and the title of the Episcopal rector's Easter sermon was "The Truth and Power of the Risen Christ" while across the street the Unitarian Universalist was preaching a sermon entitled "Upsy-Daisy." My point is simply that to my mind an "upsy-daisy" theology fails the torture test.

Sallie McFague, a theologian whose work is popular among liberals, says that "there is no place where God is not." Process theologian Marjorie Hewitt Suchocki insists that "[God is] pervasively present, like water, to every nook and cranny of the universe, continuously wooing the universe. . . . toward its greater good." But I would submit that no God worthy of the name is present in a torture chamber. I am sure that some victims of torture have found solace in their faith sufficient to sustain them through the ordeal. That appears to be the case, for example, with some of the Islamic prisoners being held at Guantanamo Bay. But I have talked to dozens of survivors of torture, read hundreds of others' accounts, and I have rarely, if ever, come across a testimony that it was faith in God that saw them through the night. For when the needle slips under the fingernails and the pliers rip them off, that pain obliterates the very face of God.

486

I am not here scoring some cheap humanist point against vapid notions of God. Over the years I have myself become increasingly comfortable using the word to describe that source of graciousness upon which we depend for our very lives. All I am saying is that, whatever our conception of God, it needs to be both complex enough and circumscribed enough to account for the fact that God's absence — true absence — is as real a phenomenon as God's immanence.

Similarly, our traditional doctrines of human nature rest uneasy in a world full of torturers. In what sense can we defend the notion that a torturer is a person of "*inherent* worth and dignity?" . . .

Who are the torturers? Are they madmen? Deviants? Hardened criminals? Sexual predators? Almost never. In fact, most police and military units weed out the psychological misfits from their midsts because they know such people have trouble taking orders. No, the horrible truth is that the vast majority of torturers are average Joes (occasionally, but rarely, average Janes).

And it is remarkably easy to turn Joe into what most of us would regard as a monster. You put him in a restricted environment like a police or military training camp under the command of a vaunted authority figure. You subject him to intense stress. . . . And then, having created an angry, bitter, but obedient servant, you provide the sanction, the means, the opportunity and the rationale for that servant to take his outrage out on a vulnerable but much despised population. . . .

Who is this creature of "inherent dignity" who is so easily led astray? Sixty five years ago James Luther Adams delivered the most heralded Berry Street Lecture of the twentieth century entitled "The Changing Reputation of Human Nature" in which, while rejecting the doctrine of total depravity, he resurrected the notion of "sin."

> . . . Whether the liberal uses the word "sin" or not, [Adams said], he cannot correct his "too jocund" [blithe] view of life until he recognizes that there is in human nature a deep-seated and universal tendency . . . to ignore the demands of mutuality and thus to waste freedom or abuse it by devotion to the idols of the tribe. . . . It cannot be denied that religious liberalism has neglected these aspects of human nature in its zeal to proclaim the spark of divinity in man. We may call these tendencies by any name we wish but we do not escape their destructive influence by a conspiracy of silence concerning them.

Have we forgotten Adams' exhortation? If we no longer think of human beings as made in the "likeness of God," are we not still reticent to dwell upon the features of the flesh that make us not just "slightly lower than the angels" but out of the angels' league altogether? . . .

Adams, like nineteen centuries of theologians before him, would try to rescue humanity from its own degradation by asserting that *freedom* was what underpinned our inherent worth. . . .

But, quite apart from arcane philosophical debates about free will or more contemporary insights into the traits of animals, is freedom robust enough a characteristic of human beings sufficient to overcome the basest of brutality? And when we speak of the "inherent worth and dignity of every person," are we really thinking first and foremost of free agency anyway? I doubt it. I suspect that we base our belief in the inherent worth of human beings on some far vaguer notion that *aliveness* itself is good and some long-outdated hierarchical assumption that because human beings represent the pinnacle of aliveness, we possess inherently some kind of merit.

Well, I don't buy that anymore. I have fought tirelessly against the death penalty in this country. I have visited death rows, spoken frequently with condemned prisoners. Some of them have acknowledged their crimes and altered their hearts. Others of them are truly innocent. Many of them are mentally ill. And some of them are vicious, dangerous killers. I oppose the death penalty not because I believe that every one of those lives carries inherent worth. In some cases their deaths would be no loss at all to anyone. I oppose the death penalty because I can't be sure which of them falls into which category and because the use of executions by the state diminishes *my* own dignity and that of every other citizen in whose name it is enforced. I need, in other words, to *assign* the occupants of death row worth and dignity in order to preserve my own. But I find no such characteristics *inherent* in either them or me.

If a loved one of mine were murdered, I would want her murderer to suffer the worst torments of hell I could imagine. No torture would be too great to satisfy my lust for revenge. But I do not want the state to indulge me in my worst impulses. . . .

So is the worth and dignity of every person *inherent*? No, inherency is a political construct—perhaps a very useful myth but a myth nonetheless—designed to cover up the fact that we all are sinners and that we are not always certain which sins (and hence which sinners) are worse than others. Each of us has to be assigned worth—it does not come automatically—and taught to behave with dignity because, as Sartre once said, "If it were not for the petty rules of bourgeois society, we humans would destroy each other in an instant."

But who does the assigning of worth? How *do* we decide that something is a sin? How do we know that torture is wrong? What is the basis for human rights?

There are only three options. Rights are established by divinity, by natural law or by pragmatic consensus. I wish we could get everybody to agree on one of the first two. But because we cannot. . . . We are left with public opinion as the basis for determining rights. Global public opinion, to be sure, but public opinion.

This is a discomfiting notion, I know. We Unitarian Universalists are champions of the individual as the source of authority for both truth and righteousness. We are well aware of all the many instances in which majority opinion has been just plain wrong. We are aficionados of the lonely, courageous soul standing up for truth, justice and Esperanto even in the face of the crowd's disparagement.

But you know something: most of the time those lonely, courageous souls are sheer crackpots. And unless they can get a whole bunch of other people to agree with them—at least eventually—we would usually be wise to keep them at a safe distance.

Was torture wrong even before anyone in the world, including the slaves being tortured, thought it was wrong? The hard answer is "No." Or if it was "wrong" in some parallel ethical universe, it was certainly no violation of anybody's rights until a significant number of people *in this world* began to say that it was. . . .

Human rights are whatever the international community—through its various declarations, covenants, treaties and conventions—say that they are. This means that theoretically at least the world could regress and torture could once again be deemed acceptable. But experience seems to show that the more people who are involved in decision-making about rights, including the victims of their violation, the less likely the backsliding. If there is one arena in which Theodore Parker's famous dictum that "the arc of the universe bends toward justice" seems to have been borne out, it is the evolution of human rights.

But what all this means is that, when it comes to deciding right and wrong, when it comes to assigning worth and dignity, the individual is *not* the final source of authority and without a reference to the values of the larger community—the *world* community, not that of any one nation alone—our judgments are fit only for a desert island upon which we ourselves are the only occupant.

But what it also means is that our job as ministers, as builders of the blessed community, is tougher and more important than ever for if we can't rely upon the inherency of human worth and dignity, if we have to *assign* worth and *teach* dignity, then we cannot escape confrontation with the forces of idolatry who would reserve worth to only a few and save dignity for their immediate neighbors, people like those children and grandchildren of immigrants, for example, who would not be where they are today if their forebears had been treated the way they propose to treat a new American generation. And if the individual is *not* the ultimate source of authority when it comes to some of the most important decisions on earth, like who lives and who doesn't, then autobiographical theology, popular as it is and tempting, is inadequate—not deleterious or to be shunned—but insufficient for a faith that would not just engage the world but transform it. What torture has taught me is that, fascinating as I find my own life, it alone is a cloudy prism through which to view Creation absent reference to the experience of others, the wisdom of community, the demands of tradition, the judgment of history, and the invitation of the Holy.

And it has taught me one thing more. If these twelve years have caused me to re-think the nature of God, the inherency of human worth and the credibility of individual authority, they have more than confirmed two other bedrock Unitarian Universalist principles, the indomitability of the spirit and the mysterious workings of an unfettered grace.

SOURCE: William F. Schulz, "What Torture's Taught Me," Berry Street Essay, delivered at the Ministerial Conference, June 21, 2006, www.uuma.org/page/berrystreetessays

"Threat of Global Warming/
Climate Change"

2006

This Statement of Conscience was the second issued on an environmental topic; the 2001 statement "Responsible Consumption Is Our Moral Imperative" addressed North Americans' disproportionate share of global consumption. The 2006 statement linked global warming to a broader ethic of responsibility to our planet. It provided the basis for subsequent "actions of immediate witness" on such topics as tax credits for sustainable energy, changes to the Clean Energy Bill, and responses to oil spills, as well as for the eventual divestment of the UUA endowment from fossil fuels.

—Dan McKanan

Earth is our home. We are part of this world and its destiny is our own. Life on this planet will be gravely affected unless we embrace new practices, ethics, and values to guide our lives on a warming planet. As Unitarian Universalists, how can our faith inform our actions to remedy and mitigate global warming/climate change? We declare by this Statement of Conscience that we will not acquiesce to the ongoing degradation and destruction of life that human actions are leaving to our children and grandchildren. We as Unitarian Universalists are called to join with others to halt practices that fuel global warming/climate change, to instigate sustainable alternatives, and to mitigate the impending effects of global warming/climate change with just and ethical responses. As a people of faith, we commit to a renewed reverence for life and respect for the interdependent web of all existence.

A Matter of Science

There is scientific consensus that the Earth's climate is changing due to global warming/climate change caused primarily by the human use of oil, coal, and natural gas. . . . The recent rapid global average temperature increase is indeed the result of human activity. While the climate is always changing, attribution studies using sophisticated supercomputer global climate models show that natural causes do not account for the recent rapid temperature increase and that human activity does. . . .

A *Matter of Faith and Justice*

As Unitarian Universalists, we are called by our seventh Principle to affirm and promote "respect for the interdependent web of all existence of which we are a part." We envision a world in which all people are assured a secure and meaningful life that is ecologically responsible and sustainable, in which every form of life has intrinsic value. In other words, Unitarian Universalists are called to defer to a balance between our individual needs and those of all other organisms. Entire cultures, nations, and life forms are at risk of extinction while basic human rights to adequate supplies of food, fresh water, and health as well as sustainable livelihoods for humans are being undermined. To live, we must both consume and dispose. Both our consumption and our disposal burden the interdependent web of existence. To sustain the interdependent web, we must burden it less while maintaining the essentials of our lives. Hurricanes Katrina and Rita are painful omens of how racism, sexism, and poverty worsen the effects of global warming/climate change. Our world is calling us to gather in community and respond from our moral and spiritual wealth; together we can transform our individual and congregational lives into acts of moral witness, discarding our harmful habits for new behaviors and practices that will sustain life on Earth, ever vigilant against injustice.

A *Matter of Policy*

Global warming/climate change is not only an environmental phenomenon; it is a hotly contested policy issue. All countries, in particular developing countries, will be unable to protect their residents from sea level increases, frequent and intense droughts, heavy rains, and violent hurricanes and tornadoes. Species worldwide face extinction from these same events. It is a bitter irony and a grave injustice that economically developed countries that are most responsible for global warming/climate change possess the wealth, technology, and infrastructure to cope with its negative effects, while those who have the least will have the largest burdens to bear. . . .

Personal Practices

- Reduce our use of energy and our consumption of manufactured goods that become waste;
- Use alternative sources of energy to reduce global warming/climate change and to encourage the development of such sources;
- Choose the most energy-efficient transportation means that meet our needs and abilities (e.g., walk, bike, carpool, use mass transit and communication technologies, and limit travel);

492

- Determine our personal energy consumption and pledge to reduce our use of energy and carbon emissions by at least 20 percent by 2010 or sooner and into the future;
- Reuse, recycle, and reduce waste;
- Plant and preserve trees and native plants and choose sustainably harvested wood and wood products;
- Eat and serve energy-efficient food that is locally produced and low on the food chain;
- Use financial resources to encourage corporate social responsibility with reference to global warming/climate change;
- Model these practices by committing to a life of simplicity and Earth stewardship;
- Consume less, choose appliances that are rated energy-efficient (e.g., by the EPA Energy Star Program), and choose products and materials that are made from renewable resources and can be recycled at the end of their usefulness; and
- Commit to continue to learn about the science, impact, and mitigation of global warming/climate change and communicate this knowledge by teaching about and discussing the problems and dangers of, and actions to address, climate change.

Congregational Actions

- Celebrate reverence for the interdependent web of existence in all aspects of congregational life;
- Treat environmentally responsible practices as a spiritual discipline;
- Seek certification through the Green Sanctuary Program of the Unitarian Universalist Ministry for Earth;
- Educate ourselves, our children, and future generations on sustainable ways to live interdependently;
- Whenever possible, plan congregational facilities around proximity to public transportation and encourage congregants, as they are able, to travel by public transportation, walking, biking, and carpooling;
- Seek U. S. Green Building Council Leadership in Energy and Environmental Design (LEED) certification for all new congregational building projects and use LEED guidelines for renovation projects;
- Use congregational financial resources to positively address the global warming/climate change crisis;
- Practice environmentally responsible consumption and encourage voluntary simplicity among members;

- Build a broader base for environmentally mindful policies and practices through congregational alliances within Unitarian Universalism, through interfaith channels, and with secular entities; and
- Maximize the energy efficiency of congregational facilities by enrolling in the EPA's Energy Star for Congregations Program.

Denominational Affairs

We call upon our denominational leaders to provide:

- Leadership, by calling upon the major political parties to develop energy and climate change policies and to make them central topics of debate in state, congressional, and presidential elections;
- Education, by providing spiritual, educational, and technical resources for congregational and individual responses;
- Justice, by seeking opportunities for public witness for environmental justice, including joining interfaith and public events promoting a just response to climate change;
- Sustainable practices, by exploring the options for performing environmental audits of all UUA properties and for modeling appropriate management and purchasing practices;
- Sustainable investing, by exploring the potential for using the ownership rights of the denomination's financial resources to positively address the global warming/climate change crisis;
- Support, by assisting congregations in evaluating and addressing the risks and challenges they face as a result of global warming/climate change;
- Recognition of congregational action, by encouraging, honoring, and publicizing the work of UU congregations, including those that achieve Green Sanctuary accreditation; and
- Ministry, by recognizing and supporting the need for UU leaders to help others understand the urgency and severity of addressing global warming/climate change, the resulting potential for despair, and places to find hope for the future.

Advocacy Goals

- Full compliance with the United Nations Framework Convention on Climate Change, with the understanding that because human activity is affecting global climate change, it follows that the greater our total population the greater the impact;
- Ratification of and compliance with the Kyoto Protocol;
- Funding for research and development of renewable energy resources and energy-efficient technologies . . . [and] to assist in mitigating the effects of global warming/climate change. . . .

*   *   *

Given our human capacity to reflect and act upon our own lives as well as the condition of the world, we accept with humility and determination our responsibility to remedy and mitigate global warming/climate change through innovation, cooperation, and self-discipline. We undertake this work for the preservation of life on Earth.

SOURCE: "Threat of Global Warming/Climate Change," Unitarian Universalist Social Justice Statements, www.uua.org/statements/threat-global-warmingclimate-change

CHRISTINE ROBINSON

"Imagineering Soul"

2008

*Christine Robinson (1952–) was ordained in 1980, becoming part of the wave
of early UU women ministers in the late 1970s and 1980s. Robinson served a
ministry in Columbia, South Carolina, for the first eight years of her career
before becoming the senior minister of the First Unitarian Church of Albuquerque, New Mexico. Since 1988, Robinson has helped First Unitarian in
Albuquerque grow and thrive, and in 2008, she presented the following lecture "Imagineering Soul" at the annual Berry Street Ministerial Conference.
Her essay, addressed to her colleagues in ministry, emphasizes the significance of spiritual revitalization and the use of language of reverence in Unitarian Universalist congregations. Robinson began by describing a visit to
Disney World with her son, in which she was "touched to the core of [her]
being" on a simulated trip to Mars.*

—Natalie Malter

I know that the Spirit blows where it will, but I hadn't expected to have a religious
experience at Disney World, and it was abundantly clear that it was no accident that
I'd had it. They put that little iconic picture of the earth in my window on purpose
and they hoped that it would do just what it did. At home, my son showed me an
article from the journal of the Themed Entertainment Association. (That's the folks
who design and engineer things like theme parks, casinos, and the Rainforest Cafe.
Disney calls them "Imagineers.") . . .

The author points out that, while people come to theme parks and other entertainment venues mostly to have fun, they are looking, even there, at least in part,
for the kind of authentic experiences and meaningfulness that museums, churches,
families and books offer, and recommends that designers strive to evoke these realities in their fantasylands. . . .

I have to tell you; the idea that even theme park designers know that it is "heart"
and "thirst" and "meaningfulness" that bring real satisfaction to a human life is hum-
bling, especially after my eyes were opened to how well they can do it. I would have
said that "heart" and "thirst" and "meaningfulness" were what *I* was supposed to be
doing. But my special effects budget is otherwise known as "flowers and candles."
I can't produce two g's in my sanctuary by any means. There are no seat belts in my

496

seats and no need of them, because the biggest physical thrills I can offer are singing, laughter, and the sound of sheer silence.

Why do people come to church? It is not to learn. People don't even go to museums to learn. It's not to be entertained. People don't even go to Disney World *just* to be entertained. They come to church, especially they come to church, to quench a thirst, find meaningfulness, to have an authentic experience, or in a more traditional religious language, to connect with mystery, to see themselves, *sub species eternitatis*, to deepen their souls. We ministers, then would be the Imagineers of soul, Sorcerer's Apprentices in the art of quenching thirst, filling voids, opening the doors of meaning.

I'm guessing that many, perhaps most of you, agree that evoking heart and depth and meaningfulness should be at the center of our ministries; and even at your most cynical moments in your ministry, you wistfully long for more. Whatever your theology, whatever your language of reverence, I'd wager that you came into this especially difficult and not well compensated profession because you'd found heart and soul in the church and in its people and you wanted to join the sorcerers who created more. Come along and join the fun! But be warned. There will be few props, and the special effects you'll create yourself, if you have the courage, out of the only thing you'll really have to work with, which is yourself and what you are willing to share of your own, precious and always threatened spiritual life.

There are lots of other interesting and worthy parts of our vocation and the ministry of our churches; teaching the children, comforting the dying, changing the world, but when we do these things in church, they, too, evoke the holy, and if they don't, we've failed at the only thing we can uniquely do. And we mostly fail.

I've been working away at these matters for my whole career, and I know I'm not alone. That's what my second wave of Baby Boomer ministers and women ministers were doing, as a whole. I think I've had some success in helping two churches do what the majority wanted to do, which was to bring spirituality, heart, and depth more fully and explicitly into our life together, and I think that that aim has had something to do with the fact that both of my churches experienced significant growth. . . .

These are all good changes but I'm not altogether happy with my career or the development of my abilities as Imagineer of soul, and the fact of the matter is that we Unitarian Universalists are failing at this crucial task of manifesting meaningfulness in our congregational life.

Heart in our Churches

How do we know we're failing?

There is our practically non-existent denominational growth during a population boom. There's the fact that pollsters tell us that between 300,000 and 800,000

Americans claim to pollsters that they are Unitarian Universalists but don't belong to a church, many of whom, no doubt, are among the two generations of our children who feel a part of the tribe but have no interest in our practice. . . .

Our children leave us because we don't give them enough to stay for. We use the precious hours we have with them to teach them everything they ever wanted to know about sex and we play "Don't ask, don't tell" about matters of the spirit. We teach them to be respectful of all the things we don't believe and don't tell them what we believe, in part because their teachers are not prepared to talk about such frightening, personal, delicate matters as spirituality. It's just too embarrassing.

Listen to one of our young people, a Northwestern University student who wrote this in her school newspaper last year.

"It wasn't that I minded Unitarian Universalism; I loved the people, the intellectualism and the freedom. But it never felt like a real religion to me. . . .—hell, I didn't even know how to pray." . . .

Peter Morales reminds us that we've tried everything we could think of to grow our churches: hospitality, social justice, restructuring, PR, everything—except religion. . . . Why not, I wonder? And in particular, what keeps us, the ministers, from being Imagineers of soul and what would help us do better?

Well, I hear you say, "I don't do it because I'd get fired." And this is a real fear. So let's talk about them, first, and what goes on in their hearts and minds, and then we'll talk about us.

Their Stuff: Shame

The sheep of these pastures—some of them, anyway, and it does seem sometimes as if they are the biggest and most ornery ones—get all bent out of shape about "spiritual." They hear the God word or the prayer word and go into reptile mode. . . . What's going on?

Some were actually hurt by traditional religion. Most were, much more profoundly, shamed. This shame, like all shame, comes from feeling or being told that there's something fundamentally wrong with you. In contrast to guilt, the knowledge that you've actually done something wrong, shame is existential. . . .

Unitarian Universalists are mostly what Martin Marty called wintery spirits; our religious experience is of doubt, shades of gray, and absence. Although there are plenty of wintery spirits in conventional religious communities, what is celebrated and held up as real is the summery, "Jesus loves me!" style of spirituality, and most of our folks couldn't connect with that in either mind or heart, and so they left, with a burden of shame.

The sheep of our pastures will be much easier to live with, my dear fellow shepherds, if we tend to this shame.

* * *

498

Our Stuff: The Scared Minister

Taking spiritual risks and being the carrier of depth and meaning and thirst into whatever we are doing, invoking and evoking the holy in the service of healing and transformation is the very heart of our calling. I know that I can teach, preach, organize, administer, conduct rituals, and lead the world to change without reference to this role; frankly, I mostly do. I can even pray without really invoking the holy in my heart, and I bet you can, too. We've all heard that kind of prayer. Probably written in a pretty way, it is read without much feeling or worse, recited in ponderous, ministerial tones, as if the weight in our voice and the length of our vowels could fool somebody, or God.

Which brings us to the minister, the spiritual leader, the Sorcerer's Apprentice, alone with all this power and all this risk. The minister, whose most important, most sacred job is bringing the light of the holy into the pasture, coaxing the people out of their rational heads, helping them understand their shame, express their gratitude, put words to the prayers they don't think they can say. What does it take to do that?

Ministry is one long, joyful, painful sacrifice of love. You enter it because you discover that a worship service feeds your spirit, that community is a vital part of your life and, perhaps, because you have a certain way with words. And then you get into ministry and what do you discover? You discover that the leader *of* worship must sacrifice their own experience *in* worship, that the minister in a community doesn't really exactly belong to the community any more, and that all your facility with words doesn't help much when you get to the things that cannot be named.

Worst of all, you come to love those counter-dependent, shame-angered folk, and it's only later that you discover that their anger, their stuckness, their inability to open their hearts to any language of reverence at all has changed your faith.

✻   ✻   ✻

Moving Towards Heart

So what shall we do, my good colleagues, to assure that we keep our feet on the ground? How do we develop as spiritual leaders, able and willing to take the risks and pay the prices?

Although I've always thought that this was the important role of ministry, that I've practiced it enough to see some of the fruits and to think I'm onto something, I have to also say that I don't think I'm very good at it, especially when I can't plan ahead. I'm impossibly tongue-tied in informal situations. I lose my focus and let all kinds of opportunities pass to pray, to point to soul, to deepen a silence. Still scared after all these years. If I'm going to do this Sorcerer's Apprentice thing well, consistently, and joyfully, I need three things: I need to tend my own spiritual life, I need my denomination to edge this quest for spiritualities authentic to our tradition more into the mainstream, and most of all, I need my colleagues.

Across the religious traditions, the recipe for a spiritual leader to nurture their own spirituality includes at least two things: daily spiritual practice of whatever kind, and somebody to talk about it with. More is possible but these two, a daily practice and somebody else, seem basic. The somebody can be a group or an individual, a companion or a guru, but apparently we just can't do this by ourselves. The time can be spent in silence, in reading, in prayer, even in certain kinds of art or writing, but we just can't be without it.

SOURCE: Christine Robinson, "Imagineering Soul," Berry Street Essay, delivered at the Ministerial Conference, June 25, 2008, uuma.org/page/berrystreetessays

"Thandeka's Change of Heart" in
What Moves Us: Unitarian Universalist Theology

2008

Thandeka is the creator of the "We Love Beyond Belief" initiative for pro-gressive congregations and is the founder of Contemporary Affect Theology, which is designed to explain emotional development in religious settings and terms. She received her PhD in philosophy of religion and theology from Claremont Graduate University. In 1984, she received the name Thandeka, meaning "beloved" in the Xhosa language, by Archbishop Desmond Tutu. Thandeka has worked as an Emmy Award–winning television producer, ordained UU minister, and congregational consultant. She has taught at Andover Newton, Harvard Divinity School, Lancaster Theological Seminary, Meadville Lombard, and Williams College and was a Fellow at Stanford University's Humanities Center. In The Embodied Self *(1995), she expli-cated Friedrich Schleiermacher's theology rooted in an affective view of the self; in* Learning to Be White *(1999), she explored the dynamics of shame and self-deception underlying white identity, drawing on original work-shop initiatives and American social history. In the narrative below, she shares her own personal experience of coming to understand "love beyond belief." Further Reading: Thandeka,* Love Beyond Belief: Recovering the Lost Emotional Foundation of Liberal Faith—A Contemporary Affect Theology Project *(Farmington, MN: Polebridge Press, 2017); Gary Dorrien,* The Making of American Liberal Theology: Crisis, Irony, and Postmoder-nity, 1950–2005 *(Louisville, KY: Westminster John Knox Press, 2006), 452–55; revthandeka.org*

—Natalie Malter

In July 2003, I went on an eight-day spiritual retreat at a Benedictine monastery in Wisconsin. The night before I left Chicago to drive to the monastery, as preparation for the journey, I made a series of decisions about what kinds of clothes I would need while on this retreat. I was thorough. I thought about the weather conditions in Chi-cago. The past few days had been quite hot. I looked up the weather conditions in the city closest to the monastery. The temperature there had also been quite warm for several days.

As part of this prep work, I remembered that the weather in Wisconsin was often colder than the weather in Chicago. I knew this fact because I had gone on a college retreat 30 years ago to a camp site in northern Wisconsin in the dead of winter and had not taken adequate clothing, so I had been cold for three days.

Not wanting to repeat this clothing disaster of 30 years ago, I decided to prepare for the worst—just in case the hot July summer weather suddenly turned unseasonably cold. So I packed a heavy winter coat, two heavy sweatshirts, a turtleneck sweater, a Polartec hat, Polartec mittens, and a heavy scarf. I also decided to take a blanket with me just in case my room at the monastery became uncomfortably cold because the heating system might not be turned on in July.

When I arrived at the monastery, I schlepped all of this stuff up two flights of stairs, neatly folded all of the winter items, placed them in the storage space facing my bed, and left them there, untouched, for eight days because the temperature never fell below 75 degrees.

I had done this before. I travel a lot in order to lead workshops, present sermons, and read papers on my theological work. So it is not unusual for me to spend two or three weekends a month on the road. And yet, more often than not, I have tended to take the wrong clothes with me on my travels. As a result I have often felt ill-at-ease in my body, while I led workshops on spiritual practices intended to help others feel more at ease in their bodies.

As I sat in my monastery room in July looking at my winter clothes, I sensed that if I could figure out why I had such a difficult time thinking about my body, I might discover something new about me. Why couldn't I make realistic decisions about my own body's future, physical needs?

The Wisconsin retreat seemed like the perfect place to answer this question. So everything I did while on my retreat was framed by this question. Thus, when I read a story in the contemporary neurologist Antonio Damasio's book, *Descartes' Error: Emotion, Reason and the Human Brain*, about a man who thought about himself "as if" he had a body, I had an "aha" experience.

The story that galvanized my attention was about a man who had suffered injury to the prefrontal lobe of his brain, which made it impossible for him to do anything internally with his body except to think *about* it. He could not think *within* it or through it. He was unaware of the emotional feelings linked to his thoughts and sensations. So he reasoned "as if" he were wrestling with his body's emotional feelings, but he wasn't. The man's mind could not grasp the actual give and take of his own emotional life—that push and pull of feelings that occur when our body reacts against a considered idea such as wearing winter clothes on a hot summer day.

Damasio's account and reflections gave me pause. Was *I* an "as if" thinker? My ability to think through and predict the probable state of my body while on retreat in

Wisconsin and my decision to pack a suitcase filled with winter clothing as well as a suitcase full of summer clothes seemed to me to be an example of "as if" thinking. No, I had not suffered a brain injury. But I seemed to have lost the capacity to make realistic predictions about my own body using the ebb and flow of my own body's affective feelings as the physical sentiments gauged to modify and limit my mind's thoughts and reflections.

I took small consolation from Damasio's observation that I was not alone in having lost the capacity to link my mind to my body through emotional feelings. This kind of disembodied thinking, Damasio has found, is endemic to Western culture. But this endemic condition of Western minds, I now reasoned, could not have come about through physical injury to each of our individual prefrontal brain areas. Surely the "fall of man" should not be explained neurobiologically as a fracture to the brain of the biblical Adam that condemned his progeny to disembodied thinking and mindless feeling. Something else must be going on. But what?

I had spent decades, first as a broadcast journalist and then as religious scholar, minister, and theologian, asking why people so often act against their own best interests or confound their own best wishes and desires. I never imagined that the practical way this spiritual question would show up in my own life would be as a clothes issue, a dress-for-success issue while on a spiritual retreat.

I knew that I no longer wanted to be an "as if" thinker and vowed to start thinking *with* my body again. But how could I achieve this end? How could I think my way back into my own body's feelings, my own emotions? How could I keep my mind focused on my own body's emotional feelings and sentiments? Clearly, it was time for me to experiment.

I had brought a small paperweight with me on the retreat, so I decided to start carrying it around in my pocket during the day and to keep it in hand at night. This way, I reasoned, my mind would be aware of something different about my body, and would thus be forced to stay focused on actual feelings within my body instead of taking flights of fancy into interesting or important ideas.

The first day was rather heady. I smiled to myself at my silly game as I carried the paperweight with me all day. Perhaps I did not suffer from a prefrontal brain injury, I thought, but I might nevertheless be addled. But I was on retreat and gave myself permission to persist with this silly game. And so I arrived at the first night of this experiment. I climbed into my small monastery bed in my small monastery room with my paperweight in hand.

I decided that if I awakened during the night, as I sometimes do, I would make my mind sink into the feeling of the weight in my hand. And so, when I awoke, I held onto the paperweight. I directed all of the attention to the feelings and sensations entailed in holding a six-ounce weight in my hand. I did this for about an hour until I fell into sleep, still focusing on the feelings of the extra weight in my hand.

In the morning, I awoke with a profound sense of a physical sadness that I had not known before. I was not depressed; I did not feel shame or guilt. I simply felt inexplicably sad.

Could it be, I now wondered, that I have such a difficult time thinking *with* my body *about* my body because it is so sad? Extravagant eating, drinking, shopping, gallivanting, even reading had dulled my awareness of this pervasive feeling in me for years. These practices had dulled my awareness of me. I resolved to hold onto the emotional sadness I now felt.

I stayed in this sea of sadness, night and day. I was now in a state of mourning, letting go of what I had already lost: an internal sense of community. Until now, I had held onto that lost sense of community *as if* real community were present in my home. My mind now understood my body's sadness. At home, I had felt abandoned and alone—but without emotionally acknowledging it. I, the mind, was a head-trip of a body at sea.

Gradually, I began to notice a shift, a letting go, a change of heart. It was subtle.

This shift was so subtle that I can only describe it by referring to an extreme example of it—a story recounted by psychoanalyst R. D. Laing during his work with a catatonic schizophrenic.

Each day, as Laing made his rounds, he would sit next to the immobile man and say something like this: "If my mother had locked me in a closet for all of those years, I wouldn't want to talk to anyone either." Day in and day out, year after year, Laing made such statements to the man and then would move on to his next patient.

And then the day came. Laing sat next to the man, told him he would not want to speak to another either—if he had been treated the way this man had been treated by his mother—and the man turned to him and said "Yeah."

The shift I felt within myself was not this dramatic. And yet, for me, it was as vividly affirming. I had finally said to myself—"I am sad and for good reason." And I heard myself reply: "Yeah."

Suddenly, I felt a childlike intensity of feeling that turns every experience of life into something unmistakably marvelous.

I felt love beyond belief. And I loved life, every moment of it.

But I could not sustain this change of heart by myself. I needed the care and compassion of my own Unitarian Universalist community to stay the spiritual course of my change of heart, my experience of love beyond belief.

SOURCE: Thandeka, "Thandeka's Change of Heart," in *What Moves Us: Unitarian Universalist Theology*, uua.org/re/tapestry/adults/movesus/workshop10/282841.shtml

PETER MORALES

"We Are One"

2009

Peter Morales (1946–) was elected president of the UUA in 2009, after serving as senior minister of Jefferson Unitarian Church in Golden, Colorado, and as UUA Director for District Services. A Texas native and the UUA's first Latino president, Morales pursued careers as a newspaper editor and government official before entering the ministry in 1999. Morales campaigned for the presidency on a platform that emphasized multicultural growth, and almost immediately confronted the challenge of responding to anti-immigration legislation, including the Arizona law that empowered local police to check the immigration status of every person they detained. Activists called upon the UUA to participate in a boycott that would have required the cancellation of its 2012 General Assembly in Phoenix. (This would have been the second such cancellation of a Phoenix General Assembly, as the 1988 General Assembly had been relocated because of Arizona's refusal to recognize the Martin Luther King Day holiday.) But the UUA chose instead to organize a "Justice General Assembly" that minimized ordinary business and engaged deeply with local partners in social witness. The result was a new emphasis on accountability to allies in all Unitarian Universalist social justice work. Morales's comments at a social justice convocation held three years before Justice General Assembly highlight the connection between denominational growth and social witness.

—Dan McKanan

We live in a new America. My colleague Stan Perea calls it the America of the moo-shoo burrito and the Korean taco. California now has more people from minority populations than it has whites. Our country is now home to more Hispanics than African Americans. In most cities, the children entering the public schools speak more than seventy languages among them.

America was once defined by the movement of people who came to the east coast and moved westward. The new American story is of people moving north from countries to the south and moving to the west coast from countries in the Far East—such as Vietnam, Korea, and elsewhere.

In the case of the recent rapid increase in immigration from Mexico and Central America, most U.S. citizens tend to think we are somehow passive victims. These aliens are pouring over our border and must be stopped.

The truth is very different. Our economic policies, which disproportionately benefit the wealthy, are helping to create wrenching economic dislocations in Mexico, Guatemala, and Nicaragua. Many of the people trying to sneak into the United States were pushed out of their homes by U.S. policies.

I am not suggesting that our country does not need to control its borders, and I do not pretend to have all the policy answers. I do know this: We cannot pretend that we had nothing to do with the creation of the problem. I also know this: We are all connected. We are in this together.

* * *

We need to see our present situation in its historical context. The border between the United States and Mexico was created to make space for slavery. We are building fences and guard towers along that border to keep Mexicans from reentering land that was taken from them. Of course, the Mexican elite, mostly of European descent, were not exactly blameless: The land that undocumented Americans stole from them was land they had previously stolen from Native Americans. It is easy to determine who has a *legal* right to be here, but who has a *moral* right to be here?

As a religious people who affirm human compassion, advocate for human rights, and seek justice, we must never make the mistake of confusing a legal right with a moral right. The forced removal of Native Americans from their land and onto reservations was legal. The importation and sale of African slaves was legal. South African apartheid was legal. The confiscation of the property of Jews at the beginning of the Nazi regime was legal. The Spanish Inquisition was legal. Crucifying Jesus was legal. Burning Michael Servetus at the stake for his unitarian theology was legal. The fact that something is legal does not cut much ethical ice. The powerful have always used the legal system to oppress the powerless.

It is true that as citizens we should respect the role of law. More importantly, though, our duty is to create laws founded on our highest sense of justice, equity, and compassion. Loud voices urge us to choose fear, denial, reactionary nationalism, and racism. We must resist and choose the better way urged by every major religious tradition. We must choose the path of compassion and hope. We must choose a path that is founded on the recognition that we are connected, that we are all in this together.

These are the teachings of every great tradition. At the core of the teachings of Jesus is the conviction that we are all one. We are all God's children, and we are all equal. We are supposed to care for one another. Jesus taught his followers that an act of kindness to the most humble human being was the equivalent of performing the same for Jesus.

The prophet Muhammad taught that the tribal divisions among the Arabian people were wrong. The symbols of those tribal divisions were the legion of tribal

506

gods, and Muhammad told the people that these gods were false, that there is only one God. We are united, and we owe our allegiance to the one creator.

Buddhism teaches that if we stop and really pay attention, we will realize that the things we think separate us are an illusion. Our connections are ultimately real, not our divisions.

We find the same message in every tradition: We are one. We are connected. We are brothers and sisters. If we truly accept that we are all part of a greater whole, that what unites and transcends us is ultimately more important than our illusion of individuality, how might that guide us? If we accept that compassion (literally "to suffer with") is the manifestation of realizing that we are one, what are the implications? What would our community and our state and our nation do if they were guided by the finest aspirations of humanity's religions? What would you and I do if we were guided by these very same ideas, as expressed in our Unitarian Universalist Principles? What future might we build if we created policies guided by our notions of justice, equity, and compassion in human relations?

I do not have all the policy answers on immigration or the related issues of public education, health care, and the economy. I do know this: Breaking up poor working families who have lived among us for years does not feel like justice, equity, and compassion in action. Refusing minimal health services to young children does not feel like the way we should treat members of our human family. Having our police forces profile brown people does not feel like breaking down the walls of tribalism. Creating a huge wall, complete with barbed wire, across hundreds of miles of border does not feel neighborly.

There must be a better way, and you and I must help build it. Barbed wire is not the answer. More border guards and more deportations are not the answer. Paranoia and panic will solve nothing.

We must remember that we are all immigrant stock, every single one of us living on this continent. Even Native Americans at one time immigrated here from Asia.

We must also acknowledge that we helped to create the situation in which displaced people look to find a home here. America has already been transformed by the latest waves of immigration. Our children and grandchildren are going to live in a multicultural society—a society of moo-shoo burritos, egg roll tacos, and whole wheat tortillas. We need not be afraid of that multicultural society. Fear leads to violence and repression.

Instead, let us embrace the possibilities before us. Let us be guided by love and hope. Let our actions emerge from the deep conviction that people from Mexico and Korea and Canada and Vietnam are ultimately part of our extended family. Surely, religious people who have learned to embrace the wisdom of Judaism, Christianity, humanism, Islam, and Eastern religions can lead the way. We are people who

507

have always affirmed human diversity. We have always looked to the future and seen new possibilities. We must to do so again. Let us be the people who break down the arbitrary barriers that divide us from them. We are one, and love and hope will guide us. Let us, together with all our brothers and sisters, build a new way.

SOURCE: Peter Morales, "We Are One," in John Gibb Millspaugh, ed., A *People So Bold: Theology and Ministry for Unitarian Universalists* (Boston: Skinner House, 2010), 84–89.

NIHAL ATTANAYAKE
"How We Belong to Creation"
2010

Nihal Attanayake (1954–), a Sri Lankan man who is married to a Filipina woman, was ordained in the Anglican Church in Sri Lanka in 1979 and accepted into ministerial fellowship by the Unitarian Universalist Church of the Philippines in 2000. He has served that church as chair of its Faith in Action program, director of its Church Partnership program, manager of its Micro Finance and International Relations Office, and as its president. He has also served on the Executive Committee of the International Council of Unitarians and Universalists (ICUU). His talk at the third ICUU theological symposium, held in Kerkrade, The Netherlands, offered an ecological understanding of Unitarian Universalist faith.

—Dan McKanan

In this paper I want to suggest three points: first, that creation and nature is one; secondly, the creator and the created is one; and thirdly, not that we belong to, but that we are one with creation.

When I use the Biblical text for our study, I am far from the majority's literal interpretations. I want to look into the texts and find minority voices there that support the proposition that Creation is one with, and is, Nature.

* * *

In the first chapter of Genesis, God is portrayed as a presence "moving over the face of the waters" (Gen. 1:2). A study of this text suggests the analogy of a mother hen brooding over her nest to bring forth life. A God who is understood as a mother hen is not something external to this world. It makes a vast difference to our sense of responsibility to our world if we proclaim God, not as the external deity who calls the world into being by divine command, but as the power that emerges within all of life.

Even when the Bible moves on to a second story of creation, the portrait is still of a deity who is not really external. God breathes into Adam. . . .

It is the prophet Jeremiah who says that the animals too are the creation of God and must therefore be regarded as holy (Jer. 27:5), and the Psalmist who asserts that all creatures look to God for their sustenance.

* * *

As Polynesians who spread out to many islands between New Zealand and Hawaii, the Maori believe that there are powers at work throughout the whole of life (a combination of gods and nature). . . .

Taoism in China portrays the world as organic, interdependent system. There is an underlying unity behind, "the ten thousand things." . . .

In Hinduism, the philosopher thinks of God as ultimate reality, the impersonal "word-soul." . . .

In the Buddhist scripture Tripitaka . . . a creation story . . . explains that the world at the beginning was covered with a primordial soup. Gradually order was established and life evolved. . . .

We know from our study of evolution that life is a single whole. All life has developed from that first cell of living matter born in the sea some four billion years ago. . . . This is one of our affirmations for promoting the interdependent web of all existence as one of our U-U principles.

* * *

Whatever is human is part of a wider cosmic order. It is by right that we let things be in harmony and whole. We are creation in the best known experiences of birth, death, and rebirth. Jesus, in his many teachings according to the Gospel writers, taught metaphorically: The seed that falls onto the ground must decay in order to change its form and to come alive clothed in a new form, the rebirth which is natural and our day-to-day experience. Becoming alive, dying, and being reborn is ever changing, making evolving the law of creation. Eastern religions provided that enlightenment as necessary for coexistence, harmony, peace, and tranquility. Today we are in search of those truths that we had disregarded.

What are the ways we find ourselves one with Creation? Can we touch the core of our inner being? Creativity begins when we are relating to that inner being. We see much more creativity around us day-by-day when who we are is one with the whole creation, one with the act of creation. We create. That is our daily experience.

This gathering has come about because of that very creativity which is with and within us.

SOURCE: Nihal Attanayake, "How We Belong to Creation," in Jill K. McAllister, ed., *Belonging: Our Unitarian Identities and the Nature of Our Relations* (London, UK: International Council of Unitarians and Universalists, 2012), 26–30, 34–35.

MARIA PAP

"Partnerships: Belonging as Collaboration, Mutuality and Accountability"

2010

Maria Pap, a minister in the Transylvanian Unitarian Church, studied in England and the United States and graduated from the Kolozsvar seminary. Following her ordination in 1995, she was appointed as minister of the congregations in Kézdivásárhely and Szentivánlaborfalva. Two years later, the Kézdivásárhely congregation entered into a partner church relationship with the Unitarian Universalist Congregation of Ann Arbor. The Unitarian Universalist Partner Church Council was established in 1993 to encourage congregations in the United States and Canada to build relationships of mutual accountability with Unitarian and Universalist congregations, orphanages, and schools around the world. The council "envision[s] a worldwide Unitarian and Unitarian Universalist community that promotes peace, justice, and liberty for all, supported by partnerships that are integral to congregational life," and has fostered nearly two hundred partnerships.

—Dan McKanan

There are identities we are born with: family, race, gender. We could change them, but most of the time that would come at great spiritual cost. But there are other identities which we assume willingly when belonging is not a given but a chosen reality. This is the case of the partner-church relation where a United States UU church and a Transylvanian church engaged in a partnership willingly. The majority of the churches in Transylvania have or had a partner church in the States. Some are thriving, some are dwindling, and some have expired. There are many reasons for this. And the notion of collaboration and responsibility play a big part.

* * *

A small Transylvanian village with mostly farmers might end up as partners with a downtown, educated, sophisticated UU American congregation. I haven't mentioned anything yet about assistance, language barriers, and so on and so forth. So many things divided us that the gap seemed impossible to fill, and in some cases it was never filled. If I look back 20 years, I realize that most of the partner-church relations survive by the grace of God and the determination, love and stubbornness of a few people who were able to drag their congregations over great difficulties and pitfalls of the fledgling program. After the initial surge of enthusiasm,

511

the eventual relationship experienced a time of restlessness and confusion. . . . It's like in a marriage. I mean after the honeymoon, I realize: My God! I am to live with this person for the next 40 years—this is a life-long commitment—what am I going to do?

So the answer came from the American side and led to the establishment in 1993 of the UU Partner Church Council which developed programs, criteria, and guidelines for partnership. In a word this gave structure to a grassroots movement.

* * *

There are partnerships which are going strong. What is the secret? Well, one is collaboration, working together in several ways, in several fields, according to their needs. But collaboration on common work is not easy.

We are aware—we, meaning the Transylvanian Unitarians—that there is an economic imbalance in this relationship. It would be foolish and unproductive not to acknowledge it. . . . This willingly or unwillingly puts Americans into a position of power which is hard to deal with on both sides. The congregation that supplies the money expects sometimes to have a say in what purpose that money will be used. The collaboration on joint projects was successful so far only when we agreed in advance on the whole process. When this was missing, lots of misunderstanding and bitterness ensued. . . .

For example, the needs of the community in Transylvania suffered a change by the time the money arrived. They used it accordingly. The partners thought that this was outrageous. What do you mean to change the destination of the gift? We thought the money was to buy a tractor, and you used it to repair the steeple. Why are you not using the tractor and the agricultural machinery we bought for you? It was your biggest dream and desire, and now they are out there rusting.

* * *

These misunderstandings arose because, on the one hand, some people were afraid or unwilling to engage in honest conversations. On the other hand, if they were able to get over the initial frustration or anger, a new level of trust and understanding arrived.

* * *

So, finally, what is the secret that makes some partnerships work and others do not? Those that do work assume the responsibility of belonging. They do it in terms of finances. They understand—I wouldn't call it their duty, but their ability, or their privilege to help those congregations in terms of finances who need it—their responsibility in terms of getting to know one another, getting to know each other's history, theology and spirituality. When I'm talking about responsibility, I'm not just talking about the American side because these transactions need to work both ways. I mean responsibility in terms of connections, in terms of community, discussions, joint projects, assuming faults and failings, and learning to tolerate, and to love.

SOURCE: Maria Pap, "Partnerships: Belonging as Collaboration, Mutuality and Accountability," in Jill K. McAllister, ed., *Belonging: Our Unitarian Identities and the Nature of Our Relations* (London, UK: International Council of Unitarians and Universalists, 2012), 129–34, 138. Corrected by the author.

FULGENCE NDAGIJIMANA
"African Perspectives on Belonging"
2010

Fulgence Ndagijimana is the founding minister of the Unitarian Church in Burundi. Raised Roman Catholic, he attended a Dominican seminary before realizing that he needed to find a new spiritual path. He discovered Unitarian Universalism through the Internet and, with the support of the ICUU, joined with others to organize a congregation in 2005. In September 2011, the seventy-member congregation dedicated its building in Bujumbura—the first Unitarian Universalist church built in East Africa—and ordained Ndagijimana as its minister. In October 2015, as political tensions escalated in Burundi, the congregation was attacked by an armed group. One month later, Ndagijimana was arrested at the church and interrogated by the police. He and many members of the church subsequently went into exile in another African country. Ndagijimana also serves on the ICUU Executive Committee.

—Dan McKanan

Let me first say that the reality of belonging can be seen as both a perception from the point of view of an outsider and also an experience of the person who belongs. I can express myself better with an example. If you drive past an African village and see a group of men, women and children looking and waving at you, you will think that they belong together, but that might be just your perception. Since you are not aware that women are not well treated, that some rules or ways of doing things are harmful to some, you won't know until an experience is shared from the people of the village themselves. This example may be true for UUs in Africa as well.

* * *

The concept of belonging is one of the deepest in our African cultures. Contact with the Western traditions and cultures is changing the way things used to be but generally speaking, the concept of belonging still holds a very high importance in the African traditions.

* * *

The identity as African is clearly present with the members of different U-U congregations in Africa. They clearly know where they belong after the service. But how do we *together* make sure we Africans also have a U-U identity and not some sort of Western identity? The first question should be, what do we mean anyway by a U-U-identity expressed through values that can be shared or passed on to others?

Simply put, the U-U principles can be the first place to tap: freedom of conscience which we all cherish; the high importance given to individual judgment in matters of faith; the worth and dignity of every person; the concern for justice and compassion in human relations; the web of life and the commitment to democratic principles, are all elements of what could be called the U-U identity.

* * *

How do we make people feel at home in their newly found religious home and call it proudly their new home, while some people close to them are not as accommodating? Transition always has something new; it also needs something of the old to keep going. Some African Unitarians still look to their former churches with some sympathy, and I sometimes enjoy some songs on Roman Catholic wedding ceremonies. U-U churches need to build a culture of established churches with everything involved like good music—you know like I do that Africans have good and lively music. Exchange of experiences from well-established churches would help this culture and this tradition to be in place. This too is part of people's identities as they gradually evolve from one religious setting to the other, and is generously called for as a sign of our belonging to one another. . . .

For the spirit of cooperation and mutual support to grow and bear fruit, we will have to be prepared to learn from one another, to seek understanding in a positive way and foster mutual growth that is real in the spirit of partnership. When you write an email to your colleague in North America who is 2000 miles away, you expect a reply probably within minutes! If you write an email to your partner in some countries, you might expect a reply in a week or two! But you can be patient, because the person on the other end is your brother or your sister. Some people in some cultures keep time better than others and sometimes we have to adjust to stubborn cultural habits.

Challenges in getting to know and work together on common goals also build partnerships. There are different approaches to use of money; many of you are used to accountability and deal with money orders and invoices, others are not used to those kinds of complex systems. By virtue of our shared faith, we are colleagues but—fundamentally in the African mentality—we are all brothers and sisters. As such, we ought to stand in solidarity with one another whenever necessary as it is reasonable and realistic.

* * *

The U-U faith has a potential to not only enrich the life of our communities, but also to challenge unacceptable ways of behaving and treating people. We must listen to one another and hear the stories of people who have barriers to belonging, are excluded from belonging or have chosen NOT to belong, so that the saving message of UUism can rise and be a light for all of us and for the rest of the world.

SOURCE: Fulgence Ndagijimana, "African Perspectives on Belonging," in Jill K. McAllister, ed., *Belonging: Our Unitarian Identities and the Nature of Our Relations* (London, UK: International Council of Unitarians and Universalists, 2012), 145, 148, 152–56.

DEBORAH J. POPE-LANCE

"Whence We Come and How, and Whither"

2011

Clergy sexual misconduct—the use of religious authority to exploit and sexually abuse those in a minister's care—has been a part of every religious institution in every historical era. Many observers believed that sexual misconduct by Unitarian Universalist clergy was most common in the 1960s and 1970s, a period when traditional mores were broadly questioned and sexual restrictions had broken down among religious liberals. However, once women entered ministry and leadership in larger numbers, breaking the silence about this history and bringing a feminist analysis of the relationship between sex and power, many came to see that clergy sexual misconduct is an abuse of power and not simply a symptom of changing mores. The Ministerial Sisterhood Unitarian Universalist (women clergy) petitioned the UUA in the late 1980s, demanding action. In the early 1990s, the Unitarian Universalist Women's Federation (primarily lay women) formed the first denomination-wide task force to advocate for survivors. Two decades later, essayists at the Ministerial Conference at Berry Street portrayed the denomination's response as still inadequate, failing to understand the extent of misconduct's harm and to stand on the side of justice for those affected. The first essay was by Deborah J. Pope-Lance (1952–), a Marriage and Family Therapist, ethicist, and Unitarian Universalist minister, who consults widely about the aftereffects of clergy misconduct. Further Reading: Gail Seavey, "If Our Secrets Define Us," Berry Street Essay 2016, www.uuma.org/page/berrystreetessays

—Dan McKanan

> *Rank by rank again we stand,* [singing, joined by all]
> *from the four winds gathered hither:*
> *Loud the hallowed walls demand*
> *Whence we come and how, and whither.*

This hymn we know by heart summons the best in us for ministry. . . .
Rank by Rank was not sung at the first General Assembly I attended [in 1969].

* * *

General Assemblies in the 1970s could feel like carnival or a Roman bacchanal. Hospitality suites doubled as hook up bars. Some ministers openly engaged in intimate same-time-next-year relationships without, shall I say, benefit of clergy.

Some brazenly. One colleague, a minister I had known when a child in the church, expressed delight [seeing me at GA] that now that I was an adult and ordained, he could pursue his long interest in seducing me. Another, on the walk over to the Service of the Living Tradition, pointed to a woman colleague walking ahead and remarked, "I wonder what she's like in bed." Years later he told me of his sexual misconducts with congregants, his terrible recklessness, and his relief not ever to have been caught.

In the 1980s a cable TV show profiled an admired colleague, calling him the Brother of Love and reporting on his sexual relations with women in his church.

In the 1990s a respected colleague's misconduct was reported in a major magazine and by a caller on a national radio show given chapter and verse. Media coverage of his indiscretion led three men in my New England parish at the time to ask, as each came through the receiving line one Sunday, "Hey, that colleague of yours is having a good time. Will you be offering the same pastoral services here for us?"

From one of our pulpits, another preached about finding love across a crowded chancel. He said all love was holy and of God. Even his love for a married member, which, yes, he admitted, did violate guidelines, a detail he prayed they'd look beyond.

*　*　*

In 2005 Oprah hosted victims of another colleague on a show whose theme was children sold into sexual slavery. Our colleague brought teenage girls from the third world to live in his home under the pretense of saving them from poverty, educating them and introducing them to a new life. Instead, he molested and raped them. . . .

Witnessing these and other events, in the 1980s we, the Unitarian Universalist Ministers Association, drafted sexual ethics into our guidelines and code. And now, we revisit these, as well we should from time to time, in search of clearer expression of our convictions. We find we are not easily of one mind.

*　*　*

But we have found it hard to talk openly about our colleagues' mis-steps, about what in specific renders their actions rude or wrong, risky or injurious, unethical or unlawful. We whisper lest we violate the guidelines' prohibition against speaking ill of a colleague, lest we say out loud what everyone already knows to be true. We minimize. . . . "They do behave badly but do we really want to sacrifice our shiniest preachers and our brightest lights on this?" . . .

We debate due process and marital status. We assert a colleague's right to a private life. . . .

What is too much missing in our collegial conversations is an acknowledgement of our humiliation and hurt. Our [own] and the humiliation and hurt of those we serve.

The hurt endured by individuals who come to their ministers for religious counsel and are instead abused. [The injurious effect of this abuse by itself ought to

518

compel us to seek compassion and justice for survivors and zero tolerance for colleagues' misconduct.] The humiliation endured by spouses and partners, families, and friends of these harmed individuals. The bruising betrayal endured by coworkers and colleagues, unwittingly drawn in to a maelstrom of lies, manipulation, and self-indulgence.

The harm suffered by congregations and organizations: the months of upset and fierce disagreement, the hours of volunteer time, the expense of investigating and deliberating and of hiring conflict experts, the loss of members, damaged public image, and disruption to mission.

And the harm inflicted upon the profession of ministry itself: the public outrage; the withdrawal of trust; the loss of respect.

*   *   *

Congregations wounded by the misconduct of their clergy can be chronically dysfunctional, conducting their business in disturbingly ineffective ways. They can lack the capacity to follow procedures, to do what they say they will do, to set appropriate boundaries, to establish lines of responsibility, to secure their building, to respond properly to unsafe behavior, to welcome new people, to run successful canvasses, to tolerate difference or to engage in productive disagreement without nasty conflict. The usual efforts—healthy congregation workshops, district staff interventions, a succession of able-enough clergy—bring no permanent fix. The least able, crankiest members remain in leadership while the mature more self-differentiated members, those immune cells [Peter Steinke tells us are] needed for healthy congregations, fed up with the craziness, bully tactics and resistance to change, withdraw.

*   *   *

Nowhere is the effect of clergy misconduct's harm more evident than in the ministerial relationships of those who serve as minister in its aftermath. These afterpastors, as they are sometimes called, commonly report that congregants relate to them in ways confounding and crazy, making their work unduly challenging. Afterpastors report their ministerial relationships lack the usual trust, respect, and interest accorded to clergy. Laity, whose trust is betrayed by a predecessor, appear reluctant or unable to trust subsequent clergy.

Afterpastors report feeling pushed and pulled. They describe leaders who manipulate and intrude, who expect too much or too little, who sometimes coerce and threaten. The boundaries of the minister's role in the aftermath of misconduct can be confused and unclear.

Afterpastors report being lied to and misled. Information is controlled. Secrets common. Interactions triangulated. In the aftermath of misconduct, secret keeping may provide an illusion of control over an escalating crisis.

Afterpastors report an unusual number of difficult people in congregations with misconduct histories, people whose functioning is impaired or inconsistent, who

519

can be abusive, unreasonable, or divisive, who routinely generate upset and drama. Now, yes, we all have endured congregants who repeatedly strain the limits of our goodwill and grace. But afterpastors report that nearly every interaction contains some element of reactivity, coercion, disrespect, and boundary pushing. . . .

In one stunning example, an afterpastor tells of a church treasurer who failed repeatedly, month after month, to pay her on time. When she finally complained to the board, they told her she was too demanding; "Remember: he's a volunteer." When some months later she complained again, they suggested she stop doing what- ever she was doing to piss him off. "Then he'll send your checks on time." More months passed. This time when she complained, she told leaders she was prepared to take a leave of absence to put her affairs in order. Only then did they confront him and he resigned from the church. And only then did she learn the story: that his mother had been the second wife of a misconducting [colleague] whose numerous indiscretions two decades earlier had ended their marriage and his ministry in scan- dal and had mortified his stepson.

Individuals and congregations in the aftermath of misconduct may behave much as those who have endured a trauma. Trauma survivors can be unable to trust. They may act unreasonably or be controlling. Ironically, they may act in ways that lead to their being re-traumatized. Understanding misconduct as a trauma helps explain the odd interactions afterpastors experience. This afterpastor did not imag- ine that she was playing the part of the betraying minister in the drama of this man's life. Understanding his behavior as detached from its traumatic origins and not about her would have suggested different strategies and these might have provided the play with a last act that healed and blessed.

Navigating these crazy-making relationships, day after day, is stressful and difficult.

☆　☆　☆

In ministry, relationships are the basic tool of the trade. Through a minister's relating pastoral care is extended, spiritual life nurtured, psychological health pro- moted, divinity experienced, and grace mediated. By virtue of our ordinations, because of our religious perspectives, and through calls extended to us, ministers have unique relationships with those we serve as minister. Regardless of our desires or our opinions about whether or not ministers should be allowed to form special rela- tionships with those they serve, we ministers already have a special relationship— a ministerial relationship.

In this special relationship, conscious and unconscious dimensions from con- gregant and minister play out. Congregants may imagine a minister, like God among the ancient Hebrews, as one who shepherds the people, who knows what they need better than they do. Or they may imagine them like their own god-like fathers who asked too much or showed them no mercy. A minister, too, may imagine a minister god-like, one to whom the sheep come for tending. Or like their own mother omnipotent and without whom nothing was ever allowed to happen. An infinite number of these dimensions enhance, distort and generally complicate minister-congregant interactions, though, I must say, another verb does come to mind.

Any minister, reasonably aware of his or her own distortions, who can remain non-reactive, non-anxious, and non-judgmental in the face of a congregant's distorted reactions can provide unique opportunities for healing. The special relationship gives us as ministers a capacity, an opportunity, a power, to deeply influence, to profoundly change, and to potentially transform the lives of those we serve.

* * *

Whither then? . . .

Two centuries after Channing imagined [the Berry Street essay so that] we might do well to speak annually with one another on the state of our ministry, we colleagues find ourselves in a profession challenging and much changed. . . .

We would be well served if we could find our way clear to be of one mind about ethical standards of practice. We would support one another better if *we would be one* behind some language that made our guidelines clear and our resolve firm.

What our collegial conversation needs is a stunning reminder of our power, a power we wield to good result or poor, whose complex interpersonal dynamics we can oft-times neither observe nor command though it be ever our responsibility to do so. What is needed is greater understanding of the dynamics of our power, our power to humiliate or to bless, to harm or to heal, our power to influence the success of our ministries, the health of our congregations and indeed the future of our religious heritage. What is needed is a recognition of ministry's power and a stirring re-conviction, by and with that power, to our call as ministers to transform. Then might clarity come, then might unity be found, and yet the world be changed.

SOURCE: Deborah J. Pope-Lance, "Whence We Come and How, and Whither," Berry Street Essay, delivered at the Ministerial Conference, June 22, 2011, uuma.org/page/berrystreetessays

"Ethical Eating"

2011

This Statement of Conscience was approved at the 2011 General Assembly. It was crafted to honor the diverse choices that Unitarian Universalists make with regard to food, while challenging everyone to act in ways that reflect the rights of animals, agricultural and food processing workers, and everyone affected by food systems.

—Dan McKanan

Aware of our interdependence, we acknowledge that eating ethically requires us to be mindful of the miracle of life we share with all beings. With gratitude for the food we have received, we strive to choose foods that minimize harm and are protective of the environment, consumers, farmers, and all those involved in food production and distribution.

Environmental justice includes the equitable distribution of both environmental burdens and benefits for populations of residents and workers. Marginalized people have often been able to find housing or work only in areas exposed to environmental pollutants, with consequent negative health and quality of life effects.

As Unitarian Universalists, we are called to address our relationship with food. Our Principles call for recognition of and respect for the other. As we search freely and responsibly for truth, meaning, and spiritual wholeness, we will make a variety of individual choices about food. Ethical eating is the application of our Principles to our food choices. . . .

Access to an adequate supply of healthy food and clean water is a basic human need and right. Many people do not have adequate food, while others have a surplus. In many locations, poor distribution of food is a major contributor to hunger and malnutrition. The effects of climate change, weather conditions, and armed conflicts can also expose many people to starvation. Paradoxically, an abundance of food does not guarantee access to healthy food.

We acknowledge that aggressive action needs to be taken that will ensure an adequate food supply for the world population; reduce the use of energy, water, fertilizer, pesticides, and hormones in food production; mitigate climate change; and end the inhumane treatment of animals. These steps call for an evolution of our eating habits to include more locally grown, minimally processed whole foods. We acknowledge that this evolution must respect diversity in cultures, nutritional requirements, and religious practices.

Minimally processed plant-based diets are healthier diets. Some of us believe that it is ethical only to eat plants while others of us believe that it is ethical to eat both plants and animals. We do not call here for a single dietary approach. We encourage a knowledgeable choice of food based on understanding the demands of feeding a growing world population, the health effects of particular foods, and the consequences of production, worker treatment, and transportation methods. We commit to applying this knowledge to both personal and public actions, recognizing that many of us might embark on a dramatic change in eating choices and some might pay more for food that is ethically produced. For congregations, helping congregants gain this understanding and supporting their choices will require a long-term collective process of engagement, education, discernment, and advocacy. Unitarian Universalists aspire to radical hospitality and developing the beloved community. Therefore, we affirm that the natural world exists not for the sole benefit of one nation, one race, one gender, one religion, or even one species, but for all. Working in the defense of mutual interests, Unitarian Universalists acknowledge and accept the challenge of enlarging our circle of moral concern to include all living creatures.

As individuals and as congregations, we recognize the need to examine the impact of our food choices and our practices and make changes that will lighten the burden we place on the world. We also recognize that many food decisions will require us to make trade-offs between competing priorities. These priorities include: taste, selection, price, human health, environmental protection, sustainability, adequate food supply, humane treatment of animals used for food, and fair treatment of farm and food workers. . . .

Calls To Action

Individual Actions

Recognizing that individual circumstances vary, we aspire to buy, raise, and consume food for ourselves and our families that:

- increases our proportionate consumption of plant-based foods, which increases the global access to calories, provides health benefits, and prevents injuring animals;
- minimizes the pain and suffering of animals by purchasing meat or seafood produced under humane conditions, for those who choose to eat meat or seafood;
- minimizes the negative environmental effects of raising animals or plants by purchasing organically produced food, and seafood certified as responsibly farmed or harvested;

- minimizes transportation-related carbon dioxide emissions by obtaining foods locally produced through home or community gardens, farmers markets, or community supported agriculture (CSA);
- provides farm workers with living wages and safe working environments;
- contributes to social harmony by encouraging communal eating;
- promotes health, consuming food in quantities that do not lead to obesity;

* * *

Congregational Actions

As congregations, we aspire to:

- provide and sell more plant-based, organic, locally produced, and fair trade foods at congregational events;
- promote economic accessibility to safe, ethically produced food by organizing members to work for food justice through activities such as: urging grocery chains to locate stores in low income neighborhoods, supporting local food co-ops, helping people obtain food stamps, advocating for increased funding to alleviate hunger, and assisting local meals on wheels and food bank programs;
- support the Unitarian Universalist Service Committee, Unitarian Universalist United Nations Office, and other relevant UU organizations in their efforts to ensure that everyone has adequate nutritious food, produced sustainably;
- provide educational programs for all ages that address the issues of environmental justice, world hunger, gardening, food preparation, and nutrition;
- become Green Sanctuary—accredited and include ethical eating in programs;
- advocate for healthful food for school and other institutional meals; and
- engage in direct action in solidarity with workers and labor advocacy groups to support agricultural and food workers.

With gratitude and reverence for all life, we savor food mindful of all that has contributed to it. We commit ourselves to a more equitable sharing of the earth's bounty.

SOURCE: "Ethical Eating: Food & Environmental Justice," Unitarian Universalist Social Justice Statements, uua.org/statements/ethical-eating-food-environmental-justice

"Immigration as a Moral Issue"

2013

This Statement of Conscience was approved one year after the Unitarian Universalist Association held its "Justice General Assembly," working in solidarity with immigrant rights activists in Phoenix, Arizona. It solidified a long-standing commitment to work for more inclusive immigration policies and to advocate for the human rights of all people regardless of immigration status.

—Dan McKanan

A belief in "the inherent worth and dignity of every person" is core to Unitarian Universalism: every person, no exceptions. As religious people, our Principles call us to acknowledge the immigrant experience and to affirm and promote the flourishing of the human family.

Our Sources "challenge us to confront powers and structures of evil with justice, compassion, and the transforming power of love." Hebrew scripture teaches love for the foreigner because "you were foreigners in the land of Egypt" (Leviticus 19:33–34). Christian scripture reports that Jesus and his disciples were itinerants. When asked "Who is my neighbor?" Jesus responded with the parable of the Good Samaritan, a foreigner who treated a badly beaten man as the foreigner would have wished to be treated (Luke 10:25–37). The Qur'an teaches doing "good to . . . those in need, neighbors who are near, neighbors who are strangers, the companion by your side, the wayfarer that you meet" (4:36). The Universal Declaration of Human Rights asserts that "everyone has the right to leave any country, including his own, and to return to his country" (article 13.2). . . .

Today people leave their places of birth and migrate for the same reasons people always have—to be safe, to meet their needs for food and shelter, and to better their lives. Thus, violence, environmental change, and economic conditions often motivate migration. Acts of violence that drive people to migrate include armed conflicts, violence against women, violence related to sexual orientation and gender expression, ethnic cleansing, political persecution, and genocide. Environmental conditions that lead to migration include climate change, droughts, floods, radiation, and pollution.

Economic factors are currently the primary driving force behind immigration worldwide. . . .

Who migrates, how they migrate, where they migrate to, and when they migrate are central to immigration policies worldwide. While immigrants find jobs, build community, fall in love, have children, and in other ways enrich a country with new ways of thinking and being, some people declare them unwelcome and label them—not just their status—illegal.

Lack of documentation and legal status can lead to exploitation. Work visas often require having an employer-sponsor, which can limit a person's freedom to change employment. Some employers are unable to find workers willing to do certain jobs under the work conditions and at the wages they offer. Other employers are stymied by onerous requirements to prove that they need people with certain abilities. When the number of work visas is fewer than the number of workers demanded by the economy, employers will fill the need regardless of workers' documentation.

Documented and undocumented immigrants alike are often denied the civil rights protections of citizens, paid less than citizens, labor in unsafe and unhealthy conditions, and/or are forced to work and live without pay under the threat of violence. In the United States, increased border security has resulted in undocumented immigrants crossing in more dangerous and remote areas where basic human needs such as drinking water do not exist.

Increased enforcement of immigration laws and the proliferation of for-profit detention centers have led to egregious human rights violations with little accountability or transparency. For example, immigrants in the U.S. detention system are not afforded the same due process rights as U.S. citizens, leading to unnecessarily lengthy detentions, and thus greater profits for the prison industry. . . .

Many undocumented immigrants and their families live in constant fear of deportation. This fear affects their use of educational opportunities and health care services, and their willingness to interact with local police officers. Enlisting local law enforcement agencies in immigration enforcement violates accepted practices of community policing and erodes trust between police and the communities they serve, sometimes resulting in racial profiling of those who appear to be foreign. Deportation results in destroyed dreams and broken families—partners separated and children taken away from their caregivers or forced to return to a place they do not know. The perceived and constructed threat of those who are different has led some individuals and nations to meet immigrants with fear. Fear has become a social and political force that incorrectly labels people as "illegals," "criminals," and "terrorists."

Therefore

Our Unitarian Universalist (UU) Principles and Sources compel us to affirm that all immigrants, regardless of legal status, should be treated justly and humanely. At a minimum, a moral immigration policy would include the following elements:

- A path to legal permanent residency and citizenship
- Work visas that
  - Require the same worker protections applicable to citizens including fair wages, safe and healthful environments, and receipt of benefits
  - Do not depend on a single employer
  - Allow multiple entries
  - Permit entry into the path for legal permanent residency and citizenship
  - Provide parity between the number of visas and the work available in the receiving nation
- Timely processing of applications for visas and timely deportation decisions
- Access to the same medical care and education available to citizens
- Evaluation of human and environmental costs and benefits of proposed barriers to immigration or other changes in immigration policy
- Due process under the law. . . .
- Alternatives to detention for those not considered a threat to society and humane treatment for those being detained
- Preservation of family unity, including same-sex and transgender couples and families
- Provision of asylum for refugees and others living in fear of violence or retribution
- Collaboration with source countries to address underlying issues that contribute to immigration, including trade policies. . . .

Affirming the inherent worth and dignity of every person, we take up this call with joy and commitment, celebrating the creative and life-giving diversity of our world's peoples.

SOURCE: "Immigration as a Moral Issue," Unitarian Universalist Social Justice Statements, uua.org/statements/immigration-moral-issue

Business Resolution on
Fossil Fuel Divestment

2014

Delegates at the 2014 General Assembly voted overwhelmingly to divest UUA investments in coal, oil, and natural gas businesses. This action built on the legacy of South African divestment and on a long tradition of environmental activism, including the 2006 Statement of Conscience on the Threat of Global Warming/Climate Change. During the years prior to this action, there was a lively debate about the relative value of divestment as opposed to "shareholder activism," in which organizations hold small shares in corporations in order to influence the policies of those corporations in a positive way. As a compromise, the resolution allowed the UUA to retain the minimum number of shares needed to introduce shareholder resolutions. The UUA was the second major faith body in the United States to pass a divestment resolution, following the United Church of Christ.

—Dan McKanan

WHEREAS, Unitarian Universalist congregations covenant by our Second and Seventh Principles to affirm and promote justice, equity, and compassion in human relations and respect for the interdependent web of all existence of which we are a part; and

WHEREAS, the climate crisis threatens Earth systems through warming, destabilization of the atmosphere and climate, sea level rise, and the acidification of the oceans, of which the brunt of the burden has fallen and will fall on the poorest people in the world, who are least responsible for the crisis; and

WHEREAS, the 2006 Unitarian Universalist Association (UUA) General Assembly approved a Statement of Conscience on the Threat of Global Warming/Climate Change declaring "that we will not acquiesce to the ongoing degradation and destruction of life that human actions are leaving to our children and grandchildren;" and

WHEREAS, member congregations have demonstrated their commitment to environmental and climate justice. . . .

WHEREAS, if all known fossil fuel reserves are burned, they will produce five times the amount of greenhouse gas emissions required to raise global temperatures beyond 2°C. . . .

WHEREAS, we have a moral responsibility to Earth, to all beings, and to future generations to do everything in our power to bring about a swift transition from fossil fuels to a sustainable energy economy; and

WHEREAS, a global and growing movement is calling upon universities, pension funds, public entities, and religious institutions to divest their holdings in the 200 major fossil fuel companies listed by the Carbon Tracker Initiative (CT200). . . .

WHEREAS, the Unitarian Universalist Association is a leader among religious institutions in shareholder activism to halt climate change by ending the use of fossil fuels. . . .

WHEREAS, the guidelines for socially responsible investment of the UU Common Endowment Fund (UUCEF) state that "The UUA seeks to avoid companies that . . . contribute in significant ways to climate change;" and

WHEREAS, the 2013 General Assembly overwhelmingly passed an Action of Immediate Witness for congregations to "Consider Divestment from the Fossil Fuel Industry;"

THEREFORE BE IT RESOLVED that this General Assembly calls upon the UUA to cease purchasing securities of CT200 companies as UUCEF investments immediately; and

BE IT FURTHER RESOLVED that this General Assembly calls upon the UUA to continue to divest its UUCEF holdings of directly held securities of CT200 companies, reaching full divestment of these companies within five years; and

BE IT FURTHER RESOLVED that this General Assembly calls upon the UUA to work with its current and prospective pooled-asset managers for the purpose of creating more fossil fuel-free investment opportunities, with the objective of full divestment of UUCEF indirect holdings in CT200 within five years; and

BE IT FURTHER RESOLVED that this General Assembly calls upon the UUA to invest an appropriate share of UUCEF holdings in securities that will support a swift transition to a clean energy economy, such as renewable energy and energy-efficiency-related securities; and

BE IT FURTHER RESOLVED that, notwithstanding any provision above, the UUA may retain investments in CT200 companies in which it is engaged in shareholder activism seeking environmental justice or transition to clean and renewable energy; and

BE IT FURTHER RESOLVED that, notwithstanding any provision above, the UUA may purchase the minimal shares of CT200 companies necessary to permit introduction of shareholder resolutions seeking environmental justice or transition to clean and renewable energy; and. . . .

BE IT FINALLY RESOLVED that this General Assembly encourages Unitarian Universalist congregations and Unitarian Universalists to review their congregational and personal investments with a view to taking action to end climate change, such as public divestment of their holdings in fossil fuel companies, supporting shareholder activism designed to end use of fossil fuels, and investment in renewable energy and conservation.

SOURCE: Unitarian Universalist Social Statements, uua.org/statements/fossil-fuel-divestment

"Reproductive Justice"

2015

The practice of solidarity with partner organizations that shaped Unitarian Universalism's "Justice General Assembly" in 2013 was also decisive for the Statement of Conscience approved in 2015. The idea of "reproductive justice" was developed at the International Conference on Population and Development in 1994, and widely publicized by the first national conference of Sister Song, a reproductive health collective for women of color. Sister Song worked closely with Unitarian Universalist activists and congregations in the development of this statement.

— Dan McKanan

As Unitarian Universalists, we embrace the reproductive justice framework, which espouses the human right to have children, not to have children, to parent the children one has in healthy environments and to safeguard bodily autonomy and to express one's sexuality freely. *The reproductive justice movement was founded at a time when the unique range of issues faced by women of color were not addressed by the predominantly white middle class women's rights and reproductive rights movements nor the predominantly male civil rights movement. Those issues have included forced sterilization, forced contraception, and higher rates of removal of children from families due to accusations of abuse or neglect. These issues, coupled with systemic racism, have frequently made parenting or co-parenting more difficult due to many factors, including but not limited to, discriminatory and unequal implementation of laws and incarceration rates, prohibitions imposed on people after incarceration, unjust immigration policies, and economic insecurity.*

Reproductive justice is the term created by women of color in 1994, to center the experience of the most vulnerable, and to bridge the gap between reproductive rights and other social justice movements. . . . We as Unitarian Universalists declare that all people have the right to self-expression with regard to gender and sexuality and the right to live free from sexual violence, intimate partner violence, and exploitation including sexual and reproductive exploitation.

The reproductive justice movement envisions the liberation of people of all genders, sexual orientations, abilities, gender identities, ages, classes, and cultural and racial identities. Such liberation requires not only accurate information about sexuality and reproduction and control of personal reproductive decisions, but also living wages, safe and supported housing, high quality and comprehensive medical and reproductive health care, access to voting and the political process, affordable legal representation, fair immigration policies, paid parental leave, affordable childcare, and the absence of individual and institutional violence. . . .

As participants in the reproductive justice movement, Unitarian Universalists commit to follow the lead of, act in solidarity with, and be accountable to communities of color and other marginalized groups, using our positions of power to support those communities' priorities. Both those affected and their allies play important roles. Unitarian Universalists are laying the groundwork for the transformative power of multicultural organizing in partnership with reproductive justice organizations and leaders, looking for leadership from those most affected. We will use our position to speak loudly in the religious arena, as the religious voice has often been used to limit access to reproductive justice. . . .

As individuals we can

- Study reproductive justice issues, including sexuality, gender identity, classism, ableism, sexual violence, immigration, and racism.
- Seek to understand and take responsibility for our personal biases.
- Risk telling our own stories, and be willing to truly hear and trust the stories of others.
- Work to accept one's own body, sexuality, and abilities.
- Adopt spiritual practices that contribute to self-care.
- Advocate for reproductive justice and related issues through op-ed pieces, letters to the editor, letters and visits to legislators, and direct action.
- Volunteer with and/or provide financial support to organizations that provide reproductive health services at little or no cost, abortion clinics, women's shelters, and child and family community support centers.
- Protest violations of basic human rights, including sexual trafficking and the inhumane treatment of sex workers. . . .
- Support reproductive justice groups as active participants or accountable allies. . . .
- Contribute financially to organizations that advocate for reproductive justice issues, including the social determinants underlying racism, classism, sexism, ageism, ableism, homophobia, transphobia, and other forms of oppression.
- Work to ensure equity and respect and eliminate discrimination and coercion for all participants in the adoption and foster care system.

In our relationships we can

- Respect all people and their decisions regarding reproduction, even those with whom we disagree.

- Minister to one another around reproductive health and reproductive justice issues.
- Be sensitive to others' stories, respecting their life experiences and lived realities.
- Accept people of all abilities, identities, orientations, and generations as sexual beings.
- Accompany anyone wanting support (e.g., while seeking government assistance, in making decisions for their families about pregnancy and adoption, during abortions, and during childbirth).
- Engage children and youth in dialogue and learning about sexuality and relationships in ways that respect their self-expression and contributions.
- Seek and accept leadership from people most affected by reproductive injustice.
- Believe the survivors who share their experience of sexual and/or interpersonal violence. Listen with compassion, offer support, and avoid victim-blaming language.

In our congregations we can
- Form a reproductive justice group, task force, committee, or interfaith coalition.
- Invite and consult with reproductive justice advocates and groups to share their understanding and expertise, and/or conduct reproductive justice trainings.
- Connect religious professionals and lay leaders with organizations and networks that promote reproductive and economic justice and human rights. . . .
- Implement Safe Congregations guidelines and practices.
- Continue Welcoming Congregation advocacy and education efforts related to gender and sexuality.
- Reach out and participate in interfaith and secular work on racism, classism, gender and/or sexual health issues.
- Welcome breastfeeding in our shared spaces.

As an Association we can
- Publicly witness and advocate for sexual and reproductive justice in the US and around the world.
- Advocate for just legislation and policies and the rights of families and individuals at the state and federal levels.
- Advocate for comprehensive reproductive health services, including contraception, prenatal care, abortion, and infertility treatment.
- Advocate for the right to access comprehensive and medically accurate reproductive health information.
- Support UU state legislative ministry organizations in their work that supports reproductive justice.

- Provide curricula, resources, current information, and networking opportunities that congregations can use in their reproductive justice education and advocacy efforts.
- Collaborate with other faith-based and secular organizations working for reproductive justice and related issues, in order to build a stronger, more intersectional justice movement.
- Present reproductive justice workshops at district/regional, national, and international meetings.

With open minds, helping hands, and loving hearts, we work toward reproductive justice, and commit to replacing insecurity with safety, fear with acceptance, judgment with love, and shame with compassion.

SOURCE: "Reproductive Justice," Unitarian Universalist Social Statements, uua.org/statements/reproductive-justice

LILIA CUERVO

"Paradigm Shifts, or Having a Taste of My Own Medicine"

2015

Rev. Lilia Cuervo (1937–) joined her first Unitarian Universalist church in 1978, drawn in by the liberal religious principles and by the care the congregation provided her and her children as they were going through a difficult period in their lives. Twenty years later, Cuervo received her Master of Divinity from Starr King School for the Ministry and became the first female Unitarian Universalist minister born in Latin America. In the course of her career, Cuervo has served congregations in California, New York, and Massachusetts. In addition to her congregational work, Cuervo co-founded the Latino/a UU Networking Association (LUUNA) and helped translate and compile the first Unitarian Universalist Spanish-language hymnal, Las Voces del Camino. *In the following sermon, Cuervo explores her experience as a Latina in the UU tradition and her encounters with racism and prejudice in the denomination and in society at large.*

—Natalie Malter

I was born in Bogotá, Colombia. My mother raised me as child of the universe; and, without knowing it, as a Transcendentalist really. Wanting to give me the best education, she sent me to boarding schools with Catholic nuns. Unfortunately, they, as well as the priests, were products of a prejudiced patriarchal society and of a very conservative church. With them I learned about "good people," those like us, and "bad or strange people," different from us and with whom we should not associate.

When in 1964 I accepted the invitation to come to the United States, along with my personal belongings, I brought a bag of prejudices against "the strange others," some of whom I even feared. As I share my list, I invite you to examine yours, translate into your context, and see how many checks you might place.

- The Colombian Indians, who should be grateful to the Conquistadores, who brought them civilization and the true religion.
- The Jews, punished to wander on earth for having crucified Jesus.
- The Protestant missionaries, then a rarity, walking on the path to hell, along with those whom they were leading astray from the one true religion.
- The blacks. A whole African continent was teeming with pagans, whose salvation depended on the Catholic missionaries and on the prayers of good girls like me.

535

- The Turkish and the Polish immigrants, who were sorry people, selling textiles from door to door.
- And of course, the Yankees, those pale, greedy, naïve gringos, tricking us into accepting their outdated tractors and arms in "exchange" for our oil, and other natural resources.

Because of my prejudices, I very reluctantly accepted the invitation to come here. No sooner had I arrived in San Francisco than my first paradigm shift began. As I was picking up my suitcase to board an airport shuttle, the driver, a burly, typical gringo descended from the bus and took it. I immediately asked: How much? Smiling he said: "nothing, just smile." I was in total shock. Did I land in the wrong country? Several kind acts later and it hit me: one thing is the government and its policies, and another is the people.

My father's ancestors were Spaniards. My mother's were Spaniards and indigenous from the Andes. In my country of birth, I grew up as a white person. Here, in my adopted country, my birthplace and my color became the core of one of the most difficult and hurtful paradigm shifts I had to undergo before regaining my true identity.

That shift began one Sunday in 1991, after I had been a UU for some fourteen years. A member of my congregation approached me saying, "The Unitarian Universalist Association wants to know how many people of color there are in the denomination; could you please fill out this questionnaire?"

At that moment I couldn't figure why he asked me. Later, driving home, my head was spinning as I started realizing that the person I thought I was all these years was not the same person others thought I was. I was stunned.

Next, I felt betrayed by my new faith. After having renounced Catholicism and having been in spiritual exile for many years, I had found my true spiritual home in Unitarian Universalism. Here, I have been encouraged to get rid of my prejudices and to be proud being a woman. I was so happy in my Unitarian Universalist theological honeymoon, thinking what freedom! No more pretensions, no more labels, we are all equal, just freedom of thought and action!

And now, this denomination—that had started showing me the devastating effects of racism, sexism, and other -isms,—this church—was labeling me, and as a person of color at that! It didn't take me long to start making petty comparisons between the color of my skin and that of others. I noticed that many of those considered whites were darker than I. I compared my education, my professional career, and my home with some of the whitest within and without my congregation, and kept wondering why on earth people thought that white skin alone made someone superior.

In the seminary I completed this paradigm shift. There, I became truly aware of the extent of prejudice and racism in the world, sadly, in our denomination, and in myself as well. Now as a person of color, I understood the twofold effect that prejudice and racism was having on me. On the one hand, remember my list? I was feeling both shame and pain realizing this ugly fact in my life. On the other hand, I was feeling humiliated and angry, resenting being labeled and put in a racial box.

I no longer could minimize or ignore the fact that on several occasions my children and I had been discriminated against; the most hurtful instance when I wanted to buy a certain house and we couldn't even see it inside because we were Latinos. I became more and more convinced that classifying people according to skin color, birthplace, or ethnicity, to put them in their place—so to speak—was not only evil, but genetically inaccurate.

Fitzpatrick, the great sociologist, and scholar of Puerto Rican life, remarked: *In Puerto Rico a drop of white blood makes a person white. In the United States, a drop of black blood makes a person black.* He was of course referring to "The One-Drop" rule, a tactic believed to be useful to strengthen segregation and the disfranchisement of most blacks and many poor whites in the U.S. South from 1890 to 1910. . . .

These things are so subjective. I myself have been asked if I am French, Greek, Italian, Brazilian, German, yes—German!, and even Californian! Last time, I was asked if I was Czechoslovakian! And yet, having been perceived as European or as a light Latina was detrimental when I was in search of a parish under the Diversity of Ministry Initiative. After pre-candidating in a certain congregation, I was told that I was one of the two finalists. With regret, a member of the search committee asked: "How can we choose you when the congregation is expecting a minister of color?"

Right then and there, I understood that I was facing another paradigm shift. Now that I was comfortable as a person of color, I had to accept that others didn't accept me as such. Welcome to the borderlands, where people belong to both sides, and sadly, are rejected by both.

The issue of blood purity was a confusing aspect of my racial Paradigm Shift. In Colombia, I had learned that my blood was a rich mixture of many bloods: Goth, Visigoth, Roman, Arabic, and indigenous. I always felt proud and thankful being so richly endowed. But here such richness made my blood impure, and a lesser person of me. . . .

It has been very difficult for me not to give in to despair realizing both how insidious and damaging racism is and how easily, like destructive viruses, we transmit prejudices of all kinds from childhood on, from generation to generation. The experience in our country, and in our denomination, tells us that antiracism work is hard work for those trying to be inclusive, and for those wanting to be included. This is because seeing the other as inferior, as the cause of one's guilt, or as one's burden prevents true friendship and acceptance. Likewise, seeing the other as the oppressor or as the cause of one's feelings of inferiority, fear, and hopelessness prevents healthy relationships as well.

* * *

In 1819, the Unitarian minister, William Ellery Channing . . . said to Jared Sparks in his ordination sermon: *If any light can pierce and scatter the clouds of prejudice, it is that of pure example. My brother, may your life preach more loudly than your lips.* Yes! *May our lives preach more loudly than our lips.* For us Unitarian Universalists, the best way to eliminate barriers to love and to help eradicate the scourge of racism is to embody our faith principles. An easy task? Of course not! But try we must! The practice of our first principle: *To affirm and promote the inherent worth and dignity of every person* —will lead us to learn the appropriate means to properly communicate with each other. The practice of our fourth principle: *To affirm and promote a responsible search for truth and meaning* —will lead us to educate ourselves about the cultures and customs of those we fear or disdain, because they are different, and to honor their values and dreams.

In my view, and increasingly in the view of others, to attain true justice and integration, we need to move beyond our impersonal top-down social justice to a personal embodiment of fairness and compassion. We need to practice spiritual justice and let social justice be its fruit. And what could be more spiritually just than to share our precious faith with the thousands, if not millions, craving a spiritual home such as ours? Do you remember your excitement finding this spiritual home? Why then deny the same to others just because we consider them different and therefore not worthy of our faith?

For many years now, our denomination has been encouraging its congregations to become more multi-culturally savvy and racially diverse. Although only a handful of them are succeeding so far, we should not lose hope. Many of us have crossed the ocean to learn about our Unitarian roots and to unite with our European faith family in Transylvania. What would it take for us to cross a few streets to meet the "strange other" face to face, heart to heart? And what would it take to invite them to our religious home?

By wrestling with multiculturalism, racism, and prejudice issues, I regained my identity as child of the universe and arrived at my last paradigm. My call is to be a bridge between traditional dividers: cultures, generations, ethnicities, religions, and age.

I invite us to individually and collectively take up the challenge of breaking all barriers; of opening our hearts and the doors of our churches to the spiritually homeless and the theologically abused. Let us do it by engaging our whole being in a vibrant, loving and fearless way. Amen and blessed be.

SOURCE: Lilia Cuervo, "Paradigm Shifts, or Having a Taste of My Own Medicine." Reprinted by permission of the author.

Bibliography of General Histories and Primary Source Collections

Ahlstrom, Sydney, and Jonathan S. Carey, eds. *An American Reformation: A Documentary History of Unitarian Christianity.* Middletown, CT: Wesleyan University Press, 1985.

Bressler, Ann Lee. *The Universalist Movement in America, 1770–1880.* New York: Oxford University Press, 2001.

Buehrens, John A. *Universalists and Unitarians in America: A People's History.* Boston: Skinner House, 2011.

Buehrens, John A., and Forrest Church. *A Chosen Faith: An Introduction to Unitarian Universalism,* rev. ed. Boston: Beacon Press, 1998.

Bumbaugh, David E. *Unitarian Universalism: A Narrative History.* Chicago: Meadville Lombard Press, 2000.

Cassara, Ernest. *Universalism in America: A Documentary History.* Boston: Beacon Press, 1971.

Emerson, Dorothy May. *Standing Before Us: Unitarian Universalist Women and Social Reform, 1776–1936.* Boston: Skinner House, 2000.

Greenwood, Andrea, and Mark W. Harris. *An Introduction to the Unitarian and Universalist Traditions.* New York: Cambridge University Press, 2011.

Harris, Mark W. *The A to Z of Unitarian Universalism.* Lanham, MD: Scarecrow Press, 2009.

Myerson, Joel, ed. *Transcendentalism: A Reader.* New York: Oxford University Press, 2000.

Miller, Russell E. *The Larger Hope: The First Century of the Universalist Church in America, 1770–1870.* Boston: Unitarian Universalist Association, 1979.

Miller, Russell E. *The Larger Hope: The Second Century of the Universalist Church in America, 1870–1970.* Boston: Unitarian Universalist Association, 1985.

Morales, Peter, ed. *The Unitarian Universalist Pocket Guide,* 5th ed. Boston: Skinner House, 2012.

Parke, David B. *The Epic of Unitarianism: Original Writings from the History of Liberal Religion.* Boston: Starr King Press, 1957.

Parker, Kathy. *Sacred Service in Civic Space: Three Hundred Years of Community Ministry in Unitarian Universalism.* Chicago: Meadville Lombard Press, 2007.

Robinson, David. *The Unitarians and the Universalists.* Westport, CT: Greenwood Press, 1985.

Ross, Warren. *The Premise and the Promise: The Story of the Unitarian Universalist Association.* Boston: Skinner House, 2001.

Wilbur, Earl Morse. *A History of Unitarianism.* 2 vols. Cambridge, MA: Harvard University Press, 1945–1952.

Wright, Conrad, ed. *Three Prophets of Religious Liberalism: Channing, Emerson, Parker.* Boston: Beacon Press, 1961.

Wright, Conrad, ed. *A Stream of Light: A Sesquicentennial History of American Unitarianism.* Boston: Unitarian Universalist Association, 1975.

About the Contributors

WAYNE ARNASON is a retired Unitarian Universalist minister. He has authored, co-authored, and edited several books, including *We Would Be One: A History of the Unitarian Universalist Youth Movements* and *Worship That Works*.

JAY ATKINSON retired from parish ministry in 2011. He served on the adjunct faculties of Meadville Lombard Theological School and Starr King School for the Ministry. Currently he is a research scholar at Starr King with a focus on Unitarian Universalist history.

COLIN BOSSEN is a Unitarian Universalist minister and Ph.D candidate in American Studies at Harvard University. He is the author or co-author of two religious education curricula, more than three dozen journal articles, book chapters, essays, and poems and a dedicated organizer for justice and liberation. He keeps a blog at colinbossen.com.

AVERY (PETE) GUEST is an emeritus professor of sociology at the University of Washington. Since retirement, he has been writing a series of papers analyzing the social history of the Universalist denomination. His most recent paper describes the growth, or lack of growth, of the Unitarian and Universalist denominations in big cities in the early twentieth century.

ROBERT HARDIES is senior minister of All Souls Church Unitarian in Washington D.C. and editor of *Blessing the World*, a collection of essays by Rebecca Ann Parker.

MARK W. HARRIS has served as minister of the First Parish of Watertown, Unitarian Universalist, in Massachusetts, since 1996. He has taught Unitarian Universalist history and polity at Andover Newton Theological School and Harvard Divinity School. He is the author of *Elite: Uncovering Classism in Unitarian Universalist History*; *An Introduction to the Unitarian and Universalist Traditions* (with Andrea Greenwood); and the forthcoming *Historical Dictionary of Unitarian Universalism*, Second Edition.

PETER HUGHES was the first editor of the *Dictionary of Unitarian and Universalist Biography* and has published articles on American Universalist history and on Reformation history in the *Journal of Unitarian Universalist History* and other periodicals. He is currently working on translations of the works of Servetus and other antitrinitarian writers. His most recent published book is *Declaratio*, a translation of the writings of Matteo Gribaldi.

is the Frank and Alice Schulman Chair of Unitarian Univer-
leadville Lombard Theological School. Her research interests
nization, technology, and commerce impacted American reli-
:tions of race and class. Her forthcoming book is on John Wana-
iladelphia department store.

EMILY MACE served from 2011 to 2016 as the director of the Harvard Square Library, a digital library of Unitarian Universalist biographies, history, books, and media. You can find her online at emilyrmace.com.

NATALIE MALTER is a candidate for the Unitarian Universalist ministry. Her research interests in American religious history include the history of the second wave feminist movement and women's ordination in Unitarian Universalism and neo-paganism as an expression of twentieth-century feminist spirituality.

SARAH GIBB MILLSPAUGH has served as a parish minister and as staff at the Unitarian Universalist Association. She helped to develop the *Our Whole Lives* sexuality education series. She works for the Pacific Western Region of the Unitarian Universalist Association.

MARK D. MORRISON-REED is an affiliated faculty member at Meadville Lombard Theological School and coordinator of its Sankofa Archive. He is author/editor of nine books, most recently *The Selma Awakening* from Skinner House Books. He is a former president of the Canadian Unitarian Council.

SUSAN RITCHIE is the minister of the North Unitarian Universalist Congregation in Lewis Center, Ohio, and the director of the Unitarian Universalist House of Studies at the Methodist Theological School in Ohio. She is the author of *Children of the Same God: The Historical Relationship Between Unitarianism, Judaism, and Islam.*

ELIZABETH M. STRONG is a retired minister of religious education and minister emerita of the First Parish Unitarian Universalist Church in Ashby, Massachusetts. She was awarded the Larry Axel Award for Excellence in Teaching by Meadville Lombard and the Angus MacLean Award for Excellence in Religious Education by the Unitarian Universalist Association.

JEFF WILSON is a professor of Religious Studies and East Asian Studies at Renison University College, University of Waterloo. He is the author of *Mindful America: The Mutual Transformation of Buddhist Meditation and American Culture* and a frequent contributor to the *Journal of Unitarian Universalist History*.

SHARI WOODBURY is a parish minister serving Westside Unitarian Universalist Church in Fort Worth, Texas, where she resides with her family.

Index of Titles and Authors

Index of Genres and Themes

Social Justice

Unitarianism

Universalism

Unitarian Universalism